DATE DUE

DEMCO 38-296

An Anticlassical
Political-Economic Analysis

A VISION FOR THE NEXT CENTURY

Yasusuke Murakami

YASUSUKE MURAKAMI

An Anticlassical Political-Economic Analysis

A VISION FOR THE NEXT CENTURY

Translated with an Introduction by Kozo Yamamura

STANFORD UNIVERSITY PRESS

STANFORD, CALIFORNIA

1996

Stanford University Press
Stanford, California
© 1996 by the Board of Trustees of the
Leland Stanford Junior University
Printed in the United States of America

Published with the assistance of the
Japan Foundation

CIP data appear at the end of the book

Stanford University Press publications are
distributed exclusively by Stanford University
Press within the United States, Canada, Mexico,
and Central America; they are distributed exclusively
by Cambridge University Press throughout the rest of
the world.

Preface

An Anticlassical Political-Economic Analysis may be too pre-sumptuous a title. The substance of this book is the search for a conclusion to the arguments I have attempted in various forms over the past 30-odd years, mainly focusing on a critique of existing arguments. In other words, in this book I was unable, regrettably, to offer a comprehensive theory of anticlassical political economy. To have named it something like *A Critique of Classical Political Economy* or *Introduction to an Anticlassical Political Economy* might have been a more accurate reflection of the contents. This is not to say, however, that I do not have any insights into the substance of a theory of anticlassical political economy. This book, I hope, will show what I have been able to accomplish to date toward developing such a theory, the substance of which will be a somewhat biological framework for discussion, which takes (what is commonly called) information as its basic concept. But I do not know whether I have either the ability or the time to complete the theory. Thus I have decided with some reluctance to publish my work to date in its present, provisional, negative form, placing the emphasis on critique. I hope readers will forgive the present title as a reflection of the intellectual bravery I still possess.

Looking back, what I have continued to feel over these 30 years is doubt toward the preeminence of Marxist social science or, more generally, the progressive view of history. While it is not impossible to say that humanity is "progressing," I do not believe that "progress" is a conquest of the physical world or a convergence toward a fixed form of society. The sense that human beings are, put in a favorable light, the most free of beings or, put unfavorably, the most troublesome of creatures has never left me. The reason I have been so interested in so-called modern economics, or what I call "neoclassical economics" in this book, is its usefulness as an antidote, a critical force, and a counterthought to this progressive view of history. But modern economics is but a discipline and its perspective is narrow and self-contained; thus by itself it can hardly be a counterthought. If one were to develop a system of thought or a view of historical change drawing on modern, or neoclassical, economics, it could not but be unduly swayed by the modern tradition and become modern in the classical sense of the term. We would thus be able to obtain only a unilinear understanding of history, which asked of everything whether it was advanced or backward, whether there was distortion and lag. In the end, therefore, both Marxist analysis and modern economics and political science are nothing more than ideologies of "progress." My dissatisfaction with this intensified over time and has been the basis for my thinking. The book's title is a reflection of this fact.

Needless to say, this is not simply an academic issue. The political-economic world system, driven by modern European ideals and thought, seems now to be facing a major turning point. Are we not coming to a period when someone from Japan, which has traced a path unlike the course of development of Western societies yet has achieved results hard for anyone to deny, will have to make an intellectual and practical contribution? I do not believe this book reaches the level necessary to respond to this question. I would like to be permitted to hope, though, that it can be a starting point from which a younger generation can make a contribution useful to the world community in analyzing societies and developing new visions. The condition for such a contribution is to have to doubt in its entirety what was promised by the march of the "modern" period. It will not be easy, but I continue to hope that someone will muster the necessary courage.

With various such thoughts as its background, this book became long —two volumes. Had I reorganized and edited to reduce its length, it might have become easier to read, and the arguments clearer for the reader. But to do so would have meant more months of delay in publication. Thus I have decided to publish the current version.* The first volume consists of six chapters presenting a general, theoretical critique. The second volume also has six chapters. Chapters 7 to 9 deal with specific, somewhat specialized, economic themes, and in Chapters 10 and 11 I make a number of proposals dealing with contemporary global political-economic problems. Chapter 12 is a little different in tone, attempting a generalized, somewhat philosophical argument. Though some readers may find it a little surpris-

---

* *Translator's note*: The remainder of this paragraph refers to the original Japanese version. See the Translator's Introduction for revisions made in the organization of chapters for the English version.

ing, I believe that in order to doubt the "modern" period, even those who are not philosophers by training must attempt this kind of inquiry. The argument in Chapter 12 may contain many inadequacies, but I have added it, since it allows me to write things I have particularly wanted to say.

Apart from this, somewhat exceptionally for a book titled as this one is, there is not one figure or graph explaining data. The main reason for this is to keep the book from growing even longer; another is that, as is customary for armchair social scientists such as myself, the materials I have used are all secondary sources, and I have merely mentioned these sources in the footnotes. This of course is an inadequate excuse to readers. I can only ask their forgiveness for the inconvenience of not being able to find pertinent data in this book.

Finally, I would like to take this opportunity to express my gratitude to the many people who have made this book possible. Since I am indebted to so many who have aided me directly and indirectly over the years, I can regretfully mention only those with whom I have directly discussed this book since beginning it three years ago. First I must thank the members of the Seisaku Kōsō Forum, a policy proposal group, of which I have been a member since 1979. They provided an opportunity for discussing the first outline of "Seikimatsu no hoshu to kakushin" (Conservatives and progressives at the end of the century) (*Chūō kōron*, January 1990), which became the starting point for this book. Subsequently, Toshio Suzuki, Kazuo Koike, and Shōichi Royama offered particularly generous guidance.

Next I would like to thank warmly former prime minister Yasuhiro Nakasone, Seizaburō Satō, and Susumu Nishibe, who participated in the small research group that discussed the part corresponding to the last six chapters of the book over the past two years. The results of this research group have been published as *Kyōdō kenkyū: reisen igo* (Collaborative research: after the cold war) (Tokyo: Bungei Shunjū, 1992). Many of my arguments in these six chapters overlap with those in this book, but other points are different.

In addition, I have received invaluable advice on specific points from Yukihiko Kiyokawa of Hitotsubashi University, Mitsuhiro Mizutani of Tokyo Metropolitan University, Mitsuharu Miyamoto of Senshū University, and Kumiharu Shigehara of the Bank of Japan's Institute for Monetary and Economic Studies. In some parts of this book, I also owe much to Professors S. N. Eisenstadt of the Hebrew University of Jerusalem, Kozo Yamamura of the University of Washington, and Thomas Rohlen of Stanford University. Needless to say, any errors or unclear points in the book are my responsibility.

I have also received valuable suggestions, in various forms, from the members of the Center for Global Communications (GLOCOM) at International University, with which I am now affiliated. I would like to thank all the members of the center, beginning with Shumpei Kumon, my companion in research for many years, and including Ken'ichi Nishiyama, Hiroshi

Deguchi, Izumi Aizu, Yoshitsugu Fujino, and Takashi Shintani. In particular, I would like to warmly thank Tatsuo Tanaka, Yasuhide Yamanouchi, George Iguchi, and Kōichirō Hirata for their work in the final editing and hunting for citations. I must also thank Mari Sasahara and Akane Yorimura for making up for my administrative inefficiency.

I would like to express my gratitude to the Japan International Culture Research Center, particularly its director, Takeshi Umehara, for having provided me with a liberal research environment for two years. Words are inadequate to express my sorrow that Keiichirō Hirata, the president of the Japan Development Bank, who encouraged my work over many years and who greeted the completion of the initial manuscript as if it were his own, died before the book reached publication. I must also thank Professor Hiroshi Obata of Tokyo Women's Medical College. Without his guidance, my ill health would not have allowed this book to be completed. Last but not least, I want to thank Kōichi Tsuge of Chūō Kōronsha, who became involved with the publication of my works over many years. Without his patience and skillful guidance, it is doubtful whether this book would have been completed.

Once again, finally, I thank the many friends who have supported me over the years.

Y. M.

June 1992

Contents

Figures

Translator's Preface

Yasusuke Murakami passed away on July 1, 1993, just after this book was published in Japan. I have translated this work because I am convinced it contains a vision supported by truly seminal, interdisciplinary analyses that should be read widely around the world. The subjects of Murakami's analyses are the fundamental challenges the world faces at the end of this century, and the central questions he deals with are equally fundamental. How and in what form can a harmonious and stable post-cold-war world order be created? How can the world maintain the economic performance necessary for the well-being of peoples both North and South and in newly industrializing economies while minimizing international economic conflicts and further deterioration of the world's environment? And what must be done to safeguard the freedoms of all peoples?

To appreciate fully the import of Murakami's vision for the decades to come and the wide-ranging analyses supporting it, open-mindedness is required of readers, especially of social scientists who are trained to see and analyze issues from the perspective of their own discipline and to rely more often than not only on their own analytic tools. To those who are open-minded and who share his concern for the future of the world, Murakami offers thought-provoking analyses of the most important issues of our time.

Yasusuke Murakami was destined to be a thinker deeply concerned with humanity. Born in 1931 in Tokyo, he graduated from the Department of Liberal Arts of the University of Tokyo in 1953 and earned an M.A. in 1955 and a Ph.D. in 1961, both from the Economics Department of the same university. He was an avid student of history, especially of English history which was his minor in his undergraduate days. In graduate work, he specialized in economic theory (welfare economics in particular) and quantitative analysis (statistics and econometrics). During his academic career he taught economic theory, mathematical economics, statistics, and, in later years, various topics in the field that can be broadly characterized as international political economy, all in the Department of Social Studies (Kyōyō Gakubu) of the College of Liberal Arts and Sciences at the University of Tokyo. In 1988 he resigned from his alma mater where he had taught for 26 years and became a research professor at the International Research Center of Japanese Studies (1988–90), moving on in 1990 to International University of Japan where he was until his death. At International University, he served as director of the Center for Global Communications, which he created in 1991.

In addition to numerous shorter visits overseas throughout his academic life to attend international conferences, he made two long visits abroad, both to the United States. One was a two-year stay (1962–64) during which he spent a year at the Department of Economics at Stanford University, where he was a research fellow, and a year as a postdoctoral researcher in the Department of Economics at Purdue University. The other was a two-year appointment (1980–82) as a visiting professor in the Jackson School of International Studies at the University of Washington.

Throughout his professional life, Murakami was much involved in public service. To note only a few of his contributions, he was senior research officer, Economic Research Institute, Economic Planning Agency of Japan (1967–70); expert member, Provisional Commission for Economic Reform (1973–87); director, Japan Association of Economics and Econometrics (1975–77); and chairman, Forum for Policy Innovations (1976–89). The last is a highly regarded and influential organization of leading economists and others, which sponsors numerous symposia and issues many timely position papers on a wide range of economic and political-economic issues of the day.

However, Murakami's most important contribution was his publications, which include highly technical works in welfare economics, especially analyses of public good and social choice, as well as interdisciplinary works dealing with broad issues of political economy and society. The following small sample of publications in English gives a glimpse of the topics he dealt with in his more technical works: "Formal Structure of Majority Decision," *Econometrica*, 34 (July 1966); *Logic and Social Choice* (London: Routledge, 1968); "Efficient Paths of Accumulation and the Turnpike of the Japanese Economy" (coauthored), in A. P. Carter and A. Brody, eds., *Application of Input-Output Analysis* (Amsterdam: North-Holland, 1969); and "Relative Stability in the Two Types of Dynamic Leontief Models" (coauthored) in *International Economic Review*, 13 (June 1977). *Turnpike Optimality in Input-Output Systems* (North-Holland, 1979), coauthored by Murakami and Jinichi Tsukui, was awarded the coveted Nikkei Prize for

Excellent Book in Economics in 1980. As an economist-econometrician, Murakami wrote no fewer than 200 articles and essays, some highly technical and others for lay readers, on many topics including those dealing with domestic and international policy issues of the Japanese economy.

Murakami's interdisciplinary works on broader political-economic issues began to appear in the mid-1970s and increased rapidly during the 1980s. Here I describe only his three major books because they contain the most important articles he published, in English and Japanese, during these years. The first of these is *Sangyō shakai no byōri* (A pathology of industrial societies) (Tokyo: Chūō Kōronsha, 1975). This book, consisting of two parts—an incisive and critical analysis of the strengths and weaknesses of modern capitalism and a rigorous analysis of the usefulness and limitations of economics (classical, Marxist, and neoclassical)—is a landmark in Murakami's scholarly life because it defined his life's work; much of this 1975 book anticipates the present work. *Sangyō shakai no byōri* won the Yoshino Sakuzo Prize, given annually to the best work in the social sciences and history, and became one of those rare scholarly works that continues to be read widely and over a long period, as attested by the fact that its fourteenth edition was published in 1992.

The second book is *Bunmei to shite no ie shakai* (*Ie* society as a pattern of civilization) (Tokyo: Chūō Kōronsha, 1979), written with his colleagues at the University of Tokyo, Shumpei Kumon and Seizaburō Satō. This 598-page book analyzing the origins and character of Japanese society was awarded the Odaka Prize for the most significant work in sociological studies in 1980. The principal content of the analyses offered in this second book, which also helped to nurture Murakami's analyses contained here in this book, was ably summarized by Murakami in English and published in the *Journal of Japanese Studies*, 10, 2 (1984).

The third book is *Shin-chūkan taishū no jidai* (The age of the new middle mass) (Tokyo: Chūō Kōronsha, 1984), which examines the changing character of Japanese society and political economy since the Meiji period but which concentrates especially on the postwar years. In this book, Murakami argues that Japan today has a "new middle mass" that is larger than those in other industrial societies and shapes Japan's political economy in distinctive ways. Murakami summarized in English the essential content of this book in 1982 in "The Age of New Middle Mass Politics: The Case of Japan" in the *Journal of Japanese Studies*, 8, 1 (1982).

I should add here that Murakami played a major role as the general co-editor, with Hugh Patrick, of the three-volume study, *The Political Economy of Japan*.[*] Murakami contributed two thoughtful and valuable essays to this study. "The Japanese Model of Political Economy" appears in volume 1, and "Social-Exchange Aspects of the Japanese Political Economy:

---

[*] Vol. 1, *The Domestic Transformation* (1987), Vol. 2, *The Changing International Context* (1988), and Vol. 3, *Cultural and Social Dynamics* (1992), all published by Stanford University Press.

Culture, Efficiency, and Change," coauthored by Thomas P. Rohlen, appears in volume 3.

The author of these many works was a genuine, warm, and unassuming man. All who knew him quickly learned that he meant what he said, that he cared deeply for others and respected their views, however contrary to his own. He was truly saddened by selfish or misconceived arguments but remained always hopeful that people would learn and would be able to see the needs of others. Murakami was a patient man with inexhaustible energy. He could debate for hours in his quiet and measured way. He argued with precision and evidence, as expected of an accomplished econometrician. At the same time, he never forgot that humans feel as well as think and that culture, history, and values matter profoundly in our daily lives. Above all else, I remember him as a thinker preoccupied with the ideas—insights, thoughts, and analyses of many disciplines and ideologies, philosophies, and worldviews—of others who lived long ago and of his contemporaries who were challenging his own. I believe that this book will attest that my perception of him is not unduly biased because of our many years of friendship.

Before turning to describe the differences between the original Japanese version and this translation, I must pass on to the readers of this book his deep regret for not having sufficient time to cite many more sources that had aided his analyses and to revise various parts of this book to react to, or benefit from, very recent works. He especially regretted not having done more on "evolutionary economics" and having failed to acknowledge the works of many scholars in the broad fields of international political economy and international economics. I still recall vividly and with sadness the day of our last meeting in October 1992, when he expressed this regret.

This book differs in a few ways from the original 910-page version that appeared in two volumes. The original title is *Han-koten no seiji keizai gaku*, which literally means "anticlassical political economics" (or political-economic analysis). The subtitle for volume 1 is *Shinpo-shikan no tasogare* (The twilight of the progressive view of history) and that of volume 2 is *Nijūisseiki e no josetsu* (Prefatory remarks for the twenty-first century). The organization, and thus the content in some instances, of this work was changed somewhat for publication in English. Murakami himself wanted to edit the book rather thoroughly for the English version. Thus, he revised and combined Chapters 1 and 2 and decided to eliminate Chapter 6 in which he offers an extended historical analysis of the English experience to support his analyses of industrialization, democracy, and social changes. (Just before his death, he expressed his wish to add a shortened version of this chapter as an appendix, but he was not given the time to do so.) Consequently, this book has only ten chapters instead of the twelve contained in the Japanese version.

The content of each chapter also differs from that in the original version. Referring to the chapter numbers by those in the English version, Murakami himself shortened Chapters 3 and 4. Under Murakami's guidance, Tatsuo Tanaka, his graduate student and a colleague at the Center for Global Communications, made some revisions, mostly to shorten the book. I also made revisions—if and only if they reduced the length without loss of content or clearly improved the exposition and if I believed restating or adding brief explanations increased the clarity of exposition. Based on my discussions with Murakami, I eliminated several subsections and paragraphs written primarily with Japanese readers in mind. I must, however, admit that I chose to retain a long subsection on Japanese pacifism that Murakami would have sacrificed in the interest of shortening the book. This is because I believed the section would be useful to non-Japanese readers interested in Japan, especially in the "Japan problem." My goal in translating this book was to make it as readable and as clear as possible while intruding minimally on Murakami's original exposition. I can only hope that I did not fail in my effort to remain faithful to that goal.

Finally, I must thank many who made this translation possible. There are no adequate words to express my appreciation to Martha L. Walsh, the managing editor of the *Journal of Japanese Studies*. Had it not been for her editorial skills and unstinting assistance, this translation could not have been completed by a nonnative English speaker who habitually overestimates his ability to undertake multiple projects at the same time. Angus Lockyer also made indispensable contributions in the translation of this book. His linguistic talents both in English and Japanese and his Cambridge education helped to shorten the time needed for translation substantially and to minimize errors. I thank also Shumpei Kumon, who read the draft, offered valuable suggestions for changes, and pointed out errors; Tatsuo Tanaka, who provided answers to many queries including those regarding Japanese sources used in the book; and Koichi Hamada and Susan B. Hanley, who made comments most helpful in clarifying the exposition of my preface and introduction. I am most grateful also to Norris Pope, director of Stanford University Press, who recognized the scholarly value of this book and took a personal interest in making its publication possible. And I express my sincere appreciation to Sohei Nakayama, chairman of the Foundation of International Education, and to George S. Ishiyama, president of Ishiyama Corporation, for the generous funds they provided to enable me to defray various costs involved in all phases of translating and preparing the manuscript for publication.

I am fully aware that, despite my efforts, this translation is not free of errors and not what it could be had it been done by someone better equipped than I. I dared to translate this book not because I felt I had the requisite talents but because of my belief in the importance of this book and my friendship with the author who left us too soon.

Translator's Introduction

It is not easy to write an introduction for this book. The task is made even more burdensome because I am painfully aware that I do not possess the breadth of knowledge necessary to undertake it with confidence. What follows is my best effort, presented without the illusion that I fully understand all that Yasusuke Murakami, whom a leading Japanese economist called "the Max Weber of Japan," offers in this book. I have no doubt that others who are better able to understand what Murakami offers would have written a very different introduction.

Although it becomes evident in reading this book what Murakami means by "classical political-economic analysis," it may be useful to begin by briefly explaining the object of his critical analysis. For Murakami, classical political-economic analysis comprises two parts. One is political analysis (or the beliefs supported by that analysis) based on the nation-state system, which sees nation-states, each having sovereignty over a territory and people sharing a common culture, as the primary units that form alliances and engage in power politics. This is well known as realist political analysis. The second part is economic liberalism, which holds that unimpeded competition and free trade are the fundamental bases for increasing wealth for the benefit of all. This analysis—or some might say ideology— is supported by classical and neoclassical economic analysis.

Murakami's closely woven anti-"classical" arguments and analyses are composed of five extensively overlapping but broadly definable parts, identified by Murakami himself either explicitly or implicitly. (In reading this book, it is important to keep in mind that the time horizon of his analyses is the medium term, by which he means the first few decades of the twenty-first century.)

Polymorphic Liberalism

The first argument, which provides the essential foundation for the book, is that today, in the last decade of the twentieth century, "progessivism" can no longer be seen as the guiding ideology or vision. Progressivism for Murakami is the quasi-deterministic belief that humans have an ultimate, unique path on which they will reach a similarly ultimate and unique—ideal—social and political-economic system. It is a vision, he argues forcefully, deeply rooted in the Western Enlightenment and nurtured by the progress of science, technology, and continuing industrialization.

Murakami believes that progressivism must now yield to a new vision he calls "polymorphic liberalism," the contours of which are revealed as the book progresses. He argues that the dominant version of progressivism, which has long anchored Western civilization and been supported by liberalism and classical economic analyses, can no longer meet today's challenges. Progressivism, with its science and technology (that is, industrialization), can no longer give the promise of relieving human beings from suffering (death, sickness, old age, and other suffering) and anxieties; also a profound friction has arisen between the progressivism of Western origin in freedom of thought and action and the traditional cultures of many non-Western societies. (Marxism, a short-lived version of progressivism, has shown itself to be incapable of remaining a guiding ideology.) This argument applies also to the core views of social democrats around the world and the Democratic party in the United States, which is groping for fundamental ideas or an ideology to replace the neoliberal counterparts of the preceding Republican administrations. In preparing to build arguments for, as well as to better explain what is meant by, "polymorphic liberalism," Murakami proposes to analyze what he calls "the three axes of the problem" he believes we confront today: the axes of nationalism-antinationalism, industrialism–anti-industrialism, and equality-liberty.

Nationalism-Antinationalism

The second of Murakami's arguments provides essential support for polymorphic liberalism as the guiding thought of the future and is provided in his analysis of the axis of nationalism—the ideology of stressing the value of the nation-state—and various forms of antinationalism that he believes have become apparent. In Murakami's view, nationalism, originally a product of the nation-states that emerged in Western Europe beginning about the sixteenth century, can exist only when accompanied by a nation-state system—that is, a regional or international order that "accommodates" nation-states, which Murakami stresses had come into place in Europe following the Treaty of Westphalia of 1648. Most significantly, the concepts of nation-states and the nation-state system of Europe were based on a multiple-justice system: no nation claimed a monopoly of justice, and wars—*bellum nonjustum* or nonjust wars—were fought to maintain the balance of power, while observing the "rules" of war. The basic concept of nonjust war was severely tested by the First World War, which required participating nations to mobilize their citizens in the name of a single, unchallengeable justice. The concept of multiple justices or of nonjust wars became bankrupt at the Nuremberg and Tokyo trials, which condemned the leaders of the vanquished for having waged an unjust war. One result was the invocation of the doctrine of just war by the United States (and NATO) and the USSR during the cold war, as was also done in the wars waged by the imperialists to establish colonies and in the wars of liberation by the colonies against the colonial powers after the end of the Second World War.

Thus, Murakami argues, what has occurred since the end of the cold war (since the end of the period during which the concept of just war defined the international order) is a search for the new doctrine that is necessary to establish a new nation-state system or a new world order. That we are searching for such an order is evidenced in the fact that wars and regional conflicts proliferate around the globe today, many due to a third wave of nationalism, following those that occurred after each of the two world wars. The nationalism of today will remain poorly defined unless and until a new world order that can accommodate it is created. The future of antinationalism or transnationalism—"some form of the denial of the nation-state before proceeding toward internationalism" as an antithesis of nationalism—remains "murky indeed" in the absence of such a new order.

Murakami also sees two other very significant obstacles to transnationalism. One is the undeniably persistent salience of "natio" (a Latin root of "nation"), which Murakami uses to mean the shared sociocultural values, consciousness, and identity of each ethnic group or people because of a common history, language, and literature. He sees this persistence despite the "borderlessness" that has increased in many dimensions. The other obstacle is the unrealistic but lingering "nostalgia" for the creation of a world-state and the "psychological inertia" due to the "happy memories" of the past century during which the creation of nation-states and industrialization proceeded hand in hand.

Industrialism–Anti-industrialism

A very crucial reason for the need for "polymorphic liberalism" is added in Murakami's third argument, the analysis of the axis of industrialism-anti-industrialism. Murakami's discussion of this axis can best be seen to consist of two segments. One is an analysis of the confrontation of values and visions between industrialism and anti-industrialism. The main proponents of the latter include some in the "new left" and in the environmentalist movement and those who see the limits of science and technology in the profound ethical and medical issues raised by continuing industrialization. The second segment is an extended analysis of the increasing conflicts now evident between two types of political economies: those that are, in principle, liberal-classical-economic in their fundamental orientation and willing to sacrifice economic growth for the sake of the orientation; and those adopting "developmentalism" (discussed further below) in which government plays crucial roles in promoting economic growth.

Murakami sees what he calls transindustrialism—an orientation that contains elements of anti-industrialism and attempts to pursue a higher order of industrialization—as a synthesis between industrialism (including superindustrialism, which is based on the production of information instead of machinery and energy) and anti-industrialism. Thus, this second segment of his analysis on this axis can be seen as his effort to examine how transindustrialization can be best achieved by solving the fundamental political and economic conflicts we observe today between the two types of political economies. Murakami analyzes these conflicts at length because they are important in developing other arguments in the book, including defining and defending the need for polymorphic liberalism. For the sake of expositional clarity and convenience, let me summarize Murakami's extensive political and economic analyses (including his somewhat technical economic analysis) of the conflicts as follows.

1. To understand the conflicts between the liberal-classical and developmentalist economies, one must be aware of the undeniable fact that the costs of industrial production have been declining, historically since the beginning of industrialization and ever more rapidly today as technological progress continues at an accelerated pace. This is why industrial economies have grown and real wages risen as a trend. Alfred Marshall was aware of this reality of decreasing cost (for reasons that are both internal and external to firms) but was not able to offer a theoretically satisfactory answer to the question that came to be known as "Marshall's problem": when costs are decreasing, why do markets remain competitive? In other words, why aren't they dominated by monopolists or collusive oligopolists? This is a question that neither classical economists, such as David Ricardo, nor neoclassical economists have been able to answer satisfactorily.

For Murakami, the principal reason for the failure to answer this question resides in the essential character of neoclassical economic theory, which is a theory for developed capitalist economies and not one that explains industrialization. In analyzing industrialization, what is central is not the stability and equilibrating trends—the homeostatic character—of markets and the economy, but decreasing cost and the dynamically changing character of markets and the economy, which necessarily result from technological progress. The ad hoc efforts made by neoclassical economists to deal with decreasing costs (such as "learning by doing") cannot but remain unsatisfactory because technological change—the most salient change in the process of industrialization—remains "exogenous" to the theory.

2. Developmentalism, as Murakami defines and analyzes it, is a political-economic system that attempts to take maximum advantage of decreasing costs by adopting various types of activist industrial policy while also implementing policies to redistribute income (intended to minimize unequal distribution resulting from industrialization), to promote education, and to achieve other social, political, and economic goals. The most critical industrial policy is "targeting" industries that are best able to adopt new technology. To achieve successful targeting, one possibly useful policy is to permit firms adopting new technology (thus reducing costs rapidly) to form price cartels under specific conditions, delineated carefully by Murakami, so that what amounts to "domestic dumping" by an early entrant to a market does not occur. The most important fact of developmentalism is that its micro- and macroeconomic, as well as social, policies enable firms and individuals to have the long-term perspective that is essential in allocating resources to maximize economic performance over time.

I should stress here that the preceding is far from an adequate summary of Murakami's analysis of developmentalism. He pays close attention to the finer technical points that are necessary in challenging the well-developed body of neoclassical theory and contrasts the performance and policies of the economies of nations in Asia and Latin America.

3. In the above analysis, Murakami does not argue that one type of political economy is "superior" to another. For him, developmentalism is a historical, transitory, "catch-up" stage of industrialization, and he believes that each type of political economy has distinct strengths and weaknesses. This is why, for example, Murakami is extremely critical of Japan's retaining various developmental policies after it is well past the "catching-up" stage. He is also aware that despite all that developmentalism can do to promote the adoption of new technology and all that this implies for the growth of an economy, political intervention, once begun, tends to increase, along with political and economic costs, and becomes difficult to terminate even after the justification for it ceases to exist. For all the very real shortcomings of the ideology and theory of liberal-classical political economies both as "paramount rules for human beings" and economic theory, nations that adhere to this liberal ideology are free of the risk and costs of developmentalism noted above and require no world government or global regulating mechanism like that required for developmentalism. What must not be missed in reading Murakami's analyses of developmen-

talism and classical liberalism is that his advocacy of industrial policy is based not on an ideological position but on a historical analysis of industrialization.

4. Murakami allocates significant space to argue that the theory of hegemonic stability, despite the valiant effort of its proponents, remains an ad hoc theory in need of substantive reformulation. The task, Murakami believes, must begin with a more rigorous analysis of what a state is and with an attempt to offer a coherent analysis of the "dynamics of changes in national power" or of the real character and significance of both the dynamics of technological change and developmentalism. The task is to deal more adequately with the implications of the ongoing political and economic conflicts between the classical economies and developmentalist economies and with the complex character and significance of the "public good" supplied by a hegemon and/or by leading nations. Part of his reformulation of the theory of hegemonic stability is found in his polymorphic liberalism and part in his discussion of American hegemony, the future of which, he believes, will be determined by whether American society "generates the ideology and ideals" needed to undertake the political and economic reforms necessary in reviving its leadership, the strength of which is no longer determined only by economic and military power.

Equality-Liberty

Murakami's fourth argument is presented in his analysis of the last of the three axes, that of equality-liberty. Close attention must be paid to his discussions of this axis because they offer underpinnings indispensable to better understanding his analyses of the preceding two axes. This analysis has two dimensions: within a nation and between nations. In the relations between nations, Murakami places substantial emphasis on the issues between North and South.

For Murakami, the most crucial issue in this axis is the ability of democracy to achieve an equality of opportunity for individuals without being transformed into a tool for bringing about equality of outcome, forced by a "mechanical system" of majority votes. Reviewing at length the histories of Western nations and the views expressed by past thinkers of liberalism and parliamentary democracy as well as reflecting on the effects of technologism and developmentalism on equality and liberty, Murakami stresses the indispensability of "debate." We should not make the mistake of justifying equality of outcome in the way typified in Marxism, which "inflicted a mortal wound to the democracy of debate" by the concept of class struggle. Rather, what must be attempted, Murakami argues, is a debate that is based on polymorphic liberalism and that includes "commensurability." By commensurability he does not mean relativism but "mutual toleration" or "understanding"; the real meanings are made clearer in his discussion of the differing worldviews of peoples.

Without such debates, Murakami argues, we will be unable to control the powerful force for equality of outcome in mass democracy, thus unable to maintain or achieve true democracy, within each nation and among the nations, especially between North and South. Reviewing the history of exploitation of the South by the industrial, imperialist North, his criticism of the latter is stinging. To recompense at least in part for their exploitation and to make the world truly democratic, Murakami suggests many actions that the leading industrial nations should take. The most important is adoption of a rule-based international trade regime that explicitly sanctions the developmentalism of the South.

East and West

No less significant in underpinning all of the preceding analyses of the three axes, and thus shaping Murakami's vision in a fundamental way for the future, is his fifth argument: (1) the basic orientation, philosophical and ideological, of the West is "transcendental" while that of the East is "hermeneutic," and each orientation in diverse ways determined its respective worldview, or *Weltanschauung*, and hence the belief systems and actions that are based on it; and (2) although the transcendental orientation in Western thought shaped the character of the dominant Western civilization with its superior technology and power in the past few centuries, the world today can best benefit if it recognizes what Murakami believes are the fundamental differences in *Weltanschauung* existing between East and West and adopts polymorphic liberalism, which can best accommodate the reality of diversity. In discussing this diversity, Murakami uses the East, typified by East Asia, and the West of Europe and North America in a very broad sense and at times almost metaphorically. The boundaries between the two change over time from the period of archaic religions to the present.

What Murakami means by transcendental and hermeneutic orientations and the thoughts and actions reflecting them in East and West can be glimpsed in the following. In its original philosophical meaning, Murakami explains, transcendental reflection meant that the "self" takes up a position that transcends "naive consciousness" and tries to relativize, or subordinate, the naive consciousness. In contrast, hermeneutic reflection means that "the higher-order (postreflective) self is recalled to the lower-order (prereflective) self in the system it has just transcended, and the new and old images of the world are made to overlap." He goes on to show that this difference has far-reaching effects on how the peoples of East and West see and interpret the world surrounding them and therefore how they think and act.

For example, Christianity has a unique structure in that Jesus was a man who actually lived, but what became the key to that faith was the absolute nature of his existence as the son of God, a man who transcended all other men. In contrast, what is fundamental in Buddhism is its abstract principle of "origin"—the principle that all beings necessarily depend on others and exist in relativity with others. In short, in the East of Buddhism (and Confucianism, which is also hermeneutic in the same sense), *Lebenswelt* (the everyday world) or the context of day-to-day existence is far more important than in the West, the transcendental orientation of which is exemplified by the structure of Christianity.

Murakami's intent in engaging in these discussions (which I am greatly simplifying here) is of course to discuss the significance of this diversity in our efforts to solve the challenges the world faces today. The point he emphasizes in his erudite comparisons and contrasts of the two philosophical orientations is unmistakable: namely, we must be aware of how human beings differ in perceiving their *Lebenswelt*; to increase "commensurability" and so be able to march into the next century guided by the vision of polymorphic liberalism, we must, Murakami is convinced, recognize and understand this diversity.

Based on these principal arguments on polymorphic liberalism, on the three axes, and on his analyses of the contrasting orientations of transcendental and hermeneutic *Weltanschauung*, Murakami offers his vision of how we must attempt to solve the challenges we face today. Murakami phrases these challenges as a single "huge" question: how is it possible for nations to continue to industrialize and still maintain a stable and harmonious world order when that process necessarily entails the danger of differing paces of development for each nation and all of the consequences? His answer consists of two specific efforts that he implores the nations of the world, especially the leading ones, to make and of his hope that the world will replace progressivism with polymorphic liberalism as its principal guiding ideology or vision.

One effort that must be made is to create a world security system based on what he calls "shared roofs," and the other is to adopt "a rule-based world trade regime." The first effort is to create regional security alliances that have a hegemonic nation (and/or its regional equivalent) as a shared roof. By this Murakami means that the United States and Russia should enter into various regional security alliances and act as the "shared roof" over regional alliances so that political and military conflicts among the members of each alliance as well as between alliances can be minimized or prevented. Although he speaks of Russia providing such a roof over alliances among republics of the former Soviet Union and others that were formerly its "clients" elsewhere, the candidate he sees able to perform this role most effectively is the United States. Murakami's vision is for the United States to provide "shared roofs" over, for example, ASEAN, Arab states and Israel, Latin American states, and Europe by extending or strengthening various existing alliances in which the United States is the principal participant.

For Murakami, there exists no viable alternative to alliances with shared roofs that are pragmatic (dealing with security as well economic issues on the basis of explicitly stated rules), pluralistic, and open (respecting "nation" and promoting "commensurability"). The United Nations, for reasons he examines in detail, is not structurally able to provide international security, and regional alliances without a shared roof are prone to intraregional conflicts. Although he recognizes many trade-offs involved in his suggestion, Murakami hopes that shared-roof alliances can be more pragmatic and open than the United Nations.

What Murakami means by a rule-based world trade regime, embodying polymorphic economic liberalism, is an international regime with the following principal rules: (1) the developmentalism of "follower" (developing) nations is explicitly sanctioned; (2) every effort, including the virtual abolition of patent rights, is made to maximize the flow of technology from the leading (developed) nations to follower nations; (3) no leading nation engages in developmentalism; and (4) no nation, be it a follower or a leader, limits access to its markets even though there may be some distinctive characteristics in each nation's rules of market. Among several other rules that Murakami would like to see adopted, one of the most important is international "sunset" rules that terminate, by agreement, developmental measures for specific industries that have become internationally competitive. As his careful discussion relating to this rule-based international trade regime reveals, he is fully aware of the ambitious nature of the regime he proposes and of the political and technical difficulties involved. In reacting to his proposal, we must keep in mind his forceful arguments on the need to recognize that fundamental conflicts exist between the liberal-classical economic system and developmentalism—as evidenced by many of the trade conflicts involving Japan, the newly developing economies of Asia, the United States, and European economies—precisely because of our inability or unwillingness to adopt a regime based on this realization.

When we have become acquainted with his closely intertwined analyses in five parts and familiar with his visions of the world with "shared roofs" over regional alliances and with the "rule-based international trade regime" that limits trade conflicts, we realize that we know what Murakami means by polymorphic liberalism. He does not define the term because there is no need for him to do so. A central thrust of this book is that polymorphic liberalism with a new and wider vision must replace the liberalism that originated in the Enlightenment, supported by science, technology, and industrialization as well as the classical economics of developed capitalism. Included in that vision are the realizations that as a transitory stage of industrialization, developmentalism must be recognized and even aided, and that the differences among peoples will continue to exist because of the diversity in their "natio" and all that implies.

All of the preceding, however, covers no more than the bare bones of this seminal work, neglecting many other substantive contributions.

Among these contributions are (1) thoughtful discussions, found in many chapters, of the United States, which reveal Murakami's deep admiration for American institutions and ideology, despite the harsh criticisms he makes of the lack of political will demonstrated in the recent failures of macroeconomic policy and the inability to rectify these failures; (2) extended historical and critical analyses of the United Nations (as noted above), the League of Nations, international regimes, and the concept of and issues relating to "international public good"; (3) careful historical analyses of "conservatism" vis-à-vis progressivism that lead him to characterize his vision of polymorphic liberalism as "meta-conservatism"; (4) broad but important characterizations and analyses of century-long "technological paradigms" providing a crucial foundation for his analysis of developmentalism and its significance to the world trade regime; (5) at times somewhat technical but illuminating dissections of macroeconomic analyses, especially relating to international trade and foreign direct investment and to Keynesian policies; and (6) broad, historical analyses that attempt to examine various political and economic problems faced by the European Union and Asian and Latin American nations.

Although I have resisted the temptation to lengthen the above list or elaborate on some items, I must extend this part of this introduction by adding the following on Japan. For obvious reasons, including his familiarity with Japan and Japan's importance as a successful developmentalist, Murakami allocates more pages to Japan than to other topics listed above. For those who are interested in Japan, this is an important book. In discussing Japan, the foci of Murakami's analyses are (1) the reasons for Japan's pursuit of developmentalism since the Meiji period and the institutions and practices developed to succeed in the pursuit; (2) the motivations for and characteristics of Japan's "instinctive" pacifism; and (3) the substantial political and economic problems due to the successful pursuit of developmentalism and pacifism—in other words, the current political confusion and the stubborn bureaucratic power at home and the "Japan problem" in the world community.

His discussion of Japan offers thoughtful explanations and justification for many of Japan's policies and institutions (including its industrial policy and many aspects of its enterprise groups or *keiretsu*) that must be carefully read by critics of these policies and institutions. It also contains strong criticism of numerous developmentalist institutions and practices that remain today in Japan. Murakami is especially harsh in his criticism of the reluctance or inability of the bureaucracy to relinquish its power and of Japan's being a lightly armed economic superpower using its official developmental assistance (ODA) to developing nations as scutage. To Murakami, the success or failure of Japan's developmentalism depends on Japan's ability to eliminate the remaining institutions and practices of developmentalism rapidly and thoroughly and to take the necessary steps, including a change in its constitution (specifically, to Article 9), to enable it to become an active, "trusted," and responsible member of the international community, discharging the obligations and responsibilities of an economic giant.

Reactions to Murakami's analyses of Japan will undoubtedly be diverse, especially because of the significant and unexpected political developments in Japan in the early 1990s. However, much is lost by reading his analyses as those offered by a Japanese scholar attempting to justify Japan's policies and institutions; rather, his analyses of Japan should be scrutinized as those made by an exceptional social scientist who happened to be Japanese. This observation applies especially to his discussions of Japan's "instinctive" pacifism and the U.S.-Japan trade conflict.

Despite, as well as because of, the scope of this book, many scholars in several disciplines, especially specialists of the numerous topics and issues analyzed by Murakami, will be stimulated to react to his analyses and visions. Among such specialists, I particularly have in mind those political scientists who study the world order and security issues, the meaning and roles of the state, the multifaceted linkages between the domestic and international political economy, and various other international political-economic issues; those economists who are contributing fresh insights to the roles of technology in economic growth and international trade and investment and the analyses of history and institutions in determining economic performance; and those social scientists and historians who have expertise in the various regions of the world discussed by Murakami.

These specialists and others (including experts on topics and issues discussed by Murakami but outside my competence) will agree or disagree with many parts of this book and criticize various parts of his analyses. Some criticisms will undoubtedly be strong and even vehement. I am confident this book will receive much attention from international scholars in several disciplines. When this happens, Murakami's determined effort, literally in his final days, to revise his book for English readers will be fully rewarded.

An Anticlassical Political-Economic Analysis

A VISION FOR THE NEXT CENTURY

CHAPTER I

On Progress

Progress and Progressivism

At the end of the twentieth century, we are confronted once again with the need to consider the question of what progress is or was. As illustrated by the English phrase "in progress," the word progress originally meant simply forward movement (together with time), and there was no judgment of good or bad. The establishment of progress as a concept with a positive value in fact happened only in the wake of Enlightenment thought in eighteenth-century Europe. Of course, if one were to denote as progress in a broad sense the advancement toward ultimate ideals such as truth, good, and beauty, then there is no doubt that believing in this possibility is a fundamental condition of human existence. Everyone has had a blissful moment. When we remember the sensation of absolute happiness and contentment felt in these moments, then surely we can see this yearning for an ultimate ideal state—commonly called something like heaven, the land of the gods, paradise, or utopia—as something that sustains human beings. Even if one is uncertain of, and thus apprehensive about, one's ability to reach the ideal state, believing that one can aspire to do so is a minimum condition for human existence. When we understand progress in this extremely broad sense, there is not the slightest reason why we should deny the validity of the concept of progress, but if we use it in this sense, it would be better to call it "idealism." In both modern and ancient times, the psychological desire for progress—the element of idealism—has usually been hidden somewhere in the human heart.

However, since the Enlightenment, what modern people have become accustomed to calling "progress" is not the aspiration toward progress in this broad sense (idealism), but something more limited, with a narrower meaning, which one should perhaps call "progressivism." *Aspiration toward progress and progressivism are not the same.* This difference is not just a matter of definitions, of interest only to scholars; in a sense, this is the essential question confronting the contemporary world. In understanding modern thought since the Enlightenment and the industrial revolution, one could say somewhat abstractly that progressivism is the belief that there is an ultimate, unique, ideal social system—or at least a unique road leading toward that system—and that this system can be understood by human beings and realized in the present world through human effort. Put succinctly, progressivism means rushing headlong, undistracted and with confidence, on the road of progress that one has designed. Putting aside abstract definitions and searching for concrete examples from human history, only one example of progressivism has had sufficient duration, geographic breadth, and strength of influence to be called "civilization." It is none other than what we call "modern civilization," with its origins in Europe.

Modern civilization in this European model vigorously developed what we know as "natural science," which seeks to understand and explain physical nature; it used that knowledge to control nature and achieved splendid results in manufacturing various kinds of artifacts, represented by machinery (the complex of appliances that use inanimate power as their motive power). In short, it enriched the extent and scope of human activity. The material aspects of these kinds of achievements are now normally called "industrialization," but it was the power of this industrialization that in fact came to support and spread modern civilization. The development of science and the spread of political freedom are also much celebrated as results of modern progress. Certainly, during the European modern period, they stood with industrialization as a harmonious whole and in fact provided the seedbed for industrialization. If industrialization (and particularly the expansion of military power that accompanied it) had not sprung up from there, then modern civilization could surely not have had the ascendancy over the world it does today. In this sense, it was industrialization and progressivism, measured by the degree of the advance in industrialization, that provided modern civilization with its historically unprecedented power and deserved recognition.

We are all aware today of the various reconsiderations and criticisms of this modern civilization. Generally speaking, first to be noted are the arguments over the limits of nature: the limits on global resources and the global scale of environmental pollution that threatens human existence. Not a few see the end of industrialization in these developments. In this book, I divide nature into *the human body* and *the rest* and call the former "internal nature" and the latter "external nature." One could say that current warnings about resources and the environment point out limits on the latter. But this kind of criticism, concerned with the limits on "external nature," though it has significance as a political issue, is not as fundamental as it seems. If one looks at concrete examples, it is reasonable to believe from experience that even these kinds of limits can be surmounted by science and technology, by piecemeal engineering, or by a substitute technology. The history of science and technology, from one perspective, is the history of the appearance of substitute technologies dealing with the damage caused by deforestation, soot and smog, sewage, mining pollution, and so on. The much-talked-about problems of acid rain and excess emission of carbon dioxide are already technologically soluble; the problem is whether the political decision will be made to impose the substantial costs involved and to compel the conversion of the industrial structures. The treatment of nuclear waste is the most troubling of these problems, but even this is fundamentally nothing more than a problem of an increase in treatment and disposal costs.

Even for problems that may appear in the future, one cannot logically deny the possibility of solutions through piecemeal engineering. For example, were nuclear fusion or superconductivity at ambient temperature to be realized, almost all the problems with which people are now concerned could be solved. Even the science fiction dream of expansion into space cannot be completely dismissed. Of course I am not here arguing for easy optimism in science and technology. It is obvious that there is no guarantee that these new supertechnologies will materialize. However, it is equally the case that no one can scientifically deny the possibility of nuclear fusion or superconductivity at ambient temperature. In short, we human beings are as yet unable to make an infallible judgment as to the general tolerance levels of external nature, much less give concrete examples.

Those who advocate making scientifically precise judgments on these kinds of limits and taking appropriate countermeasures should perhaps remember Ludwig Wittgenstein's aphorism, "By having come to believe that they 'have seen the limits of human knowledge,' people then delude themselves that they can see beyond those limits."[1] That is to say, with this kind of advocacy, criticism of science and technology has returned once again to scientific and technological thought. The arguments that are being made at present about the limits of external nature are an amalgam of scientific judgments and revelational visions; though they may heighten to some degree our psychological anxiety, they may also stimulate our efforts at piecemeal engineering. It is possible that the arguments about the limits of external nature may contribute to changes in the present political-economic system. Yet I cannot believe that these arguments alone have the power to deal an intellectual death blow to modern civilization.

The limits of modern civilization are detectable not only in external nature. In internal nature too—that is, in the human body—different kinds of limits are appearing, and one can believe that it is there, rather than in external nature, that the limits of "progressivist" thought are more quickly becoming critical. Certainly science and technology have come to respond well to the physical demands of human beings, and it seems that a happy and harmonious relationship has been established. But in the advanced consumer societies we have recently begun to hear that no human desires remain unfulfilled. Of course such an as-yet limited perception of society will not be a force for change in our fundamental thinking. This perception, however, is a serious omen of deeper disharmony yet to arise.

For human beings, physically speaking, the most serious concerns are old age, sickness, and death. Modern medicine, which has celebrated remarkable achievements in these areas, continues to deal with vexing problems related to induced abortion, organ transplantation, irreversible comas, euthanasia, and genetic engineering. When does a fetus become a human being? Is a person who has had most of his or her organs replaced the same person? Is a person who survives by relying on life-support apparatus a human being? Is the ability to preserve life by interfering with genes and immune systems evidence of progress? The problems connected with internal nature, evident in these examples, do not have the same quality as the problems associated with the limitations on external nature. It is not a matter of running up against limits, but of becoming unable to define what is meant by humans (and human life) unless we ourselves place limits on the definition. As the philosopher Martin Heidegger has observed, technology destroys the inherent nature of living things.[2] The problems humans face are far from illusory. Among old people, patients, and doctors, for example, there is no doubting the acuteness of the problem. Good evidence is found in keen debates on medical ethics, which show that the concept of progress is running up against a certain ideological wall.

Gradually becoming apparent, as I mention again below, is a suspicion toward the "subject-object dichotomy" established by René Descartes, or the "mind-body dichotomy"—that is, an anxiety about the "anthropocentrism" of the European modern age, which posits that all objects may be used as means for the ends of human beings. Is it acceptable to regard fetuses, organs, and even genes as tools for human subjects—that is, for human minds? The propriety of the conception of modern progress that believes subjects and objects need to be separated, and for the former to control the latter, is being questioned today in the medical field where subject and object, and mind and body, are most intimately intertwined.

This problem of the intertwining of subject and object is not confined to medicine. In the field of political economy, to use the approach of G. H. Mead, the intertwining of the subjective "I" and the objective "me"—that is, of the individual nature and group nature of human beings—points to the heart to the problem.[3] Even the most extreme advocate, however much he averts his attention from the reality of political economy, is not permitted to completely ignore either of the two natures; each society or civilization has its own systematic method for striking a balance between them. In modern civilization, this systematic method appears in the twin frameworks of a market economy (capitalism) and the nation-state, and these sustain industrialization. No one can deny this central fact of modern civilization. However, as I show below, a contradiction is buried in these two systematic frameworks. While people can differ as to whether this kind of contradiction exists, in this book I want to make clear that this contradiction is being disclosed above all in the area of international relations. The limits to modern civilization and to progressivism are coming into sight. I believe that modern civilization, the motive force of which has been industrialization, and the progressive thought that has sustained it are both clearly faced with an extremely difficult set of circumstances.

There may be those who note that the meaning is very broad when I argue about "progressivism" in this manner. For example, when progressivism is mentioned in everyday conversation, many—at least in Europe and Japan—are reminded of Marxist-Leninist socialist thought. (In postwar Japan there were many occasions when *kakushinteki*, meaning "progressive" or "reformist," was used as an equivalent for "revisionist," containing a strong nuance of "revolutionary.") This Marxist-Leninist socialist thought advocated the adoption of a planned economy in place of a market economy and insisted on the need for the abolition of the nation-state as a tool of class control. As the collapse of the Soviet Union and the East European bloc has demonstrated, this way of thinking has disclosed tragic contradictions when confronted by liberalism, environmentalism, and industrialization. Given that much ink has already been spilled on the subject, it should not be necessary to explain that progressivism in this narrow sense has come to a dead end. By completely repudiating the twin pillars of a market economy and the nation-state, the attempt at progressivism that tried to oppose the transformation from the nineteenth to the twentieth century has come to an end. Whether in the former Soviet Union or in China, the possibility of reverting to the old system is nil.

However, the twentieth-century version of progressivism was not limited to the extreme form of the planned economy under a one-party dictatorship, as in the Soviet Union and the Eastern bloc. Socialist thought, in the diluted form of an equalization of income distribution and a welfare-state policy, had substantial influence on the advanced industrial countries; one could say that, particularly after the Second World War, it played a leading role in policy formation. Among political parties, the Labour party in the United Kingdom, the Social Democratic party (SPD) in West Germany, the Socialist party in France, the social democratic parties in northern Europe, and, though somewhat irregular (inasmuch as it does not itself acknowledge the influence of socialist thought), the Democratic party in the United States, particularly its so-called liberal wing, are all examples of this. These parties have not always had a long hold on political power, but the policies they advocated have had strong influence even on conservative administrations and have effected the phenomenon of "big government" common to the advanced countries. In short, progressivism, transformed from its nineteenth-century incarnation, with the market economy and the nation-state as its foundations, into a twentieth-century version that had as its aim the overcoming of its weak points, and while involving various trials and errors, has given rise to every sort of hybrid. However, the consistent theme among all these, as mentioned above, is the belief that the realization of an ideal society with a set of predetermined characteristics is possible. We now face the general question of whether or not we can maintain this unambiguous future orientation.

In order to proceed, let us recall again the abstract definition mentioned above: progressivism has been the belief in the uniqueness, cognizability, and realizability of an ultimate order (and/or a path toward that). Putting together these three characteristics generates a mode of thought close to determinism about the history of humankind and society. To insist that progress converge on a single path is to deny completely the possibility of its branching out in multiple directions. But for human beings, given the problems and dilemmas of freedom (for example, the problem of consciously subverting predictions), the logic of determinism cannot be foolproof. Thus it is better to separate the views based on progressivism and the strict determinism seen in classical physics. In this sense, it is probably better to talk of progressivism as "quasi-determinism."[4]

Either way, however, progressivism is close to determinism. And what has been generated from it is a belief in unitary—unilinear—progress that results in raising expectations of a promising future society and dismissing the past as uncivilized and ignorant.[5] In comparative social theory, this belief in unitary progress leads to so-called convergence theory, which holds that all societies are approaching a single ideal form. In the context of synchronic comparative social theory, a theory of diachronic developmental stages is translated into a rank ordering of countries. That is, all countries are given a rank corresponding to their degree of developmental progress, and between the various countries there is established a one-way relationship from the imitated to the imitators—a unitary rank ordering of civilization(s) from developed to developing. This has been and still is the dominant image of international relations.

For example, even the Japanese, under the strong influence of progressivist thought in the century since the opening of the country, have continued to say, "We are inferior to the advanced countries, we are premodern and thus backward; let us learn from the example of the advanced countries." Intellectuals, who had little direct influence over those holding political power in postwar Japan, saw in relentlessly exposing the backwardness and deformity of Japanese society both a reason for their own existence and a chance for greater political influence; but even among bureaucrats and managers, this inferiority complex was deeply rooted. Of course, such phenomena are not limited to Japan; given that they are typical indications of the influence of progressivism in late-developing countries, the same tendency can be seen to some extent in all countries that are late in modernizing. In many cases this ideological pressure generates serious friction with the traditional culture in countries with non-Western origins, and frequently it can determine the success or failure of catch-up development. However, given that progressivism itself is now being forced to reflect on its own intellectual foundations, we may have to discard the existing stereotypical response that sees the source of various evils in premodern remnants and keeps repeating, "Let us learn from the example of developed countries."

This is not because—at least not solely because—Japan is now sufficiently "advanced." Rather, given that modern civilization continues to confront serious transformation, it is because there is a strong possibility that the road that directly, unilinearly led toward the advance of industrialization—which was the motive force of that civilization—is already no longer open for humanity. Thus, a farewell to progressivism may well have to be prescribed, not only for Japan but for all countries. Regardless of whether they are developed or developing, all countries will have to emerge from progressivism, grope for their own, pluralistic paths forward, rooted in their various individual experiences, and, in doing this, recognize the validity of each other's actions. Of course, there will still be many occasions when so-called late-developing countries will have to learn from developed countries, mainly in industrialization and science and technology. However, in their fundamental orientation, the international relations of imitator and imitated have no choice but to change gradually from a one-sided to a reciprocal model. That is, international relations too will have to change, as I discuss in the chapters to follow, from the existing one-sided and unifaceted pattern to a reciprocal and pluralistic form. For these changes to occur, the advanced countries must, above all else, discipline themselves to refrain from forcing on others the path they themselves have followed.

The Unrealism of Neoprogressivism

The momentum of the progressivism that has controlled us for two centuries or more is powerful indeed. The pattern of progressivist thought is deeply ingrained in the minds of all modern people. However, Marxist-Leninist progressivism (the twentieth-century pattern of modern progressivism) will disappear, as did the former Soviet Union that represented it. The combination of one-party dictatorship and a planned economy has clearly failed on almost all counts—including industrialization, liberalism, democracy, and environmentalism. There is still strong anticipation of the reappearance of progressivism in a new disguise. A number of fumbling attempts are being made at "neoprogressivism," trying to protect the logic of progressivism. In the advocacy of carrying democracy through to its conclusion (from an egalitarianism of rights to an egalitarianism of outcomes), of environmentalism, and, as a drastic example, of anti-industrialism, there is frequently a desire to bring about a revival of progressivism. There are a number of "new left" movements trying to inherit the mantle of progressivism from the "old left." In my opinion, however, today when industrialization and the progress of science and technology have become increasingly destabilizing, these kinds of advocacy are unable to provide us with a vision of an ideal order and have little likelihood of being realized. At the end of the twentieth century, we must believe that the conditions for establishing a new progressivism do not exist.

Though I am anticipating the argument I develop, let me comment simply on the examples of "neoprogressivist" advocacy mentioned above. For example, fully implementing democracy cannot but be the same as equality of outcomes (see Chapter 6), but is equality of outcomes something that can lead as expected to an ideal social order? Certainly there is usually majority support for equality of outcomes. This is almost the logical conclusion of a distribution curve of outcomes usually being an asymmetric distribution skewed to the left (for example, a normal logarithmic distribution). At the same time, however, it is certain that very few consider perfect equality of outcomes as an ultimate ideal. First, this is because people are keenly aware that the free action of each person generates unequal outcomes. Second, a large part of the advocacy of equality of outcomes is sustained by psychological difficulties with ostentation and envy, but, in fact, no one would try to build an ultimate ideal state on the basis of sentiments about envy and ostentation. Even so, for argument's sake, let us focus on the achievement of a perfect equality of outcomes. We would have to restrain each person's actions (particularly in industrialized economies) with a complicated, delicate system of regulation. Achieving equality of outcomes and liberalism in action is a contradiction. To eliminate this contradiction, in the end equality of outcomes cannot be mired in such secondary problems as those faced in determining the amount of the guaranteed minimum.[6] But there will be any number of opinions as to which is the appropriate minimum level of equality. Even the ordinary citizen, who may expect moderate equalization, does not want perfect equality. A unique ideal state (or its cognizability and realizability) does not follow from the logic of equality of outcomes.

As a second example, let us consider environmentalism. Here too opinion is confused as to what might be the ideal ecological environment for humankind. Even within present-day ecology, which is supposed to produce for us valuable knowledge on this issue, there is strong skepticism about the existence of a "climax" (a state of equilibrium among the various species) and encouragement to reconsider the simple hypotheses that posit that the diversity of species will bring about an equilibrium of ecological groups.[7] There is no ecological basis for the attempts—like those advocated in the natural history magazines—to save all species and exterminate none. The movements that advocate giving priority to and saving specific animals (such as whales and dolphins) have no theoretical foundation. Ecology cannot endorse the realizability of a unique order in which an equilibrium has been achieved among the species. It seems there are environmentalists who would regard an agricultural society as an ideal state, but in fact even an agricultural society is a state achieved to a great extent by human agency and certainly is not an unchanging ideal order. If we were to abandon agriculture, then relations between organisms would be thrown into upheaval. The preservation of the tropical rain forests is much talked about at present, but it was the former agriculturists who destroyed the forests on the Eurasian continent, and it is their descendants who have built today's industrial civilization.

Thus, because of the appearance of humanity since the agricultural revolution—a species that is willful and capable of altering ecological order—the existence of a "climax" cannot but be even more uncertain a possibility than in a world of nature with no human beings. However, in recent years there seem to be too many hasty arguments advocating harmony with nature while failing to give due recognition to the disturbing, active nature of this human species. Environmentalism is possible and meaningful if one means by it only "partial engineering" to make the world a little greener or a little less polluted, but one should not expect it to be capable of providing a concept of a unique and ultimate ideal state that could be used to make environmentalism the basis of progressivism.

In a similar sense, there are also a great number of meanings of anti-industrialization. There are not a few who believe that one can see a modification of industrialism in the shift from the production of physical assets, which takes nature outside human beings as its object, to the production of services, which caters to the physical desires mostly of human beings, and even from this to the production of information, which caters to human thought.[8] However, it seems there is no agreement on the exact form the development of information production should take. For example, is the production of information centered on natural science or on humanistic culture, or should it be focused on something far more abstract? And even if we are certain of a desired form of the production of information, can there be a dynamics of thought that guarantees convergence toward that form? If convergence does not occur naturally, are we to be allowed to bring it about forcefully by adopting measures to control thought? Above all, would not a choice of a specific desired form of information production mean the death of human intellectual activity? When thought about in terms of centuries, I agree that an ideology will appear that will in some sense replace industrialization. But the ideology that follows industrialization will not be an anti-industrialist progressivism; it must be an ideology that has in some form evolved from progressivism itself.

In general, to describe a unique, ideal order—emerging as a direct extension of democracy, environmentalism, or anti-industrialism, inasmuch as it is premised on freedom of thought—is very difficult. I have already mentioned that carrying democracy through to its conclusion (a society of equal outcomes) may well be nothing more than a fearful anticlimax. Again, in environmentalism and anti-industrialism—at least at the level spoken of today—even if one can explore single issues, the ability does not exist to describe persuasively a unique order. It was Marx who proudly proclaimed he had raised progressivism "from a fancy to a science," but all the above-mentioned attempts to establish a neoprogressivism get no further than a somewhat irresponsible "fancy." Of democracy, environmentalism, anti-industrialism, and, if one were to add to these, pacifism (though one might object to their characterization as "fancies"), none can "scientifically" prepare a plan for an ideal state. There is not even rough agreement on, let alone a scientific basis for, the cognizability and realizability of a unique order that transcends our modern concepts.

In short, there is increasing likelihood of conflict between the attempts to establish a new progressivism and freedom of thought in its intrinsic sense, and these "fanciful" propositions lack strict awareness of this fact. In other words, we are once again faced with a dilemma in which the essential human impulse toward self-transcendence (explained below) continues to set back the unconditional convergence of thought. The greatest "fancifulness" in the various propositions of the new progressivism lies in the fact that confrontation with this dilemma is being avoided. This is another way of saying that the conflict between progress and freedom is once again becoming a problem. In modern progressivism to date it has been believed that the advance of science and industrialization would increase human freedom (in fact, freedom of action). Now, however, doubts have begun to surface as to whether the advance of industrialization or science and technology is connected to the spread of the freedom of human action, and, beyond this, there are even more serious doubts about freedom of thought. Bringing about a revival of progressivism as something above the advance of industrialization, and of science and technology, will require fundamentally reexamining the existing relationship between freedom and progress, on which little careful analysis has been done. If we decide to produce forcibly a new progressivism, we shall get stuck in the rut of advocating an order that can be sustained only by exercising strong political power, and we shall be confronted with the fundamental dilemma of whether to throw out progressivism or true liberalism.

However, when we talk about transcending or discarding progressivism—here to be understood in a broad sense—there may well be resistance if there is nothing left but a future in which the desire for progress has been extinguished. But let me repeat: the renunciation of progressivism is not the renunciation of progress or the renunciation of ideals. The reckless pursuit of a present utopia, as seen in progressivism, is not the only form of idealism. If we are to think of *progress that is not progressivism*, there has to be a mega-concept that can transcend the swarm of ideas surrounding progress. Without this, the renunciation of progressivism can be nothing but the renunciation of progress. Traditionally, the *Weltreligionen* (world religions) or "historical religions" that appeared around 1000 B.C. supplied this kind of mega-concept. Many scholars, such as Arnold Toynbee, emphasize the need for a revival of the world religions in order to overcome the modern progressivism. Islamic fundamentalists may well now hold the same opinion, and the springing up in all countries of new religions is probably a symptom of this. Having a feeling of reverence not only for the "profane" of this world but also for the "sacred" that transcends this world is perhaps a necessary condition for achieving a progress that is not progressivism.[9] However, even if we were to seek such a mega-concept among the world religions, at least in the existing sense, our prospects of success are at best meager. This is because those religions have been intolerant of freedom of thought.

Reconsidering Liberalism

To repeat, progressivism was optimism about the cognizability and realizability of a single order. A progress that is not progressivism, even if the ideal ordered state is something indistinct and the prospects of its being realized in this world are weak, is surely nothing other than a pseudonym for the feeling of tension sensed in the pursuit of ideals. However, this seeking too can only be within the limits (ability) of human nature. To believe that some kind of road toward the ideal will open up, even in the midst of those natural limits, is what I believe to be the smallest necessary optimism for human beings. What then is this human nature?

Once again I wish to emphasize that human beings are characterized by the impulse toward freedom, particularly the impulse toward freedom of thought. It can also be called the impulse toward self-transcendence, and many philosophers call it "self-reference." That is, it is the labor of trying continually to overcome the world image one holds and to make it anew; it could also be called the impulse to reflection or self-examination in the broadest sense. It is this labor of self-examination that separates human beings from other creatures. What enables human beings to do this is the development of the frontal lobes and expanded memory capacity. In a very broad or somewhat loose sense, this labor is one kind of human activism toward the world. Whether a blessing or not, it is the case that human beings cannot accept the world as it is but must inevitably try to make their world image anew. I believe that inasmuch as human beings are human, this active nature is something that cannot be extinguished, and when one tries to deny this, human nature itself becomes something one can no longer define. Whether for good or evil, there is no truth for

human beings other than creating and preserving this distinctive characteristic. In this sense, liberalism (or more precisely, as I say below, liberalism of thought) is the most important trait characterizing human beings.
To speak of liberalism may sound terribly old-fashioned. Certainly, even in
the nineteenth-century modern progressivism already mentioned, given
that liberalism in politics and economics was one of its critical supports,
liberalism was one of the most overused concepts. However, liberalism
in this nineteenth-century model, I believe, was still not liberalism in an
absolute sense. I am not trying to advocate classical liberalism as it was.

To turn again to history, liberalism in Europe was mainly defined in the
context of human action and thus was liberalism of action. In the context
of action the definition of freedom has a clarity that did not allow for pre-
varication, and there is a strong correlation between liberalism of action
and liberalism of thought. For example, when one is confined and tor-
tured, the movement of the human mind is usually severely restricted, and
one is deprived of freedom of thought. Intellectual activity is a phenomenon of both mind and body, and so it cannot usually be separated from the
body. In this sense, there is sufficient meaning in the European definition
of liberalism. The Anglo-Saxon thinkers in particular came to develop en-
thusiastically the theory of liberalism—Isaiah Berlin is an example in the
present age—but they emphasized strongly the freedom of action, so-called
negative freedom.[10] However, even if freedom of action is guaranteed, freedom of thought, or freedom of the mind, is not necessarily guaranteed.

For example, Buddhism advocates that, since the cause of suffering is
in voluntarism (this is in fact karma), discarding "adherence to self" is
necessary for true freedom of spirit (nirvana). Given that the world image
held by those who pursue wealth, seek power, and cling to passions is
narrow and rigid, they are ensnared by "negligence and diversion,"[11] and
there is a danger they will stray far from the pursuit of understanding the
ideal world (supreme Enlightenment). As everyone is aware, when people's
active nature is neglected in this way, one cannot deny the possibility of a
deviation from an ideal understanding of the truth. However, there is still
room for argument as to whether or not, according to Buddhism, one can
achieve true freedom of thought by depending solely on an effort to discard adherence to self. This is because this dependence signifies a great or
even excessive expectation in the potential of consciousness. For example,
Kūkai's concept of "this-worldly attainment of Buddhahood" in esoteric
Buddhism and Dōgen's "slipping-off of mind and body" in Zen are both
generated from this kind of expectation. However, as the struggles of Hina-
yana Buddhism show, at least for ordinary people, these are not things that
can be achieved easily. It is clear that both the European concept of behavioral freedom and the Asian concept of "intellectualistic" (Max Weber)—
or rather gnostic—freedom are approaches that one can take in the pursuit
of true freedom.[12]

To repeat, the fundamental condition for human existence is liberalism of thought, or liberalism of the mind. First, the self-transcendence of one's world image is an innate, uniquely human act. Second, however, with this there is usually a danger of bias or distortion, which people normally have a desire to escape.[13] In other words, though indistinct, there is for human beings a sense of direction toward an ideal order of truth. With this sense of direction, liberalism of thought becomes an ideal. But third, there is no guarantee that the results of this striving toward the ideal will converge directly—in this world—toward a single world image; contrary to expectations, they may diverge. The clear awareness of this fateful truth is still a serious problem for liberalism of thought. The advocacy of this liberalism of thought originates in human nature; it has deeper roots than merely modern thought and has surely been an undercurrent throughout human history. Progressivism, or a European-style active nature of human behavior, may or may not bring this fate to an end; liberalism of thought could be a universal guiding principle for humankind.

The argument presented in the following chapters is, one might say, a preliminary sketch that attempts to examine the kind of system or pattern of conduct in which such a true liberalism might be expressed. The contents of true liberalism should include nineteenth-century classical liberalism, but the two are not the same. After examining the contents of "modern progressivism," I draw out the implications of what form liberalism should take in future societies.

Conservatism is usually thought of as the opposite of progressivism. At first glance, it may seem that the aforementioned proposal of a parting from progressivism means a recommendation of conservatism. But it is not so simple. As Karl Mannheim pointed out, conservatism is a modern concept, established in the nineteenth century, and is not merely the principle of preserving the status quo, or anachronism, but a reaction against progressivism.[14] Conservatism does not deny that an ultimate ideal order can be imagined, and in that sense it is not antiprogressivism. Rather, its difference from progressivism is on the point that this ideal state cannot be thought to be instantly cognizable or realizable by human beings. Though people can progress, they may also occasionally regress. Thus humans look not only to the future but live with an affection for the past; they do not think of the past as a period of ignorance that must always be conquered by the future. This is conservatism as an intellectual position. The difference between optimism and pessimism about the possibilities of human potential—the difference between denial and approval of skepticism—is rooted in the opposition between progressivism and conservatism, and these two intellectual positions sum up the vicissitudes of the human intellect. While there is certainly antagonism contained in this relationship, the relationship between progressivism and conservatism is not one in which the retreat of one would mean the victory of the other, but rather a rivalry or dialectic, in the original sense of the word.

However, as I have mentioned before, one cannot deny that the driving force of modern society has been progressivism—the progressivism whose specific and substantial content has propelled industrialization. As Mannheim says, conservatism was established as a reaction to this. Modern progressivism began with the Enlightenment in the eighteenth century, took the form of an advocacy of nationalism and capitalism in the nineteenth, and in the twentieth changed into an emphasis on socialism—particularly of the Marxist school. Among these there was a consistent belief that human society was advancing toward a single ideal state. Though this progressivism changed its appearance, conservatism also changed the content of its emphasis in reaction to this, playing the role of critic to and brake on progressivism. In this sense, conservatism, as an intellectual position that reacts to change, is not something with a fixed content or something that ends with the principle of preserving the status quo.

In the United Kingdom, for example, the contents of policies changed among the very parties that represented conservatism—the Tory party, which opposed the Whig party, and the Conservative party, which opposes the Labour party. Even the conservative political parties introduced progressive ideas into their policies. The Conservative party led by Benjamin Disraeli, for example, legislated genuine electoral reform in the United Kingdom. Even after the Second World War, in the advanced industrialized countries the conservative parties for the most part skillfully prolonged their hold on political power while introducing progressive policies. Though one should perhaps note that conservatism in itself would not have assumed a major role, it played an indispensable supporting role in modern progress; progressivism and conservatism, together as a whole, sustained progressive civilization. In this sense conservatism too was an associate in the project of modern civilization.[15]

If one believes that progressive civilization will leave the stage, what will take its place? Two answers spring to mind. One is the formation of a neoprogressive civilization—that is, a revival of progressivism filled with new wine. However, as mentioned before, there is an extremely small possibility of this happening, and there may well be a need to change the wineskins themselves. Another answer is the possible appearance of something called a "conservative civilization." However, as I have been saying, given that conservatism in the strict sense is a supporting player to progressivism, it cannot take the leading role in a new antiprogressive civilization. Thus, this answer too is incorrect. One cannot, however, leave the discussion of this question at this, for the problem is surrounded by several subtle questions.

Among the stable societies in the premodern period, in many cases there was a strong tendency toward maintaining a static order. One can well imagine China, India, and Greece and Rome among the examples of this, but it is not appropriate to call these great civilizations conservative. As I argued earlier, an ideology that aims to maintain a fixed static order is not conservatism, or at least there is no need to call it conservatism.

In order to make the distinction, let us here call this tendency toward a static order "orthodoxy."[16] The so-called historical civilizations such as the Greek and Roman, the Indian, and the Chinese were all orthodox societies of this kind, and one can think of the Islamic empires and medieval Europe also as belonging to almost the same pattern.

In orthodox societies, criticism of the order was not permitted. It was stifled as heresy and so was not provided with a forum. In general either an indifference toward history (in the cases of India and medieval Europe) or a cyclical view of history (in the cases of Greece, Rome, and China) was dominant in these kinds of society. On the other hand, for conservatism, as a critical ideology in a society in which progress is being realized, the source of the critique is mainly found by looking back over history, and it does not slide into a reactionary ideal that seeks the revival of a static order. One can clearly distinguish between orthodoxy and conservatism in their receptivity to the dynamism of history. Thus, though premodern societies were orthodox, they were not conservative, and there has never yet been something called a "conservative civilization." Certainly, conservatism and orthodoxy share the common characteristic of pessimism or skepticism toward change brought about by human hands, and respect for those things inherited from the past; one can say that an orthodox civilization carries that characteristic through to completion and sees it as the highest ideal of a society. From the other angle, conservatism may play the role of preserving in the midst of modern culture that which could be said to be the germ of the culture nurtured in the orthodox civilizations of the past.

Thus, to date, one can be reasonably certain that a society that has been stable is either orthodox or progressive. However, there have been societies not optimistic about realizing an ideal order, even while they could clearly recognize that order. There were many examples of these societies, in which an eschatological way of thinking held sway, during the period when orthodox societies were declining. One might say that negative orthodoxy also belongs among these—such as that of Jewish society, which did not decline but continued to battle without discarding its beliefs in orthodoxy in the face of numerous misfortunes. In this case an ideology of a thousand-year kingdom and an eschatological view of history remained dominant. However, these declining societies or societies unavoidably subordinated cannot possess the stable influence that could be said to be equivalent to the authority of a civilization. In short, it is no exaggeration to say that the civilizations that have heretofore embellished human history are limited to the two cases of orthodoxy and progressivism—though there is only one example of the latter in modern civilization.

However, given the subtle relationship between progressivism and orthodoxy, they are not as antagonistic as they seem. On the point of believing, in some sense, in the realizability of an ideal order in this world, the difference is frequently very slight, and this difference may well be much smaller than that between conservatism and orthodoxy. To use a concept that I will explain gradually, both progressivism and orthodoxy are "transcendental." For example, when a certain country that has experienced a sudden rise to power believes it is continuously advancing toward an ideal order, that country, on a historical axis, is a progressive country striving toward progress. When that country believes it has fundamentally achieved an ideal order—at least in comparison with other countries— the belief gradually becomes orthodox *within the country*, and the country tries to build an "empire" *outside the country*, by spreading that order throughout the world. This historical dynamic can be easily seen in the great civilizations throughout history; it is "imperialism" in the original sense, and in this there is support for the concept of an ideal order, beyond mere military authority. In this sense, imperialism originally had to be an "imperialism of civilizations." Thus, a society that has experienced a sudden rise to power, and that has a progressive character, on reaching its peak gradually tries to transform into "orthodoxy + imperialism." In short, the dynamic of progressivism contains the possibility of turning from a temporally dynamic progressivism into a temporally static and spatially expansionist imperialism. This is possibly the general pattern for the creation of a civilization's imperialism; recently, the Soviet Union before its collapse was a good example of this, and one can also see similar symptoms in its antagonist, the postwar United States.

Thus, we should think of an orthodox and imperialist civilization as having the potential to replace a progressive rather than a conservative civilization. There have been recent attempts to suggest this progression. For example, the neoconservatism that appeared in the 1980s in the advanced industrial countries, with Ronald Reagan, Margaret Thatcher, and, similarly, Yasuhiro Nakasone, as its representatives, provides one prototype of this. This neoconservatism developed from the three pillars of an emphasis on advanced technology added to a respect for the classical framework of economic liberalism and nationalism. The neoconservative governments in the United States, the United Kingdom, and Japan, in aiming at superiority or victory in the cold war, continually emphasized a return to the "pure model" of capitalism and strengthened their ideological weapons, and they increased their military and economic superiority by attaching great importance to advanced technology. All of this was to strengthen or maintain the hegemonic system dominated by the United States.

This political style on the one hand projected great results after exposing the negative bequest from previous progressive policies (for example, big government and particularly the accumulation of budget deficits) and on the other decisively contributed to the economic and psychological collapse of the Soviet Union and the East European bloc. The historic significance of having put a stop to the post-1945 era dominated by a gentle progressivism is recognized in neoconservatism. However, the three central pillars of neoconservatism are not necessarily able to coexist without contradiction. In fact, the Reagan administration could not ensure simultaneously the enrichment of general national resources, centered on the military, and a reduction in the budget deficits. More generally, neoconservatism was nothing other than an emphasis on reviving the dynamism of industrialization, symbolized by advanced technology, from within a classical framework of economic liberalism and nationalism. However, as I will show below, its chances of success were low.

Despite this, following neoconservatism, a strong global chorus, even in Japan, has insisted that not only deregulation within the country but freedom of trade internationally should be carried through to completion. This emphasis on a pure capitalism (or neoconservatism) clearly means a return to the classical image of the order of modern civilization, and it is an attempt to seek a point of departure for a new orthodoxy. A representative example of this is the argument of Francis Fukuyama, in "The End of History?"[17] that the progress of history fundamentally achieved its goal in the nineteenth century and now there is nothing left but the "technical problem" of planning its realization and dissemination. This means a proclamation of the end of progress rather than the end of history, and what is suggested is no longer conservatism but simply orthodoxy. However, not only Fukuyama in the United States but a number of people in Japan are satisfied by emphasizing only the realization of the principles of the market economy (the opening of markets and the end of administrative guidance). If this is advocating the general validity of the pure model of capitalism for a country's internal and external affairs, then it is nothing more than an attempt at a new orthodoxy. However, whether this pure capitalism can materialize as expected—particularly in international relations on a global scale—is a question that contains substantial difficulties.

Capitalism has captivated people by initiating and developing industrialization, and especially by driving forward material progress. However, as I show in the following chapters, industrialization in the future will develop into new forms (such as what I call the phenomena of "developmentalism" and "informatization") and will probably generate concrete economic and political problems that pure capitalism cannot deal with. In short, it is very doubtful whether industrialization and this kind of orthodoxy can coexist. However, one cannot imagine that industrialization will die easily. Orthodoxy, at least from the present point of view, is an inappropriate ideology, even though one cannot completely deny the possibility of its reappearance in the future. There is little expectation that neoconservatism will turn from a supporting part to a leading role in civilization by becoming an orthodoxy. Thus neither a new progressivism nor even a new orthodoxy (in the field of international relations, as I note later, a quasi-imperialism in the name of a dominant national system) is an appropriate prescription for what is to come. The absence of ideas is clear, and even, for example, in the Clinton administration, which was established to reject the Reagan-Bush orthodoxy, the confusion of ideology is readily apparent. Similar symptoms are common to all the advanced countries.

If this is the case, then what mode of civilization will follow the end of progressive industrial civilization? What can be the prescription? Taking a very long-term, philosophic view, the industrial civilization, which has lasted two centuries, may itself have possibly been nothing more than the initial phase of a long-lasting mega-civilization. It is not impossible that this mega-civilization has a strongly orthodox nature. However, to imagine its nature is far beyond our capacity at the present. We are clearly in a period of transition between civilizations. What is possible in this state, though intending not to lose sight of our main direction, may be nothing more than to search, through trial and error, for a soft landing that would avoid the destruction of the human race.

An important hint on this point is the pattern of past antagonism between progressivism and conservatism. To repeat, conservatism, inasmuch as it is an orientation toward change, does not differ from progressivism. If this is the case, then we must realize that the antagonism between progressivism and conservatism suggests a contrast in intellectual positions hidden in the very depths of human conduct. For example, a difference between pessimism and optimism about change brought about by human hands, a difference between respect and hostility toward the achievements of people in the past, can clearly be observed between conservatism and progressivism. How will this difference in intellectual positions be involved in the formation of the civilization of the future? How should we arrange and summarize the difference in intellectual positions among people in order to think about this? I believe that Mannheim's analysis, which stopped at discussing the antagonism between conservatism and progressivism, is not sufficient for this. To discuss this point fully would require another book.

Moving Beyond Conservatism and Progress

I have shown the distinctive characteristic of modern progressivism as having a unique ideal order and the conceivability and realizability of a unique path toward it, but it can be restated more simply as the belief in the existence of "objective laws." In short, the standpoint of modern progressivism is that a universal proposition, valid regardless of time or place or individual, can be found in analyzing societies as in natural sciences, thus "social science" is possible. However, in order for the pursuit of objective laws in this fashion to be possible, it is necessary to establish a position for an observer who has transcended human beings and the self. Let us call this the establishment of the transcendental subject. In short, the subject and the object must be perfectly distinguished. Descartes's famous subject-object dichotomy provided a solution for precisely this point, and so modern natural science flowered on the basis of this Cartesian premise.

Various experiments in modern social science have been made in conformity with this method. Needless to say, Descartes is the greatest source of modern progressivism.

However, even at first glance, social phenomena are more complex than natural phenomena. This is because the "objective" object among social phenomena naturally includes the observer (the social scientist?); and if the "objective laws" become common knowledge, then everyone cannot but be both observed and observer. If at that time people, aware of the results of thinking about these laws, were all at once to change their behavior, would not the laws collapse? This is the famous problem of predictions being broken, or of self-denying predictions; it is because of this breaking of predictions that there cannot be established objective laws for stock prices or scientific predictions about when revolutions will occur. That is, revolutions always come from unexpected directions.

One can think about the problem more generally. When people have an image of the world, that image includes an observed self, seen by an observing self. One can call this an epistemological split in the self. The observing self reconsiders its image of the world, including the observed self, and makes this image anew—more comprehensive and (so it thinks) with fewer contradictions. This is the fundamental structure of cognition common to human beings and is nothing other than the structure of self-transcendence or self-reference mentioned above. Simply expressed, this could be called self-examination or reflection in the broadest sense. Human beings are above all reflecting animals. It is clear that the rules for human beings such as Aristotle's "zoon politikon," Friedrich Engels's "tool-using animal," or "homo faber" can all be derived from the rules that define this reflecting animal.[18]

Though the function of this reflection is in a sense the attempt to prevent the dissolution of the self, broadly speaking, it has two modes. On the one hand, there is the standpoint from which one gives serious consideration to the observing self; on the other, there is the one from which one does not ignore the observed self. From the former standpoint, the transcendental self becomes an established entity by taking as correct the image of the world held by the observing self, and the image of the world held by the observed self before reflection is discarded as a mistake. This is the standpoint of Descartes and of modern science. From the latter standpoint, which gives serious consideration to the observed self, the image of the world before reflection is not necessarily abandoned, and the two images, before and after reflection, overlap and form an amalgam.

For example, in the course of everyday life, people do not give priority to the image of the world created by the observing self but compare it with the image held by the observed self (the observing self of the previous stage) and obtain a picture in which the two images are indistinct and overlapping. In this there is no absolute standard for judging which is the correct image; the process continues without end in what philosophers have

called a "hermeneutic circle." Thus, people live their daily lives while reinterpreting the world. In this case, the self floats between observing and
observed (going this way and that) and comes to a mutual coexistence with
the "others" external to the self and the "nature" external to human beings.
This is because, as the self is returned to its former state as an observed
self, so its connection within its image of the world to others and nature is
habitually confirmed. Let us call the way in which the image of the world
is thus formed and transformed "hermeneutic"—in the sense found in
philosophical hermeneutics since Wilhelm Dilthey.[19] What is pivotal here
is that this is a process of interpretation (hermeneusis) that is not transcendental. We should take note that the original meaning of hermeneusis
was thinking as if one were another, in order to understand them (particularly the past authors of scripture and classics). An example familiar to
economics is Adam Smith, who in *The Theory of Moral Sentiments* was
thinking of a similar hermeneutic process in the concept of sympathy.[20]

If the expression "hermeneutic" is too awkward, what this means, in
short, is the creation of an image of the world for everyday life and of how
that is organized. Though there may be some danger of misunderstanding, it may be acceptable to call this "*Lebenswelt* thought" (thought of the
everyday world). Since *Lebenswelt* thought is something that enables one
to establish one's own daily life, usually it must be something that in its
own way provides a complete image covering the whole world. However,
given the limited abilities of human beings, it is in fact a "rough sketch"[21]
that naturally makes some allowance for this—which is to say there will
be some defects in expression. But even if this is the case, this hermeneutic or *Lebenswelt* thought is not something that should be looked down
on. In people's lives it will be forever indispensable.

Diametrically opposed to this is the position that sets up the above-
mentioned transcendental subject, based on the subject-object dichotomy,
and tries to grasp the world "scientifically." Let us call this transcenden-
tal/scientific thought. In transcendental/scientific thought, the observing
self (the scientist, so to speak) habitually has to break away from and tower
above the objectified world. Connected to this, the observing self must
be separated from the observed self. On the other hand, in hermeneutic/
Lebenswelt thought, the observing self and the observed self should habitually overlap. But in transcendental thought, it is not easy to endure
the splitting up of the observing and the observed selves.

One way of coping with this is the method of dealing with only one
part of the objective world; and this method has certainly been effective
for "nature," from which human beings have been excluded. If one defines
one's object well, then one can make one's image of the world increasingly accurate. With the advance of what Shōzō Ōmori calls "the making
of detailed drawings," language was made more rigorous, and there was
a growth in quantitative expression. This development of natural science
lent weight to the authority of transcendental/scientific thought, and it

is no mistake that this was what established the basis of the modern age. However, if we were to attempt to develop a similar line of thinking about the whole world, including human beings, then the path that relied on the process of definition and the making of detailed drawings would not open up easily.

This is why sciences that take society for their object evolve only with difficulty. Thus, scientific thought has been established only in a number of "disciplines" that have been skillful in limiting the fields of their endeavor, the most successful example of which is economics. However, even in economics, to broaden the scope of the object of one's examination—for example, from partial equilibrium analysis to general equilibrium analysis—will necessitate imposing additional restricting conditions on analysis. A result is to make the scope of the examination even narrower. There can be no objection to saying that transcendental/scientific thought is an approach that has been developed in the most recent stage of human history and to which we should pay attention, but it is not something that can completely replace hermeneutic/*Lebenswelt* thought. Transcendence and hermeneusis are thus two methods of controlling the impulse to self-transcendence. These two modes of thought should be mutually complementary and should support each other. This, I believe, is what occurs in human lives and history.

As should be clear, progressive civilization is founded on the idea of the superiority of transcendental/scientific thought. If there is going to be a civilization to replace this one, it must place greater emphasis on hermeneutic/*Lebenswelt* thought. Simply put, transcendental/scientific civilization has plowed onward in its pursuit of a new image of the world and has tried to destroy or break up the old image of the world; in contrast, one can say that hermeneutic/*Lebenswelt* civilization, in addition to having recognized the simultaneous existence of multiple worldviews, has allowed their overlapping—even though there are conflicting details. My argument here is somewhat rough, but I believe it is acceptable to perceive that, even outside a progressive civilization characterized by an exclusive activeness, we could have something that might be called a civilization with an inclusive activeness, or a hermeneutic/*Lebenswelt* civilization. This corresponds precisely to the liberalism of thought mentioned above, or perhaps liberalism of thought is something that can lead to this civilization. Unlike property or money, thought is something everyone can possess. Liberalism of thought is certainly an activeness peculiar to human beings, but this does not usually make the establishment of a transcendental subject inevitable. The activation of hermeneutic thought must again be included in this. From this is generated the polymorphic liberalism advocated in this argument.

The argument beginning here is very wide-ranging. It is connected to the problems of justice and religion, and so also to the problem of war and peace. For example, one can see that religion is a transcendental attempt to provide the image of a pertinent rough sketch of all the possibilities in the world. In this sense the transcendental nature of the historical religions is strong. The germ of this kind of attempt to capture an ultimate ideal state is always in the human spirit. However, it is necessary to emphasize that so far the only concrete results have been in providing rough sketches with the idiosyncrasies peculiar to each religion. I am not trying to discuss here the problem of religion itself, but if one looks at its effects on society, one cannot but be struck by the fact that there has been nothing as violent and bloody as the antagonism between religions. More generally, there is nothing as troubling as "just wars" (as will be discussed fully in Chapter 2) between nations. Putting this problem of war and peace on one side, and the problem of liberalism on the other, I believe that in order to try to cope with today's world it is necessary to weaken the force of transcendental/scientific thought and increase the importance of hermeneutic/Lebenswelt thought. For example, the same considerations are necessary both in the struggle between the various forms of "capitalism" and in what is called ethnic conflict.

In order to make the argument easier to understand, I define hermeneutic/Lebenswelt thought as meta-conservatism, and transcendental/scientific thought as meta-progressivism. One could say that we are entering, or must enter, a new age in which the guiding principle is not meta-progressivism but rather meta-conservatism. In a present in which we continue to run up against the limitations of human transcendental/scientific thought, it is probably only this direction that will open up our path to the world yet to emerge. To enforce our progress toward a single order solely by relying on scientific or pseudoscientific thought is like sailing a straight course across an unknown sea filled with many reefs. The argument I advance is structured to demonstrate the application of this idea to concrete political and economic problems. Certainly there are now problems in both "progressivism" and "conservatism" in the accustomed meaning of each term. Inasmuch as the antagonism between these two terms itself structures the paradigm of modern thought, overcoming this existing paradigm is the task that faces us today. How can we discharge this task in practical terms? This is the central theme to which I now turn.

The Three Axes of the Problem

What is the most fundamental factor that will determine the future of the world and one's nation? The answer to this question can be defined in terms of orientation toward industrialization and the nation-state. Two axes of the problem can be shown provisionally as industrialism–anti-industrialism and nationalism-antinationalism. This is not to say that there is no connection between the two axes, but fundamentally they exist in independent dimensions. Many people may question whether these two axes exhaust the fundamental question, and some may argue, for example, that another possible axis—freedom-equality—is crucial. As I have mentioned before, the problem of freedom is the ultimate subject matter of human beings and is the decisive condition for what it means to be human. Also, equality of rights or equality of opportunity is an ultimate condition leading from the requirements of freedom. However, what is being debated at present in the advanced industrialized countries is not freedom or equality in this ultimate sense but mainly the confrontation between freedom of economic activity (especially business activity) and equality of distribution, meaning equality of outcome. In fact, this is a lingering symptom of the confrontation between capitalism and socialism. Of course, freedom of economic activity is merely one aspect of freedom of action and naturally is not freedom of thought.

Thus, I think that freedom-equality, though often viewed as such by many, is not really an axis of confrontation. When compared with the first two axes, it lacks importance as a subject in the advanced nations. As already mentioned, one cannot envisage equality of outcomes as an ideal order. When one thinks clearly about the economic problems (such as income and assets) in the so-called advanced nations, the problem of freedom and equality diminishes in size. Nevertheless, the force of "democracy," driving toward equality of outcomes, is very strong today. How we are to control this powerful force will be a serious problem for the world in the future.

I have reasons, of course, for choosing the specific order in which to discuss these three axes. First, let us remember that people's images of the world are constructed from three elements: things (which I will provisionally call nature), other people, and the self. When we try to represent the problems of the present within the structure of this image of the world, the following framework results. The axis that indicates the fundamental human orientation toward nature is industrialism–anti-industrialism. The axis that indicates the fundamental human orientation toward others is, between countries, nationalism-antinationalism and, within countries, economic freedom–economic equality. The distinction between "within countries" and "between countries," as I mention below, is due to the fact that one cannot but give serious consideration to the present reality that is the nation-state. The three axes correspond to the fundamental structure of the image of the world that people construct.

But perhaps these three confrontations do not sufficiently capture the complexity of the problems we face today. For example, industrialization, since the latter half of the 1970s, has entered a new and higher stage, and, supported by the new technologies of microelectronics, genetic engineering, and new materials, has brought about the phenomenon known as "informatization." I would like to call this newest stage of industrialization, which seems dominant at least for the present, "superindustrialization."

It has now been decades since some began to speak of a great turning point for the industrial society that has lasted for two centuries. For example, Daniel Bell was already using the expression "postindustrial society" by about the mid-1960s,[22] but what Bell hypothesized was the tendency toward what I here call "superindustrialization." In contrast to the classical image of industrialization, the use of powerful machines and the consumption of great quantities of energy, it is the image of expanded high-speed processing of information that has symbolized the most advanced phenomena in industrialization since the second half of the 1970s. In short, it is an image of information carried by tiny material structures, processed in great quantities and at high speeds, and transmitted. There is no wearing down of machines and a remarkably small consumption of energy. The general concept of information is unusually vague; it might be redefined as that which is arranged and systematized under a fixed system of cognition—that is, knowledge that belongs under a fixed system.[23]

Historically speaking, machinery, energy, and information are the holy trinity of industrialization, and lacking even one of these, industrialization would not have occurred. However, the history of industrialization is a tale of alternating leaders. The leading force in the nineteenth century was machinery; beginning with the spinning machine, new machines were gradually manufactured, bringing about a change in people's lives. In contrast to this, the leading force in the twentieth century was energy. The use of petroleum, and especially electric power, with the remarkable diversification in and increasingly efficient use of energy, expanded the possibilities of machinery, and energy's influence permeated every inch of daily life. For example, one can imagine the situation were electricity to be removed from present-day life. To continue the analogy, beginning now, the leading force in the third stage will be information. It will change fundamentally the uses of machinery and energy and a certain aspect of human life (the aspect that uses various intermediations, such as machines, energy, and information). Using "production" in the economic sense, we have advanced through three phases centered on the "production of machinery," the "production of energy," and now the "production of information." Let us here call this third phase "superindustrialization."

In contrast, let us call the orientation that contains elements of anti-industrialism, and attempts to rebuild industrialization under an order with somewhat higher standards, "transindustrialism" and distinguish it from superindustrialization. Perhaps one could say that, in contrast to the thesis of industrialization (which of course contains superindustrialization) and the antithesis of anti-industrialism, transindustrialism indicates a synthesis that transcends these. For example, the reconciliation of science and anti-industrialism has been an important theme among those of the so-called "new left," and, at the present, there are fewer environmentalists who are simply anti-industry than previously.

At the same time, internationalism is normally thought of as the polar opposite of nationalism, but internationalism in the end takes the nation as its unit of analysis and is a concept that deals with the relationship between ("inter") nation and nation. The nation (or, more precisely, the nation-state) is at present a very powerful reality, but recently it has seemed as if the dissolution of the nation-state might be possible. In fact, the idea of the extinction of the nation appeared quickly in the old pre-Leninist Marxism, and if one reexamines the past, then until recently political bodies similar to the nation-state have been the exception rather than the rule. Thus it is appropriate as a depiction of the present situation to place opposite nationalism a concept of transnationalism that does not take the nation-state as its basis but that includes as well as transcends nationalism and internationalism. Transnationalism too, like transindustrialism, is a synthesis. I have already suggested that the confrontation between economic freedom and equality is an overly narrow formulation of the problem. Thus let us advance the argument by superimposing the three axes of the problem and keeping in mind the following somewhat dialectical schema: [superindustrialism–anti-industrialism] ↔ transindustrialism; [nationalism-internationalism] ↔ transnationalism; and [economic freedom–economic equality] ↔ freedom of thought in a broader sense. Depending on the circumstances—particularly, for example, in the case of the second axis of nationalism—it may seem that the opposition within the brackets that symbolizes the primary opposition is becoming indistinct and that the synthetic viewpoint has already grown strong.

One can show that various choices are possible within the space plotted by these three axes. But what could act as a guide for choosing between them? It should be emphasized that there cannot be only one key leading to only one solution. To expect an explicit solution as in mathematics or engineering is to return to the position of rationalist progressivism that has been in place since the eighteenth-century Enlightenment. As history since the Enlightenment has already shown, conditions are expected to advance even while various approaches confront and influence one another. When we try to organize these processes in an analytic fashion, we see once again a kind of dynamic confrontation between the hermeneutic and the transcendental that is rooted in the duality of the structure of human cognition, or that between meta-conservatism and meta-progressivism.

Among the possibilities of the various choices shown along these three axes, we cannot simply make the choice of one direction. On the first axis of industrialization, in the developed countries, the question of global environmental protection, the limits of medical science, and genetic engineering are becoming problems, and transindustrialism will be debated; but at the same time the increasing desire in developing countries for industrialization cannot be overlooked. On the second axis, dealing with nationalism we must be concerned with the existence of various possible choices, such as creating a global state (world federalism) or a state consisting of multiple former states (multinational regionalism). Again, on the third axis of freedom-equality, at the same time as the excesses of equality in mass democracy are becoming a problem in the developed countries, in

various places in the world a minimum level of equality in order to realize freedom (human rights) is still urgently needed. If we cannot order our
choices among these many directions, it is the same as confessing that
human thought on ideology plays no role in determining our collective
future. The meta-conservatism that is expected to reassume the leadership
will have no choice but to conquer its antipathy toward environmental
problems, break away from classical economic liberalism and nationalism, and overcome the existing conservative beliefs that have come to rest
on the achievements of industrialization. For example, in Japan, the late-
developer conservatism that became a tradition in the politics of the Liberal Democratic party (LDP), which dominated Japanese polity until 1993,
is in some ways a subspecies of the old progressivism and has a strong attachment to industrialization. The politics of the LDP and other conservative parties too must undergo a great conversion. More generally speaking,
what is crucial is how the developmental dictatorship will be brought to
an end.[24] We can call the future an age in which meta-conservatism in this
new sense takes the lead, but this uncharted ideological voyage cannot but
be a very rough and trying one.

CHAPTER 2

Nationalism and
Transnationalism

Nationalism

Of the three axes of the problem outlined in the previous chapter, probably the most critical is what the international society of the future should be like. A number of problems, such as the so-called decline in U.S. hegemony, the breakup of the Soviet Union and the Eastern bloc, and the Persian Gulf War, have arisen. A mistake in dealing with any one of them could plunge the world into a serious crisis. In the following, I take up the axis of internationalism-nationalism, focusing our attention on these problems in international relations. As I have stated before, however, if one were to include the various symptoms that have already appeared, one could call this the axis of confrontation: transnationalism-nationalism.

Let us begin with a definition of the nationalism that lies at one pole of this axis. The word is used with a good degree of flexibility, but nationalism in the strict sense is an ideology that sets much value on the "nation-state," or the "modern sovereign state"; in other words, it is "nation-statism." When we discuss nationalism, we are dealing with a nation-state or a modern sovereign state and not with a nation as the natural development of a tribe or an empire of the past that was created in an attempt to realize its own concept of a historical civilization. Nationalism is a unique historical inheritance of European history and has a complex character. It is not a natural development of the self-assertion of a community.

At the other pole, there are various aspects to internationalism and transnationalism, and one cannot define them easily. In recent history, the forces that have promoted and sustained internationalism from behind the scenes have been the trade that linked countries across national boundaries, and the ideology of economic liberalism advocating ever-expanding trade. Thus, until now this axis of the problem could be translated to a certain extent as the sometimes contradictory, sometimes harmonious relationship between nationalism and economic liberalism. I predict, however, that in this new historical phase on which the curtain is being lifted, these two historical ideologies will bring about an imperfect adjustment to reality, and the contradiction between them will deepen. I am not announcing the advent of a much talked-about cosmopolitanism (a principle of particularly cultural nonnationality) or of the principle of a planned economy, but rather the reverse. To cling to a classical understanding of nationalism and liberalism is too ahistorical, but the cosmopolitanism and the principle of a planned economy that are their conceptual opposites are nothing but an antihistorical flight of fancy. What is needed now is to reexamine and reconstruct the core of nationalism and liberalism. Let me be brave and challenge this very difficult subject. To do so, I begin by first exploring the ideology of nationalism—that is, of the nation-state— and examining its essential form.

THE NATION-STATE AS A HISTORICAL EXCEPTION

As historians have widely recognized, the nation-state, or the modern sovereign state, is a historical phenomenon peculiar to Western Europe since about the sixteenth century; it is a unique condition in which the nation, the sovereign state, and the territorial state are all three coterminous. First, the nation is a natural unit based on the identity of race, language, and history—a communal unit in the normal sense. "Natural" here does not have the biological sense (of a genetic human characteristic) but means something not consciously created that has developed naturally in history. In Latin, "natio," the etymological root of "nation," means something generated spontaneously, and in that sense, it might be clearer to use the expression "natio" rather than "nation." In fact, it is a common argument that a "nation" is an ideological creation. But however powerful the ideological propaganda, without sufficient foundation in natural developments a nation can never exist.

Second, "state" designates a social order that has achieved political and economic unity. When this is a sovereign state, the state has an absolute authority ("sovereignty") unrestricted by any other power (either within or outside the country). In a "territorial state," the state's authority has been established over a fixed territory. The nation, the sovereign state, and the territorial state are not usually coterminous. As I explain in detail below, the fact that these three organizational units came by chance to be identical is due to the peculiar historical conditions Europe faced on escaping from the so-called Middle Ages. Japan too was one of the few societies in which it was possible, for reasons such as geopolitical isolation, for these three elements to come together. In European societies the existence of the nation-state is considered normal, and Japanese people too think of the nation-state as something as natural as air. Generally speaking, though, even if the "natio" (the natural unit) has existed throughout history, it is not inevitable that this should become the territorial sovereign state.

However, as I will argue below, the idea of the nation-state, and of the system that developed from the nation-state, is a key that is for the most part effective only in understanding Europe since the Middle Ages. When the European civilization came to dominate the world, this political order too became widespread and the legal fiction of the nation-state was gradually and forcibly introduced even into countries whose geographical and political-economic conditions were substantively different. A good example of this is the Treaty of Versailles in 1919, which described the principle of national self-determination. In reality, the powerful countries of Western Europe had already taken on the character of colonial empires; and even today it cannot be said that the United States, Russia, and China, for example, are nation-states or that the new multitribal states in Asia and Africa possess the essential character of nation-states. The present world system is at most nothing more than a quasi-nation-state system. However, inasmuch as the countries with European origins have assumed the leadership, the European system of nation-states has been established as the stage for world politics and, as a consequence, the nation-state system has maintained its status up to the present as the rightful doctrine with regard to the world system. For example, the functional inadequacy of the United Nations is largely due to the inherited consequences of this political myth (such as the system of one country/one vote in the General Assembly). Thus, in reexamining the present world system, the ideology that gives great importance to the nation-state—nationalism—cannot but be one pole on the axis of our problem, or a natural starting point.

Let me emphasize once more that the nation-state is a historical exception. The early states known as chiefdoms, kingships, and theocracies were gatherings of people drawn together by kinship or religion, and the concept of territory was at most only a secondary consideration. The various historically renowned, great imperial civilizations that appeared in their wake—such as the Empire of the Middle Kingdom and the Roman Empire—given that they incorporated many races, were not nations; and since they considered the whole world as their own, they did not give much consideration to the concept of national boundaries or territory. It was probably in the medieval feudal societies of Europe and Japan that the concept of dominion or territory was most clearly established. There, the core human relationship (vassalage) was expressed in terms of land (*beneficium*), there were fierce struggles between the lower- and higher-ranking lords over territorial control, and even the lower-ranking lords had established authority over their own territories. However, the territorial sovereignty of the king (or the Holy Roman Emperor, the Japanese *tennō*, or the *shōgun*)—the highest lord—was far from absolute.

This situation changed as the Middle Ages came to an end. The early modern period that followed was an age of so-called absolute monarchy, and as that name suggests, the authority of the king became absolute. In the sixteenth century, some countries were unified by means of marriage and inheritance among the royal families (for example, the Hapsburgs in Spain and Austria). These unified nations were man-made and composed of many races and cultures and so cannot be called nations. Through the strengthening of the bond between an absolute monarchy and a fixed territory in the modern period, the three characteristics of natio, sovereign state, and territorial state came to be united. The Treaty of Westphalia in 1648 symbolized this process.

One of the main factors bringing to an end the feudal society of medieval Europe was the appearance of firearms (cannons and muskets); their overwhelming power made meaningless the security capacities of the feudal lords, which had until then depended on castles and cavalry. A mobile standing army (in the earlier period, mercenaries had been the main force) and the large economic power to support it became necessary, and from this developed a movement toward the political unification of greater areas. "The transformation of the medieval into the modern . . . in one sense . . . represents the trend toward the consolidation and strengthening of the territorial state. National units coalesce and begin to compete for power, influence, and territory."[1] The territorial authority of the monarch became gradually stronger and approached a form one could call sovereignty. This early modern period began in the fifteenth and sixteenth centuries.

Given the circumstances of their formation, these territorial states were based on military power and expansionism. As a general tendency in human history, a power that subjugates and unifies the whole has appeared from the midst of such quarrels. In the case of Japan, for example, the disputes over territorial acquisitions by the *sengoku daimyō*—the regional lords of the warring states period of the late fifteenth to late sixteenth centuries—and the appearance of firearms led to the unification of the country by the military powers of Oda and Toyotomi and then by the Tokugawa. However, in the early modern period in Europe, no one country—whether Spain or the Austria of the Hapsburgs or France—could unify the whole. Why was this so?

This difficulty of unification can be explained by the fact that Europe as a whole covers a large area, in contrast to Japan. But area is not clearly a decisive factor. The central Eurasian steppe, an area far larger than Europe, was characterized by the formation, rise, and fall of the great empire of mounted nomads who swept across the steppes. Thus what was important was clearly not merely geographical extent but Europe's natural environment and the complex realities of its history.

First, perhaps, the natural environment of Europe, covered with forests and divided by mountain ranges, allowed numerous tribes to coexist. Second, the feudal system, which evolved closely tied to the ownership of land, developed from the early situation of coexisting tribes and established a number of mutually competing language areas. Third, though at first glance this may seem a contradiction, one cannot ignore the influence of the homogeneity of religion and culture (the catholicism of the Roman church and a fraternity among the upper classes based on Latin). The secret of the continuation of this coexistence—neither a perfect unification nor a complete division—is probably in the fact that a delicate balance was maintained between the dissimilarity of languages and tribes on the one hand, and the cultural similarity of religion and education on the other. In this sense, the Christian church had decisive significance for the system of coexistence in medieval Europe, and this dual structure especially played a large part. In short, in the Christian society of Western Europe, spiritual authority (the Roman church) and temporal authority (the Holy Roman Emperor) were split, but the clerical and the secular subverted each other's authority, thereby diminishing their respective authorities. As a consequence, the dominance of the authority of the Christian church was not unchallenged, unlike the case, for example, of Islam. On the contrary, this weakness produced the balance of dissimilarity and similarity.

However, when religious revolution loosened the hold of Roman Catholicism, which had extended over the whole of Europe, this balance disintegrated. A rift separating the regions appeared; powerful monarchies (the nascent version of so-called absolutism) appeared in many places, based on the main language areas and adopting new military technologies; and the Holy Roman Empire gradually began to lose its essential character as an empire. But the tradition from the Middle Ages of the body of Christian belief—the "corpus Christianum"—never disappeared. There was a search for a new system of coexistence, and as a result, the international system peculiar to Europe was created, in which a fair number of middle-sized states competed, and maintained a balance of power, among themselves. In this book I call this the "nation-state system." Its starting point was the famous Treaty of Westphalia. This treaty, concluded in 1648, brought to an end the Thirty Years' War between the countries that were adherents of the new and the old religions, deprived the Holy Roman Emperor of real authority, and, by settling the territorial sovereignty of the monarchies, established the framework for the nation-state system. Thus, though I stated above that nationalism is the ideology of a nation-state, to be precise, in the classical nationalism in Europe established by the Treaty of Westphalia, two conditions are indispensable: the existence of the nation-state itself and the existence of the nation-state system.

For somewhat different reasons, in Japan too it was easy for the characteristics of the nation, the sovereign state, and the territorial state to become coterminous. I do not attempt a detailed comparison here, but Europe and Japan have in common the experience of feudal society and a strong attachment to land. For example, both European and Japanese historical sources on legal relationships in the Middle Ages record countless disputes that demonstrate this attachment. In this sense, the nation-state is to some degree a legacy of the feudal system, and, to the same degree that the feudal system is an exception, the nation-state too is an exception in world history. In the societies of Europe, the existence of nation-states is considered natural, and the Japanese also think of the existence of the nation-state as inevitable. Generally, however, the nation-state is a historical rarity.

In particular, the establishment of the nation-state system that must complement the nation-state is a rare occurrence limited exclusively to Europe. Japan's modernization had to proceed without the benefit of the nation-state system. The transformation of Japan into a nation-state at the end of the nineteenth century was carried out in an isolated fashion in the absence of any regional (East Asian) international system. The fact that nationalism in modern Japan has shown a tendency toward confusion both in policy and in ideology is not unconnected to this fact. This is not something unique to Japan. The lack of an international system capable of sustaining the nation-state is a phenomenon common to the non-European world and has become a factor making so-called modernization difficult and one of the greatest problems in the contemporary world.

The arguments about nationalism, however, have been continued, leaving the crucial fact ambiguous; that is, they fail to pay due attention to the absence of an accommodating international system. Europeans assume that the nation-state (condition 1 above) is sustained by the international system (condition 2). In this sense, we can call the classical nationalism of Europe "systemic nationalism." In contrast, in the non-European world, tribal or linguistic communities trying to escape European colonialism are trying to achieve independence by borrowing a form of nationalism. But since its contents are at most only the pursuit of the nation-state itself, we can call this "naive nationalism." The distinction between these two nationalisms—systemic nationalism (classical, European, containing both conditions 1 and 2) and naive nationalism (often rebellious, non-European, containing only condition 1)—will have great significance in the following argument.

Many accept the concept of the nation-state unconditionally, and most of them see nationalism as "systemic nationalism"—nationalism within an international system—which suits their notion of a nation-state. Certainly it is natural that tribal or linguistic communities should assert themselves politically—through so-called popular self-determination. But such assertive actions are not justifiable unconditionally. If these actions become self-righteous and aggressive, communities that engage in such actions will become renegades and a threat to others. The classical nationalism of Europe has lasted because the international system restrained the self-assertion of each nation-state so that all could coexist. In this sense, the existence of an international system (satisfying condition 2 above) will be decisive, particularly from now on, in determining whether the phenomenon of nationalism can continue to exist. To be able to discuss this further, we must first study the historical experience of the European system.

THE THREE PHASES OF CLASSICAL NATIONALISM: THE TRANSFORMATION IN THE DOCTRINE OF THE NONJUST WAR

As noted above, the nation-state is, above all else, a "sovereign state," whose fundamental characteristic is not being subject to any higher authority within the territory delineated by such things as race and language. When an effort was made to construct an international system with this "self-evident truth of sovereignty" as its premise, what logically followed was the theorem of nonjust wars (*bellum nonjustum*).[2] First, the nation-state, given that it did not recognize a higher authority, could not but emphasize itself as more righteous than any other earthly justice. Thus, as in Europe, in trying to maintain a system in which the nation-states might coexist (the nation-state system), it became necessary to recognize the coexistence of a number of justices. That system, in other words, could not sanction between states wars that were fought proclaiming the validity of the justice of each belligerent—so-called just wars (*bellum justum*); the system had to be based on the principle of nonjust wars. The antithesis to this is the "empire" as a system that recognizes only a single justice or order (for example, the order advocated by the historical religions), a system based on the doctrine of just war. In fact, the nation-state system in Europe could not but bring to an end the authority of the Holy Roman Empire. Thus the history of the nation-state system is also the history of the rise and fall of the doctrine of the nonjust war. Certainly, there were occasions when this doctrine faltered, and the doctrine of the just war (or even, as I mention below, the doctrine of the holy war) appeared on the stage. However, the fundamental trend of the past 500 years can rightly be summarized as the development of the doctrine of the nonjust war.

More concretely, the doctrine of the nonjust war continued in the form of a power game in which middle-sized states mutually restrained each other. The most direct indication of this characteristic was war as a legitimate means of balance-of-power diplomacy. A balance of power exists when countries are at all times allied with each other in order to restrain the aspirations of any particular country to become a great power, and war in the nation-state system is a legitimate extension of this balance-of-power politics; thus there cannot exist "war criminals" accused of having used war as an instrument. A system based on the doctrine of the nonjust war is not an antiwar or pacifist system that makes war illegal. "Modern international law," the set of rules of this power game, illustrates this characteristic well, and through this the legal rules of war are established. However, it is difficult to say that modern international law is the only set of rules with universal applicability for human beings (so-called natural law). Developmentally, the efficacy of this modern international law was supported in its first period by the individual loyalty among the European monarchies, cemented by long-lasting family ties and the similarity of culture and education in each country's courts. In this sense, modern international law has been heavily dependent on the European historical context. For example, the *jus gentium* that was the international law of the Romans was not at all comparable to European law, and if the Arabic or East Asian peoples were to create an international law, its contents would surely be different. The history of Europe from about the middle of the seventeenth century has been the history of a unique international system; it is the story of balance-of-power diplomacy and legal war that takes as its theme the transformation in the doctrine of the nonjust war.

The first period of the doctrine of the nonjust war was from the Treaty of Westphalia (1648) to the end of the eighteenth century. War did not decline in this period in Europe, and the acceptance of the doctrine of the nonjust war did not bring about an antiwar doctrine. Beginning with the Anglo-Dutch Wars (1652–54, 1666–67, 1672–74), the Spanish war of succession (1701–14), the Austrian war of succession (1740–48), and the Seven Years' War (1756–63), war continued virtually without interruption. A new characteristic of the wars following the Treaty of Westphalia, though, was that they could no longer take place under the banner of religious justice, and their character as private quarrels between rulers (wars of succession are of this type) grew stronger. These private quarrels contained the danger of becoming drawn out and vicious, in a quite different sense from religious wars. What provided rulers with the rules to avoid this was international law based on the doctrine of the nonjust war, with Grotius as its founder; and his 1625 book, *De jure belli ac pacis* (The rights of war and peace), was in fact dedicated to the rulers (as is evident in its preface). In reality these wars were battles between mercenary forces composed of many foreigners, and the common people were merely spectators or victims. That this system based on the doctrine of the nonjust war functioned in its own way was one of the main reasons nationalism did not up to this point spread among the masses.

The second period of the doctrine of the nonjust war corresponded closely to the nineteenth century, from the Napoleonic Wars to the First World War. After the industrial revolution (industrialization) and the French Revolution (democratization) at the end of the eighteenth century, the state began to play a role in representing the interests and ideals of the common people. Particularly after the Napoleonic Wars at the beginning of the nineteenth century, the concept of nationalism spread among the common people, and through the conscription system wars began to develop into large-scale clashes between national armies. From this time, wars between rulers were transformed into wars between peoples or nations, and so the banner of "justice" gradually became necessary in order to mobilize the common people for war.[3] Throughout the nineteenth century, however, the framework of the doctrine of the nonjust war and the balance of power continued to work. The Council of Vienna in 1815 reaffirmed the doctrines of the nonjust war and the balance of power, and international politics in nineteenth-century Europe operated under this conceptual framework. With the balance-of-power system in effect producing an efficient set of fixed controls, the wars in this period—such as the Crimean (1853–56), the Franco-Austrian (1859), the Prusso-Austrian (1866), the Prusso-French (1870–71), and the Russo-Turkish (1877)—were short-lived, local affairs and did not lead to the impoverishment of the warring parties. In a sense, this period was the golden age of the doctrine of the nonjust war, and from the end of the 1870s to the First World War, no war broke out anywhere in Europe.

However, a series of changes was proceeding beneath the surface of politics that would weaken this nineteenth-century framework. As it spread among peoples, nationalism gradually became more difficult to control. There began to be cases, such as the Crimean War, in which the people, rather than the government, were advocating war. Above all, with the technological revolution in the second half of the nineteenth century (what some people call the second industrial revolution), the equilibrium among the national powers collapsed and the balance-of-power framework began to be greatly disturbed. When the balance-of-power mechanism (which allowed a changing alignment among the leading countries) became inflexible, the shot at Sarajevo plunged the leading countries of Europe into war and so caused the outbreak of the First World War. The countries that took part in the war suffered huge losses, and the resulting impoverishment was extreme. No country gained anything, and all that was left was a deep sense of wasted effort.

The third period of the doctrine of the nonjust war was the so-called interwar period, and beginning with the First World War, the signs of the decline of the classical nation-state system became clear. However, in this process of decline, there was a mixture of two contradictory aspects. First, the Paris Peace Conference, held at the close of the First World War, attempted to rebuild the postwar world by making the principle of popular self-determination a new doctrine to be accepted not only by the nations in Western Europe but also in other parts of the globe. The principle of popular self-determination, inasmuch as it recognizes the "natio" of the people as a territorial sovereign state, is nothing more than official recognition of what we are calling "naive nationalism."

The universalization of this principle of popular self-determination demanded the systematization of the logic of the nonjust war, and the concept of "the justice of self-preservation (or self-defense)" became the core concept for this process. With the premise of naive nationalism, in recognizing the coexistence of multiple forms of justice in different countries, the easiest issue on which to obtain agreement was the right to self-defense against aggression. This did not mean, however, that, in having accepted the rule of constraint or compromise such that its own justice could not override another country's right to self-preservation, each country had recognized an order of justice superior to its own. In this sense, the phrase "the justice of self-preservation" is not sufficiently apposite. The expression "the rule of self-preservation" better describes the actual situation. Justice and rule are frequently confused, but even etymologically they are not the same. For example, "keep to the left" is a rule but not justice. In other words, justice is something derived from an abstract value system (transcendental thought), whereas rules are the products of the accumulation of historical experience (hermeneutic thought). Of course, given that it is possible for rules to be transformed into justice over a period of many years, it is in fact difficult to discriminate between them; but one can say that the concept of the right to self-preservation created by the Versailles system is something closer to a rule than to justice.

Thus, after the Treaty of Versailles, the various efforts from the establishment of the League of Nations (1919) to the Kellogg-Briand Pact (1928) were attempts to make once again a clear statement on the minimum rule of self-preservation that is believed necessary in rebuilding the system based on the doctrine of the nonjust war. That the Kellogg-Briand Pact was not simply a product of nonbelligerency doctrine is clear if one looks at the famous speech in which Frank Kellogg explicitly stated the right of self-preservation to be a natural fact and any stipulation about it unnecessary. This was the so-called Versailles system and can be seen as an attempt to rebuild the postwar world by extending the former logic of the doctrine of the nonjust war beyond Western Europe.

However, the damage suffered in the First World War was much larger than that of wars of the nineteenth century. The advent of such things as machine guns, long-range artillery, tanks, airplanes and airships, poison gas, and submarines changed the mental image of war, and the loss of human lives was immense. As a result, the victors, particularly France, tried to inflict on Germany severe reparations that went beyond the existing understanding based on the doctrine of the nonjust war. However, as J. M. Keynes pointed out, these huge reparations threatened the existence of Germany itself and were likely to further destabilize the international economy, which had been in an unsettled period of transition since the end of the nineteenth century.[4] The appearance of the concept of this kind of retaliatory justice was symbolically demonstrated by the clause on war responsibility in the Treaty of Versailles (clause 231); this clause, by pinning the responsibility for the war only on Germany, violated the rule of the doctrine of nonjust war.[5]

This retaliatory justice breached a hole in the existing logic of the doctrine of the nonjust war, which had come to support nationalism, and the dike began to collapse. Thus in the interwar period ideology faltered, swaying between the doctrines of just war and nonjust war, and international politics came to be haunted by an uncertainty about its principles. Some historians view the efforts to establish a peaceful system following the First World War with undisguised cynicism and call the interwar period simply "a twenty-year truce."

But the interwar period was not merely a period of truce. Beginning at Westphalia in 1648, there wormed its way into the hearts of people a distrust toward the European system that was to be perfected at Vienna in 1815. To borrow the words of the famous British historian, A. J. P. Taylor: "This old, tried system failed to work after 1919. The great coalition dissolved. There was a reason of high principle for this. Though the victors had acted according to the doctrine of the Balance of Power, they were ashamed to have done so. Many men believed that the Balance of Power had caused the war, and that adherence to it would cause another."[6]

This feeling of distrust was connected to the sense of a "twenty-year crisis" (E. H. Carr), or even "the downfall of Western Europe" (O. Spengler). There was certainly something like a crisis within Europe. What one can call "a modified system based on the principle of the nonjust war"—the Versailles system in the sense that it had contained the germ of the League of Nations—supposedly reinforced by the universalization of the principle of popular self-determination, began to destabilize European politics. In practice, the most significant aim of the concept of self-determination was the establishment of independent nations in Central and Eastern Europe. This had the objective of trying to check the reexpansion of Germany, and from the outset the concept of self-determination had the appearance of a rhetorical flourish on this. As a result, however, as was seen in the problems involving Danzig and Sudeten, these independent nations increased the agitation in European politics. It is well known that these problems finally became the trigger for the Second World War.

IMPERIALISM AND THE DOCTRINE OF THE NONJUST WAR

The problem was not confined to Europe. Popular self-determination was a time bomb that would lead to the collapse of the international system. The problems in Central and Eastern Europe were a local example of this, but far more serious in the long term was the influence of the concept of popular self-determination in the colonies of the various European countries.

From the very beginning there was a double standard concealed in the logic of European-style international politics. The doctrine of the nonjust war was applicable only within Europe, and toward the non-Western world the European countries behaved mercilessly as "empires."[7] The ideology supporting this was the principle of civilization, or the principle that civilization had a duty to enlighten the savages. The European system of international politics was supported by the doctrine of the nonjust war within Europe and the imperialistic doctrine of the just war outside Europe. However, if one were to apply the principle of popular self-determination to the whole world, then this double standard could not but be abandoned.

It is common knowledge that through such things as the European seizure of mines in Central and South America of the sixteenth and seventeenth centuries, and the slave trade and land expropriation of the eighteenth, the history of European colonialism was a long one. However, it was only from the beginning of the nineteenth century that colonial rule was systematically integrated with that of the home country, thus beginning the period historians call "imperialism." For example, the British administration of India had for a long time—since the time of Elizabeth I—been entrusted to the private company known as the East India Company, and it was in the first half of the nineteenth century that Britain officially assumed control of India. France's hurried colonization of Indochina and Holland's notorious compulsory cultivation system were also products of the nineteenth century. With the establishment of imperialism as a system, the colonial struggles among the European countries were more or less concluded, and with the virtual disappearance of any blank spaces on the map, imperialism took on the aspect of a zero-sum competition. Unlike inside Europe, globally the partition of the map at that time was unbalanced. The German overseas territories and the Arab provinces of the Turkish Empire were all repartitioned after the First World War, but the result only increased the imbalance.

What followed was a conflict between the early and late colonizers that took the form of the "have-nots" challenging the "haves." The Japanese administration of Manchuria, the Italian conquest of Ethiopia, and the repeated German violations of the Treaty of Versailles are examples of this. However, the European haves, who themselves had a history of imperialist aggression, did not possess a logic sufficient to deny the assertions of the have-nots. For example, Britain, while appeasing Japan, Italy, and Germany, tried to keep them within the League of Nations but was finally forced to abandon the policy in the face of opposition from the United States, which prided itself on not being an imperialist, and the newly independent nations of Central and Eastern Europe. With the secession of these "imperialist have-nots," the League of Nations became powerless. This was not simply a failure in the system's construction. From the beginning, the (primary) characteristic of the doctrine of the nonjust war was the maintenance of the status quo, in the sense that it did not recognize the "justice" of hostility toward the established pattern of territorial holdings. The real cause for the failure was the fact that this European, or excessively European, logic could not survive being applied to the world as a whole, including the many colonies.

The imperialism of the have-nots, however, came too late, just when the anticolonialist movement that was prompted by the concept of popular self-determination adopted in the Treaty of Versailles was gaining momentum and the age of imperialism was coming to an end. In Central and Eastern Europe, people's resolve for popular self-determination was strong. The League of Nations' refusal to recognize the Japanese rule of Manchuria was due crucially to the vote of small European countries. Outside Europe, with the appearance of influential anticolonial activists such as Sun Yat-sen in China and Mahatma Gandhi in India, the independence and antiforeign movements intensified. Anticolonial movements also gained strength in such places as Egypt, Tunisia, Indonesia, and Vietnam. Objectively speaking, it is difficult to say that these countries met the criteria for a classical nation-state—one people, one nation. Moreover, these movements for popular self-determination were undoubtedly naive nationalism, unconcerned whether there existed an international system that could support and integrate them.

However, it was the intellectuals in the late-developing countries who had studied in Europe and the United States—such as Sun and Gandhi—during this period who led the anticolonialist movements with indomitable enthusiasm. Their ideology was popular self-determination, and their model was European nationalism. The European countries and the United States, having themselves paraded the idea of popular self-determination, could not in principle deny the independence of the natural cultural units —the "natio"—within the colonial empire. Thus, "reactive nationalism" took root in the colonies in the interwar period, supported by the importation of ideology. An anticolonialist literature emerged, and there gradually began to appear signs of theories of cultural resistance toward Western civilization—that is, theories that went beyond the mere importation of Western nationalism.[8] One should perhaps, however, say that before the Second World War these movements had not achieved any visible results.

PREWAR JAPAN

Japan, for reasons of historical timing, was placed in a unique situation. In the second half of the nineteenth century it could well have become the last object of Western colonialism, but it opened up and modernized using reactive nationalism as the motive force. But because the cultural (particularly the linguistic) area and the territorial unit were coterminous in Japan, naive nationalism was established as easily as it had been in Europe. There was no change in its fundamental character of naive nationalism, and there were strong undercurrents running through Japan's modernization, such as a reaction to Western colonialism, an antipathy toward racial discrimination, Asianism, and a skepticism toward Western thought.[9]

For example, it was a commonly held belief that the Japanese should help modernization efforts on the Korean peninsula and in China, and advance with them hand in hand; some tried to offer staging bases and funds for the revolutionary movements of Sun Yat-sen and Jin Yujun. In the end, however, in Asia during this period only Japan actually became "a rich country with a strong army," and in the other late-developing countries the formation of the nation-state and industrialization did not proceed easily. There was no likelihood that an Asian international system into which the Japanese nation-state could be accommodated would emerge. And Japan did not have the ability to create such a system unaided. As a result, having checked the imperialist advance of Europe and the United States into Asia, the view gradually grew stronger that Japan had no choice but to oppose the power of Europe and the United States by taking an imperialistic path of its own. Yukichi Fukuzawa's argument, "escape Asia to join with Europe," typifies such a view.

Thus the Japanese people began to oscillate between resistance to Western colonialism and emulation of Western civilization. This confusion reflected the double standard (dual character) inherent in Europe and the United States, and it is thus unjust to pin this label on Japan alone. Unlike Europe and the United States, however, where the concept of the righteous civilization helped justify the use of the double standard at home and abroad, Japan never managed to develop a system of thought on a scale equivalent to civilization that might have made it possible to cope with the confusion it faced vis-à-vis the West and to deal with the realities it experienced during its emergence as a nation-state. When such a thought is lacking, people are always swept along by the force of vested interest— as is shown throughout Japan's modern history.

In one example from the interwar period, this absence of thought was symbolically demonstrated at the time of the Paris Peace Conference. Mindful of President Woodrow Wilson's long-standing assertions, the Japanese delegation proposed a supplementary clause on "the termination of racial discrimination," and for a time the proposal looked as though it would be adopted with majority support. However, as chair of the conference, Wilson was under pressure due to the internal circumstances of the countries of Europe and the United States, and he retreated to the position that the proposal had to be adopted unanimously. Within the Japanese delegation, in contrast to the senior delegates who argued that Japan must not yield from its original demand, the leading officers of the Foreign Ministry, fearing that Japanese rights and interests in Asia might be harmed, called for a compromise; after a heated discussion, the Japanese delegation finally agreed to withdraw the supplementary clause. On the one hand it is possible to see this as a prudent compromise with political reality, and on the other it is possible to criticize Japan, which had colonized Formosa and Korea, for demanding the termination of discrimination. Whichever position one takes, this episode clearly reflects the confusion of thought characteristic of prewar Japan that was manifested in its effort to be a late-starting imperialist and to oppose Western colonialism at the same time.

This is not to say that, in the interwar period, no one tried to unravel this confusion. A small number of Marxists were consistent in seeing all imperialism as evil. Even if their view had not been suppressed, it is most unlikely that the intellectual cosmopolitanism of the Marxism of that period would have become widely accepted by the average Japanese, who then was embracing reactive nationalism. There were also right-wing intellectuals such as Ikki Kita and Shūmei Ōkawa; however, in failing to understand the actual conditions and desires of the neighboring countries in Asia, their views converged, in the final analysis, on ultranationalism. One product of the poverty of thought was the slogan of the "Greater East Asia Co-Prosperity Sphere," which took as its motto "hakkō ichiu" (literally, the eight corners of the world under one roof) meaning to make one great *ie* (family or household) for all from every last corner of the world. The thought reflected in this motto has frequently been seen abroad as representing the thought system or national ideology of prewar Japan, but that view is incorrect. The motto and the thought it expressed were no more than products of their times, created in the environment of impending world war.[10] Many of the "atrocities" committed by the Japanese army during the war had their roots in the ideological confusion of the officer class.

The imperfect development of this kind of thinking, however, was not only a prewar phenomenon. In postwar Japan, nationalism has been regarded as anticivilized thought, representative of all the evils that surround war, and has long been an emotional taboo. As discussed below, the counterargument to nationalism, advanced by most postwar progressive intellectuals and political parties, has depended heavily on these antiwar sentiments and continued to do so until very recently.[11] Thus from the prewar period until several years ago, few reasonable intellectual arguments about nationalism or its significance were forthcoming. The postwar Japanese, while enjoying affluence by free-riding on the Pax Americana, have failed to discuss openly and thoughtfully the two issues that continued to fester: their lingering attachment to the ethos of Japanese culture and their feelings about being victims of racial discrimination. Nationalism, even if one criticizes it, is not something one can avoid by attaching the label of militarism or fascism. Thus, until now, I believe there has been no change in the situation of having abandoned the intellectual effort of dealing with the mixture of emulation and repulsion. I take up this problem in the following sections.

SIGNIFICANCE OF THE SECOND WORLD WAR

On the eve of the Second World War, there was conflict among three ideas: the modified doctrine of the nonjust war as seen in the League of Nations, the anachronistic doctrine of the just war espoused by the have-nots, and the simple doctrine of the just war of anticolonialism.

The latter two were unexpected by-products of the first, and the competition among them was settled by the Second World War. Fought on a massive scale, this grim and total war could not have been waged without the banner of justice to mobilize the common people. From an early stage the fascist governments in Germany and Italy and the cabinets dominated by the army in Japan from the second half of the 1930s all repeatedly used the rhetoric of a restoration of justice in their efforts to prepare their citizens for war. In contrast, the decision to plunge into war was difficult for the Allies, who wanted to maintain the status quo. But once the decision was made, they waged an all-out war, repeatedly using indiscriminate large-scale bombing and aiding guerrilla warfare, in the name of resistance. It is natural to see both of these strategies as violating the existing international law, which was based on the doctrine of the nonjust war. To justify such strategies, a new logic of a just war against anticivilization (fascism) was needed. The symbolic result of this was the war crimes trials in Nuremberg and Tokyo. One has to say that the classical doctrine of the nonjust war, which had symbolized modern Europe, was made conceptually bankrupt at this point. I discuss the developments from that time to the present in detail in Chapter 4, but the bankruptcy of the classical doctrine of the nonjust war has until now been hidden in the opposition based on the doctrine of the just war in the U.S.-Soviet cold war. As a result, even today, in the early 1990s, the collapse of the nation-state system is not yet sufficiently recognized. As this reality becomes clear, classical nationalism will have to take on a fundamentally changed appearance.

Transnationalism

What is the substance of transnationalism, as it contrasts with nationalism? There are various images of transnationalism, and the situation is murky indeed. In fact, we have only various undefined and mixed images of internationalism, which is the stage preceding it. The confusion results from not having distinguished the three elements of nationalism—"natio"-ness (cultural individuality), sovereignty, and territoriality. Many people think that if one places emphasis on transcending "natio"-ness, then separating from one's unique cultural tradition and turning toward a universal, cosmopolitan culture will be "internationalization." If one focuses on sovereignty, then transferring sovereignty to an international organization or to an alliance will be internationalization. This happens in monetary policy and macroeconomic policy under the name of international cooperation, and the U.S.-Japanese negotiations on structural impediments that began in 1989 are one example of this. If one aims at transcending territoriality, then, for example, there will be no basis on which to restrain the activities of multinational businesses. At present these forms of internationalization are advancing in their separate ways, yet in parallel. However, to determine the substance of internationalism or transnationalism, or which form is desirable, we must first distinguish among three elements—sovereignty, territoriality, and cultural individuality—and consider which of these is the easiest, and which the hardest, to change.

To begin with, though transnationalism is in some form a denial of the nation-state, as a minimum necessary condition it cannot be anarchy. In realizing transnationalism, some kind of political economic system on a global scale—that is, a world-state—is clearly necessary. One can imagine various definitions for a world-state, but defining it as a political-economic system on a global scale, in which national boundaries have disappeared, perhaps comes closest to the commonly held image. That is, let us begin our discussion by imagining the world-state to be the stable, continued existence as a political-economic system of a borderless society in which people can go anywhere irrespective of anything like nationality; in which money, too, can be used anywhere, no longer known as dollars or yen; and in which knowledge and technology disseminate everywhere without hindrance. This is clearly a definition focusing on territoriality. This world-state is still a kind of state, but it does not necessarily have absolute sovereignty. That is, it can be imagined as including something like a "United States of Earth," which goes along with the decentralization of power. For the time being let us leave it undecided whether this is a state that has transcended cultural individuality.

What we are here calling the world-state can take various, specific forms, and one can imagine various administrative methods. For example, one can say that there are two kinds of boundaries that must be overcome in order for the world-state to be formed. The first kind includes the visible boundaries, symbolized by such things as barbed wire along national borders, border garrisons, exchange control laws, and passports. It is this type of visible boundary that people normally call a border. More important in a certain sense, however, is the second kind, the invisible boundaries in our minds, which develop from such things as the unique structure of thought developed through child-rearing and language, the knowledge and contents of information produced by education, and the images handed down through the historical and literary classics. One could say that this is what we broadly call ethos and tradition. The first kind of boundary corresponds to territoriality and the second to cultural individuality. As I note below, there is a great difference in the staying power of these two types of boundaries, and our vision of the world-state will change depending on the position we take in dealing with that difference.

Since the horrors of the two world wars, the arguments for a transnationalism that takes peace as its objective have gradually become influential. However, the world empires of the past, through their preoccupation with justice, had a character close to that of transnationalism. Throughout human history we come across two positions, depending on whether peace or justice is primary. In the present, which is the appropriate attitude vis-à-vis transnationalism? Or, how is the argument focused at this time?

THE TRADITION OF THE DOCTRINE OF JUST WAR

Certainly the twentieth century has been a prosperous time for the theory of the world-state, advanced by those devoted to an idealistic pacifism. Even in prewar Europe there were examples such as Henri Barbusse and Roman Roland, but after the war, particularly since the advent of nuclear weapons, the idea of world peace above all else has come to be the core concept supporting transnationalism. The intellectual situation in postwar Japan is a typical example of this. However, peacekeeping as a chief aim and the belief that the world-state can be a means toward peace are phenomena only of the past two or three centuries in world history. Before this period, the mainstream opinion in the historical civilizations had been that peace must be achieved as a result of the victory of a particular form of justice (for example, the justice founded on the teachings of a religion such as Christianity or Islam). The center of the debate had been rather a theory about justice, and pacifism was its by-product.

For example, it is hard to say that the Pax Romana was created by taking peace (*pax*) as its objective. The Roman efforts at expansion, such as the Punic wars, the Illyric wars, and the Macedonian wars, were not guided by the idea of a fixed peaceful order. For example, during the Punic wars, which ended with the destruction of Carthage, two arguments were heard in the Roman Senate: to destroy Carthage, or to let it continue to exist. Among the minority faction, which argued that Rome should co-exist peacefully and competitively with Carthage, there was a lingering affection, like that of Scipio Nasica, for the concept of an association of city-states, derived from Greece, but the argument made by the Elder Cato, that "we must destroy Carthage," won. In taking the opportunity of the Punic wars, the Roman people subsequently could not but leave behind the tradition of the city-state and stumble into the unfamiliar problem of imperial rule. The Roman methods of rule, which greatly increased the authority of citizens, adopted the tradition of the city-state; and given that they were both more reliable and effective than the previous methods of the Persians and the Macedonians, it was easy for the conquered to accept them too. However, the Romans, who did not have a world religion, could not call the numerous wars that had brought about the expansion of the imperium (Roman authority) "just wars." For example—as is often seen even today—they waged war on such shallow pretexts as the protection of allies and violation of treaties. Rome was an exception among world empires in that it did not have a sufficient concept of the just war.

It was not until the appearance of Christianity as a world religion that the concept of the just war was developed in a clear form. Augustine, who built the foundations of Christian theology during the breakup of the Roman Empire, tried to provide simultaneously a proof of Christianity (the question of the kingdom of God) and a proof for the existence of the Roman Empire (the question of a kingdom on earth). On the point of a kingdom on earth, he defined a war against an unjust country as a "just war," and he believed that Rome, because of its moral stature in prizing freedom and order, was a more just country than others. Thus he declared that "the Roman Empire is ordained by God, from whom every power is derived, and by whose providence all things are governed."[12] Incidentally, he shrewdly pointed out how the Roman gods (which were, for him, pagan gods) were beside the point in making sense of Roman history. His argument, however, in praising the "good conventions" of Rome, was not all that different from the typical arguments of Romans before him (such as Cicero). The decisive difference was in his insistence on such points as that in kingdoms on earth "peace is but a doubtful good,"[13] and that justice and injustice are relative. His true concern was with "the everlasting blessings that are promised for the future," and "earthly peace" was nothing more than an imperfect reflection of that.[14] Precisely because of this, however, he passed conclusive judgment on justice in kingdoms on earth and so could support just wars. The construction of this argument makes it suitable for Augustine to be known as the founder of the doctrine of the just war. Recent pacifism, which easily confuses peace on earth and true everlasting peace, can surely learn much from his argument.

With this argument of Augustine in the medieval Christian world, the doctrine of the just war, as represented by Thomas Aquinas, for example, became the dominant opinion, and efforts advanced to concretely prescribe the concept of justice. Together with the establishment of the feudal order, justice within the Christian world was defined as maintenance of the status quo, with necessary premises such as: taking retaliatory action for injuries suffered was just; justice should not be based on revenge or a lust for power; and the ways in which military power was used should be fair.[15] These conditions did not apply to wars against pagans. Thus, for example, in the great capricious undertakings known as the Crusades, merciless, unlimited military actions were taken against pagans. These should be called holy wars rather than just wars. This medieval doctrine of the just war had the double character of maintaining the status quo within one's own culture while allowing holy war toward different cultures, and this has exerted a strong influence on the Western world to the present day.

In contrast, in other areas of agrarian civilization, such as India and China, there are no such clearly thought-out examples of the doctrine of just war. China is typical in believing that a comprehensive order existed naturally in the agrarian civilizations of Asia and in defending rather than extending that order, or in assimilating foreign aggressors to that order over a period of time. Within this order, war was not condoned in any shape or form. An exception was the revolution against a dynasty that had lost the mandate of heaven, but besides this, there was no room for a doctrine of just war, and an ideology of holy war was of course also impossible. For example, the Han Chinese, the bearers of Chinese civilization, never set out to establish a permanent colonial administration. In particular, after the Tang dynasty there are no examples of attempted expeditions, except the fifteenth-century overseas expedition by the Ming, led by Zheng He, which reached as far as Zanzibar; this did not have the objective of territorial conquest, however, but was rather a huge show of force. (The Mongol dynasty is an exception, but it was a dynasty of Mongolians, not Chinese.) In contrast, the Portuguese, Spanish, Dutch, and British who advanced into Asia from the sixteenth century plundered and massacred and seized every opportunity for conquest. At the bottom of this contrast is not the difference between the humane and the inhumane but that between the presence and absence of a tradition of just war.

GENEALOGY OF PACIFISM

Among the schools in this line of thought are two contrasting positions on the theory of the world-state. In the just-war model, the world-state symbolizes justice, and war must be waged against the forces of injustice. In the pacifist model, the world-state symbolizes order, in which peace must always be maintained. The two positions may (as Augustine said) converge in the end. However, in the present, justice and peace almost always contradict each other.

The idea of the nation-state on the pacifist model was systematized in Europe. Its genealogy begins with Bernardin de Saint-Pierre, Jean-Jacques Rousseau, and Immanuel Kant. As I have already mentioned, sixteenth- and seventeenth-century Europe was embroiled in religious wars—which one should call holy wars—within the Christian church. With the Treaty of Westphalia in 1648, Europe gradually escaped the quagmire of religious war and entered, so to speak, a period of nonjust war, which did not emphasize justice; but even in the eighteenth century wars between countries (or rather between monarchs) had not stopped. However, the reaffirmation of homogeneity of Christian identity in the seventeenth century soon developed into Enlightenment universality in the eighteenth, and with this change came other new developments. Saint-Pierre, Rousseau, and Kant, accepting the guidance of rationality, expected the advent of a world-state "in the cause of everlasting peace" (Kant) and believed that this would put a stop even to nonjust war. Since then, arguments have been advanced within this pacifist tradition that see the formation of the world-state as the primary means of achieving peace. This argument, however, was generated against the background experience of the system of nonjust war between the relatively homogeneous countries of Europe and cannot appropriately be extended in this form to societies that contain heterogeneity. For example, substantial problems remain as to its applicability to the entirely heterogeneous non-European world that has been under colonial rule.

Many people refer to a world-state, but this intellectual endorsement is not enough. The Enlightenment approach represented by Kant is also not sufficient. Certainly it seems as if the concept of a universal humanity has already been established. If this is the case, then the concept of a world-state as human community would follow as a necessary conclusion. Without calling up the ghost of racism, it seems that we cannot in principle resist the concept of a world-state. All ideas, however, have a history as ideology, and limitations because of this. It was the eighteenth-century Enlightenment that established the concept of a universal humanity, and in its background were anthropocentrism and rationalism, which is rooted in industrialization. The world-state derived from these was a community supervised by the enlightened and civilized; and given that the measure of the degree of civilization was the gauge of rational progress, therein a logic discriminating between the uncivilized and civilization was to be found. For example, even Kant, who criticized colonialism, expected a role for the civilized in instructing the world-state.[16]

Of course, Enlightenment thought had the good intention of extending the blessings of civilization to all the uncivilized peoples and did not try to fix in place the distinction between civilized and uncivilized. The civilized were given nothing more than a role as leaders, with good intentions. This is greatly different from racist discrimination. However, by giving careful thought to the contribution of the non-Western cultures, and to the possibility of anti-industrialism, the human race today seems to be trying to fundamentally rethink the concept of unitary rational progress; at least the number of people who think in this manner is increasing. If this is the case, it will be difficult to gain consent for an approach that sees the world-state as the climax of rational progress. Support for the leadership of modern civilized man (the anthropocentric rationalist) will weaken. He will be hindered by his own history of erasing "uncivilized" culture in order to achieve progress. The pacifist model of the world-state, which began with Rousseau and Kant, has an unspoken common theme, running through the ideologies of Christian belief, the Enlightenment, and rational progress, and contains the possibility of degenerating into a holy war against the non-European world that rejects progress. If from now on we are going to make transindustrialism our subject, and so try to fundamentally rethink the ideologies of anthropocentrism and rationalism, then our scenario for the world-state cannot be the logic of unitary progressivism but must describe a design premised on the coexistence of diverse cultures. This is because the logic of progress, which made all the "natio" (the natural cultural units) converge in one climax, is already nowhere to be found. The Enlightenment theory of the world-state, in that sense, has ceased to be persuasive.

LIMITATIONS OF INSTINCTIVE PACIFISM

Many people are beginning to believe that the concept of the world-state supported by the idea of unitary rational progress is losing its meaning. If they are correct, is there something that can take its place? Some would respond by saying that it is instinctive pacifism,[17] which they would define as the idea that one's own life, the lives of one's children, and the lives of one's family are much more important than anything else; thus the condition—peace—that maintains it must be preserved above all else. Certainly these feelings resonate with the feelings of war-weariness, particularly in Japan (and so perhaps also in Germany), and are firmly shared irrespective of political ideology. Throughout the postwar period teachers in Japan have consistently taught the value of peace. They have done so, I believe, not because of the influence of the Japan Teachers' Union, with a leadership long dominated by members of the Communist party, but because of the psychological legacy of having been defeated in the war. As a result, the young generation in Japan has come to display revulsion at the mere mention of war and relief at the mere mention of peace.

But can we achieve a world-state by relying on such instinctive pacifism? To anticipate my own conclusion, the answer is no. Such a pacifism creates a logic of self-preservation that would deprive others of their lives in order to protect one's own life and the lives of loved ones. Self-love, under the pretext of affection, and indifference or cruelty toward strangers are but two sides of the same coin.

It has often been said that in order to defend one's existence, "self-preservation" or "legitimate self-defense" is permitted. But whatever one calls it, to justify such defense is to justify killing others. Those who disagree should consider the debate over the rights and wrongs of capital punishment. Those who favor capital punishment are judging that it is possible to deprive another person of her or his life in order to protect one's own life and livelihood.[18] (Even many of those who are against capital punishment base their argument on the possibility of a miscarriage of justice or of the rehabilitation of the criminal; they do not always hold the unconditional belief that we should not deprive others of their lives.) And once one has taken up this position of approving of capital punishment, it becomes difficult to discount the argument that, if one's way of life and livelihood are threatened, one should not reject even war.

In thought, there is a distinction between a threat to one's way of life and livelihood and a threat to one's existence; and legitimate self-defense, or self-preservation, is permitted only when faced by a threat to one's *existence*. In this way, the distinction between existence and livelihood corresponds to the question of where to place the limits on legitimate self-defense, or self-preservation—a question that has long troubled legal specialists. One can never deny the possibility, however, that threats to one's livelihood are connected to threats to one's existence. This is a powerful concern especially in the minds of the ordinary citizens who are not well-off. Thus, the argument for being allowed to live in peace by removing any possibility of a threat to one's existence always has a considerable degree of persuasive power. (This kind of argument is often used in opposing nuclear power or pollution.) In this way, a threat to one's existence is given an extended interpretation as a threat to one's livelihood. (This is why in Japan there is strong pressure to reread the right to life guaranteed in Article 24 of the Japanese Constitution as a right to livelihood.)

In domestic law, many of the limits on legitimate self-defense, or self-preservation, have been established by judicial precedent, and what constitutes a threat to one's existence has also been settled to some extent. In international relations, however, no court exists that might establish those limits. (The jurisdiction of the so-called International Court of Justice is established only when the persons involved make a declaration to accept it.) For example, many international treaties (such as the U.S. government's official document on the 1928 Kellogg-Briand Pact and Article 51 of the United Nations Charter) recognize a war in self-defense, but opposing interpretations of the definition of self-defense always make such treaties nothing more than worthless scraps of paper. The traditional understanding of self-defense, for example, is the defense of a country's territory; but given that this understanding takes as its premise the classical concept of the territorial state, it is not an ahistorical absolute. (In the future, for example, many countries' interests will change from being concerns with territory to concerns about trade and investment.) To borrow Benedict Anderson's expression, the concept of territory itself was originally something "imagined," and so it is easy for nations to expand the image of their *Lebensraum*.[19]

Many recent international incidents, for example, such as the military rescue operations in Mogadishu and Entebbe airports, and the Israeli destruction of the Iraqi nuclear reactor, have not involved territorial infringement. Similarly, one can easily imagine that, if oil tankers bound for Japan were to be sunk, or if Japanese living abroad were to be massacred in great numbers, the limits on the theory of territorial self-defense would be felt keenly, and the Japanese people's concept of legitimate self-defense would be severely shaken. Prewar incidents such as the U.S. expulsion of Japanese immigrants and the murder of Japanese living in China suddenly inflamed public opinion in Japan. When faced with these kinds of incidents, can instinctive pacifism—especially the Japanese version—provide a logic with which to extricate oneself from the crisis? The concerns of such pacifism are with one's immediate environment, but how far can this environment be expanded so that it can be an integral part of a logic of international politics? Is it to the limits of the physical national boundary? Or, going beyond the concept of the territorial state, does it go so far as to include the Japanese who are scattered throughout the world? The logic of instinctive pacifism cannot answer such questions. This very inability invites the risk of expanding the concept of self-defense.

More important, no human life is lived only in a narrow sense—satisfied with food, clothing, and shelter. There are many in the world, even now, who put ideals or religious faith at the center of their lives. Even those who do not talk about ideals and faith have ideal images of the world, or images of their lives (as already discussed in Chapter 1). The most cynical of individuals in fact lives by being consistent in terms of his own world image, and the attachment to that world image is an indispensable part of life in the broad sense. For example, personal things such as one's clothing, way of keeping house, relations with others, attachment to one's hometown, taste in food, and hobbies appear trifling. But for the person concerned, all of them together form the image of a certain consistency or create what we call an ethos, or culture in the broadest sense. Human beings live, to a certain extent, steeped in an ethos. For example, that many Japanese feel about rice differently from all other foods may well reflect the lingering ethos of Japanese farmers. Of course, a crisis in ethos (life image), unlike a problem such as a lack of food, is not directly connected to a crisis of existence in the biological sense. However, anger at having lost an ethos has deep roots and festers without easily disappearing from memory.

This is the question of "a life worth living for" and, moreover, the question of freedom in the fundamental sense, discussed in the first chapter. Generally speaking, even those of the young generation in Japan, who seem unconcerned with matters such as faith, ideals, and ethos, are searching for their own lifestyle niche in the midst of the kaleidoscope of contemporary consumer civilization. These young people, who reject anything to do with war with a feeling similar to that they have toward "3K" work—that is, work that is *kitanai* (dirty), *kurushii* (difficult), or *kitsui* (strenuous)—expect that the core component of their lifestyle will be being able to live in a peaceful Japan. To be satisfied merely with a guarantee of one's existence is to be an animal. Though there is room for argument as to whether this is a blessing or a curse, to be human is to be particular about the faith, ideals, ethos, or lifestyle one has built up through the course of one's life. Any threat to these human attachments is felt as a threat to one's existence. This tendency to expand the concept of a threat to one's existence is a fundamental human characteristic.

What we are searching for here is the definition of peace. It is not enough to define peace merely as a state in which there is no threat to one's existence; human beings cannot find any meaning in merely existing. One can imagine a state in which life as existence is guaranteed to all, but freedom of action or thought beyond this is not allowed. A number of actual circumstances are close to such a situation in offering little that makes life worth living. A state in which there is no threat to one's existence is merely the negative condition for freedom: the problem is the substance of the life one can find in this state. Social systems that do not provide something worth living for, or an ethos, frequently collapse through internal disorder. This is why the rebellions in the colonies occurred despite the extreme hardship they inevitably entailed. Clearly, what provides meaning to peace is a positive substance, such as faith, ideals, ethos, or lifestyle; and so rebellion is in fact a safety valve that corrects a contradiction between the negative condition and the positive substance.

For peace in the international sense, the situation is the same. Is it possible to define peace in this case merely as a state in which there is no war? If the world were to become a single state system, by definition wars between states would be impossible, and peace would result. If, however, this world-state included a colonial system, or were a repressive system like that envisioned by Aldous Huxley or George Orwell that crushed cultures differing from the one that is accepted, how much sense would there be in calling the order thus achieved "eternal peace"? Peace without justice and traditions for all is meaningless. Historically, no single ideology has been satisfied in calling peace merely a state in which there is no war. On the one hand, in religions such as Judaism, Islam, and Christianity, war has been something brought about because the realization of the divine will was obstructed or disturbed, and in this sense, the ultimate antithesis of war has to be what Augustine called "peace . . . as everlasting life in the kingdom of God." For example, famous expressions such as the Jews' "shalom" and Islam's "islam" are sometimes translated as peace, but originally they signified an absolute belief in God the Creator.

On the other hand, in India and China, social peace is a reflection of the original cosmological order and should naturally go together with peace of mind. In this case, the opposite of a state of war is in the end a harmonious order that incorporates tranquillity of mind. The Greek and Roman concept of peace (*eirene* and *pax*) was in fact nothing more than a concept resulting from a compromise between two contrasting concepts. In all of these ideologies, there is not one that talks of peace without reference to justice or order. The few exceptions are cases such as the Jain religion of India, and minority Christian sects such as that of the Quakers, to whom any injuring of life is considered evil.

In short, it is easy for instinctive pacifism to fall into the trap of taking as absolute and universal one's feelings about one's own life image that is to be protected, and not recognizing the narrow-mindedness and the relativity of one's own life image. Even instinctive pacifism does not usually deny the concept of self-defense. What is ambiguous, however, is how to determine the sphere of self-defense. The concepts of self-defense that have a visible dimension, such as territorial self-defense and defense of a country's nationals (those who have citizenship), do not determine definitively the sphere of self-defense. Above all, self-defense has the problem of an invisible, or psychological, dimension. For example, if, for the Japanese, the object of psychological self-defense includes their unique way of thinking about nature and human relations—such as their particular view of rice—to people in other countries this will seem nothing more than an unjustifiably extended interpretation of the concept of self-defense. This way of thinking could not but cause the Japanese to be less than sensitive toward the feelings of people in other countries.

In contrast, those who belong to Christianity or Islam and hold transcendental beliefs may perceive religious persecution as a grave threat to their own lives, even when it is caused by events outside their own countries. The strong reaction of an average American to an infringement of freedom and equality is an analogous phenomenon. For many people, the pursuit of justice is an indispensable principle in their life image. If we were to call American feelings about justice an ideology, and the attitude Japanese have toward rice only a true feeling about life, then that in itself would be a manifestation of the structure of the Japanese consciousness. This kind of Japanese ethos has its own significance, and there are also problems in the excessive American feelings about justice. What I want to point out here is that the instinctive pacifism of the Japanese can never, in its present form, become a theory of peace for the whole world.

Certainly, instinctive pacifism exists in the broad sense not only in Japan, but in all countries in various forms, and it is indispensable as the general motive force of pacifism. Included, unconsciously, in this pacifism, however, is an attachment to the ethos that supports one's own life image, and this in itself is a desire to defend justice in the loosest sense. Instinctive pacifism, though, contains a fundamental dilemma, in that the logic of self-preservation, which it seeks as a minimum, and the freedom of action to protect one's own life image frequently harm such freedoms of others. As Augustine would say, in "the kingdom on earth" the theory of peace and the theory of justice cannot in fact be perfectly separated. Readers may already have noticed that this problem is a special example of the dilemma of freedom of action mentioned earlier. One cannot explain a theory of peace without explaining a theory of justice. Without facing up squarely to the dilemma of freedom, pacifism cannot be an ideology that will give rise to a world-state. The attempt to see pacifism as a new concept of progressivism, as with efforts to achieve the most complete possible democracy or environmentalism, cannot but confront the question of its underlying basic incompatibility with liberalism.

PACIFISM IN THE POSTWAR ORDER

In Japan, the postwar progressives (the Marxists and others on the left in the spectrum of ideology) have advocated a pacifism based on unarmed neutrality and so have garnered the sympathy of the instinctive pacifists. It was in fact often Marxism, however, that provided the theoretical background for this argument of unarmed neutrality. According to the theory, war was a necessary attribute of capitalism and a socialist world revolution the only means of eradicating war. The fact that people's instinctive pacifism was not resulting in world peace was also due to the evils of the capitalist system. Putting aside the question of its realism, this Marxist theory of world revolution was an ideology and as such provided a consistent explanation across the board, from economics to politics. It was the logical consistency of Marxism that secretly supported pacifism in postwar Japan. However, given that Marxist logic was in fact a theorizing of a just war against capitalism, a contradiction with pacifism was inescapable. Many of the acts of aggression of communist regimes were explained as just wars undertaken to stop capitalism. As these aggressive acts were repeated, however, in Hungary, Czechoslovakia, and Afghanistan, for example, people's suspicions began to mount. And socialist progress, which was expected to be made at the high price of such aggressive acts, was not being realized in any way. Thus people began to stop believing in the communist utopia, and instinctive pacifism had no choice but to abandon any effort to save Marxism. Faced with this situation, even those who were influential proponents in postwar Japan of a pacifism based on unarmed neutrality from a certain time on stopped depending on Marxist thought, at least on the surface, and tried to make up for it with what one has to call a "strategic analysis of peace."

Naoki Kobayashi has stated: "If we persist on remaining unarmed, then however bad things turn out to be, the worst that can happen is a military occupation of Japan. . . . It is impossible, at least in a country of courageous people determined to preserve freedom and independence, for an occupying [force] to deprive the people of their culture or spirit, let alone to be able to commit genocide."[20] Such words reveal simultaneously a disregard for the lessons of history and intellectual confusion.

Many times courageous people have been massacred, in the tens and hundreds of thousands, from ancient Carthage to the modern Soviet Union under Joseph Stalin, and in these cases, when culture loses its core (a large number of persons able to transmit culture), it degenerates and frequently is destroyed. There are those who cite the American postwar occupation of Japan as an example of when this was not the case; but because this outcome was due to the particular character of American hegemony (see Chapter 3), one cannot generalize from this event either. If one rejects arms in opposing an invasion, then logically one must also reject military resistance after the occupation. Can a country that submits weakly in this way to a degeneration of its culture and does not put up any resistance really be called "a country of courageous people determined to preserve freedom and independence"? "Courageous people" here means people who remain faithful to their own thought, however much they are compelled to change it, but few such strong people ever exist.

To answer yes to this question, in the context of liberal thought, would mean assuming that human beings can completely separate freedom of action and freedom of thought. (Western mystical philosophers, devotees of Hinduism, and followers of Buddhism, Taoism, Lao-tse, and Ze huang-zi [Chuang-tzu] are examples.) One cannot perhaps say that such people never exist. This belief, however, is an extreme argument on one side of liberalism, and in reality, there are almost no people who can have their actions restricted and yet have complete freedom of thought. Japan could not be among the countries that had as its subjects only people with such strength. By positing such an extreme hypothesis one cannot overcome the fundamental dilemma of freedom. In the end, I believe, the pacifism

based on unarmed neutrality in postwar Japan did not—after its disasso-
ciation from Marxism—attain the level of a consistent ideology. Or rather,
one should say perhaps that it was an extreme intellectual carelessness,
indulged by the fact of peace, in which the U.S.-Japan Security Treaty isolated Japan from the threat of war.

I am not saying that an argument for demilitarized neutrality can
never become a consistent ideology. But *unconditional nonviolence*, in
which one would never harm another's life, even in self-defense (the unconditional argument against capital punishment belongs to this category)
is not a sufficient basis for a coherent ideology. Merely by saying that they
will not use violence, human beings will stop thinking and sink into an
enervated state. The absence of action almost always signifies a poverty of
thought. In not using violence and yet demonstrating one's defiance, for
the first time the argument for disarmament and peace can have consistency as an ideology. In this way, the argument for disarmament and peace
converges with the principle of *nonviolent resistance*. In fact, if we hypothesize a situation in which Japan has been occupied and put under an
oppressive rule—that is, the same situation in which Gandhi was placed
in India—then the argument of unarmed neutrality as an ideology cannot
but come extremely close to the rigorous theory of nonviolent resistance.
The standpoint of the "courageous people" above can only be of this form.

Even if the principle of nonviolent resistance can be the motive force
for a revolution that will bring down the existing system, there is a strong
possibility that it cannot be a sufficient guide with which to build and
maintain a new political-economic system. (For example, even if one could
overthrow a colonial system with nonviolent resistance, would it in fact be
more or less practicable to create a new independent state from a gathering
of tribes under the restriction of an absolute prohibition on violence?) The
reason is that the overwhelming majority of people are not strong enough
to sustain the principle of unconditional nonviolence to the extent of sacrificing their own livelihoods and ethos. If after the war Gandhi had had
to bear the responsibility of building an independent Indian state, then a
different Gandhi would have had to appear. The problem is the same in
creating a world-state from a gathering of nations. It is impossible for all
countries to martyr themselves to the principle of nonviolence by sacrificing their own disparate ideals and interests. For example, opinion cannot
but be divided as to how the use of violence by a nation is to be punished.

This is not the only problem. The market economy and parliamentary
democracy are often cited as examples of nonviolent social institutions.
These institutions, however, as some people point out, do not bring about
equilibrium or homogeneity or guarantee peace. Even in these institutions, there are factors that can lead to a polarization of opposition and
spark violence. That these institutions have been chosen is not simply because their dependence on violence is limited but because they give strong
support to the concepts of liberalism and democracy. Let me reiterate: lib-

eralism and democracy are not means by which to guarantee peace but are a different kind of ideology, with different origins, and so there is a possibility of hostility between these and pacifism.

In international relations, the democratization of the United Nations or the liberalization of trade will not necessarily lead to equilibrium and harmony. Even if one tried to build a world federation with these concepts, it would be difficult to escape the outbreak of military clashes. If one were to plan a world-state with the sole idea of eradicating war, it would be possible that such a plan could bring into existence a heartless autocrat whose only concern was minimizing violence. In fact, what justified the Roman imperium was the concept of protection of allies. There would probably have been fewer lives sacrificed in Africa if European colonialism had remained there. Nowadays, when nuclear war has the capacity to wipe out the human race, there are no objections to saying that one of the most vital objectives for a world-state is to stave off full-scale war. But if there do not exist ideas that one must defend, even at the cost of one's life (such as national independence or freedom of thought), then what meaning would there be in achieving world peace under the direction of an autocrat?

We must not think of the world-state as a utopia. The world-state is not a final destination. If we are going to try to give concrete form to a world-state, then the process must be one of trial and error in which multiple ideas quarrel, including not only peace but also freedom of thought. The purely pacifist argument for a world-state—that is, the belief that we should build a world-state only in order to achieve peace—is nothing but a symptom of an overly constricted field of vision. In this sense, whether one looks at the Kantian, Enlightenment argument for the world-state or at Japanese-style instinctive pacifism, there has not yet been formulated an ideology that might lead to a world-state. Attainment of such a state is still only an empty promise.

Of course this is the case not only in Japan. Globally, the idea of the world-state is in a confused condition. The mainstream history of the Western world has long included the idea that through the nation-state system based on the doctrine of nonjust war one might adequately restrain the evil influence of war. There has also been considerable support for the idea that if one advanced the doctrine of the nonjust war, one would soon arrive at a doctrine of no war. It is also clear, however, that these ideologies of the nonjust war have been repeating their cycle in vain: from the rule of the doctrine of the just war in the Middle Ages; to the schism of the doctrine of the just war between the old and new churches before the Treaty of Westphalia; to power politics based on the doctrine of the nonjust war from the eighteenth century to the First World War (colonialism, however, was justified by the doctrine of the just war); to the loss of power by the doctrine of the nonjust war following the First World War, and the reappearance of the doctrine of the just war (the anticolonialist doctrine of the just war, the doctrine of the just war held by the have-nots); to the

bankruptcy of the doctrine of the nonjust war during and after the Second
World War (the doctrine of the just war against the Axis powers), and the
schism in the doctrine of the just war (the anti-Soviet doctrine of the just
war and the socialist doctrine of the just war).

During this time, the scenario of a world-state along the lines of the
League of Nations or the United Nations was envisioned as an extension of
the doctrine of the nonjust war, but in the end the double structure of the
doctrine of the nonjust war (in the system of collective security treaties)
and the doctrine of the just war (in the U.S.-Soviet cold war) became established as the mainstream and so supported the relative state of peace after
the war (as is discussed fully in Chapter 4). In this sense, what redeemed
the doctrine of the nonjust war from a final bankruptcy was, ironically
enough, the doctrine of the just war as seen in the U.S.-Soviet cold war
and not, as some people had expected, the doctrine of no war. However,
the period of revival of the doctrine of the just war, generated by the cold
war, did not last either. The failure of the wars against Vietnam and Afghanistan weakened to a remarkable extent the morale of the just war in
both the United States and the Soviet Union. The socialist just war that
made a leader of the Soviet Union has suffered an internal collapse, and
correspondingly, and ironically, the anti-Soviet just war that made a leader
of the United States has also lost its foundations. Since it now looks as
though the complete prosecution of a just war would lead to the destruction of the human race, in ideology the center of gravity is shifting from
holy war to the mundane battles of economic wars. As Europe groped in
the seventeenth and eighteenth centuries toward coexistence among the
competing religious dogmas, so in the present world are we not searching for a new agreement on nonjust war that would make it possible for
disparate cultures to coexist? What is required—as seen in the Treaty of
Westphalia, which recognized both the new and old religions—is a tolerance of a polymorphism of ideologies and not the creation of any single
ideology as absolute. The minimum condition for transnationalism is perhaps nothing but this idea of tolerance.

The Obstacles for Transnationalism

The concept of the world-state is thus still immature, and a scenario
to achieve it has not been described. Even supposing, however, that the
concept and clear scenario of a world-state were provided, there would
obviously be huge obstacles to its realization. Given that the nation-state
is indeed a sovereign state, it is the strongest existing political and military
unit, and in most normal circumstances neither a larger unit (some kind
of international organization) nor a smaller one (a region within the country) could possibly defy it. At the end of the twentieth century, nationalism has not yet surrendered its position as the most influential of political
myths. It is supported by the conflicts of interest between existing states

and the differences between communal cultural "natio," particularly languages; these differences have their roots in all aspects of everyday life, and given that they contain a multitude of historical memories, they will continue to oppose the dissolution of national boundaries. If transnationalism is to create some kind of unified system in place of the nation-state, then the indispensable condition for this will be the appearance of a real incentive strong enough to crush the historical inheritance of nationalism.

In the first place, for a polity of fixed domain including transnationalism, certain conditions—not only the establishment of concepts with which to achieve this but also conditions in reality—will have to be fulfilled. For example, considering the question of the scale of the polity, be it large or small, there are actual pluses and minuses (connected to benefits realized in people's lives) in spheres such as the economic (per capita production), the military (the strategic ease of attack or defense), and the cultural (the degree of heterogeneity among lifestyles or education). For each union there will be an optimum size that will maximize the total benefits. Thus, to make the union successful, it will be important to choose a size for which the total benefits will at least be positive, or to approach as nearly as possible a size that maximizes the benefits. The ideological force of such things as religion may make one forget for a moment these actual advantages and disadvantages, but one cannot completely disregard actual conditions. The union that is the nation-state has been no exception in this regard.

NATIONALISM AND INDUSTRIALIZATION ONCE IN HARMONY

As I mentioned in the first section, following the sixteenth and seventeenth centuries in Europe, the midsized political union in the form known as the nation-state, founded on a linguistic identity, was perhaps close to the optimum as an actual solution. The revolution in firearms had made the feudal union too small (taking what we call the fiefs of the nobility as the typical unit of feudal integration), but at the same time cultural (particularly linguistic) pluralism made large-scale unification as an empire problematic. Far more important, however, than these military or cultural factors was the economic development of capitalism, which began from about the sixteenth century. This was proto-industrialization, the economic development between the first period of industrialization and the full-fledged industrialization that began in the second half of the eighteenth century.

I discuss the relationship between proto-industrialization and capitalism in detail when I give a strict definition of the latter in Chapter 5, but there is no doubt that the development in this period, as Karl Polanyi and many others have pointed out, necessitated a market that clearly went beyond the scale of the local market or the regional market.[21] And yet what was made necessary was not merely the scale of the market.

Production under capitalism systematically generates huge quantities of manufactured goods. In order to make the most of the advantages of this new means of supply, there must be continuous public order and peace, to guarantee the systematic flow of goods and to make the fulfillment of business contracts reliable. That is, a stable market with a high density of transactions must exist. This is the creation of what one might call a high-quality market, and in order to achieve this, using the cultural community with common language and customs as the basis for the state was most expedient. This was one of the main reasons for joining together the "natio" and the "state."

One method of improving the quality of the market was to increase the density of transactions by investing in such things as a legal system, police, a military, roads, bridges, canals, and harbors. The scale of investment in these public goods had to be sufficiently large to guarantee significant benefits; at the same time, the scale of investment could not be so large that the costs of the total investment exceeded the benefits it yielded. As Richard Rosecrance noted, the cost effectiveness of the investment in public goods is best raised when it is made within a fixed territory, and this was a reason for creating the territorial state.[22] Thus in the initial period of the capitalist economy, the conditions required for political unification took the form of a conformity between the natio and the territorial sovereign state, and these came together in the form of the "nation-state"—what Polanyi so appositely called the appearance of the "national market."[23] For example, the concept of the commonwealth (a people and territory who held their wealth in common) that appeared in sixteenth-century Britain was different from the concept of the national market. These nation-states of Western Europe, with Britain as a forerunner, offered a political union to support a good-quality market. Numerous national markets appeared, and the balance-of-power system following the Treaty of Westphalia allowed both quarrels among, and the continued existence of, these national markets, or nation-states.

Of course capitalism relies not only on the domestic market (the national market) but also on overseas markets. This fact is an important reason for its development. During the initial period of capitalism, mercantilism frequently emphasized this fact. However, capitalist industry cannot easily develop without a stable national market. Only Portugal and Spain were able to prosper as trading states, depending mainly on overseas markets. There will be an opportunity below to discuss the newly industrializing economies (NIEs) as trading states, many of which can be seen at present in East Asia.

Particularly in the capital-intensive industry that followed the industrial revolution, the demand for stable returns on investment grew still more strict, the search for a homogeneity within the labor force grew ever stronger, and so the need for political union increased still further. The midsized nation-states of Western Europe already provided the national market that was the minimum necessity during the industrial revolution. In this sense, the fact that Western Europe had already devised the nation-state and a corresponding nation-state system was a lucky historical accident for industrialization, and as industrialization proceeded, the significance of the accident became even better appreciated. Thus, one could say that one of the main factors that actually strengthened the nation-state was industrialization.

At the beginning of the nineteenth century, the creation of nation-states and industrialization were advancing hand in hand. Certainly, military factors also played a large role, and, as noted earlier, the wars following the appearance of Napoleon became wars between nations. In the background, however, was a fierce trade war between Britain and France, and the British victory was also a victory for the economic liberalism Britain advocated as well as for British industry. Along with this, the growth of productive capacity in each nation, and the provision of the public goods supporting it, came to be regarded by the general populace as a sign of national strength and a source of national pride. The Great Exhibition of 1851 at London's Crystal Palace and the Paris Exhibition of 1889 that rivaled it were both events that displayed the might of the great industrial nations and strengthened national consciousness. During the nineteenth century, nationalism mobilized all classes of individuals (the people) and grew stronger, indissolubly linked to industrialization: nationalism and economic liberalism (market economics) were in harmony.

Into the twentieth century, however, when both productivity and technology have changed (especially in recent years), the nation-state no longer necessarily offers the optimum market size, and the connection between the territorial state and industrialization is no longer indispensable. The economic changes resulting from the continuing progress in productivity and technology—as seen for example in "informatization" (a veritable revolution in our ability to create and use information), the international transfer of capital, the multinationalization of business, and the environmental destruction across national boundaries—are creating a strong, real incentive toward transnationalism. The optimum market size exceeds the nation-state and is expanding toward the whole world. This is well demonstrated by the present activity of multinational businesses and by the remarkable rise of trading states especially prominent in East Asia. Solely as an economic condition, the connection between the territorial state and industrialization is no longer necessary. The remarkable present-day developments (superindustrialization) are surely becoming a decisive incentive toward internationalism, or rather transnationalism. At the same time, the happy memories of the time when industrialization and nationalism were in harmony are creating a psychological inertia and becoming a primary cause for resistance to transnationalism.

ADVANCE TOWARD A BORDERLESS ECONOMY

What form will transnationalism take? It is not likely to be the world-state, the concept of which is as yet underdeveloped. And we must note that resistance from the mythologized reality, that is the nation-state, is strong. Thus transnationalism, though driven by powerful economic factors, will probably advance only incrementally. Which of the three aspects discussed in the opening of this chapter—sovereignty, territoriality, and cultural individuality—will be the first to change? Changing the perspective somewhat, let us separate the changes into those affecting the economic constituents within the state (typically, businesses), the state itself, and the relationships between states.

1. As superindustrialization progresses, rapidly increasing amounts of the economic activities of businesses and all kinds of organizations are being conducted across national boundaries. There is a major reason why the phrase "borderless economy" has been much used recently. Certainly, the ties between economic actors, whether individuals or corporations, and their countries of origin are weakening, and there is a tendency for the former to disregard the latter's control. Already, countries can no longer control investment. This of course is a result substantially influenced by the remarkable advance of transportation and communications. Today, vast amounts of capital flow, freely and instantaneously, across national boundaries with no regard for the national interest and are strengthening as never before the ties among national economies. This, above all, has been why nations are being forced to coordinate their economic policies ever more closely.

Many world leaders among businesses are energetically establishing factories, research centers, and affiliates outside their own countries (the countries where the businesses were originally founded); in short, there is a great trend toward the multinationalization of business. As a result, powerful companies in cutting-edge industries frequently act in ways contrary to their own countries' national interests. For example, a multinational company invests abroad, thereby lowering employment opportunities in its own country and increasing domestic anxiety. Of course, one's own country's government and political connections (for example, defense expenditures and other government contracts) are a large source of economic interests, and in many cases even a multinational company takes its links with its own country very seriously. However, multinational businesses already operate beyond the control of their countries' governments. Economically, there are certainly signs that point to a dissolution of national boundaries.

2. The character of the nation-state itself is changing. In particular, there are signs that the territorial character of the state is changing because many countries have acquired interests beyond their own borders. As Rosecrance has shown, each country's economy is increasingly depen-

dent on the world market, and the territorial state may well be gradually changing into a trading state. But this is true not only for trade: each country's overseas investment—and not just the investments of advanced countries—has reached levels that can no longer be protected by colonial rule or gunboat diplomacy. The Asian NIEs too are actively investing overseas. In one respect, this fact is a result of the multinationalization of business mentioned in change 1, above, and, for the nation-state, some kind of effort toward transnationalism is unavoidable. The territoriality of the state, however, will not be easy to change, only inasmuch as it has come to play an important symbolic role. Thus, we may well choose the trend toward "groupism," mentioned in change 3, which follows, as an easier path to lead us through the transition.

3. With the decline in the independence of the state, there is a trend for relations between states to become more intensive. Clearly, throughout the postwar period there has been an increase in groupism between various states, and this trend will not change in the future. Many sum up this groupism as "bloc-ism" and warn that it is a retrogression; but their view is not well thought out. One can imagine groupism between countries as an intermediate stage between the system of independent states under the nation-state system and an inclusive, comprehensive system along the lines of a world-state. The general characteristic of this groupism is cooperation achieved to lower the barriers among a number of countries, and, if cooperation improves, sovereignty is abrogated to a certain degree. The most obvious postwar example is the system of collective security treaties—such as the North Atlantic Treaty Organization (NATO); the network of treaties between the United States and Korea, Japan, the Philippines, Taiwan, and Australia and New Zealand; and the Warsaw Pact organization. These are clearly far more enduring than the prewar military alliances, and technological cooperation between the participant countries has developed to a high degree.

Though some are more intensive than others, various kinds of economic (policy) groups have been created, such as the Organization for Economic Cooperation and Development (OECD), the Organization of Petroleum Exporting Countries (OPEC), bilateral free-trade agreements, and summit meetings of the advanced nations. The prewar economic blocs were nothing more than examples of this economic groupism with a strong degree of exclusivity. Another distinct phenomenon of the postwar era is the systematization of international cooperation on particular issues—that is, the establishment of what theorists of international relations would call "regimes." There are countless examples of regimes, beginning with the General Agreement on Tariffs and Trade (GATT), the International Monetary Fund (IMF), and treaties on the law of the sea, but because the degree of systematization and cooperation among the participant countries is high, they have garnered particular attention. These too, however, are a weak kind of groupism, inasmuch as not all countries participate.

The characteristic of the postwar world has been the overlapping of these networks of treaties and cooperative relations, or, to borrow the words of systems theorists, the formation of not a tree system but a rhizome system. These networks differ in their degree of exclusivity, and there are various ways in which the system can be formed—where economic factors are important, where cultural motivations are strong, or where both factors are mixed together. Although economic factors connected to industrialization might indicate a large, world-scale network, cultural factors would probably suggest a different size. Even economic factors, such as the supply of resources (oil, for example), the market for manufactured goods, and the supply of capital, may well suggest differences in the desirable scale.

Again, as can be seen frequently in the examples mentioned above, groupism is not just a regional phenomenon or incompatible with high-ranking international organizations. Groups formed before the war were limited in number and were readily classified according to the bloc to which each belonged. In contrast, the formation of groups since the war has been a mixture of a great division into East and West and something that has even gone beyond that. Thus, what we see is a clear contrast between the prewar tree structure and the postwar rhizome structure.

The fundamental factor has been the accelerated advance of relationships of mutual dependence in the postwar world, and in this the emphasis of scholars on interdependence theory is correct. In the economic arena, superindustrialization is proceeding; militarily, it is doubtful whether any country independently has the ability even to defend itself (particularly when one thinks of economic cost); and against this background there is the remarkable information revolution in the international arena. In the midst of this advancing dynamic of interdependence, groupism among countries will become even more prevalent in the future as a handy means of coping with increasing interdependence. This is because groupism can be adopted without compromising the fundamental principle of the nation-state. It is difficult to predict, however, which among the complicated possibilities of groupism will be chosen, and it is doubtful whether its rhizome character guarantees a convergence to some kind of global order. Whatever the case, groupism will progress, and if it has a unique character that it has not had until now, then the sovereignty of the nation-state may well in fact grow weaker.

TRANSITION TO A BORDERLESS CULTURE

Among those who emphasize the phenomenon of the borderless economy, there are quite a number who believe the exchange of people, information, and knowledge will increase as borderlessness proceeds in the economic arena. The opinion that the transition to a completely borderless world is a long-term natural tendency is being accepted too uncritically. In the theory of international relations, interdependence theory, since about the middle of the 1970s, has stressed that the natural development of an increase in international exchange will by itself lead to a harmonious world order. That is, the proliferation of regimes will converge in a world order. However, Ernst B. Haas, who was the father of interdependence theory, has grown remarkably pessimistic about this theory on the basis of empirical research.[24]

The most important point at issue is the huge difference between the dissolution of visible national boundaries and the dissolution of invisible national boundaries. One cannot imagine that the movement toward a borderless economy is naturally linked to a transition to a borderless culture. This is because if we are to move toward a borderless culture, then an exchange of people and information alone will not be sufficient; some kind of common denominator or what philosophers call "commensurability" that will serve as the interpretive framework (our worldviews, our value systems, or in short, our image of the world) will be essential in achieving this exchange.

In order to understand this, let us compare it with the case of economic activity. The interpretive framework for the aspect of human action known as economic activity (for example, an understanding of such things as money and contracts) is common property that is shared throughout the world. This is why the transition to a borderless economy has progressed easily. In comparison with the dissolution of the visible national boundaries related to such things as the economy, however, the dissolution of the invisible national boundaries in people's hearts and minds will clearly not be easy.

Since long ago many diverse cultural groups have lived in the same place and engaged in active economic transactions and exchange of information. The Jews who have been in European countries for centuries, the African-Americans in U.S. society, and the guest-workers in postwar Europe are good examples, but they are also good examples of how increased social contact alone does not effortlessly bring about cultural agreement. In contrast, exchange through the education abroad of the elite, for example, is effective only to a limited extent, and learning through overseas travel is more for amusement than for enlightenment. In many instances the foreign-educated elite even become antipathetic toward the countries where they study, and the behavior of tourists often causes citizens of the host countries to think less of the tourists' home countries. Without an agreement between countries on the interpretive framework, knowledge, information, and emotions will only be seen through a distorted lens.

It is often observed that the world has come to share the same information because of mass communication, especially television. Certainly in the narrow sense the common nature of information has increased. However, an exchange of *information* does not necessarily mean an exchange of *interpretation* or the communication of *knowledge* or *wisdom*. Although the same information is disseminated throughout the world, it is always surprising how greatly the interpretation differs by country. Newspaper headlines, or one word from a television reporter, can completely change the complexion of the news. In every country, the mass media pick and choose information to conform with the interpretive framework of the citizens, thereby letting them see what they want to see and read what they want to read. It is extremely difficult to break through this framework. In the long run, as the exchange of people and information eventually influences the interpretive framework, the situation in which the boundaries of a polity and those of one's worldview are identical will gradually disappear. This will be a slow process over generations if not centuries, and during this phase contact may well heighten cultural animosity and thus could bring about a reversal. What is crucial is that one should distinguish between the move toward a borderless economy and the transition to a borderless culture, at least in terms of tempo of change.

Further, culture is becoming a means of opposition to the change to a borderless economy. The transition to a borderless economy is generating a massive influx of goods and capital and is demanding difficult changes in domestic industry and firms. The existing domestic interests try to resist the economic invasion by insisting on an indigenous life, lifestyle, and culture that cannot be converted into an economic value. Faced with the transition to a borderless economy, they try to raise barriers along cultural boundaries. For example, in the present economic tensions between the United States and Japan there are clear signs of this in both countries. Thus at least in the transitional period, the transition to a borderless economy may well heighten cultural borders. We must understand that the transitions to a borderless economy and a borderless culture, for different reasons and following different paths, will proceed separately.

Whether we call it interdependence or the creation of a borderless economy, the trend toward transnationalism in the visible dimension is a logical result of the nation-state's having been a historically unique phenomenon, and the strength of superindustrialization provides an impetus to that trend. That is, at least in the visible dimensions, it seems as if the shift from the pole of nationalism to the pole of transnationalism is already happening. But this movement is not a smooth one that can be left to take its natural course; it will probably require resolute intervention from us as human beings. For example, as I explore in detail below, will it be enough to live with a set of principles centered on the United Nations, will there be a revival of U.S. hegemony, or will it be possible to have an international system besides these? Depending on our resolution on this point, there will be disturbances, including deviations from the trend many people have assumed, reversals, and maybe even a world catastrophe. Moreover, this resolution will depend greatly on how we think borderlessness should be achieved in the invisible dimensions.

From the beginning, through what kind of dynamic has the human interpretation of the world changed? There is no easy answer to this question. Some believe convergence to a single, scientific or rational worldview will occur, as was predicted by the Enlightenment. But others believe that, just as each person has his or her own individuality, each culture will continue to have its own worldview, exhibiting its individuality in some core element (for example, in what I would call the different weight put on a transcendental orientation or a hermeneutic orientation). There is no need for the individuality of this worldview to be tied to the specific systematic framework of the nation-state. It is surely natural, however, that there should be differences in interpretation of the world between those who live in the tropics and those who live in the cold regions, between oceangoing peoples and inland peoples, and between those who live in the desert and those who live in the humid deltas. If there are peoples who have variously developed these multiple worldviews, then humanity may be able to get some kind of grasp on the world as a whole. And if there are people who can look back on the lives of people in the past with empathy, then we may be able to understand human history as a whole. Beginning with (what social scientists call) this synchronic and diachronic spread, human beings can exist as reflecting animals.

Up until now, the communal "natio" has had a significance and the nation-state has played a large role as bonds that hold in common the lives of both the past and the present. Of course there is no reason why the unique historical entity that is the nation-state should have a monopoly on the role as such a place. However, it is surely indispensable for human beings, having a historical sense of time, that some kind of "natio" should offer such a place and for there to appear there some kind of regionalism. What has come to be called nationalism is probably weakening. However, what we must call "natio-ism"—some kind of cultural individuality—will not disappear, and it should be preserved. To return to the argument made at the beginning of this chapter, there is a high possibility that in the respects of sovereignty, and then territoriality, nationalism will disappear. But cultural individuality in such things as ethos and tradition will not collapse easily, and it may even be desirable for it not to disappear.

Our task must then be to accept the shift to borderlessness in the visible dimensions and to build a world in which much cultural individuality can exist. Even if these units of cultural individuality are for a time weighed down by the inertia of the nation-state framework, they cannot forever be fixed in their historical existence as Japan, the United States, France, and so on. The world system in the political-economic sense must also be created so as to preserve cultural individuality.

CHAPTER 3

The Theory of Hegemonic Stability

A COMPROMISE BETWEEN ECONOMIC LIBERALISM AND NATIONALISM

Economic Liberalism

The relationship between the two dimensions of the problem, one encompassing industrialism-transindustrialism and the other nationalism-transnationalism, is not a simple one. Some may think that as industrialization advances, trade and overseas investment flourish, and so transnationalism progresses; but whether one looks at it logically or in the light of past experience, the story is not that simple. For example, in the nineteenth century, there was a tendency for nationalism and industrialization to reinforce each other. It was only after the Second World War that the power of industrialization steadily weakened nationalism and became an engine for the transition to transnationalism. Over the course of their historical development, the relationship between the two has made a 180-degree turn, changing a positive correlation into a negative one. Many people, however, still believe it is possible for the two classic modern ideologies of economic liberalism and nationalism to be, in theory or at least in practice, in harmony with each other (interdependent). In the future, however, a serious reconsideration of this optimism will be necessary.

Let us examine this problem in the context of recent arguments. As is well known, the debate on the so-called decline in American hegemony is thriving in recent analyses of international relations. I want to emphasize here, in a form that anticipates the argument below, that the "theory of hegemony" in the background of this kind of argument is an attempt—perhaps the last attempt—to effect a compromise between the two classical ideologies of economic liberalism and nationalism. In this sense, the theory of hegemony is an ideal case study for my argument here. I begin by clarifying the position among the existing theories occupied by the theory of hegemony, or more precisely, the theory of hegemonic stability.

To borrow the argument of Robert Gilpin, a leader among those developing these theories, the political-economic theories that appear in analysis of international relations can be broadly divided into three models: the liberal theory of economics (a theory of free trade); the realist theory of politics (a theory of power politics); and the theory of hegemonic stability. By taking the third standpoint, which strives for a synthesis to make good the deficiencies of the first and second theories, Gilpin's aim is to elaborate a theory of hegemonic stability.[1] Certainly, there have been no previous attempts to tie the first and second theories together at the level of a theory of international relations. The two classical ideologies of economic liberalism and nationalism have never been satisfactorily integrated. Scholars such as Susan Strange have recently advocated the need for a broader-based political economics,[2] but its actual substance has not been sufficiently developed. Again, those of the Marxist school have developed a consistent political-economic analysis, but they try to dismiss both classical ideologies out of hand.

In contrast, the theory of hegemonic stability is the first actual attempt to tie together liberal economic theory and the realist theory of politics—whether one can go so far as to call it a synthesis is another question. However, as any number of individual cases already indicate, economic liberalism and nationalism have their own peculiar characteristics, and given that there are points of contradiction between them, a synthesis will not be easy. In order to identify these points, we must once again examine the characteristics of liberal economic theory and the realist theory of politics—that is, the theory of free trade and the theory of power politics. Let us begin with the theory of free trade.

Standard economic theory has become the closest thing to a foundation for the model based on economic liberalism. Only comparatively recently have specialists in international relations shown an interest in economics, and one could say that this began as a link to the interdependence theory that appeared in the 1970s. But the economic understanding of specialists in international relations in fact stops at accepting standard theory as it is. The present standard economic theory, which can be learned from any textbook, provides a kind of elegant model of an ideal state, resembling one in classical mechanics, and provides a point of departure for thinking about the complicated, interdependent systems that are the economy. In fact, however, in order to create this model, many strict conditions—which I discuss below—are necessary, such as an unchanging environment (of technology and people's preferences), fixed quantities of resources, an increase in marginal costs, and perfect competition. Thus it becomes a substantial problem whether this model of an ideal state can apply as expected to reality—that is, whether the many premises hold in reality.

Of course there are circumstances in which one can apply this model to reality. For example, under the condition of *ceteris paribus*, in so-called partial equilibrium analysis, it is easy to observe whether the preconditions are in place, and thus one can expect the analysis to be useful. However, when one goes beyond this partial analysis and aims at a comprehensive analysis (for example, so-called general equilibrium analysis), it becomes difficult to observe whether the preconditions exist and thus whether the model is applicable to reality. Despite this, there is a tendency for many economists, attracted by such a comprehensive model, to create an image of the world, and when the image does not conform to reality, to believe that reality (actual policy administration) is at fault rather than the preconditions. For the sake of simplicity, in the argument below I call this image of the world, created by this pseudoexpansion of standard theory, the neoclassical school; it is not simply a theoretical model but points to a particular interpretation of the world containing an implicit value judgment, including the ideal of attaining a peculiar form of economic liberalism. In this is contained a type of "progressivism," which is in fact very nearly an "orthodoxy."

According to the economics of this neoclassical school, international changes in industrial structure are explained by the classical concept of comparative advantage (in its original sense a relative scarcity of resources such as labor, capital, and land), and derived from this is the central thesis that free trade is most desirable. This kind of thinking stood behind the postwar free-trade regime of the IMF and GATT. But the neoclassical theory of international economics has any number of weak points. First, according to the neoclassical school, factors such as resource endowments, technology, and people's preferences, which bring about changes in comparative advantage, cannot be treated "scientifically" by economics and so are considered givens external to the economy. Changes with regard to resources and the advance of technology are nothing more than shocks from outside the economy. Thus, structural changes in international relations are also in principle distinct events based on these external shocks. What explains structural change and development are not economic but rather extraeconomic factors. Neoclassical economics does nothing more than provide an explanatory framework by treating development and structural change, one might say, as exogenous variables.[3]

This explanation, however, does not grasp sufficiently the reality of an industrialization that proceeds on its own momentum. For example, the technological change we observe at present is not a distinct event generated intermittently but a continuous process, like waves breaking on the shore; it is not an event unconnected to the economy but to a certain extent is clearly a reflection of circumstances within the economy. If this is the case, given the continuous nature of technological progress, before the economy can fully adjust to the progress, more progress occurs; thus the economy is never able to attain equilibrium. The continuing disequilibrium in the economy will cause further technological change. This means that, as is fully discussed in Chapter 5, the path leading to equilibrium can only be described as a line connecting a series of disequilibria. Certainly, the long-run dynamic theory endogenizing technological change is in principle beyond the reach of human ability. In addition, technological change itself always contains a certain unpredictable shock. Even so, a theory of development and structural change based on neoclassical economics cannot escape the criticism that it neglects endogenous and disequilibrating aspects of economic development. This is why Gilpin observed that "the basic problem is that economists lack a theory of economic change."[4] What is needed to overcome these limitations is a dynamic analysis that gives serious consideration to endogenous and disequilibrating aspects, and particularly, as I mention below, a dynamics of technology.

A second weakness of economic liberalism is that it does not have a theory of the state. In the neoclassical school, following in the tradition of economics since Adam Smith, the state is seen as a passive, neutral entity, providing a minimum of public goods and not interfering in the everyday market. As what we today call public goods, Adam Smith (using the expression the "duty of the sovereign") cited defense, a judicial system, public utilities (roads, bridges, canals, harbors, and so on), and education, but he considered that the latter two could be supplied by the people in some instances and so were intermediate cases. As is apparent in Smith's argument, public and private goods cannot be distinguished a priori, and many goods have an intermediate character. One cannot determine a priori the minimum extent of public goods or settle on only one mechanism to provide them. If one follows up on these points, one has no choice but to return to a general theory discussing why the state is necessary and what the functions of the state are. Clearly, the concept of public goods is economists' jargon. By forcing the indispensable functions of the state into the economists' concept of a good, one can come up with the concept of a public good. To define the state as the supplier of public goods is, in economics, and only because of economics, an argument that confuses means and ends.

Public goods have the two qualities of being possible to use in common (consumable in a nonrivalrous manner) and of being impossible to deny to someone who tries to use them (nonexcludable). The concept of private goods was created after the appearance of the concept of public goods, as its antonym; private goods thus are defined as nonpublic goods. They are goods that are either impossible to use in common (not commonly consumable) or possible to deny to a potential user (excludable) (or both). However, if the users of a good that cannot be used in common were not restricted, then disputes would be endless, and the utility of the good would be lost. That is, for goods that cannot be shared, a social system must be established to limit the number of users (such as a system of private property or a system for collecting a charge for use). Thus, in a society that does not neglect building an intelligent system to perpetuate its stability, there must be a switch from noncommon consumability to excludability. In most societies it is generally enough to agree on the following: private property consists of goods one can deny to a potential user, and public property consists of goods one cannot deny to a potential user. These definitions conform to common sense.

While these definitions are logical, it is not easy to determine what is meant by common consumption. For example, the benefits of receiving assistance from the police or the fire department are greater for those who live near a police box or a fire station than for those who live far away. The latter therefore bear the costs for the former. Many durable consumer goods can be used in common by users who coordinate the times when each uses them. Information can be used in common, if the users pay the costs of copying. In short, with a small expense many people can enjoy the benefit of goods that otherwise would not be commonly consumed. Such common consumption is conceptually the same as a so-called external economy, and depending on the individual, this conceptual similarity is why public goods are defined as goods with externalities. Moreover, one can think of most goods as having, to some degree, the effect of an externality. One cannot a priori draw a clear line separating those goods that can be used in common and those that cannot.

One can, however, name countless social systems that deny potential users. In fact, many limitations on and denials of use are not only concerned simply with things that cannot be used in common but extend to things that can be (for example, entrance fees to art museums or private beaches). In fact, the system of private land ownership may be another example. The various systems handle these restrictions differently, but frequently their particular histories determine their methods.

Thus the concept of public goods takes the actual past of the society and the system as givens. The concepts of common consumption and excludability discussed above provide a practical basis on which to discriminate between private goods and public goods, having taken the system as a given, and are not a priori or universally applicable as a theoretical basis for judgment. For example, one can easily imagine societies in which there are only private police or private fire services, or societies that collect tolls on all roads. It is also possible that there are circumstances in which the scope of common consumption is very large, exceeding the variations of every social system (for example, the concept of justice in the abstract sense), but this is an exception; even with this justice there are various concrete contents. In fact, in the end, depending on the choice of system, there are various degrees of common consumption, and there are many intermediate goods, between public and private. "Public goods" is not an a priori category.

Despite the above, neoclassical economists neglect the problem of the state. This neglect derives from a value judgment based on economic liberalism, to the effect that politics should not intervene in economics, and the less government the better. There are perhaps societies where it is comparatively easy to apply the model of economic liberalism, such as Britain in the nineteenth century or the United States in the twentieth. In these cases, one can understand that the value judgments of economic liberalism dominate the society, and there is a strong insistence that the state and the government should play a minimal role.

Further, this economic liberalism is often extended to international relations, and its adherents insist on free trade. At least in the leading countries, free trade at this point may well become a demand for the government to minimize its provision of public goods—that is, for the "liberal state" to restrict the functions of government to a minimum. If such a demand were not made, the neoclassical model would clearly not be applicable to the world situation. However, it is no wonder that the function that government must serve—the substance of the things demanded as public goods—changes according to society and international conditions. In fact, as is discussed in Chapter 5, some countries adopt protectionism and others developmentalism, depending on the differing conditions they face. Whether or not one thinks this a good thing, one cannot ignore protectionism and developmentalism from the outset as aberrations. In exploring the reasons for protectionism or developmentalism, one will naturally come to reexamine the extent of the state's role (the substance of public goods). From this one should generate a valid general theory of the state. It is necessary that the theory of public goods, founded on such a general theory, be reconstructed so as to be appropriate to the new circumstances from now on. This is especially necessary in relation to the international public goods I discuss below.

A Theory of International Relations Based on Nationalism from the Perspective of Power Politics

The realist theory of politics also mentioned by Gilpin has a long history of dealing with international relations, and until the 1970s most analyses of international relations were of this type.[5] This approach regards the nation-state as intent on the pursuit of its own interests and depicts international relations as the dynamics of coldhearted confrontation and bargaining between such countries. This approach emphasizes the role of military power as a direct means of resistance—that is, it is an analysis of military/political power politics. Traditionally, those adopting this approach mainly relied on historical narrative, but recently game-theoretic analysis has begun to be used increasingly. There are two important premises for this power politics approach.

First is what one has to call the premise of nonpermeability. The qualified participants in power politics are limited to nation-states (in fact, to their governments). The nation-state negotiates in the international arena by coordinating and representing the interests and opinions of its domestic constituencies, such as businesses and individuals, who can interact only under the conditions determined by their respective governments. In principle, it is impossible to gain knowledge of, or affect what happens inside, each country. As is often said, the system depicted by the realist theory of politics is a series of collisions between hard balls, as one sees in a game of billiards. Of course the hard balls are the states, and we cannot understand their internal mechanisms, which have certain habitual, fixed responses to certain stimuli, or in other words, are like black boxes.

Second is the premise of homogeneity. For such a game of billiards to be played, there must be a certain degree of homogeneity among the states. When all of the billiard balls are a certain fixed, common size, then the game becomes possible for the first time. The size and strength of the nation-states must also be equal to a certain degree. The realist theory of politics is often called the balance-of-power theory, which means that the emergence of an overwhelming great power is prevented by a coalition of other countries. But to be able to expect this kind of strategic action there must be attitudes and practices held in common among the countries. There must in fact be at least a commensurability of perception (see Chapter 2).

Specialists may appreciate all of this more readily if the framework of game theory is used. In game theory there is the well-known analytic tool known as the payoff matrix (a diagram that shows how one's own and another's payoff changes following an interaction between the two strategies). However, when we try to determine the actual elements of this matrix, we tacitly assume a commensurability of perception toward the way we calculate the payoff and the range of strategy. This is because game theory assumes that all the players (participants) share a single payoff matrix and have a certain degree of knowledge about its contents. If this is not the case, the central themes of coalition and the cooperative game are excluded from the analysis from the outset. The substance of balance-of-power politics is nothing but these kinds of coalitions and cooperative games. Thus power politics has as its premise a weak form of commonality of perception (commensurability) such that though one cannot know how one's opposite is going to choose, one can know the factors that affect his choice. Without this premise, power politics cannot be established as a system. A power politics that does not have some common foundation has no way of preventing an escalation of mistrust or the advent of catastrophe.

This second premise of homogeneity is equivalent to the existence of the nation-state system mentioned in the previous chapter, and the realist theory of politics was clearly created as a reflection of European reality following the Treaty of Westphalia. As already mentioned, the nation-state system had its foundations in the acceptance of sharing a civilization with

Christian origins and tried to formalize war on a model of the doctrine of the nonjust war, which was based on that system. For example, there was a common understanding of such things as the diplomatic etiquette for declarations of war and surrenders, distinguishing between combatants and noncombatants, treatment of prisoners, limitations on the kinds of weapons, and the extent of the demands the victor could make. Given that there were some rules, these were gradually made into treaties and then became international law. As long as it conformed to these rules, war was a fair means of international politics. Otto von Bismarck's comment on the Prusso-Austrian War captured the essence of this system: "Just as we did not err in making our demands, neither did Austria err in rejecting our demand." Thus the nation-state system worked as a balance-of-power system maintaining a fixed framework. As long as the idea of the nation-state and its system was preeminent in the world, the realist theory of politics demonstrated a certain degree of validity.

I pointed out in the previous chapter, however, that beginning with the First World War, cracks began to appear in this framework. The Treaty of Versailles had already placed responsibility for the war exclusively on Germany and thus violated the existing rule based on the doctrine of the nonjust war. Then with the Second World War, the concept of so-called total war began to spread, guerrilla war waged by the people and indiscriminate bombing became frequent, and the previous rules began to exist only in name.

The very fact that from the first the Allies had defined this war as a war of civilization against anticivilization had itself already denied the existing premise of homogeneity. Again in the cold war between East and West, the understanding that this was an ideological war of justice against injustice dominated both sides. Moreover, in the colonial wars for independence that followed the Second World War there was no room for ideological compromise, and rules were broken in increasing numbers. Beginning with the Japanese aggression in China in the 1930s, and in the anticolonialist wars in Indonesia and Algeria, the colonized, who waged all-out guerrilla warfare, emerged as the final victors. In these examples, the premise of homogeneity completely collapsed, totally unexpected strategies were often adopted, and the payoff matrix became unsettled. The belief in a commensurability of perception weakened, and although the nation-state existed, if only as a fiction, the international system that supported it is becoming nothing but an empty shell.

With our existing concept of the international system, we seem unable to deal with problems such as the confrontations over the cold-war offspring of divided countries, numerous ethnic conflicts, wars in the Middle East where the legacies of colonialism since the nineteenth century are still evident, and the disintegration of the Soviet Union. In the future, will thought based on the doctrine of the just war take over, or will a new concept based on the doctrine of the nonjust war appear? The world in the twenty-first century may well agonize as it gropes for a shared understanding of the conduct that states are to observe.

Together with this, the usefulness of game-theoretic analysis is reduced. As a tool of analysis for balance-of-power politics, game theory is most appropriate. After the Second World War, game-theoretic analysis was frequently used by specialists in international relations, with the U.S.-Soviet cold war providing useful material to be analyzed. Certainly the United States and the Soviet Union at least shared an awareness of the possible disaster of the outbreak of nuclear war. Both the West and the East, however, more resembled alliances welded together by ideology than coalitions based on interests. In pursuit of ideology, strategic choice and its effects (or in the jargon of game theory, strategy and payoff) extend beyond their expected limits to include anything from the annihilation of one's opponent in the cause of justice to taking on suicidal ventures at the risk of becoming a martyr to one's ideology. The just war generates an escalation of mutual distrust about the opponent's attacks and cannot be settled within the framework of a game-theoretic analysis defined in terms of strategy and payoff. Unlike the nation-states of Europe, which had common understanding and an agreement about the rules of war, in the cold war both sides were doubtful that there was any such common understanding or rules. In the future, the same problem may well come up in conflicts with the Islamic world, for example. There are transnational rules in the Islamic world, but they are not the same as the traditional rules of Europe.[6]

Generally speaking, there are limits to the mechanical application of a game-theoretic analysis that disregards historical background. Recently, elaborate analyses that apply the concept of a "supergame" have attracted interest, but supergames also require a commensurability of understanding. In that this is premised on an infinite number of plays, the substance of this requirement is rather strong.[7] Whichever one uses, one of the main factors supporting a balance of power is cultural commensurability between nations, and it cannot be reduced to the technical concept of game-theoretic stability. The theory of games is only effective in a world based on the doctrine of nonjust war and supported by commensurability. In the world of the future, in which the existing framework has dissolved, it is doubtful how effective game-theoretic analysis will be.

I have referred frequently to the points at issue with the first premise of nonpermeability or nations as hard balls—that is, the premise that only nation-states are the subjects of international politics. Today when we can see the unimaginable development of transportation and communications, businesses, all sorts of organizations, and individuals are actively developing their activities beyond national boundaries. With the various manifestations of borderlessness, such as the trade and investment activities of multinational companies, the international exchange of information between organizations, the emigration and overseas travel of individuals, and the extensive transmission of television and radio, the hard shell of the state is being weakened. In short, the state is becoming porous or developing cracks. The fact that the Tiananmen Square prodemocracy incident and the Soviet coup d'état ousting Mikhail Gorbachev reached an international audience through television is a symbolic example of a new kind of crack. The state is already no longer a black box. The first premise of the realist theory of politics was in considering the nation-state a completely impermeable unit of analysis, but this has now become a limit to the theory. The limits to nationalism are also becoming obvious.

Finally, let me mention one more weakness in the approach based on political realism. This approach—like that of economic liberalism—has a strong character of exogenous explanation. In this approach, changes in international relations are explained by the rise and fall of the power of individual states. But on questions such as what is national power and what are the factors for the rise and fall in national power, political realism always provides only ad hoc explanations. For example, changes in economic power, which is an important dimension of national power, decisively alter international relations, as we can see today. If this is the case, then the realist theory of politics must be supplemented by some kind of economic theory (a theory that can explain the rise and fall of economic power).

However, if we try temporarily to supplement the realist theory of politics with liberal economic theory, we will notice a difference in the intellectual backing for the two theories that could be called incompatible. In contrast to the optimism behind economic liberalism, which believes in equilibrium and harmony, in political realism there is—even if one does not call it pessimism—a skepticism toward world harmony. That is, unlike economics, which pays attention to a positive-sum world that generates forms of cooperation such as divisions of labor and trade, the traditional conception of politics has been disposed to a zero-sum world in which people struggle for possession of the same territory. The problem of this contrast or conflict has been habitual over time up to the present. The two ideologies of economic liberalism and nation-statism have never been integrated but have coexisted in the midst of the reality of many Western nations in the modern period. Inasmuch as it looks as if the interests of the nation-states are in harmony, economic optimism is dominant. But when economic conflicts become evident among nations, the so-called mercantilist responses and the fear of war increase, giving rise to political pessimism. The two ideologies, alternating in relative dominance, have until now supported industrial society. This intellectual situation, though, is nothing more than an unprincipled compromise.

Now, however, with the remarkable changes in the distribution of national power and the increase in economic interdependence, we can no longer neglect the easy coexistence of these two ideologies. The realist theory of politics and liberal economic theory are opposed in a tangle of interests; and in that they mutually repel each other like oil and water in international politics, there is even a fight between them for the leading role. For example, views differ widely as to whether Japan and the United States will collide with each other as nation-states or have a harmonious relationship through their economic interests. There is now a need for some kind of compromise or synthesis between these two theories or ideologies.

The Theory of Hegemonic Stability

The third theory, that of hegemonic stability, is an attempt at a comprehensive theory to overcome the deficiencies of the theories of political realism and economic liberalism. The first deficiency is the problem of not dealing straightforwardly with the question of political unions (namely, the state). In the theory of economic liberalism this deficiency is clear, but even in political realism a narrowness of vision has seen the problem of political union only within the framework of the nation-state. In other words, there has not been an adequate attempt to deal with the state (or its functional equivalent) on a global scale. Certainly the world-state does not exist. But the political agenda of providing a common foundation for world governance throughout the world does exist, if only for the sake of the ideal of free trade. As mentioned above, the theory of economic liberalism has a theory of public goods as an imperfect substitute for a theory of the state, and one can at least imagine a similar approach to the discussion of international relations. In short, if a liberal theory of international relations is to apply the theory of the domestic market economy to the international economy, then the suppliers of public goods who are tacitly assumed to exist in the domestic economy should also be assumed to exist in the international economy. The mainstream of existing theory on international relations has in fact ignored this necessary requirement. However, we must consider the question of public goods in an international sense.

That is to say, in order that the operations of an international economy on the liberal model should not be destabilized or distorted, some mechanism must function to maintain the international market environment. For example, it is natural that in a situation where war is recurrent, trade stagnates; and if the value of what serves as an international currency changes, then again trade is suppressed. (As I mention below, in this sense it is important to think about the significance of a floating exchange rate system.) Keeping the peace and supplying an international currency are in this sense international public goods; a model of an international market economy that ignores these questions loses its qualifications as a model of reality and becomes nothing more than a description of a liberal utopia with such utopian conditions as perpetual peace and always-stable international currency. In this sense, there was great significance in Gilpin's and his predecessor Charles Kindleberger's raising the question of international public goods in the explicit way they did. Even a liberal international economy is not something that alone naturally leads to a world order. Certain kinds of international public goods, and an international political system to provide them, are needed as well.

The second deficiency that must be overcome is the weakness of analysis of the dynamics of changes in national power, common to both the realist theory of politics and liberal economic theory. Since the beginning of industrialization the most important factor in determining each country's national power has ultimately been economic power. Particularly since the Second World War, as colonialism and large-scale wars have become impossible, the significance of military power in itself has gradually declined while the importance of economic power has risen. A change in relative economic position alone has come to have the capacity to change the existing international political system. Clearly, in order for the international political system to be stable, each country's economic position should be disposed in a certain way. Thus the argument comes full circle. A liberal international economic order requires a certain kind of international political system, and this international political system requires international economic power to be distributed in a certain way. Describing a solution that fulfills these two requirements thus becomes the subject for a theory of international relations. In order to do this, an analysis of the dynamics of economic power is indispensable.

Kindleberger and Gilpin assert that it is the existence of a hegemon that can provide, without contradiction, a solution to these requirements, and at the same time they point out that in our present circumstances, when the United States as hegemon is growing relatively weaker, it is extremely difficult to maintain the stability of the world system.[8] "Hegemon" is a neologism that has been in use since the eighteenth century; taken directly from the Greek ηγεμον, it signifies a substantial leader who does not possess a formal authority but does have overwhelming actual power. More concretely, "hegemon" signifies a state established through force, which has an advantage in national power in many dimensions such as the military, political, and economic and is determined to exercise this force in the world. If there is a need for a supply of international public goods, then certainly the hegemon is a strong candidate to be the supplier.

The supply of international public goods is not simply a theoretical requirement but partly an existing fact. For example, there have appeared many international rules dealing with particular individual problems and institutions to maintain what theorists of international relations would call "regimes"; but regimes clearly supply international public goods only case by case—that is, for each regime.[9] There are at present countless specific regimes playing various roles, such as the IMF dealing with international currencies; GATT dealing with trade rules; the "regime of the sea" dealing with the use of the ocean; regimes dealing with national airlines, post, and telecommunications; U.N.-sponsored regimes dealing with global environmental protection; a regime dealing with the protection of animals; and others. Some scholars in the interdependence theory school expect that as these individual regimes develop and become connected to each other, they will naturally lead to a comprehensive system for the supply of international public goods. Their expectations, however, are overly optimistic.

First, it is easy to neglect something that has not already been formalized as a regime because it is difficult to reach agreement. For example, on the question of economic development, which in a certain sense is vital (I discuss in Chapter 7 the reasons why aid for this purpose should be regarded as an international public good), although there have been created organizations and new ideas such as the United Nations Conference on Trade and Development (UNCTAD) and the New International Economic Order (NIEO), at present these do not have the substance of a regime. Second, in a number of cases the individual regimes contradict each other on points of ideology. For example, between the United Nations Environmental Plan and NIEO (assuming that this becomes a regime), there is an ideological discrepancy between the environmentalism of the developed countries and the industrialism of the developing countries. Third, without the positive participation of the powerful countries, regimes cannot be maintained. NIEO does not operate effectively because the influential developed countries show little active interest in this regime. As even Ernst Haas, the elder statesman of the school of interdependence theory, has now acknowledged, the increase in interdependence and the proliferation of international organizations will not naturally lead to the formation of a comprehensive system providing international public goods.[10]

Note that international public goods are provided without creating a regime. The most important example is security, and there have been almost no instances in which the limited military capabilities of the United Nations have been deployed effectively in a major incident. (I discuss the Persian Gulf War later.) What should we do in order to make up for this crucial deficiency, or to get rid of the ideological contradictions between regimes? Here too, the closest solution one can imagine is for a great power that is predominant among existing states in terms of national power in many dimensions to voluntarily assume the responsibility for providing international public goods. In other words this great power would provide international public goods mainly at its own discretion. This may not be the ideal situation for the other countries, but inasmuch as there are some advantages, there is no reason for those countries not to free-ride. Of course for each international public good the circumstances will be different. There may be cases in which countries complain about being disadvantaged or refuse to comply from the beginning, saying that they cannot submit to the ideology. In order to appease or silence these objections, economic or military power alone will not be sufficient. There will have to be political power that can work skillfully to build up a majority who are in favor and a force of conviction that can finally persuade or at least silence those who are opposed.

Thus, finally, one should say something about that country's ideological, intellectual, and cultural authority. Usually, the principal connotation of hegemony is force or military power. But in today's world, and in the future, there can be no hegemon without a persuasive ideology. This will become an important point in the following argument. A hegemon must assume the responsibility for the provision of international public goods and maintain preeminent power in several dimensions over other countries. If these conditions are not fulfilled, it will be because the system of international public goods cannot be maintained because of the interference of another great power. Thus a hegemon can again be defined as a powerful country that can maintain its preeminence in all dimensions of national power, and do so with a comfortable margin even while incurring the costs of supplying international public goods.

The theory of hegemony, however, is not the only conclusion that can be drawn from the theory of international public goods. Even though the need for international public goods is generally recognized, the theory of hegemony is not the only solution; another is for powerful countries to supply them jointly, and yet another, at least theoretically, is the above-mentioned systematic convergence of individual regimes. Again, for the same reason mentioned with regard to domestic public goods, the extent or substance of international public goods is not settled in advance. Thus the solution will vary depending on global circumstances. For the time being, however, let us follow what has become the common understanding in the postwar Western world and state that the following are necessary as international public goods: politically, the observation of the international rule of liberalism; militarily, the maintenance of international security and peace; and economically, the maintenance of the value of international currencies and the provision of markets and capital to developing countries. Moreover, in attaining these, the following are extremely important: technologically, to take the lead in the world in science and technology; and culturally, to take the lead in the world intellectually. In fact, the postwar United States was the only country with the power to assume the function of supplying these international public goods, and it is persuasive to argue that the world system in the twentieth century was a Pax Americana centered on the United States as hegemon.

Similarly, there is a plausible argument that Britain was the hegemon that maintained the nineteenth-century Pax Britannica. One could go further and say that a powerful country has appeared in each century, such as Spain under the Hapsburgs in the sixteenth, Holland in the seventeenth, and Britain in the eighteenth. In looking back at these periods, however, it is not clear which was the preponderant great power. George Modelski identifies Portugal in the sixteenth century, and one cannot disregard

France under the Bourbons in the seventeenth and eighteenth.[11] Paul Kennedy's best-selling *Rise and Fall of the Great Powers* has been remarkably popular as a description of the prosperity and decay of, and alternation among, these kinds of powerful countries. In all cases, however, there were differences in historical conditions and correspondingly clear variations in the substance of the international public goods. For example, from the sixteenth to the eighteenth centuries, the international system had not yet been completed, industrialization had not yet arrived, and the idea of free trade was weak; thus it is meaningless to think of the concept of international public goods as a means to free trade. Though one can name the hegemons in this period, they had no significance other than as political-military powers.

In contrast, in the nineteenth and twentieth centuries following the industrial revolution, international public goods for free trade became significant. In order to avoid confusion, therefore, let us limit the concept of the hegemon to the period since the industrial revolution and think of it as signifying a supplier of international public goods as a means to free trade. In short, "hegemons" must be those who came into existence as a result of free trade and who sustained free trade. The word carries a slightly different significance, however, for the periods before and after the First World War.

Until the First World War, the European rules of the nation-state system for the most part restrained the great powers. Thus the burdens placed on the political power of nineteenth-century Britain were small in comparison with those borne by the United States in the second half of the twentieth century. Because of this fact, the "international public goods" offered by the Pax Britannica were smaller both in extent and scale than those of the Pax Americana. For example, Britain's army was certainly not overwhelming, and Britain's preeminence in GNP and total trade declined comparatively early. Britain's navy, however, was superior to all other countries'. And prudent international investment by Britain's major banks and investment firms and skillful British management of the gold standard made a contribution as an international public good to the global market economy. In contrast, the international public goods provided under the Pax Americana have been accompanied by an unprecedented expansion in extent and scale, in order to deal with the functional decline of the nation-state system and the acceleration in industrialization. As these examples show, the substance of international public goods varies greatly with changes in historical conditions. And under future conditions too, there will be changes in what international public goods are necessary. For example, it will be particularly necessary to reexamine the significance of international currencies and aid to developing countries (in a very broad sense).

Going Beyond the Theory of the Hegemon

The attempt at synthesis in the theory of hegemony is a slightly mechanical joining together of liberal economic theory and nationalist political theory and as such stops at something incomplete. This is because the dynamics of changes in national power, which must be the common foundation for both, are still analyzed in an ad hoc manner. To cite a symbolic and at the same time instructive example, it is impossible to explain the birth (or change) of a hegemon without analyzing the dynamics of changes in national power. Hegemony here refers to the power that supports free trade. Thus it must have arisen naturally from the operations of the global market economy. If this did not occur, then military and political domination would have generated economic domination, and so the hegemon itself would provide a bad precedent in violating the principles of economic liberalism. However, at this point cracks become apparent in the mechanical welding together of these two theories. The liberal economic theory of the market (neoclassical theory) does not provide an argument that allows for the rise of only a single economic power great enough to be called a hegemon, through the normal working of the global market economy. Of course, given resources and other conditions, disparities in economic scale (for example, GNP) will appear among the various countries. But this does not mean that a single great power will tower above the rest in terms of technology and standard of living (for example, per capita GNP). The problem is not only with the rise of a hegemon. As Gilpin says, "uneven growth" among the various countries is a fundamental fact in the industrialized world, but neoclassical economics has nothing to say about why this should be so.

In fact, if neoclassical economics is correct, the rise of an economic power that dominates the rest in terms of living standards is an impossibility. According to the Heckscher-Ohlin theorem of factor price equalization, which has become the core of standard international trade theory, real wages in the various countries will become equal through international free trade (except in those nations where there is perfect specialization in production). Thus disparities in the standard of living should disappear (except where there is perfect specialization in mineral products, agricultural products, and so on). This conclusion is the international version of the standard thesis that in the domestic economy free market competition will equalize the real wages of all workers.

In fact, there are problems with any number of the assumptions that are necessary to establish this factor price equalization theorem. The assumption that all countries have the same technology (identical production functions with constant returns to scale) ignores international differences in technology. Clearly, the existing neoclassical trade theory, which has this theorem at its core, is not capable of explaining disparities between countries. I know of no examples that successfully explain these disparities by relaxing the assumptions of the theorem.[12] In fact, most of the free trade theory that depends on neoclassical economic theory lives at peace with itself in the tacit optimism that if the ideal of free trade were realized, then the world would become homogeneous. In order to explain the unchanging fundamental fact of uneven growth, it is necessary to overcome the limits inherent in neoclassical economic theory, dependent on exogenous variables and on equilibrium analysis.

Broadly speaking, there are two possible ways to use economic theory to explain disparities in national power. One is based on market imperfections, and the other is based on technological dynamics. Most economists will on the whole attribute the existence of disparities to imperfections in market competition. This is to argue that the causes of disparities between countries are such imperfections in market competition as domination of the world market by huge businesses or cartels, protectionism and dumping, and regulation of the colonial economy by the colonial power. But if one considers that these imperfections alone are the cause of these disparities, then the proposition would follow that poverty in the developing countries would disappear if only the wealthy developed countries would open their markets and the firms of these countries would compete fiercely. Is not this proposition overly optimistic and impracticable? For example, in the 1950s and 1960s, when international trade was increasingly liberalized, the developing countries became increasingly discontent about the growing economic disparity between themselves and the developed countries.[13] (This fact is nothing more than supporting evidence, however.)

Even if we allow this optimism for the moment, it does not dispose of the problem. Monopolies, cartels, and dumping may be profitable management strategies for private businesses and yet have a negative effect on a country as a whole. Similarly, protectionism and colonial rule may weaken the private businesses in that country unless they are managed skillfully. Marxists have often used the expression "state monopoly capitalism" and emphasized that the state and the businesses in the country act together as a team to benefit the advanced nation at the cost of other nations. Without making this Marxist assumption, the disparities in wealth between countries do not follow easily from imperfections in market competition.

Going back a step, let us examine whether the standard economic theory of imperfect competition can explain to some extent the appearance of disparities between countries. It is not easy, however, to move from this to an explanation of why only one country becomes powerful and emerges as hegemon. This cannot be explained without assuming that this country has the substantial political power necessary to control other countries by intervening in the market. At this point the theoretical explanation of the hegemon reverts to the old theory of great political and military powers and separates from economic theory. If politically and militarily great powers can achieve great economic power by using their political and military powers to the full, in a world where such a country has seized hegemony, it is not possible for free trade to remain the ideological orthodoxy. Thus if one looks for the causes of disparities, or "uneven growth," and especially for the causes of the formation of a hegemon, in imperfections in competition, then eventually the discussion cannot but go beyond the realm of economic analysis.

In a sense, the most complete form of the theory of politically and militarily great powers is found in Marxist economics, which emphasizes that the state is nothing more than a tool with which to realize the theory of capital. In the theory of imperialism in particular, stretching from Rosa Luxemburg to Lenin, capital, which strives for world domination, generates violent disputes over colonial possessions through its political-military control based on the state. A recent example belonging to this tradition is Immanuel Wallerstein's center-periphery theory. He explains that the economic division of labor between the developed countries at the core and the developing countries on the periphery is established through the political-military domination and continuous exploitation of the latter by the former. That is, Wallerstein's theory is the theory of class warfare applied to international relations, and one could call it neo-Marxist, together with dependency theory, which has the same ideas.[14] However, the relationship between core and periphery does not seem to be as fixed as these theories imply. As is shown by the recently much-discussed decline of the United States, and the rise of Japan and the NIEs, the most striking fact in the world economy today is the lack of correlation between political-military and economic ability. This shows that political and military power do not guarantee economic power, and that economic power does not necessarily lead to political and military power.

In the language of economic theory, the reason Wallerstein's theory and dependency theory lack persuasive force is because their assumption, that there is a perfect specialization of manufacturing industry in the core and primary industry in the periphery, has not held true. If one could assume this kind of perfect specialization, then it would be comparatively easy to explain disparities. One could even explain the existence of disparities as examples of perfect specialization that resulted following the neoclassical factor price equalization theorem. The problem is that reality continues to refute this well-worn assumption. For example, the NIEs, which are developing rapidly, are not exporters of primary goods but of manufactured goods, and they do not conform to neo-Marxist assumptions. In Wallerstein's scheme of things, the NIEs may be classified as semiperipheral countries—countries that are rising above the rank of peripheral countries but are not yet fully core countries; but in fact the NIEs are not following in the paths traced by the old core countries.

As I mention below, what distinguishes the development of the NIEs is a new industrial strategy one may call a "flying-geese" pattern of specialization, and a new structure of the state one might call the developmentalist trading state. The former refers to Kaname Akamatsu's analysis that the higher level of technology used by the developed "lead goose" will be, over time, adopted by the less developed geese following in close formation behind the lead goose.[15] Today's NIEs, with these new characteristics, even in the future will probably not become a "core," at least in the sense that the word is used today. To imagine that a new world system, in which these rising nations will play an important role, will become an imperialist order in the neo-Marxist sense is to show a poverty of imagination. The proportion of quasi-peripheral countries in the world is already high and getting higher. This world situation, in which the international "middle class" is expanding, cannot be explained by the arguments of Wallerstein or dependency theory.

As is shown by the above argument, uneven growth cannot be sufficiently explained by imperfect competition. If one were to follow this kind of explanation through to its logical conclusion, one would have to resort to the old theory that emphasizes political and military domination. But reviving, for example, the theory of imperial cycles from ancient Rome and classical China, or the theory of the rise and fall of civilizations, does not take sufficiently into account the importance of the role of economic factors seen since industrialization. The Marxist theory of international class war and the neo-Marxist theory that is its modern version do take economic factors into account, but neither is capable of explaining the extremely rapid rise of Japan and the NIEs. We must abandon explanations that rely on imperfections in the market and move on to an explanation based on the dynamic of technological change, a factor whose importance everybody must recognize.

The Dynamic of Technological Change

Technological change is a theme that economists until now—apart from such great heretics as Thorstein Veblen and Joseph Schumpeter— have not dared to analyze. Technological change is certainly difficult to analyze. One reason is that several heterogeneous phenomena can easily be lumped together as technological change. Following this practice, let us here think of technological change as something that arises from the following series of stages: theoretical research → basic research → applied research → development (development of processes or products). As we follow these arrows, we are moving to a stage that is increasingly more "applied," less "basic." Theoretical research is distinguished from basic research in order to show that there is a difference, within science in a broad sense, between research whose theoretical nature is paramount and research that has a high applicability. For example, nuclear physics would be theoretical research, but theories concerned with physical matter (for example, a theory of semiconductors) would be basic research, and the invention of a new semiconductor would be applied research. And the stage of development would include, for example, the know-how necessary to create a huge, stable crystal of silicon, the learning of skills, and all the management efforts involved. *Technological change is a social process in which everyone participates, from the most learned scientist to managers and workers.* When discussing the technological transformation of developing countries, this social character of technological change comes into question. Below, we will come to understand technology in this very broad sense.

Any social-scientific analysis of the development of research in these stages reveals clear differences in the relative difficulty encountered at each stage. The reason for this is primarily differences in inventiveness. For example, it is almost impossible to predict the development of basic research in the sense just given because it is conducted by a path-breaking scientist who defies the common understanding of everyone else (especially fellow scientists). A science that would predict scientific creation is in principle impossible. But this is certainly not true in more applied stages.

Let me advance the argument by presenting my provisional hypothesis on the dynamic of technological change. In this book, I mean by "dynamic" a model of development that has a strongly endogenous character and that is not restrained by an equilibrating mechanism. I sketch only the gist of this hypothesis, and thus the following provides only a basis for a possible hypothesis. I begin by presenting the following five broad (in the sense of statistical rules of large numbers) general observations-*cum*-theorems:

1. The closer the technological progress is to applications, the higher the predictability of the direction of further progress and the lower the risk. In other words, the more basic the technological advance, the lower the predictability and the higher the risk. This is because the accumulated results of research in the more theoretical stages are able to provide more guidance on the direction of advances in the more applied stages. This is also to say that determined and patient efforts at research and development as a continuous endeavor increase the possibility of realizing the fruit of the total effort.

2. The more basic the technological advance, the greater the possibility of developing a wide range of applications. Thus in the choice between basic and applied research, there is a trade-off between the possibility of developing applications and predictability (low risk). Technologically advanced countries (or leaders) are countries that have discovered an optimum balance between the possibility of developing applications and development risk—that is, between basic and applied research—and were the first to decide to take up this challenge. In each century there are probably only one or two such countries.

To become a technological leader, a sensible strategy is not to aspire solely to the most theoretical research. The optimum strategy is to aspire to basic research only when the possibility of applying its result can reasonably be hoped for, or in other words, to attempt to strike a balance between basic research and efforts at application. In the eighteenth century, from the point of view of theoretical syntheses, one could say that France was preeminent among all other nations, including Britain, having as it did Pierre Simon Laplace and Joseph Louis Lagrange in physics and Antoine Laurent Lavoisier in chemistry. However, in this period it was not France but Britain that built a position for itself as a technological leader. Then in the second half of the nineteenth century, Britain took the lead in theoretical research. Such British scientists as Michael Faraday, William Thomson, and James Maxwell were representative figures of the period. At this point, though, Germany had already shown a determination to best Britain, and one could not ignore the achievements of France. But it was the United States, with almost no achievements in theoretical research, that rose in the second half of the nineteenth century to become the technological leader of the twentieth. The biographies of Thomas Edison and Alexander Graham Bell represent the situation in the United States at this time. Only later, after the Second World War, did the United States achieve results in theoretical research. It has been the historical rule up to this point that after a country has established its position as a leader it begins to make a priority of the pursuit of high-level theoretical research.

3. The risks in technological advance for technologically backward countries, or followers (countries other than the leaders), are even lower than those for the leaders. The very fact that they know that a particular technology has been developed by an advanced country in itself already helps the followers. A technology developed by a leader will be imported in some form and copied by the followers, tactics that reduce their risk in technological progress. Here, following R. P. Dore, let us call this kind of effect, emphasized long ago by Veblen and recently by Alexander Gerschenkron, the "late-developer effect."[16]

4. In order for followers to succeed, however, the late-developer effect alone is not enough. Also relevant is the level of technological advance to which the follower decides to allocate limited resources (talent and capital). According to the above proposition, in terms of diminishing risk, the more applied the technological advances the easier it is for followers to exploit, and the more theoretical the advance the more likely that it will remain with the leader. Insofar as the followers attempt to realize the gains from their technological efforts as soon as possible, the optimum choice will be for them to make application-oriented investment.

5. Thus, from the historical perspective of technological advances that are predominantly applied in nature, backward countries can catch up quickly, but from the perspective of technological advances that are predominantly basic in nature, the advanced countries can easily maintain their lead.

Little of what I have just presented is original. However, by emphasizing the differences between basic and applied research, and connecting these differences to the question of advanced and backward countries, the preceding may be useful in better understanding the process of the dynamic of technological change. The process of technological change as a whole consists of both *discontinuous* breakthrough-type change that occurs when the results of basic research are successfully applied, and *continuous*, maturation-type change that takes place as the breakthrough-type change is adapted or digested. The two types of change make up a cycle. I believe that, at least as far as the past is concerned, the larger cycles have been in units of a century and have consisted of the cycle of the nineteenth-century technological paradigm, based on iron, steam, and the railroads, and the cycle of the twentieth-century paradigm, based on electricity, chemicals, and consumer durables. Within these cycles, other smaller cycles center on changes in basic research and changes in applications (corresponding to the cycles of the so-called Kondratieff wave), but it takes about a century for the fruits of a high-risk, breakthrough-type technological change to be fully enjoyed. This has been the fundamental pattern for the past two centuries. This point is discussed again below.

Which specific country achieves a technological breakthrough and becomes the leader is determined accidentally by historical circumstances; but the period in which the advance in basic technology is relatively important lasts quite some time, and during this period the dominant position held by the leader is not yielded. This dominant position sustains the leader's military power, increases its economic power through trade, generates material wealth domestically, and nurtures a certain culture (including theoretical research), and so gradually establishes its position as hegemon. However, as the potential of the technological paradigm is gradually used up, applied technological advances become predominant, and the catching up of the followers becomes noticeable. In the nineteenth century, British dominance reached its peak in the third quarter of the century, but at the same time Germany, France, and the United States had almost caught up and were beginning to exhibit their own characteristics in the technologies of the textile industry and railroads. As a result of a number of conditions, from among these powerful followers, in the last quarter of the century the United States and Germany became powerful candidates for leader of the next paradigm. A similar phenomenon can be seen to have occurred between the third quarter of the twentieth century (what we would call in Japan the postwar high economic growth period) and the last quarter, when Japan caught up with the United States in the field of applied technological advance.[17]

Thus the development of the industrial countries is not simply uneven but has a fixed pattern. Once a leader has emerged, it soon develops into a hegemon; eventually a number of followers catch up to it, and from among these will appear the leader of the next era. That is: (1) first there is unevenness in the sense that an advanced country takes the lead, and (2) this is followed by unevenness in the sense that the follower countries catch up; together these two stages form a cycle. In the background, (3) there are countries that do not (or cannot) participate in the race as either leaders or followers, and as they are left behind the disparities between them and those that do participate in the race grow larger. These three kinds of unevenness have been noticed by many theorists of long-term cycles and have been particularly emphasized in the theory of the flying-geese pattern discussed earlier and the theory of the center-semiperiphery-periphery of the Wallerstein school.[18] If one does not distinguish between these three kinds of unevenness, it is impossible to explain the emergence of a hegemon and the mechanism of its rise and fall. In the dynamic of technological change, the existing economic and political sciences are combined, economic liberalism and political nationalism are joined together, and the theory of the hegemon becomes more complete.

However, we should notice that in the midst of this process of taking into account the dynamic of technological change, the economic liberalism that was a pillar for the theory of the hegemon has been forced to change in character. Each country's technology (production function) is, generally speaking, not homogeneous. The dynamic of technological change is a furious race in which the leader tries to maintain the lead and the followers try to catch up; it is not a process in which the levels of technology of countries converge to one internationally standard level. As is shown typically by the Heckscher-Ohlin theorem, homogeneity of technology is frequently a fundamental tacit assumption of neoclassical economics. However, when the heterogeneity of technology among countries continues, there is no guarantee that factor prices (wages or interest) will be equalized internationally, and there will be differences in wealth among countries. A liberal market economy is not a functioning mechanism for homogenization of countries. If international homogenization is to be its mission, then the aim of economic liberalism can be nothing other than to spread technology as quickly as possible throughout the world. From this would emerge, for example, the idea of bringing the system of patents to an end.

In that economics at its core is the analysis of price competition over private assets, it lacks the wherewithal to take up the question of competition over technology. Technology, originally, was an asset supplied monopolistically by the inventor. (Here, an asset is not something that has been quantified or standardized but has a very indefinite character.) At the same time, technology is an asset that can be reproduced at virtually no cost and thus is almost an asset for common consumption. That is, technology has a bipolar character: there is a monopoly on its supply, and it has a potentially public nature (the characteristic of being a public good). The patent system is nothing but a system that places more importance on discarding, from this impacted character, the public nature of technology, and tries to provide incentives for technological development by providing a reward to the inventor. Through this system, technology becomes a quasi-private asset (an asset whose common use is restricted). As a result, there has developed in the world of technology a kind of price competition in the form of the buying and selling of patents. But because the monopoly on supply remains in place, the market in patents clearly cannot be perfectly competitive. Thus there is no guarantee that technology as a resource will be efficiently managed through the market in patents.

Moreover, it is important to note about competition over technology that, since market competition over patents is a competition over the development of technology, there is no comparable form of competition in the market for normal goods. Thus competition that involves technology falls outside the framework of the model of market competition in the normal sense; competition over technology, in a general sense, is a special example of what Hayek calls competition over knowledge and thought. The question that arises from this is, what would a liberal system appropriate for technology competition be like? In particular, if in the future we predict that competition over technology will intensify, then this question will become of prime importance. I discuss this question again in detail in Chapter 5.

The introduction of the dynamic of technological change also changes the classification of states. Normally, we use the classification "developed countries–semideveloped countries (NIEs)–developing countries," but this classification is based on a snapshot of the effects of industrialization taken now. If we adopt the argument here, the classification of "leaders, latecomers, and countries that are not even followers" becomes important—a classification not based on effects as seen at this point in time but on the process of development up to this point, and thus a dynamic classification. The leader by definition is a single but indispensable exception. Thus, to give an example, with the exception of Britain all countries were followers. Though Germany, France, and Japan are developed countries today, they were not leaders. The United States, too, had the appearance of a follower in the nineteenth century and was not a true leader. Thus the economic development of the world has for the most part been the story of followers. Liberal economics was created in the context of the country that was closest to being a true leader, namely Britain, but in that form it cannot apply to the vast majority of countries. It is the political economy of what one could call developmentalism, which takes catching up to the leader as its object, that has real significance for the majority of countries. Few have attempted this kind of analysis, however, and those that have, such as the German historical school, have been treated as heretics. It seems that this fact has confused analyses of societies to date. The existing theory of the hegemon, too, does not face squarely up to this question of developmentalism.

Redefining the Concept of Hegemony:
Is U.S. Hegemony in Decline?

The above argument emphasizes the limitations of the theory of hegemonic stability, but one should recognize that it has made a great contribution to the political economy of international relations. The concepts provided by this theory, such as international public goods and hegemony, are adequate as means of analysis. These analytical concepts, however, gradually began to take on lives of their own in the mass media as useful rhetorical tools, and under the sensational headline, "Is U.S. hegemony in decline?" arguments began to flourish in newspapers and magazines. As many will have noticed, in this journalistic debate, terms such as national power, great power, and hegemony were used whenever it was convenient. But the concept of hegemony, so popular at present, has its origins in the particular model of the theory of hegemonic stability, and however one looks at it, it is a concept designed for analytical use. It is not as if something like this either has or does not have a real existence. Depending on what one takes it to mean, one could say either that U.S. hegemony has declined or that it is continuing. The fundamental point is the explanatory power of the model of the international system based on this concept as a whole; and the contribution of the theory of hegemonic stability should rather be sought in having precisely defined the concept of hegemony so as to provide a new explanatory model.

In the original formulation of the theory of hegemonic stability, a hegemon was solely a country that had sufficient national power so that, while letting other countries behave freely in both the economic and political arenas, it could also provide on its own an international environment (what we are calling international public goods) for that purpose. This is a strong requirement that is only indirectly or incompletely referred to in describing the roles of the leader of a unipolar system or a superpower system. For example, a number of people have recently given a narrower definition of a hegemon, as "a superpower that in terms of national power is preeminent *in all dimensions*, and having sufficient power can single-handedly supply *all* international public goods."[19] This, however, is an extremely strong definition, and if one were to take conditions such as "national power in all dimensions" and "all international public goods" at face value, the possibility of such a hegemon's appearing would be extremely low. Only the United States in the period following the Second World War, when all the other countries had been exhausted by war, comes close to fitting this definition. Britain in the Victorian era led other countries in industrialization and naval power but was in no way the most powerful country militarily. Even in terms of industrialization, other countries had caught up with Britain within a matter of decades. Thus the decline of the hegemon is a conclusion that follows almost directly from the strict definition. This theory of hegemonic decline is a result of the overly rigorous definition of the concept of hegemony. For the time being I will call this the first type of theory of hegemonic decline, but this argument does not lead one to a meaningful conclusion. The theory of hegemonic stability was surely not meant for such an argument.

The second theory of hegemonic decline places more importance on economic power than on any of the other dimensions of national power; that is, this theory argues that the economic power of the dominant country will not be able to weather the costs of that dominance. Certainly, if its economic power is weakened, the hegemon will not be able to maintain the other dimensions of national power. To give a recent example, Paul Kennedy has predicted the decline of U.S. hegemony, using an explanation "so familiar to historians of the rise and fall of previous Great Powers," namely that of "imperial overstretch." Certainly, the changing of dynasties in the classical empires and the transfer of hegemony between monarchies in many cases took the form: overstretch → bankruptcy of the government purse → impoverishment of the domestic economy.[20]

This kind of argument, however, which focuses on the balance between the extent of the hegemony and its costs, is a general observation, valid to varying extents for East and West, ancient and modern. But I do not believe it is sufficiently rigorous to be used for a discussion of the question of hegemony under superindustrialization. To take the present example of the United States, solving the problem of excessive economic burden should not be too difficult if its domestic politics are managed intelligently. For example, if military expenditures are kept under, say, 5 percent of GNP, and the propensity to save (or the tax burden) is increased by more than 2 percent, the macroeconomic balance will return, and the United States will be able to escape economic ruin created by its military burden. There is still a strong possibility that a courageous president might accomplish such a policy change.

The third theory of hegemonic decline is frequently confused with the above-mentioned theory that emphasizes economic power but is rather a theory that attaches greater importance to technological power. Certainly, even if the macroeconomic balance had returned—for example, if a country had a low growth capability—then its economic power itself would deteriorate, and its position relative to other countries would move downward. This problem did not exist for empires before industrialization and is peculiar to modern hegemons. The most important factors in determining growth capability are a country's strength in technological innovation and its ability to provide capital for industrial investment—for example by increasing its propensity to save and/or by changing tax burdens.

As mentioned in the previous section, technological innovation includes theory and applied results, and it extends to the development of manufactured goods and the maintenance of their quality. Thus the capacity for technological innovation is intimately connected to techniques of business management—such as motivation of employees—and to the level of education. The trends in the saving and tax rates are strongly dependent on the general atmosphere within the society and on domestic politics. Many have been pessimistic recently about the U.S. microeconomic structure in the sense just described, and also about its technological ability, including that in manufacturing industries. Certainly it is no mistake to see technological ability as a decisive factor in hegemonic rise and decline. But it is no less important to realize that technological ability is determined by such factors as education and organizational structure of institutions, as well as by the strengths of ideology and ideals. That is, the question of technology cannot be solved in isolation. Whether American hegemony revives or declines will be determined by whether American society generates the ideology and ideals that can push through the necessary reforms.

To sum up, whether one emphasizes the macro balance or the micro structure, a revival of American economic power will not by itself signify the return of American hegemony. A revival in economic power is simply an effect. The point in question with regard to a return of hegemony is rather how responsive the American political style will be and what ideals Americans will have in dealing with new world realities. Economic power can be transformed into national power in other dimensions, but doing so is difficult except for military power. This is because transforming economic power into technological capacity, political power, and the persuasive force of culture will require, as just noted, changes in the political style and ideals of the United States. On this point, Paul Kennedy and many of today's theorists who attach great importance to economic power and technological capacities are not exempt from criticism. At present, even among the theorists of hegemonic stability, there are those such as Gilpin who are cautious about placing any great emphasis on economic power.

All of the preceding needs to be stressed. If new realities announcing a turning point in civilization are indeed appearing today at the end of the twentieth century, then the quality required of a hegemon will not be military and economic power, but rather the insight needed to see the significance of these new realities.[21] Great Britain, as the hegemon of the nineteenth century, learned much from its lengthy experience from the Anglo-Dutch Wars to the Napoleonic Wars, particularly from the delicate maneuvering required during the trade wars. The success of the Pax Britannica owed a great deal to the calm historical insight of the British. The United States, too, as the hegemon in the second half of the twentieth century, learned much in the interwar period from its experience of the Great Depression and retaliatory protectionist policies and so was able to construct a new system. Unless the lessons of history are learned in an attempt to build a new international system appropriate to the present and the future, hegemony can be neither established nor lasting. Spain in the seventeenth century misread the tide of history, which was turning toward industrialization, and so hegemony slipped out of its grasp. Military and economic power, too, can only be the power of a hegemon if a country possesses the ability to learn from, and see the changes in, history.

The structure of domestic society is not unconnected to this discussion. Even powerful countries experience periods of upheaval from time to time. In the present-day United States, one can see many serious symptoms of a society in turmoil, such as the use of drugs, the decline in the standard of education, and the prevalence of crime. The problem, however, is not these symptoms in and of themselves, but the direction and sustaining of the effort to try and solve them. These are determined by the ability to learn from history and to see the problems in a historical perspective, and also by the power of ideology and ideals. Here let me again define a hegemon as a country that understands the tide of history, has the intellectual capacity to suggest the way the world ought to be, and possesses the economic power to provide the international public goods necessary for the world to reach the future the country envisioned for it.

There may well be those who want to respond cynically to this argument, saying that there is nothing new in this, that it is merely the return of power politics to international politics. Everyone recognizes, though, that history occasionally undergoes great changes in direction. If the present new realities are changing the direction of history in a fundamental sense, then it is not simply power politics that is at work. Or at least it is no mistake to say that both the meaning of power and the pattern of its interactions are changing. We must therefore ask ourselves whether these phenomena, which we are calling the new realities—the transition to a borderless economy, the information revolution, the sudden rise of the NIEs, the relative decline of the U.S. economy, and the disintegration of the cold war system—are really signs of a new direction in history. We must again determine whether there is a need for a new conceptual framework that can go beyond the old power politics. This—and discussion of what this new conceptual framework might be—is the subject of the following chapter.

Let me summarize the points made in this chapter. One could evaluate the theory of the hegemon as an attempt to synthesize the two existing orthodoxies—liberal economic theory and nationalist political theory—by developing the concept of international public goods. Its conclusion, however, stopped at the diagnosis that a hegemon was necessary in order to maintain or revive classical economic liberalism. If one looks at the actual circumstances parallel to this argument, it is clear that the real prescription offered was to wait eagerly for the maintenance of the Pax Americana or its revival (a Pax Americana II). The pessimistic feeling of helplessness that haunts Gilpin's final chapter well expresses this intellectual state.[22] If we are to discover some kind of positive prescription, then we must create a more general perspective that includes the theory of the hegemon as a particular case. To use the argument made thus far, this more general perspective must include the dynamic of technological change. The fundamental component of the dynamic of changes in national power centers on an analysis of the market mechanism (there is a need to expand this analysis itself to include the possibility of declining costs and the effects of expectation functions); but this fundamental component encompasses both the dynamic of technological change and the dynamic of politics as indispensable elements. Such an attempt to generalize the theory goes beyond existing neoclassical economics and the works on the nation-state in political science and will be a very difficult task. However, in the following chapters, I offer a number of preliminary results of my efforts to date.

One example is the dynamic of technological change and the theory of developmentalism that can be deduced from it. This theory is a criticism of neoclassical economics, inasmuch as it ignores differences in wealth and developmental capacity among the nations. This does not mean, however, that we must return to the old Marxist or neo-Marxist theory. Marxist theory, which dwells on the relentlessness of exploitation, is premised on the immutability of the structure of class domination. What we are observing now is a pluralism of structures that cannot be reduced to class domination; there is both a confrontation between ideologies burdened with the history of the past and an emerging confrontation between differing perspectives on the future. As mentioned in the first chapter, the twin confrontations between classical liberalism and Marxism, and between capitalism and socialism, are themes that must now be overcome. In doing this, the experience of Japan, and of the NIEs, will be important.

Another example is the question of the dynamic of politics, scarcely mentioned so far. The political dynamic contains at least two important themes. One is the reexamination of the concept of international public goods, which symbolizes the politics between countries; more concretely, it is a focus in particular on international currencies and more broadly on foreign aid and investment. The other theme is the question of the changing character of democracy within the advanced industrial countries—the theme of mass democracy. The preliminary results of my study of these themes are presented in Chapters 7 and 9.

CHAPTER 4

The Demise of the
Classical Belief

Two Dynamics

As I have already explained to some extent, the "new realities"—including the transition to a borderless economy, the relative decline of the U.S. economy, the sudden rise of the NIEs, the information revolution, and the end of the cold war—are products of the two dynamics of industrialization and nationalism, and of their interaction. One can believe that these dynamic "new realities" are a sign that industrialization and nationalism are, at least in part, being forced to undergo great changes. In this chapter, I offer an analysis of this situation, focusing on the problems we face today. However, since it is impossible to explain it fully with a static analysis of market competition and power politics—that is, within the classical framework of economic liberalism and the nation-state system—I present further analyses of the new realities in the following chapters.

In beginning the analysis of the new realities, we must note the huge expansion in the destructive capabilities of the military, particularly the repercussions of the development of nuclear weapons. The invention of nuclear weapons during the Second World War was, from the perspective of the history of energy, one of the greatest events in human history. The subsequent appearance of nuclear power generation owing to this invention is of course important, but of particularly great significance is the accumulation of military nuclear capability, which increased the possibility of human annihilation. One cannot say that the development of nuclear weapons was in itself a necessary product of industrialization or nationalism. But one can ask whether it was not almost inevitable that when the development of the modern nation-state, which had begun with the firearms revolution, was linked to the dynamic of industrialization, it would eventually lead to the appearance of weapons of mass destruction—if not nuclear weapons, then perhaps biological weapons, chemical weapons, or an as yet unknown X weapon. In this sense, the development of nuclear weapons was not merely accidental but symbolized the fate of industrialization and the nation-state in the sense that these terms are ordinarily used. In other words, it suggested that the combination of the two dynamics of industrialization and nationalism might even be self-destructive.

With the common knowledge that nuclear capability holds the potential for human annihilation have come various efforts to control its use. However, no new ideology of world peace capable of changing the course of history has emerged in direct response to the rapid developments of this situation, and there is little hope that such an ideology will emerge for some time. Even so, since the appearance of nuclear capability, the great powers have begun to exercise self-control over all aspects of the use of military force, and as a result, belligerency when it occurs has come to be rigorously localized. For example, the Korean War, the Vietnam War, the wars in the Middle East, the war in Afghanistan, and the recent war in the Persian Gulf were all waged locally so as not to plunge the whole world into a state of war. Thus world trade was not disrupted but prospered because of those wars. That is, the *modus vivendi* among the nuclear powers of maintaining an equilibrium in nuclear deterrence has sustained a certain level of peace and security. That economic activity has flourished under the *modus vivendi* means that the significance of military power has declined relative to that of economic power. Below I demonstrate that this fact has been a secondary but substantial factor in the emergence of the trading state and the developmentalist countries.

Thus, generally speaking, it seems that, for a long time to come, it will not be possible for the dynamic of military technology to be the main driving force of history. It will not be impossible for the Russian Republic to rebuild its nuclear arsenal or for China to become a nuclear power, but it will be impossible for them to rival the capabilities of the American nuclear arsenal. Again, it is not impossible that nuclear weapons will be used as a means of intimidation by adventurist small countries, but such intimidation will be effective only when the world order has been weakened below a certain critical level. Thus the interaction between the two dynamics of industrialization and nationalism will continue to determine the course of history. Only when their interaction leads to a catastrophe will the significance of nuclear weapons reemerge. The drama of the Second World War, of the interaction between industrialization and nationalism, was played out with nuclear weapons as the sword of Damocles. The fact that the sense of oppression felt at that time will be retained or even amplified in the political psychology of the future may well be a handicap to making calm judgments about the world. There is a danger that the impatient new progressivism, which seeks even the immediate elimination of the use of nuclear energy, will aggravate prevailing political realities.

Decline of the Nation-State System: The Demise of Classical Nationalism

Many historical interpretations since the nineteenth century have attached much importance to economic factors. Marxism is typical, in considering politics to be nothing more than the superstructure of economics. I believe, however, that political factors have been unduly slighted. In fact, even for modern society, an interpretation that regards politics as a "superstructure" is not generally tenable. Nationalism, which has been the most important political factor in the modern period, has a powerful dynamic that cannot be derived solely from economic factors such as capitalism and industrialization. Here, taking up the argument in Chapter 2 that explained the development of nationalism up to the Second World War, let me add the following on the dynamic of politics since then.

BASES OF NATIONALISM IN THE POSTWAR WORLD

Politics is the making of decisions as a collectivity while influencing people's way of thinking. Thus it includes a number of dimensions, such as supplying information needed to make decisions, placing emphasis on justice (or a set of rules) in order to give authority to decisions, and choosing a means by which to carry out the decisions. In politics, the concept of justice and the means of war have come to play a most remarkable role. As I mentioned in Chapter 2, the international political history of modern Europe is a story of balance-of-power diplomacy and war as a legitimate means for a nation-state to achieve its goals. The fundamental principle was a striving toward the doctrine of nonjust war as a mechanism for coexistence—that is, an attempt to circumvent the concept of just war. Retrospectively, what dominated the dynamic of nationalism was mainly the confrontation between the doctrine of just war and the doctrine of nonjust war, although the doctrine of the *un*just war occasionally put in an appearance in a supporting role. This confrontation formed the main thread of international political history up to the Second World War, by which time, as mentioned in Chapter 2, it had developed into a confrontation between three groups of thought: the modified doctrine of nonjust war as seen in the League of Nations; the anachronistic doctrine of just war by the have-nots; and the simple doctrine of the just war of anticolonialism.

As shown in Chapter 2, the war brought a clear conclusion to this confrontation and the reemergence of the doctrine of just war. The classical doctrine of nonjust war had been violated and proven conceptually bankrupt in fighting a war against an anticivilization (fascism).

A major power in this theoretical shift was the United States, a nation built on ideals and aspirations and possessing natural affinity with the doctrine of just war. The United States, as a multiethnic state comprising various immigrant groups, is not, strictly speaking, a nation-state. In place of the unity of the natural unit (the "natio"), it is a semination-state that has depended on a common ideology (free competition and democracy), or rather, to use an expression of Samuel Huntington's, a transnational state.[1] The thirteen original states provided a natural cultural unity derived from Puritanism; however, with the rapid increase of immigrants from the mid-nineteenth century, the role of ideology in unifying the nation was enlarged, and the original idealism of the Founding Fathers was stressed even more. As was symbolized by the Statue of Liberty that welcomed immigrants at the entrance to New York harbor, the land of America was established on the concept of freedom itself.

In attending the Paris Peace Conference at the end of the First World War, President Woodrow Wilson was very much aware that he represented this American idealism, and others at the conference expected that he would do so. However, he was not able to destroy, single-handedly, the framework of the nineteenth-century game played by European politicians. Outmaneuvered by Georges Clemenceau, Wilson returned home a disappointed idealist, and his political battles to defend the League of Nations and U.S. membership cost him both his health and his political power. This can be seen as signifying that the American people had chosen isolationism. At least among the leaders in the United States, however, the desire to try to show their determination as a great power in idealist diplomacy had not been snuffed out. While American intervention in the continental advance of Japan had the direct aim of checking Japan, it also showed the American determination to challenge the Anglo-French diplomacy of double standards, based on a maintenance of the status quo, and to defy the classical doctrine of nonjust war, which was taking its dying breaths. It was not easy, however, to encourage public opinion in the United States in this direction, and prewar American diplomacy had not attained the authority to control the confusion surrounding the three confrontational perspectives on justice and war mentioned above.

The Second World War changed this situation. The complete victory of the Allies was clearly due to the entry into the war of the United States, and its national power was overwhelming. For the countries of Europe, which had become the battleground for both world wars, the outcome of the balance-of-power diplomacy had been devastating, and Europeans themselves had lost their faith in it as a time-honored means of diplomacy. The postwar attempt to rebuild the nation-state system based on the doctrine of nonjust war amounted to nothing more than a repeat of the wasted effort following the First World War. Without the military, economic, and ideological intervention of the Americans, the postwar reconstruction of

Europe would have been impossible. Europe had no choice but to follow the American policies.

The policy of Britain, in playing the role as hegemon in the previous international system, had been maintenance of a balance-of-power diplomacy based on the doctrine of nonjust war and tacit approval for colonialism. In short, the policy had been to maintain the status quo, based on a double standard. It was lucky for this British policy that until the First World War there had been but one influential new player on the stage of international diplomacy. To deal with this newcomer, Japan, cautious steps were taken, including establishing the Anglo-Japanese alliance and holding the Washington and London conferences on naval arms limitations. As long as British leadership persisted—that is, as long as the League of Nations fell into line in its criticism of Japan's Manchurian policy— then Japan, too, cooperated with these British policies.

With the U.S. assumption of hegemony following the Second World War, however, the situation changed, and the number of new entrants rapidly increased. With the anticolonialism of the newly independent countries and the reappearance of the Soviet Union as a great power, it is clear that the new entrants were diverse and noncooperative. The British policy of maintaining the status quo was inadequate as diplomacy, and there was a need for a theory that could overcome its inherent double standard. In contrast to the British hegemony, whose foundation was post-seventeenth-century European thought, American hegemony had to stand on new ideals. This historical necessity and the fundamental idealist characteristics of the United States as a state fit nicely with each other. In this sense, one might say that the United States became a hegemon at just the right moment in history.

One strength of the United States as the new leader was that its hands had not been dirtied by colonialism, or only to a comparatively small extent. The possession of the Philippines following the Spanish-American War of 1898 is always somewhat arguable, and one can interpret the U.S. Open Door policy as nothing more than the skillful strategy of a late entrant into imperialism. American expansionism, however, was different in character from classical colonialism, and Huntington has an important point when he emphasizes that "the American 'empire' . . . was an empire of functions, not territory."[2] For example, the United States, which had itself formerly been a colony, was certainly consistent in its criticism of European-style colonialism (and of the Japanese imitation of it). At present, the United States frequently subjects itself to self-criticism by saddling itself with all the historical debts of Western colonialism, but it is unconvincing to regard the Korean War, the Vietnam War, or the recent Persian Gulf War as imperialism in the service of the interests of monopoly capitalism, or the military-industrial complex. Presidents Harry Truman, Lyndon Johnson, and George Bush all prudently avoided territorial imperialism. This, of course, reflected the fact that these wars were fought under a strict limitation: American ideology must not be compromised. It is perhaps not impossible to call this ideology cultural imperialism or functional imperialism.

Certainly one can call American diplomacy imperialist, in the sense that it tried to propagate a unitary or universal idea of justice. However, this attempt lacked the characteristic of territorial domination that the previous five centuries of European imperialism had possessed, and thus the extent of American economic domination was also limited. To call this American position "transnationalism," as Huntington does, is perhaps to go too far, but there was a good reason why even non-Western peoples more readily accepted American hegemony. The American proposal for the United Nations was more innovative in its treatment of the colonies than those of Winston Churchill and others. In its attitude to the Suez crisis and the immediate postwar issues involving Indochina, the United States efforts to go beyond the existing colonialism were welcomed by many nations. Clearly, the Pax Americana was not only the result of American economic or military power. The most important element was the idealism of American diplomacy, which seemed to provide new rules for a postwar world in which colonialism had become impossible to sustain. However, in that the basis for this idealism was the belief that Europe and the United States should educate the world, it was not in the least different from the British position—if one ignores the fact that Britain was more explicit in emphasizing this point. Perhaps the most important determinant of the shape of the world to come is how this American idealism will change, or whether it will change at all.

Together with the United States, the Soviet Union, as the "fatherland" of socialism, was also engaged in a fight to the finish, using the doctrine of just war in the form of a war against capitalism. These two great powers, which in their respective ways had been isolationist during the interwar period, increasingly took the main roles on the postwar international stage, and there the two doctrines of just war met in ideological confrontation. Given the limitations created by the potential of massive nuclear holocaust, the form this confrontation took was the cold war. This cold "war" was neither accidental nor the result of the individual characters of Stalin and Truman. Rather, it was the final expression—by two countries at the periphery—of the ideological division that had lain dormant throughout the modern period in Europe. Thus a new logic of the doctrine of just war was born: to "contain" another anticivilization (namely, Soviet-style communism) and thereby maintain the order of the so-called Western world (those countries with market economies), centered on Europe and the United States—and the order of the Eastern bloc as well.

Putting the United States to one side, what would have happened had the postwar rebuilding been entrusted to the workings of the balance-of-power mechanism based on the doctrine of nonjust war? There is no doubt that the world would have been plunged into a confusion the Western world would not have been able to control. This is because the sustained strategy of intervention by the Soviet Union, based on the doctrine of just war, would have been aimed at destroying the existing capitalist order and so would have continuously disturbed the balance of power. And the gaps created by the disruption of that balance would have been exploited, bringing chaos to every region by the new have-nots intent on redistributing vested interests. Given that the complete submission of either the East or the West was impossible because of each side's nuclear capability, the division of justice into two differing worlds was the only viable solution for avoiding this chaos.

In this sense, what saved Europe from the deadlock of the framework based on the doctrine of nonjust war following the First World War was the moral diplomacy of the United States, which produced the cold war, and in fact the existence of the "evil" that was the Soviet Union was indispensable in maintaining this American order. It is inappropriate to criticize the crudeness of the idealism of U.S. diplomacy up to the present by looking at it only through the lens of nineteenth-century European diplomacy.[3] The question is whether the idealism of the American people can successfully cope with the flow of history yet to unfold.

The relative peace after the war was a product of a system based on the doctrine of just war, with two sides, which to be accurate should be called the Pax Russo-Americana. This relative peace was maintained by the unrelenting idealism of the United States, which was ready to wage war against a Soviet Union claiming to be a nation of "scientific" socialism. This kind of power could not have been generated within the intellectual world of postwar Europe—as is readily seen in the works of, for example, Bertrand Russell or Jean-Paul Sartre. Hegemony has various dimensions, but in the complex postwar situation generated by the interaction of nationalism and industrialization—such as the intertwining of the East-West question and the North-South question—it was the force of American ideology that acted as an engine. The theory of hegemonic stability is easily apt to be interpreted as a concentration on economic power, but the most important support of postwar U.S. hegemony was its ability to supply this political orthodoxy.

AN ASSESSMENT OF THE UNITED NATIONS

Thus the classical nation-state system, which had aimed at the doctrine of nonjust war, turned under U.S. leadership toward a system based on the doctrine of just war. The ideological leadership of the United States cut through the long-lasting confusion in the doctrine of nonjust war. The idealistic diplomacy at Versailles following the First World War was forced into retreat by the weak support it received within the United States. But as the Second World War drew to a close, the American leaders were determined to build a postwar system, and early on, in collaboration with

Britain, they prepared a proposal for a United Nations. As was symbolized by the victory of Cordell Hull's American proposal over Churchill's, the formation of the United Nations signified the passing of hegemony from Britain to the United States. But what was the United Nations when it was created? Even today, answers to this question are frequently confused.

The United Nations seemed to inherit the tradition of the doctrine of nonjust war, as had the League of Nations. Certainly the Covenant of the League of Nations and the Kellogg-Briand Pact seemed to extol antiwar spirit and tried to disavow war in general, but their substance was not antiwar. Both recognized wars waged by countries in self-defense. That is, in the sense that this was a system that did not recognize a justice that went beyond the rule of self-preservation, both documents aimed at a system based on the doctrine of nonjust war. An official statement of the U.S. government recognized that even under the Kellogg-Briand Pact there was a right to self-defense, and this became the standard interpretation of the pact. The League of Nations, too, in Article 10 of its covenant, made its first objective the protection of its member nations from foreign aggression, and this can be interpreted as having justly recognized the right to self-defense, whether individual or collective.[4]

The problem after the First World War was finding answers to questions such as what is self-defense, what is war, what sanctions can be used to prevent wars that are not fought in self-defense, and how can rules be formulated on these points. However, the Kellogg-Briand Pact, for example, consisted of only two articles and was nothing more than a moral prescription that did not determine what means should be used as sanctions. Rule making in the League of Nations was also not a success. The fundamental principle of the league was the unanimity of all its members in decision making (Article 5 in the covenant),[5] and as a result it was difficult to make effective decisions. The league was weaker as an organization than the United Nations that followed it, and its provisions, especially for sanctions on violations of rules, had many faults. It appears that the league thought mainly in terms of nonmilitary economic sanctions (a prohibition on "financial, commercial or personal intercourse," called for in Article 16.1 of the covenant),[6] but without the participation of the United States, as the most important economic power, these economic sanctions would have been ineffective.

The two processes provided by the covenant for dispute resolution—arbitration and dispute enquiry—sought conciliation by different means. Arbitration was more powerful in that all parties involved had to consent to the process before it could begin. Dispute enquiry, however, was more effective in producing League of Nations recommendations because it allowed for investigation of disputes without the agreement of all parties concerned.[7] In cases where a country rejected a recommendation, and initiated or continued military action, the covenant provided means of initiating sanctions (in Articles 15.6 and 16.1), although it was doubtful that the league would have carried them out.

The covenant made it relatively easy (in contrast to the United Nations) to resolve dispute enquiries by majority decision, but this also enabled the doctrine of just war to enter by the back door, so to speak. Given this situation of the competing doctrines of nonjust war and just war, the delicate balance between them largely dominated the outcomes of dispute enquiries, and the smaller countries who greatly feared the prospect of invasion in general held the casting vote. Originally, dispute enquiry was perhaps the outcome of earnest efforts made in hopes of peaceful consultation and the pressure of international opinion. In general cases other than dispute enquiry, however, the fundamental rule of the League of Nations was unanimity. The disparity between the ease of decision making on dispute enquiry and the general character of the League of Nations caused confusion in understanding the essential characteristics of the league. As a result, the league wavered between the doctrines of nonjust war and just war and heightened rather than diminished the risk of aggravating international confrontations. This risk became a reality in 1933 with the withdrawal of Japan and Germany from the league, followed by the withdrawal of the Latin American countries. Even its agonized efforts at dispute investigation were not enough to redeem the weakness of the league as an organization.[8]

The charter of the United Nations demonstrates a strong desire to go beyond the Covenant of the League of Nations and to move from a doctrine of nonjust war toward a renunciation of war. Idealist pacifists—particularly "instinctive" pacifists in Japan—have frequently emphasized this point and have tried to call for a world led by the United Nations. There are even some who fancy that the United Nations contains the seeds of a world state. However the U.N. Charter does not renounce war; having learned from the failure of the League of Nations, it clarifies and greatly strengthens the possible sanctions that can be placed on those countries that violate it. Though the charter states that countries should refrain from using military force (Article 2), it recognizes that military actions may be undertaken to maintain or restore international peace and security in accordance with the recommendations and directions of the Security Council (Articles 39, 42) and makes various provisions for taking such actions, including a role for a Military Staff Committee (Article 47 and others). The approval of military sanctions in the Gulf War was one example of these provisions in action. The basic logic is that, with collective sanctions available within the United Nations, there is no need for individual countries to have recourse to military expedients.

But this logic is not adhered to throughout. For example, there is no clear resolution in the charter on the question of whether, in the absence of any recommendation or direction from the Security Council, a particular country can independently use military force, while insisting that it is following the spirit of the U.N. Charter. Certainly there are provisions that acknowledge individual military action when it is recognized as the exercise of the right of self-defense (Article 51), but even here there are less-than-unambiguous stipulations such as "until the Security Council has taken necessary measures." (What about those cases in which the Security Council never takes the necessary measures?) But it is difficult to judge what should be regarded as an act of self-defense. For example, although international opinion strongly approved of the German evacuation of the Mogadishu (Somalia) airport and disapproved of the Israeli evacuation of the Entebbe (Uganda) airport, the difference between them was in a sense very small. The 1981 Israeli destruction of an Iraqi nuclear reactor was problematic, but it is not impossible to understand the Israeli aim of self-defense. It is difficult to judge where the limits to self-defense lie, in those cases, as at the time of the Arab-Israeli war in 1956, when a country (Israel) has been attacked and invaded, and so counterattacks by invading and occupying another country's territory. The problem of indirect aggression, in which a country secretly supplies arms and troops, has frequently been an issue in Central America and Africa. In neither place, however, has the Security Council been able to produce an effective resolution.

Unlike the council of the League of Nations, the U.N. Security Council plays a very prominent role. Indeed, the significance of the United Nations as a system is determined by the work of the Security Council. The United Nations is neither the ideals expressed in the articles of its charter nor simply the reemergence of the League of Nations. In the latter, the fundamental principle was unanimity—all member nations had equal veto power—and as a result it was difficult to make effective decisions. The role of the assembly was rather strong in the league (except in dispute enquiry, as I have noted). In short, the system of the League of Nations sacrificed efficacy for the ideal of egalitarianism. Having learned from this experience, the United Nations created a mechanism to reflect the actual distribution of national power. As is shown by the right of veto held by the five permanent members of the Security Council, the United Nations was designed as a system led by an alliance of the victors in the Second World War, and a process for implementing military sanctions was clearly provided in order to ensure collective security.[9] One of the expectations held of the United Nations was that under a kind of international guided democratic system it might effectively suppress military disputes.

Even this system, however, inasmuch as there was no unity among the leading countries, was unable to support effective decision making. Where there was a sharp division of interests and opinions among the leading countries, veto power was exercised and it was impossible to initiate military sanctions. For example, the military conflicts in Nicaragua and Afghanistan were symbolic cases for the interpretation of self-defense and aggression, and the United States and the USSR, themselves involved in these instances, did not yield their respective positions. Throughout the 45 years since the war, "guided democracy" under the United Nations has been impracticable given the dissension among the leading countries (particularly the intensification of the confrontation between the United States and the USSR) and the forceful self-assertions made by the numerous newly independent states. As a result, the U.N. General Assembly has become a forum where "justice" as seen by various members is debated. The United Nations could neither restrain the cold war doctrines of just war nor suppress the anticolonialist doctrine of just war. Perhaps the United Nations can be a place for communication and contact, but there is no prospect of its becoming the core of an emergent world-state. Idealists who advocate a world led by the United Nations must be reminded of this fact.

COLLECTIVE SELF-DEFENSE AND COLLECTIVE SECURITY ALLIANCES

The relative peace after the war was brought about not by the United Nations but by the U.S.-Soviet cold war system, which was centered on a complex system of collective security, itself based on the right to collective self-defense. The Western countries formed a global ring of collective self-defense, with the United States as hegemon at its center, advocating an anti-Soviet doctrine of just war. Thus was established an order that both confronted the Eastern bloc and made the use of military force between the advanced Western nations impossible.[10] In other words, it was the system of collective security based on the right of collective self-defense that incorporated the doctrine of nonjust war among the principal countries within the larger framework of the anti-Soviet doctrine of just war. It is possible to see this dual structure as one terminus for the 300-year-old confrontation between the doctrines of nonjust war and just war (in which, admittedly, the former had originally played the leading role). (This does, however, leave unresolved the question of how to deal with the nationalistic doctrine of just war espoused by the newly independent states.) Whether one looks at NATO, the U.S.-Japan Security Treaty, or the U.S.-Korea Treaty, the system of collective security founded on the right of collective self-defense has a double character as a military alliance in the face of potential enemies such as the USSR and as a covenant prohibiting the use of military force among the member nations.

It is easy to overlook the latter part of its character, but the fact that no war has broken out among the major powers during the nearly 50 years since the Second World War cannot, historically speaking, be ignored. Since the end of the war, the last occasion on which major powers directly confronted each other with military force was when the United States and China clashed during the Korean War, between 1950 and 1953.[11] This is the longest peace among major nations at least since the beginning of the sixteenth century. In Europe, no war broke out in the 44 years between the

Franco-Prussian War of 1870–71 and the outbreak of the First World War in 1914. In this period, however, there were many incidents such as the Russo-Turkish War, the Sino-French War, the Sino-Japanese War, and the Russo-Japanese War, which one could call wars between major powers. And in the period after the Korean War, there have been the Vietnam War, the war in Afghanistan, and the Gulf War, but it is difficult to call these wars between major powers. Historically, the major powers have never managed to succeed in realizing such a long period without war.

The member nations of the postwar collective security treaties collaborated in dealing with the potential for mass slaughter and participated in joint military operations. In NATO a system somewhat like a division of labor emerged, in which each major power supplied troops and weapons according to its expertise and capabilities. Even within the framework of the U.S.-Japan Security Treaty, which had a strongly unilateral character, beginning in the 1980s, a system of collaborative military operations gradually emerged, focusing on the northwest Pacific. In the American dispatch of troops to the Persian Gulf, the American bases in Japan can be seen to have played a decisive logistical role. As these cooperative relationships deepened, for the first time in history a war between member nations became next to impossible, and the relationship among the member nations took on the character of a political and economic cooperation that went beyond military questions.

Of course, this does not mean that there was no political or economic friction between these countries. If the economic friction between Japan and the United States that grew particularly acute during the 1980s had occurred half a century earlier, it would have broken off economic relations (we should remember the abrogation of the U.S.-Japan trade treaty in 1939). Probably the most important factor in preventing such a catastrophe has been the concern for maintaining the cooperative security relationship between the two countries. And the relationship between Japan and the United States is no exception: it has also been the most important factor in limiting economic friction between the United States and Europe.

Whether one likes it or not, security issues and economic issues have become closely intertwined. The so-called economic summits provide a symbolic focus on this linkage and are not merely conferences of the leading economic powers. Were Japan to abrogate the U.S.-Japan Security Treaty, it is doubtful whether it could be a participant at the summits. Although the system of collective security based on the right of collective self-defense has lost its original purpose with the end of the U.S.-Soviet cold war, the realities of the multifaceted cooperative relationships between member states will not easily be disentangled within NATO or in the U.S.-Japan Security Treaty. At present, in the Council for Security and Cooperation of Europe, efforts are being made to develop a multifaceted cooperation that goes beyond the military character of NATO. The alliances for collective self-defense have left a substantial bequest of nonmilitary cooperation.

With the collapse of the socialist bloc and the disappearance of an order based on a dichotomy in the concept of justice, at first glance it seems as if there is little need for collective self-defense. Because of this, some Japanese have recently argued for the abrogation of the security treaty. Certainly, circumstances since the height of the cold war have changed substantively. During the cold war, it would have been impossible for Japan or West Germany, each of which had a substantial industrial capacity and an important geopolitical position, to choose neutrality. Had such a country announced a policy of unarmed neutrality, all the political energy of the cold war would have been directed at that country. There would have been a high possibility of a chain reaction, in which its domestic politics would have been destabilized by the immense pressure exerted by both the United States and the USSR, a revolutionary government would have been established by one of the two, indirect aggression would have intervened in the confusion, and a fierce war would have broken out. Nonalignment was an option only for countries that were not geopolitically or economically important—such as India, Indonesia, Yugoslavia, and China—or for countries that had both a sufficient defense capability and the fortitude— philosophy—to remain isolationist. Unlike in this situation at the height of the cold war, it seems increasingly possible that there could now be a Japan without a security treaty.

However, what the proponents of the abrogation of the security treaty are unconsciously—or perhaps consciously—ignoring is the double significance of the postwar collective security system. That is, the security treaty is not only a part of the anti-Soviet cold war system but has become symbolic of an economic and political cooperative relationship within what used to be the West, which went beyond the merely military. Thus, the abrogation of the security treaty would be a rejection of military cooperation and would be interpreted as a challenge to the U.S.-Japanese policy of political and economic cooperation. The United States and all other countries would interpret it in this way (regardless of whether they were friendly with the United States). The position of many of the Japanese who argue for the abrogation of the security treaty is inconsistent in that they do not deny the singular importance of the economic interdependence of Japan and the United States. Thus these Japanese add that a rejection of military cooperation does not necessarily mean political-economic noncooperation. These people, however, are either obstinately adhering to an argument they know is invalid or simply ignorant.

When one takes a position of military noncooperation, one is inviting the economic friction between the United States and Japan to grow worse. The economic relationship between the two countries today is not one of free trade; the protectionism and voluntary export restraints that began in the days of the cold war fetter the bilateral economic relationship, and political negotiations maintain the trade relationship. Within the U.S. Congress, a weakening of the existing cooperative relationship would surely deny Japanese manufactured goods access to the U.S. market. Thus an abrogation of the security treaty could only damage the Japanese economy and would be much more destructive than Charles De Gaulle's withdrawal from military cooperation within NATO in 1966 or than criticism of the United States from Canada and northern Europe.

Certainly one can separate military and economic cooperation in the abstract. Diplomacy, however, must consider real current and historical conditions. Today, the historical condition is the evolution, in the more than 45 years since the war, of the collective security treaties into a network of cooperation that goes beyond the merely military. Only when one can devise the framework of a new international order that could go beyond this historical achievement can one dare to advocate this kind of abstract argument. That is, only when one can suggest a better system to replace the collective security system based on the right of collective self-defense, and also convince the world that the proposed security system has the capacity to realize its goal, will the argument for the abrogation of the security treaty be valid. For present-day Japan, which cannot persuasively propose such a world system, advocating abrogation of the security treaty is nothing more than expressing incoherent, immature, and inarticulate criticism of "servitude to the United States" and "dependency on the United States." No doubt, the world would interpret an abrogation of the U.S.-Japan Security Treaty not as a manifestation of pacifism but as the expression of naive nationalism.

Even though Japan currently labors under a belief in the need for a new world order, abrogating the security treaty would produce feelings of uneasiness in East Asia and the Pacific far greater than those occasioned by Japan's dispatching minesweepers to the Persian Gulf or Self-Defense Forces to the peace-keeping operation in Cambodia. Japan's abrogation of the security treaty would surely be greeted throughout the world with suspicion and fear, and Japan would have to pursue a foreign policy of isolation, welcomed and understood by no one.

Should Japan choose to pursue such an isolationist foreign policy, Japan's domestic politics, as well as peace in East Asia and the western Pacific, would likely be thrown into confusion. Even if the dismantling of the system of collective security treaties were desirable (which I do not believe), Japan's seceding from that system before anyone else would be unwise and very costly for both Japan and the rest of the world. Anyone familiar with the management strategy of Japanese business would find it difficult to believe that the course of diplomacy of a nation that includes such shrewd managers could be determined principally by the desire to vent the psychological frustration of the nation. If such a policy were adopted, some would suspect its motivation to be some hidden global strategy. This is because other countries too are today experiencing similar frustration with the system of collective security.

That is, the experience of member nations with the unprecedentedly close-knit system of postwar collective security treaties has been a series of concessions and dissatisfactions; not only Japan has experienced discontent and frustration. France has articulated this most clearly and has also expressed its dissatisfaction by partially withdrawing from NATO. Even the United States, which is supposed to have had the most freedom in its behavior, has not been an exception. Fundamentally, the concessions and dissatisfactions are manifestations of the weakening sovereignty of every advanced industrial country, and this exacerbates naive nationalism. Whatever the case with newly independent states, naive nationalism cannot be a self-prescription for the developed countries, which have surely accumulated many bitter experiences since the First World War. Certainly the system of collective security treaties has not been an ideal solution, from the perspective of world peace. Although it utilized to some extent the experience of the doctrine of nonjust war, it did not come sufficiently to terms with the self-assertion of the newly independent countries based on the doctrine of just war, and above all it had to assume the psychological risk of taking the cold war doctrine of just war as its governing framework. However, in emphasizing the negative aspects, one must not forget the achievement of the system of collective security in nearly erasing the mentality of just war among the advanced countries of the West. We will discuss the future of collective security alliances in Chapter 8.

REACTIVE NATIONALISM AS A DOCTRINE OF JUST WAR

Together with the positions of the Soviet Union and the United States, another postwar doctrine of just war was the anticolonialist position on justice, which in a sense has had even greater historical significance. The anticolonialist movements that resulted from the concept of popular self-determination came to fruition after the war in the form of independence for many new countries, and the world changed rapidly in ways not even imagined before the war. The primary factor in this was that Western civilization, which had proclaimed the concept of popular self-determination an integral part of its beliefs and believed in the universality of its own civilization, had no choice but to recognize popular self-determination/reactive nationalism in the colonies. In addition, there were any number of secondary factors. Even the Japanese wartime invasion of Southeast Asia waged under the slogan of colonial emancipation —despite the vast inconsistencies between Japanese word and action—became a factor in demolishing the foundation of the European system of colonialism.[12]

More important as a secondary factor was the U.S.-Soviet cold war, which reinforced this anticolonialist doctrine of just war. In various senses, the United States and the Soviet Union, in trying to develop a new system of justice with equality as one of its pivotal tenets, competed to enlist the nationalism of the developing countries into their own camps. This provided an advantageous bargaining position for those seeking emancipation from colonialism. The United States in particular, which took pains to distinguish its foreign policy from prewar colonialism, exasperated the British and the French, as can be seen by its direct and indirect interventions in the Suez crisis and the Indochinese and Algerian questions, and made it impossible to go back on colonial emancipation. It is possible to criticize the inconsistency between word and action in U.S. foreign policy toward developing countries (as it is in regard to the question of domestic racial discrimination). U.S. foreign policy does change. However, because it has to pay serious attention to domestic public opinion, U.S. foreign policy cannot wander too far from the ideal of equality (that is, it must continue to fight colonialism and racism). This is the strength that has made U.S. hegemony unique.

It is well known that the effect of this complex of factors was the elimination of colonialism. The colonies had for the most part achieved independence by 1960, and even the last French colonies (Vietnam and Algeria), and almost all British and Portuguese colonies in Africa, achieved independence after going through violent civil wars. The elimination of colonialism has been, and will be, an irreversible trend in the world.

Of the various consequences produced by this change, the fruitlessness of military investment is the most important in determining what is to come. One could say that colonialism was a mechanism for recovering investment in military power from economic interests. Military expenditures protected the capital investments in one's colonies and thus were an economic investment that would increase one's returns. Examples of this are the East India Companies established by Britain and other European countries. The British East India Company possessed an increasingly extensive administrative organization and substantial military power, but the costs of maintaining these were seen as a necessary part of investment by the company. Until the Second World War, it was accepted that building up armaments and dispatching armies was the normal means of securing the overseas economic interests of one's country.

However, with the disappearance of colonialism after the Second World War, a country's investment in military power did not generate direct economic returns—apart from fostering its own military industries and some degree of technological spillover to private industries. Or at least the chance of generating returns declined remarkably. Military expenditures were made to achieve security or hegemony or to maintain "justice." In particular, the huge military capabilities of both the United States and the Soviet Union had little likelihood of being used. Nuclear capability could not be used, and even the escalation of electronic military capabilities was a competition to develop a technology that had little chance of being used. (I discuss the significance of the Gulf War below.) The United

States certainly had substantial overseas interests, but as an investment to protect them, its military expenditures were far too large and inefficient. For example, how useful is the Seventh Fleet in protecting U.S. overseas investments? (How effectively has it in fact protected oil interests in the Middle East?) From an economic standpoint, U.S. military expenditures are a huge waste. Since the age of colonialism, the economic burden of sustaining a hegemony has gradually become unendurable. This excessive burden was one of the most important reasons for the collapse of the Soviet bloc. It goes without saying that military power is an important component of hegemony, but the economic burden needed to maintain it is now becoming overwhelming. Without exceptional economic power, it has become impossible to sustain a system of hegemony.

We examine this problem for the United States and the Soviet Union again below, but let us now turn to the problems that have followed the disappearance of colonialism. The newly awakened postwar nationalism was triggered in reaction to Western (and Japanese) colonialism and was forcibly created, without waiting for "natio" and state to attain fully overlapping identities. In Asia and Africa, there are many multiracial and multilingual states, and there are even a number where the concepts of territory and national boundaries were not established at the beginning. Thus, although the system of the nation-state was put in place, this does not mean the substance of the nation-state came into being. In many cases, tribal divisions threaten the continued existence of the nation-state, and frequent military actions protest national boundaries established haphazardly at the time of independence. The attempt to unite a country through religious identity already has a precedent in the Islamic world (the attempts to unify Egypt and Syria between 1958 and 1961).

As these phenomena show, although reactive nationalism is flaring up, it is not easy for the newly formed nations to establish and stabilize the structure of a nation-state. Particularly important, and unlike in classical Europe, there has been no provision for an international system that could accommodate, as it were, this nationalism. Of course, it is possible for these nations to do such things as adopt an official language to make progress toward the classical nation-state on the European model and gain membership in the United Nations. But these actions do not result in the formation of genuine nation-states and, as less than genuine nation-states, the nations have a latent demand for an international system that permits their nationalism to coexist with other evolving nation-states. Thus in the Islamic world, Africa, and Southeast Asia, before these nation-states can develop fully, there will have to be rapid progress toward the formation of a new type of nascent nation-state. Instead of observing the gradual formation of nation-states, we may see nations that appear either to leapfrog over others in the process of forming nation-states or to retrogress.

As an example, let us consider Southeast Asia. This region includes the Indochinese peninsula and the surrounding ocean, which has the greatest number of islands in the world; since long ago this region has seen a repeated cycle of the rise and fall of countless kingdoms. Some were prosperous and left behind splendid religious monuments or city ruins, such as the ruins of Borobudur built by the Sailendra dynasty (in the eighth and ninth centuries), and the ruins of Angkor Thom and Angkor Wat built by the Khmer kingdom (from the ninth to the thirteenth century). Many of these wealthy kingdoms were not European-style kingdoms based on territorial rule but what we would today call trading states. (The Khmer kingdom, however, seems to have been an exceptional territorial state.) Trade on the Indian Ocean developed early, exploiting the semiannual change in the direction of monsoon winds, and in the fifteenth century kingdoms such as Malacca, Ayutthaya, Champa, the Le dynasty of Vietnam, and the Ryukyus at the eastern edge were prospering as bases in a trade network that stretched from Arabia to the Far East. But these were all trading states, or port states, not territorial states.[13] In this period, too, Chinese emigrated to Southeast Asia in huge numbers, and the Japanese, who were positioned at the easternmost edge of this trade network, crossed to Southeast Asia, and Japanese merchants began to appear in the main trading ports. In the fifteenth century, Southeast Asia was a world in which various races and religions were mixed together, with trading activity as their main concern.

However, this self-generated Indo-Asian trading world was incorporated into the global trading world of the European armed merchant fleets, led by Portugal. The Portuguese capture of Malacca in 1511 symbolized this development, and in quick succession Spain, Holland, Britain, and somewhat later, France occupied the main trading ports using the same means. Soon these European states turned to territorial acquisitions, and by the nineteenth century the whole of Southeast Asia, with the exception of Thailand, had been colonized. The present-day nation-states of Southeast Asia were created using the geographical framework left by this colonial partitioning. As many people have pointed out, even now a long-lasting cultural tradition extending over the large region of "the single ocean" is held in common throughout Southeast Asia.[14]

The present ASEAN (Association of Southeast Asian Nations) forms a unique coalition relatively free of the memories of past territorial conflicts, while incorporating many cultures with differing religions. (The problem of the Sabah territory between the Philippines and Malaysia is not sufficiently serious to be considered an exception.) The fact that most Southeast Asian countries have been successful in simultaneously embarking on trade-led industrialization, seen in a global perspective, is worth noticing, and it seems that there is a historically unprecedented possibility of a group of states being formed.

Finally, there is the problem of rekindled nationalism. Somewhat distinct from the above-mentioned newly independent states are movements for independence in the last remaining empires, or pseudoempires, of the former Soviet Union and China. Rekindled nationalism in those nations will surely become a substantial political problem in the future. Under the strain of the cold war, the communist governments had powerful authority, and minority peoples were resigned to accepting it. Now, however, there are increasing movements for democratization, and it appears inevitable that this movement will further encourage the self-assertion of the minority peoples. All the republics of the former Soviet Union proclaimed their sovereignty, and in December 1991 the Soviet Union finally disintegrated. At present, the republics, including the Russian Republic, seem to have a double nature, one that is pushed by the centrifugal force of wishing to create a state based on ethnicity and another that is pulled by a centripetal force wishing to maintain the republics as they exist today.

China too, at least in the Sinkiang and Uighur regions, and in Tibet, has similar problems. Thus, even the two last empires—the former Soviet Union and China—will have no choice but to accept the demands of these movements and carry out some kind of reform of the political system. However, once released from the empire, these potential nation-states will have difficulty existing as classical nation-states because of their geopolitical position. They will probably have to choose between joining a group or forming a new group. This may be the Commonwealth of Independent States, which announced its formation in December 1991, or a new structure along the lines of an Islamic federation. Such a process of organization and integration has just begun and will continue, repeating trials and errors. Even within those countries that have established their structures as nation-states, there is the explosive problem of minority peoples, such as the tensions in Sri Lanka, Kashmir, the Punjab, and Northern Ireland. Thus nationalism remains a complicated subject. Beginning with the newly independent countries, and with the independence movements of minority peoples within the former empires, one might say that naive nationalism is flaring up, but one cannot say that nationalism within a system is being created. At present, naive nationalism is struggling to find some kind of international system that might accommodate and help stabilize it.

A SUMMARY OF THE DYNAMIC OF THE NATION-STATE SYSTEM

The historical facts stated so far show that the modern nation-state system has a characteristic dynamic. It was originally a pluralistic system, premised on the coexistence of multiple similar polities. In contrast, the former empires of the great civilizations were grounded in the belief that they were unique entities, and although they were vaguely aware that there existed other political entities equal to themselves—Rome knew of China, for example—it was an essential condition for a great civilization that it should possess the confidence in its power to ignore this fact. Small countries, though, which did not possess the power to initiate a pluralistic system, could not ignore the existence of great powers that had the ability

to absorb them. Europe, at the end of the Middle Ages, was in an intermediate posítion, neither dominated by an empire nor merely a collection
of small countries. What was distinctive was the fact that each nation was
clearly aware of being in the intermediate position. There have been instances in which multiple polities have coexisted but few examples of a
political system in which the concept of pluralism has been commonly
accepted by its members. (The exception is ancient Greece, which was
premised on the pluralistic nature of the polis.) This is the singularity of
the dynamic of the modern nation-state system. Thus the dynamic of its
transformation has been determined, first, by the attacks on and defenses
of the concept of pluralism in justice, and second, by abrupt shifts in power
between the multiple states.

The question of pluralism has been manifested primarily as a question
of pluralism in justice. For example, the nineteenth century was fundamentally an age in which the doctrine of nonjust war was dominant. But
the same period was also an age of increasing popularization of nationalism, and so the concept of a justice of peoples was fostered. It was also an
age of imperial justice, in which there appeared the concept of a justice
of civilization—that is, Western civilization obligated itself to educate the
heathen. The First World War was, in a sense, a settling of accounts for
this nineteenth-century state of affairs, and the Treaty of Versailles was
burdened with the issue of how to incorporate both concepts—a justice of
peoples and a justice of civilization—into an international system based
on the doctrine of nonjust war. The concept of popular self-determination,
however, which was promulgated as a solution to this issue, triggered the
"people's" criticism of "civilization" and instead exacerbated the problem.
In the interwar period, the experiment at a modified doctrine of nonjust
war in the League of Nations foundered on this contradiction and, after
the experience of the Second World War, was reorganized in a postwar system that transferred emphasis to a justice of civilization. In other words,
the confrontation between the three groups of thought identified at the
beginning of this chapter changed in the postwar period to a three-tiered
structure, which was the (partially functional) doctrine of nonjust war as
espoused by the United Nations: (1) the doctrine of just war as exemplified
by the U.S.-Soviet cold war; (2) the doctrine of just war within collective
security alliances; and (3) the doctrine of just war of the newly independent
states. The doctrine of just war of the have-nots had failed. The system
based on the doctrine of nonjust war disintegrated because it was unable
to withstand the challenge by the concept of justice.

Second, the system based on the doctrine of nonjust war was fundamentally a system aimed at maintaining the status quo, and the key to
its continued existence was how it could absorb substantial changes in
the distribution of power, or alterations in people's worldviews. When it
became difficult for it to absorb the impact of these changes, the system
based on the doctrine of nonjust war eventually had to be reorganized. For

example, among the developed countries, the distribution of power gradually changed, as follows, and each time a reorganization of the balance-of-power system based on the doctrine of nonjust war became unavoidable.

> *Nineteenth century*: Rise of the United States and Germany, riding the crest of a wave of technological innovation
>
> *Interwar period*: Overpowering development of the United States; defiance of Germany, Japan, and Italy; expansion of the power of the Soviet Union
>
> *Postwar period*: Immense increase in the political and military power of the Soviet Union
>
> *End of the twentieth century*: Rise in the economic power of Japan and the Asian NIEs; bankruptcy of the socialist economies

The Versailles system following the First World War (including the League of Nations), the transfer of hegemony from Britain to the United States during the interwar period and the Second World War, and the postwar cold war system (which had the effect of enfeebling the United Nations) were all products of this kind of reorganization. The recent rise in the economic power of Japan and the Asian NIEs and the collapse of the Soviet bloc will surely be severe challenges for thought based on the doctrine of nonjust war.

At the same time, one cannot ignore the problems connected to the developing countries. As has often been discussed, the peoples outside Europe have limited historical experience with a coterminous cultural community and territory and no experience with many similar coexisting polities. Thus, the politics of the colonies emancipated and the new countries born following the Second World War continues to be unstable because the conditions necessary for their political stability have not yet matured. Although it seems as if naive nationalism has exploded everywhere, there exists today no international system that can deal with this fact. The United Nations has tried to extend the existing nation-state system in its efforts to stabilize the newly independent states, but it has not been successful in coping with the nationalism of these new states, their advocacy of distributive justice, and the impact of their economic power. The system based on the doctrine of nonjust war, in the shape of the United Nations, has not been effective in dealing with the problems of the developing countries.

Ironically, the bankruptcy of this doctrine of nonjust war has been hidden until now by the structure of confrontation between the United States and the Soviet Union. The so-called theory of hegemony is nothing more than an analysis from a mainly economic perspective of this kind of structure of international relations, supported by the doctrine of just war, only with regard to the West. The United States (like the Soviet Union) has played a positive role as hegemon, supplying international public goods, beginning with security, to its allies, and both countries have produced stable collective security structures. Seen only from the perspective of the provision of international public goods, the hegemony of Britain, stretching from the nineteenth to the twentieth century, had a similar character, and the theory of hegemonic stability attempted to analyze all of these cases in a similar way. But from the perspective of the political transformations in the doctrine of nonjust war, there is a substantial difference between British and U.S. hegemony. In contrast to Britain, which attempted to hold fast to the principle of nonjust war, the United States built an international system founded on the doctrine of just war. In terms of the theory of hegemonic stability, this was the growth in importance of ideological or cultural authority among the dimensions of international public goods, but this difference had a substantive content that went beyond changes in the relative importance of particular dimensions. However much one emphasizes the need for an analytic approach that pays attention to both economics and politics, when one refers to U.S. hegemony one must acknowledge both its continuity of the Pax Britannica in the provision of international public goods, and its discontinuity in the appearance of the doctrine of just war.

The latter aspect is apparent in the following. Under the pressure of the doctrine of just war, in the name of the cold war, a part of each country's territorial sovereignty was in effect transferred to collective security alliances such as NATO or the Warsaw Treaty Organization, where it was exercised by the hegemons, the United States and the Soviet Union, by proxy. These unprecedentedly close-knit collective security alliances maintained and strengthened the notion of nonjust war *only among the developed countries*. The result was the illusion that the classical nation-state system still existed. However, the sovereignty that had been transferred and was being exercised by proxy was illusory. To participate in a collective security system was, for example, to accept U.S. military bases, to be under U.S. leadership in the event of a crisis, and to lose some territorial sovereignty. Postwar Japan, which had renounced the use of military force (according to its constitution), was an extreme example of this, and in this respect Japan had lost the character of a classical nation-state. However, more or less all the advanced countries of the West, and of course the Eastern bloc countries who were members of the Warsaw Pact, were in similar situations. The Brezhnev doctrine nicely symbolizes this fact. With the doctrine of just war established as the primary framework, national sovereignty was already being compromised.

Looking back, it was the respective doctrines of just war espoused by the United States and the Soviet Union that prevented the doctrine of nonjust war from disappearing by incorporating it into the lower levels of their structure. However, a fear of nuclear war always existed during the cold war. Thus it is natural that the end of the cold war in 1989 brought psychological relief. But the most significant result of the end of the cold war was the disappearance of a stable system. This was apparent, for example, in the Gulf War, but generally speaking, any number of scenarios may occur now that the framework of the cold war has been removed. As already noted, once the primary framework of the triple-tiered structure of the cold war has been removed, without the primary framework of the doctrine of just war that enclosed them, the doctrine of nonjust war within the collective security alliances (mainly among the developed countries) and the doctrine of just war latent in the newly independent states will begin to take their respective uncharted courses. With no mediating structure, there is an increasing possibility that the tendency of the developed countries to maintain the status quo and the self-assertion of the developing countries will confront each other. This is the new North-South problem. Further, the system based on the doctrine of nonjust war among the advanced countries may not be as stable as it has been up to now. This is the new East-West problem, as seen in the relationship between Japan and the United States. The post-cold-war world will be structurally the most unstable since the seventeenth century (and the signing of the Treaty of Westphalia).

Recently, many of the arguments emphasizing the explosion of nationalism have only paid attention to naive nationalism and have not considered the problem of a system that can support nationalism. Nationalism always needs an international system that can support it. Naive nationalism in the developing countries is taking an increasingly high profile, but one cannot realistically expect the classical nation-state system to reemerge and hold this in check. The United Nations, which was expected to have the form of an extended nation-state system, also is not capable of dealing with this issue. This is an age in which the concept of nationalism, which supported the Western countries for five centuries, is being expanded and has become confused. This means that we now must search for a new direction. One can perhaps best summarize the current circumstances as a decline in the classical nation-state system.

Unable to bear its own weight, the seventeenth-century doctrine of nonjust war yielded its place to the doctrine of just war of the cold war. Now, however, the cold war has been abandoned, and the doctrine of just war has lost its foundations. In this situation, there are three choices that could be made about the dynamic of nationalism in the future: (1) a world with a unitary justice (the reemergence of the Pax Americana); (2) a system of multiple justices Type I (a model centered on the United Nations); and (3) a system of multiple justices Type II (a model based on regional groupism).

I discuss the question of choosing among the three again in Chapter 8. Whichever we choose, however, it is no mistake to say that in meeting the twenty-first century, the time has come to take a new first step away from nationalism.

Development of the Trading State: Mediating Phenomena

In which direction should we step away from nationalism? This choice will be influenced primarily by the impetus of industrialization, which has seen no decline throughout the postwar period. The economic growth that was achieved up to the 1970s is bound to determine both the general trend of future changes and the direction of changes in the distribution of national power. Thus we must review the pattern of postwar industrialization in the West up to the present.

THE DYNAMIC OF INDUSTRIALIZATION

In my thinking on the dynamic of technological innovation, there have clearly been wave cycles, in a distinct pattern, over the past 200 years of industrialization. Here let me succinctly sketch the main elements of an analysis I presented once.[15] Nikolai Kondratieff's wave cycle of on average half a century is well known, and Joseph Schumpeter, Fernand Braudel, and Immanuel Wallerstein all subscribe to his theory.[16] This half-century wave, seen from an economic perspective, is made up of an upswing of a quarter of a century characterized by prosperity and rising prices, and a downswing of a quarter of a century with the reverse characteristics. The technological aspect, however, is in a sense the reverse. That is, a phase of economic recession becomes a creative phase in which new technology appears, and a phase of economic prosperity becomes a phase of application, in which the application of technology is linked to the creation of demand; on this point the above theorists seem to be in agreement. This can be interpreted as meaning that it takes 25 years for technology to be applied in the economy, or that it takes 25 years for economic stagnation to call for the development of new technology. It is difficult to establish which of these interpretations is correct, and there is no need to do so here.

Let me summarize these wave cycles as simply as possible (see Figure 1). The years in the figure indicate only approximate dates. The half-century wave takes as its unit the progression from one peak, through a trough, to the next peak (a Kondratieff wave is the reverse); but it is not enough to observe this half-century wave cycle. For example, the first half-century wave beginning in 1775 and the second beginning in 1825 were clearly technologically similar in their use of iron machinery and in steam being the primary source of energy. Whereas the first wave was a stage of breakthrough, which occurred only in the cotton industry, the second wave was a period in which related technologies that had gradually accumulated around the cotton industry were developed for other industries, particularly railroads, steamships, and machine tools—what one might call a stage of maturation for these technologies.

The same pattern is repeated a century later. The third wave was supported by a new technological system, which took as its axis new forms

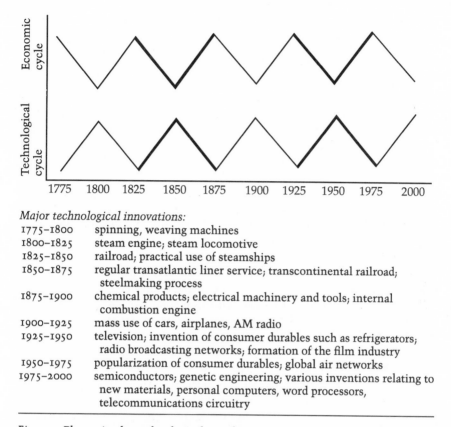

Major technological innovations:

1775–1800	spinning, weaving machines
1800–1825	steam engine; steam locomotive
1825–1850	railroad; practical use of steamships
1850–1875	regular transatlantic liner service; transcontinental railroad; steelmaking process
1875–1900	chemical products; electrical machinery and tools; internal combustion engine
1900–1925	mass use of cars, airplanes, AM radio
1925–1950	television; invention of consumer durables such as refrigerators; radio broadcasting networks; formation of the film industry
1950–1975	popularization of consumer durables; global air networks
1975–2000	semiconductors; genetic engineering; various inventions relating to new materials, personal computers, word processors, telecommunications circuitry

Figure 1 Phases in the technological paradigms, 1775–2000. The thin lines represent what I call the breakthrough phase and the thick lines the maturation phase.

of energy (such as electricity and petroleum), and artificial materials (such as cement, glass, rubber, and artificial dyes). In the fourth wave, beginning around 1925, these technologies were applied across the board and generated mass demand, particularly in consumer durables, transportation, and communications. I combine these waves and call the first and second the nineteenth-century system, and the third and fourth waves the twentieth-century system. (Note that these systems begin a quarter of a century earlier than calendrical centuries.) As others have done, let me call the watershed between the second and third wave the second industrial revolution. Thus the wave cycle is made up of three parts: a quarter-century wave, a half-century wave, and a century wave.

To be precise, this cyclical character should not be regarded as simple repetition but rather as a spiral movement. During the initial period of the twentieth century, many industries that were inherited from the nineteenth-century system had already finished developing, and the break-through came not from a single industry as with the nineteenth-century system from the cotton industry in England, but simultaneously in many industries. New manufactured goods appeared, such as cars, electric lights, and telephones; in every industry the use of alternating electric current produced epochal changes in factory machinery and the organization of labor. Moreover, many countries in Europe and America were able to adopt the new technologies. With the advance of industrialization the break-through could occur in an increasing number of countries and a range of industries. What one might call the depth of industrialization grew with the overlapping of the wave cycles.

If one applies this cyclical perspective to recent history, one can explain how it was that the last quarter of a century, when the effects of the Second World War had just faded, could have been an unusually fortunate period of economic prosperity. That is, in that it was the second phase of the fourth half-century wave, it could be compared to the Victorian period, which was the second phase of the second wave; it belonged to the half-century wave of maturation and to the quarter-century of prosperity and technological application that formed the second half of this maturation phase. It was a period in which the conditions were established for a prosperity that exceeded even the prosperity of the Victorian period (because of the additional power of the spiral upswing).

The technologies put to practical use during this period had for the most part been created before and during the war; those that have come to characterize the twentieth century include: radio broadcasting networks (1926), facsimile (1926), refrigeration using freon (1931), polyvinyl chloride (1935), television (1936), FM radio (1936), nylon (1938), fluorescent light (1938), polyethylene (1941), penicillin (1942), the jet engine (1942), rockets (1943), nuclear energy (1945), and photocopying (1950). The discoveries and inventions of a fundamental nature that were made and created during this postwar period—such as transistors (1951), the structure of DNA (1953), solar cells (1955), lasers (1958), and optical fiber (1970)—were not used commercially until 1975. The third quarter of the twentieth century was an age of reaping the gains of the technological harvest, an age of application, in which the main emphasis was on the systematic and wide-ranging application of the discoveries of the previous period on a large scale. This provided momentum for further technological innovation and produced unprecedented prosperity.

And what is happening in the last quarter of the twentieth century? On many points there is a remarkable similarity to the situation one century ago. The last quarter of the nineteenth century produced a continuous stream of inventions, such as the internal combustion engine (1876), the telephone (1877), electric light (1879), the electric locomotive (1879), and the automobile (1885); the second industrial revolution had indeed arrived. However, although these inventions were used in particular regions and classes, the development of necessary infrastructure lagged, and they failed to generate broad-based demand. With the invention of the transmission of alternating current (1886) and the alternating current motor (1888) the use of electricity spread rapidly in industry, but a life transformed by electricity was still beyond the reach of the general populace. For mass demand to be generated by the technology of the twentieth-century system, an infrastructure that included paved roads and transmission networks for electricity had to be provided.

Like those of a hundred years ago, the inventions and discoveries of the past half century—such as the computer, the transistor, optical fiber, DNA research, and new materials—have had an impact worthy of being called the third industrial revolution. However, the invention of the transistor, for example, although an event with great significance inasmuch as it promised the possibility of a machine capable of analysis, so far has only been used commercially as a component to increase the performance of existing machines. The exceptions to date include supercomputers, mainframe computers, and circuitry dedicated to telecommunications, but these are used in only a limited number of businesses and important research centers. Of course, as transitional machines going beyond the existing concept of machinery, robots, word processors, and personal computers have been used increasingly. Even robots and personal computers, however, are as yet used mainly to increase the efficiency of the existing pattern of industrial activity. Once again, not until an infrastructure of large-capacity communication circuits and satellites, and particularly a global communication network, is created will there be a true information industry or information society. Only when information for the masses becomes available and is used widely can there be a large enough demand for information to create an information society. As C. Perez notes, there is still a mismatch between the system and the technology.[17]

An inauspicious aspect of the analogy with a hundred years ago was the occurrence of a recession, long absent from the economy, from 1873 until the mid-1890s. Fundamentally, it was the first half of a breakthrough phase, in which demand had not caught up with supply. From about the middle of the 1890s until the First World War, the European economy was comparatively prosperous, but this prosperity was largely due to an arms race embarked upon simultaneously by the great powers of Europe. As a result, there was a clash between Britain, which had been the hegemon up to that point, and Germany, which was both an imitator and a challenger; the arms race escalated into the twentieth century, eventually bringing on world war. The end of this century is also an age of stagnation (in the sense that no large-scale high mass consumption is seen today). Thus there is a high likelihood that it will be an age of confusion in international politics. Although the ends of the two centuries have unfortunate similarities, the end of this century has unique characteristics. First, the possibility of an escalating arms race has been checked by the appearance of nuclear weapons, and since the end of the cold war it has become almost nil. But the resulting decline in the demand for arms is also a contributing factor in the world recession.

THE POSSIBILITY OF A FLYING-GEESE PATTERN

A second important difference between this century and the previous one is the remarkable increase in the number of countries able to assimilate the new technologies. The rapid diffusion of these technologies has suddenly increased the number of countries that can achieve, or immediately adapt to, technological breakthroughs and achieve economic growth. A pattern is becoming apparent in which not only one country (Britain at the end of the eighteenth century) or a few countries (Britain, Germany, and the United States at the end of the nineteenth) are technologically prominent, but in which many countries develop in a flying-geese formation.[18] The ability to achieve a technological breakthrough can be seen in Europe and North America as well as in Japan and Russia; countries in Eastern Europe, East Asia, and Latin America have the potential to exploit the new technologies immediately. This flying-geese division of labor, in which the developed countries are in the vanguard and the developing countries follow close behind, has the potential, if well managed, to create a complementary structure and to generate demand in all countries for each other's products.

Moreover, as a large number of countries adopt new technologies, the possibility of the practical application of fundamental inventions increases, and the likelihood of a wave of mass demand spreading from the developed countries to the developing countries also increases. For example, from the beginning of the 1970s, Japan, which was not a technological front-runner at the time, made a contribution by creating mass demand around the globe. Examples of goods that generated such demand include the transistor radio and the automatically controlled high-speed railway (in the 1960s), and the Walkman, video equipment, the auto-focus camera, copy machines, and high-definition television in the 1970s and 1980s. Of course the United States also made a substantial contribution (with such products as the word processor and the personal computer), but had it not been for Japan, with its enthusiasm for mass-use technologies, the global demand for electronic goods of the past fifteen years would not have been as great. This is another example of the flying-geese pattern of the division of labor.

If, however, technology stagnates in the countries leading this flying-geese pattern, then the formation might well be forced to return to a horizontal pattern of competition. Alternatively, the fear of the follower countries working to catch up might increase more than is justified by reality. Should this occur, the leading countries might resort to the sort of protectionism that existed before the Second World War. The situation would be different, however, if the countries that lead the formation transfer technology by following what I call the new rule of polymorphic economic liberalism, and create new technologies.[19] Moreover, we could escape stagnation in the world economy if, as for technologies, we could create a pattern of demand such that, when demand in a certain industry is satiated in the leading countries, the baton is passed to the follower countries, and these nations then help sustain the demand. Current developments in East Asia, centered on Japan, approximate the pattern just described. For example, when demand for cars stagnates in Japan, capital, instead of cars, is exported to produce cars in Asian nations to meet their growing demand. The United States does not yet seem to be utilizing this situation as well as Japan.[20] There is a need to give serious consideration to the advantages of such a flying-geese division of labor instead of restricting ourselves to the traditional vertical and horizontal divisions of labor. I examine this question again, more theoretically, in Chapter 8.

As long as the gap between leaders and followers is not too large, we can expect such a desirable chain reaction of technology and demand. The model of the long wave cycle of a quarter or half century applies only to the developed countries, but if more and more developing countries pursue the developed countries in a flying-geese pattern, the reality will change. The model of the long wave cycle cannot be applied to the developing countries in its present form. There is a slight lag between the long wave cycle—the internal dynamics of technology and demand—in the developing and the developed countries. The Kondratieff long wave cycles now become less pronounced by superimposing, in effect, the wave of the developed countries on top of that of the developing countries; the result is that the global economy may be able to avoid great undulations in global recession and prosperity. To achieve this, reducing the gap between the developed and the developing countries becomes desirable. That is, it seems desirable for the United States, the European Community (EC), and Japan to consciously promote this flying-geese division of labor. High mass consumption is about to begin in the follower countries (the NIEs) in the flying-geese formation. This situation would have been unimaginable at the end of the nineteenth century, when colonialism was dominant. The flying-geese pattern of consumption in step with technology has appeared only at the end of this century, and it may well be the key to helping the world economy ride over the seemingly recession-prone end of this century. Thus there is sufficient possibility that the economic liberalism of the developed countries, and the developmentalism of the developing countries (which I discuss in detail later), will be able to coexist, enabling all countries to sustain economic growth.

During the recession in the first half of the fourth half-century wave (that is, in the 1930s), there was unfulfilled mass demand in countries such as Germany, which was suffering from war reparations, and Italy and Japan, which were still developing. As sources of demand, these countries might have played a role similar to the current role of the NIEs. At that time, however, the major powers such as the United States, Britain, and France, fearing competition from these countries, turned to protectionism under the pretext of creating respective political-*cum*-trade blocs. International politics prevented the establishment of complementary economic relationships, and inasmuch as this was a bloc-ism that sought to preserve its own sphere of influence, it became embroiled in quasi-imperialist conflicts over the recovery of territory and colonial acquisitions. Today, however, there is reason to be hopeful because imperialistic military disputes have become impossible. Though the lessons from the end of the previous century may not be directly useful, we should not mechanically apply the theory of the long wave cycle and thus forecast economic stagnation in the developing countries. The question, to which I return in Chapter 9, is whether the developed countries, particularly the major powers, will have the willpower to choose polymorphic economic liberalism in order to generate development of the flying-geese pattern.

THE DEVELOPMENT OF A TRADING STATE

The foundations for the technology that sustained the postwar period were, for the most part, laid before and during the war. In the postwar period until the 1970s, technological advances were made primarily in applications, especially in the scale of production and systematizing existing technology, rather than in new innovations. Technological innovations occurred steadily and the optimum scale of production continued to increase. A number of countries began aiming at the global market rather than their domestic markets and took the risk of large-scale production. Even those countries that relied on the small-scale production of goods found that their niche in the market expanded with the global increase in the number of "rich countries" and the diversification of demand. What made this dependence on overseas markets possible was the relative peace and free-trade system achieved under the Pax Americana. The relative significance of international vis-à-vis domestic markets thus increased, and various aspects of international economic activity grew rapidly. This increasing importance of trade for many countries was new in the postwar global economy, and has grown steadily; if the flying-geese pattern of technological transfer and economic growth is established firmly, the period of increasing trade will be further prolonged.

Richard Rosecrance was the first to point out the phenomenon of the development of the trading state. However, he does not make it clear whether he believes it will be limited to one period or become a historical trend. On the premise that nationalism has not yet died, Rosecrance says that there are only two means by which a country can increase its relative standing: military force to increase its territory or economic development and trade to increase its wealth. He calls a country that mainly uses force a "military-political state" or a "territorial state," and one that mainly uses the economy a "trading state."[21] According to Rosecrance, with the establishment of collective security systems and the spread of anticolonialism following the Second World War, it became virtually impossible for a country to expand its territory, and so each country was restricted to expanding its existing trading relationships. His argument seems to be that the degree of decline in the significance of military power motivates countries to a corresponding degree to become trading states. As mentioned above, however, the problem is not the relative increase in economic power but how a country mobilizes its economic resources internationally and what direction its foreign policy takes. It is dangerous to say definitively that the development of the trading state is a historical trend, even though this has been a marked tendency of the past half century. For example, although the United States and the Soviet Union, as the leading advocates of justice, with huge military power, undertook actions that resemble territorial expansion, in the end even these superpowers have seen their territories or spheres of influence diminish throughout the postwar period.

Clearly, the advanced industrial nations have enjoyed a peace during the postwar period that is unprecedented for nation-states. As a result, the importance of economic factors has increased and the greatest beneficiaries have been the lightly armed, middle-ranking advanced nations—in Europe, Germany and Italy rather than Britain and France—and this is apparent in the differences between their growth rates throughout the postwar period. Of course, the most evident beneficiary is Japan, which is extremely weak in military power but the most successful in achieving rapid growth of its economy and trade. Japan exemplifies what a trading state can accomplish. Though not to the extent Japan did, other advanced nations too are developing into trading states. And as is shown by the development of Japan and Germany, with the changes in the distribution of economic power, the balance between East and West has collapsed, and the balance *within* the two areas is becoming unstable. The adoption of the floating exchange rate, the economic friction between the United States and Japan, Germany's *Ostpolitik* diplomacy, and the dismantling of the Soviet bloc are all elements in a chain of events that originated in the collapse of this balance. The most immediate cause for the collapse of the primary framework of the U.S.-Soviet cold war was the relative decline in the economic power of the Soviet bloc. The cold war system helped to accelerate industrialization and brought about the advent of superindustrialization, which in turn hastened the collapse of the cold war system. Clearly the interaction between politics and economics has been a motive force in recent history.

But not only the developed countries enjoyed the benefits of postwar industrialization and the Pax Americana. In many respects, Japan, immediately following the war, was an intermediate case, somewhere between a developed and a developing country. Once Japan had already demonstrated the possibilities of the trading state, those countries known as the Asian NIEs—Hong Kong, Singapore, Taiwan, Korea, and also Thailand and Malaysia—pursued those possibilities more consciously and developed their economies while heavily dependent on foreign markets. For example, Taiwan's trade dependency (the ratio of exports plus imports divided by GNP) at times exceeded 100 percent. Countries adopting the same pattern may well soon appear in Central and South America and quite possibly within the former Soviet Union and Eastern Europe. The remarkable acceleration in the catching-up of the developing economies in the last quarter of the twentieth century is due to this trading-state developmentalism, of which Japan is the precursor. At the same time, because these developing countries are not always the classical nation-state of "one people, one state," they have an even weaker attachment to the concept of the territorial state than do the developed countries. This is another important trend leading away from the territorial state and to the trading state and, since the 1970s, it has been even more vigorous than the impetus that leads to the development of the trading state in the developed countries. (Japan has been subject to both forces, as a developed and a developing state.)

A trading state does not rely on military force but has to trust in interdependencies as a means of protecting itself.[22] Thus, with a continued increase in the number of trading states, it is natural to expect the emergence of security-trade groups, whose members share trade interests. In the Europe of the past, examples of this kind of group are limited to a few alliances formed by city-states, such as the Hanseatic League. Often, those formerly powerful European trading states such as Portugal, Spain, Holland, and Britain had huge naval powers and were intent on acquiring colonies and spheres of influence. Those countries were both trading states and strongly territorial in character. In contrast, in the Indian Ocean and East Asia before the invasion of European forces, there were many lightly armed trading states that prospered in an extensive trading network stretching from the east coast of Africa to Japan. This prosperous network was destroyed at a stroke by the heavily armed European merchant fleets, and particularly by the firepower they carried. Today, however, similar conditions may be reemerging in East Asia. The formation of a group of trading states in East Asia would be a replication of history.

The trend toward trade-*cum*-security groups will probably occur among the countries of Asia, Africa, and the Middle East that lack the conditions for being nation-states. Also, it is not impossible that the former Soviet Union and China will come to see their last hope in a loose trading group rather than in a strong, "imperial" political union. The EC as well is not aiming to become a "superstate" but a trading group. Many of these trends are only in the earliest stages, but there are strong incentives for the countries of the world to compete as members of such economic groups. What will become a problem, however, is the paradoxical fact that the primary framework that has until now supported the development of the trading state, whether among the developed or the developing countries, has been the system based on the doctrine of just war. The doctrine was supported by military force—in other words, the U.S.-Soviet cold war system of collective security (or what I earlier called a double structure in which the doctrine of just war supports the doctrine of nonjust war).

What will happen now, with the end of the cold war and the loosening of links in the system of collective security? The trading states, which must protect themselves in alliances, have no choice but to endeavor to create some kind of group to replace the cold war system. But the formation of such groups will not proceed rapidly. We should expect these groups to reorganize and proliferate as well as to compete and conflict with each other. One cannot therefore draw a facile conclusion that as more states become trading states, the world will become more peaceful and the international system will become increasingly stable. The trend toward trading states, or, more generally speaking, the trend toward increasing political and economic interdependence cannot alone provide an ultimate solution to the world's problems.

All countries, of course, were not beneficiaries of this cold war peace. Many did not manage to build a nation-state system, such as those that were incorporated into the Soviet Union or China by the cold war system, those that were divided, and those that were wracked by internal conflicts reflecting the East-West confrontation. With the end of the cold war, these countries may begin to make earnest efforts to revive their residual nationalism. Again, many countries have established the form of a nation-state but failed to benefit from the postwar trade liberalization under the cold war peace. Feeling they have been unjustly denied the benefits of the free trade that enriches others, these countries may instead be tempted to seek control of the resources of neighboring countries, or of industrialized regions, by using military force. These countries will not aim at anything more than localized wars, but it will be comparatively easy for them to stockpile nuclear or chemical weapons to use as a threat. Thus popular justice and religious justice may be preached in this cause, and the territorial state may reemerge. In most cases, these attempts at a mini–military state will be localized and will not last long, but in those cases where similarly inclined countries create an alliance with access to indispensable economic resources (such as oil), there is a chance that this will become a trigger for global disorder.

Iraq's invasion of Kuwait may have been the germ of such a scenario. Fortunately or unfortunately, Saddam Hussein seems not to have the leadership ability to unite the Arab world, but it may well be possible for some kind of Arab federation to emerge in the future that would attempt to dominate the world using its control of the oil supply as a weapon. There have already been a number of such attempts, including the attempted Egypt-Syria union and Khomeini's vision of a pan-Islamic federation. Such a problem—a negative by-product of the trend toward trading states—will be an important issue in the future.

Dissemination of Industrialization: The Factors That Lead to Superindustrialization

The postwar phase of industrialization was over by 1980. Since about the middle of the 1970s, industrialization has become superindustrialization, and this brings with it particular effects. For expositional convenience, I will divide superindustrialization into its quantitative and qualitative aspects. For the time being, I will summarize these as the trend toward a borderless economy and the information revolution, respectively. Of course, these two aspects influence each other, and in the advanced countries in particular they generate various multiplier effects, most notably, the multinationalization of cutting-edge industries, the vast increase in international transfers of capital, the transition to flexible manufacturing, and massive increases in both speed and quantity in the communication of information. However, in considering the multiplier effects, it seems that what will gradually become the focus of attention is not their effects on the developed economies but whether economic development in the developing countries will be accelerated or retarded by the effects. The remainder of this chapter concentrates on this topic.

The increase in quantity (or the trend to a borderless economy) signifies the vigorous increase in international activity. After the Second World War, the international flows of trade and capital increased absolutely and rose visibly more rapidly than did domestic production and assets. Capital and technology, as well as trade, linked countries together, and the development of the trading state has made national borders decreasingly significant. The ties between economic actors—individuals and corporations—and their home countries were weakened, and the actors showed a tendency no longer to submit to their own governments' control. Evidence of this includes the brain drain and the exodus of professional athletes; but most apparent is the multinationalization of business. In the prewar period, corporations and individuals that moved overseas maintained strong ties with their home countries and expected protection in time of crisis; in the postwar period economic activity has come to operate with little attention to national boundaries.

Since the introduction of the floating exchange rate in 1973, vast amounts of capital can flow across national boundaries in an instant, without consideration of national interest, strengthening as never before the linkages between national economies. Capital flow is the most important reason why today a close coordination of the economic policies of nations has become necessary. Moreover, many of the largest firms in the world have become multinationals, making direct foreign investments and establishing factories, research centers, and subsidiaries outside their home countries. Such multinationals have already begun to operate beyond the control of their home governments, and their entry into the developing countries will increase even more in the future. As they spread, the formation of intermediate organizations (such as subcontracting firms) centered on the multinationals in the host nations will also increase. Finally, and in a sense most important, the environmental destruction that industrialization has caused extends beyond national boundaries and has become a problem of global dimensions. In sum, the latent pressures leading to a borderless economy will be inescapable in the future: they will generate friction with territorial nationalism (that is, classical nationalism) and will come into conflict with the social system unique to each country (rooted in cultural individuality to some extent) that has been the basis for nationalism.

The information revolution will qualitatively change industrialization at the deepest level and will be the trend that dominates the twenty-first century. The information revolution signifies the development of technologies that take knowledge arranged under a fixed system (information) and process and transmit it in great quantities and at high speed. What we normally mean today when we say information revolution is the advances in the application of microelectronics that began in the 1970s. However, the improvements in the technology of transportation and communications from the second half of the nineteenth century—such as ships, railways, telegraphs, telephones, and airplanes—also incorporated the transmission of information and clearly should be seen as precursors to what I am here calling the information revolution. Over a century ago, Friedrich List observed that the railways would have the epochal effect of "creating harmony among peoples."[23] It is certain that without these advances in the technology of transport and communications, today's information revolution would have been impossible.

It is widely recognized that the information revolution will have a great influence on society in general into the twenty-first century. In the economic arena, it is already apparent that the revolution is changing the nature of the production process and the style of management. As for Japan, it may be appropriate to say that this revolution has occurred. There is a change under way from "Ford-Taylor-ism," characterized by the large-scale production of standardized goods, high energy consumption, and pollution emission, to flexible manufacturing, characterized by the small-scale production of differentiated products, energy conservation, and pollution control. Consumption patterns and purchasing methods are also changing substantially. Undreamt-of consumer durables are appearing, and epochal changes are taking place in the way services, differentiated by specific demand, are provided. Politically, the information revolution, through the medium of television, for example, has come to have a significant influence on people's political judgments. The information revolution will provide the voters in democratic polities with more and more information, which should enable them to make better-informed judgments. In Chapter 9, however, we will see that this is not necessarily what is happening.

We can speculate on the influence of the information revolution not only in the short term but also in the long term because it will have a profound influence on the way people live well into the future. In order to think about these long-term questions, we must understand the concept of information in a broader sense, as knowledge in general (what I called in Chapter 1 the world image that people have), and extend the meaning of the information revolution to include the ways knowledge in general is processed and used. Thus, we should call the information revolution a "knowledge revolution." The road that leads from the information revolution to the knowledge revolution (and possibly beyond) will not necessarily be a smooth one. For example, cultural incommensurability (not only among countries but among differing world images) will be the largest obstacle for the knowledge revolution. Sooner or later, though, the question of the knowledge revolution will arise as the next step after the information revolution. There are even arguments (seemingly most prevalent in Japan) that the knowledge revolution is already becoming a principal force in determining the course of history. I shall not, however, in this book deal directly with the question of the information society in this long-term sense.

What we cannot overlook, however short-term our perspective, is that information (and trailing behind it, knowledge) trickles through all levels of society and spreads to all countries. Thus the two trends—the information revolution and the transition to a borderless economy—are clearly related and reinforce each other in their global diffusion. The information revolution is also clearly an important element in the changes discussed in connection with this transition, such as the international flows of capital and the multinationalization of business. At this point, however, we should notice the acceleration in the international transfer of technological information—in other words, the phenomenon of the globalization of technology as an indication of the way in which the information revolution and the transition to a borderless economy reinforce each other. The greatest problem for the world of the future will be this increase in the rate of technology transfer from developed to developing countries.

In the past, technology was transmitted from teacher (master) to pupil (disciple), and the process rarely relied on written words. The emigration of artisans had been the only way technology could be diffused internationally. (One cannot ignore, however, the historical significance of events such as the emigration of Protestants to Holland, or the emigration of the Dutch and Huguenots to England.) But with the development of the steamship and railways from the second half of the nineteenth century, the advances in international communications from about the beginning of the twentieth century, and the development of the airplane in the second half of the twentieth century, human exchange gradually began to flourish.

Particularly with the appearance, from the 1970s, of telephone networks, photocopying and fax machines, computer networks, televisual conferencing, and close-knit networks of communication circuitry using fiber optics and satellites, there has been a phenomenal increase in exchanges between people without actual physical encounters, and nowadays knowledge and information can fly across the world in an instant.

Of course there have also been remarkable recent developments in human exchange in the narrow sense. International academic and other conferences are held frequently, and not only leading scholars but also middle-ranking technicians are afforded opportunities for discussion. The international exchange of scholars has become a part of every country's educational system; common international vocabularies and standards of measurement are being established for those working in the same academic field or technology; and internationally shared databases are being quickly established. Further, through the mass media the ordinary consumer too is becoming aware of the benefits of advanced technology. The acceleration of the international transfer of technology—particularly from developed to developing countries—cannot be stopped.

The transition to a borderless economy, in the sense that it is usually understood, involves only goods (trade) and capital. Now, however, technology must be added. As the globalization of technology continues, the trend of borderlessness promoting superindustrialization and the information revolution are converging. This convergence is the most significant development in the present stage of superindustrialization, and the future political-economic system will be substantively shaped by the way this development is dealt with.

TWO PATTERNS OF INDUSTRIALIZATION

This trend toward global—or borderless—technology can only bring great changes to industrialization. The common understanding of industrialization for many years has been an elitist one: only those countries that have made the necessary social and cultural preparations can industrialize. The modernization theory of the 1960s and 1970s also emphasized the difficulty of the "takeoff" and, indeed, foreign aid that was intended to initiate industrialization in countries in Central and South America and Asia failed in many cases. Sometimes developmental aid was denied to worthy projects. Japan, which did not fit well into this widely accepted analysis, was explained as an exceptional case. The explanation could be accepted as long as there was only one exception. But the appearance of the NIEs in the 1970s forced a change in this analytic framework. With the acceleration in the transfer of technology (and the decline in the significance of military power), the elite countries no longer have a monopoly on industrialization, and many other countries are succeeding in industrialization.

Industrialization is said to be difficult because of the preconceptions we have developed by focusing on the Western (or Anglo-American) pattern in which political democratization preceded industrialization. The NIEs, following the road first taken by Japan, are developing in an opposite pattern: industrialization is preceding political democratization. As Rose-crance remarks, "It is clear that internal democracy is not the minimum requirement for adherence to a trading system. Authoritarian regimes in many Third World and developing nations have made the transition to a trading world."[24]

To return to a long-term perspective, one could perhaps say that the countries in the former Soviet Union and Eastern Europe, where the sys-tem of one-party dictatorship is disappearing, have also followed this pat-tern—but to this point their sacrifice of democracy has been too great. Here let us call this pattern developmentalism, in the broad sense. Chal-mers Johnson has recently emphasized the contrast between the two pat-terns of democratization → industrialization and industrialization → de-mocratization. He calls these, respectively, "the regulatory state" and "the developmental state," but in this book, I would rather emphasize their eco-nomic aspects and call them instead "classical economic liberalism" and "developmentalism."[25] In the following chapters I discuss the economic-analytic significance of each.

Many Europeans (and the progressive individuals in developing coun-tries who imitate them) are skeptical and frequently even dismissive of developmentalism in this sense. However, there is no basis for dismiss-ing developmentalism in neoclassical economics, for example. There can be such a basis only in the political or rather philosophical belief that re-gards democratization as a categorical imperative. Even some economists, however, try to reject developmentalism on the grounds of economic effi-ciency; but their position has no basis under general conditions that in-clude a dynamic state (see Chapters 3 and 5). What forces one to reject developmentalism in principle is a distrust of nondemocratic politics—in other words, the belief that, whatever the sacrifice, democratization must be placed first.

The word "democratization" is ambiguous. In normal usage, one most likely has in mind a democracy premised on liberalism—that is, liberal democracy. In this sense, democratization means the systematization of liberal democracy, or more concretely, the establishment of pluralist, par-liamentary democracy. In fact, there are problems in linking democracy and liberalism as a matter of course. As has long been said, and more re-cently pointed out by such leading figures as Friedrich von Hayek, the two are not the same, and there are even points of contradiction between them.[26] As already argued in Chapter 1, the core of freedom is freedom of thought. Given that liberalism is essentially a mental attitude, a system that guarantees freedom of action is a necessary condition for freedom, and a liberalism that is unaware of this fact will be no more than the inertia of the system. For example, since free thought is something that should not be restrained even by a constitution, it is more liberal for a constitution to be composed of nothing but clauses that guarantee minimum human rights. In this sense English common law is more liberal than the Napoleonic code.

In contrast, democracy's fundamental demand is that it be made transparent as a system. This is because democracy is a concept founded on equality (in which discrimination among individuals can be based only on objective standards, such as qualifications for suffrage). In achieving a systematization of liberal democracy, democracy therefore becomes the active element in many cases, and liberalism becomes the passive element suppressing democracy. What I here call "democratization" or "the effort toward liberal democracy" places more emphasis on the process of democratization. From the beginning, however, democracy in the narrow sense, distinct from liberalism, has frequently been regarded with skepticism in classical Western political philosophy, by those ranging from John Locke, Jean-Jacques Rousseau, and James Madison to Hayek. The critique of democracy is the fundamental question with which this book deals, and I take it up repeatedly. Let me here point out the following. The belief that regards democratization as its ultimate goal, and that values the process leading from democratization to industrialization, does not have an indisputable foundation even within the European intellectual tradition.

In looking back over the past, there is something vital that everyday historical common sense overlooks. The industrialization → democratization pattern—that is, the pattern that resembles developmentalism—has been widespread even within Europe. This fact is frequently pointed out with reference to France and Germany, but even Britain, which is considered the cradle of modernization, is no exception. In the European countries between the sixteenth and eighteenth centuries, the phenomenon frequently referred to as industrialization before the industrial revolution, or proto-industrialization, made progress under absolute monarchy hand in hand with mercantilism. As I argue again below, mercantilism was not merely a simplistic policy intent on accumulating a trade surplus. Friedrich List talked of "the industrial system (falsely termed . . . 'the mercantile system')," but though the theory of mercantilism was in many respects underdeveloped, it was effective policy (under certain conditions) in promoting industrialization of a country, and the pursuit of a trade surplus was its easiest indicator and means (though in fact limited).[27] J. M. Keynes was one of those fully aware of the fact I just noted.[28] Many have noted the similarity between this historical mercantilism and the export-oriented policies of the present-day NIEs, who themselves are frequently called neomercantilist.

Politically, as already mentioned, the period following the sixteenth century in Europe was one of the gradual formation of the nation-state. The absolute monarchies created the nation-state by depriving the nobles, the church, and the medieval towns of the feudal privileges they had enjoyed and, ultimately, allying themselves with the middle class, whose economic base was the new industries (such as sheep-rearing, commercial agriculture, various aspects of the textile industry, and the manufacture of consumer goods). It was not easy to deprive the nobles of their privileges, however, and the vagrant poor rose visibly in number. Democratization under absolute monarchy was slow in coming. But the sudden economic rise of the middle class increased their political influence, and with the English Revolution (referring to the English civil war and the Glorious Revolution), for example, parliamentary democracy was created. In this sense, a movement from proto-industrialization to democracy is clearly visible. Moreover, even after the eighteenth century, during which the European countries had gradually adopted parliamentary democracy, democratization was finally realized in the form of universal suffrage only after the beginning of the twentieth century. To complete the process of democratization, at least a century was needed after the American and French revolutions, and it was a century that saw bloody revolutionary disturbances.

Thus even Europe and North America followed a path from industrialization to democracy, in the form of progressions from proto-industrialization to the political participation of the middle class, and from the industrial revolution to universal suffrage. When Europeans and Americans urge the non-Western countries to democratize quickly, they are being amnesiac about their own past. Over the long term, industrialization and political democratization have advanced in tandem, and there is not much sense in criticizing the precise order in which each is achieved. One cannot explain the tide of history by condemning developmentalism as a distorted pattern of history followed by the late developers. An appropriate explanation requires a new kind of conceptual framework, one not based on classical economic liberalism, just as the political sphere needs a concept that goes beyond classical nationalism. In order to come to terms with this issue, we must fundamentally reexamine industrialization, democratization, and the nationalism that seems to have mediated them.

Toward a Pluralist View of History: Reconsidering the Concept of Industrialization

The "new realities" discussed in the preceding sections of this chapter necessitate revisions in the classical explanatory framework. The substance of the nation-state system, one of the pillars in the classical explanation, is weakening, and the system is no longer able to follow the road leading to the doctrine of nonjust war. Our vision has been clouded, both by the economic dynamic that has brought about the transformation to a world without borders, and by the dynamics of politics and thought that are manifested in the appearance of a rising tide of naive nationalism and a doctrine of just war in the United States (the results of which seem paradoxically to be based on the doctrine of nonjust war). As for economic liberalism, the other pillar in the classical explanation, the market economy is being forced to undergo a systematic pluralization because of the appearance of the new hybrid, developmentalism. The theory of hegemonic stability was the last attempt to keep the classical explanation intact. But it can no longer explain the changes.

Here, by beginning with a discussion of developmentalism, let us try to develop a new analytic framework to replace the classical one. To examine developmentalism, we must reexamine the two fundamental concepts of industrialization and democratization. Industrialization is usually regarded as synonymous with the development of European capitalism (economic liberalism). But is this accurate? What is the relationship between industrialization and capitalism? Recently, the concept of proto-industrialization has been much used, but is this an apposite concept? In any case, there is a need to look once again at the historical background of the concept of industrialization.

There are also many unclear points in the development of the phenomenon we know as democratization. Of course democracy itself has ancient origins, considered to stretch back to classical Greece and Rome. However, the democracy we see today, which incorporates all members of a society, is quite different from Greco-Roman democracy, which took the family (*oikos* or *familia*) as its basic unit and began to appear in the European nation-states only in the sixteenth century. This form of democratization is clearly related to nationalism, but its substance has not been made sufficiently clear. In order to resolve the central questions raised in this book, or indeed to better understand history, it is necessary to examine the historical relationship between these four fundamental concepts: industrialization, the development of capitalism, democratization, and the development of the nation-state.

INDUSTRIALIZATION AND CAPITALISM

Industrialization is a term often used to express a stage of development in a society. Unexpectedly, though, the precise meaning of this frequently used word is rather vague. The word "industry" is nowadays usually used to refer to the manufacturing industry, as is "industrialization" in a broader sense, but today there is little sense in distinguishing among manufacturing industry, agriculture, and the service industries. Noting this fact, modern economists such as Simon Kuznets and W. W. Rostow have provided the clearest definition of this word; they define industrialization as a continuous growth in per capita GNP or income. Most people understand industrialization in this sense to have been a phenomenon limited to the 200 years since the industrial revolution at the end of the eighteenth century.[29] As a macroeconomic definition this is clear enough, but this definition alone cannot explain the corresponding microeconomic social structure (concerned with individual economic actors). Faced with the question, for example, of how to deal with microeconomic phenomena such as the emergence of firms and the trading of factors of production (labor and land), the image provided by this definition is not necessarily a clear one.

There is not even any good basis for why industrialization defined thus macroeconomically should be a phenomenon limited to the period since the industrial revolution. For example, Douglass North has pointed out that per capita income grew "in fifth century Athens, in the era of Rhodian domination in the third century B.C., and in the first two centuries of the Roman Empire."[30] As I discuss later in this chapter, in Britain per capita income grew, however slowly, in the eighteenth century, and—though good statistics do not exist—one cannot deny the possibility of a similar growth even before the seventeenth century. In recent economic history, the concept of proto-industrialization has begun to be used to describe this period, and some call this industrialization before industrialization.[31] Expressions such as this are eloquent testimony to the extent of the confusion about the concept of industrialization.

The concept of capitalism, which is intimately related to industrialization, is defined more in terms of microeconomic social structure. There are definitions of various strengths for the concept of capitalism, but in its weakest definition, capitalism is the establishment over a reasonably large area of a system that supports actions in pursuit of profit (gain). This definition is much used in the German neohistorical school by scholars such as Lujo Brentano and Max Weber, and is also close to the definition used by Werner Sombart.[32] In this definition, capitalism becomes something that can be seen in almost all periods and in all societies, at least since the appearance of something that can be called money. Most common nowadays is a stronger definition that appeared under the influence of Marxism, which defines capitalism as a system (an aggregation of individuals) that satisfies the following three conditions: the existence of wage laborers (a proletariat) who live by selling their labor; the existence of firms (capitalist firms) that seek profit by employing these laborers; and the prevalence of market transactions (including the trading of factors of production such as land and labor).[33] For simplicity, I will call these the three conditions for capitalism. The weak definition above requires only the second of these and does not make an issue of the first and third.

At first glance the three conditions seem complicated, but in substance they are almost equivalent to what we would call the establishment of private property rights. To borrow the words of Douglass North, well known for his studies of economic history that adopt the so-called property rights approach, it is almost equivalent to "better specified property rights."[34] A property right is the right to use (including the right to dispose of) a particular object without any restrictions by others—in other words, a right that guarantees perfect freedom of action with regard to a specific object. In medieval society, agricultural laborers (the so-called serfs) were unable to sell freely what they themselves had produced, and they could not even use their own labor power with perfect freedom (they were required to provide labor to the lords of manors, and their movements were restricted). Instead, there was a specified right to use the common (grazing land and forests), and the right to expect a certain degree of mutual support from the community to which one belonged. At the same time, even the lords of manors in the Middle Ages were bound by the rules of the feudal system and could not freely dispose of their own domains or use or exile their own serfs at will. Under the feudal system, both freedoms and restraints were bound together, with an object (such as land) serving as an intermediary, and these were not thought of as object-specific.

In contrast to the situation under the feudal system, under capitalism there is perfect freedom of action with regard to objects acquired through contract or inheritance. Above all, there is freedom with regard to one's own body. Apart from one's own body, however, there are no rights to objects other than those acquired through contract or inheritance. Workers under capitalism have lost any right to the common, or to products they produce, and instead have perfect freedom to use their own labor. They are an unpropertied class who have no property other than their own bodies, or what the Romans called a proletariat.[35] Firms under capitalism have perfect freedom to buy and sell or dispose of products or assets but must purchase land, raw materials, and labor under contract. Thus under capitalism, workers and firms clearly have object-specific property rights.

The first two of these three conditions for capitalism provide a concrete definition of the private property rights held by two social classes. The third condition, the prevalence of market transactions, signifies the spread of contractual relationships and thus the dominance of private property rights. The basis of capitalism is precisely private property rights, and in this sense, Douglass North's approach closely resembles Marx's. Unlike Marx, however, he stresses the desirable results private property has brought about, and perhaps because of this he consistently avoids using the expression "capitalism." In any case, one can say that the popular view that capitalism is a system of private property rights is unexpectedly accurate.

For the sake of the argument that follows, it is important to note that the freedom of action permitted with regard to a particular object has a substantial direct influence on other objects or other economic actors (an influence other than that exercised through market exchange). This influence is called an externality, and the objects involved are called public goods (including both positive and negative varieties). A negative public good might be what we call pollution. In fact, there are probably very few kinds of property (objects) for which there is no possibility of creating externalities. In part, the system of private property is based on an invalid assumption that there are no externalities even when property has some kind of externality—that is, a potential public good. But this is not the only assumption. There are many examples of potential public goods, such as land (or the earth itself), or technology, and there is no way of deciding a priori which of these should forcibly be made, and to what degree, into private property. Thus, ultimately, a system of private property becomes pluralistic. This fact is a focus of the following argument.

THE UNITARY AND PLURALIST VIEWS OF HISTORY

Industrialization and capitalism are thus distinct concepts, or at least concepts with distinct ancestries. What consistent explanation will enable us to understand the relationship between the two concepts? Common sense would say that a strong candidate is a unilinear view of history, and a primary example of this is Marx's schema of historical stages: Asiatic → ancient → feudal → capitalist → socialist. For a long time the argument about the Asiatic → ancient → feudal progression has had critics even among Marxists, and with the collapse of the system in the Soviet bloc in 1989, the argument about the capitalist → socialist progression has had its foundations overturned. But to this day many theorists still tend to use the term capitalism to refer to a stage within a unilinear view of history, even if not within the Marxist schema itself. As is clear from the above definition, however, the concept of capitalism is simply a concept for classifying a system and does not include historical irreversibility.

Our thinking is influenced by unilinear views of history, great numbers of which appeared in nineteenth-century Europe—not only Marx's but also those of G. W. F. Hegel, Comte de Saint-Simon, Auguste Comte, and Herbert Spencer. Put another way, this unilinear view of history has been progressive, anticipating a convergence to a fixed form of society; ultimately, it is a unitary view of history that posits that a single great force determines the course of history. Now, however, the forced nature of this unitary view of history is gradually becoming clear. To begin with, human beings are not simply economic entities but have many different aspects— political, religious, and so on. Of course when we look at a society as a whole, a particular aspect may be dominant at a certain time. At least at first glance, though, the dominant aspect changes with each period. Thus if one wants to provide a unitary explanation for the whole of human history, one has to propose a highly abstract "prime mover," such as Hegel's "freedom," or Marx's "productive capacity." But when one tries to identify what we observe in reality with these prime movers, there is room for countless interpretations giving rise to endless and sterile doctrinal disputes. In fact, among the many concepts that make up Marxist theory, the most vague is "productive capacity." This is perhaps evident in the fact that sympathetic commentators always try to get by without using the concept.

Given that theory based on a prime mover is so abstract, it is difficult to develop in concrete terms. The usual form the unitary view of history takes is of a "theory of single factor dominance," which holds that one particular characteristic of society becomes the primary cause and all the other aspects are reduced to effects. An influential and typical example of this is theory in which the economic factors are dominant and the other aspects—political and cultural—are determined by them. In the unitary Marxist view of history economic factors are dominant, and the political, cultural, and other noneconomic factors are seen as superstructure. In a theory of single factor dominance, it becomes necessary to explain the dynamic between the dominant factor (for example, the economic factor) and the dominated factors (the noneconomic factors). The most-used concept in such explanations is the concept of "revolution." For example, the force of the economy, as the dominant factor, cannot in the end be prevented, but the political and social structure tries to counter the force. If it is premised that the counterforce resists the force of the economy, and that this resistance becomes increasingly determined, then unless one assumes that this resistance is eventually crushed and a new political and social framework appears, the theory of single factor dominance becomes untenable. Revolution, in the modern sense, is nothing but the stubborn resistance by the counterforce and the destruction of the dominated factors. Thus a unitary view of history can easily become a revolutionary view of history. But this is not inevitable.

If one examines historical phenomena carefully, one sees that the various aspects of a society move independently. The modern unitary view of history seems to have been generated from observation of the relationship between politics and economy since the early modern period, but, when freed from abstract formulism, even for this relationship, it is difficult to provide a unitary explanation. The most important political fact of the modern period is nationalism, but Benedict Anderson observed, for example, that for Marxism, the political fact of nationalism "has proved an uncomfortable *anomaly* for Marxist theory and, precisely for that reason, has been largely elided, rather than confronted."[36] And as was mentioned in Chapter 3, the existence of the state is treated as an unwelcome intruder even in liberal economics and history. Certainly it is comparatively easy to explain in economic theory why capitalism or industrialization requires political integration (see the explanation in terms of public goods in Chapter 3, for example). But this same theory does not explain the formation of nation-states in Europe or the emergence of what we today call nationalism. (In the first place, the nation-state has a longer history than industrialization, not to mention capitalism.) It is more persuasive to view the development of politics and the development of economy during the modern period as independent phenomena.

Seen this way, it is natural to expect the political aspects of a society to change under a different dynamic from that which causes changes in the economic aspects. The difference between the political and economic dynamic may in fact be of limited significance. This is because religion and ideology are always able to see critically the mundane affairs of the world, and so changes in either one of them (or both) at times overwhelm politics and the economy. For example, though somewhat ironic, it was Marxism as an ideology that, in greatly changing the course of capitalism and industrialization, ensured their continued existence. Generally speaking, changes in society as a whole are affected by the accumulation of multiple forces in the economy, such as politics, ideology, and religion.

The unitary view of history certainly provides an easy first understanding of history by using the stages divided by revolution, and it has played a role in lauding the achievement of progress. But this simplistic view leads one to overlook the subtleties of the changes in each aspect and to underestimate the importance of nonviolent, continuous change. And today, at the end of the twentieth century, human society is gradually being besieged by seemingly independent changes, such as the stockpiling of nuclear weapons, the development of electronic information technology, the acceptance of genetic engineering, the overcrowding of the global environment, the collapse of the sexual division of labor, and the demise of the planned economies. All of these changes, however, are great changes with very few violent elements, or what one might call nonrevolutionary revolutions. Their impact seems to be in their penetrating and settling in, rather than diffusing or expanding, the depths of our consciousness. The dominant transformations we observe in society have become those that can be characterized as shifts in the earth's crust rather than volcanic explosions. Our image of the world is therefore being expanded in unusual and distinctive ways. This may be an omen that the balloon will soon burst.

It is possible that we are today standing at the gateway to a period of great changes that cannot be comprehended under the accustomed rubric of "revolution for the sake of progress." No longer will anyone accept the naiveté that explains this situation solely in terms of a single factor such as the undesirable consequences of capitalism (or socialism). The unitary view of history, dependent on the concept of progress, is becoming less valid with the progress of knowledge. The historian's task today is to advance toward a rich, pluralistic interpretation that is at the same time highly complex. As the human image of the world becomes larger and more complex, so we are approaching a period in which we must advance from the unitary view of history we have held since the nineteenth century toward a new pluralistic view. In setting forth an argument that uses industrialization in the economic sphere and nationalism in the political sphere, I am attempting to make a first step toward a pluralist (or in fact dualist) view of history. How we understand the processes of the seemingly interdependent industrialization and democratization will also surely determine whether we should adopt a unitary or pluralist view of history.

GREAT BRITAIN AS A COUNTEREXAMPLE

Of course it is not my intention to deny that, in thinking about what we call modern society, the economy is extremely important. There is surely a logic to distinguishing periods, as Marx did, on the basis of the development of capitalism (though there is a need for a careful argument as to its strict definition), but as I have already pointed out, there are clearly other views. For example, if one takes a religious viewpoint, the religious revolution in Europe in the fifteenth and sixteenth centuries would be a great historical watershed. Max Weber's famous thesis on protestantism attributed to this religious revolution a role in starting capitalism. Again, if one sees things from the viewpoint of sociological structure, it is possible to believe that historical stages can be divided by changes in the organization of sanguinous relationships. For example, it is frequently believed that the development of the nuclear family occurred at the same time as capitalism (as exemplified by the well-known sociological principle for dividing the premodern *Gemeinschaft* [community] stage from the modern *Gesellschaft* [society] stage). And from the political viewpoint, much attention is given to the transition from absolute monarchy to the system of parliamentary democracy. But until now, all these issues—protestantism, the development of the nuclear family, *Gesellschaft*, and the system of parliamentary democracy—have been tied to capitalism or to the theories of industrialization. The multiple viewpoints have thus been reduced to the unitary view of progress.

With the results of recent specialist research, much evidence has been offered against such a reductionist unitary view. Historians are increasingly critical of Weber's thesis. And on the development of the nuclear family, too, there are powerful arguments that in Britain the development of the small family was already occurring around the middle of the thirteenth century.[37] With the division between *Gemeinschaft* and *Gesellschaft*, the division of periods changes greatly depending on how one understands the concepts. For example, if the nation-state is a *Gemeinschaft*, then the transition to an age of *Gesellschaft* is still not complete. Clearly in this case, the singularity of the *Gemeinschaft* that is the nation-state would become the focus of attention. In any case, there are various changes in dimensions other than the economic; these are not necessarily contemporaneous with the beginning of capitalism (changes that would satisfy the three conditions described earlier) and are not easily incorporated in the theory of capitalism. What is being suggested here is the principle of pluralism.

Why was it, though, that among these various viewpoints, it was the unitary, revolutionary view of history that has been dominant until now, and the three economic conditions that came to be regarded as the most important? This was due to many wide-ranging reasons reflecting the sociology of knowledge, and it would be impossible to discuss them all here. To give just one of the most evident, for the modern individual since the industrial revolution, the power of the economic dynamic has been so strong that interest in the accomplishments of market forces has become an *idée fixe*. But with a shift in people's interests, this situation also changes. It is natural that materialist interests increased with the appearance of industrialization, but in entering the phase of "transindustrialization" discussed in Chapter 3, there will be a complete change in the situation, with new *idées fixes* such as the information/knowledge revolution, the conservation of energy, and the global environment. There may well appear such things as an information-based view of history (of which perhaps Marshall McLuhan was the first proponent), an energy-based view of history (of which perhaps Leslie White was the originator), or some kind of ecological or meteorological view of history.[38] Moreover, our view of history will change as our vision of the future changes.

However, it will still be necessary for our view of history to conform to the facts of the past. In the unitary view of history as a theory, the most attention is paid to synchronization of the changes in society. One of the main reasons the unitary view of history has been dominant until now was the vague impression that the great religious, sociological, and political changes all occurred at almost the same time that economic changes took place. But there is little basis for this impression. Even if we forget non-European societies for a moment, the history of Europe itself does not support such an impression. And even in Britain, considered to be the cradle of modernization, the changes were not synchronized.

Of course, whether or not one can say they were synchronized is to some extent a question of periodization. But in Britain in the sixteenth century the three conditions of capitalism had already been satisfied, and so it is possible to say that capitalism was already established. If this is the case, why was there an almost three-century lag between this and the industrial revolution? In contrast, only two centuries have passed between the industrial revolution and today. What is more, even feudal society lasted no more than five centuries, from about the middle of the ninth century to the beginning of the thirteenth century; and in Britain, however long the feudal period seemed to have lasted, it was no more than three or four centuries after the Norman invasion. Historians call the sixteenth to eighteenth century the early modern period (for convenience, I also use this designation). This was surely a period of preparation for the modern period; but is it not a little too self-serving of the unitary view of history to see the early modern period merely as preparation for the true modern period that followed the industrial revolution? Were not the capitalism of the early modern period and the industrialization that followed the industrial revolution two distinct developments?

In his famous essay, "The Crisis of the Seventeenth Century," E. J. Hobsbawm, even as a representative of the Marxist view of history, felt he had no choice but to pose the question: "Why did the expansion of the later fifteenth and sixteenth centuries not lead straight into the epoch of the eighteenth- and nineteenth-century Industrial Revolution? What, in other words, were the obstacles in the way of capitalist expansion?"[39] Clearly this long period of preparation in the early modern period was a serious problem for the Marxist view of history. During this period there was a succession of major events—the Reformation, the age of the great voyages, the formation of the nation-state, the emergence of science, transformations in the political system, rampant colonialism, and the industrial revolution. It is hardly acceptable to reduce all the momentum generated by these various events, represented by Martin Luther, Christopher Columbus, and René Descartes, to developments due only to economic factors.

It is much more reasonable to regard each of these aspects—the economic, the sociological, the political, the intellectual, and so on—as having its own particular dynamic; each changed to some extent independently but still affected the others. Given that there were time lags in the changes in the various aspects, the change from what we call feudal society to modern society can be seen only as a continuous change consisting of superimposed changes of various aspects that occurred with time lags, and it may not be altogether possible to identify clear, absolute breaks in all the aspects (revolutions).

Thus there is a paradox. The incongruency in the revolutionary view of history in fact appears most clearly in the case of Britain, regarded as the classical example of modernization. In British history, there were successive waves of changes great and small, slow and rapid, such as the development of the small family in the thirteenth century, the advent of consumer society and entrepreneurs in the sixteenth century, the political revolutions of the seventeenth century, and the industrial revolution of the nineteenth century. Seen as a whole, these seem, somewhat unnaturally, to have been continuous rather than abrupt. In fact, there is a strong tendency among British historians generally to be rather proud of this continuity. Regardless of this, somewhat pointless intellectual acrobatics are necessary if one is to try to interpret British history from the unitary-revolutionary point of view.[40] This observation is connected both to the developmentalism mentioned above and to the suggestion for a new framework of historical analysis.

CHAPTER 5

An Economics of Decreasing Cost

A Definition of Developmentalism

Two conclusions can be drawn from the preceding chapters. First, we must distinguish between capitalism and industrialization. And second, there are at least two forms of industrialization: classical economic liberalism and developmentalism. Until now, the majority view has been that industrialization is merely an extension of capitalism and that developmentalism is a deformed variety of classical economic liberalism. In this chapter, I show that this dominant view is inadequate.

On the first point, economics in most instances does not distinguish between industrialization and capitalism. In essence, it is an analysis of pure capitalism, dependent on a static equilibrium analysis. In other words, the questions of technological innovation and motivation or incentive are not introduced into the theoretical framework. Clearly, however, it is almost constant technological innovation and a universalization of pecuniary incentive that have sustained industrialization (which we will understand for the time being as a continuous growth in per capita output). Oddly, up to this point there has been no economics of industrialization that genuinely incorporates these elements. In a sense, Adam Smith—who died before the industrial revolution began—came closest to doing so, as if he had anticipated something like the industrial revolution. David Ricardo, Thomas Malthus, and Alfred Marshall were aiming for an economics of industrialization, but their insights were not followed up by later economists (except, in the case of Ricardo, by Marx). The current mainstream of neoclassical economics provides only a patchwork of ad hoc analysis of industrialization.

If a genuine economics of industrialization had been created, a different perspective on a number of economic phenomena, including developmentalism, would have been possible. Seen only from the standpoint of the economics of pure capitalism, developmentalism is a deviation from the basic form of capitalism, or an exception only recognized as transitional. But seen from the standpoint of an economics of industrialization, developmentalism—together with classical economic liberalism—becomes one form that industrialization can take.

In reality, developmentalist development, or development that takes the form industrialization → democratization, is not at all exceptional. As explained in the previous chapter, developmentalism, or developmentalist aspects, have been seen frequently since the early modern period even in Western countries, beginning with Britain, and also in Germany and France. But these examples are analyzed only within the confines of the theory of infant industry (discussed below) and not in their own right. Even the visible success of Japan is commonly explained as an exception. However, what has occurred since the Second World War, particularly since the 1970s, has taught us that Japan's success is not an isolated example.

In East Asia, the developmentalist Asian NIEs have succeeded one after another in the takeoff to industrialization. These countries have sustained high rates of growth in the secondary and tertiary industries for more than fifteen years, and with the growth of entrepreneurial talent it is apparent that they are not likely to retrogress. The possibility of developmentalism has been sufficiently demonstrated in Mexico and Brazil and in the ASEAN countries of Thailand, Malaysia, and Indonesia. More than the success Japan achieved, the continuing success of the NIEs is an event of global significance. The theory that sees developmentalism as an exception is clearly contradicted by the facts. Thus, in order to preserve the viewpoint of classical economic liberalism, there is no choice but to adopt, in place of the theory of exception, a theory of transition that posits developmentalism as a transitional stage leading toward classical economic liberalism. But again we have to examine whether developmentalism is more than merely a transitional stage. This question must be asked in thinking about the world system of the future.

Let us start by giving a specific definition in place of the vague industrialization → democratization we have used up to now.

> Developmentalism is an economic system that takes a system of private property rights and a market economy (in other words, capitalism) as its basic framework, but that makes its main objective the achievement of industrialization (or a continuous growth in per capita product), and, insofar as it is useful in achieving this objective, approves government intervention in the market from a long-term perspective. Developmentalism is a

political-economic system established with the state (or a similar polity) as its unit. Thus in many cases some restrictions are placed on parliamentary democracy (such as a monarchical system, a one-party dictatorship, or a military dictatorship).

The qualification of "intervention from a long-term perspective" is added in order to make it clear that the use of short-term policy to counter the business cycle—that is, Keynesian policy—does not alone qualify as developmentalism. Because Keynesian policy by itself does not contribute to economic growth, it cannot be characterized as developmentalism.

The above definition contains an important implication. Developmentalism is premised on the existence of the state or a similar integrated polity. In other words, developmentalism is the theory, or policy, of industrialization from the standpoint of nationalism and is thus an advanced form of mercantilism or the views held by the German historical school. In developmentalism, the interaction between politics and economics plays a central role. In contrast, classical economic liberalism held that an economy must be independent of politics and seemed to hold that an economy is also independent of nationalism. In fact, as shown in the preceding chapters, industrialization cannot proceed free of the interaction between politics and economics. Even classical economic liberalism is no exception to this and has been supported by the nation-state system peculiar to Europe. The recent theory of hegemonic stability too—at the level of the world as a whole, though not at the level of individual states—is an attempt to recognize the linkage between politics and economics. It is now necessary to discard the classical concept that divided politics and economics and to analyze the relationship between industrialization and nationalism, or between industrialization and democratization. In this chapter I first provide an economic analysis of developmentalism and, on that basis, analyze in Chapter 6 the interaction with politics.

The Neoclassical Analysis of Decreasing Cost: A Critique of the Theory of Infant Industry

Let me sketch the framework of an economics of developmentalism. Its starting point is with the following proposition of decreasing marginal cost, which is one of the main pillars of this book's argument. Decreasing marginal cost (increasing marginal returns) is an important phenomenon, particularly in those cases where there are long-term issues such as growth or development.

This proposition is in direct conflict with the law of increasing marginal cost, which is the foundational premise of neoclassical economics. As is well known, the law of increasing marginal cost has become the source of the elegant microeconomic theory concerned with the equilibrium and stability of the market and has been placed at the heart of neoclassical textbooks. Thus there are likely quite a number of people who will wonder why I object to this law.

Before going further, let me clarify a few expressions:

1. Rather than increasing marginal cost, it may be better to talk of non-decreasing marginal cost, including fixed marginal cost, but I will not be particular about this difference here. Economists often employ the assumption that marginal cost equals average cost and that both are fixed, but this assumption is justified only in those cases of perfect competition in partial equilibrium analysis where the supply of capital is infinitely elastic. In those cases, as below, where one is trying to analyze not only a part but the whole of an economy, such an assumption should not be used.

2. A decrease (or increase) in marginal cost is somewhat different from a decrease (or increase) in average cost, but in the analysis to follow, ignoring this difference matters little.

3. Thus, for simplicity's sake, I have decided to call increasing marginal cost and increasing average cost both simply increasing cost. Decreasing cost is treated in the same way.

Forgetting the circumstances surrounding past developments in theory, there is no empirical basis for the law of increasing cost. Certainly, firms attempting to increase output in the short run do at times encounter a visible increase in cost. Agriculture is an example that has been often cited since Ricardo, and in many cases marginal return on investment of labor and capital in a fixed area declines. But if one makes a statistical analysis of the industries and firms that play leading roles in industrialization, it is hard to identify examples of increasing cost (both here and below, I refer to real, not nominal, costs). In particular, changes over time in the per unit real cost of industrial manufactured goods are usually decreases.

This is natural because industrialization is a continuous increase in per capita productivity, seen macroeconomically. Generally speaking, an increase in productivity brings decreasing cost. The results of most analyses that account for growth have shown that less than half of the economic growth rate can be explained by the growth rate of labor and capital.[1] Without assuming a trend of decreasing cost (or increasing returns), it is impossible to explain the remainder of the growth. Believing that industrialization means a trend of decreasing cost is a straightforward economic judgment based on what we observe. An economics of industrialization has to be an economics of decreasing cost.

In the history of economics, however, a majority of scholars opposed the view that cost decreases. The best-known have been those who followed the analytic tradition of Ricardo to Marx and were pessimistic about the future of capitalist industrialization and did not even recognize the fact of increasing returns. Ricardo was the first to grapple with the question whether returns would increase or decrease and developed a long-term analysis that took as its starting point diminishing returns in agriculture; he finally concluded that the profit rate had a tendency to decline in the long term. This is not to say that Ricardo did not also recognize the possibility of increasing returns, but after being shocked by the Luddite movement and the financial panic, he concluded that diminishing returns was the principal trend. The explanation that led to this conclusion is the most equivocal—though interesting—part of his theory.[2] For Ricardo and Marx, what made the development of capitalism possible was in the end only the increasingly intensive use of capital, and they thought that this would lead to a decline in the profit rate and the stagnation or collapse of capitalism. They clearly underestimated the capacity for growth in industrial capitalism, but as pessimists, the logic of their argument was in its own way consistent.

In contrast, the logic behind the argument against decreasing cost offered by the neoclassical school, which came to occupy the mainstream following the Second World War, is unsatisfactory. While acknowledging the fundamental fact of industrialization as a rise in per capita productivity, the neoclassical school sees that this is due to two factors—technological innovation and changes in cost excluding those due to technological innovation—and has continued to maintain that the law of increasing cost applies to the latter factor. As I argue below, however, dividing the reason for the rise in productivity into these two factors is arbitrary and artificial. We must critically examine the validity of this neoclassical mode of analysis. One way to do so may be to return to the beginning of economics—that is, to the economics of the period of the marginal revolution from which the neoclassical school evolved. Alfred Marshall, one of the founders of the neoclassical school, provides us with the best starting point.

MARSHALL'S PROBLEM

Although usually neglected, Marshall, in *Principles of Economics*, unequivocally states that the law of decreasing cost (increasing returns) is predominant in modern industry.

> We say broadly that while the part which nature plays in production shows a tendency to diminishing return, the part which man plays shows a tendency to increasing return. The *law of increasing return* may be worded thus:—An increase of labour and capital leads generally to improved organization, which increases the efficiency of the work of labour and capital.
>
> Therefore in those industries which are not engaged in raising raw produce an increase of labour and capital generally gives a return increased more than in proportion; and further this improved organization tends to diminish or even overrride any increased resistance which nature may offer to raising increased amounts of raw produce. . . .
>
> In most of the more delicate branches of manufacturing, where the cost of raw material counts for little, and in most of the modern transport industries the law of increasing return acts almost unopposed.[3]

In those industries where nature plays a large role (agriculture, for example) a tendency toward diminishing returns is seen, and in those industries where the human role is important the tendency toward increasing returns is dominant. Marshall made this clear, but nowadays the fundamental problem, as thus proposed, has been for the most part forgotten. Certainly Marshall's argument is ambiguous, and it does contain theoretical difficulties, which I discuss below. One can also understand why his theory has been respected but given much less than due recognition in the neoclassical "paradigm" that has made great progress especially in the postwar United States. We cannot but realize in the 1990s that Marshall's economics contained many valuable insights. He was attempting to develop an economics of industrialization, and he understood fully that in order to do this it would be impossible for economics to remain a science. He was also probably the first to point out the similarity between biology and economics. Though he left unresolved many of the problems he himself had proposed, the importance of the issues he raised has not disappeared.

Among the problems he left behind, of particular importance is the puzzle of competition under decreasing cost. In other words, if, as he puts it, we understand modern industry as operating under a condition of decreasing cost, then there would be no guarantee of a stable market equilibrium, and as a result one would expect monopoly to appear and competition to die out. In actual economies, however, one does not usually see competition ceasing in growing industries, and there are almost no examples of true monopoly (one industry, one company). This problem of how to explain the puzzling coexistence of a tendency toward decreasing cost and market competition is what later economists, following Piero Sraffa, have called "Marshall's problem." Marshall himself seemed to have been aware of this problem, and at the end of the chapter summarizing equilibrium theory, he wrote: "The statical theory of equilibrium is therefore not wholly applicable to commodities which obey the law of increasing return."[4] But Marshall was unable to solve this problem, as was incisively noted by Sraffa, a distinguished economist interested in broad ideological issues. The difficulty of dealing with this point, however, is not an excuse for ignoring the importance of the problem, and anyone trying to stress the importance of the tendency toward decreasing cost must work hard to solve this puzzle.

At Cambridge, Sraffa and Joan Robinson, on inheriting Marshall's mantle, tried to solve "Marshall's problem." Sraffa created a concept halfway between perfect competition and perfect monopoly, but it was Joan Robinson and E. H. Chamberlin who, accepting Sraffa's suggestion, developed in the 1930s the theories of imperfect competition and monopolistic competition.[5] They hypothesized that, in the major industries in which product discrimination is commonly observed, each company could become a monopolist through product discrimination and, by exploiting the tendency toward decreasing cost, could obtain a monopolistic profit. However, they believed that the mobility of capital and the existence of substitutes (similar manufactured goods) would indirectly provide a competitive character to this phenomenon of monopolization. Their model was precisely the intermediate model between monopoly and competition that Sraffa had suggested and also does not lead to unstable competition in each market. One could say that, because of the dismal background of the 1930s, they concentrated their attention on monopolization and failed to give due attention to competition. Unlike at the Cambridge in Massachusetts, at Cambridge in England an interest in decreasing cost was not lost.

From a different perspective, Kiyoshi Kojima in Japan, inheriting Kaname Akamatsu's flying-geese theory of development, has been interested in cases of increasing returns and has tried to devise the economics of foreign direct investment that is lacking in the neoclassical school. Recently, noting the large proportion of industries with increasing returns in today's world trade dominated by cutting-edge technological innovation, the American economist Paul Krugman has also shown a strong interest in the role of increasing returns. The Italian economist Giovanni Dosi and his group are involved in a similar attempt, starting from the question of technological innovation.[6] Although I do not delve into the theories of Kojima, Krugman, and Dosi, one can say, I believe, that some economists continue to maintain a latent interest, as it were, in decreasing cost. Despite such recent attempts, however, Marshall's problem has still not been adequately solved.

In this book I propose a different way of approaching the problem. I incorporate the question of developmentalism already discussed, or more specifically, the question of whether government intervention in the process of economic development is right or wrong. One of the conclusions I reach is that under decreasing cost, the basis for rejecting government intervention is not as evident as it is commonly believed to be. To better understand the problem of developmentalism, we must be better able to explain the phenomenon of decreasing cost.

THE PRODUCTION FUNCTION

In discussing decreasing cost, it is convenient to start with a critical examination of the clearly formulated neoclassical concept of decreasing cost. One of the main theoretical pillars of neoclassical economics is the stylized analytical concept of the production function. As is well known, the production function is a functional relationship in which the amounts of input are independent variables, and the maximum output that can be obtained from those inputs is a dependent variable; in other words, the function expresses the maximum possibilities of a given technology, or a technologically ideal state. In a sense, the most important point at issue here is what this "technology" is, but this is examined in detail in the analysis I develop below.[7]

Neoclassical economics usually assumes that marginal productivity decreases with an increase in output, or that marginal cost increases. This is the famous law of increasing marginal cost, or—the same thing—the law of decreasing marginal return. In other words, this law posits that productive efficiency (average productivity or marginal productivity) declines with an increase in scale. This is equivalent to assuming the existence of a negative feedback effect from an increase in output. The law of increasing marginal cost implies the existence within a firm of a kind of automatic break.

As is also well known, this law says the scale of production can be increased only when real wages are reduced (profits are maximized when the value of marginal product is equal to real wages). In a short-term analysis where one can assume that technology is fixed, many phenomena can be explained with this argument, but in an analysis of long-term phenomena, one cannot explain an increase in production that occurs together with a rise in real wages—that is, economic growth. Even neoclassical economists acknowledge the possibility of continuous economic growth due to increasing returns. That is, because the law of decreasing returns is postulated, they have only one explanation for economic growth: technological progress. This is why neoclassical economists carefully distinguish changes along a function (the production function, the supply function, and so on) and changes in the function itself (due to exogenous factors such as technological progress). The latter, in particular, is known as a shift, but it is mainly shifts in exogenous factors such as technological progress that cause cost to decrease. One perhaps is correct in observing that in calling technological progress a shift and making it exogenous to their theory, neoclassical economists have abandoned the analysis of continuous economic growth in order to protect instead the convenient analytical tool that is a production function with decreasing returns.

VARIOUS CONCEPTS OF DECREASING COST:
AN EXTENSION OF THE THEORY OF INFANT INDUSTRY

Even those of the neoclassical school, though, have recognized that there can be exceptional cases in which the premise of increasing marginal cost does not hold. Infant industry is an example, and for such industries they have even recognized, as an exception, the rationale for government intervention in the form of subsidies and protective tariffs. The theory of infant industry is closely connected to the question of developmentalism and is also the best way of making clear the significance of decreasing cost. Thus, let us critically reexamine the theory of infant industry.

Since J. S. Mill and C. Bastable, the classical argument has been that an infant industry is one that, given its small scale of production and high average or marginal cost, cannot possibly compete in the world market but can be expected to be self-reliant in the long term, by being protected for a certain length of time. In other words, the textbooks define an infant industry as one in which, through government intervention to a certain minimum level, the level of production is raised and the supply function

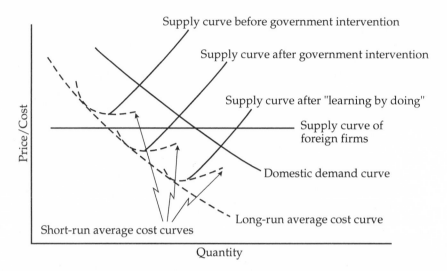

Figure 2 Demand and supply curves of an infant industry (or firm).

(actually its marginal cost function) shifts downward, thus making the industry competitive in the world market (see Figure 2).[8] Factors commonly mentioned as contributing to high costs are inadequacies in the social infrastructure, the inability to use technology fully, the lack of a skilled workforce, the inexperience of management, and the burden of a large initial investment. In other words, in the view of theorists of infant industry, there is a trap of high costs in the initial period, and unless an industry can exceed a certain minimum scale of production the road to industrial development will remain closed. It is thus necessary to seek government intervention to escape the trap; once it has escaped this trap, the industry will thereafter expand smoothly. Infant industry is the exception to the general neoclassical rejection of political intervention. As can be seen in the above-quoted textbook definition of an infant industry, the concept of such an industry was created with competition with the advanced nations in mind, and the theory of infant industry seemed to be a neoclassical attempt at an economics of development.

The core of the definition of infant industry is the part that says "if its level of production could be raised to a certain minimum level, its marginal cost function would shift downward." There have been a great number and variety of attempts made at explaining this crucial "shift." For example, such theories as Marshall's "external economies," "learning by doing," and "dynamic economies" have all in their own, independent ways been attempts to explain how the shift would occur; but there is little connection among them. To rectify this weakness, we can change the above definition of infant industry as follows: in contrast to the high marginal cost before the shift, the marginal cost after the shift must decline to the international level. In other words, an infant industry is one in which an increased level of production results in reduced marginal cost, and the industry thereby becomes internationally competitive. This is nothing more than saying, ex post facto, that there has been a decrease in marginal cost. The problem of infant industries is an example of the problem of decreasing cost.

But this ex post facto decrease in cost is not the same as what I will call a decrease in cost in the neoclassical sense. We must reconceptualize the significance of decreasing costs more broadly. Generally speaking, one can think of the following as frameworks for understanding marginal cost and average cost: (1) a neoclassical analysis of the long-run production function; (2) a nonneoclassical analysis of the long-run production path (an analysis that includes technological progress and uncertainty).

This division is approximate. For example, an analysis using Marshall's external economies, discussed below, or learning by doing are roughly speaking somewhere between (1) and (2). Below I look at the two analyses in order. There is also a neoclassical analysis of the short-run production function, but since it is of little relevance to the argument here, I mention it below only in passing, when necessary.

A Substitute for Infant Industry

First let us discuss the analysis of the long-run production function. I hypothesize that the long-run marginal cost curve (and the long-run average cost curve) moves downward to the right. In other words, there is a phase in which the long-run cost curve declines as capital investment in-

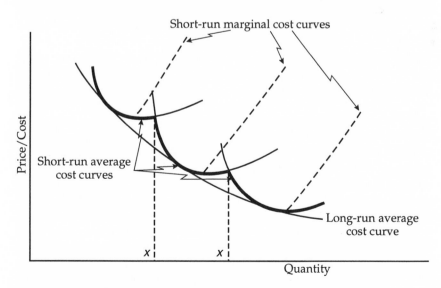

Figure 3 Average long-run cost path of decreasing-cost industry (or firm).

creases. Productivity rises as a result of an increase in capital investment but not in output (see Figure 3). In this case, the short-run supply curve (the short-run marginal cost curve) shifts downward with an increase in capital investment, and the break-even point also moves downward and to the right. This for the most part corresponds to what is dealt with in the standard diagram of infant industries (compare Figures 2 and 3).

DECREASING LONG-RUN MARGINAL COST

In the above definition of an infant industry, I did not specify the actual substance of the central concept—a level of production above a certain level—but if I define it to mean a level of production that could pay rent for capital investment on an international scale, then an industry realizing decreasing long-run marginal cost would satisfy all the requirements for the definition of an infant industry. (The x in Figure 3 is the intersection between the old and new short-run average cost curves and shows the minimum level of production needed to avoid losses and move to the new level of investment.) As is evident when we focus on the short-run cost curves, an industry that achieves decreasing long-run marginal cost but operates with investment on a scale that would be inadequate by international standards fits precisely the definition of an infant industry. Good examples of this are the automobile and petrochemical industries in developing countries.

At this point, however, the meaning of infant industry has gone beyond the existing understanding of that term. There is a tendency to think of infant industry as the extremely small-scale industry found in developing countries. One should, however, call infant industry all those industries, even in developed countries, that have decreasing long-run marginal cost but are unable to compete internationally because of inadequate domestic demand or capital. It is impossible to distinguish between industries with decreasing long-run cost and infant industries on the basis of theoretical analysis of the cost function. Thus, if one is to distinguish infant industries, one will have to do so by raising questions about surrounding social conditions, such as the inadequacy of the infrastructure. (Marshall's theory of external economies and the theory of learning by doing, discussed below, belong to this type.) But however small-scale the industry in question is when seen internationally, if it has already entered a phase of increasing long-run marginal cost, there is no sense in the government's seeing it as an infant industry and intervening. This is because, even if it receives government subsidies and makes investments (and even if in the short term its costs decline), its long-run cost only increases, and its international competitiveness does not improve. In this case, the concept of infant industry loses any meaning. In the end, it is only the concept of an industry facing a decreasing long-run marginal cost that has meaning.

Because capital investment can be made only at discrete intervals, firms cannot move accurately along their long-run curve. Thus, the actions

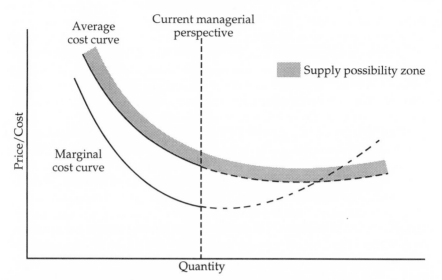

Figure 4 Cost curve of decreasing-cost industry.

of a firm attempting to follow the long-run curve are to increase its capital investment periodically when it strays too far from the long-run average cost curve in order to jump to a new short-run supply function. This is to say, its investment pattern will follow the sawtooth pattern shown by the thick line in Figure 3. (The line is the path traced by the coordinates of output and cost determined by the average or the unit cost function.) It is this path followed by the unit cost, including investment, that managers actually use as a basis for their decisions; below I call this the long-run average cost path.

What form will competition take where marginal or average cost is decreasing? (For the sake of simplicity, I call long-run average cost simply average cost.) As is evident, in a phase when average cost is decreasing (moving downward to the right), the profits of a firm reacting to a given price (what economists call a price taker) will increase as output does. To use the expression of a mathematical model, profit would be maximized when output is infinite (see Figure 4).[9] In other words, profit maximization will take the form of *market-share maximization* or competition for a demand that is always insufficient. When cost is decreasing, market-share maximization will be normal practice for firms. Recall that increasing cost has an automatic stabilizing function. Decreasing cost itself is a destabilizing factor.

Firms' efforts to maximize market share of course conflict with each other, and each firm has no choice but to follow the strategy of expanding capacity through investment and cutting prices. This investment or price-cutting can take various forms. Thus it is not easy to construct a generally effective analytical model for cases of decreasing cost. One might expect neoclassical analysis, which focuses on cases of increasing cost, to be ineffective, but as discussed below, Marshall's analysis, which attempted to incorporate cases of decreasing cost, was also not adequate. Even Robinson and Chamberlin's analysis of monopolistic competition, which in some respects refined Marshall's, is not satisfactory. The focus of their analysis was on product differentiation, but their analysis of the competitive relationships between these differentiated products was inadequate.

One alternative is a general application of game theory. For example, frequently analyses are made of businesses that act passively, by taking other companies' actions as given; these are analyses of what are called Nash equilibria. One could call a Nash equilibrium a solution that includes a comparatively large amount of compromise and cooperation. The simplest examples of analyses of this kind of cooperative solution are the classical theories of duopoly of Antoine Cournot and Joseph Bertrand. But as Heinrich von Stackelberg, for example, emphasized in his theory of duopoly, there is no guarantee that a firm will act passively and that the parties will converge on a cooperative solution. Although, as a solution to a noncooperative game, a Nash equilibrium may have some significance as a natural expansion of a perfectly competitive equilibrium, when perfect competition has failed, there is no basis for a Nash-style passive strategy to be adopted. Also, there is no guarantee that a Nash equilibrium is stable. And further, the market-share maximization I am discussing here is clearly incompatible with a passive strategy.[10] (Will a firm submit tamely to increases in another firm's share?) Thus one must believe that it is unlikely that the investment and price-cutting competition in a phase of decreasing cost will generate a cooperative situation such as a Nash equilibrium.

In fact, this problem of the instability of equilibria under decreasing cost is not always a long-term phenomenon; it can appear even in the short term, where capital investment is fixed. In the case of public utilities such as electricity and gas, which require huge fixed investments, competitive equilibria are impossible to maintain.[11]

Last, in firms that have underused capacity because of recession, one can frequently expect to observe the phenomenon of decreasing short-run marginal cost. In this sense, the Keynesian problem too can be regarded as a part of the economics of decreasing cost.[12] Moreover, the dimensions of a firm's strategy are increased by the fact that, in the long term, there is an element of price competition and competition to increase capacity. That firms make competitive investment is very significant; investment irreversibly changes the situation because it constitutes a threat to competitors. A new entrant can also counterattack with investment, but given the disparity in its ability to procure capital, it is at a disadvantage and will fall behind for the length of time it takes to complete its capital investment.

A similar policy of offensive investment is possible among the many existing firms. But such a policy is most likely to meet retaliation. In this case, the firm that first made the investment is clearly at an advantage. If this price and investment competition is allowed to continue, it will prevent the entrance of new firms, a number of existing firms are likely to go bankrupt or merge, and collusive oligopoly between a small number of firms, or monopoly, will likely emerge. Where a firm fails, a part of its capital may be absorbed by a surviving firm, but most of it will be wasted, and there will be a large sunk cost.[13] The unemployment created by bankruptcies is certainly not a phenomenon one can ignore. Though it is at present difficult to provide closely argued theoretical proof, is it not the case that with investment competition, price competition becomes more severe and compromise and cooperation become less likely? In a phase of decreasing long-run marginal cost, joint bankruptcy through price-cutting competition is perhaps more likely than when costs are only decreasing in the short term.

One can see that when costs are decreasing it is difficult for competition to produce an equilibrium, but naturally one wants to be able to analyze this in a little more detail. Unfortunately, though, there has not yet been developed a new analysis of competition that can deal with decreasing cost. In what follows, I attempt a provisional, though inadequate, analysis using the tools at hand. The argument is somewhat technical, so some readers may wish to skip it. The main thrust of the conclusion of the argument is as follows.

When costs are decreasing and price is a given, maximizing profit is identical to maximizing output. From this one can conclude that competition under decreasing cost is competition in maximizing market share and that it will generate intense investment competition and price-cutting competition. There is thus little likelihood that either stable equilibria (in price and quantity) or the rule of cooperation within an industry will appear through game-theoretic bargaining. The result will be the appearance of collusive oligopoly, and eventually of monopoly. This can be avoided only through intervention from outside the economy (legal or administrative). From the first, the tendency toward decreasing cost is the source of strong potential pressure to cut price. Thus strong intervention to promote a reduction in prices, such as a policy of subsidies, is not usually necessary. In many cases intervention that demands controls on profit rates and acts as a break on price-cutting competition is sufficient. This is easy to understand when one thinks of the example of the public utility industry, which has decreasing costs in the short term. For example, where two electric companies compete in the same region, the possibilities are that one company will gain a monopoly, the two companies will collude, or the government will intervene.

TECHNICAL ANALYSIS: THE POSSIBILITY OF RESTRICTIVE COORDINATION

Let us begin by considering some standard firm activities, so as to classify the possible scenarios. When a firm is expanding its output, if it can follow the declining average cost curve and cut its prices, it can maintain a state of zero profit. Let us call this a "restrictive action." (The outline of the following argument does not change even if, instead of zero profit, the firm makes some profit by marking up its prices, for example, or if it makes a loss but still recovers variable costs.) When all firms have agreed to take such restrictive action, let us call it "restrictive coordination" and consider such coordinated action to be standard in industry. When there is a prospect that demand will increase soon and capacity will be sufficiently large, there clearly is a significant long-term rationale for maintaining such restrictive coordination until demand appears. In this standard situation, the total of all the firms' average cost curves acts as the "restricted pseudosupply curve" for that industry. If we regard this as a "supply curve," we can use the usual analysis of price theory. In this sense, the analysis of supply and demand under restrictive coordination provides a standard theoretical model. (In fact, this model also becomes a way of understanding the industrial policy I define below, but I discuss this later.) We should note that this restrictive coordination is not a game-theoretic cooperation generated from shortsighted bargaining, as in a Nash equilibrium, but what one might call a policy-based coordination founded on a unanimous recognition of the long-term situation.

However, even when this restrictive coordination is functioning well, the standard conclusions of normal price theory cannot apply as they stand. First, the slope of the pseudosupply curve for this industry is negative. Even if one follows the standard Walrasian analysis of price, if the slope of the supply curve is negative, a number of peculiar features are present. In particular, there is no guarantee of an equilibrium or (standard Walrasian) stability.[14] Second, the supply as shown by the quasi-supply curve is the supply when restrictive coordination is being maintained, and so the original supply, which took the form of market-share maximization, has been suppressed. However, this pressure toward market-share maximization is always present, though dormant, and there is no knowing when it will disturb the restrictive coordination. We must, however, attempt to see under what conditions a disturbance of the coordination will occur. Therefore, let us divide the various possibilities into two main categories, depending on whether the restricted supply or demand is larger.

First, there is the case of what we might call pseudoexcessive supply, where even restricted supply outstrips demand. (This corresponds to the area below the intersection of the supply and demand curves in Figure 5, and the area above the same intersection in Figure 6.) At this point, even if prices are cut, demand will continue to be inadequate for the restricted supply, and a firm will have no choice but to cut prices even further, below its average production cost. Other firms will have no choice but to follow suit. It will become impossible to maintain the restrictive coordination yielding zero profit. Instead, there can be only an ultrarestrictive coordination, with the firms agreeing to a negative profit rate, but such

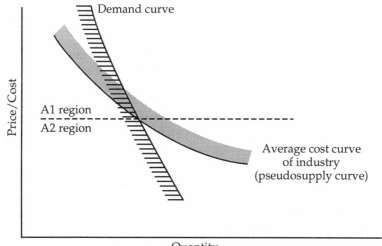

Figure 5 Pseudosupply zone of decreasing-cost industry: the case of nonelastic demand (case A).

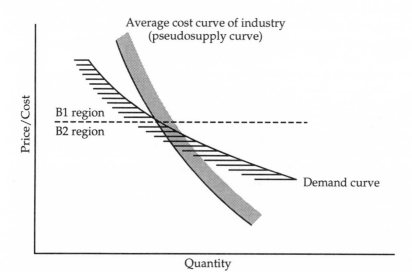

Figure 6 Pseudosupply zone of decreasing-cost industry: the case of elastic demand (case B).

an agreement contradicts the raison d'être of capitalist enterprise. Thus coordination will become impossible, and, even knowing this, firms will continue their mutually harmful investment and price-cutting competition. The negative profit condition continues, and because they are able to implement a restrictive strategy, the firms will likely be bankrupted

one by one. To avoid this predicament, collusive oligopoly may appear between the few survivors, or eventually monopoly. I call this the case where
restraint is impossible.

Second is the case of pseudoexcessive demand, where demand outstrips
the restricted supply. (This corresponds to the area above the intersection
of the supply and demand curves in Figure 5, and the area below the same
intersection in Figure 6.) In this case, restrictive coordination is clearly possible. However, excessive demand creates the possibility of positive profits
that stimulate an incentive for market-share maximization. The incentive
becomes a motive to destroy the restrictive coordination. Thus without
some kind of outside pressure (government intervention, for example), it
will be difficult to maintain the restrictive coordination yielding the zero
rate of profit for its participants. A candidate to replace it as a coordinating mechanism might be agreement on a fixed positive profit rate, but this
would not change the fundamental incentive of firms to maximize market share, thus jeopardizing the coordination. Even in this second case,
where a pseudoexcessive demand exists, there will be no move to raise
prices. This is because the natural reaction of any firm motivated to maximize market share is usually to lower prices. In the end, even in this case
of pseudoexcessive demand, there is a high possibility that the restrictive
strategy will collapse and price-cutting competition will intensify. This
shows that agreement on the restrictive coordination—a policy-based coordination—is difficult both to initiate and to sustain. Let us call this the
case where restraint is unstable.

It may be easier to understand these two cases if we link them to
the shape of the demand curve and the supply function. If we follow the
normal method of analyzing stability, we can distinguish between two relationships of the two curves of Figures 5 and 6, depending on whether
demand is sufficiently elastic in response to changes in price, or in other
words, whether the slope of the demand curve (more precisely, the absolute
value) is more moderate or steeper than that of the pseudosupply curve.
In case A (Figure 5), the slope of the demand curve is steeper than that of
the supply function—that is, demand is more inelastic than pseudosupply.
Above the intersection between the demand curve and the pseudosupply
function, demand outstrips restricted supply, and thus this is the region
where restraint is unstable. But even here prices will come down in response to the pressure of market-share maximization, and we will move
into the area below the point of intersection. In the region below this
point, demand is lower than restricted supply, and this is where restraint
is impossible. The cases of A1 and A2 below where demand is inelastic are
made up of these two regions.

In case B (Figure 6) the slope of the demand curve is more moderate
than that of the supply function, or demand is elastic. This time, the area
above the intersection between the demand curve and the pseudosupply
function is the region where restraint is impossible, and below the inter-

section is where restraint is unstable. Cases A and B occupy contrasting places. We can summarize this as follows.

A: demand is inelastic
  A1: above the intersection—pseudoexcessive demand, restraint is unstable
  A2: below the intersection—pseudoexcessive supply, restraint is impossible
B: demand is elastic
  B1: above the intersection—pseudoexcessive supply, restraint is impossible
  B2: below the intersection—pseudoexcessive demand, restraint is unstable

In cases A2 and B1, where restraint is impossible, competition is extremely unstable. Because a situation of negative profit is dominant, the chances of establishing coordination are extremely low, many firms will go bankrupt, and the emergence of a monopoly or a collusive oligopoly seems inevitable. Only in these cases is government intervention justified. In cases A1 and B2, where restraint is unstable, unlike normal coordination under increasing costs, coordination is unstable to the extent that firms pursue market-share maximization. But since positive profit is possible, there is a relatively high likelihood of achieving coordination. Thus the way to avoid the emergence of monopoly is for industry to stay in regions A1 and B2, where restraint is possible but unstable, and to try to establish coordination. If it enters regions A2 or B1, mutually harmful price-cutting competition will be unavoidable without government intervention. In either case, however, market-share maximization will cause prices to continue to decline, and industry will inevitably move from A1 to A2, and from B1 to B2. Thus:

1. In case A, where demand is insufficiently elastic, A2 is an inevitable outcome, and without intervention, competition will cease.

2. In case B, where demand is sufficiently elastic, B2 is an inevitable outcome, but even in this case, without government guidance or the strong pressure of a consensus within an industry, for example, restrictive coordination may collapse. But government intervention will not help coordination.

In summary, an analysis of industries with decreasing costs leads us to note the possibility that price-cutting competition may become a suicidal strategy. Competition among firms takes an abnormal form, unlike the neoclassical image of competition. The same conclusion applies to the utility industry, but in this case, as is well known, natural monopoly is permitted and prevents the collapse of the industry.

A POLICY FOR FOSTERING INDUSTRIES FACED WITH LONG-RUN DECREASING COST

In industries faced with long-run decreasing marginal cost (or infant industries in the broad sense of the term), there is thus a high possibility that price competition will lead to monopoly or collusive oligopoly. According to the neoclassical analysis, a standard policy for infant industries would be for the government to maintain the level of production by making up firms' losses with some kind of subsidy (typically price subsidies or protective tariffs), and as a result to plan to facilitate lowering prices to international levels. Here, however, we now see that this description is not sufficiently precise. More precisely, because infant industries face long-run decreasing marginal cost, from the beginning there is a latent impulse to lower prices. The neoclassical school has stated that subsidies should be provided only to those industries that have the potential to be independent (Mill-Bastable's criterion). If this were common practice, and if the capital market were perfect, even a firm that received no subsidy could procure capital in the market and should be able to realize its potential for independence on its own. Without imperfections in the capital market, the latent impulse to lower prices might be unleashed at any time. Thus the problem of infant industries is reduced to the problem of fostering a capital market. Even if it is not easy to do so in one's own country, it should be possible to entice foreign capital (which Latin America has done, as I discuss below). In other words, if we assume the ideal neoclassical model, including a capital market, the problem of infant industries is nothing more than an illusion.

This, however, only makes apparent the deficiencies of neoclassical analysis relying on moving from equilibrium to equilibrium (an analysis of comparative statics). And this is not the end of the problem. A substantial problem that remains is the losses firms incur during the process of price-cutting competition while trying to reach an equilibrium (what I call below the undesirable consequences of excessive competition). The neoclassical school ignores these kinds of losses because it optimistically assumes a stable equilibrium at the destination and regards the move from one equilibrium to the next as a momentary process. But inasmuch as the deadweight loss at the equilibrium point, with which the neoclassical school is so concerned, and the losses that occur during the process of trying to achieve an equilibrium are both a loss of resources, there is no difference between them. If a shift in equilibria is neither a momentary nor a rare phenomenon, there is no good reason to ignore the losses that occur during this process.

The preceding analysis of industries faced with decreasing cost has demonstrated theoretically that the process of price-cutting competition will continue over a long period, ending perhaps only with the emergence of a monopoly, and that we cannot ignore the frequent business failures that will occur during that period. In fact, the fear of these losses may cause the supply of capital to come to a standstill; in other words, the concept of a perfect capital market contradicts the facts during the initial period of industrialization. As long as an idealized framework of comparative statics is used, a policy for infant industries is unnecessary. Even neoclassical economists have recently begun to say that except in those cases where there are effects from "dynamic economies," a policy for infant industries is unnecessary. The problem is how we are to identify these dynamic economies within a neoclassical framework that is essentially static, but I discuss this again below.

The misunderstanding that a policy for infant industries is a policy of subsidies and of trade protection also arises from the inadequate analysis of the instability of price competition. First, it is a mistake to think that a policy for infant industries must include the provision of subsidies. When one distinguishes between cases in which demand is inelastic (case A in the technical analysis above) and those in which demand is elastic (case B above), then one sees that government intervention is justified only when the former case is expected to persist. Second, it is also a misconception to believe, as we have until now, that protectionism is a policy for infant industries. The main reason for protectionism (tariffs or import quotas) is the fear that large companies from advanced countries will enter the domestic market and, by setting lower prices, prevent the entry of domestic firms or drive them to bankruptcy; and one can certainly not ignore this possibility. The entrance of large foreign companies can be compared to a particular domestic company's becoming dominant in a market. But foreign firms and domestic firms do not necessarily behave in the same way. Unless they have a particular political interest in that country, large foreign firms are unlikely to pay much attention to that country's market and engage in strategic bargaining. At least, they are less likely to do so than a dominant domestic firm. It is highly likely that large foreign firms will remain price-takers, taking the international price as a given.

Suppose large firms from the advanced countries were to adopt an aggressive management strategy of preventing new entrants into the market. If the long-term prospects for that industry were bright (and if they were not, why would large foreign firms be interested in that country's market?), it should be possible for domestic firms to borrow capital to enter the market and repay it in the future. Thus, the problem returns to the disparity in the abilities of domestic and foreign firms to obtain capital— that is, imperfections in the capital market. Only when foreign firms have a demonstrably superior ability to obtain capital is it justified to provide domestic firms with some assistance, such as subsidies for initial investment. Thus, there is not as much need for protectionism to prevent the entry of foreign firms as is often argued. For example, immediately after the opening of Japan in the late nineteenth century, its domestic cotton, raw silk, and tea industries were exposed to severe international competition because Japan did not then have tariff autonomy. But they rallied, changing the structure of their industries, and Japan's takeoff proceeded.[15] The danger of a domestic market's being completely dominated by foreign products does exist, but it is going too far to believe that protectionism is a policy for infant industries. Protectionism and subsidies are nothing more than a backup policy for infant industries.

Ultimately, the primary objective of a policy for industries faced with decreasing cost must be to remove such undesirable consequences of price-cutting competition as business failures, unemployment, and the rise of monopoly. I am not the only one who has recognized that some kind of coordination is an effective means of preventing these consequences. For example, Marshall offered the following insight:

> The aggregate satisfaction . . . could be much increased by collective action in promoting the production and consumption of things in regard to which the law of increasing return acts with especial force. . . . The divergence between individual and collective interests is *prima facie* less important with regard to those things which obey the law of diminishing return, than with regard to those which obey the law of increasing return: but, in the case of the latter, there is strong *prima facie* reason for believing that it might often be to the interest of the community directly or indirectly to intervene.[16]

As we have seen so far, however, coordination under decreasing cost does not seem to reach the game-theoretic Nash equilibrium. What is possible is perhaps a policy-based coordination founded on an agreed understanding of the situation. Given that each firm can be expected to have its own independent prospects, it is hard to hope that the industry as a whole will independently agree on an understanding of the situation. This means, therefore, that the government does its part to foster an agreed understanding by supplying information that goes beyond the perspective of each firm, and that the government engages in "indicative planning" as to how coordination is to be implemented. But indicative planning for individual industries is a difficult task; a more important problem is how to prevent violation of the coordination.

Indicative planning has long had its skeptics. Today, however, indicative planning for the national economy as a whole (mainly for macroeconomic policy) has become common. But there may be doubts about the wisdom of adopting policy for individual industries mainly to guide prices because in order to do so one should ideally have detailed information from individual firms. More specifically, when one is setting a schedule for price reduction, it is essential to know the aggregate average cost curve for the industry (what I called the pseudosupply curve in the section on technical analysis). But the structure of average cost differs by industry, and even within an industry each firm's investment and management strategies differ. Without information about individual firms, indicative planning will lack precision. However, to legally compel firms to provide the necessary information would be to violate the freedom of management of capitalist enterprises.

Even more difficult is preventing violations by individual firms (such as lowering prices before the planned date) once a schedule for lowering prices has been indicated. Of course violations can be effectively controlled if laws are enacted to punish violators. Regulations against dumping, against the proliferation of monopolies, and covering securities dealing, as seen in the West and particularly in the United States, have been enacted, and government has the right to investigate and punish violators. But generally speaking, an economic theory is usually necessary to make a legal interpretation of the phenomenon of the market economy (for example, dumping regulations are based on an economics of increasing cost). Thus, legal judgments on economic phenomena, in the sense that they are made by relying on a particular economic theory, are frequently highly subjective and even close to being unreasonable. Despite this, though, there is a reason why laws regulating dumping, prohibiting monopolies, and restricting securities dealing are usually accepted. These laws are like criminal laws: they see the violating firms as evil and punish them. Such punishment frustrates the desires of the management of offending firms and may even purge the management. For example, in the case of dumping regulations, even if foreign firms are banished, nationalism will justify the action. In the case of antitrust laws and laws on securities dealing, the justice of the masses, who believe themselves to have been injured, accepts the downfall of the violating firms.

The situation is different, however, for industries facing long-run decreasing cost. Consumers who do not see the undesirable effects of price-cutting will frequently welcome lower prices and are not likely to consider evil the firm that violates the restrictive agreement. Also, often the firm violating the agreement is an efficient firm. If the aim of policy in the first place were to foster domestic firms, purging or ruining superior firms would be contrary to the original objective. In this case, legal regulations are not justified and would interfere with the original intention of developmentalism. When legal regulations are impossible, the government must be a mediator or arbitrator and bring about autonomous cooperation among firms through indirect means. Theoretically, at least, the central part of policy for industries facing long-run decreasing cost is to prevent suicidal price competition through government intervention as a mediator. The result is a kind of price cartel under government leadership, and a policy of subsidies or protectionism is nothing more than a subsidiary means of achieving the same goal.

In the traditional Western understanding, there exist the two alternatives of absolutely no government intervention or intervention through legal regulation. But in postwar Japan, the government (ministries) provided "administrative guidance," a form of intervention that was somewhere between mediation and arbitration. There must be a set of conditions under which this intermediate form can continue to exist and, as I mention below, this is particularly related to the way the bureaucratic system operates. What is necessary is not an economics of protectionism or subsidies but a political sociology of coordination and mediation.

LEARNING BY DOING

Before continuing, let me discuss two well-known attempts at a theory of infant industry. As already noted, if we assume a textbook neoclassical model, including a perfect capital market, then from the very beginning a theory of infant industry is impossible. But a body of economic theory that has no theory of development for developing countries and developing industries is, in effect, confessing its inability to deal with the reality of industrialization. Neoclassical theory needs an independent theory of development. The recent frequent appearances, as a form of theory of infant industry, of the approach that calls itself a "dynamic economics" might perhaps be a response to this need. Here let me mention the model of learning by doing as a representative example of this approach. This model also provides an introduction to the nonneoclassical analysis in the following sections.

The theory of learning by doing is the theorization of the phenomenon of the learning curve discovered by business economists. The learning curve points to the fact that technological know-how, workers' skill, and methods of administering the organization are acquired by participating in production, and as a result, productive efficiency is increased (neoclassically speaking, the cost curve is shifted downward). In mathematical terms, this means that the cumulative value of output automatically shifts the cost curve downward, without incurring any additional costs.[17] As is symbolized by the shift in function, the substance of learning by doing is improvement in skill, technology, and/or organization, and this is connected to, and cannot be distinguished from, what we have been thinking of as technological progress in the broad sense. In fact, the first application of the concept of learning by doing to economic theory was Arrow's explanation of standard technological innovation.[18] Clearly, the theory of learning by doing endogenizes technological progress, in taking the cumulative value of output as a variable. Thus, if we were to adopt the theory of learning by doing, we would be outside the neoclassical framework for which technology is an exogenous given.

Let me demonstrate that there are a number of antineoclassical results if one adopts the theory of a model of cumulative value. Cumulative value, it goes without saying, is a quantity (output) that does not decrease. Thus, unless production is curtailed, the production function will indefinitely shift upward, and productive efficiency will continue to increase. In relation to infant industries, as long as production continues even at a low level the results of learning by doing will accumulate, and eventually there will be a shift sufficient for the industry to grow out of the stage of infancy. This is to say that the unbreakable barrier or trap that kept an industry in the stage of infancy will disappear.

More broadly, one has to say that learning by doing is not unique to the stage of infancy but appears naturally even in mature industries. Every time one adds to capital equipment, learning by doing becomes both necessary and effective. Thus, under the theory of learning by doing, output at each point in time changes depending on the cumulative value of past output, and it becomes impossible to determine the ideal technology that is supposedly expressed by the production function. In other words, the production function is a temporal function that includes the history of the firm—its cumulative output—and clearly is different in character from the nontemporal neoclassical function that expressed the potential of technology. The same is true for marginal cost. Marginal cost is a function of the cumulative output and can be expressed only as a dynamic aggregate path, in the sense that it is determined by historical time. The theory of learning by doing stands at the gateway to a dynamic analysis incorporating technological innovation and investment.

MARSHALL'S THEORY OF EXTERNAL ECONOMIES

The argument of Alfred Marshall was a little more advanced in that it made more factors endogenous and was dynamic. As mentioned before, Marshall saw increasing returns (decreasing costs) as a central tendency, but he explained this in terms of two factors, internal economies and external economies.

> Looking more closely at the economies arising from an increase in the scale of production of any kind of goods, we found that they fell into two classes—those dependent on the general development of the industry, and those dependent on the resources of the individual houses of business engaged in it and the efficiency of their management; that is, into *external* and *internal* economies.[19]

> An increase in the aggregate volume of production of anything will generally increase the size, and therefore the internal economies possessed by . . . a representative firm; . . . it will always increase the external economies to which the firm has access; and thus will enable it to manufacture at a less proportionate cost of labour and sacrifice than before.[20]

This does not mean that what he is calling internal and external economies are essentially different in quality. As is evident in *Principles of Economics*, Marshall made a clear distinction between external economies, which depend on such things as technological diffusion and the development of related industries (particularly the transport and communications industries), and internal economies, which rely on improvements in management and organization. But he also noted that core features such as division of labor or specialization, training, and mechanization are common to both. The two types of economies are at least connected in substance, and the difference is nothing more than whether these developments occur inside or outside a representative firm of an industry. Marshall, having surveyed the British economy of his time, placed particular importance on external economies and emphasized that the tendency toward increasing returns came about mainly as a result of external economies.

If one were to restate Marshall's argument as it would be incorporated into a neoclassical framework, external economies would demonstrate the phenomenon of marginal costs decreasing in the industry as a whole. In detail, this means that though the marginal cost curve for each firm might be rising (where that situation for other firms is constant), with the entrance and simultaneous expansion of a large number of firms, there would be a general rise in the quality of the labor force and an improvement in the infrastructure; the positive effects of these external economies would be shared among the firms, and the marginal cost curve for the industry as a whole would decline. However, if external economies have such an important effect, the concept of the supply function for individual firms loses its meaning. The basic concept in the analysis is the supply function for the industry as a whole and not that of individual firms. Marshall's famous concept of the "representative firm" was the best he could do to represent the supply function of the whole industry on a smaller scale at the level of the firm and to analyze the effects of external economies on the actions of a firm. In order to do this, however, his "partial equilibrium analysis" became an analysis of the relationship between the supply of a representative firm and the (perhaps hypothetical) demand faced by that firm. In this series of analyses, he was in effect abandoning the method of neoclassical methodology, which started from the individual firm and moved to an industry as an aggregation of firms.

When the substance of Marshall's external and internal economies is analyzed, his concept of cost (for the representative firm) must be seen as a long-term concept, including technological and organizational innovations, learning by doing, and investment. But there are still doubts as to whether he relied on his concept of internal and external economies as the deciding factor in determining whether long-run cost decreases or increases. There is no doubt that the industrial infrastructure developed with remarkable rapidity in the latter half of the nineteenth century, and this fact led him to emphasize the effects of external economies. But this was nothing more than a peculiar characteristic of the age in which he lived. To analyze the present economic situation, a different perspective is necessary. We must, however, give due recognition to his efforts to come to grips with the reality of industrialization, without being in thrall of the elegance of neoclassical theory.

An Anticlassical Analysis of Decreasing Cost

This section deals with analysis of the *nonneoclassical* aggregate long-run production path, focusing on technological innovation and uncertainty, particularly the former. As emphasized earlier, technological innovation is a wide-ranging concept that includes technological breakthroughs and innovations in application and involves organizational innovation. Not all technological innovation is achieved through a high degree of creativity. From the Second World War to about the middle of the 1970s, innovative activities were limited to those involving genetic structure, the semiconductor, and lasers. That quarter century was one of the most fertile periods of technological innovation, but the seeds had been sown for the most part before and during the war, and it was the accumulation of innovations in application that supported the rise in productivity during this period. In short, it was the countless applied innovations that had substantial economic results.

DECREASING COST IN ITS BROADEST SENSE: TECHNOLOGICAL INNOVATION AND UNCERTAINTY

Applied innovation itself is a wide-ranging phenomenon. According to Taylor's famous theory of scientific management, management is supposed to adopt technological innovations achieved by scientists or engineers, which workers on the shop floor then implement by following a manual of procedures. But if these workers are adequately trained and accumulate experience, and if the scientists and engineers are directly involved in problems on the shop floor, there will be a mutual exchange between research and production, and many innovations will be generated at the point of contact. This is often seen in Japan, as in the well-known example of quality control circles, and there is no reason not to count these cooperative shop-floor innovations as technological innovations. Finally, let me emphasize once again that organizational innovations are nothing but technological innovations in the broad sense. Any technological innovation, as it is adopted, will produce a new organization, and an improvement in organization—like technological innovation in the narrow sense—will increase productivity. Here let us recall once again the earlier citation from Marshall: "The *law of increasing return* may be worded thus:—An increase of labour and capital leads generally to improved organization, which increases the efficiency of the work of labour and capital. Therefore in those industries which are not engaged in raising raw produce an increase of labour and capital generally gives a return increased more than in proportion."[21]

As noted in the previous section, an increase in capital equipment actually includes some element of technological progress. So-called capital-embodied technological progress is a well-known attempt to formulate this idea.[22] Theories of capital-embodied technological progress, learning by doing, and Marshall's external economies succeeded in endogenizing actual technological innovation. Thus, the concept of technological innovation has been extended to include applied innovations, and this extended applicability—unlike the highly original technological breakthrough—increases the likelihood of predicting such innovation. On the other hand, as technological innovation is endogenized to a certain degree, it merits serious consideration by management. As technological progress becomes a part of management decisions, those decisions are reflected in the aggregate marginal (or average) cost curve, that is, they contribute to achieving reductions in the cost of production (if this were not so, technological progress would have no significance). When there is a strong tendency toward decreasing cost in such ways, it becomes easier to explain the robustness of industrialization.

In contrast, the distinctive characteristic of neoclassical analysis is to deal with technological innovation by using a dichotomy between technological innovation as something uncertain and the movement along the production function as something certain. Of course, dividing reality that seems to be a continuum into two clearly contrasting poles is a recognized analytical method. But the neoclassical school, in regarding technological progress as something uncertain and impossible to predict, excludes it from the main body of neoclassical theory (the production function) and posits it merely as a given (a factor that causes a shift in the production function). This is tantamount to ignoring one of the two aspects that make up reality. But what propels the reality that is industrialization is precisely this uncertain, dynamic aspect. Can we adequately analyze industrialization from a perspective of certainty and regularity? Put differently, can we use the concept of constant equilibrium, or the assumed stability that is expected in the process of reaching the equilibrium? The deciding factor here will be the fundamental image we have of the past two centuries of industrialization in all parts of the world. This image must rely on observation of actual fact and on a judgment as to the importance of technological progress in industrialization. But when they see the main developments since the industrial revolution, and particularly the vigor of constant technological innovation since the Second World War, surely even neoclassical economists cannot regard the fact of technological progress merely as a given.

To be sure, technological progress in the past was an intermittent or discontinuous phenomenon that relied on a small number of dedicated individuals and was difficult to predict. Because of this, economists in the eighteenth and nineteenth centuries did not explicitly deal with the question of technological progress. For Adam Smith, who lived before the industrial revolution, this was unavoidable, but he thought of the progress of technology as the single pattern that was the advance of the division of labor. Ricardo was aware of the phenomenon of technological progress, but after pondering it at length, he decided that it did not have the capacity to stave off the inevitability of the stagnation of social progress. Marx and the Marxist economists did not consider the possibility of a technological progress that might blunt the sword of their pessimistic analysis. It was Marshall, having experienced the second industrial revolution in the latter half of the nineteenth century, who clearly recognized the power of the impetus of technological progress, but as I noted above, he was unable to produce a satisfactory theoretical analysis. However, technological progress after the second industrial revolution was integrated with science and began to accelerate, and since then technological innovation has almost become a steady stream. Thus, management decisions, and subsequently investment, have been made in the expectation of this fact. And since the Second World War, this practice has become even more pronounced.

For today's entrepreneur, the profit-maximizing point is a moving target, and when an objective is reached, the technological frontier has already moved further away. The aggregate output path is no longer a line connecting a series of points of profit maximization on the production function. Rather, it is a second- or third-best path, chasing after a series of profit-maximization points. Corresponding to this path, the path of average production cost too is a second- or third-best series of points. In fact, the general characteristics of capital investment during the period from the Second World War until the 1970s were its adaptability, large scale, and systematic nature. Thus, applied technological progress has advanced and has created a tendency for the average cost path to decline. Moreover, economies of scale in capital investment have also further strengthened the tendency of the path to decline. At present, what managers have in mind in making medium- to long-range management plans is naturally this aggregate per unit (average) cost path and not some theoretical average cost function. And when they are confident about the prospects for a decline in this per unit cost, they invest.

If technological progress shows no signs of coming to a standstill, the average cost path will continue to decline indefinitely; it will not be reversed and start to rise. Managers, who must concentrate on short- to medium-term issues, do not need to give any thought to a phase of reversal in the long-run marginal cost path. What is necessary, therefore, is an economics of decreasing cost (or increasing returns), but this will not be an economics of economies of scale, premised on the neoclassical production function. An analysis of economies of scale may be incorporated as a part of it, but this is an economics whose nucleus is an analysis of technological progress and its uncertainty. In the end, the greatest point of divergence will be whether one broadens the analytical framework into the world of uncertainty and sees technology as an expectation variable, or whether one regards it as a given that is quite unpredictable. Today, however, when R&D is organized and technology is diffused as if there were no borders, one could hardly adopt a theory that sees the evolving path of technology as unpredictable. At least the developing countries, which have the advanced countries as a precedent, must adopt an economics of decreasing cost, based on technological diffusion.

But we should be aware that in the developed countries too, following the Second World War, continuous technological progress (or the possibility of importing technology) was anticipated, and demand was also expected to increase rapidly and steadily. Many of the industries in the developed countries were in the stage of development, and their prospects were bright. The relative political stability under the Pax Americana greatly enhanced their prospects. The heavy and chemical industries—iron and steel, synthetic fibers, oil, petrochemicals, and automobiles—in Japan during the 1950s and 1960s are typical examples in which these conditions, both technological and demand, were satisfied. In these industries, the economies of scale in capital investment could clearly be seen, but beyond this, there can surely be no argument that constant technological innovation was the main driving force. The size of blast furnaces increased sharply, oxygen furnaces were widely adopted, continuous casting was perfected, new synthetic fibers appeared one after another, oil refineries increased in size and became petroleum plants incorporating all related processes, and the quality of cars visibly improved in many dimensions. As various aggregate data show unmistakably, the characteristic of the advanced economies in the postwar period has been a trend of decreasing cost, supported by continuous technological innovation. In the superindustrialization since the latter half of the 1970s, the main role has been taken over by the microelectronics industry, but technological innovation in this cutting-edge industry shows no sign of coming to an end as a new industry based on an unanticipated technology always seems to emerge to take the lead. Thus it appears that there will be no end to technological progress as a macroeconomic phenomenon or to the phase of decreasing cost. One can speculate about future trends, but even in the advanced countries the present age clearly needs an economics of decreasing cost.

EXCESS COMPETITION AND ADEQUATE COMPETITION

The preliminary attempt I have made thus far at an analysis of competition under economies of scale can also be applied in outline to a phase of decreasing cost that includes technological innovation. In this case too, market-share maximization is a firm's basic strategy. Each firm aware of the trend of technological innovation competes fiercely to improve capital equipment and attempts to maximize market share even at the cost of lower profit, or to make up for the loss that results from inevitable price-cutting competition. Incidentally, Japanese firms' seeming preoccupation with market-share maximization, which has often been criticized, is due to economic motivation (decreasing cost) and to a cultural characteristic of the Japanese. Until now, the situation has been similar to the two cases of restrictive supply exceeding demand and demand exceeding restrictive supply that were discussed in the above section on technical analysis. But from now on, going beyond such cases, competition to invent, import, and develop new technology will play an important role. As technological and investment competition are integrated, they may well become an effective weapon to prevent new entrants into the market. This kind of aggressive investment and technological competition is also possible among a number of existing companies and can develop into retaliatory responses. In this case, which firm takes the initiative—the question of timing—is decisively important.[23] However, the projection each firm makes of technological progress is largely subjective, and there is no guarantee that all the projections will be the same. Thus it is difficult to predict the response of other firms (the response function in Cournot's model is an example of this). The possibility that a game-theoretic, Nash-equilibrium-type coordination could be achieved under these conditions is even lower than in the case of a simple decline in long-run marginal cost with no technological innovation.

Thus, under dynamic competition, in a phase where technological progress of a predictable type is dominant, there is little likelihood of compromise or cooperation, and if efforts to achieve them are abandoned, there is a high probability of collusive oligopoly, or even monopoly. When firms go bankrupt in the process of this competition, much of the capital invested in them is wasted. The comparative statics of static equilibria have ignored the problem of the unemployment caused by bankruptcy, but in an industrialized world where there is no guarantee that such equilibria will ever be achieved, this position is untenable.

We should note that the theoretical myth of the survival of the fittest, which posits that the most productive firm wins the competition, does not necessarily apply in this dynamic competition. The argument that competition is equivalent to efficient resource allocation can be proved only under a static equilibrium. Under the dynamic competition with which we are dealing here, any firm can abandon (theoretical) profit-maximizing (the infinite output) and survive solely through skillful strategic maneuvering for market share (for example, in its timing of product releases or investment) or its ability to gain access to capital (for example, the strength of its connections to banks). In developing countries, a number of foreign firms have used substantial amounts of capital from their home countries to establish a monopolistic position. In postwar Japan many firms connected to the former *zaibatsu* grew successfully because they had ready access to capital. Again, there are large firms, supposedly the most technologically advanced, that lack cost consciousness. Thus competition under decreasing cost not only cannot guarantee that a stable equilibrium will be achieved but is inadequate as a mechanism for choosing efficient firms. I would like to call market competition under decreasing cost, thus characterized, "excess competition."[24]

The concept of excess competition is the antithesis of the concept of "adequate competition" or "appropriate competition." Accepted analysis has considered only the optimality of competition in terms of resource allocation in the final equilibrium state. This is an integral part of the idealized perfect competition model. In this case, the desirability of competition is judged only by the results achieved at a final state. In reality, however, there is a waste of resources at the final state and in the process leading to it. Generally speaking, the desirability of competition must be considered in at least two dimensions: the process and the final state (or many dimensions if one thinks of the process as divided into subperiods). If there is a trade-off in resource allocation between the process and the final state (improvement in one coming at the cost of decline in the other), then there will be a situation of adequate competition, at an intermediate point that is not biased toward only one of the two. This will be a dynamic phenomenon that does not conform to a static optimality, in the sense of the optimality of the final state as understood by the neoclassical school. Moreover, if there is no stable equilibrium, then there will be no final state, but the neoclassical ideal of competition relies completely on the stability of equilibrium. Generally speaking, it is necessary to go beyond the neoclassical framework and to see the concept of optimality in competition in the two dimensions of process and final state; this is especially true when there is no guarantee of a stable equilibrium. But even when the emphasis is placed on the process, as in this book, it is necessary to clearly understand what occurs in the final state. The above discussion has underscored the high likelihood of monopoly or collusive oligopoly in the final state.

ON MONOPOLY

It is rash, however, to conclude that monopoly is undesirable. Although the majority opinion has for a long time rejected monopoly and censured the injustice of "excessive profit,"[25] this opinion is for the most part based on an emotional argument. The critique of monopoly during the modern period first appeared to protest monopoly as political privilege created by absolute monarchy. Therefore it is inadequate as a critique of the phenomenon of monopolization since industrialization, produced in the midst of vigorous technological innovation. Note also that some arguments defend monopoly or say monopoly can be ignored because, if left alone, it will disappear.

Monopoly (or collusive oligopoly) is often discussed as if all monopolies are identical, but there is a great difference between monopoly in a period of semistagnation, when there is almost no technological progress, and monopoly in the midst of a ferment of technological progress. Joseph Schumpeter emphasized the distinction between these two and raised the debate on monopoly to a new level.[26] As he said, a firm that has developed a new technology is expected to earn a profit that somewhat exceeds the average level (for example, because of royalties from a patent). And the bankruptcy of a firm that has continued to use old technology in the midst of intense investment and technological competition performs a significant role in allocating resources more efficiently. The old-fashioned theory of excessive profit overlooks the significance of this process that Schumpeter called "creative destruction." One cannot criticize the trend to monopolization in dynamic competition on the basis of a theory of excessive profit.

However, there were some unclear points even in Schumpeter's view of the relationship of cause and effect. He was correct in pointing out that the process of creative destruction tended to generate monopolistic firms, but he created a misconception by suggesting that this process might not advance without monopolistic firms. On the latter point there is a great deal of room for argument.[27] Although it was not sufficiently clear in Schumpeter's time, contemporary technological progress is made mainly through competition among firms rather than by the inspired idea of a specific individual or firm. In this sense, the existence of a number of firms is indispensable for the process of creative destruction. Furthermore, given that every industry has a life-cycle, it will in time reach a saturation point for technological progress, and in due course the tendency of decreasing cost will disappear. At that time, the old-fashioned—and neoclassical—arguments against monopoly and collusive oligopoly will again become valid. But it will not then be easy to eliminate monopoly or collusive oligopoly, given the entrenched power base they have already created within society. Finally, but most important, for all kinds of competitive mechanisms—that is, not only for economic competition but also for technological and intellectual competition—a monopoly that prevents the emergence of what is new cannot be allowed. This is because monopoly, of whatever type, denies equal opportunity to all. As discussed in Chapter 1, equality of opportunity is one of the conditions of true liberalism.

On the other hand, the naive, supposedly empirically supported optimism, which maintains that monopoly will not last, is held more widely than one would expect. Even Marshall mainly had in mind a firm dominated by one individual and believed that as his entrepreneurial spirit declined, so would the firm, and that it was unlikely the children who followed him would be successful. That is, Marshall was little concerned with the undesirable effects of monopoly.[28] Milton Friedman, similarly unconcerned, also seems to have in mind an image of the same nineteenth-century firm. Since the beginning of the twentieth century, however, rather than an individual managing a firm, there has been an increasing tendency for the firm as an organization to employ managers, and recently, in particular, the managerial view has become increasingly long term. The firm has increasingly become a lasting corporate entity. Unlike in the nineteenth century, or even the first half of the twentieth, I believe firms from now on will show a tendency not to be linked to a specific individual manager but to seek their continued existence as an organization (see the second section of Chapter 9). If this view is correct, a firm, once it has achieved a monopoly or collusive oligopoly in a certain industry, will pursue a long-term strategy in order to maintain its position. From now on, once a firm has entered a phase of stagnation, it will be even more likely than it was in the nineteenth century to become outmoded. This is one paradox produced by the superindustrialization of the future, which seems as if it might put everything into flux.

The existence of monopoly is not simply an economic phenomenon but also a political phenomenon. Particularly in the present age of mass democracy, monopoly is a hotbed of political instability. For example, though it is easy to exaggerate, a typical pattern when industrialization fails in developing countries is for a monopolist or a small number of oligopolists to exert their power over the impoverished people. Until a certain period, in the Middle and Near East and in Latin America, there were frequent instances of a foreign firm's achieving a monopoly through its ability to obtain capital (particularly from its own country). In contrast to this, in the successful East Asian NIEs, there are almost no examples of a monopolistic national firm's (whether foreign or domestic) dominating an industry. If monopoly is established during the early stages of a country's industrialization, it may hinder the workings of the market economy and block the progress of developmental industrialization. More important, however, monopoly frequently invites inequality in income distribution; it thus becomes an object of political resentment and can even erode the minimum political unity necessary for a takeoff into industrialization. Politically, also, it is undesirable for competition under decreasing cost to lead to monopoly.

Here we can turn the usual understanding of monopoly completely around, as follows. If monopoly or collusive oligopoly is established as the final outcome of price-cutting competition, the actions taken to achieve it can be seen as something akin to domestic dumping, exploiting a time lag. As is well known, international dumping that exploits a lag in the stage of growth between two economies and monopolies or oligopolistic cartels within the exporting country is often criticized. All nations pay close attention to international dumping, but domestic dumping, which exploits a difference in the situation at different times, is not usually recognized because its negative effects appear only after a time lag. However, both seek excessive profit and exploit the difference between a competitive market and a monopolistic market and eliminate competitors to establish a monopoly in the end. If we protect the firms in the nation subjected to international dumping, then surely we should also protect competing firms in the industries with decreasing costs that suffer from domestic dumping. In order to prevent domestic dumping, there is a need to guarantee in advance the survival of a number of firms in order to ensure the continued existence of a competitive market after the end of the phase of decreasing cost. This is to say that we must come up with a policy that can restrain excessive competition. Of course it is not absolutely certain that excessive competition will bring about monopoly or collusive oligopoly. But in reality, even normal antitrust regulations, in prohibiting some mergers and ordering divestitures, in some cases are preventive measures often founded on a similarly arguable judgment. Government intervention to restrain excessive competition is the equivalent of preventive antitrust measures.

A RECONSIDERATION OF MARSHALL'S PROBLEM: LONG-TERM AND SHORT-TERM DECISIONS

In the above sketch of an economics of decreasing cost, I emphasized that price, investment, and technological competition all intensify, and it is highly probable that in this process a monopoly will be established. Here, though, let us recall once more "Marshall's problem." If decreasing cost is from the first an extremely common phenomenon, then in the advanced countries with a long history of capitalism we should expect the repeated appearance of monopoly or collusive oligopoly and the suicide of the market economy. Why is it, then, that this has not always been the case? Our economics of decreasing cost must also be able to answer this puzzle of competition under increasing returns, known as Marshall's problem.

The easiest solution is the explanation that posits that the instability inherent in the market economy is restrained politically, or rather socially. Very broadly speaking, the force of human habit and the inertia of institutions keep the instability of capitalism within certain limits. By and large, during the period after the 1930s when the memory of the Great Depression had not yet disappeared, arguments pointing out the instability of capitalism and denouncing the evils of monopoly were made widely, and interest grew in social systems that would be able to correct these deficiencies. Anticapitalist political parties were formed and grew in strength, and in the United States antitrust laws were enacted. Joseph Steindl, for example, believed that systematic factors relating to technology, the market, and currency were suppressing perfect monopoly.[29] Keynes too clearly saw the "stickiness" of price and wage as indispensable stabilizing factors.

One can see so-called Keynesian policy as an attempt to rectify the deficiencies this stickiness caused. Generally, politics and the economy intervened in each other's spheres more strongly than expected and this was why capitalism stabilized. But it is going too far to believe that the solution for economic instability can be entrusted entirely to the working of noneconomic factors. Certainly politics must intervene in catastrophic circumstances such as the Great Depression or dire resource shortages. At least in the nations of economic liberalism (such as Britain and the United States at the height of their prosperity), one does not observe intervention of noneconomic forces, for example, in the activities of industries. The view that economies can be stabilized by the social system outside the economy is no less ideological than classical economic liberalism, which holds that the economy is self-regulating. What occurs in reality is that, before the political and social system begins to work, some specific stabilizing mechanisms—not market forces themselves but those closely connected to them—are already at work. It is facile to try to solve Marshall's problem with noneconomic factors.

An attempt to reach a policy solution that relies on economics is the already-mentioned solution of Robinson and Chamberlin using product discrimination. They believed that in general there were dominant monopolies in individual discriminated markets, but that there were direct (for Chamberlin) or indirect (for Robinson) substitutes for the products of these discriminated markets; thus there existed effective crossmarket competition. However, rather strong conditions must be met for this equilibrium to be maintained. And their solutions did not provide an answer for the problem of intermediate goods (as in the heavy and chemical industries of postwar Japan, which had many markets in which competition existed among similar, nondiscriminated products). Another solution involves Marshall's distinction between external and internal economies. If the trend of decreasing cost is mainly attributable to external economies, this is because a firm's actions do not necessarily lead to instability in the market or the dominance of a monopoly. Recently, however, "external dis-economies," such as pollution, have become a problem, and at present "external economies" do not seem strong enough to overwhelm "internal economies."

But what other explanations are possible? One I would like to put forward here is the short-term character of decision making in businesses. Marshall thought in terms of a distinction between external and internal economies, but in place of this let us think of a distinction between short-term decision making and long-term decision making. Firms that make decisions based on a short-term view—except for investment decisions—will set prices as equal to short-run marginal cost. As explained above, one can say that the short-run marginal cost function (in the short term, the same as the cost path) usually rises. Thus, the more firms conduct their business with a short-term view, the more stable the market will be in the short term (or will be believed to be stable). But this shortsightedness will naturally reveal itself as long-term inefficiency, and soon there will be failures (recession or the decline of an industry). Even so, as long as many people think in the short term, these failures too will be seen as unexpected, unfortunate happenstances or as the outcomes of the dynamic of the economic process following a chain of short-term equilibria. (This interpretation corresponds precisely to neoclassical comparative statics.) In Western countries and typically in the United States, prewar management traditions linger, and it seems that many firms' decisions are made from a short-term perspective. This fact undoubtedly contributes to maintaining competitive markets.

Since the Second World War, however, in various dimensions of firm activities the trend toward adopting long-term perspectives in economic decision making has been observed. Technological innovation has largely changed from creative to applied, thus becoming more predictable. Forecasts often use macroeconomic models, and Keynesian policies are employed to reduce short- and mid-term economic fluctuations. One could say that the validity of Keynesian theory rests on an agreement that a situation of decreasing cost exists (due to surplus capital investment). More and more management decisions on firm investment and employment are also being made from a long-term perspective fundamentally because technological innovation and demand trends have become easier to forecast since the end of the Second World War.

No less important are the effects of the trend toward the organizational development of firms as long-lasting entities in which ownership and management are separated. Edith Penrose's theory of the development of the firm and Robin Marris's "managerial capitalism" reflect this trend.[30] The importance of the human capital within a firm is now widely recognized, as is readily seen in firms' increased interest in training their employees and then in retaining them. Given the experience of the developed countries, the importance of a long-term perspective for both firms and government has become evident for the developing countries. For example, the appearance of this trend calls global attention to the long-term Japanese management strategy, which is based on permanent employment and on-the-job training. Thus, since the Second World War, decreasing cost and the adoption of a long-term perspective in decision making have occurred in tandem. In terms of this book's analysis, however, this means excessive competition and the danger of monopolization. In its formative period, Japanese management avoided any worsening of excess competition through administrative intervention made in the name of industrial policy. Generally speaking, though, we are probably being confronted with the paradox of market competition's becoming unstable with the global spread of a long-term perspective in decision making.

Clearly the developing economies and the postwar Japanese economy are not the only economies of decreasing cost. A recent example of competition that has had a powerful international impact is in RAM (random access memory) semiconductors, which presents features not seen before. This competition is based on the trend toward a huge increase in memory capacity that is virtually predictable, and so the decrease in cost is extremely rapid. Competition in technological development, strategy in the timing of investments, and ability to obtain capital are frequently matters of life and death. This intense competition has the potential to create a huge international monopoly or collusive oligopoly. Of course, the problem may be solved naturally to some extent because firms manufacturing semiconductors attempt to engage in product discrimination, as seen in the case of U.S. semiconductor manufacturers who seem to have adopted the strategy of surviving by specializing in specific products. In contrast, Japanese manufacturers are intent on increasing memory capacity, and one can imagine the possibility of the Japanese manufacturers oligopolistically dominating the world market.

Thus, in the case of semiconductors, it is highly likely that there will be a need for a policy solution of international "administrative intervention," and this seemed to be an element of the U.S.-Japanese negotiations on structural impediments. The United States has frequently intervened in international semiconductor competition and protected its own semiconductor manufacturers on grounds of national security. Japanese manufacturers too have shown a willingness to agree to international cooperation. The present situation is still confused, but it may be that the curtain is rising on an age of borderless industrial policy. If this is the case, seeing the U.S.-Japanese Market-Oriented Sector-Specific (MOSS) talks as merely a collision of national interests may be too narrow a perspective.

The trend of decreasing cost is at present most clearly apparent in the developing countries. These nations are pursuing their long-term objective of takeoff into industrialization. In the past, there were no models to emulate, however, other than the general short-term view of capitalism of the developed countries in the West, where the mechanism for restoring order was recession. This is why the developing countries have been repeating the cycle of growth and recession. Ultimately, though, the developing countries do not have the strength to endure recession as a mechanism for regaining momentum for growth. There are many such examples in Latin America. But if they are determined to follow the development example of the developed countries, it is evident which industries they must promote and which technologies they must import. Since the Second World War, it has been particularly easy to predict the future trends of technological progress and the world market, whether at the firm or national level, and conditions have existed for developing countries to adopt a long-term view of capitalism. This long-term view could exploit the advantage of decreasing cost to achieve high economic growth. However, those countries or industries that consciously adopt this long-term view will confront the latent instability of the market, will be embroiled in excessive competition, and, if they close their domestic markets, they will confront the problem of monopolization. These are the reasons that many NIEs rely on administrative intervention. This is none other than developmentalism, in the sense that I have defined it.

Up to now, two theories have coexisted as to where monopoly can easily develop: the neoclassical theory warning that stagnant industries are the most likely candidates, and Schumpeter's theory identifying industries that are adopting new technologies. Each theory reflected its respective interests: the results of competition (the theory of equilibrium) and the process of competition (the theory of creative destruction). We must give priority to our concern about the development of monopoly in those industries or periods in which there could easily be decreasing costs rather than to stagnant industries. In other words, we must shift our priority from the results of competition to the process of competition. It becomes necessary to identify the industries or periods faced with decreasing cost (that is, the principal industries) and to adopt measures to maintain competition. In order to do this, the government (or an international agreement) must intervene or provide guidance in order to prevent the emergence of monopoly or collusive oligopoly and to maintain what one might call a state of "polipoly."[31] This is the main goal of what we know as industrial policy. Industrial policy may at times resemble short-term regulatory policy, but its true character, seen in the long term, is a policy for maintaining competition. The common belief that competition would be maintained only if government intervention were removed is not a universal truth. Under the two conditions of decreasing cost and long-term perspective in economic decision making, administrative intervention is necessary to maintain competition. But if either of these conditions is missing, administrative intervention will cause harm. Further, the way the political system operates holds the key to administrative intervention. One can expect various problems because of the working of the social system as a whole, one of which is friction with the concept of liberalism. I return later to this last problem.

The various economic theories of the past dealt with the phenomenon of decreasing cost. The classical and Marxist schools did not recognize technological progress or decreasing cost. Thus their understanding of the fundamental impact of the industrial revolution at best provided only an economics of the capitalism they saw. In contrast, among those who initiated the "marginal revolution," Marshall at least came to grips with the reality of industrialization and tried to create an economics of industrialization. In this sense it is extraordinary that the neoclassical school, which was generated from the marginal revolution, for some reason regarded the case of decreasing cost as an exception and returned to the classical model of capitalism. (The reason for this must be understood as a problem in the sociology of knowledge, but I will not go into that here.) Clearly the mainstream of economics until now has been an economics of capitalism, not an economics of industrialization. In other words, economists have talked of the economy as if it were fully developed (thus, as if the likelihood of observing increasing cost is high).

The full development of an economy is only one phase of industrialization. Industrialization is surely a whole life-cycle in which various industries are born, pass through infancy, broaden their activities in their youth and adulthood, and eventually reach old age. If this is the case, the period of infant industry (a period of decreasing cost) is a phase through which every industry must pass. In particular, when developing countries try to catch up with developed countries and import a technology for large-scale production, they operate under a condition of decreasing cost. At least for developing countries, infant industry is not the exception but the rule. If we continue to deal with infant industry as an exception, a consistent analysis of the industrial life-cycle will be impossible. This is true not only of developing countries. Industrialization as a whole, as mentioned in Chapter 1, is an expression of anthropocentrism vis-à-vis nature, and cannot develop indefinitely.

We cannot know whether in the twenty-first century the world as a whole will be in a stage of young or mature adulthood or of old age (or at least in this book I do not go into this question beyond those reflections I offer in Chapter 9). But we clearly see today many economies around the world one after another attempting to reach adolescence. In order to deal with this development, there must be a political economy of industrialization in the true sense. From this perspective, the analysis in this chapter is extremely inadequate in that it has not made a methodological breakthrough. However, I would like to believe that I have shown that economics to this point has been the owl of Minerva for capitalism—but not for industrialization.

CHAPTER 6

Developmentalism as a System

Industrial Policy

The purpose of this chapter is to describe developmentalism as an integrated system. Let me start by discussing, on the basis of the economic argument of the previous chapter, how the government should intervene when long-term decision making is dominant in the industries faced with decreasing cost. Such intervention, called industrial policy, is defined in terms of individual industries as follows (the position occupied by industrial policy in the political economy as a whole is discussed in the second section):

> Industrial policy attempts to realize the advantages of decreasing cost. Its objective is to maintain competition appropriate for industries faced with decreasing cost. Without such a policy, these industries would be unable to realize their latent potential for growth.

There are various ways of understanding industrial policy, and many interpret it as a policy that increases an industry's growth rate through forcible, government intervention.[1] Some even think of it as nothing more than passive economic planning that indicates the wishes of the government. If industrial policy were a means of implementing economic planning, it would not need to be discussed. But as is clear from the argument already presented, when cost is decreasing, it is difficult to maintain market competition and some kind of government intervention becomes necessary. This need, clearly stated in the above definition, is particularly acute in developing countries that are attempting to catch up with the advanced countries. In this sense, industrial policy provides the central policy instrument of developmentalism.

As discussed in the previous chapter, the significance of competition is not merely in allocating resources efficiently within a static framework. In both market and planned economies, if the people who work in them play their parts as they ideally should, static efficiency in resource allocation can be achieved. Thus, in principle, neither economy is superior or inferior to the other on this point. In promoting industrialization, the advantage of a market economy, absent in a planned economy, is that it is a powerful system providing firms with incentives to reduce costs, increase product quality, and make technological and organizational innovation.

The most important direct cause for the collapse of Soviet-style socialism (the indirect cause was the repression of freedom of thought) was that the direction given by the bureaucracy did little to motivate people to exert themselves or to innovate. Market economies are no different, in that government intervention in itself does not have the ability to strengthen a firm's motivation to grow. The motivation to do everything possible within the limits imposed by an increasing cost curve and then to shift that curve downward (through technological innovation or improvement) is generated by the desire for profit. Even if production or capital investment is increased for a period because of subsidies, protectionist policy, or a policy to stimulate investment, the original situation will resume once those policies are suspended.

The case of decreasing cost is similar, but the motivation is much stronger. A firm's desire to grow is strengthened by the opportunity to decrease its costs, and not by government intervention. In some cases subsidies and protectionism make sense, but these are merely the first push to provide momentum. The main role of government intervention in cases of decreasing cost is to control the desire for excessive expansion. When the failure of Soviet-style socialism and the success of industrial policy in Japan (and East Asia) are compared, it is not difficult to see that the substance of industrial policy is competition that is not found in economic planning. And competition strengthens the incentives for growth. This is the lesson of the half century since the Second World War. Industrial policy seeks to maintain a competitive environment in those industries that already have a latent potential for growth (in decreasing cost); in other words, it seeks to sustain the motivational force of competition. Unless administered in this spirit, industrial policy will degenerate into an incomplete version of economic planning. In its basic concept, industrial policy must be antieconomic planning. This fact is usually not well understood.

The first to adopt this policy consistently was probably Japan after the Second World War. It is doubtful whether the Japanese authorities concerned with policy during the postwar decades were fully aware that their policy was antieconomic planning in character. But it is certain that they were trying to produce Japanese firms capable of competing internationally, and in this sense there is no doubt they were thinking of a market economy. For example, they were consistently opposed to management of firms by the government. With the miraculous (for that period) development of the postwar Japanese economy, this kind of government intervention became well known around the world. The widespread use of the term industrial policy was also due to this Japanese postwar success.

The definition of industrial policy I am attempting here, though, goes beyond a description of the Japanese experience. Japanese-style industrial policy included much unnecessary government intervention, and the specific character of the Japanese experience seems to have prevented a satisfactory theory of industrial policy from being advanced. Here I will try to define the substance of industrial policy in its minimum form, having removed the extraneous elements peculiar to Japan.

The aim of industrial policy is to restrain excessive competition, or to sustain sufficient competition. This does not mean that its substance is unidirectional, but that it seeks to strike a balance between the two requirements of minimizing the costs of bankruptcy or unemployment during the competitive process, and not weakening the motivational power of competition. To fulfill the latter requirement, equal opportunities for individual firms (including potential entrants)—a condition that would be violated by monopoly—are needed most, and in this sense intervention that differs by firm is undesirable. Thus, as a means of intervention, regulating price equally for all firms is clearly preferable to allotting specific quotas to individual firms. Keeping this point in mind, one can define industrial policy as consisting of the following four policy instruments, focusing on regulation of price. By also describing additional instruments, which preferably should not be used, let me sketch the outlines of industrial policy.

POLICIES THAT ARE FUNDAMENTALLY NECESSARY

1. *Designation of priority industries.* By evaluating the future of technology and demand, the government designates particular industries facing situations of decreasing cost as promising industries. This is "targeting," and below I call it the designation of priority industries. Industrial policy should be distinguished from macroeconomic policy in that it targets specific industries.

2. *Industry-specific indicative planning.* Important information is to be shared among all firms. The government makes known to all firms in an industry the standard forecasts, technological predictions, and macroeconomic findings that are relevant to the industry and ensures that firms receive the same forecasts. If firms had differing forecasts, each would respond differently to regulated prices, thus making it difficult to maintain uniform rules relating to prices. In other words, industry-specific indica-

tive planning, or educative planning, is necessary. Designation of priority industries—(1) above—can also broadly be thought of as a part of indicative planning.

3. *Policies to promote technological progress.* The government promotes the import and development of technology and so maintains a situation of decreasing cost. The international diffusion of technology does not always progress smoothly if left to market forces. Specific examples of such promotion include subsidies for research and development (government contracts frequently play a role as subsidies), a tax system that favors research expenditures, and the organization of R&D associations. Unless technological progress is maintained through the import and development of technology, industries on their own have difficulty remaining in the international competition waged by firms making constant technological progress. Without government aid to promote and import technology, developing countries cannot take off into industrialization.

4. *Regulation of excessive price competition.* In order to restrict excessive price-cutting competition, the government authorizes price cartels. As noted earlier, these cartels regulate domestic dumping; when exports are involved they restrict cheap exports. One guideline to be followed in regulating prices might be the restrictive price strategy discussed above. This strategy reduces prices by enabling firms to follow the average cost path and also keeps firms' profit rates below a certain level (profit here is the balance left after paying the rental cost of capital). A restrictive quantity strategy might achieve the same results by setting quotas, but the undesirability of this strategy has already been discussed.

I think these four options are the indispensable components of industrial policy. In other words, the indicative planning of (1) and (2), the promotion of technological progress in (3), and the government-authorized cartels for restricting excessive competition in (4) compose the basic framework of industrial policy. But are there other policies one should add? For example, the five frequently debated policies below (5–9), surely are at least worth examining. Protectionist policies and the policy of subsidies (5 and 6), in particular, have been a topic of debate since mercantilism in the seventeenth century. To anticipate my own conclusion, however, the policies that follow are at best no more than supplementary policy options.

SUPPLEMENTARY POLICIES THAT MAY BE NECESSARY

5. *Protectionist policies.* Unless foreign firms engage in dumping specifically aimed at the economy pursuing developmental policy, there is no need to exclude products from its market on the grounds that they are foreign. However, it is necessary for foreign suppliers of products also to participate in the restrictive price coordination mentioned in (4); their compliance with the schedule for lowering prices must be requested. Foreign firms, though, may not comply with such a request, and in this case the imposition of protective tariffs should be recognized as an unavoidable

policy instrument. A policy to limit the quantity of imports is undesirable for the reasons already discussed.

6. *A policy of subsidies.* Subsidies could take various forms, such as price subsidies for manufactured goods or subsidies for factors of production (a favorable financial policy would be part of this). Favorable tax measures are also a kind of subsidy, and depending on how the tax is levied they become a subsidy for finished products, a subsidy for investment, or a lump-sum subsidy. A lump-sum subsidy is impossible to implement because the amount cannot be calculated given that the final competitive equilibrium is uncertain. A subsidy for finished products (or for factors of production) has the same effect as raising the demand function (or lowering the average cost path), and thus increases profits. This could be applied in cases where profit is always negative because of inadequate demand (what in the previous chapter I called cases where restrictive coordination is impossible). Strict guidelines would be set on restrictive coordination to enable firms to earn limited but sufficient profits to change a situation in which restrictive coordination is impossible to one in which restrictive coordination is unstable. Thus some cases may call for a policy of subsidies, but usually it is unnecessary. Export subsidies are relatively disadvantageous to the domestic market and are a mixture of a balance-of-payments policy (acquiring foreign currency) and industrial policy. Such a policy may occasionally be necessary from the viewpoint of the balance of payments.

POLICIES THAT ARE UNNECESSARY AND/OR UNWISE

7. *Regulation of investment competition.* Theoretically, if restrictive coordination of prices effectively controls the profit rate, there should be no need for coordination of investment. In other words, the danger of bankruptcies due to simultaneous excessive investment arises when price-cutting competition is not restrained. Thus, as long as such restraints are effective, increasing investment should have a positive effect (lowering the average cost path and thus allowing industries to escape from a situation where restraint is impossible). In practice, there are no methods of regulating investment other than allocating investment to each firm in the industry; but as already mentioned, quotas are undesirable. In particular, because allocating investment has a long-term influence on a firm, it weakens a firm's incentives as an autonomous actor and makes it difficult to end industrial policy. Regulation of investment should be avoided.

8. *Regulation of the financial sector.* John Zysman sees regulation of the financial sector as an indispensable part of industrial policy.[2] Actual methods could include guidance on interest rates (on deposits and loans), the issuance of stocks and bonds, and bank lending. As is discussed in Chapter 9, the financial sector is a unique industry in that it is difficult to formulate a policy on the basis of whether returns are decreasing or increasing; that is, there is no adequate basis for designating the financial sector itself as an object of industrial policy. Regulation of the financial

sector might make sense as an instrument of macroeconomic policy, but as industrial policy, it is an indirect means of forcing firms to comply with guidance, or a kind of threat. As Zysman says, it is an extremely powerful instrument, but it is not indispensable, and there is a danger that it may compromise firms' independence. It has the side effect of strengthening the ties between the financial sector and industry, making it difficult to end industrial policy. Also, it is difficult to regulate the financial sector in an economy that relies on the import of foreign capital.

9. *Regulation of entrants into an industry.* In postwar Japan, administrative guidance was used to a significant extent to regulate new entrants to an industry being promoted by industrial policy. (In particular, the entrance of foreign firms was strictly regulated by law.) Entry restriction creates closed groups, which may be useful for the ministry responsible for guiding firms. Theoretically, however, it makes no sense, since the number of participants in an industry does not fundamentally change the nature of the problem. The authorities in postwar Japan frequently attempted to regulate the number of firms in view of what they judged as the optimum scale of production, but technological innovation and rapid increase in demand are always changing the predicted optimum scale of those industries faced with decreasing cost. That is, there is no sense in limiting entrants. Moreover, regulation of entrants is also fundamentally anticompetitive and thus contradicts the original goal of industrial policy. The same applies to regulation of the entrance of foreign firms. However, when there is a distinct danger that foreign firms will contravene an agreement of restrictive price coordination, regulation may be needed (such as making joint partnership with a domestic firm a condition of foreign firms' participation in the market). Such a policy, however, is a type of protectionism.

One thinks often of industrial policy as protectionist measures such as subsidies, import restrictions, and tariffs, and in many cases a policy of export promotion is implemented in the name of industrial policy. However, in terms of the original goal of industrial policy—to realize the economic benefits of decreasing cost—protectionist policy or a policy of subsidies is not, theoretically, at its core. These are nothing more than effective second-order instruments depending on time and place, and as such, even when they are used, they should be discontinued as quickly as possible. The attempt to allocate investment, the regulation of the financial sector, and the regulation of entrants into an industry that characterized the postwar Japanese economy are surely extraneous to the essence of industrial policy.

The emergence of these extraneous elements did, however, have its reasons. As already noted, it is difficult to legislate intervention in the economy, and when industrial policy requires restrictive price coordination it is difficult to prevent violations. In postwar Japan, no strong laws were enacted to support intervention, and no explicit penalty was imposed against violations. Instead, measures targeted at individual industries—

such as import quotas (there were many during the 1945–60 period), investment allocation, so-called window guidance in the financial market, licensing of entrants into an industry, and (small) subsidies—acted as carrots to protect the system of coordination in the industry as a whole. (We should note that this system could also punish an industry by withholding the carrot.) This was the substance of the well-known Japanese administrative guidance, and it was difficult for the industry-specific nature of these measures to coexist with the impartiality of the authorities concerned.

Clearly the Japanese methods are not the only ones possible. Although there might have been political difficulties, it might have been possible to regulate cartels to prevent excessive competition, to promote technological innovations, and to prohibit the extraneous policy instruments noted above. Thus industrial policy as here defined, though making reference to the Japanese experience, is only an ideal, made on the basis of the analysis of excessive competition presented earlier. The essence of this ideal pattern is (1) indicative planning for each priority industry, (2) promotion of technological progress, and (3) restraining excessive competition in price and investment; the combination of these is the core that maintains a system of compartmentalized competition in each priority industry.[3]

A Policy Framework for Developmentalism

Industrial policy provides the basis for the developmentalism defined in the opening paragraphs of the previous chapter, but originally it was an economic policy for fostering individual industries; thus, seen in terms of the developmentalism that is the basic strategy for a whole country, it can be only a supporting pillar. Supplemental policies are necessary for developmentalism if industrial policy is to serve the economy as a whole, and these in turn need the support of various institutions and practices. One could even include the country's culture and system of values among these institutions and practices. The economy, politics, and culture are to some extent each independent, and they also overlap in various ways. Thus there can be no such thing as a fixed model of developmentalism, but it may be possible to provide a sketch of its essential characteristics. Here I call this a prototype for developmentalism. Let us begin by noting its essential elements.

    1. Its guiding principle is market competition based on a system of private property (capitalism).

    2. The government implements industrial policy. (In other words, it aims to foster promising new industries with decreasing marginal costs, and to guide the prices of the products of these industries as an arbitrator and mediator. The policy includes promotion of the import and development of technology.)

    3. Export-oriented manufacturing industries are included among the promising new industries.

4. Much importance is attached to fostering small firms.

5. Equality of distribution of income and domestic demand centered on mass consumption are sought.

6. As a means of promoting equality of income distribution, it undertakes measures to achieve equal distribution of agricultural land.

7. It provides a comprehensive educational system, at least through secondary education.[4]

8. It creates a fair and competent modern bureaucracy (unaffected by nepotism).

Industrial policy prevents what one might call excessive disparities (such as frequent bankruptcies and the rise of monopolies) from arising within the priority industries. But the development of those priority industries may well bring about disparities between them and other industries and generate a problem for the economy as a whole (and political discontent caused by frequent bankruptcies and unemployment in the other industries). These problems will likely become more serious than they would have if an industrial policy had not been implemented. Thus, a policy to distribute income in a way that eases these disparities is necessary. As I argue below, without such a policy, industrial policy will probably always fail. Industrial policy and distributive policy must be seen as one. Finally, mechanisms are required to set up and implement these policies according to the foreign and domestic environment of the country. The above prototype of developmentalism is a way of putting these together.

For convenience I divide the eight essential elements of developmentalism into three parts: industrial policy in the narrow sense (1–4), distributive policy (5 and 6), and intangible social infrastructure (7 and 8). As I note below, the classification is not a rigorous one. For example, the policy for small firms (4) also has an aspect of distributive policy. In addition, the public goods normally required by an industrialized state (a legal system, national defense, public utilities, and so on) are also necessary. Below I elaborate on each of these eight essential elements of developmentalism.

1. *The principle of capitalism.* Among the fundamental public goods are the system of private property and the principle of market competition. In other words, the prototype of developmentalism is a kind of capitalism. It is a characteristic of capitalism to provide maximum economic freedom to enable individuals to increase their income, or not to constrain their pecuniary incentives. Developmentalism shares this characteristic and should be clearly distinguished from economic planning, in that it relies fundamentally on the entrepreneurial spirit and energy of *homo economicus.*

2. *Industrial policy.* However, this prototype is not optimistic, as is classical economic liberalism, about the "self-regulating" ability of market competition, or what would now be called the stability of the market equilibrium.[5] As I pointed out above, there are economies of scale in industrialization, and technological innovation is very rapid; thus effec-

tive marginal cost (the cost path) will decrease, the market equilibrium will become unstable, and a high possibility of excessive competition will emerge. Industrial policy endeavors to take maximum advantage of the strengths (while rectifying the shortcomings) of capitalism, which continues to progress aided by steady industrialization. Industrial policy is effective only vis-à-vis promising industries in a phase of decreasing cost. Thus the key of industrial policy is to limit its application to industries with promising technological and demand possibilities, or in other words, to undertake targeting. For example, the Ministry of International Trade and Industry (hereafter, MITI) in postwar Japan used two criteria in its industrial policy: rising productivity and income elasticity.[6]

Generally, however, it is not easy to identify the industries that are promising. In fact, since the age of mercantilism in the seventeenth century, governments have made numerous mistakes in choosing which industries to foster. Following the Second World War, the industrial policy (at least until about the 1970s) of many countries in Latin America (dependent on primary industries such as oil, copper, silver, sugar, coffee, cotton, and rubber) helped to achieve import substitution only in manufacturing industries. This is perhaps an example of the mistake of choosing industries based on the criterion of static comparative advantage, which does not give serious consideration to the dynamics of technology or demand. From the perspective of developmentalism, this was the wrong choice.

After the Second World War it became comparatively easy to identify the promising industries. Until about the middle of the 1970s, it is beyond dispute that technological innovations consisted not of creative breakthroughs but of realizing the gains of large-scale production and systematization, and most of this was being done in the U.S. economy. Demand continued to rise in response to the increased output.[7] Thus it was not difficult for a developing country to choose and imitate technology and to predict demand. It is also largely due to these historical circumstances that postwar Japan and the East Asian NIEs were successful in establishing priority industries.

The difficulty with industrial policy, though, is not so much in designating priority industries as in revoking this designation—that is, in having an effective "sunset" provision in the policy. When technological innovation comes to the end of a cycle and the rate of increase in product demand decelerates, the period of decreasing cost comes to an end. At this point industrial policy no longer has a raison d'être. Once established, however, the relationship between industry and government becomes difficult to terminate; thus industrial policy continues, becoming nothing more than protectionism, and maybe even hampering the development of a competitive environment in the economy as a whole. The greatest danger of industrial policy is this inertia in the relationship between industry and bureaucracy. I return to this topic below.

3. *Export promotion policy*. This policy consists of designating indus-

tries that are qualified as export industries and can also be seen as a kind of targeting, but it contains the following unique problems. First, for almost any country it is impossible to imagine industrialization without export industries. A trade surplus is necessary in order for the country to import the resources it lacks (energy resources and food are often mentioned as examples) and/or to make interest payments on or to repay the capital inflows from other countries. For example, the third criterion used by MITI to designate priority industries was the trade account criterion—that is, the industry had to be able to generate a trade surplus. Without an increase in exports, the limits on a country's ability to import would make it impossible for economic growth to continue. In this sense, some kind of promotion of export industries is all but a necessary condition for developmentalism. In other words, among priority industries in the broad sense, there must be industries that have the ability to export.

Second, the criterion of this ability to export must basically be the same as that for industry in general. In the classical theory of comparative advantage since David Ricardo, it was believed that the uneven distribution of natural resources generated the flows of exports and imports. This theory—the so-called staple theory, which posits that a country that enjoys a unique climate will export the agricultural products appropriate to it, and that a country that happens to possess underground mineral resources should export, for example, oil or copper—still has influence today. But in a world where technological innovation is constant and patterns of consumption are continuously changing, the effects of decreasing cost and changes in demand overwhelm any comparative advantage based on natural resources. When the effects of decreasing cost are substantial, there is no reason to give particular attention to the exports of industries that are natural-resource intensive or to consider industries that produce only for the domestic market.

In other words, a policy that promotes the export of primary products and import substitution at the same time is often inappropriate as a long-term policy. For example, the difference in the recent progress in industrialization between Latin America and the East Asian NIEs seems to have arisen from the fact that the former have tended to emphasize such a targeting strategy while the latter have focused their energies on exporting manufactured products. In short, there is no need to create a special standard for exporting industries—except when an industry might cause a large trade deficit through indirect spillover effects.

4. *A policy of fostering small and medium-sized firms.* In a sense, fostering small and medium-sized firms is also targeting. This is because the phenomenon of decreasing cost in individual small and medium-sized firms can also be promoted by fostering economies of scale in their production and/or by nurturing their abilities to innovate. (Some argue that small and medium-sized firms have greater abilities to make technologi-

cal innovation than do large firms, but my argument does not rely on this assertion.)

From the first, industrial policy recognizes, and helps increase, the difference between priority industries and nonpriority industries. This is what one might call the dark side of industrial policy, and it naturally includes the problem of differentials in the wages and incomes of those involved in the two kinds of industry, but no less important is the problem of technological disparities. (The question of income distribution is dealt with in the following section.) Technological disparities may well generate differences in the breadth of scientific knowledge, the ability to adapt technology, and product quality. As a result, they may isolate from each other what we might call the cutting-edge industries, which have been given a priority designation, and what we might call the stagnant industries outside these. A way of seeing this disparity mainly from an economic perspective is as a dual economy between the modern and traditional sectors, which is always discussed in relation to the question of developing countries. We must not, however, forget that the two sectors operate in fundamentally different technological modes. A dual economy brings about a division in patterns of behavior and a confrontation between modern and traditional values, and there is a danger that it may generate political problems. It may even spawn what we would have to call a dual culture.

There are various dimensions to the confrontation between cutting-edge industries and stagnant industries. The confrontation between manufacturing industry and agriculture is sometimes accepted as the most serious problem, although the confrontation between large companies and small and medium-sized firms is also important. Let us take as a typical example the confrontation within manufacturing between large companies and small and medium-sized firms.

Of course even cutting-edge industries need services and peripheral parts that do not require particularly advanced technologies. But the requirements the cutting-edge industry makes of the parts industry, in relation to methods, quality, and delivery dates, will probably change and become ever stricter with technological innovation. Unless suppliers of services and parts can meet these requirements, the cutting-edge industry will have no choice but to supply all the parts and services in-house. That is, the vertical integration of all related industries would become inevitable. However, for the cutting-edge industry to integrate all the peripheral industries would be, first, a substantial waste of resources. It would be more desirable for a group of small firms to respond to the requirements of various industries, acting as a basic resource for the whole economy. The growing technological and managerial abilities possessed by such a group would vary for the different cutting-edge industries. The concept of external economies could include the development of related small and medium-sized firms. The development of a small-scale parts industry could provide external economies to cutting-edge industries and, by raising the technological standard of the economy as a whole, sustain the situation of decreasing cost faced by the cutting-edge industries. Even cutting-edge industries do not exist in isolation. These changes would solve the problem of what I have called technological disparities, and they are the key to avoiding the creation of a dual culture. This problem, more than the problem of resource allocation, will be critical in determining the success of developmentalism.

The question of the dual structure has also been much discussed in postwar Japan. The government has consistently adopted a policy of protecting small and medium-sized firms, and many large firms have developed flexible, informal, cooperative vertical relationships, known as the subcontractor system. As a result, Japan has the greatest proportion of small and medium-sized firms among the advanced industrialized countries. Japan's policy of protecting these firms has, perhaps unintentionally, played a significant role in supplementing industrial policy. When East Asia (Korea, Taiwan, Hong Kong, and other nations) and Latin America are compared, the strength of the small and medium-sized firms in the former is often noted. To return to Alfred Marshall's terms, a policy fostering small and medium-sized firms, even under the present situation where internal economies tend to occur independently, will support external economies and help maintain the balance of the social infrastructure. In this sense this policy has points in common with developmentalism's elements of education (7) and the bureaucratic system (8).

There are by-products in fostering small firms. Small firms provide a place from which highly motivated and creative individual entrepreneurs can start out. Sometimes small firms transform themselves into the most energetic large companies. There are countless examples of such transformation in the United States, beginning with the automobile company of Henry Ford. In Japan too, Matsushita Electric, Sony, and Honda were initially very small factories. Countries eagerly pursuing developmentalism tend to make the mistake of concentrating their efforts solely on the large, cutting-edge firms, with the inevitable result that these firms must either develop in-house parts industries or import parts. This means that developmentalism soon ends in failure for lack of the growth of supporting industries. The most instructive example is the difficulty faced by planned economies in developing small firms. An important reason for this difficulty is the increase in the tasks that a bureaucracy in a planned economy must undertake if it is to involve itself in developing small firms. The superiority of a market economy in entrepreneurial ability is most clearly symbolized by the energy of the small business sector. A developmentalism that has an industrial policy only for large business cannot but face the same difficulty that is encountered by economic planning: being unable to ensure the supply of entrepreneurial vitality. The most capitalist part of capitalism is the small and medium-sized firm, not the large firm.

(The large firm is representative of industrialization.) A policy for fostering small firms also has substantial effects on income distribution, but I
emphasize that in character it is somewhere between industrial policy and
distributive policy.

5. *A policy of distributive equality.* Though not limited to economies
that have adopted developmentalism, the Achilles heel of any effort to
take off into industrialization is the outbreak of social discontent caused
by distributive inequality. Where developmentalism is adopted and industrial policy implemented, there is a danger that distributive problems will
be further aggravated by an increase in disparities. Such disparities are not
limited to wages but extend to lifestyle and values. In the megalopolises of
developing countries, we see a dual structure of large, imposing, modern
factories and offices standing in proximity to wretched slums. One can no
longer ignore distributive inequality. According to the classical argument,
labor was supposed to move from old industries to new industries in search
of higher wages, and the disparities were supposed to disappear. At least
for developing countries, however, the inadequacy of such an argument
has now become widely recognized. Beginning with Arthur Lewis's model
of the "unlimited supply of labour," countless theories of economic development have appeared, but all of these recognize that a certain amount of
surplus labor will remain in agriculture or in the "informal sector" in the
cities, and in this sense the theories of economic development are in fact
a partial critique of the neoclassical school.[8] In the end, one can explain
the emergence of such a surplus labor only by positing that what moves a
worker is not simply the motivation of individual income maximization.
The counterhypothesis, that the family has become the decision-making
unit and that the principle behind its decisions is not simply income maximization, is perhaps the most influential theory at present.[9]

More generally, thinking about labor only from the perspective of
wages is itself the characteristic mentality of capitalism. In transitional
societies where the older way of thinking still remains, leaving the home
or workplace to which one has become accustomed is a substantial negative incentive that hampers the transfer of labor. Thus disparities in wages
do not disappear easily, and with the development of new industries the
existing disparities may well increase. As a result, political unity will be
endangered and developmentalism itself will be set back. The traditional
way of dealing with this problem has been to establish policies to make
labor mobile, such as training programs or schemes promoting migration,
and there have been many examples of this since the poor-relief laws of
sixteenth-century England. In the present environment, however, when
democratic equality is a powerful ideal, even promoting migration might
itself cause strong discontent. A policy to supplement in some way the
shock of changes in the structure of the labor force must be an indispensable part of present-day developmentalism.

This supplementary policy will be a policy of distributive equality, in the broad sense, but there is more than one way to achieve this equality. Inheriting the tradition of J. S. Mill, the neoclassical school has emphasized that distributive policy should take a form that has no connection to production activity or to price formation—in other words, some kind of lump-sum subsidy. This is because it is believed that redistribution linked to prices or output (for example, the Japanese system of price supports for rice) distorts the working of the market and makes resource allocation inefficient. On the other hand, income supplements that are not tied to production—unlike wages—do not increase the desire to work. Welfare payments to the unemployed, for example, have the effect of making the unemployed state permanent. This argument is much used by critics of the welfare state, but one cannot deny that it has a degree of truth. (It is an extreme example, but if income redistribution were undertaken such that perfect equality were always achieved, probably no one would work in factories and offices apart from a few unusual altruistic individuals.) Depending on the country, an increasingly important phenomenon is that of people who show no enthusiasm about seeking employment as long as their unemployment insurance continues, or who consciously combine unemployment and work.

As a second means of achieving distributive equality, one can imagine an anticlassical redistribution corresponding to changes in prices and output. In the case of industrialization in developing countries, if old industries in relative decline were kept going by means such as price supports, this would clearly have a negative effect on resource allocation. On this point there is no room for doubt. If, however, the desire to work of the people working in those old industries were preserved, the policy might have the effect of contributing to the economy as a whole. The existing family unit would be maintained and might become a stable source of consumer demand. It would also have the positive effect of stabilizing the polity. The question is whether there would be net gains or losses. In postwar Japan, each year huge sums have been paid in price supports to sustain agriculture (particularly rice farming). In the current U.S.-Japanese trade negotiations, criticism has focused on the distortions this agricultural policy has created, and many economists are critical of the policy. It should be recognized, though, that at least up until a certain period, this policy stabilized Japanese farming villages, which have been the source of an industrious urban labor force. As this example of the policy on the rice price shows, however, there are great difficulties in bringing to an end this kind of antineoclassical distributive policy—as there are with industrial policy.

Equalizing distribution had another important effect after the Second World War: creating demand for the rapidly increasing products of mass production. The effects of this are particularly remarkable when mass production technologies are being developed, as they were at that time. The automobile, for example, is supplied most efficiently when a single standardized model is produced in large quantities. The most desirable demand structure for this supply structure is mass demand—in other words, the demand created by a huge number of households with similar income levels. If society is divided into a minority of rich and a large majority of poor, the demand for cars will be limited to a small number of high-grade cars, such as Rolls Royce or Mercedes Benz, and general demand will be directed toward, for example, huge numbers of bicycles. But if the same national income were distributed more equally, there would be a demand for large numbers of Hondas or Toyotas, making it possible for large, mass-production car manufacturers to emerge and prosper. The spillover effects of this would profit the whole economy. Europeans invented the car, but they thought of it as a luxury good for some in the upper class, as was the case for the horse-drawn carriage. It was Henry Ford's Model T that broke through this prejudice.

The same pattern is true of the domestic appliances and electronic goods that followed the automobile. This kind of high mass consumption has supported the economy of the twentieth century, particularly since the Second World War. As discussed in Chapter 4, this phenomenon can be detected in all noteworthy periods of economic development since that of Britain in the sixteenth century. When developing countries embark on industrialization, the creation of demand through equalization of income distribution should not be ignored. As already mentioned, antineoclassical methods can have the positive results of maintaining the desire to work and creating demand. When technological innovation also becomes vigorous, sustained by this impetus, in many cases the results of such a policy will outweigh the distortions in resource allocation. At these times, an anticlassical distributive policy is the one that should be adopted—under the condition that it is possible to bring such a policy to an end.

6. *A policy of equality toward farmers*. The instruments of allocation for agriculture and farmers are the most difficult aspects of distributive policy in developing countries. In societies on the eve of industrialization, farmers usually make up much more than half the population, and the ways they live and form groups constitute the backbone of society. The general desire to work and the response to politics is generated from a rural view of life. Preventing the farmers from becoming a politically discontented class or disinterested in their work—thus ensuring their participation in industrialization—is a necessary condition for the success of the takeoff. In this sense I discuss this item independently from (5).

In sixteenth-century England, industries such as the wool industry were concentrated in farming villages and provided farmers with the chance of a side job and gradually allowed them to abandon farming. During the Japanese industrialization, too, in the second half of the nineteenth century, rural industries had already taken root in many regions during the latter half of the Tokugawa period, and from the opening of the country the export-oriented production of tea and raw silk linked together agriculture and industry. From our present perspective, the speed of industrialization in the nineteenth century was slow, and the pace of structural change from agriculture to industry was also unhurried. Western and Japanese industrialization was in fact fortunate in that the question of income distribution for farmers did not become serious.

Today the speed of industrialization is much faster. Only large firms can survive the fast-paced competition in product development in the world market. At least for nonluxury products, the rural, domestic woolen industry in England produced a good-quality product at one of the lowest prices in all of Europe. The cultivation of tea and raising of silkworms in Japan, when the country was opening up, also were able to survive international competition. It was possible for both these industries to acquire global markets. Now, however, there are few industries based on raw materials produced in villages or the cultivation of commercial products that have the power to compete globally, and it has become extremely difficult for developing countries to survive the initial period of takeoff by relying on rural industries. Thus the need for a distributive policy for the rural farming community (and for various traditional industries) has increased.

One example is provided by postwar Japan, which had its industrial capacity destroyed and in a sense had to go through the takeoff stage again. At that time, mainly because of the policy of the occupying forces (the Supreme Command of the Allied Powers), Japan undertook a reform of agricultural land that was extraordinarily thorough for a capitalist country. All absentee landlords lost their land, and all tenant farmers became independent cultivators. As a result, even throughout the period of continued rapid development in the industrial sector, there was not the slightest change in the industriousness of the farming community. Given this economic base, the children of rural communities found employment outside agriculture in huge numbers; the heads of farming households also tended to work in nearby cities during the week, or even in distant cities. Thus the proportion of farming families for whom nonagricultural income is greater than agricultural income is now as high as 80 percent. But even today many farming families hold on to their land and have their psychological roots in the rural community. And during the 40 years of sustained economic growth, unprecedented in the industrial history of the world, the farming class did not feel left out of Japan's economic success. The farmers' feeling is readily understood when we learn that since the 1970s the average income of farming households has been higher than that of a city worker.

Here too, the problem with the anticlassical distributive policy, as with industrial policy, is the difficulty of bringing it to an end. In the 1970s, when Japan's economic growth was proceeding and its industrial capabilities were beginning to outstrip those of other developed countries, one might have expected Japan to consider shifting to neoclassical policies, such as liberalizing the buying and selling of land or providing a lump-sum payment for those who gave up farming. Preventing such policies were the electoral considerations of the ruling Liberal Democratic party, the interests of the ministries concerned, and the wishful thinking that the situation could be solved by shifting the focus from rice farming to other pursuits (such as cattle raising, tangerine cultivation, and the cultivation of luxury produce in greenhouses). Because these efforts failed, the ethos of the farming community survived unscathed in the midst of industrialization, or rather superindustrialization.

In adopting antineoclassical policy, the question of possible obstacles —political, bureaucratic, and even mass psychological—must always be a serious consideration. The problems encountered in Japan provide a good lesson. I emphasize again, however, that if Japan had not adopted an antineoclassical policy toward the agricultural sector in the 1950s and 1960s, the people who had been forced to give up farming would probably have lost their motivation to work and would have voted for various political parties. The latter would have created instability in domestic politics and made it impossible for Japan to achieve rapid economic growth. Slow growth of its economy would have made Japan a society full of conflict. For developing countries in the future, an anticlassical distributive policy should be adopted during the initial period of an attempt to industrialize; in terms of agricultural policy, price supports, redistribution of farming land, or promotion of by-employment may be appropriate instruments if the timing for each is chosen carefully.

7. *Education policy.* There is perhaps no need to explain that education is necessary for industrialization, but let me briefly sketch why I emphasize education up to and including secondary education. For industrialization, the necessary educational level is a level adequate for learning about and using industrial technology. The education necessary for students to understand such systematized technology requires what is learned in the first two stages—primary and secondary—of the normal educational system. In contrast, higher education provides students with the ability to deal with and criticize the existing system of ideas (in science and technology, and in society). Thus, in an industrial society, higher education serves as a source of scientists and engineers who have, to a greater or lesser extent, the ability to make technological innovations, and of bureaucrats and managers who are trained to deal objectively with concepts (formal, rational systems)—in other words, specialists. But the existence of specialists does not seem to be a sufficient condition for the continued existence of industrial society. This is because the need for people who are not specialists—the cultured?—does not disappear even in industrial society. But it is surely clear that the existence of specialists is a necessary condition (see the following section on the bureaucratic system). Thus, both secondary education and higher education are fundamentally necessary, and this creates the problem of the balance between them.

As is well known, many of today's developing countries in effect entrust the higher education of superior talent to universities in the advanced industrial nations. Although this method is not free of problems, it is certainly one way of supplying the talent necessary for industrialization. One problem is that this method makes it difficult to clearly establish the cultural identity of the developing country, or in other words, to form a nationalism (or at least it complicates the process). The method may, however, be effective in preventing a narrowness in this nationalism. Thus relying on foreign countries' higher education—like relying on foreign countries' capital—is a possible choice. Therefore, let us consider the minimum requirement for developmentalism to be secondary education that gives the large majority of people the ability to use the existing systematic technology. Without this, developmentalism cannot be successful. To cite but one example, in contrast to East Asia, where there is generally a strong tradition of respect for education and where adequate educational systems developed quickly, in Latin America adequate educational systems are developing more slowly. This fact has perhaps substantially influenced the different rates of progress of these two regions toward industrialization.

8. *A fair and competent modern bureaucracy.* No analysis of the modern bureaucracy has appeared to date that surpasses Max Weber's classic study. According to Weber, the modern bureaucracy was established by the development of the money economy and the social and political needs of an industrializing society and economy. In short, using the terms of this book, Weber clearly indicated that when the three dynamics of industrialization, nationalism, and democratization were at work, the modern bureaucracy, as a *legale Herrschaft* (legal authority), was an indispensable mediating element. He defined the modern bureaucracy in terms of the following systematic characteristics: a hierarchy in which power and authority are strictly defined and distributed; a document-based performance of duties; a full-time profession with no side employment; selection through specialist education and special examination; public provision of the means for performance of duties; remuneration by salary (and a guarantee for old age through pension); and a position for life.[10] And he pointed out that formal rationality (observation of the law and other fixed forms) and impartiality, that is, *Sachlichkeit* (a rejection of subjectivity) or *Unpersönlichkeit* (impersonality), were typical of the patterns of bureaucratic behavior generated from these characteristics. I concentrate mainly on the characteristics of these behavioral patterns.[11]

As I have emphasized a number of times, the economic and political systems work independently, and intervention by the administration plays the crucial role in connecting the two systems. Of course, legislation in the national assembly, or legalism, is an established route by which parliamentary government may intervene in the economic system. Even this legalist intervention, however, usually requires some kind of administration. To cope with changing situations, what we call today social and economic laws become necessary, but even supposing that a legal judgment were provided as a formal document, under these laws (unlike civil or criminal law) it would usually be impossible to judge the situation in the abstract, without interpreting social or economic realities, and such an interpretation cannot be based on any single principle. It is impossible to deduce, solely on the basis of the stipulations of the law, how a law is to be applied.

There is therefore room for discretion in the enforcement of the law, and decisions by bureaucrats, who are supposed to be nothing more than executors of the law, will play a substantial role. Thus the law-dependent and the discretionary character of the bureaucracy make each other necessary, and at the same time they dispute each other's domain. At one extreme is the image of the bureaucracy as automatic executor of the law, and at the other one can imagine a *Kadi*-esque, precedent-based bureaucracy.[12] "*Kadi*-justice" refers to making decisions not on the basis of a formal legal rationality but on the basis of "informal judgments rendered in terms of concrete ethical or other practical valuations."[13] This tendency can be seen in the former "administration by notables" in England and in the Japanese bureaucracy.[14]

Thus, under the dynamics of industrialization, nationalism, and democracy, bureaucratic intervention will be very widespread; Britain and the United States, usually thought of as strongly antibureaucratic, are no exceptions. For example, the sixteenth to eighteenth centuries were a period of great change for Britain, but it was "administration by notables" from among the gentry class that supported the establishment of capitalism. The justice of the peace in each district was entrusted with the enforcement of the prohibition on enclosures, the supervision of rural industries, and the adjudication of the Poor Laws, the laws on craftsmen, the laws on vagrants, and other laws. The justices' shared concept of the "commonwealth" as an esprit de corps, and their forming of what one might call a unified, part-time bureaucracy, in an invisible form, led Britain in the direction of capitalism and the formation of new industries. The emergence of a class of "notables" with this esprit de corps, however, depended greatly on the historical conditions peculiar to Britain (see Chapter 4). Naturally France and Germany also had men of regional repute, but they were hostile to the transitions to the nation-state and capitalism and could not become administrative pillars aiding the process of transition.

The formation of a modern bureaucracy in both the regions and the center was one of the historical roles of absolute monarchy; Jean Baptiste Colbert was one of its designers, and Otto von Bismarck carried it through to completion. Britain and the United States, in becoming great states, also had no choice but to create a bureaucratic mechanism, but the tradition of administration by notables tended to work against the establishment of a modern administration.[15] Until comparatively recently, the British bureaucracy was well known for the vagueness of its selection mechanism, and the United States for the peculiarity of its spoils system.[16] Needless to say, in socialist industrialization too the establishment of a bureaucracy is essential. In the end, except for the Anglo-American societies and

small countries, there are no countries that have successfully industrialized without first establishing bureaucracies.

The increasing complexity and rapidity of economic development is
making bureaucracy more indispensable than ever, and all countries are
being compelled to make even greater provisions for their bureaucracies.
Trying to implement developmentalist policies increases the importance
of a modern bureaucracy still further. This is because, under a developmentalist policy, the bureaucracy is not simply the executor of the law
but is expected from the first to implement discretionary administrative
intervention. The designation of priority industries, guidance in price setting, and choosing objects for subsidy are all dynamic issues that must
be entrusted to the authorities in charge. Distributive policy under developmentalism, too, assumes the *Kadi*-esque character of something that
depends on administrative discretion, and because of this it unexpectedly
gathers mass support.

The success or failure of this administrative intervention depends on
how the two behavioral patterns mentioned above—impartiality and rationality—work out. Generally speaking, it is difficult for the impartiality
of administrative decisions (their not discriminating between individuals)
to coexist with their discretionary nature. It is inevitable that individual
cases of discretion will occasion a disparity in advantages and disadvantages among the industries or classes concerned. Over a long period, however, as discretion becomes something that profits the interests of a specific industry or group, it becomes difficult for administration to retain its
impartiality. Because of its nontransparent character, "*Kadi*-justice" can
perform only a limited role in legitimating its impartiality. The ties grow
stronger between the bureaucracy and the industry or class that benefits
from the discretionary uses of bureaucratic judgment, and go beyond the
point where they could be legitimated. Should these ties become corrupt,
the social prestige of the bureaucracy is severely damaged. Such corruption
may be controlled by, on the one hand, the sense of mission of individual
bureaucrats and, on the other, the system of personnel management (such
as frequent rotation), but if corrupt relations continue for a long period,
there will likely be limits even to this control. The collapse of impartiality
will paralyze the original function of the bureaucracy, invite distrust of the
administration, and set back the development of the society.

Particularly in developmentalist countries where the higher education
system is inadequately developed and there are extreme disparities between rich and poor, the source of supply for the bureaucracy is frequently
limited to a particular, wealthy class from the period before industrialization; because of this, nepotism is created and certain kinds of policy
are sabotaged. Many say that this kind of sabotage has brought the policy
of land distribution in many Latin American countries to a standstill. In
contrast, in the East Asian countries, the old Chinese tradition of a bu-

reaucracy of literati is said to have played a large part in creating a sense of mission in the modern bureaucracy. Although not fully proven empirically, the view that the bureaucracies in Japan, Korea, Singapore, Thailand, and elsewhere are free of corruption enjoys considerable support.[17]

Bureaucratic rationality is also a problem. Bureaucratic rationality originally was formal rationality based in law and in itself was not supposed to be either conservative or progressive. In fact, though, inasmuch as discretion plays a part, this rationality is mingled with *Kadi*-esque, precedent-based characteristics. In other words, there is a tendency to observe a framework made up of accumulated legal interpretations and records of the actual legal process, and so formal rationality comes to be transformed into something based on experience. In this sense, the patterns of bureaucratic behavior are conservative or defensive and not progressive or creative. Thus, if the policy implemented by a certain ministry or bureau has favored a particular industry, the favorable—protective— measures often remain in effect, regardless of changes in the position of that industry. To justify the continuation of the measures on the grounds of efficiency, the logic of formal rationality is frequently mobilized.

In the bureaucracies of developing countries a practical, purposive rationality is often at work. In these bureaucracies, the achievements of the developed countries are held up as models of "progress," a practice that plays a role in conquering simple formal rationality. In this sense a developmentalist bureaucracy is enterprising or aggressive and plays a more creative role than politicians. Its progressive character is well demonstrated where the bureaucracy is united with an influential political power supporting it. Robert Cecil in Britain, Colbert in France, and Bismarck in Germany are representative of such political power.

Under developmentalism a bureaucracy is also charged with the special task of bringing industrial policy to an end at the appropriate time. The conservative, defensive character of the bureaucracy may well become a factor preventing it from achieving this task. In Japan, for example, the organizing principle of the bureaucracy limits the transfer of personnel (within a single ministry in most cases, and exceptions are very few), and the authority to intervene in a certain industry is concentrated (within a single ministry in most cases). As a result, the tendency to defend organizational "turf" (in order to protect rights of supervision once acquired) easily becomes allied with the interests of the specific industry. There is thus a danger that ministerial partisanship that favors industries designated as priority industries in the past will prove fatal for the original purposes of developmentalism. When a developing country has succeeded in becoming a developed country because of its developmentalism, the creative role its bureaucracy can play becomes smaller than that that can be played by the firms themselves. Successful developmentalism has to weather a second revolution in its system, the reformation of the bureaucracy. This is an important issue faced only by developmentalism and not by classical liberalism.

The prototype of developmentalism presented under the preceding eight headings is only one possible sketch, and there is of course room for modification in its details. Even in this sketch, though, the basic framework of developmentalism has perhaps been adequately indicated. First, it is a mode of capitalism under the decreasing cost condition and is clearly distinct from economic planning. If the bureaucracy were forcibly to carry out its mission on a legal basis, managers would lose what J. M. Keynes called their "animal spirit," and developmentalism would be indistinguishable from economic planning. For example, the idea of nationalizing firms is not something that belongs in developmentalism in the sense that we are talking of it here. Second, under decreasing cost, unrestrained capitalism is extremely dynamic; at the same time, it is an extremely high-risk system and thus difficult to sustain. The industrial policy at the core of developmentalism controls this risk—that is, it aims to restrain excessive competition and maintain oligopolistic competition, what I call "polipoly." Subsidies, protectionism, and investment controls are at most nothing more than secondary means to this end. In other words, the essence of industrial policy is to lower the risk of the collapse of competition by putting in place a framework of compartmentalized competition for each industry. Third, the aim of the distributive policy, also at the core of developmentalism, is again to avoid the risk of any confusion that might derive from the implementation of industrial policy. For this reason there is no need to be particular about the sharp neoclassical distinction between production and distribution. Fourth, an impartial, competent bureaucracy controls the fate of developmentalism.

In the end, industrial policy and distributive policy are at the center of developmentalist policy, but common to both is a concern with the process of change; concretely speaking, they both take very seriously phenomena such as price reduction, firm failures, and difficulties in labor mobility, which occur during the process of change. At the base of this is the understanding that industrialization is not changes in equilibria but a constant process of self-organization to which instability is endemic. If one focuses analytic attention on equilibria, as the neoclassical school does, the state of a market that seems to be excessively competitive and the large movements of labor that occur during the progress toward industrialization are seen as nothing more than transitional. There may be room for argument about the details of the prototype that has been sketched here, but we have to construct a model that deals with all the implications of the system that is dynamic, high-risk industrialization. This chapter is my attempt at such a model.

Examples of Nondevelopmentalist Failure

Under present circumstances, can developing countries successfully industrialize by means of classical—or rather neoclassical—economic liberalism? It is usual for capitalism to alternate between prosperity and recession. In an economy of classical economic liberalism, recession is a great test for what the neoclassical school calls infant industries, in other words industries that have good prospects in the long term (industries faced with long-run decreasing cost). When demand slackens in industries with decreasing costs, price-cutting competition becomes more intense than in other industries, and there will likely be a large number of bankruptcies. Thus, since recession cannot be avoided, participation or investment in industries that are promising in the long term (that is, that face long-run decreasing cost) comes to be avoided as a highly risky enterprise. Only firms with both an exceptionally long-term view and the ability to obtain capital will last; the majority of entrepreneurs will choose ordinary industries with increasing costs. The alternation between prosperity and recession may well leave behind as aftereffects a short-term orientation in management and the dominance of the principle of static comparative advantage.

In this way, the effort to industrialize in a developing country is more troubled by negative changes in business conditions than is a developed country. (As I argue in the following chapter, the present international economic system contains a mechanism that amplifies expansion and retrenchment.) To make matters worse, the already unstable politics of a developing country is further destabilized in being unable to cope with an economic slump (recession, inflation, and trade deficits), and the effort to industrialize frequently comes to a standstill. Moreover, the classical/neoclassical policy position is comparatively indifferent to the question of distribution during the initial stage of industrialization. Even if one did adopt a neoclassical distributive policy, making a strict distinction between production and distribution, the financial burden during the great social changes that characterize the stage of takeoff would be far too large, and there might even be a danger of creating a displaced urban population that has lost the motivation to work. Developmentalism, taking a long-term view and attempting to develop those industries with good prospects, clearly has a greater possibility of success.

THE PROCESS OF DEVELOPMENT: THE CASE OF LATIN AMERICA

Since the nineteenth century (and particularly since the 1870s), many countries in Latin America have paid much attention to such export-oriented primary industries as sugar, coffee, wheat, meat, raw cotton, saltpeter, copper, silver, and oil. Emphasizing these industries became a kind of Latin American economic tradition, for good reason. Natural conditions in the region are favorable for the production of these primary goods, and there are economies of scale to be realized in these industries, which provide incentives for the large-scale development of farms, plantations, and mines. When world demand for these products was high, capital from both inside and outside the country flocked to these industries, attracted by the economies of scale. But much domestic capital was frittered away as a result of competition, and strongly conspiratorial oligopolistic systems or actual monopolies were established. Quite a few foreign firms, backed by substantial capital in their home countries, established monopolistic positions. During the competition in the phase of decreasing costs, brought about by the economies of scale, the foreign firms had an advantage in being able to raise large amounts of capital from their home countries.

In addition, a remarkably large number of domestic, oligopolistic firms forged financial ties to foreign capital. One could say that an inclination to import foreign capital—what we would call today a tendency toward capital liberalization—has been the historical characteristic of a Latin America turned toward Europe and North America. But the benefits of this kind of large-scale development were soon exhausted because, unlike in manufacturing, in primary industries the element of technological innovation is clearly limited. Thus the effects of decreasing cost were comparatively short term, and a stagnant structure of oligopoly or monopoly became rooted in the economy. With oligopolistic dominance based on substantial agricultural lands and mining interests, and the monopolistic positions held by foreign firms, the economies of Latin America came to be characterized by the disparities between industries and between rich and poor.

Many have tried to find the cause for such an economic structure in the traditions of colonial rule. But the characteristics of the Latin American economies are a product of economic management that has relied on primary goods. This is indicated by the fact that the United States industrialized rapidly, despite having a similar structure in the South. Furthermore, even in Latin America, it is Mexico, where the institutions left by the colonial land system are strong, that continues to industrialize, rather than Argentina, where the structures of colonial rule are weak (and the population is mostly Caucasian). We should also note that foreign capital and foreign firms played a large part in the survival of these Latin American characteristics. Although foreign firms were concerned about their interests in the primary industries, they were not always cooperative in the development of the country as a whole. The experience of many of the Latin American countries will be an instructive example for developing countries in the future—particularly for developing countries that decide to throw open their doors to foreign companies—in demonstrating the danger of neglecting excessive competition involving foreign firms as well.

Dependency theory has argued that this phenomenon is a result of the political global domination by the capitalism of the developed countries, but such an analysis is simplistic. This phenomenon was a result of the autonomous policy choice of the Latin American countries; in fact, at one time this choice enabled them to achieve a comparatively smooth development, and the democratization that proceeded during this period (the "populismo" discussed below) is also noteworthy. But the characteristics of the primary industries, particularly their economies of scale (albeit with little possibility of technological innovation) led to various economic effects, including a widening of the existing disparities, and as a result had a malign influence on economic development. The problem is the inability of these countries to change their policy choice and not the historical inevitability of global capitalism.

Let us retrace and review their historical development. Though the various problems mentioned above existed in the Latin American countries between the 1870s and the Great Depression, exports of primary goods were vigorous, and the traditional structure of rule by the wealthy (whose wealth was accumulated through exports) was created. A policy that placed great importance on the export of several specific products became established as political tradition. On the other hand, with the development of large agricultural estates the number of those who could not find work in the rural areas increased, as did the number of those displaced to the cities. Added to these were European immigrants. Thus one could say that in a short period an urban proletariat was formed, and the general manufacturing industry began to grow as if to take advantage of the low-cost labor offered in the cities. But following the Great Depression, Latin American countries suffered a serious stagnation in exports of primary goods. Their responses were surprisingly similar. Politically, in many countries, "populismo," based on urban middle classes and workers, succeeded in electing governments and overcoming the power of those who had accumulated wealth by exporting primary products. This Latin American populism was characterized by its basis in parliamentary democracy, its fundamental support for capitalism, and the emphasis it placed on distributive policy; in many respects it was similar to the developmentalism discussed in this book.

However, this populism differed from developmentalism in two significant ways. It adopted a policy of industrialization through import substitution—in other words, a strongly protectionist policy toward a manufacturing industry whose only objective was the domestic market. It also vigorously pursued a neoclassical policy of redistribution that focused on the urban middle class and workers—almost a policy for a welfare state. This distributive policy was only for the benefit of the urban residents who supported populism; it did little to aid farmers or those displaced from rural villages. To be sure, distributive policies for the farming community were adopted in a few instances (such as that implemented by the Cardenas government in Mexico, 1934–40). But these were exceptions. It is evident, however, that Latin American populism was a democratization sprouting from the unique development of capitalism through many years, and a genuine industrialization appeared to begin in capitalism. Industrialization started early in Latin America, nearly half a century before that in East Asia.

Why is East Asia then considered a successful example of industrialization and Latin America regarded for the most part as a failed example? (This judgment of success and failure is relative, but for the time being let us think of success as attaining the level at which a number of the core industries of today can survive in international competition.) The most important factor seems to have been that, in the final analysis, the Latin American countries have not changed their policy of emphasizing the export of primary goods together with industrialization through import substitution; in other words, in disregarding the long-term, global trends in technological innovation and demand, they have observed the rule of static comparative advantage. In short, they have not adopted what I am calling developmentalism. The policy of the Latin American countries has a long tradition stretching back to the nineteenth century, as I noted above. Thus, even populist governments succumbed in a sense to this tradition and relied on the export of primary goods, tried to achieve industrialization through import substitution, and adopted a redistribution policy of the welfare state. From before the Second World War until the 1950s, populist governments generally succeeded in promoting economic growth. But all depended on the export of primary goods, which was subject to sharp fluctuations; when exports stagnated they expanded fiscal expenditures (to compensate for declining revenues from exports). When import restraints and cuts in the exchange rate were added to fiscal stimuli, the inflationary tendency became unavoidable. The populist governments failed to seize the new international economic opportunities in a postwar period characterized by steady technological innovation.

Thus, in the 1960s the populist governments fell one after the other and there emerged conservative governments dominated by the traditional wealthy class. Even these governments, however, could not substantially change the course that populism had set, lest they lose the support of city residents. In many cases, a course of modified populism was adopted. In following industrialization through import substitution and redistributive policy, the only novel policy adopted by these governments was actively reviving the policy of importing foreign capital, which had been suspended for a time during the period of nationalist populism, and trying to break out of the framework of export dependency. But inasmuch as they depended on industrialization through import substitution, under generous protectionist measures, productivity did not rise; to make matters worse, the domestic market also began to show signs of saturation. As a result, there was no change in the fundamental structure of the economy, and these additional policies led to an extra problem of accumulating international debt. This was to be the background for the appearance of the Prebisch Report and dependency theory.

From the 1960s, military governments seemed to appear frequently in an attempt to get under control the political confusion created by populism and the modified populism that succeeded it. Though all military governments attempted to repress mass movements, their economic policies differed. Some tried to continue the populist economic policies, but others made efforts to return to prepopulist policies. In both cases, though, the failure of industrialization brought democratization to a standstill. But since the root cause of the crisis was in economic performance, unless the military governments could make their new economic policies succeed they had no raison d'être. Ironically, were their economic policies to succeed, the military governments would become unnecessary. In fact, in many cases it was under the military governments that new economic policies were attempted. Brazil and Mexico took a new course and adopted a developmentalist policy that depended on the import of foreign capital. (Mexico, though, did not have a military government.) From the beginning of the 1980s, some countries tried to adopt thorough classical economic liberalism, including Chile, Argentina, and Peru. One could say that these countries became, so to speak, a testing ground for the Chicago school led by Milton Friedman.

The latter experiment in liberal policy provides a useful example for policy comparison. When trade was liberalized in these countries, the influence of short-term comparative advantage came into play, dependency on exports of primary goods grew still further, and the proportion of consumer goods in imports increased. Both exports and imports concentrated on those goods that had a short-term advantage. In domestic industry, competition was stressed and subsidies, protection, and nationalization were abandoned. As a result, development of domestic private firms, particularly small and medium-sized firms, was stalled, and there reemerged a tendency for the large firms with access to foreign capital and foreign firms to become the leaders in the basic industries. The proportion of industries that seemed to have had favorable long-term prospects declined when they had difficulty increasing their exports. Thus when the world market for primary goods became sluggish, budget deficits tended to increase and inflation followed. In addition, there were tendencies for the flight of capital to foreign countries and for the burden of interest payments on foreign debts to increase the current account deficit. Distributive policy was also in retreat, as was symbolized in Chile by the return of land to former owners. At present, those countries such as Argentina, Chile, and Peru that adopted the policies of economic liberalism are in an even worse state than Latin America generally. Their experiments with these policies have all met with failure.

The situation in countries such as Mexico and Brazil, which adopted policies close to developmentalism, is also not a positive one. The problems of budget deficits and inflation are relatively minor, but the accumulated debt is as worrisome as it is for Argentina, Chile, and Peru. The main reason is that—contrary to what we defined as the ideal model of developmentalism—because there are many inefficient nationalized companies in the priority industries, policies of subsidy and protectionism have naturally become prominent. The proportion of foreign companies in priority industries is also high. This fact in itself is not a defect, but it is not easy to gain the cooperation of foreign firms, particularly American firms, for developmentalism. The fact that distributive policy is not pursued effectively, particularly that toward farmers and the fostering of small and medium-sized enterprises, is also an important reason why industrial policy is not progressing smoothly. Unless these problems are solved, the Latin American efforts at development may well not measure up to the ideal model of developmentalism I have described. As long as no fundamental change occurs to enable promising industries to develop, it will be difficult to start on the path toward industrialization.

EAST ASIA AND LATIN AMERICA

In contrast to Latin America, countries such as Korea, Taiwan, Hong Kong, and Singapore (Thailand and Malaysia are also now trying to enter this group) fortunately did not have major primary industries and chose from the start to foster industries seen to have good long-term prospects, especially as major exporters. Indeed, this was the only course they could take. (It is noteworthy that countries with primary industries, such as Indonesia and Malaysia, have lagged behind in industrialization.) In designating priority industries, East Asian countries have rarely been distracted by classical preconceptions, and they have been quick to respond to changes in the global economy. They have been much more active than the Latin American countries in targeting industries with good long-term prospects and have not overexerted themselves in a populist-style, welfare-statist distributive policy, thus enabling them to adopt policies to promote small farmers and small and medium-sized businesses. Furthermore, they have clearly been more active than Latin America in promoting the spread of education.

We can also compare the two regions from a political perspective. As already mentioned, when developing countries aim at developmentalist industrialization, a policy to ensure distributive equality, supplementing industrial policy, is the key to maintaining political stability. In Latin America, there have been many cases where the great landlords or those connected to the modern sector (many of whom tend to be either foreign companies or connected to the government) have occupied privileged positions. Among those cases where such a government, dominated by the upper classes, has espoused economic liberalism and opposed any distributive policy, there has not been one example of the basic industries developing smoothly and the country successfully reducing its dependency on primary industry, or any clear signs of genuine industrialization. Populist governments emerged to replace these traditional governments, but their welfare-statist distributive policies, which placed priority on organized labor and the urban middle class, did not seem to have achieved their goal. Neoclassical distributive policy (which makes a sharp distinction between production and distribution) succeeded only in creating a displaced urban population that suffered from disguised unemployment, because the policy was adopted when the economy, dependent on primary products, was in recession for the benefit of organized labor. When the economy as a whole suffered from recession and inflation, politics was destabilized (witness the frequent military coups d'état in Latin America) and the effort to industrialize accomplished little. That is, destabilization in the political system made industrialization hopeless and caused the Marxist movement to be imported to developing countries. In Latin America, once democratization, in the form of populism, had advanced ahead of genuine industrialization, this fact ironically worked as a disadvantage. In a rapidly changing international economy, it is clearly difficult to expect a democratic decision-making process to have long-term wisdom and patience.

The East Asian NIEs, even the so-called development dictatorships, placed priority on a distributive policy for the premodern sectors, and this provided the depth and stability for domestic demand that is necessary to promote economic growth. In East Asia (apart from the Philippines) the phenomenon of a large, displaced urban population did not materialize. Instead, a kind of middle class—what I call a "new middle mass"—emerged.[18] If developmentalism continues to support the distributive policies that supplement it, developmentalist societies will tend to become more classless, or become more of a mass society than other societies. For example, in the social democratic societies of Europe, although income equality is progressing, there remain differences in prestige (between employers and employees) and in lifestyle. If developmentalism advances sufficiently for democratization gradually to become genuine and systematized, this tendency toward a classless society may perhaps generate a unique mass democracy. This tendency is clearly apparent in Japan, and there are also signs of it in both Korea and Taiwan. I discuss this point in Chapter 9, but let me suggest here that developmentalist society may well have a historically unprecedented political character.

This does not mean that the reasons development in Latin America has generally failed have been exhausted by the preceding explanation. There is the question of the social structure created over the many centuries since the beginning of colonial rule; and there is the critical problem of accumulated foreign debt. I discuss the latter in connection with the floating exchange rate in the following chapter. But the former question of historical setting has a significance that cannot be ignored. Just as classical economic liberalism depended on historical conditions in Europe, particularly the unique historical background of Britain (the character of the medieval English monarchy, the expansion of rural industry, the early emergence of nationalism, the development of a mass consumer society, and so on), so it is possible to argue that developmentalism too would be impossible without a certain kind of historical setting.

Recently, for example, the argument has flourished that the success of the East Asian model of industrialization, as seen in Japan and the Asian NIEs, was supported by certain unique historical conditions. Some people have asserted that a set of values unique to East Asia, such as industriousness, thrift, and organizational loyalty, was generated from the Confucian tradition, and thus in a sense the Confucian tradition has been the key to the success of industrialization.[19] Although such values may be useful once a country is already on the road toward industrialization, there is insufficient ground for asserting that these traditions are the key to its succeeding in the takeoff to industrialization. For example, it is likely an exaggeration to say that the ethnic Chinese inhabitants or the influence of Chinese culture in Thailand and Malaysia were decisive in those countries' present success in rapid development. Again, why was it that on the Chinese mainland, in which the Confucian tradition might be expected to be strongest, economic development lagged behind in the decisive period from the 1910s to the 1920s? That Japan is a Confucian country hardly explains its economic performance. I discuss these points later, but there are surely too many problems with the argument for Confucian industrialization.

Even supposing that historical setting is a factor, it is undeniable that the greatest difference between Latin America and the Asian NIEs is in whether they adopted an economic policy of classical liberalism or of developmentalism. Differences in historical background and several other factors too could have influenced their choice of policy. For example, in contrast to the Latin American countries, which are influenced by the United States (and in various ways pressured by its classical economic liberalism), the Asian NIEs have been encouraged by the nearby example of Japan's success. The developmentalism of the Asian NIEs, though, is not a direct copy of Japan's. Generally speaking, the East Asian countries opened and followed their own path. In any case, the conclusion from a rough comparison of the two regions at this point is clear. The Asian NIEs have succeeded and the Latin American countries have failed in sustaining industrialization. One lesson from this is the paradox that abundant primary resources can hinder industrialization.

Developmentalism and Classical Economic Liberalism

To summarize as well as to add further reflections, let me again compare classical economic liberalism and developmentalism. This comparison is not easy because it involves both static and dynamic dimensions. In the sense that they are both modes of capitalism (meaning a system of private property and a market economy), classical economic liberalism and developmentalism are similar. But when one tries to discuss their differences, the story begins to be more complicated. Many people try to distinguish between the various modes of capitalism on the basis of the degree of political intervention. The principle behind this is the belief that the degree of liberalism in economic action determines the modes of capitalism. But this is ineffective as a basis on which to gauge the difference.

Even classical economic liberalism does not completely reject intervention by a political authority. In fact, it too has two strands, a *neoclassical* interpretation and a *purist* interpretation; let us start with the former, which the majority of contemporary scholars accept. As is well known, the neoclassical school tends to admit that a minimum of government intervention is necessary for the continued existence of the market economy, though this is explained as an exception. Public goods and public utilities are well-known cases, as are the infant industries discussed in the previous chapter. Neoclassical economics has disposed of this case of infant industries as an exception, but the story does not end there. As I have already noted, it is driven toward a nonneoclassical perspective (toward theories such as learning by doing or Marshall's external economies). Moreover, most neoclassical economic liberals tolerate both antitrust regulation and the existence of a central bank (at least its authority to regulate the money supply). Internationally, too, at the time when the system of fixed exchange rates was adopted, many neoclassical economists recognized governments' authority to decide the exchange rate. But it is not self-evident that these systems, which must be considered political intervention, are the minimum necessary to ensure the continued existence of capitalism.

This is not self-evident, for example, from the purist point of view. As discussed in Chapter 1, at one time Milton Friedman considered the prohibition of monopoly to be unnecessary. And Friedrich von Hayek believed that there was no need for a central bank to be the sole issuer of currencies.[20] Under the present floating exchange rate system there has been a global decentralization of the function of note issuing, teaching us that even without a central bank a national economy is at least not impossible. Purists such as Friedman and Hayek have tried to make the concept of liberalism (in my terms, liberalism of action) consistent, and they hold firmly to the principle of criticizing any and all government intervention, certainly including that needed by developmentalism. But the majority of neoclassical economic liberals, who acknowledge as inevitable infant industry protection, antitrust regulation, a central bank, and a system of fixed exchange rates, do not hold this principle. In their minds, the principles of efficiency in resource allocation, nationalism, democracy, and liberalism, among others, coexist, and they do not fully examine possible inconsistencies or conflicts among them. Such a mixture of concepts cannot provide a basis from which to criticize government intervention itself.

For example, when a strong demand is made for government intervention, from the standpoint of democracy advocating equality of outcomes, neoclassical scholars have no argument to offer in opposition to the demand. A good example is Keynesian policy, which was often adopted to reduce unemployment. Neoclassical scholars, calling it a neoclassical synthesis, once tried to acknowledge Keynesian policy as a legitimate part of a liberal economy. But as is shown by the strong opposition of Hayek and Friedman, who prize the principle of liberalism of action, this attempt at a synthesis is nothing other than intellectual inconsistency. Many neoclassical economists, oblivious of all intellectual inconsistency, may insist that efficiency in resource allocation is paramount. If they believe this, however, they should not reject government intervention in those cases where it would increase efficiency. This position also does not entitle them to criticize democratic socialism or developmentalism on the grounds of excessive administrative intervention. Neoclassical economic liberalism does not itself possess a means of judging when and how to sacrifice freedom of economic action for the sake of efficiency in resource allocation or democracy.

Intellectual confusion is even more evident among the supporters of democratic socialism, who are influential in Europe and in Japan. In principle, they approve of the system of private property and the market economy, and in this sense democratic socialism is a mode of capitalism; but it is usually distinct from classical economic liberalism in that it recognizes the usefulness of strong political intervention, such as large-scale redistribution of income (a welfare state system, a graduated income tax, property taxes, and so on) and nationalization of certain enterprises. It is doubtful, though, whether the blueprint drawn by democratic socialists has any inherent intellectual consistency. They describe democratic socialism as a combination of the good aspects of economic planning (socialism) and the good aspects of parliamentary democracy. On the one hand they have explained that, in achieving distributive equality and avoiding recession, democratic socialism can rival socialism (economic planning), and so they have justified discarding the tradition of the planned economy. On the other, they have laid great stress on the presence or absence of parliamentary democracy in the political sphere (whether or not the system recognizes multiple political parties) as the difference between Soviet/East European socialism and democratic socialism.

Thus, generally speaking, democratic socialism is a combination of the principles of efficiency and distributive equality in the economic sphere, and liberal democracy in the political sphere. Theoretically, these two aspects are compatible. (We should remember the prewar debate on the planned economy, which posited that economic planning and liberal democracy were compatible.) Clearly, though, in the economic aspect, the element of liberalism is not indispensable for this combination. When economic growth or distribution suffers, democratic socialists will not hesitate to sacrifice freedom of economic action. Unless this is the case, there can be no explanation for their willingness to nationalize industries. Democratic socialists frequently say that entrepreneurs ought to act in the best interests of their workers and that worker participation in management is to be encouraged. But when they say these things should be legally enforced, they are showing their antiliberal character in the management of the economy. In democratic socialism, the expansion of interventionism cannot be contained.

As I stress repeatedly, though, developmentalism is also a mode of capitalism. It is clear that developmentalism sanctions administrative intervention in the economy, but it is not easy to determine the relative scope and degree of intervention. The common understanding is that developmentalism is strongly interventionist, involving subsidies and protectionism. But it is difficult to say that developmentalism is any more interventionist than democratic socialism or even the neoclassical version of economic liberalism.

There are two points at issue here. First, as mentioned above, democratic socialism and the neoclassical version of economic liberalism do not sanction interventionism, but neither do they possess any principle that might prevent it. Between them and developmentalism, the only difference is whether interventions are tacitly approved or openly sanctioned. Second, the theory and practice of developmentalism have been confused. As explained in the previous sections, the minimum administrative intervention required by developmentalism is some kind of antitrust measure and an occasional policy of subsidies and protectionism, and one cannot necessarily say that it is strong intervention. The impression that developmentalism is especially interventionist has been created by the actual examples of developmentalism (such as that in Japan). The intervention required in developmentalism can be far weaker than that seen in these examples if it is pursued as closely as possible to its ideal version. Among the various derivative types of capitalism, one cannot say that developmentalism is particularly interventionist.

In truth, one can perhaps say that a comparison of strength is not meaningful because there are many dimensions to interventionism. For example, there are two kinds of political intervention in the economy, one through administration and the other through legislation. It is difficult to gauge the strength of interventionism only by the strength of administrative intervention. In the United States, for instance, where the Congress represents existing interests and enacts many laws in favor of protectionism and subsidies, the effects of these laws can only be to restrain freedom of economic activity. In other words, interest-group democracy and bureaucratic interventionism are equally hostile to economic liberalism. Even if developmentalism tends to rely more on administrative intervention (though as noted above, developmentalism may also be implemented in the form of legislative intervention), one cannot say that for this reason it is particularly interventionist.

Despite this fact, many who studied neoclassical economics regard developmentalism as particularly heretical—more so than the economic liberalism that accepts Keynesianism, or even than democratic socialism. To some extent this view is a reflection of the dominance of the neoclassical paradigm, but it also has deeper causes that cannot be disposed of simply as the conflict between different academic schools. There is clearly a difference between the view that sees developmentalism as the basis of the capitalist system and the view that does not; this difference causes developmentalism to be isolated from the various existing theories of capitalism. One has to say that attempting to define and discuss developmentalism along the spectrum that stretches from classical economic liberalism to democratic socialism—a spectrum made up of positions that are fundamentally similar in character—is itself already inadequate.

Both democratic socialism and neoclassical economic liberalism regard the economy through the theory of equilibrium, or statics; in other words, they are fundamentally analyses of a capitalism before industrialization. On this point, even the intellectual framework used by theorists of economic planning is based on the theory of equilibrium, or statics, as is seen in the work of Enrico Barone and Oskar Lange or in the Soviet "material balances." As Hayek has scathingly pointed out, whether they support capitalism or criticize it, in that they treat the concept of market equilibrium as if it were realistic, there is no difference between these positions. In short, their differences of opinion are on nothing more than simply whether it is possible, or desirable, to maintain this equilibrium.[21] Putting to one side purists such as Hayek (there will be an opportunity to examine the purist position below), all these positions, from classical economic liberalism to Soviet-style economic planning, are similar in that they take classical capitalism, in which both technological and managerial innovation are absent, as their standard model (the socialist model is nothing more than the reverse image of this).

In contrast, developmentalism analyzes the economy by adopting a dynamic viewpoint of industrialization that includes technological innovation. Unlike the debate between capitalism and socialism, which in a sense was engaged in a single arena, the confrontation between classical economic liberalism and developmentalism is a battle over whether we should be discussing the economic order that is maintained by the convergence of economic activities or an economic process in which change is never-ending—a battle over the arena for debate. One could call it a battle over whether we should adopt an economics of capitalism or an economics of industrialization. One could also say that the difference between the two viewpoints arises from the difference in their respective objects of analysis: capitalism as an ahistorical concept of a system, or industrialization as a historical concept. What causes developmentalism to be regarded as heretical when seen from other perspectives is its historical perspective.

For the developed Western nations that have dominated the world through the power of capitalism, it is not easy to discard the theory of a stable equilibrium that promises a harmonious economic order. From the traditional Western perspective, industrialization and economic growth are nothing more than by-products of liberalism of economic action — that is, capitalism. Interest in continuous economic growth is a very recent post–Second World War phenomenon; prewar economists, including Keynes, did not use the concept. What gave rise to the interest in economic growth was probably the challenge of the developing countries. The competition over growth rates between the United States and the Soviet Union, initiated by Khrushchev, was one example of this, as was the emergence of Japan — and East Asia — pursuing a strategy of catch-up development. On the other hand, industrialization or economic growth as a means of catching up with Europe and North America was an issue the developing countries could not ignore, and both capitalism and socialism were no more than means to achieve that end. For developing countries aware of their historical backwardness, and particularly for the non-Western developing countries acutely plagued by the knowledge that their civilization lagged behind that of the West, the historical characteristics of industrialization were self-evident. There was no room for doubt; Western civilization had created the history of industrialization and by so doing had dominated the world. But the intellectual orthodoxy in Europe and North America was unable to deal with the actual fact of industrialization.

Nevertheless, sustained industrialization became an undeniable fact, particularly after the Second World War when the possibility of continuous economic growth was widely acknowledged and the phenomenon of decreasing cost gradually came to be recognized. Nowadays, many countries and individuals are trying to exploit this knowledge. As I said before, this fact implies that long-term decision making will become the normal state of affairs in both government and management. The direct effects of this will appear when countries or firms that have long-term views overtake those that have adopted a short-term view. However, there will inevitably be competition among those with long-term views, and, as I explained in the previous chapter, this competition will not produce equilibria and thus will be unstable. Economic competition between countries will assume a similar character. The paradox of this increasingly long-term view in decision making will be that the market economy will be destabilized. Economic competition between countries will intensify, the developing countries' efforts to catch up will increase, and global harmony will become difficult to achieve. Thus, the fundamental question of whether we should stay wedded to economic liberalism is raised. One indication of this was (and is) the adoption by the developing countries of socialism (economic planning), and another is that even in the developed countries the choice between classical economic liberalism and developmentalism — whether or not to adopt an industrial policy — is debated.

Our choices on this issue can be made only within the existing historical dynamic. For most developing countries, the effort to industrialize cannot be abandoned. Military threats continue, and the competition of national economic power will be a great pressure spurring countries onward. Most developing countries, in searching for a more effective way to speed up industrialization, will probably adopt developmentalism. The failure of the experiments at liberal economic policy in Latin America cannot but have a great influence. The East European countries and the former Soviet Union are in a sense beginning industrialization all over again, but these countries too, if they are going to try to rapidly catch up with the West European countries, will have no choice but to adopt a developmentalist strategy. If the West European countries follow the classical ideal and impatiently urge them to liberalize trade and capital, there may well be substantial unemployment and huge pressure on their citizens to emigrate to the West. In the developing countries, classical economic liberalism will not be adopted. Instead, various kinds of developmentalism will likely be attempted.

In a delicate position are the so-called developed countries of Europe and North America, which until now have developed by following classical liberalism, and Japan, which has gained the economic status it enjoys today through developmentalism. These advanced countries seem to have come to a crossroads. For advanced industrial countries, which from the first have led the race to industrialization, technological innovation is more difficult to predict. Thus their long-term decisions are more difficult than those of the developing countries, and it is therefore difficult for them to be thorough in their developmentalism. On the other hand, at least for specific industries (such as the semiconductor industry), short- to medium-term technological prediction is possible, and so in these industries developmentalist policies can be applied. The intense national debate about the advisability of industrial policy in the United States is a sign of the confusion on this point. But if each country's nationalism gains strength and the competition for national power continues, it is natural to expect that developmentalist thought will gradually spread even among the advanced industrial nations.

Let me put it another way. If nationalism and technologism (the ideology of placing emphasis on technological innovation) are combined, developmentalism will become the inevitable solution. Here, though, there is a contradiction between classical economic liberalism and nationalism. If in the present circumstances we decide to preserve classical economic liberalism, we will face the fundamental choice between discarding our attachment to nationalism (the prestige of the nation) and adopting anti-technologism (some kind of anti-industrialization). At least this will be the basic pattern. (We should remember that this was indicated by the problem of "neoconservatism" in Chapter 1.) Will we replace nationalism with transnationalism, or technologism with transindustrialization? Or, a third alternative, will we replace economic liberalism with a broader form of liberalism? This is our final question, discussed in the last chapters of the book. Before that, though, let us return to the problem raised in the opening paragraphs of Chapter 5 and examine the relationship between developmentalism and democracy. This problem can generally be restated as the difficult relationship between industrialization and democratization.

Developmentalism and Democracy

Democratization was defined above as the institutionalization of liberal democracy (some combination of liberalism and democracy), with some form of parliamentary democracy the only possible way to realize it. But parliamentary democracy too is a broad concept. Let us start by discussing the most standard elements of its definitions.[22]

1. *The scope of suffrage.* In its classical definition, democracy is thought to include the right of a large majority of citizens to participate in the political process, or suffrage (both the right to vote and the right to be voted for), with regard to the country's highest decision-making body, the national assembly. Seen historically, the scope for suffrage has gradually expanded from a limited electoral system to a universal electoral system. In Britain truly universal suffrage, including women, was realized only in 1928. The claim that suffrage should be as broadly based as possible is not always recognized (see Chapter 9).

2. *Pluralism, or the existence of more than one political party.* The view that democracy requires expanding suffrage and that the electorate be presented with various choices (parties) is nowadays the majority opinion. This means that there should be more than one political party in name as well as in fact. Even though more than one party was recognized in name in the Soviet bloc, these countries should be understood as having had one-party dictatorships.

Those who are not satisfied with (1) and (2) may, for example, list two more conditions. Let me mention these so as to demonstrate the variety of images of democracy.

3. *The possibility of alternating governing parties.* Among those who regard a two-party system as ideal, there is a tendency to judge a country as a "genuine democracy" only if the party in power changes. Using this criterion, it becomes doubtful whether countries such as Sweden, India, and postwar Japan, which had continued one-party dominance, and Italy, which has had a conservative coalition in power throughout the postwar period, are in fact democratic. This understanding of the dynamic of democratic politics is too narrow, however. Even if the governing party does not change, as long as opposition parties can persuasively present alternative policies (that is, as long as there is policy contestability), then there is potential party competition. Also, a change in the leadership within a party can provide an adequate breadth to policy choice. The two-party system is a mode of politics established under specific social conditions; in particular, one cannot ignore the influence of the electoral system.

4. *The degree to which economic liberalism has been achieved.* Among Anglo-American conservative parties, it is often argued that parliamen-

tary democracy should choose a classical market economy and that parliaments that permit administrative intervention are not genuinely liberal or democratic. In other words, a democratic parliament is expected to support classical economic liberalism. According to this argument, developmentalism, of course, but also the postwar democratic socialist governments in Britain, France, and the Scandinavian countries would be regarded as deviations from liberal democracy (these governments frequently advocated the nationalization of industry and firms), and Keynesianism too would be looked at skeptically. This position may seem too narrow, but I present it for the sake of the argument that follows.

THE COMPATIBILITY OF INDUSTRIALIZATION
AND DEMOCRATIZATION

It is clear that industrialization also requires a certain minimum political integration. As already mentioned, industrialization requires, first, the minimum system necessary to support a market economy or public goods in a broad sense, and second, redistribution, also broadly understood. And without some kind of political integration it is impossible to resolve these issues. Merely specifying a minimum role, however, does not determine the substance of this integration. Historically, there have been various examples of political integration supporting industrialization in its initial stages, including absolute monarchy and systems of one-party or military dictatorship, and there have also been differences in the various degrees of restraint provided by a parliament. Of course, in other examples, such as Britain and its white colonies (for example, in North America and Australia), political integration for the sake of industrialization has been provided from the first by a fairly developed parliamentary democracy.

But is it always possible for the political integration necessary for dealing with the great changes that are the initial stages of industrialization—changes that for any country are a historical watershed—to be achieved through parliamentary democracy? The basic premise of democratic politics is, it goes without saying, that the decision of the majority should be made the decision of the society as a whole. This condition, though, is not easily satisfied in the large-scale group that goes under the name of a "state." Added to this is the fact, of which there are many examples even in the developed countries, that parliamentary democracy easily drifts toward a compromise among existing interests and thus is generally unsuitable as a system for dealing with wide-ranging changes in society. For example, if the question of whether to start on the road to industrialization is to be decided politically in a preindustrial country in which all classes have the right to vote, support for industrialization is not likely to emerge through majority decision. Even in Britain, for example, had universal suffrage been established in the eighteenth century, it would probably have been difficult for industrialization to develop smoothly (think of the Luddite movement). Without at least a leadership that adopts a redistributive policy (for example, via the redistribution of agricultural land), there will be no easy path to industrialization under parliamentary democracy.

But the problems are not usually resolved simply by redistribution of income. The aim of redistribution in this case is, in short, to change people's opinions by using money, but the insecurity and discontent of classes of people who lived with the established ethos or the view of life to that point cannot be erased by money. In particular, the class that is the main bearer of a preindustrial system of values is not swayed by money but rather is repelled by it. Even supposing that they were the minority, their power is frequently sufficient to bring about a civil war and set back industrialization. Civil war is the expression of a determination to reject the consensus that the decision of the majority should be made the decision of the society as a whole. In the end, when a preindustrial society aims at rapid industrialization, there is a high possibility that democratic decision making will become a mechanism for rejecting industrialization. Given that industrialization is not the supreme objective of humanity, this is, in a sense, inevitable. This inevitability is perhaps why there is a tendency for parliamentary democracy to be avoided where, for example, the ruling class in a developing country is attempting to promote industrialization in order to raise the position of the country and prevent colonization. Not as a question of good and evil, but as a matter of fact, overcoming the takeoff stage in industrialization through democratic government is usually either impossible or unlikely. At least in the initial period of industrialization, developmentalism achieved results without parliamentary government's being adequately established in relatively backward countries in Europe such as Germany and Italy, or in Japan, the Asian NIEs, and elsewhere. Today, as might be expected, there is no one who denies this fact.

Opinion is divided, however, on what happens once industrialization is under way. Capitalist industrialization broadens the range of individual action and raises living standards, or at least increases the likelihood of both. This generally raises the demand for political participation. In fact, the tendency for capitalist industrialization gradually to strengthen parliamentary democracy is widely recognized. Of course there are also examples of retreats from parliamentary democracy, such as the setback of "populismo" in Latin America. But given that developmentalism is also a form of capitalism, the tendency is for democratization to be strengthened. Thus the question becomes whether developmentalism in the economic sphere and parliamentary democracy in the political sphere can coexist in a society that is on the road to industrialization. Opinions are divided on this point as well. At one extreme, there is the position, introduced as (4) above, that the spirit of parliamentary democracy can coexist only with classical economic liberalism—that is, that parliamentary democracy leads to classical economic liberalism. This position implies that the coexistence of developmentalism and parliamentary democracy is limited to the initial stage of industrialization, and soon one of them (probably developmentalism) will be abandoned.

As I have frequently said, however, there is no inevitable connection between the two dynamics of politics and economics. The argument that parliamentary democracy and economic liberalism are inevitably linked surely undervalues liberal democracy's ability to accommodate a wide range of ideologies and ideas and probably defines economic liberalism too narrowly. For example, in the half century since the war Japan has been a textbook democracy, at least in the sense of the first two definitions above, yet at the same time it has been a developmentalist country, characterized by political intervention in the economy. The majority of Japanese people have supported a conservative party that pursued the goal of economic growth (to catch up with the developed countries), and this political consensus permitted developmentalist policies. Recently, such developing Asian nations as Korea, Taiwan, and Singapore have been striving to normalize parliamentary democracy. Clearly, parliamentary democracy and developmentalism do not *inevitably* contradict each other. But this does not mean that, in fact, there is no friction between them. This friction is one of the greatest problems for developmentalism.

The debate on economic planning that flourished in the 1920s and 1930s focused on the same type of argument. The majority opinion at that time was that socialism inevitably meant political dictatorship. Against this, defending socialism, Enrico Barone, Oskar Lange, Joseph Schumpeter, and others made the counterargument that economic planning could coexist with parliamentary democracy. As an argument in abstract theory, their position (using a static, neoclassical model) was not incorrect.[23] But subsequent developments taught that merely debating abstract possibilities is insufficient. In the former Soviet bloc (including Poland, where Lange was in the first generation of leaders), parliamentary democracy and socialism did not coexist in reality. A one-party dictatorship of the communist party was convenient for getting a planned economy off to a start, yet instead of loosening, this system of one-party dictatorship became an inflexible, self-aggrandizing system. Entrepreneurial spirit and ambition for technological innovation were stifled, becoming a direct cause for the defeat of socialism in economic competition with the West. The first generation of socialist leaders may have dreamed of days when it would become possible for many differing opinions to be debated freely, but it was not to be as economic planning continued to reject parliamentary democracy.

I predict that in the future the debate on developmentalism may come to occupy a position similar to that of the former debate on socialism, and the latter may well provide a good lesson. Clearly there is no inevitable link between parliamentary democracy and classical liberalism. And certainly, politics and economics work independently; thus, as a matter of abstract theory, parliamentary democracy and developmentalism can coexist. Having noted this, we must also recognize that each individual political or economic system has its own particular dynamic, which cannot easily be changed, and, within the context of this dynamic the political and economic systems sometimes support each other and sometimes clash. The dynamic of the party and bureaucratic system created by economic planning in the end has continued to reject parliamentary democracy. And one can perhaps imagine a similar range of possibilities in the relationship between parliamentary democracy and developmentalism, from coexistence to confrontation. Certainly it is possible for parliamentary democracy and developmentalism to coexist. They do in postwar Japan. Maintaining this coexistence, though, requires a fixed set of conditions. These conditions are likely to be less rigid than those required for a parliamentary system and economic planning to coexist, but they are, nevertheless, necessary.

As can be anticipated from the preceding argument, these conditions are related to the dynamic of the bureaucratic system, as in the case of economic planning. Essential conditions are how neutral, and how flexible in responding to domestic and international changes, a developmentalist bureaucracy can be. If the bureaucracy becomes integrated with the various interest groups that developmentalism creates and becomes a vast interest group, and parliament loses the political power to control the organizational interests of such a bureaucracy, then developmentalism will either become an empty shell no longer able to pursue its original goal of realizing a potential for growth, or conversely, will provoke a rebellion among those who are alienated from the existing interest groups and cause parliamentary politics to become dysfunctional. In this case, developmentalism has no advantage over classical economic liberalism. Those who believe in classical economic liberalism object to developmentalism because of their distrust of the bureaucracy, which they believe is likely to be integrated with—or coopted by—the interest groups it created in pursuit of developmentalism. Analytically, though, even the above scenario is only one possible outcome of the interaction between developmentalism and democratization. Today, when the impetus toward superindustrialization is strong, many factors encourage the adoption of developmentalism. Also, the various possibilities of developmentalism itself have as yet not been well understood. Without an adequate analysis of these points, we will not solve many of the most important political and economic problems of today. Below, to help us solve these problems, I discuss two of the most important issues inherent in successful developmentalism.

THE DEVELOPMENT OF MASS DEMOCRACY

The first issue is the trend toward mass democratization. One characteristic of developmentalism is the importance it places on a distributive policy whose principal goal is to not weaken the incentives of workers and entrepreneurs in nonpriority sectors. The policy is a necessary outcome of the theory of developmentalism that emphasizes the *process* of unstable competition rather than attaining equilibrium from competition. In contrast, in the static theory of equilibrium, the concern is only with producing equilibrium, and no serious attention is given to the problems of frictional unemployment and weeding out inefficient firms that occur during the process of reaching equilibrium. In equilibrium theory, the problem of distribution is a policy issue of income equalization, adopted after resource allocation in the production sphere has been completed—that is, a welfare-state policy or graduated income tax.

Clearly apparent here is the contrast between the two aspects of the question of allocation and distribution. On the one hand, there is the aspect of helping to bring about equality of opportunity in choosing work or a style of life; on the other is the aspect of increasing equality of outcome as regards income. Developmentalism protects the farming community and fosters small-scale producers because its aim is that even in the noncutting-edge sectors to which they belong there should be technological opportunities (the opportunity to adopt new technologies or to make more efficient use of old ones) and lifestyle opportunities (mainly the opportunity to preserve the old way of life). As a by-product, it can be expected that many people, by remaining small-scale entrepreneurs, will participate actively in the market economy and that large numbers of people will create demand as consumers with long-range plans for their lives. (The disadvantage is that the problem of inefficient small-scale production is maintained.) In contrast, equilibrium-based economic liberalism takes the form of weeding out old lifestyles or technologies through market competition and compensating for this through income redistribution. Although equal opportunity to participate in the market is provided for all, from the first there is no chance that activities that are inefficient, calculated solely in monetary terms, will survive. Here, the narrowness of classical economic liberalism as liberalism is evident.

A characteristic of this kind of developmentalist distribution is not creating a rootless class completely removed from its past way of life or ethos. To take the example of agriculture, in that there will in the end be a substantial decrease in the proportion of the labor force working in agriculture, there is no great difference between the paths of developmentalism and economic liberalism. The issue is whether to disregard the disruption and try to achieve this change as rapidly as possible, or try to achieve it over a few generations while preserving a continuity in people's way of life. In postwar Japan, for example, the farming community was protected by a policy of price supports and thus was able to adapt slowly to rapid industrialization by gradually finding by-employment. It is Laslett's opinion that even in Britain before the industrial revolution, taking on by-employment helped farmers adapt to capitalism. These workers, who had maintained continuity in their way of life, did not become a proletariat, in the original sense, that had lost all resources other than their own bodies.

That is, to the extent that a continuity in lifestyle was maintained, a rootless, unproductive class did not emerge and no classes of winners and losers in industrialization were created.[24]

In postwar Japan, farming families kept possession of their farming land and their houses (which were larger than those in urban areas), and their income (much of which came from by-employment) increased at the same rate as that of workers in the cities. The majority of their children received educations and found employment in cities. After a generation or two, all those who wished to leave agriculture have finally done so. Yet during this period there has been no decrease in the number of farming families, thus enabling the parents (who are now advanced in age) of those families to maintain their way of life. Even today, many urban wage-earners who came from farming communities take their families to visit their villages and towns during the New Year and summer holidays.

Surprisingly, there has been no decrease in the number of small retail stores in the cities, despite the appearance of supermarkets and stores that are open around the clock. Though there have been changes in their activities, there has been an increase in the number of small and medium-sized firms. A large majority of the farming families, shopkeepers, and small and medium-sized firms from before the war have not become bankrupt and disappeared, and they are still an important segment of the middle class in present-day society. (No large urban slums have appeared in Japan.) This class, including those who have moved into the cities since the war, form what I call the "new middle mass" and continue to be an inexhaustible source of demand for mass-produced consumer durables. Present-day Japanese society takes the historically unprecedented form of a high-level mass consumer society that has not been structured along class lines.

If this were only a Japanese phenomenon, one could regard such a tendency as temporary and accidental. But a similar tendency seems to be appearing throughout East Asia, beginning with Korea, Taiwan, and Singapore. The developmentalism accompanied by distributive policy, in the sense being discussed here, may thus create a kind of high-level mass society. What will happen in such a society in the future is extremely hard to predict, given that it has no precedents. Will such a society become devoid of ideologies and original thoughts as a mass society is often said to become? I discuss this question in Chapter 9. For now I note that there is a possibility that adopting developmentalism may have unforeseen negative consequences.

THE INCREASING RIGIDITY OF THE BUREAUCRACY

The second issue inherent in successful developmentalism relates to the bureaucracy, which plays the central role in implementing developmentalist policy. As already noted frequently, the problem with industrial policy is the difficulty of ending it. When technological innovation in industry slows down, or the prospects for the political-economic system in the country become uncertain (for example, because the party supporting industrial policy loses power), one can no longer expect decreasing costs and industrial policy loses its validity. Also, the policies that protect and foster agriculture and small and medium-sized businesses may no longer be effective with changes in the industrial structure and a rise in the standard of living. But even when there are such changes, it is highly improbable that bureaucrats will easily relinquish their rights to intervene or alter their practices of intervention.

In postwar Japan, because of the vertical divisions of the bureaucratic structure (the cohesive and closed organizational nature of each bureau of each ministry), the symbiotic relationship between individual industries and the ministries in charge of them has grown stronger; thus there is a danger that the industrial policy implemented for a growing industry may, with the slowing of growth in that industry, become a protectionist policy for a stagnant industry. For farming households and small and medium-sized businesses (small shopkeepers, for example), protectionist political intervention continues over many years because of politicians' fears of losing votes. The restriction on rice imports is a representative example of such prolonged protectionism; here too the time has come for protectionism to be brought to an end, given the aging of the farmers and the divergence of the supported prices from international prices. This is the natural conclusion in terms of classical economic liberalism; but also in terms of the theory of developmentalism, the protectionism has lasted beyond justifiable limits. Changes in industrial structure, the diversification of firms' activities into several industries, the internationalization of the economy (particularly the entrance of foreign firms), and so on, have made industrial policy toward the leading postwar industries unnecessary and impossible to implement. Each ministry, however, is attempting to preserve as far as possible the limits of its authority of administrative intervention. Administrative guidance toward the financial industry is still strong, under the pretext of protecting depositors.

Japanese neoconservatism, as represented by the Nakasone administration, tried to overcome this resistance, but the opposition was extremely strong. If Japan fails to end industrial policy, its postwar developmentalism may be judged a failure. Japanese developmentalism, in many aspects, has depended on informal, *Kadi*-esque administrative intervention—so-called administrative guidance. This kind of informal intervention makes it doubly difficult to bring industrial policy to an end because it is difficult both to terminate it and to verify that it has been terminated. The Japanese experience provides a valuable lesson for future developmentalist countries. Industrial policy must include in advance a rule for bringing itself to an end. One way to facilitate this is to make the bureaucracy more flexible and less exclusionary (for example, by controlling vertical divisions or appointing external talent). Another way is to ensure the development of interest groups with political power that is strong enough to counterbalance or control the bureaucracy.

DEVELOPMENTALISM AS A WORLDVIEW

The image of the world that lies behind developmentalism resembles biology or ecology more than mechanics. Its central concern is the life-cycle of each industry and the process of evolution and finding the respective niche of each industry. Each industry is born, experiences rapid growth in its infancy, is vigorous in its youth, and in due course enters adulthood and then old age. Technological and organizational innovations during this period can be compared to mutation or changes in character due to heredity. Industrial policy in developmentalism is intended to foster development during the stage of infancy in this life-cycle (the phase of declining marginal cost), and we can say that distributive policy usually maintains a particular niche for the various "species" (industries and firms). In developing countries, this period of infancy will appear, simultaneously and unmistakably, in a majority of industries. But even in the advanced countries, specific industries (for example, the semiconductor industry at present) are clearly recognized as being in the stage of infancy.

The reality of industrialization is a composite of all the life-cycles of the various industries. This life-cycle does not emerge by aggregating all the responses of all the economic actors to the stimuli provided by the environment. Why does industry have an infancy, an adulthood, and an old age? If one explains it as a result of the creation, application, and stagnation of technology, then why does technology have this kind of life-cycle? Technology is, clearly, an endogenous factor of development, which at its birth is planted within a particular industry, changes with the development of that industry, and gradually declines. Without a dynamic analysis that follows this development, one will not be able to understand the life-cycle of industry or, in its turn, industrialization. One could say that economics since the classical school, and particularly neoclassical economics, has analyzed mature economies in their adult stages and thus has evaluated other phases of the life-cycle from the perspective of such an adult economy. This is acceptable for advanced industrial countries that have achieved adulthood. But if, in forgetting their own periods of infancy, the advanced industrial countries try to enforce their own formulas on developing countries, the development of the latter will be hampered. To use such a rough analogy is dangerous, but for developing countries striving to industrialize, developmentalism is more appropriate than classical economic liberalism.

The problem with developmentalism or, rather, the problem common to all phenomena of growth is perhaps how to change behavior with each phase of the life-cycle. Concretely speaking, this problem will become apparent when each economy has overcome its backwardness. To repeat, it is not easy for a country that has industrialized sufficiently to bring industrial policy to an end. Even in the most advanced countries, there may be industries suitable as objects of what I am here calling industrial policy. But to designate individual industries appropriately, and in due course to bring such a policy to an end at the appropriate time, is a difficult task. In contrast, classical economic liberalism, unconcerned with this kind of industrial life-cycle, prescribes that administrative intervention should be minimized. It is doubtful that the prescription can be followed, and it may even be accurate to say that it is unrealistic, but there is no doubt that the prescription is most concise. Of course, were one to follow this prescription, one might have to sacrifice the growth rate to some degree and engender discontent over distribution. There may be a balance between the advantages and defects of the two economic modes; in contrast to developmentalism, which can achieve higher growth rates but suffers from the difficulties of controlling policy, classical economic liberalism takes pride in the simplicity of its prescription, which is maintained by sacrificing the growth rate. In the final analysis, to manage developmentalism well is to control the bureaucracy, and the difficulty of doing so becomes a burden for parliamentary democracy. In this sense, the success or failure of developmentalism depends entirely on the workings of parliamentary democracy.

In other words, the fundamental problem in managing developmentalism is determining what kind of liberalism of economic action is possible under the conditions of a trend of decreasing cost and with a long-term view in decision making. From the perspective of classical economic liberalism, one can think of two responses. One is that even the trend toward a long-term view in decision making is a temporary phenomenon that has been observed since the Second World War, for example, and so classical economic liberalism works efficiently as ever. This is the passive response. The other is the positive response, that classical economic liberalism is one of the paramount rules for human beings and so must be preserved, even at the cost of economic growth or anything else. The bases of these two responses are different. I discuss them beginning in Chapter 8.

CHAPTER 7

The Increasing Complexity
of the International Economy

The International Implications of Developmentalism

In the preceding chapters I discussed developmentalism mainly from the standpoint of the domestic economy. It was, of course, the international political-economic environment of the twentieth century that generated developmentalism, and I devoted many pages to this subject. I have not, however, adequately examined the effects of developmentalism on the global economy as a whole. The goal of this chapter is to attempt to examine these effects, if only in part.

Three important international issues relate to developmentalism. The first is the problem of the effect successful developmentalism exerts on the international monetary system. The second is the question of foreign aid and investment, which has a direct and significant connection to the bases on which developmentalism can be maintained. One could broadly rephrase these two issues as a question of international public goods. The third is the theoretical problem of industrial organization in those industries most technologically advanced by international standards. To adapt a developmentalist perspective, it may be possible to achieve international cooperation within each industry, but it is also possible that the risk of international confrontation may be increased when nations protect their most technologically advanced industries. Whichever of these possibilities materializes, it will surely have a strong effect on international politics, ever in thrall to nationalism. Before discussing these points, however, I briefly review the history of international relations from the following perspective.

THE ECONOMIC CHARACTER OF MODERN CIVILIZATION

Modern civilization, born in Europe, is the first example of a great civilization that does not have an integrated political order, or a great civilization not based on a global empire. Politically, the dynamics of a balance of power was expected to maintain orderly international relations. However, most political scientists analyzing international relations have been cynical or at best half-hearted toward the effective uses of the balance of power in maintaining the international order. In regard to economies, the optimism of economic philosophy since Adam Smith—that free trade will bring about international harmony—has been influential, adequately compensating for the pessimism toward international politics. That is, while politics has been seen as prone to disintegration, economies have been seen as capable of achieving harmony. In this sense the weapon of ideological unity for modern civilization has been the economics of free trade. That is, seeing the economic aspect of modern civilization from a unidimensional perspective of liberal economics made integration of a global civilization possible. This unidimensional perspective on modern civilization has not changed since the sixteenth and seventeenth centuries, when modern civilization was in its embryonic stage.

Within the history of modern civilization, it was perhaps the Pax Americana during the cold war that depended most on an integrating role for noneconomic, political-military power. Even this Pax Americana, however, did not aim at a global empire. Samuel Huntington probably was making this observation when he said that the United States was attempting to create not a "territorial empire" but a "functional empire."[1] Other than the antagonistic U.S. relationship with the Soviet Union, which did aim at a global empire, U.S. military interventions were always restrained. For example, had the United States used its full strength in Vietnam, a military occupation would have been possible. But both the American people and leaders well understood that political-military territorial rule of other nations by the United States would have meant the ideological suicide of the United States as a civilization. Thus, for the Pax Americana, the irreplaceable mainstay of its civilization is economic logic—that is, the ideology of free trade. As exemplified in the IMF and GATT, the economic liberalism of the international system created and led by the United States was the realization of this ideology. When seen in this light, it is also perhaps understandable why American economic diplomacy persists in maintaining this rule of economic freedom.

The theory of hegemony, examined in Chapter 3, is in a way the stirring of the owl of Minerva for this Pax Americana. The theory of hegemony is an attempt to integrate a classical (or rather neoclassical) liberal economy and nationalism. However, given that the economic liberalism of the former is expected to play the positive role in creating the international order, the international public goods that are the central concept in this theory are defined as the tangible and intangible institutional environment necessary to support free trade. In shaping the international order, the leading role is played by the global market, and military power plays only a supplementary role. The theory of hegemony contains this kind of message; the success or failure of the Pax Americana depends on whether we can expect the unidimensional control of classical economic liberalism. Scholars often seek to attribute the reasons for the decline of the Pax Americana to the decline in U.S. economic ability to supply international public goods, but this is only a surface understanding. A deeper cause is that from the first, the reality of industrialization has been at odds with the unidimensional world depicted by classical and neoclassical economic liberalism.

Today, constant and continuous technological innovation and an increasingly long-term orientation in decision making have irrevocably complicated the realities of the liberal economy (capitalism). In our terms, the well-established trend of decreasing cost has created a mosaic of classical capitalism and developmentalism. Thus, the problems created by an economics of decreasing cost cannot be readily comprehended by the precepts of classical economic liberalism, and this fact intensified the conflict between economic liberalism and nationalism. In the previous chapter, I discussed at some length developmentalism's implications for the domestic economy, but its implications for the international economy are just as important. Developmentalism causes certain kinds of nations to develop rapidly and intensifies international conflicts, but it also invigorates and expands global trade. As discussed in Chapter 4, global trade is now actually emerging as two trends, toward the spread of industrialization (the developmentalist growth of the NIEs) and toward the trading state. These trends are difficult to understand within the classical schema, whose pillars are economic liberalism and nationalism.

A further problem with the classical liberal model has become particularly apparent recently (since the adoption of the floating exchange rate system). This is the problem of money, finance, and investment produced by the spread of industrialization and the trend toward the trading state. Of course, since the beginning of industrialization, these have been fundamental issues. With economic growth through industrialization becoming an incontrovertible fact, several problems cross national borders and affect the course of the economy of the whole world in significant ways: controls on the supply of money for growth, portfolio selections of increasing financial assets, foreign direct investment, and the like.

Both the classical theory of economic liberalism and the neoclassical theory that is its modern variant, in that their main concern is with a static theory of the "real" economy, have been unable to deal adequately with the problem of the "monetary" economy. There has already been much criticism of and self-criticism within the classical and neoclassical "veil of money" approaches, and there are now few economists who accept

the neoclassical "neutrality hypothesis," which posits that the real economy and the monetary economy can be analyzed separately. It was J. M.
Keynes, the greatest economist of the first half of the twentieth century,
and Knut Wicksell who explicitly incorporated into theory the linkage between the real and monetary economies. Generally speaking, these problems of money, finance, and investment cannot but exert a great influence
on the international economy, and no one today doubts that they are of
critical importance. Their influence has been particularly great since the
1970s and the adoption of the floating exchange rate system, the sudden acceleration in the international transfer of capital, and the rapid increase in
investment by multinational companies. Below I discuss the most important among these issues, including the function of the floating exchange
rate system.

THE DEMISE OF THE PAX AMERICANA

In reviewing the history of the Pax Americana we come to realize that
the problems of money, finance, and investment have received inadequate
attention. The political and economic stabilization of the Western world
achieved through the Pax Americana created two major but unexpected
trends, toward the trading state and toward developmentalism. The system
of free trade guaranteed by the Pax Americana provided newly independent nations with a favorable environment for the takeoff to industrialization, but the trend of decreasing costs seen during the period of takeoff
usually generated a strong desire to depend on exports. If a certain critical point is passed and they become internationally competitive, developing countries using price cutting as a weapon are able to flood the world
market with their exports. The most striking examples of this have been
Japan and the Asian NIEs, which developed by relying on developmentalism; exports from these countries poured into, particularly, the wide open
American market.

    This is not to say that the benefits of the economic liberalization
brought about by the Pax Americana were confined to the newly emerging
economies. The European countries too, as represented by Germany, were
generally more dependent on trade than they had been before the war. During the prewar period the Japanese economy had already almost reached
the level of the developed countries, and after the war its economic policy
became distinctively developmentalist, exhibiting characteristics of both
Europe and the Asian NIEs. As Richard Rosecrance observed, the general
trend in the postwar world economy was toward the "trading state."[2]

    This trend of nations toward becoming trading states, however, was an
unexpected and in a sense irritating development for the United States
(and for the Soviet Union). Of course, an expansion in world trade was what
the Pax Americana had hoped to achieve. But another principle of the Pax
Americana was the doctrine of a just war against the Soviet Union, and
it was impossible for the United States to maintain a balance of military

power with the Soviets. The preoccupation of the trading state with economic growth perhaps implies, in terms of resource allocation, an inclination to be lightly armed, but from the American perspective, this trend toward abandonment of military concerns was unwelcome. Japan was the first to exhibit this preoccupation, but not the last, as seen in the Asian NIEs. The preoccupation with economic growth in these developing countries could be called "free-riding" on the security system provided by the Pax Americana. That is, the consciously export-promoting policies and "industrial policy" of these countries was nothing more than a violation of the rules when seen from the standpoint of classical economic liberalism.

Of course the Pax Americana was, so to speak, paternalistic in its concern with the progress of the developing countries. Clauses in the articles of the IMF and GATT, for example, provide exceptions for developing countries. But nobody expected that the trading-state developmentalism of the developing countries would be as successful as it has been, or that there would be countries (such as Taiwan) whose degree of dependency on trade would exceed 100 percent (exports and imports ÷ GNP). That there would even be countries that would threaten U.S. economic hegemony (Japan was the first example of this) was beyond everybody's expectations, including those of Japan and other developmentalist countries. This became an important factor in forcing a rearrangement in the basic structure of the Pax Americana.

In the end, it was the superpowers, who were the fundamental supports for a framework of peace centered on military force (in my terms, based on the doctrine of just war), that lagged in their awareness of this situation. The Soviet Union, before *perestroika*, paid scant attention to the expansion and increasing interdependence of the global economy. Good evidence of this is the fact that Brezhnev, during the period of détente in the 1970s, built up Soviet military power and neglected to improve the economic structure. But one cannot say that the United States was sufficiently sensitive to the structural changes in the world economy either. In the perceptive words of Rosecrance:

> This recognition dawned gradually, and the United States may perhaps have been the last to acknowledge it, which was not surprising. The most powerful economy is ready to make fewer adjustments, and America tried initially to pursue its domestic economic policies without taking into account the effect on others, on itself, and on the international system as a whole. . . . Finally, in the 1980s two American administrations accepted lower United States growth in order to control inflation and began to focus on the international impact of United States policies. The delay in fashioning a strategy of adjustment to international economic realities almost certainly made it more difficult. Smaller countries actively sought to find a niche in the structure of international comparative advantage and in the demand for their goods. Larger countries with large internal markets postponed that reckoning as long as they could.[3]

This argument demonstrates well the significance of the trend toward the trading state. It is historically ironic that the United States, which itself had depended little on trade, promoted the trend toward the trading state through its support of the system of free trade; this trend, though, cannot but extend in due course to both the United States and the former Soviet Union. Even in the United States the situation has recently been changing rapidly; total exports as a proportion of GNP have increased particularly since 1987, and the degree of trade dependency has exceeded that of Japan since the beginning of the 1990s. This may be a sign that the United States, too, is becoming a trading state.

I expect these trends, toward the trading state and developmentalism, to continue in the future. There is virtually no risk of military clashes between the great powers. The likelihood does exist, however small, for the world to split into politically and economically isolated blocs, creating the danger of war between them. However, even if this situation were to arise, it would not be in the foreseeable future. In any case, this is the worst possible scenario, and it is probably more likely that relative peace will continue, enabling world trade to continue.

Given this situation, the trend toward the trading state will strengthen. (There may be cases, though, where a particular country is ostracized by a trading bloc and faces a crisis.) And, as already mentioned, it is hard to imagine developmentalism weakening. The number of developing countries that try to adopt developmentalism will surely increase. There are any number of strong candidates for this in Asia and Central and South America. Furthermore, one cannot imagine the countries in the former Soviet Union and Eastern Europe proceeding directly to classical economic liberalism; they are more likely to adopt some form of developmentalism. Developmentalism will occupy the greater part of the map of the world—as long as reindustrialization in the countries of Eastern Europe does not fail.

The spread of developmentalism is not confined to developing countries. There is now in process a great wave of technological innovation that we could call the "third industrial revolution." This is connected to transindustrialization and may, or probably will, create a new stage of human civilization. But during the transitional period of indeterminate length leading to the new stage, technological innovation will be incorporated in the existing system of industrialization and will likely intensify competition in the cutting-edge industries. The trend of decreasing cost will become dominant in those industries, and firms will be more likely to make decisions on a long-term basis. As discussed in the previous chapter, if this happens, even the developed countries can no longer expect equilibrium to be maintained through classical competition. There are already a number of such cases.

For example, had IBM been able to expand, without any restrictions, it might have achieved a monopoly in the world computer market. But

IBM was restrained by the silent pressure of domestic U.S. antitrust regulations. In addition, several countries, with IBM in mind, tried to protect and foster their domestic industry, and Japan was successful in doing so. Had Japan not protected its own computer industry, its electronic industry might have become an industry of subcontractors, supplying semiconductors and accessory machinery and tools to IBM, or Japanese firms in the industry might even have been acquired by IBM. At that point IBM might well have become invincible. Had this kind of monopoly been established, Apple Computer, integrated circuits at the megabit level, and notebook computers might not have appeared.

There have been in the past and may well be in the future many similar cases. For example, the spread of high-definition television will probably not proceed on the basis of market competition because the government in each country intervenes. Thus in this and in many other industries there is little likelihood that gains due to an explosion of new demand will be captured by a global monopoly of a particular firm in a particular country. These examples show that it is clearly possible for a firm that achieves cutting-edge technological innovation ahead of other companies to dominate the world market. But policies to prevent this from happening are already in place.

The problems, on the one hand, of the trading state and developmentalism, and on the other, of global finance and investment, generate issues beyond the capacity of the classical system of economic liberalism to control. Of course it is not easy to devise an international economic system that can deal with these issues, but one can suggest the minimum requirements for such a system. I make such suggestions in the following sections.

A Reexamination of International Public Goods, I

In thinking of an international economic system for the future, let us take the view that an expansion of trade is fundamentally desirable. (If this were not the case, any continuity with the trend of history to this point would be lost. I discuss the possible collapse of this system below, but in doing so I refer to the possibility of a different objective.) If we determine this as our objective, tangible and intangible international institutions and agreements that help to expand trade become indispensable. For the time being, following the argument in the first half of this book, let us call this an international public good. But, as already mentioned, the concept of international public goods is inadequate; in particular, there are many dangers in the analogy with the neoclassical concept of domestic public goods. Characteristics specific to the nation-state, such as a common language or customs, or territorial sovereignty, for example, do not exist in an international system. Thus it is inevitable that international public goods and domestic public goods differ in substance. I postpone discussing this difference, however, to the end of this section, and for the time being use the expression "international public goods." The international public goods under a new international economic system must naturally be different from those we have had up to now. Below, I focus particularly on international money and on aid to developing countries (in a broad sense), two topics that have not been dealt with adequately in the conventional theory of domestic public goods.

INTERNATIONAL MONEY

The supply of money is often talked of as a public good. But whether copper coin, gold coin, or fiat money, money itself is not a public good (since it is impossible to use in common, and possible to restrict its uses). What makes money more than a mere piece of metal or paper are its functions as a unit of account, a means of payment, and a means of wealth accumulation. The supply of money is regarded as a public good because these functions benefit spenders and recipients.

We should, however, note that its functions as means of payment and wealth accumulation depend on money's actual value—its purchasing power—being constant. This is because nobody will accept or try to save something whose value is declining. It has been recognized since the sixteenth century that as long as there is no substantial change in the economic condition, there is a strong correlation between the total amount of money supply and the price level (the inverse relation between the former and the purchasing power of money as held by the quantity theory of money). Thus, unless there is a system controlling the total money supply, money will not retain its value. If there is too much money there will be inflation, and if there is too little, deflation; either will throw the valuation of goods into confusion, and both will interfere with the workings of the market economy. In short, not money, but a system that maintains the value of money—a system that controls the amount of money supplied—is an indispensable public good for a market economy. I call money supported by this kind of system "currency."

STABILITY IN CURRENCY VALUE

One of the greatest questions for the international economy at present is whether the current system of floating exchange rates really does qualify as an international currency system (an international public good). It is well known that opinions are divided. On the one hand is the negative assessment that once the system of fixed exchange rates could not be sustained, there were no other possible choices; this is probably the majority opinion at present. On the other is the argument often made by scholars before the system was actually adopted: the positive assessment that the system of floating exchange rates is the ideal international currency system. Here I attempt to compare the floating and fixed exchange rate systems, keeping in mind the choice between developmentalism and classical economic liberalism.

If one emphasizes stability in currency value, the system of floating exchange rates is a failure. In view of our experience so far, we must expect that the range of fluctuation for the exchange rates of leading currencies (dollar, yen, and mark) will be 3 to 5 percent annually, and as high as 20 percent over a five-year period. Such figures are higher than an ordinary profit-to-sale ratio; in other words, they could change profit-making firms into money-losing ones (or vice versa).[4]

Whichever currency one takes—dollar, mark, or yen—one cannot expect price stability in international transactions.[5] Trade under a floating exchange rate system cannot avoid this risk. Even covering this risk in the futures market is inadequate as a solution because the period covered in the futures market is limited to six months; thus the costs of sunk investment, as well as even those of employment and raw materials of export-oriented industries, remain exposed to exchange rate risk. The system of floating exchange rates, therefore, creates a situation similar to that encountered by the domestic economy that experiences frequent and significant changes in prices. Such changes cannot but diminish the desire to export (and the enthusiasm to produce exportable products), and cause firms to become more interested in the domestic market. One might call this the trade-reducing effect of a floating exchange rate system. Since the adoption of the system of floating exchange rates, there has been a clear reduction in the macroeconomic performance of the advanced industrial countries and in the growth of international trade, and it is probably no accident that trade friction has intensified.

Countless models have attempted to explain the behavior of the system of floating exchange rates, but unfortunately their results differ widely, making us acutely aware of "the imperfection of economic knowledge," especially in the analyses of the floating exchange rate system.[6] One of the most important reasons this model building yields unsatisfactory results is that one has to include portfolio selection behavior (including speculation), and particularly the international portfolio selection, as a factor in the fluctuation in exchange rates, as I discuss in greater detail below. Models that include speculation have to incorporate forecasts, but the general solutions provided by such theoretical models (not forecasting models) almost always seem to be unbounded.[7] I do not claim to have the ability to go into a specialized discussion of such models, but we may be allowed to conclude that in our experience up to this point and in the theoretical results as a whole, there has been nothing to suggest whether fluctuations in the exchange rate are convergent or cyclical. At present, firms throughout the world are operating without any insight as to whether exchange rate fluctuations are cyclical or move toward restoring equilibrium. In short, the system of floating exchange rates has not succeeded in stabilizing the value of international currencies.

AN EXPORT-ORIENTED, LONG-TERM VIEW

An important conclusion from this is that, under the increasing uncertainty inherent in exchange rate risk, the motivation for long-term management, at least in connection with trade, is weakened and probably encourages short-term orientation in management. Short-term planning is the opposite of the trend toward "long-termism" in decision making discussed as a general historical trend in the previous chapter, and the trend toward long-term planning will be severely tested under the regime of floating exchange rates. In other words, if the system causes firms' horizons to become short term, it will have a market-stabilizing effect, in the sense that it will check the instability of competition under decreasing costs. But it is unclear how substantial this influence will be.

We can say, however, that exchange rate fluctuation acts as a filter, distinguishing companies and countries on the basis of their predisposition to be export-oriented. Only companies with a management predisposition to overcome exchange rate risk will set about exporting. Standard economic theory, in classifying attitudes toward risk, distinguishes between risk-averse and risk-loving economic actors, but this is only a formal distinction. The attitude of a firm that ventures into exporting regardless of exchange rate risk contains elements not captured by calling it risk-loving. Keynes said that it was an "animal spirit" that inclined an entrepreneur toward investment; I believe a similar animal spirit is necessary to set about exporting.

This kind of argument may run counter to the mainstream of economics. For example, one can imagine an argument to the effect that the difference between domestic supply and demand will be made up by exports and imports. Certainly in those cases where the products are homogeneous (not highly differentiated), as is often true of primary products such as agricultural products, oil, coal, minerals, and metal ores, there is no difference between foreign and domestic markets, and any surplus products will flow naturally, so to speak, to foreign markets. But today, when there is a high degree of product differentiation in manufacturing, and a flourishing horizontal division of international labor that has become dominant because of this, exporting industries must tailor their products to the requirements of foreign markets, make efforts to advertise their differentiated products, create a sales network, and maintain an inventory. In other words, exporting nowadays requires very large investments. Thus, whether a firm can adopt export-oriented management is determined by whether it has the "animal spirit" necessary for this kind of investment.

That is, the system of floating exchange rates separates those firms that have the animal spirit for such investment from those that do not. For example, it is sometimes said that while the clearly export-oriented firms in the NIEs and Japan will take action to establish and maintain a beachhead, U.S. firms, which until very recently depended largely on the domestic market, are more likely to withdraw at the first sign of a disadvantageous exchange rate. Given this difference, their respective long-term export performances cannot but differ as well. And the effect of a reduced motivation to trade, attributed to the floating exchange rate system, does not work in the same way for all countries. The proportion of export-oriented firms differs from country to country, and a country itself may adopt policies to promote exports. The interest and motivation of the people themselves will have a controlling influence on these policies. The difference between whether a country is a trading state or not becomes clear at this point.

Whether the export industries are in a phase of decreasing cost is vital in determining the motivation to export—that is, to make "product differentiation" of exported products. In this phase, what firms require above all is demand. If domestic demand is buoyant, their need for demand will be satisfied within the country (and during this time prices will be reduced). But if a recession hits the domestic economy, firms with decreasing cost will turn to exports to find demand, and at this point will reduce their prices. The increase in exports that goes with this price reduction will be criticized as dumping. It is not that there are no elements of classical export dumping in this (that is, a cartel for maintaining domestic prices); but in industries faced with decreasing cost it is inevitable that with an increase in exports there will be a decrease in costs (marginal or average cost). Thus firms under the pressure of decreasing costs are firms full of an animal spirit toward exports. Developmentalism attempts to sustain the situation of decreasing cost, and developmentalist industries or countries are at least intermittently export-oriented (or trading states) and are often export-oriented at all times.

Thus one can think of three effects created by the system of floating exchange rates: a trade-reducing effect in the sense explained above, a market-stabilizing effect, and a filtering effect. First, speaking in general, the system of floating exchange rates increases the risks associated with trade, thus reducing trade. Second, the system may stabilize the market when management in the world as a whole, fearing the increased risk, begins planning for the short term. Although these shortened managerial horizons do not exploit the benefits of decreasing cost as much as they could, market instability, generated by the trend of decreasing cost, is generally alleviated.

Third, this effect does not work everywhere in the same way, and the uncertainty of fluctuations in the exchange rate acts as a filter for countries. The presence or absence of an animal spirit toward exporting creates a difference in whether decision making is long term or short term, and this difference substantively determines each country's export performance. Schematically, and somewhat simplistically, the system of floating exchange rates further exacerbates the difference in export performance between trading states (particularly developmentalist countries) and countries that espouse classical economic liberalism and do not become active trading states (as can be seen, for example, in a comparison of the Asian NIEs and Japan with the United States, until recently, and the Latin American countries). The preceding is to say that there is a conflict between the first two effects and the third. If in the midst of a general stabilizing trend, only trading states (particularly developmentalist countries) increasingly focus their energies on exports, then there will be an increasingly striking contrast with those countries that espouse classical economic liberalism. Therein lies a significant reason that cannot but intensify international political friction.

BURDEN-SHARING AMONG
INTERNATIONAL CURRENCIES

Let us examine the system of floating exchange rates from the slightly different perspective of controlling the supply of international currency. Under the gold standard or the dollar standard, it was necessary to control the supply of international currency—that is, the amount of gold being used as currency or the amount of dollars issued—in order to stabilize the value of the currency. Under an ideal system of floating exchange rates, however, the problem itself will disappear, theoretically. This is because, when exchange rates are adjusted instantaneously, a demand for any country's currency is expected immediately to be matched with a supply. The leading currencies, at least, can be obtained almost instantaneously, thanks to advances in the technology of exchange transactions made possible by the information revolution; and currency reserves, once needed to facilitate smooth exchange transactions, have become unnecessary. The system of floating exchange rates as a theoretical model seemed to have solved this problem of controlling the supply of international currency, if at the cost of fluctuations in the exchange rate.

In reality, all governments share the concern that excessive fluctuations in the exchange rate cannot be ignored. One reason for this is their concern about the trade-reducing effect mentioned above. Indeed, all countries, and particularly the leading trading nations, have no choice but to maintain adequate amounts of other countries' currencies with which to intervene in the markets to control exchange rate fluctuations. The policy of intervening in the exchange markets has become a substitute for the policy of controlling the supply of international currency.

To continue international trading, there must be something that functions as an international currency as a means of transaction, and the problem of how to control this will not disappear. Under a system of floating exchange rates, one country can always use its own currency to buy another country's products. Even if the value of a particular country's currency fluctuates, it will never be completely rejected internationally. In this sense, every country's domestic currency is also potentially, or partly, an international currency. If, for example, an important trading power were to increase the supply of its domestic currency very rapidly, this would create global inflationary pressure. Because that kind of situation is undesirable, a rule for controlling the system becomes necessary.

It is difficult to define such rules specifically, or to enforce them strictly, and therefore the leading countries anxiously monitor the supply of domestic currency and cooperate with each other in exchange rate intervention. Thus, international currency under the system of floating exchange rates no longer takes the form of a single currency. It can be provided only in the form of a highly complicated system. Applied to the international arena, the quantity theory of money can be formulated only in an ambiguous form. In this sense, it is possible to say that controlling international currency has thus become a burden to be shared by the leading nations. That is, the international currency system—an international public good—is being supplied collectively by the leading nations.

The nature of this burden-sharing merits attention because, as is well known, the most difficult problem of public goods is the problem of so-called free-riders, those who shirk their burdens. As mentioned above, the system of floating exchange rates seems quite naturally as if it should decentralize the burden of responsibility for supplying international currency; and if it did so the problem of free-riding would be overcome naturally. In reality, however, it is unclear how the burden will be distributed because it depends on how the exchange rates fluctuate—in other words, on how the system of floating exchange rates is organized. (One can say, though, that because of this uncertainty countries will not object to sharing the burden.) In order to make this point clear, we must understand the mechanism that determines exchange rates; most important is the relationship between the exchange market for settling trade accounts and that for transferring capital.

TRADE AND INVESTMENT: PRODUCTS AND FINANCIAL ASSETS

International economic activity includes trade as well as the transfer of capital (both direct investment and financial investment). Each of these operates to some degree according to different factors, and through different mechanisms. Imports and exports of products (and so the trade balance) are determined by the level of the exchange rate, but exports and imports of capital are determined by changes (more accurately, the expectation of changes) in the exchange rate. Of course, other factors, such as differences in interest rates, differences in investment risk, a country's policies (particularly those related to foreign aid and reducing accumulated foreign debt), and even the general social situation of a country also influence the transfer of capital. Consider for the time being, though, only the exchange rate changes; in this case, unless there is a change in the exchange rate, there will be no transfer of capital.

Thus, a system of fixed exchange rates makes a theory of exchange rates that concentrates on the trade balance possible. But a system of floating exchange rates requires us to consider the capital account. For example, the theory of purchasing power parity—that is, the theory that the exchange rate is determined across currencies to make their respective purchasing powers (toward tradable goods) the same and to make the trade account balance—is representative of theories that center on the trade balance, but it is inapplicable under a system of floating exchange rates.[8]

With a floating exchange rate system, the exchange rate changes continually, and both the trade balance and the capital account also change in response to the changes in the exchange rate. The exchange rate fluctuates depending on the total supply and demand for exchange—that is, whether the sum of the current account (which in the following argument I consider to be equivalent to the trade balance) and the capital account (the balance of international payments) is positive or negative.[9] An important corollary of this is that under a floating system, the exchange rate brings the balance of international payments into equilibrium, but not the current account. This argument is well known among specialists, but let me provide a simple illustration for the sake of emphasis.

Following standard economic theory, let us assume that exports of goods are determined by the global business climate and the exchange rate, and that imports of goods are determined by the domestic business climate and the exchange rate. From this we can theoretically calculate the exchange rate at which exports and imports would be in equilibrium, but let us posit that by chance the exchange rate has settled at exactly that level, and that this is 120 yen to the dollar. If, however, Japan at that point has an excess of capital (for example, an excess of savings over investment, corresponding to what economists call loanable funds), then that rate will not be maintained. There will be an outflow of capital to other countries—for example, to the United States (thus necessitating the purchase of dollars and the sale of yen). As a result, the yen will weaken against the dollar, moving to a rate of perhaps 140 yen to the dollar, an exchange rate at which exports will be invigorated and the current account will have a surplus just large enough to make up for the capital outflow.

During this period, even though the exchange rate changes, Japanese investment and saving behavior does not change fundamentally. For example, unless there is a change in the returns on Japan's U.S. investments, the investment plan when the rate is 120 yen and when it is 140 yen will be exactly the same as long as the return on the investment in the United States remains the same. The dollar value of Japanese investments may drop to $\frac{6}{7}$ of the original value, but the yen value of the returns (and that of the investment itself) will go up to $\frac{7}{6}$ of the original value; thus there will be no change in the rate of return measured in yen. Though there may be speculation on the exchange rate during the change from a rate of 120 yen to 140 yen, let us suppose that this speculation is only a peripheral phenomenon and does not have the power to change the working of the basic mechanism.[10] Needless to say, in capital-deficient countries—the United States, for example—precisely the reverse phenomenon would occur.

Simply stated, the capital account is a quasi-given in exchange rate supply and demand, determined in advance by capital surplus or shortage within the domestic economy and the exchange rate changes in a way that enables the current account to eliminate surplus or shortage of capital in the domestic economy. At this exchange rate, the current account will not balance and purchasing power parity will not hold. For capital-rich countries, the exchange rate will be lower than the level at which the current account would be balanced (thus aiding exports); for capital-deficient countries, the exchange rate will be high (thus hindering exports).

The above analysis, simplified here, is widely accepted by international economists, although one can think of a variety of complicating possibilities. The main point of this simplification is the Keynesian hypothesis that shortage or surplus of capital flow within a country (savings – investment + tax revenue – government expenditure) can be equilibrated not by the domestic profit rate but only by the income level. On the other hand, this argument assumes that asset selection (as stocks, changes in the amounts of which involve international transfer of capital) responds sensitively to the interest rate. This is also Keynesian in spirit in that it places emphasis on asset selection. As is well known, the basic formula of Keynesian economics is savings – investment + tax revenue – government expenditure = exports – imports. Rewriting both sides of this equation, we obtain the relationship: deficit in the capital account = surplus in the current account. As noted above, a surplus in the current account will make up for net export of capital. In any case, as long as we recognize the logic of the Keynesian analysis, my conclusion is that in capital-deficient countries, the exchange rate will be a handicap to exports and an advantage for imports, and vice versa in capital-rich countries. Under a system of floating exchange rates, there will be what one could call distortions in exports and imports (instead of, for example, purchasing power parity).

For example, two solutions have been proposed to deal with the problem of the large U.S. trade deficit. One centers on the capital account to solve the capital deficiency in the United States—specifically, to increase the saving rate, increase tax rates, or decrease government spending. The other proposal centers on the trade balance—to improve the U.S. ability to export and other countries' ability to import. Liberalization of the Japanese market is often emphasized as a concrete proposal in the latter. Which proposal gets to the heart of the problem should be evident from the preceding argument. It is not the case that both the first and second proposals would be effective in their own ways; it is the first proposal that is decisively important.

Let us assume that the U.S. current account deficit has been reduced by careful attempts to follow the suggestions made in the second proposal. As is shown by the Keynesian equation cited above, however, unless there is a change in the deficiency in U.S. saving, there has to be a decrease in the level of investment (and in government spending). Without an increase in saving, the only thing that will occur is a shift in emphasis from investment to exports in the United States. In the long term, the decline in investment, which prevents an increase in the ability to export, is the important problem. The United States at present is strongly urging liberalization of the Japanese market, but this will only result in diminishing investment. Inevitably, unless there is an increase in saving or taxes, nothing will enable the United States to increase both exports and investment at the same time. (I return later to a discussion of the liberalization of Japanese markets as an issue relating to the rules of international economy.)

Although most economists agree with this argument, the problem is its actual implications. Capital deficiency under a system of floating exchange rates tends to increase structural trade imbalances. This is because, in capital-deficient countries, export industries are handicapped by the comparatively high exchange rate (whereas industries producing for domestic demand are not). Thus industries will turn their backs on exports and gradually withdraw from the world market. Conversely, in countries where there is a surplus of capital, as in Japan, exports will gain an advantage. This asymmetry is an important problem for floating exchange rate systems generally. That is, when some countries have significant shortages of capital while others have large surpluses of capital, their respective efforts to export and import are weakened, and one result is an even larger trade imbalance.

As long as we are using this system, in the long term all countries (except when they are affected by the business cycle) will need domestic policies to prevent a shortage or surplus of capital. The United States, and developing countries too, will not be able to escape the trap of accumulating debt unless they eliminate their capital deficiencies. Quite symmetrically, one can also imagine a proposal that capital-rich countries such as Japan must eliminate the situation of having surplus capital. Looking at the world as a whole, however, we should not require perfect symmetry. This is because, as long as the world is in a phase of industrialization, including those developing countries for whom saving is difficult, there will probably be a basic deficiency of the capital necessary for development and investment. Given that throughout the nineteenth and twentieth centuries the major developed nations acted as a source of capital, this kind of conjecture may well be quite valid. The leading developed countries have a responsibility to supply capital. (To be noted explicitly, however, is that if there is a capital surplus globally, it is the responsibility of the capital-rich countries to reduce their excess saving.)

A Reexamination of International Public Goods, II

In this section, I consider the question of international public goods from a perspective that focuses on developing countries. As already mentioned, the classical model of free trade does not seem adequate to analyze the present international system. The reality of industrialization is far too different from the ideal of global homogenization, as envisioned in the Heckscher-Ohlin theorem. Throughout two centuries of industrialization, the only unchanging reality has been increasing, rather than diminishing, differences in economic performance between the developed and developing countries due to what I am calling the dynamic of technology. If the diffusion of technology fails to occur, global inequality will widen between the leaders and the laggards. But if, for example, countries appear that consciously import, imitate, and develop technology, then such countries can catch up with the leaders. By catching up with the leading nations, such countries will do more than change the existing ranking of the countries because their success will create new inequalities and instabilities. Developmentalism is a model that unsettles the order that had prevailed in the industrialized world.

Until now, international public goods have been thought of as sustaining the classical system of free trade. But the reality behind this view has generally been a world based on a strict ranking, even if changes occasionally occur in the ranking. This is what the concept of the theory of hegemonic stability symbolizes. In our times, however, when a fundamentally different situation emerges, due to the effects of developmentalism and the catching up of the developing countries, the way the international system is ordered cannot but change. And with this, the substance of the concept of international public goods must also change.

OVERSEAS INVESTMENT AID

In view of the foregoing discussion, let us here consider again the question of aid or subsidy to disadvantaged regions or industries, which I have called nonneoclassical distribution. From a classical or neoclassical perspective, aid or subsidy to specific regions or industries that are disadvantaged in productive activity is rejected on the ground that it leads to inefficient resource allocation. As mentioned in the previous chapter, though, people who decide to leave farming and move to manufacturing or service industries in the cities must confront difficulties in finding work and in getting used to different kinds of work, and they must change their style of life and discard their previous culture. They must become, in effect, a proletariat (people whose only property is their own bodies). Anticipating these difficulties and sacrifices, many people will avoid moving and may well choose to remain in a semiemployed state. The process of adjustment will be long, there will be many unused resources, and there may well be mounting political discontent among those forced to move.

Certainly, in those cases where exogenous changes that yield advantages and disadvantages occur only once (such as technological innovations), and where a long time can be taken to adjust to them, then neoclassical theory may be seen as an approximation. But when technological change continues almost uninterrupted, as it did after the Second World War, and there is continuous high economic growth, decreasing cost becomes the basic trend. In such a nonneoclassical situation, developmentalism becomes a distinctively effective policy instrument. If this policy is adopted, technological innovation will proceed and the growth rate will increase. But at the same time, the pressure on people to move grows stronger, and the sacrifices that accompany the move cannot be avoided. As already emphasized, developmentalism without a distributive policy will do more harm to the society than classical economic liberalism, and there may be a danger of destroying that country's culture.

What characterizes a developmentalist economy is excessive competition within industries and uneven growth and wage disparity among industries. Such uneven growth and wage disparity does not occur, as the neoclassical school suggests, because of imperfections in the mobility of factors of production (labor and capital). Disparities among industries (or regions) are characteristic of a developing economy that is being pulled along by industries with decreasing cost. Classical competition does not have the capacity to solve this problem. Both the friction that attends the mobility of labor and disparities among industries and regions, however, can create political discontent and endanger the unity of a society. For example, in the countries attempting to industrialize, the phenomenon of large-scale abandonment of farming has continued over several decades. Because of this, in not a small number of developing countries, there have emerged megalopolises with huge semiemployed populations and striking disparities between rich and poor, and these have become a cause of political instability. Thus—contrary to neoclassical belief—aid or protection for stagnant regions and industries is indispensable for societies with developmentalist economies.

As already mentioned, public goods should not be defined on the basis of the attributes of common consumption and nonexcludability. Public goods are the minimum necessary institutional basis to ensure a society's continued existence. The two attributes mentioned above are the translation into economic terms of the characteristics displayed by such an institutional basis. If this is the case, aid and subsidies are indispensable in ensuring the continued existence of a state industrializing through developmentalism. This is to say that such an institutional basis is public goods, or that the concept of public goods has to be expanded to include such an institutional basis.

THE PITFALLS OF FREE TRADE

Turning from domestic to international questions, the problems become even more deeply rooted. Envision the following situation. There exist both "leading countries" in which technologically innovative industries faced with decreasing cost are dominant and "follower countries" in which such industries are not yet dominant. In such a situation, the problems that arise within a domestic economy—unstable equilibria, uneven growth, and the friction and disparities that inevitably accompany them—will also occur between countries. By analogy with the domestic situation, we can infer that these problems will not be solved through the influence of free trade. In addition, because international mobility of human resources is nil, adjustments in industrial structure can be achieved only through the mobility of labor within each country. The transfer of capital is another possible solution, but it is clear that international capital transfer is more difficult than domestic. The instruments for resource allocation are thus substantially limited. The effects of free competition in reducing disparities will be less than within a single country, or at least they will be indirect and slow.

Objections to the premise that there will be no international labor mobility include the argument that such mobility (temporary or permanent) is a means of solving the problems. Certainly recently there has been the remarkable phenomenon of a short-term migration of people from follower countries working away from home, between Europe and the area surrounding it, and among the countries stretching from East Asia to the Middle East; and many governments have formally established systems to facilitate such labor mobility. Such a phenomenon has begun to occur even in Japan, in the form of the illegal employment of foreigners. But for now it is unlikely that large-scale permanent migration will be used to solve economic problems. Such a trend would mean that nationalism had already disappeared. Even the United States, which has been somewhat of an exception on this point, is no longer eager to accept immigrants. Temporary migration will certainly come to be recognized in the future as an extremely effective form of economic aid, but it cannot solve economic problems permanently. If the migrants' own countries lag behind economically, temporary migration will grow indefinitely, but as long as a country and its people try to preserve their cultural identity, migration cannot be an effective policy. The problems of cultural friction that go with migration may even become a cause of international clashes.

Another influential counterargument suggests that the international transfer of capital is a means of adjusting resource allocation. Although the international mobility of capital has rapidly increased recently, it has not quickly helped to achieve efficient international resource allocation. First, the recent vigorous activity in capital transfer has been to acquire assets speculating on the exchange rate, and not always direct investment for production. Second, where there is direct investment, when the activities of the foreign companies are not restricted (as with some examples in Latin America), there are many cases where monopolies are established and the development of the recipient country is hindered. Third, as argued in the previous section, we cannot ignore the problem of the system of floating exchange rates working at a disadvantage for follower countries with trade deficits—for example, countries with large accumulated debt. Thus if we optimistically implement classical principles of free trade in a world that is a mixture of countries enjoying the benefits of decreasing costs and countries mired in a phase of increasing costs, there is a high possibility that international economic disparities will increase rather than disappear.

As I examine in more detail in the following chapter, a reduction in these disparities seems to be a necessary condition for the existence of a future world system. As long as the impression of a widening gap between the wealthy leading countries and the poor follower countries does not disappear, there will be a possibility of military actions against the leading countries by follower countries that have grievances against the former, and it is even possible that such actions will escalate into a united front against the rich leading countries. At present, however, it is almost impossible to believe that an international military force could be mobilized to suppress such a challenge. It is also possible that the world system will be threatened by the follower countries' noncooperation on the global problems of pollution, resource scarcity, and the population explosion. To create any likelihood of reducing these disparities, the best strategy is surely for a large number of follower countries to attempt to exploit the benefits of decreasing cost by becoming developmentalist countries. This requires a favorable international environment.

In a sense, the following is the most important. Free trade destroys inefficient industries (particularly in follower countries) as well as the ethos that supported them and the soul of the cultural community—the natio—that was based on this ethos. This scenario has frequently been seen in countries supported by agriculture or traditional industry. Free trade is often a machine, violently destroying cultures under the pretext of industrial civilization; it is functional imperialism. If it occurs only within a single country, then the decline and disappearance of an industry or ethos may contribute in some way to forming a new culture or natio, helping to maintain a continuity of tradition. But when economic power crosses borders, is allowed to operate unconstrained, and destroys the ethos of a follower country (for example, the ethos of work), then cultural tradition is callously eroded. Until recently, this break from cultural tradition has been considered the advance of industrial civilization. It has been a matter of historical fact that, when follower countries have resisted the "invasion" of industrial culture, their resistance has been crushed militarily.

Now, however, at the end of this century, it would be almost impossible to mobilize an international military force to suppress such resistance, and many have also come to doubt the unifaceted nature of industrialization. Today we have circumstances that enable differing cultures to contribute to a reexamination of industrialization. In view of this, Francis Fukuyama's argument forecasting a "universal" convergence to a "homogeneous state" is an incomprehensible pronouncement.[11] Without the international institutionalization of policies that provide the prospect of reduced economic disparities and preserve the cultural uniqueness of individual natio—a distributive policy in the broad sense, or an aid policy—it may not be possible to maintain the world system in the future.

The neoclassical—or democratic socialist—view of aid in this sense is surely wide of the mark. First, the equalization of international distribution cannot be a useful concept because equality itself is a concept that differs by culture. Even an international minimum level of welfare cannot be defined because the understanding of what constitutes it also varies by culture. The minimum standard of living is not the same in the tropics and the colder regions, in forested countries and desert countries. In the end, the only useful standard for international distribution is what can be defined in physical, or biological, terms. This would lead only to aid for disaster, famine, and disease.

Many approach the question of aid with a cynical attitude and view it as no more than an expression of emotional "humanism." There is some basis for this cynicism in that aid is not provided on the basis of a necessary minimum agreed on by the international community but is often nothing more than what the donors believe is appropriate. Aid given only on the basis of judgment made by the donor's culture is surely an insult to the recipient's culture. Aid also requires some kind of common understanding or consensus between donor and recipient. The only justifiable aid is that provided to deal with problems on which such a consensus is possible.

For example, on what problems is consensus possible between the leading and follower countries? Unlike during the cold war, aid is no longer military, and it should be neither cultural nor political. Using aid to intervene unilaterally in the social customs or politics of another country (each of which has deep-rooted traditions) is to act condescendingly—except when the fundamental definition of what it means to be human (freedom of thought) is clearly being greatly violated. Relatively speaking, consensus is most likely to be reached on economic issues. Industrialization—leaving aside its ultimate meaning for now—is a goal on which an understanding is most readily reached and discussion is possible between leading and follower countries. In this case, aid will likely be in a form closely related to productive activity, thus determining the strategy of industrialization. Such economic aid, in that it interferes with resource allocation, runs counter to the neoclassical/democratic socialist principle of distribution. However, should aid take as its principle the promotion of income transfer *à la* welfare states, the follower countries would be turned into countries of masses demanding equality of economic outcomes and would lose their cultural pride and diversity. A global welfare policy is no more than an illusion, but its rhetoric has continued to confuse aid policy to no purpose. We must not repeat this mistake again.

THE DIFFUSION OF TECHNOLOGY AS AN INTERNATIONAL PUBLIC GOOD

The most effective nonclassical allocation with regard to production, in the sense mentioned above, is probably the transfer of technology. The neoclassical critique of nonmarket allocation that affects productive activity is that the industries benefiting from such allocation will remain inefficient. But given that new technology is such an important factor in raising productive efficiency, follower countries that assimilate the technology transferred under a developmentalist system will likely enjoy a rapid increase in efficiency. The institutionalization of technology transfer is perhaps the first thing that should be added as an international public good.

One obstacle in doing so is intellectual property rights. If there were no intellectual property rights and diffusion of technology were totally unconstrained, it is highly possible that every country's production function would be the same and that classical free trade and trade involving developmentalism would be identical. At this point, for the first time, extreme arguments such as the Heckscher-Ohlin theorem would become valid. In this sense, one could say that classical economic liberalism anticipated a situation in which there were absolutely no obstacles to the diffusion of technology. But at the same time, many economic liberals consider patents, or more broadly, intellectual property rights, to be indispensable in providing incentives for invention. In fact, it is here that the dilemma of classical economic liberalism becomes apparent. I discuss the basic problem of freedom again below; in terms of pure liberalism, though, there are no reasons why the transmission of the knowledge that is technology should be restricted. Technology is knowledge, or even thought, more than it is property. Property rights are preserved for the sake of maintaining the familiar old economic freedom. What should be deduced from the concept of freedom, in its most fundamental sense, is not monopoly but unrestricted use of technology.

As I said, technology is not something to be commercialized (patented) and owned as a property right. Put strongly, technology is a public good and thus not something optimally allocated through market competition. It is therefore not possible to justify patents or intellectual property rights by the same theory that is applied to market competition in commodities. An argument justifying intellectual property rights is that motivations to develop technology would be weakened without them. This argument, however, is not as convincing as is usually believed. If we believe that technological progress is to some extent predictable, and firms do constantly compete to develop technology, then firms' desire to avoid all the negative consequences of lagging behind in this competition will provide an adequate motivation to develop technology.

One cannot deny, of course, that guaranteeing rewards for developing technology increases the pace of technological progress. The optimum route is probably somewhere between strengthening intellectual property rights and ignoring them. But from the perspective of the international economic system as a whole, unless new technology flows in significant amounts to follower countries, it is highly possible that the basis for the future world system will collapse. (I discuss this point again in the following chapter.) Recent attempts in the United States to interpret intellectual property rights as broadly as possible (to the point of expanding them to include those relating to mathematical techniques and the structure of genes) are a result of impatient efforts to improve the current account and are contrary to the ongoing general direction of changes in the international economic system. Not only the United States, but Japan too, must be active in transferring technology to follower countries. As emphasized in Chapter 3, technology includes the minor peripheral technology known as know-how and related management techniques. Unless it includes technological and management guidance, technology transfer will in many cases proceed only very slowly. In this sense, technological and management guidance are important international public goods.[12] (We should note here, however, that the recipients of technology must be the principal actors in that the essence of technology transfer is opening up opportunities, not transferring results.)

The argument about technology has further implications. Behind the above argument is the expectation that all aspects of industrialization will inevitably spread to most parts of the world. Industrial activity will likely increase rapidly, not only in Asian NIEs and ASEAN nations but also in Central and South America, Eastern Europe, and China and India. This activity would be accompanied by a rapid increase in global environmental pollution, discussed earlier in connection with anti-industrialization. At that point, it would be desirable for investment and aid from the leading countries to include technology for the prevention of such pollution. It is possible to adopt a policy of prohibiting the import of products not produced using such technology (and there are already signs of this among the developed countries—as seen, for example, in the issue of growth hormones between Europe and the United States). The costs that the follower nations will have to bear in such a case will be substantial; but the transfer of environmental preservation technology, in addition to helping industrialization in the follower countries, also has the external effect of preserving the global environment, and so has significance as an international public good in a double sense.

CAPITAL AID AS AN INTERNATIONAL PUBLIC GOOD

What we must consider next as a form of allocation connected to production is capital aid to follower countries. As already discussed in connection with the theory of infant industries, if capital is abundant, even for follower countries, there is really no need to adopt a policy of protectionism or subsidies. But usually in follower countries capital is deficient. To generate domestic capital, a change in social structure or substantial political determination is required, but neither is easy to achieve. Thus, as long as the shortage of capital continues, it becomes necessary to import capital from countries that have surplus capital.

Japanese foreign investment, for example, whether in the United States or in follower countries, involves a substantial exchange rate risk. When the accumulated U.S. deficit does not disappear, because of a mistaken policy that continues to be implemented, we cannot dismiss the possibility that the dollar value of the debt will decrease as a result of inflation or a de facto moratorium. To forestall the risk of such a possibility and to prevent the international economy from collapsing, the countries supplying capital, such as Japan, have shouldered other countries' burdens. A de facto moratorium has already been declared on the accumulated debt of some follower countries, imposing a burden on Japan, the United States, and other leading countries. To repeat, this kind of burden is particularly heavy under a system of floating exchange rates; because capital-deficient countries are continually handicapped with regard to exports, it is highly possible that these countries' debts will continue to increase and their economies continue to stagnate. In the sense that the capital-exporting countries, including Japan, prevent these things from happening (or prevent de facto moratoria from being declared) they are already discharging in a substantive way the responsibility of sharing the burden of an international public good.

Economists are likely to question the preceding argument because the majority of foreign investment is made by private companies and thus would seem to have no connection to the concept of public goods. For example, Japanese foreign investment (including both direct and portfolio investment), whether in follower countries or in the United States, is based on the decisions of private companies. Note, however, that foreign investment is possible only by overcoming the difficulty of crossing national boundaries.

To be specific, making international investment requires much direct or indirect support from the governments concerned. For example, there cannot be a regulation or "guidance" restricting investment abroad (as was the case when the Japanese Ministry of Finance restricted the foreign asset holdings of Japanese life insurance companies); domestic interest rates should not be high (the prewar United States, for example, paid attention to the effects of its own interest rates on international investment).

And today many countries maintain various types of restrictions on investment from abroad. Most are followers, but leading countries also have de facto restrictions. Economists call these difficulties the risk premium that goes with foreign investment. The question is, who pays this risk premium, these costs of overcoming the tangible and intangible obstacles created by national boundaries? The simplest answer is that governments pay, in the form of aid or by creating an institution that promotes such investment. If we think of the problem in this way, it becomes easier to accept the view that an increase in foreign investment is a public good.

For example, already under the Pax Americana (and the Pax Britannica) foreign investment played the role of an international public good. One reason the world (or at least the Western world) enjoyed prosperity after the Second World War was that there was vigorous private foreign investment, accompanied by technology and management techniques, in the countries that had been damaged by the war and in the follower countries. Because of such investment these countries could aspire to escape their impoverishment of the years directly after the war, or of the prewar monoculture economy. Had the follower countries remained economies of labor-intensive monoculture, the world today might well be divided into a group of rich advanced countries enjoying the benefits of material wealth and information, and the NIEs and other follower countries suffering from lingering poverty. There would be incessant civil wars in the follower countries (yet military intervention by the leading countries would be impossible, given the present climate), and these wars would soon be joined into a major war that could plunge the world into chaos. In certain respects, this would be the world as predicted by dependency theory.

In addition, private direct investment overseas is very risky, particularly under a system of floating exchange rates. And given that capital-deficient countries are disadvantaged in exports, this risk is compounded. Unless governments or private companies in leading countries assume this risk, a collapse of the industrialized world is possible. Contrary to neoclassical common sense, most or at least part of investment in and aid to capital-deficient countries must be counted as an international public good.

A RECONSIDERATION OF INTERNATIONAL PUBLIC GOODS

In ending this section, let us reexamine two terms, "international public goods" and "allocation." As mentioned in Chapter 3, the concept of public goods is jargon from neoclassical economics and is not a concept in which the two necessary criteria—"common consumption" and "excludability" (particularly the latter)—can be established a priori. A definition of public goods might be that they are whatever institutions are necessary for a particular society to exist. The definition of international public goods is similar, but because there is no international institutional framework that corresponds to the state, the common consumption and excludability must necessarily be even broader. Charles Kindleberger has said that investment or aid from creditor countries has been, to the present, an indispensable international public good for the international system, but if one accepts his argument, all the institutions, regimes, and agreements that are indispensable for this system would be called international public goods.

Security and international currency, however, which have been the main topics of the discussion on international public goods, cannot be encapsulated in the concept of a "good." It may be possible to say that the Pax Americana supplied the international public good of security, but this "good" was nothing more than the strength of U.S. influence as a military superpower, or rather, a belief in that strength. The system of floating exchange rates, too, is nothing more than the aggregate of a linkage among all countries' currencies and the determination of the leading countries to cooperate in their intervention. Today, when the Pax Americana has lost much of its ability to maintain and mobilize military power, when the fixed exchange rate system has been replaced by the more uncertain floating exchange rate system, and when developmentalist countries have grown in number, new institutions and regimes must emerge to ensure the stability of the international system.

I am arguing that the most important task to be accomplished in order to maintain the stability of the international system is to ameliorate the conflicts of economic interests between the leading and follower countries, or between the advanced countries and the NIEs (and those countries that have achieved a level near that of the NIEs). To do this the flow of technology and other benefits must increase from the leading to the follower countries (particularly the NIEs). In this chapter, I have dared to argue that international distribution is necessary because, I believe, without it the world's political and economic system cannot be maintained. In other words, this international distributive policy is not based on egalitarianism. Within a single nation-state, perhaps (though even there it would be doubtful), but in the whole world it is simply not possible to obtain equality unless one were to create a uniform world by demolishing diverse cultures with the bulldozer of civilization. Even supposing that one could obtain worldwide equality, realizing worldwide redistribution would require vast, complicated, economic planning—and probably dictatorial rule to implement it. Naturally such a system would be contrary to liberalism. What is required is equality of opportunity, or more specifically, open and free opportunities to gain access to technology and capital.

The problem is opportunities, not results. The opportunities for follower countries to gain access to technology or capital are certainly not great. Their access to technology is restricted by the patent system, and they and their firms are not blessed, as are small and medium-sized firms in leading countries, with access to capital. An important reason for this is that international institutions are based on the perception that there are few successful industrializing follower countries. This perception raises the risk premium for foreign investment—that is, it increases the cost of capital to the follower countries. Another important point that needs to be stressed is that investment and aid must be implemented only on the basis of consensus. Aid and investment should be provided only if the donors or the investors fully understand the strength of the desire on the part of the recipients for the projects to be financed by the aid and investment. Such an understanding will certainly reduce the risk premium demanded by investors.

Therefore it is desirable as a principle that, at least on the recipients' side, the major roles in aid and investment be played by private firms that assume responsibility for executing a project. Thus, aid or investment should take the form of international financial institutions subsidizing private business only for the risk premium. This is nothing more than typical redistribution connected to production. I should also add that, since each international financial institution has its own specific characteristics, it will be necessary for there to be many of them—for example, more than one World Bank and development banks for each region. In short, the goal is not to equalize income throughout the world but to overcome existing barriers—the concerns about the risks of providing aid and economic development—and thus to give equal opportunity for participation in the global market economy.

Let me add one further note. Humanitarian aid for famine, disease, and disaster is surely desirable because in these unfortunate situations the needs of human beings are fundamental and virtually universal (and in these cases "free" aid—that is, aid not related even indirectly to development—is surely appropriate). But what about capital or technological aid provided to undertake specific infrastructure-building projects? The leading industrial nations have a common fixed image of what infrastructure is, but it is not clear that this agrees with the image held by follower countries. In particular, we cannot be certain whether social capital such as roads, harbors, canals, drains, railways, industrial sites, and communications networks will be appropriate for a twenty-first-century society. Third, there are projects such as pollution prevention and population control that are desirable for the leading countries themselves, but it is very difficult to establish a consensus on these issues between the leading and follower countries.

The preceding demonstrates that both international public goods and distribution are inadequate as ways of addressing the problem of maintaining international stability. International public goods are not goods, but regimes, rules, and a search for consensus. Distribution is not equality of outcomes but aims only at equality of opportunity. Even if, for the time being, we talk here about international public goods and distribution, we must consider the genuine heart of the problem in these terms: what are the institutions or rules that are indispensable for the existence of the future international system?

The Possibility of an International Industrial Policy

The international problems brought about by the trend of decreasing cost are not limited to the problems between leading and follower countries. Among the leading countries, too, for those industries that have endogenized the trend of decreasing cost, there is the global problem of competition and the instability of these industries. The semiconductor industry is a dramatic example of this. With the increase in the number of RAM chips sold, their price has declined rapidly, and through technological innovation their capacity has increased fourfold. If one plots quantity on the x-axis and price on the y-axis, the curve keeps moving sharply downward to the right, from 16 KB to 64 KB to 256 KB to 1 MB to 4 MB to 16 MB. This almost exactly resembles what I am calling the long-run average cost path. It is well known that semiconductor makers in every country have been engaged in life-or-death competition. Without the antitrust regulations in each country, this is the condition that would allow a global monopoly to emerge. The Japanese companies compete among themselves, but there is also a possibility that they might drive manufacturers in other countries out of the market. In any case, it seems that, in those industries faced with a trend of decreasing cost, a situation is developing throughout the world that cannot be explained by the existing theory of competition.

Let us look at a few more examples. As mentioned earlier, at a certain point it seemed possible that IBM would monopolize the computer industry, but domestic U.S. antitrust regulations intervened. Control of the global market by Japanese semiconductor makers is being prevented by European and North American protectionism. Japan's MITI also seems to be exerting pressure on these Japanese firms to defuse trade tension and promote international cooperation. But in comparatively small industries, some Japanese firms have monopolized the global market.

In the motorcycle, camera, and home video industries, Japanese firms at one time did achieve virtual monopoly. In Europe and North America there are conspiracy theorists who say that the Japanese are following a strategy to achieve domination of the world market in all industries. This view, however, is nothing more than a misunderstanding that arises from knowing nothing but classical theory. Japanese firms achieved near-monopolies in those markets because they made appropriate investments and a consistent effort under a situation of decreasing cost. According to the classical understanding, such monopolistic dominance in various world markets can be achieved only because Japan has closed its domestic market, created a collusive oligopoly, and is dumping below cost in foreign markets. But as the many examples cited below make clear, such a view is untenable. Even after Japanese firms have achieved a controlling position in the world market, they continue to engage in fierce price-cutting and quality improvement. Such behavior cannot be understood with the classical concept of dumping. Unless we shed the outmoded analysis of classical theory, we will make serious mistakes in thinking about the future world economic order.

Recently the Schmiegelows have pointed out that, in Japan, domestic competition seems to have been preserved.[13] For example, in the Japanese motorcycle industry, Honda, Yamaha, Suzuki, and Kawasaki have jointly achieved a virtual monopoly in many segments of the world motorcycle market, but this does not mean that they have formed a collusive oligopoly to gain control of the world market, or that they have engaged in dumping. There has been fierce competition over both quality and price among the Japanese motorcycle manufacturers; one result is that almost all of the manufacturers in other countries can no longer effectively compete with the Japanese firms. It seems that manufacturers in other countries believed it was neither possible to make as many technological innovations nor necessary to invest as heavily in motorcycle manufacturing as the Japanese firms did. Reviewing their behavior, we find that the motorcycle industry offered opportunities for both substantial scale economies and technological innovation (even if one thinks only of transferring automobile technology). In short, it was rediscovered as a cutting-edge industry. Only the Japanese manufacturers actively exploited the possibilities, with the results we see today. A similar thing occurred in the camera and video industries.

To repeat, it is not as a result of a domestic system of collusive oligopoly that Japanese firms have dominated the world market. In none of these industries has there been suspicion of a cartel, and none received preferential treatment through subsidies or taxes. Put simply, Japanese firms became dominant in these markets because they made the most of the opportunities for technological innovation.

There are doubts, however, as to whether this situation has benefited the world's consumers. It is clear that Japanese motorcycles are well made, long-lasting, and satisfy the needs and tastes of many users. But the loss of motorcycles possessing the distinctive characteristics of a Harley-Davidson or a BMW cannot be compensated for no matter how high the average quality of Japanese-made motorcycles. Not only for the enthusiast, but also for the general buyer, the range of choices has been narrowed by the dominance of Japanese firms. With more producers, more motorcycles of varied designs and characteristics would have been produced. The motorcycle industry is comparatively small and has been the object neither of MITI industrial policy in Japan nor of protectionism in other countries (although the U.S. government did rescue Harley-Davidson with a one-time subsidy). Because of this, the effects of decreasing cost become evident. One can perhaps say the same thing about the camera and video industries.

In those large, leading industries that no country can ignore, however, the response was quite different despite the similarity of the situation. It is quite possible that without protectionism on the U.S. side, the Japanese steel and automobile industries would have controlled over half the U.S. market. After failing to adopt the most advanced converting process in the 1960s, the U.S. steel industry continued to lag in technological innovation and in the 1980s was one of the last to adopt the technology of continuous casting. These industries, though, were not neglected. From the 1960s, Japanese steel makers adopted "self-imposed (export) controls," and after 1984 when the third iron and steel export restraints went into effect, the export restraints became comprehensive and detailed, applying to nineteen countries and the EC. The situation was the same in the automobile industry, and without the Japanese export restraints introduced in 1981, the worldwide small-car market, which makes up at least half the total automobile market, might well have become totally controlled by Japanese manufacturers. In the home electronic goods industry (televisions, tape recorders, VCRs, and so on), the situation has in fact developed in the same way as the motorcycle industry, and almost all U.S. firms have given up domestic production.[14] Though I have cited only U.S. examples, Europe has clearly embarked on a course of protectionism and is restricting exports from Japan and the NIEs.

This situation, from the 1970s on, goes beyond the framework of a classical understanding. The new protectionism that has appeared since the 1970s is not identical to protectionism in the sense that the term is customarily used. For example, in the 1920s, leading firms such as Harley-Davidson, US Steel, Chrysler, and RCA did not need protection. There was no need for them to be obsessed with technological innovation, and even if they did lag behind in investment, they had ample time to make amends. This situation changed when technological innovation became continuous and constant after the Second World War, the trend toward decreasing cost became a fact of industrial life, and developmentalist countries such as Japan began to consciously exploit this fact. As I emphasized earlier, even if the principle of free competition were applied to industries with decreasing cost, no equilibrium would be achieved. Instead, it would generate the possibility that those firms, actively and successively adopting new technology and long-term views, would succeed in exploiting the fact of decreasing cost and achieve an oligopolistic, or monopolistic, position in the global market. Any lag in the timing of investment (investment both in R&D and in production facilities) would cause even the best established firms in any country to fall by the wayside, and the monopolies that would arise because of the disappearance of such firms would restrict choices for consumers. There is no doubt that the new protectionism that has appeared since the 1970s originally sprang from naive nationalism. But seen from a global perspective, it now has a new significance and some justification as a means of reacting to uncontrolled developmentalism.

At the same time, exports from Japan and the Asian NIEs are not unfair; they are not supported by cartels or aided by preferential treatment in subsidies, financing, or taxes. When these countries first embarked on developmentalism they received preferential treatment, but even after such treatment had been discontinued the exporting strength of these countries did not diminish. Even in the Japanese automobile industry where this treatment remained in place the longest, import restrictions were removed by the first half of the 1960s. (At that time, Japan's automobile exports were still very small in number.) In short, it is difficult to discover violations of the classical principle of free competition among firms that increased exports by actively exploiting the trend toward decreasing cost.

Thus, just as it is a mistake for exporting countries to criticize on classical grounds what is at present called protectionism, it is also a mistake to attack on neoclassical grounds what is called dumping. The United States, for example, is making a mistake in criticizing Japan's exports as violating the rule of liberalism and, because of American unwillingness to adopt protectionism, in trying to rely on self-restraint by its trading partners. Japan is mistaken in asserting that as long as it protects the rule of liberalism, there are no points on which it can be criticized. A political tragedy (or rather, considered dispassionately, a comedy) has resulted because the economic theory of increasing cost is being used in attempting to deal with the fact of decreasing cost.

A theoretical policy solution might be derived from an economics of decreasing cost—in other words, from an analogy with domestic industrial policy. In those industries that, seen globally, are priority industries, there is a need for an agreement on international indicative planning and on the international scheduling of export price-cutting. The import quotas presently implemented by the United States and by European countries, or the export restraints by the developmentalist countries, can be seen as an extremely inadequate substitute for this kind of price scheduling. Even within a country, however, the implementation of industrial policy is always extremely difficult. Of course, there already is an international *price-fixing* cartel in the iron and steel industry. It is often stated that agreements on price are necessary in primary industries. Internationally, though, there are no obvious examples of cartels that have a principal intent of reducing price by controlling the speed of reduction. To borrow a term from works in international relations, doing so would require forming a "regime" to control the pace of price reduction in cutting-edge, priority industries. However, it would be difficult for leading and follower countries to reach an agreement on the pace of price-cutting, and it would be extremely difficult to form such a regime.

Thus it is quotas, either explicit or implicit (self-imposed quotas), that are nowadays much used as substitutes for such a regime. There is a strong danger that this method will cause firms (particularly those in the protected country) to lose their incentive to innovate. But even with quotas, achieving a consensus is not easy. Whether a cooperative agreement on price-cutting or a consensus on quotas, it is quite possible that establishing agreement will be easy among some countries and difficult among others. In this case, there is a danger that those countries that can reach an agreement will combine to form an exclusive group, as Paul Krugman has warned, and that a new kind of trade bloc will emerge. But I do not believe the likelihood of this happening is as strong as Krugman does.[15]

The strongest possibility is that the countries that espouse classical economic liberalism will form a group and exclude the developmentalist countries; this, though, would not be an advantageous choice for the former countries. These two kinds of countries have already developed a close interdependence benefiting both sides. For example, many cutting-edge industries in the United States depend on a supply of parts or machine tools from Japan; and many U.S. multinationals have set up important production bases in Asia. Even if the countries adhering to a classical, liberal view of trade were able to endure such a disadvantage, there is the fact that the markets of the developmentalist countries will grow most rapidly in the future. If, as I predict in this book, developmentalism generates advanced mass consumer societies, the trading bloc of the classical-liberal countries will deny themselves access to the most promising markets.

For example, the former Soviet Union and the East European countries will perhaps, to a greater or lesser extent, adopt developmentalist policies, but it will be impossible for Europe to exclude these countries or not to trade with them. If Latin America becomes an important market, then it too will probably be developmentalist. Over the next 25 years, the Asian NIEs and ASEAN nations, with a population of 500 million, will be the fastest growing market in the world. If the coastal regions of China and the former Soviet Union are added to this, the size of this market becomes even greater. Even here, though, given the domestic political pressures in the classical-liberal countries, one cannot ignore the possibility that a "new bloc-ism" will emerge because of the differences in attitude toward developmentalism. I discuss this point further in the following chapter; here I say only that Krugman's predictions are too one-sided.

Under what conditions is it possible to maintain the international system, given a system of floating exchange rates? As I have stated before, this system is not necessarily a desirable one in terms of resource allocation. But if one thinks in terms of its function in ensuring the smooth international transfer of capital, then it is not immediately possible to think of another, more effective system. In this sense, there is in fact no other road we can take but to strive to maintain this system. In order to do so, the following circumstances are necessary: (1) ideally, no country, particularly no leading country, should have a surplus or shortage of capital; (2) second best, investment should be made, as required, in the leading countries (particularly the United States); and (3) foreign investment in, and aid to, developing countries should be made and should be accompanied by the transfer of technology (particularly technology to prevent environmental pollution). In other words, under this system, a discipline in macroeconomic policy among the leading countries, sharing the burden of risk involved in foreign investment and aid, and technology transfer are the new, indispensable international public goods, and it is the leading countries that must provide them. It is more difficult for these new international public goods to take the form of easily defined institutions than it was for what were commonly thought of as international public goods up to now—the IMF and military power. But the world has already entered the era of this new system, and in fact the United States, Europe, and Japan have already assumed the burden of providing the new international public goods.

Generally speaking, this system is "polymorphic." Unlike when classical economic liberalism was taken as the premise, not all countries will be dealt with equally and without discrimination. (Even in the postwar liberal system, some countries that did not follow the rule of free trade received only qualified treatment from the IMF and GATT.) Under the floating exchange rate system, four groups of countries—leading capital exporters, leading capital importers, follower capital exporters, and follower capital importers—perform different roles. (Even among the leading countries, there is a distinction between capital-deficient countries such as the United States, and capital-rich countries such as Japan. And among the follower countries, too, countries such as the Asian NIEs, which have succeeded in developmentalism and have become capital-rich, are divided from the large number of countries that are capital-deficient and suffering from accumulated debt.)

On the whole, there is an important current leading beyond the framework of the nation-state and toward what one might call trading regions. Furthermore, cultural differences, particularly differences in political-economic thought and ideology, have the potential of igniting international conflicts. We have to say that this system recognizes the existence of these pluralistic groups. Robert Gilpin called the system that might appear in the future a "negotiated system," but it is highly likely that any negotiation, rather than being something carried out as necessary between two countries, will be worked out between heterogeneous groups, in the sense described above. The trump card in such discussions will not be military force but investment, aid, and technology transfer.

From the perspective of the existing concepts, what is occurring today cannot but give rise to resentment and conflict. As I discuss in the next chapter, the countries that are developed but have become capital importers will surely resent the fact that those countries that cannot be said to have developed sufficiently become capital exporters, thanks to their seemingly privileged position of being developmentalists. The developed countries that have been rapidly caught up to by the developmentalist trading states (or regions) will want to call their competitors "adversarial states." This designation, though, discloses the existing unidimensional way of thinking, one result of which is the current friction between the United States and Japan. To create a new set of rules, we must first abandon the existing conceptual framework.

Cultural confrontation arises readily from this kind of existing concept. Communication difficulties are often said to result from cultural differences. For example, Japanese economic behavior tends to be long term, multifaceted, and informal, while American economic behavior tends to be short term, specific, and formal, or in other words, based on legal contract. This difference in style is based on differences in historical and social experience, and each style has its own raison d'être. One is not superior to the other. For example, in many cases, in terms of employment or long-term investment under constant technological change, the former style of economic behavior will achieve better results. But this style of behavior raises the risk that the power of entrenched interest groups will become dominant. Of course, were an ideal world state to be established, and were there a period in which technological innovation was not that rapid, there might be established a system in which equal world citizens were tied together through contracts. As long as this is not the reality, we must be prepared to recognize the coexistence of multiple patterns of behavior. This recognition is necessary for the future system. The distortions in the present world economy and misunderstanding about the reasons for, and the effects of, these distortions will alone make it impossible to establish a new system. Together with many other real and conceptual obstacles, there is a possibility that the issue of polymorphism in the present world economy will cause much troublesome friction—such as the current friction between the United States and Japan.

CHAPTER 8

A Scenario for a New International System

THE RULES FOR
POLYMORPHIC LIBERALISM

Reexamining the Experience of Nationalism

In this chapter, I attempt to sketch the international system that must emerge in the world of the future. My sketch is not a description of historical inevitability or a "progressive" answer to the question of what the future international system should be. I also do not believe we should return to a combination of classical economic liberalism and democracy or imitate the Anglo-American system. This system must contain a multi-dimensional choice: which among the three axes of the problem mentioned in this book is to be chosen, and how much emphasis is to be placed on each of the axes? In other words, the core of the answer will be found by overcoming the unitary, unidimensional perspective of the modern progressivism that has dominated the past few centuries. The means of accomplishing this must be not "transcendental" but "hermeneutic," but I postpone discussing this until Chapter 10. To outline the new international system, I discuss the question here from two perspectives: how to deal with nationalism (the first three sections), and how to deal with developmentalism (the last two sections). I begin by reexamining the experience of nationalism.

THE SIGNIFICANCE OF THE GULF WAR

In looking at the world today in 1991, following the end of the Persian Gulf War and the surprisingly quick collapse of the conservative coup d'état in the former Soviet Union, we find that everywhere movements for national independence are growing stronger, and at first glance it seems as if there has been a revival of nationalism. In the press one can find, here and there, the opinions that there has been a revival of the nineteenth-century nation-state and the nation-state system, as well as the interpretation that, as before, power politics and military capability continue to play the leading role. But such interpretations are superficial. For example, the interpretation that the Gulf War reaffirmed the role of military force in international politics is overly simple.

First, we should regard the Gulf War as having been not so much a victory of U.S. military power as a triumph of diplomacy, which could be achieved because of the existing international situation. In dispatching troops to the Persian Gulf, the Bush administration, exploiting the extremely unstable situation within the Soviet Union, developed its foreign policy with a caution unprecedented in U.S. diplomatic history. Had the United States not obtained the approval of the U.N. Security Council, it would have been impossible to deploy an offensive military force against Iraq, or at least the United States would not have obtained the cooperation of the Arab countries (other than Saudi Arabia). Without powerful international support, if not by the United Nations at least by a wide international consent, the use of military power would not have been possible because of the "democratic" public opinion in each of the developed countries, including the United States. Thus the Gulf War taught us that a single country's military capability has no significance.

Second, in contrast, the diplomacy and war leadership of Iraq's dictatorial president, Saddam Hussein, was far too self-serving and less than competent. In war many mistakes are inevitable, and the side that makes more mistakes is defeated. Even so, Hussein made too many mistakes. For example, let me make the following three-part counterfactual hypothesis. Had Iraq's invasion of Kuwait been somewhat more justified, had the multinational force suffered considerable casualties, and had Israel incurred large numbers of civilian casualties and thus been forced to retaliate, there would have been a substantial change in global public opinion (especially in the United States). Such a development could have caused the disintegration of the multinational force and would have made it difficult to bring the war to a rapid conclusion. Clearly, to further his interest, Hussein should have prolonged the war to inflict a cumulatively large loss in the human resources of the multinational force, but he does not seem to have adopted such a strategy. Because the complete facts of the Gulf War have not yet been made public, we cannot be certain of many details; but at least the following is clear. Future aggressors are unlikely to repeat Saddam Hussein's foolishness.

The Gulf War was a diplomatic rather than a military problem, which in the end was settled by the slightest of margins. The multinational force, shackled by international and domestic politics—particularly the U.S. force—was compelled to achieve a clear result in a short period and with the fewest possible casualties. That this result was, quite miraculously, realized was due to an accumulation of factors: the international situation restricting the Soviet Union and China, the existence of a de facto security alliance between the important power in the region (Saudi Arabia) and the United States, Saddam Hussein's poor judgment with respect to the international situation, the internal fragmentation of Iraq (the Shiite faction and the Kurds) which made guerrilla warfare impossible, geographical conditions, and others. Where this unique set of conditions is absent (as it was in Vietnam and Korea, for example), even if U.S. military technology is overwhelmingly superior, it is unlikely that a war would be over as quickly as it was in the Gulf. Any future aggressors will likely learn from the Gulf War and adopt other strategies: using political devices such as indirect aggression before the event or installing a puppet administration; waging a thorough guerrilla war in which the people are forced to participate; or throwing international politics into confusion by using or threatening to use long-range ballistic missiles or nuclear weapons.[1] In the face of such an aggressor, it will be difficult for a great power or coalition army to be dispatched and solve the problem quickly.

Thus there is a double lesson from the Gulf War. First, there seems to have been no reversal in the basic trend in recent years (particularly since the end of the cold war) toward a relative decline in the significance of military power. To see U.S. hegemony as having reemerged because of the use of its military power in the Gulf War is to misread reality. Gone is the cold war period, during which the doctrine of just war distinguished black from white unequivocally. It has become impossible to exercise military force on the basis of the doctrine of just war; military force has become something that can be exercised only if first endorsed by sufficiently broad support within the country, and at the same time by a sufficiently broad consensus among nations (that is, by a de facto collective security agreement). The concept of justice is in retreat, and the trend is toward a search for a rule that can validate such a consensus. Even President George Bush exercised military force only within the limits of the international consensus in the United Nations and did not go on to overthrow the government of Saddam Hussein. Once the temporary excitement of the "television war" had died down, it must have been clear to everybody that, globally, there had been no change in the basic trend.

Second, we have learned that *local* acts of aggression are possible with the lesser military capacity possessed by many countries. It is common to think of areas that have a long history of disputes, such as the area surrounding Israel, or the India-Pakistan border, as the regions where it is most likely that problems will occur, but the problems in these regions have to some extent become predictable and are dealt with more readily within the existing international framework. From now on, there is a need to pay attention instead to the possibility that wars will be caused by disputes resulting from the breakup of the quasi-empire of the Soviet Union and by struggles over leadership in the reorganization of regional alliances (for example, leadership within the Islamic region). The Korean peninsula is a region of East Asia that holds this possibility; the domestic situation in China can become unstable and domestic disturbances may occur, and one cannot say that there is no likelihood of the Chinese engaging in a kind of foreign adventurism involving Taiwan and Hong Kong. The military buildup in India is also worrisome.

None of these regions, however, fulfills the particular set of conditions present in Iraq's invasion of Kuwait, particularly the unique fact that this area is the principal source of the world's oil supply. Formerly, almost all disputes were linked to the cold war and thus led to military intervention (or at least the threat of military intervention) by both sides. From now on, it will be hard to imagine that, as local conflicts break out around the world, the United States, Europe, and the other major countries will spontaneously and vigorously take military action to punish aggression. The effort needed to generate the domestic and international support necessary to do so will be too great and too time-consuming. (For example, in the future will the "pacifist" Japanese be prepared to pay $10 billion to solve disputes in far-off countries that produce no oil?) We today have the vacuum that has been created by the end of the cold war; that is, there is no longer the somewhat paradoxical effect that war had in guaranteeing security. Almost the only solution for this situation, which will invite more international disputes, is perhaps a collective security alliance among the countries that fear invasion; I discuss this possibility below.

THE THIRD WAVE OF NATIONALISM

In one respect, the assertion that the age of nationalism has reappeared is correct. Today, movements for popular self-determination are gaining momentum in various places. Beginning with the three Baltic countries, all the republics in the former Soviet Union demanded their independence, and with Byelorussia and even the Ukrainian Republic making the same demand, the Soviet Union finally disintegrated. The countries in Eastern Europe too have become independent one after another. And in what was once Yugoslavia, military conflicts continue among ethnic groups in their attempt to create a nation of their own. It seems appropriate to call this succession of events an explosion of nationalism.

But these movements are not identical to past nationalism. Even if the classical European nationalism up to the First World War is in a class by itself, we should generally distinguish between three subsequent waves in nationalism. These three waves are similar in that they were all, more or less, "reactive" in character—reacting to the imperialism or expansionism of the great powers—but in their respective historical phases they are distinct.

The first wave was marked by the birth of independent states in Eastern and Central Europe following the First World War. This was a by-product of the collapse of the classical nation-state system brought on by the Treaty of Versailles and anticipated the support of a modified nation-state system under the name of the League of Nations (or the Versailles system). The second wave brought the independence of colonies throughout the world following the Second World War. This was a result of the collapse of the colonial system, but because the support expected from the United Nations was inadequate, the cold war system played the main supporting role. The American-led system of security and economic aid, on the Western side, and the quasi-imperial system of the Soviet Union, on the Eastern side, kept each other in check and contributed to the continued existence of the newly independent states. But some unfortunate countries were divided by East-West conflicts. The third wave came with the attempts at independence by the republics and satellites within the socialist federation (mainly the Soviet Union). This was a result of the disintegration of the quasi-empire founded on socialist ideology, and at present efforts are being made to form some kind of group in its place.

We are now observing this third wave of nationalism. The secession of Slovenia and Croatia from the multiethnic former Yugoslavia occurred because the latter, once supported by a unique, quasi-socialist ideology (self-governance by workers), rapidly lost its ability to remain united because (1) it has been shaken by the decline in ideological unity among surrounding countries, and (2) its constituent ethnic groups are attracted by the greater unity of the EC or the idea of a possible Central European federation. This, in short, is a small-scale version of the situation in the Soviet Union. China, another quasi-empire, could potentially disintegrate for similar reasons. It is not only that China has ethnic problems in Sinkiang and Uighur provinces and Tibet; to paint an extreme scenario, there is even a chance that China might disintegrate into its territorial units of the past.

Generally, the third wave of nationalism is an expression of the fact that the ideological quasi-empires that unified many ethnic groups through socialist ideology have collapsed. Looking back, the first wave of nationalism symbolized the failure of the classical nation-state system, and the second wave of nationalism demonstrated the bankruptcy of the colonial system. Thus the classical nation-state system, the colonial system, and now the socialist quasi-imperial system have, one after another, been eliminated.

Those countries in which we today see this third wave of nationalism have for many years been prevented from expressing their own identities; in other words, the legitimacy of the natio has not been recognized. However, during these years, they have accumulated political experiences and institutional capabilities similar to those of a nation-state. Perhaps this third wave of nationalism is no longer under an illusion that the nation-state might lead to perfect independence, a mistake made by the first wave within the Versailles system. The third wave is also free to some extent of the impatience demonstrated during the second wave, as countries attempted to be rid of the yoke of colonialism. That is, the third wave is not as naive as the first and second. The nationalism of secession from the quasi-empires will perhaps go toward establishing a cultural identity in such things as language and customs; but those involved in the third wave possess the political experience that also encourages them to search for a federation of states that can provide support for their own nationalism. Thus these countries may behave as pure nation-states for perhaps only an extremely short period. The countries in the former Soviet Union, for example, have in mind the possibility of an economic federation centered on the Russian Republic (now known formally as the Russian Federation, although in this book I use the former designation), but they may well try to form a new federation of states. In the latter, they are likely to explore the possibility of participating in the EC or NATO or of forming some kind of Islamic federation.

In the countries of Eastern Europe, too, beginning with East Germany's rapid reunification with West Germany, one can see movements seeking participation in the EC and a "Central European federation" (as proposed by Czech president Václav Havel). Slovenia and Croatia are perhaps aiming to participate in the EC sometime in the future. In both cases, unless they make steady progress toward joining an existing group or forming a new one, these countries may come to an economic standstill; and it seems they are aware of this fact. In the third wave of nationalism, all seem to be aware that they can ill afford the luxury of believing that the United Nations or some international alliance will come to their aid. It is not enough to summarize this situation as an explosion of nationalism because it is clear that this third wave is the self-assertion of the natio, and that, from the start, it has held the implication of an emergence of a new international system that is capable of integrating all states.

A Successor for Nationalism

Independence is always a coercive political action. To achieve independence, the differences (territorial and cultural/linguistic) within a political unit, or natio, must be overcome. Today, despite the waves of nationalism, these differences exist everywhere. Although I will not enumerate here the countless examples throughout the world, let me simply note that cultural sphere and territorial sphere do not always coincide. By cultural sphere, I mean a group of people who share a distinct language or ethos. The degree to which a people has accumulated a set of classic texts in its own language, for example, is a strong indication of the degree to which they share a cultural identity.

Of course, the countries that have until now promoted the nation-state and the nation-state system are those in which there is a high degree of correspondence between cultural and territorial spheres. These are the countries in Western and Northern Europe, most of the East European countries, and a majority of the former white colonies. In Asia the degree of such correspondence is highest in Korea (though at present Korea remains divided), and Japan is perhaps the next closest. These, though, are exceptions, and in both Asia and Africa many countries are multiethnic (multicultural) states that have inherited unchanged the national boundaries of the colonial period; since their independence, they have made a conscious, continuing effort to increase the degree of correspondence, taking the developed countries as a model.

THE CONDITIONS NECESSARY FOR INTEGRATING STATES

Playing the most important role in this effort is the education system, which has established a national language. Some countries have adopted an explicit cultural policy, with a clear slogan, such as what the Indonesian people call *Panca Sila* (the five bases) or the Confucianism advocated in Singapore. There is room for doubt, however, as to whether a cultural identity can be crystallized through such conscious adoption of policies. It cannot be said that once an education system is established, cultural unity will continue to increase. For example, all that is left now in the former Soviet Union, which was supposed to have been unified through ideological education, is a desolate, 70-year cultural void.

Noteworthy also is the fact that many of the countries in Latin America have long histories as independent territorial states, but the upper classes are oriented toward Western Europe, and the Indian, mestizo, and African populations lack cultural identity (though this is a result of the success of policies to meld native cultures). These groups exist side by side, with little contact between them. Thus it is hard to say that they have formed an adequate cultural identity as a country. The pursuit of "Brasilidade"— a love of Brazil—espoused by President Getulio Vargas, President Lazaro Cardenas's emphasis on Mexico's indigenous culture, and the criticism of the Western European lifestyle of the upper classes by the Peron government in Argentina are all attempts to promote individual national cultures. These efforts, however, symbolize the lack of a cultural community, or natio.[2] Countries do not have a strong cultural identity simply because they have a long experience as independent states.

This situation in Latin America invites the following question. Is it impossible that countries that share the Spanish language and classics written in Spanish might turn toward a broader regional integration, rather than protecting the existing territory of the nation-state? In a world dominated until now by the system centered on the nation-state, the countries of Latin America too have naturally made efforts to become nation-states. At the same time, Latin America has made repeated attempts at regional unity and economic cooperation, in numbers not seen anywhere else. Among them are the well-known Organization of American States (1941-), created under U.S. leadership, and LAFTA (the Latin American

Free Trade Association, 1960–80); its successor, the Latin American Integration Association (1980–); the Andean Common Market (1969–); the Central American Common Market (1961–); the Caribbean Common Market (CARICOM, 1973–); and the somewhat anti-U.S. Latin American Economic System (SELA, 1975–). Since the second half of the 1980s there have been further attempts to form a Central and South American common market, mainly by Brazil, Argentina, and Mexico. These attempts have achieved some success, at least in intraregional industrial exports, thus contributing to some extent to industrialization.

In those states, therefore, where cultural unity, or the natio, is comparatively weak, there may be a possibility of leapfrogging, without waiting for the nation-state to be completed, and advancing to a different kind of political unity (for example, a federated system with other countries). To see this as a lag or distortion in development is nothing more than preconception bound by the classical idea of nationalism. Given the present situation in the world's political economy, the formation of nation-states cannot be our only objective. This is not only the case with Latin America. As I discuss again below, similar possibilities can be seen in East Asia. In the Arab region too, since the area that shares the Arabic language is larger than the territorial states, an Arab regional association might incorporate many states. Some believe that the Gulf War ended any chance of an Arab federation, but even if a pan-Arab federation has become problematic, the possibility for a somewhat more restricted regional association, focusing on the economy and security, is perhaps growing steadily.

The Arabic Federal Republic of Egypt and Syria was an extremely short-lived effort (1958–61), but in Europe and Japan any similar effort is unimaginable. The concept of the territorial state is weak in Arab countries, in sharp contrast to countries whose origins were in agricultural societies.[3] In sub-Saharan Africa where the multiethnicity of states is even more striking and nation-states have not fully developed, there is an even greater likelihood of moving toward forming a regional federation if an effective proposal for it is forthcoming. Though not widely known, Senegal and Gambia formed the Sene-Gambian Federation (1982–89) and Guinea Bissau and Cape Verde once had a plan for integration (abandoned in 1981). Several attempts at economic cooperation are also being made today throughout the sub-Saharan region, and they include the economic community of West African countries, the Southern African coordination conference for development, the economic community of Central African countries, and the East African preferential trading region.

Let me emphasize again that, even if some kind of federation is formed politically and it assumes to some extent the role of the state, the individual cultural communities, or natio, will not disappear. Natio will exist as long as people do. This is because the image of the world and life that people have are what philosophers call "intersubjective"; they are generated only at those points where individual experiences interact. This is most clearly demonstrated by the fact that people share languages and customs, an ethos or cultural tradition based on a common language. Without language there would be no way of creating a human view of the world.

What I am calling natio was originally nothing more than the place where these communal experiences were accumulated. As the techniques and skills humans used in their lives increased, the natio, as the basic site of such experience, expanded from the band of hunter-gatherers to the village of cultivators, and then to cities and the state. In this history, the imperial system was unique in that it aimed at creating an integrated political entity that included many heterogeneous natio. The nation-state that appeared at the end of this history was an attempt to combine once again the natio and the political unity. But given that the various natio are based on different common experiences, there always is a possibility that they will confront each other. This confrontation will be lasting because it is deeply rooted in the everyday experience of life of each natio.

As discussed in Chapter 2, there are two approaches to dealing with this confrontation. One is a transcendental justice-based approach, and the other I choose to call a hermeneutic rule-based approach. One could also call the former an approach based on the doctrine of just war and the latter an approach based on the doctrine of nonjust war. The great empires, based on the historical religions, adopted the former approach, as did the nations of the Middle Ages in Europe, which followed these empires. Throughout the early modern and modern periods, people have shifted any number of times between justice and rules (between the doctrines of just war and nonjust war). But generally speaking, with the increase in communication and improvement in transportation (recently including the information revolution), perhaps we have moved in the direction of a rule-based approach. In the future, however, it will surely be necessary for us to make a decisive choice of direction. I will not repeat the argument of Chapter 2 here, but I believe that as long as the human race is determined to avoid a collapse of its civilization, it will have no choice but to adopt a rule-based approach from now on, as distinct from a justice-based approach.

A rule-based approach recognizes the individuality of each natio, or the differences among them, and searches for "commensurability" among natio in order to evolve common rules, to the extent possible. To make it quite clear, seeking commensurability between cultures is not the same as sharing a culture; it is using one's power of imagination so that it becomes possible, to some degree, to empathize with what it is like to live in another culture. The foundation of this rule-based approach, of course, is the acknowledgment of the individuality of each natio.

The justice-based approach is an attempt to homogenize every individual's life and world, and thus the world image of every natio, by making all observe a universal justice. One could call this an attempt to "communize" culture. Sometimes this approach can resolve what seem to be unresolvable confrontations between cultures. For example, I consider the emergence of the historical religions and the historical civilizations they founded in the first millennium B.C. to be a systematization of a set of common rules, in terms of a universal justice, that made it possible for agrarian and nomadic cultures to coexist. Generally speaking, however, a justice-based approach is accompanied by an ideology of bloodshed (the doctrine of just war) that enables the eradication of injustice and tends to eliminate the individuality of the natio. In the present, when nuclear weapons are held in many parts of the world, the doctrine of just war has the potential to bring about the annihilation of the human race. When one thinks of the long history of nationalism to the present, to attempt suddenly to eliminate the individuality of the natio would be an outrage. The justice-based approach, with its tendency toward an "imperial" system, might even exacerbate, not solve, the world's problems. The human race has no choice but to adopt the rule-based approach and to move forward by recognizing the existence of the natio.

Of course, the natio is not unchanging or motionless. If economic interests coincide over the long term, they can become a means of increasing commensurability. And as the information revolution advances, the cultural sphere itself will likely expand. A quasi-community of experience will emerge among peoples in different countries who watch the same television programs. Hypothetically, if people used a single language across national boundaries, there would be a rapid increase in cultural commensurability. Thus the cultural sphere, or natio, is fluid and, one might say, always in the process of development. In order to establish a rule-based approach, while respecting the existing natio, we must attempt to increase commensurability. Occasionally however, because the extent of commensurability is limited, cosmopolitanism, a belief that the whole world is one natio, will call for a justice-based approach while indulging in elitism. It is most fitting for us to seek a commonality among ourselves to the extent that our abilities enable us to do so. In practice, this means making specific efforts to achieve a limited degree of integration of, or cooperation among, states.[4]

A FURTHER CRITIQUE OF UNQUALIFIED DEPENDENCE ON THE UNITED NATIONS

What would an international system dependent on a rule-based approach be like? The empires of colonialism and the quasi-empires of socialism were clearly grounded on justice-based approaches. There is no likelihood that these will reemerge. In contrast, the League of Nations and the United Nations were modeled on a rule-based approach, copying parliamentary democracy within countries. Certainly, as long as the independence of each country is recognized, a rule-based international system is what we might call liberal democracy between states. But there are differences here not wholly captured by an analogy with parliamentary democracy. The most important difference is that, unlike individuals, many states, in being sufficiently capable of supporting and defending themselves, can exist independently, and thus can withdraw from the system comparatively easily. The lessons of the past concerning liberal democracy among states are harsh. Thus, as has been argued above, one cannot say that the League of Nations was or the United Nations is a success.

What form could liberal democracy between states take? For comparison, let us imagine the extreme case, in which a world-state has emerged and national boundaries have lost their significance. This world-state would perhaps be governed by an "ideal world parliament," copying a typical parliamentary democracy. In this democracy, everybody would have an equal right to vote, and those who lived in particular regions would not have special privileges (such as the right of veto enjoyed by members of the U.N. Security Council). In this model the democracy between countries would be the same as the democracy among people. At the moment, there is little likelihood that this model will become a reality, but it can be a starting point for comparison.[5]

Let us return to the precedents of the League of Nations and the United Nations as the germ for democracy between states. The league took countries as its member units, and its founding principle included a respect for each country's sovereignty. Thus it was determined that "decisions at any meeting of the Assembly or the Council shall require the agreement of all the Members of the League represented at the meeting" (Covenant of the League of Nations, Article 5). This meant that all member countries had the right of veto. As already mentioned, when sanctions against a member country were on the agenda for deliberation in the council of the league, this principle of equal right to veto was restricted. But the elaborate principles in the league's covenant, fundamentally respecting such egalitarianism, restricted the effectiveness of the league.

In contrast, the United Nations has a clearly institutionalized dual structure. In one respect the United Nations also adopted the principle of equality, giving to all member countries, regardless of population, an equal right to vote in the General Assembly.[6] Authority for implementing action, though—the most important being to restore peace—was given to the Security Council, and veto power was given only to the five permanent members of the Security Council. This two-tiered structure, of Security Council/General Assembly, was an innovation of the United Nations adopted with the expectation that the five great powers, as the permanent leaders, would take necessary, effective action. This was an attempt at a kind of "guided democracy."

There may be "democrats" who are opposed to the very idea of this kind of "guided democracy." Historically, similar political systems have achieved substantial success. For example, in the bicameral parliament adopted by many Western countries, this kind of guided democracy survives in the form of the upper house. Historically speaking, this concept has its distant origins in the two-tiered structure of the *senatus/comitia tributa* in republican Rome. The history of this Roman system has any number of lessons that apply to the present age.

In Cicero's pithy words, the characteristic of this Roman system was that "this compromise, by which supreme power is granted to the people and actual authority to the Senate, will make possible the maintenance of [a] balanced and harmonious constitution."[7] But Roman guided democracy was tested during its expansionist period following the fourth century B.C., when the power of the *comitia tributa* expanded and thereby challenged the traditional authority of the senate, which was based on the noble families. The problems were, first, in the senate, to what extent the noble families, not elected by popular vote, could make decisions that transcended their own private interests, and second, how differences of opinion and conflicts of interest between the two houses could be resolved. To some extent, the two problems were related.

If one compares the five permanent members of the U.N. Security Council to those noble families, and the other countries to the general Roman populace, the United Nations and Roman democracy clearly resemble each other. In Roman society, however, the famous *patrones-clientes* relationship (simply, the relationship between leaders and followers) worked effectively. As Rome expanded and the number of those who gained rights as citizens increased, the unifying force of these patron-client relationships, seen in all parts of the Roman territory, averted a split between senate and *comitia tributa*. Roman history evolved with these relationships at its core, and it is well known that this political system was transformed from a democracy to a *principate* following Augustus, and then to imperial government. Ultimately, the dominance of the vertical ties of the patron-client relationship over horizontal ties among the general populace allowed the empire to survive for a number of centuries.

To return to the United Nations, until the Gulf War the cold war relationship between the United States and the Soviet Union maintained a situation in which the Security Council, the upper house, was a forum for the exchange of vetoes; the more important the issue, the less likely it was that the Security Council would make a decision on it. One could say that the dysfunction of the Security Council was more serious than the one in Rome.

Since the end of the cold war, the opinion has been heard that the Security Council has recovered its effectiveness and that the United Nations has begun to play a substantial role. In my opinion, though, the reason the United Nations has not fulfilled its function is not merely the dysfunction of the Security Council. Another important problem is the composition of the lower house (the General Assembly), which increases friction with the upper house (the Security Council), and which further causes the two problems to be linked. Unlike in the one-person, one-vote "world parliament" described above, in the most extreme case in the United Nations there is a disparity of 1 billion to 50,000 (China to Saint Christopher and Nevis), or 20,000 to one, in the different weights attached to the opinions of the world's people. In a more meaningful comparison, between Indonesia and Malaysia (whose past relationship cannot be said to have been friendly), the "weight" of Indonesia is disadvantaged by a proportion of 170 million to 17 million, or ten to one. There are ten U.N. member countries with populations greater than 100 million, and about 60 with populations greater than 10 million, but the populations of most of the remaining 100 countries are far smaller. There are also many structural differences in the sociological character of the member nations. Moreover, since each country's financial contribution to the United Nations is calculated in terms of its economic capability, eight countries—the G-7 and the former Soviet Union—alone are responsible for 75 percent of total contributions, and each of the 80 lowest-ranked countries contributes the minimal 0.01 percent of the total (in other words those 80 countries together contribute only 0.8 percent).

Unlike in the hypothetical world parliament mentioned above, in the U.N. General Assembly the small countries and the nondeveloped countries are overrepresented. The gap between this situation and an ideal world parliament is striking. There is reason to be concerned with this overrepresentation of the interests of the weak, however pleasing one may find it. If the General Assembly were to become the final decision-making body, operating by majority decision, the division between the General Assembly and the Security Council would deepen, the permanent members of the Security Council would probably withdraw, and the United Nations would come to a functional standstill. The possibility of withdrawal, as seen also in the case of the League of Nations, is a crucial weakness peculiar to international organizations and is not present in domestic parliaments. In fact, it is the right of veto provided in the Security Council that prevents such withdrawal, and it is this right of veto that emasculates the United Nations. Thus the problem of the composition of the General Assembly and the dysfunction of the Security Council are linked.

Let us consider the problems that could arise if the General Assembly became the final decision-making body of the United Nations, operating by majority decision. Most likely there would be an increase in demands relating to economic issues (including issues of resources) on which it is easy for those Southern (developing) countries who control the majority in the General Assembly to agree. In short, what has been called the North-South confrontation would constantly preoccupy the United Nations. Signs of this have already been seen even in the present system, in the Treaty of Lomé (negotiated 1965–79, which gave products of 69 African, Caribbean, and Pacific nations tariff-free access to EC markets), the NIEO (the New International Economic Order), the activities of Group 77, and the workings of the so-called AA Group (the African-Asian Group). In recent years the reaction of the North (including the former Soviet Union) to these kinds of mass-movement demands has generally been negative, stretching from benign neglect to boycottlike actions (such as withholding their contributions). In regard to such demands, the discontent of the powerful countries in the North is apparent. As is well known, the Economic and Social Council of the United Nations, unlike the Security Council, has no powers of implementation. This has become a safety valve, perpetuating the situation in which the South makes demands and the North ignores them. The economic issues between the North and South are probably among the most important problems facing the world today, but the present structure of the United Nations does not have the power to deal with these issues.

During the cold war, both the United States and the Soviet Union were comparatively active in aiding economic development as one means of increasing their supporters in the Southern world. France and Great Britain made similar efforts because of their ties to the South as former suzerains. The military and economic assistance provided by the Soviet Union was also substantial. The end of the cold war, however, is likely to lessen these countries' motivations to provide aid to the South. This way of acquiring supporters is reminiscent of the Roman patron-client relationship mentioned above. In Roman history this relationship gradually came to predominate. As the political system changed from democracy to *principate* and then to imperial government, it prolonged the life of the Roman Empire. Nowadays, however, when the memory of colonial rule has not disappeared, it is unlikely that a majority of the member countries in the United Nations would accept an increase in the influence of the leading countries, which would recreate a de facto patron-client relationship. It will be impossible to follow a dynamic like that of the Roman Empire.

A theoretical solution is to limit the role of the United Nations. In other words, one could imagine precluding U.N. involvement in economic issues and limiting it to security issues (such as sanctions against aggression). But this too is unlikely to be a solution. With economic issues, a possible solution is to split the difference between the Southern demand for and the Northern willingness to provide aid, but the heart of the question of sanctions is deciding whether a specific country is an aggressor. In short, there is no middle ground. It is well known that, during the cold war, serious conflicts broke out on the Korean peninsula, in Vietnam, and in Afghanistan, but—except on the Korean peninsula where, unusually, the Soviet Union was not involved—the United Nations never provided any sort of solution. As already mentioned, though, the ending of the cold war is not likely to lessen the danger of conflict within or between countries that have not yet become bona fide nation-states. Particularly with the dismantling of the quasi-empires such as the Soviet Union, the danger of military intervention in the newly independent states or internal civil war will increase, as it has between the republics of the former Soviet Union. These countries and regions contain the time bomb of various minority peoples within their borders. China is still trying to preserve its form as a quasi-empire, but it is extremely difficult to predict what kind of policies the Communist party will adopt after Deng Xiaoping. There is not only the issue of the minority peoples in Sinkiang and Uighur provinces and Tibet; there may be internal divisions due to the unevenness of economic development, and we do not know what attitude China will take toward Hong Kong, Taiwan, or the unification of the Korean peninsula. To some extent, the problems of the countries in Central America, which the United States has come to regard as its own backyard, are similar. There have already been many instances of forceful intervention by the United States in El Salvador, Nicaragua, Grenada, and Panama.

It is highly possible that, faced with problems such as these close to their own countries, the three main permanent members of the Security Council—the Russian Republic, China, and the United States—will continue to exercise their respective rights of veto, even if they must do so against the majority opinion of the General Assembly.[8] At such times the justifiability of the composition of the Security Council will be tested. During the cold war, the logic of protecting the power balance between East and West (for example, between the Brezhnev doctrine and the domino theory) was to some extent commonly accepted, at least among the clients of the respective camps; but such justification is no longer valid. The Security Council may be revealed as a forum for disputes among the three great powers, all protecting their own interests, or as a forum for tacit complicity between the great powers. In particular, there is no anticipating the behavior of the Russian Republic and China. Once the "distortion" of the cold war has been removed, the limits of the United Nations may be exposed as a structure designed only to maintain the status quo. We cannot expect that rules will be established in the near future so that, faced with an act of aggression, the United Nations will make a prompt decision and implement sanctions (or a peace-keeping operation, PKO). A PKO can be implemented only when an agreement on a ceasefire exists and the parties concerned have agreed to the PKO. Thus one can argue that a PKO is nothing more than a salve for the conscience, possible only when the conflict is unimportant (or has become unimportant).

Clearly, the United Nations cannot bring about great change. In that it takes the existence of the nation-state as an unchanging given, it has adopted the rule of collective self-defense and maintains the status quo. For example, the Southern countries may well demand a revolution to ensure international equality in income distribution, and the Northern countries a revolution in the supervision of resources (oil, tropical rain forests, rare metals, fishing resources, and so on), the international regulation of pollution, and population control. Both sides, however, are equally conservative in that they resist each other's demands for reform. Any possibility of change in the present situation is contained, not so much by decision making within the United Nations, but by a country's participating in, or withdrawing from, the United Nations. And the participation of the large number of newly independent states since the Second World War has increased the egalitarian character of the United Nations.

The possibility of withdrawal, however, usually acts as a brake on any rapid change. If the aim is to include all the countries in the world, there is no choice but to introduce the right of veto as a way of avoiding such withdrawal, but this further increases the tendency toward maintaining the status quo. As long as the nation-state is taken as the basic unit and dealt with on an equal basis, there will be no avoiding this tendency, whatever form of pseudodemocracy among states one designs. In prolonging the United Nations premised on the independence of all countries, it is impossible to construct an ideal world-state that takes the individual as its basic unit. To better reflect population and the scale of the economy, some proposals have been made to change the way voting rights are allocated, but it is not likely that such radical reform of the United Nations would be accepted by the General Assembly.[9] It is impossible to entrust the dream of a world-state, or the fate of the world, to the present United Nations, fundamentally a structure that maintains the status quo.

In Japan, there is a tendency to idealize the United Nations as a forum for internationalization, world peace, and impartial diplomacy, and many Japanese thus attach great importance to the organization. Among postwar progressives, this image has played an important part in their self-righteous position opposing the U.S.-Japan Security Treaty. The image also enabled the LDP government to adopt "multidirectional diplomacy" as a cloak hiding its single-minded efforts to pursue economic growth. The Japanese people's understanding of the reality of the United Nations, however, has been clouded by this kind of opportunism. The actual substance of the United Nations Charter is not the idealistic preface (or clause 1 or the first part of clause 2). The charter as a whole sets forth a single rule, not an unchanging justice. This is similar to a "constitution" on which parliamentary democracy is based. The charter provides a set of rules and not justice itself. The British constitution has not been systematically codified, but it is a good demonstration of the original, rule-based character of liberal democracy. With the United Nations, too, we must understand its limits as an imperfect system of rules. In seeing the United Nations as an instrument providing infallible justice, one commits a number of mistakes. For example, it is not logical for those who argue for unarmed neutrality to stress the importance of the United Nations. The argument for unarmed neutrality is not compatible with the U.N. Charter, particularly clause 43, which stipulates that military force should be provided by the member nations. Even in the Liberal Democratic party, which supports the U.S.-Japan Security Treaty, there are those who view the United Nations as an all-important international institution, but their view and the security treaty are not always consistent.[10]

As such inconsistencies show, the view of many Japanese regarding the United Nations is nothing more than an incantation mouthed when the Japanese come to an intellectual impasse in dealing with diplomacy, or an excuse offered when they wish to avert their eyes from reality. The postwar Japanese have continued to suffer from schizophrenia, alternately repelled by and attracted to the West, from a sense of guilt about their having invaded the Korean peninsula and China, and from a sense of frustration caused by their defeat in the Second World War. Many Japanese have tried to avoid confronting these psychological conflicts and to seek refuge in their view of the United Nations. But the fear of international issues the Japanese have had for a hundred years will not dissolve the elevated importance of the United Nations in their minds.

I am not arguing that the United Nations is useless, however. Seen globally, it is useful in various ways, even for the leading industrial nations, including Japan. The General Assembly of the United Nations, as a world forum in which the follower countries and the smaller countries can argue for and make public their positions, should continue to exist. The various subsidiary organizations of the United Nations are very useful in their respective areas and contribute to the formation of so-called regimes for international society. As I argue from a different perspective in the following section, however, we will not be able to depend on the United Nations to provide leadership on what I believe will be an increasingly important issue in the coming few decades, the issue of international public goods— in other words, security, technology, and investment. Even if we were to create a substantive international system separately, the United Nations may be usefully maintained as a secondary system.

If the regional security alliances I discuss below are created, it may even be possible for the United Nations to act on the basis of the activities of such alliances. (For example, the efforts of the ASEAN countries played a large part in the United Nations' dealings with the Cambodian issue; this can be seen as a precedent for such a development.) I see no reason to object to Japan's cooperating actively in U.N. forces and peace-keeping operations or to its asking for a permanent seat on the Security Council. But the United Nations itself does not have the power to break through the confusion in the world today. In Japan's case, as long as it does not have a clearly articulated and systematized foreign policy, a simply emotional overestimation of the capabilities of the United Nations is harmful. This is because it increases the Japanese people's antipathy to ideology or systematic thinking and reduces Japanese diplomacy to a vacillating situational opportunism.

The Possibility of Regional Security Alliances

If the United Nations cannot be effective as the principal actor, then what kind of international system should we be thinking about? I have already suggested a rule-based approach instead of a justice-based approach. Thus the actual form of the international system I propose should meet the following three conditions.

1. Practicality, or pragmatism: the system should provide practical rules for solving conflicts over security or economic issues.
2. Pluralism: the individuality of all cultural spheres, or natio, should be recognized.
3. Openness: at the same time, consideration should be given to encouraging an increase in the minimum level of commensurability between cultures.

Of course, there is no place for the idea that all countries should share a single, transcendental ideology or justice. The basis for the rules is in a minimum level of commensurability.

There is a trade-off here. If the requirements for a minimum level of commensurability are rigorous (or the level of the minimum is high), then it will be possible to establish a powerful set of rules for solving problems, but only at the cost of significantly reducing the number of countries that will participate in the system. If, as in the United Nations, all the countries in the world are to participate, then what is meant by commensurability becomes devoid of content, and solvable problems will be limited to cases where there has been a clear territorial violation, as in Iraq's recent invasion of Kuwait. If it is thus the case that the rules of the United Nations are ineffective, one can imagine two possible directions for reform. First, there is the possibility of creating more narrowly based alliances of states in order to achieve stronger commensurability. Here, an alliance of states refers to a group of nation-states that maintain specified relations and are regarded as legitimate (hereafter "alliance" will include weak forms that could be called "cooperation," for simplicity). Thus, this is not necessarily the same as regionalism in the usual sense.

Second, there is the possibility of limiting such a system for the most part to dealing with those problems that must be solved. Concretely speaking, it might be sensible to distinguish clearly between security issues and economic issues. Obviously, a security-oriented alliance of states and an alliance of states oriented toward economic issues are different in character. Naturally, these two models of an alliance of states in fact frequently overlap, and there is no way of predicting which should take precedence. Generally speaking, the conditions for economic cooperation are troublesome (see the following section), and it usually takes time to create the basis for such cooperation. At present, when the cold war system has collapsed so unexpectedly and abruptly, the rebuilding of the security system has become urgent.

THE EXPERIENCE OF REGIONAL SECURITY ALLIANCES

Let us first take up the question of security, the greatest responsibility of any political union. Various international systems have been devised to ensure security. One can say that the nation-state system, the League of Nations, the United Nations, and the cold war system all had security as their main objective. And this reflects an undeniable fact: security issues continue to weigh large among international problems. The pacifists in postwar Japan have tried to avoid facing this fact, and in doing this they even overlook the following important fact that has allowed Japan to take advantage of the peace: perhaps the greatest successes in terms of security since the early modern period (that is, since the formation of the nation-state) have been the regional collective security alliances in the West since the Second World War. Examples include, on the one hand, NATO, and on the other, the U.S.-Japan Security Treaty, the U.S.-Korea mutual defense treaty, the U.S.-China mutual defense treaty (abrogated in 1979), and the Pacific security treaty. During this period of almost half a century, there has been no aggression against these alliances and no situation that could have given rise to military conflict within them. There has also been no danger of the balance of power politics malfunctioning, as it did in the nineteenth century.

In fact, during this period, there has been no war between major powers, including any between the East and West camps. Since the end of the Second World War, the last time major powers came into direct military confrontation was when the United States and China clashed at the time of the Korean War (1950–51).[11] As noted earlier, this remarkable 40-year period is the longest without war between major powers since at least the beginning of the sixteenth century. For Europe, this state of peace is a record not achieved in the previous 2,000 years, and as a result, economic development has enjoyed favorable, historically unprecedented conditions. Japan too has been so blessed by peace and prosperity that it has forgotten its singular fortune. This state of peace between the major powers is half a result of the U.S.-Soviet mutual deterrent but half an achievement of the collective security alliances. The postwar progressives in Japan have maintained that the U.S.-Japan Security Treaty is the incarnation of evil, aggravating the tensions of the cold war, but given the present situation there is a need to reevaluate and discard this kind of cold war prejudice.

Let us abandon this prejudice and compare the accomplishments of these regional security alliances with other foreign policy options. What was the outcome of the principle of "nonaligned neutrality," whose objective was to alleviate cold war tensions?[12] There were frequent conflicts among the countries advocating the principle (the countries in the non-aligned conference or the African-Asian conference). In Asia, thé Sino-Indian War, the Indo-Pakistan War, the Sino-Vietnam War, Vietnam's invasion of Cambodia, and the Iran-Iraq War, and in Africa, the various conflicts involving Ethiopia (the Ogaden War against Somalia, the conflict against Eritrea, and the intervention in Sudan), the conflict in the western Sahara, and Libya's invasion of Chad were all conflicts between participants in the nonaligned conference (or the African-Asian conference).[13]

From a global perspective, these can be seen as insignificant incidents, but for the various countries concerned they were cruel wars. I am not saying that the cold war had no influence on these conflicts, but their origins were clearly in the situations of the involved countries; while advocating the great objective of nonalignment, they trampled on security and peace among themselves.

The movement for nonaligned neutrality does not seem to have been helpful even in its original objective to ease tensions between the United States and the Soviet Union. On the issue of disarmament, emphasized during the initial period, beginning with China and India possessing nuclear weapons, many nations of the African-Asian conference turned to building up their military capabilities and lost any right to appeal for disarmament. A principle of nonaligned neutrality that cannot prevent "internal" conflicts even among those who advocate it surely cannot be expected to help reduce "external" conflict (between the United States and the Soviet Union). Nowadays, the substance of this kind of movement has been reduced to the activities of the African-Asian group within the United Nations, united principally to vent their discontent over economic disparities. The group no longer plays a role in security issues.

Next, there is the example of the Warsaw Treaty Organization (WTO). This collective security alliance is different from the Western NATO. In the sense that it established a defensive force capable of opposing NATO, the WTO too may have been a success. However, two internal military conflicts—the uprising in Hungary and the disturbances in Czechoslovakia—occurred among its members. Thus, the WTO failed to ensure peace among its members, primarily because it did not stop with maintaining an agreement on the issue of collective defense but attempted to broaden its control over the economy, politics, and ideology of the member states (that is, to enforce an increase in commensurability). That the Soviet bloc nations had COMECON (Council for Mutual Economic Assistance) in the economic sphere is well known, but its value was substantially limited because of interstate control of the political and ideological spheres. For example, the so-called Brezhnev doctrine of 1968 advocated a theory of limited sovereignty, which argued that the sovereignty of individual socialist countries was subordinate to the interests of the socialist camp as a whole. In NATO, countries were free to secede, as evidenced by France's withdrawal from its military organization in 1966, but even so, the substance of NATO remained unaffected. In contrast, were it not for the threat of military force made in the Brezhnev doctrine, the WTO could not have survived. The WTO was an excessively rigid, constraining, involuntary alliance, perhaps because of the nature of Soviet socialism, whose direction was determined in its initial period by Stalinism; but the quasi-imperialistic nature of socialism, which depended on a unitary justice and a centralized power structure, is also surely responsible.

In many parts of the world, particularly Japan, the collective security alliances in the West came to be considered the root of evil. Of course, from the Marxist viewpoint, opposition to a military alliance with the United States, the global headquarters of capitalism, is an ideological position that transcends the issue of war or peace. Depending on the circumstances, opposing the military alliances with the United States was justice that should be advocated even at the sacrifice of a state of peace. Nowadays, however, when the end of the cold war has undermined the Marxist mythology, there is no longer any ideology that can act as an alibi for failing to consider how to achieve peace. We should realize that the existence of the U.S.-Japan Security Treaty has probably been decisive in maintaining relative peace in East Asia and the Pacific; in this sense, the influence of the U.S.-Japan Security Treaty has extended beyond Japan to the rest of Asia and even, indirectly, to the world as a whole.

The U.S.-Japan Security Treaty is only one example. NATO and the alliances in East Asia and the Pacific region, as already noted, have played a role close to that of a large-scale collective security alliance centered on the United States. Of course these alliances were originally formed to resist the Soviet Union (and to some extent China); however, they have not completely lost their meaning with the disappearance of the background of the cold war (or with China's trend toward modernization). As already pointed out, there has been the substantial achievement of maintaining peace within the alliances for almost half a century and relationships within the alliances have become unusually close. Other than those fanatics who are prepared even to sacrifice peace for a certain kind of "justice," there is surely no one who would be willing to do without the achievements of this half century. In Europe in particular, there are no voices calling for the abandonment of the collective security system. (In Japan too, those calling for the annulment of the U.S.-Japan Security Treaty are no more than a small minority.)

We can draw the following lesson from the "failures" of the principle of nonaligned neutrality and the WTO: in order for a security-oriented alliance to succeed, a great power (or several great powers) with the ability to punish violations must participate, but at the same time the influence of this great power should be limited to the field of security. If the experience of such cooperation on security issues is accumulated sufficiently, it is possible that the economies and political systems of the member countries may by themselves come to resemble each other. If, however, it is taken as a basic principle that a collective security alliance is not formed unless the economic and political systems are similar, then there will be a movement to enforce such a homogenization within the alliance. When this occurs, it is highly likely that the alliance will fail as the WTO did. During the cold war in the West too there was a tendency to think (especially on the part of the United States) that political and economic homogeneity—freedom of markets and a democracy similar to that in the United States—should be a criterion for membership. However, with the end of the cold war, if the idea of justice embodied in the system loses its hold, then it will be possible for regional collective security alliances to form that pay little attention to the differences between great and minor powers or to the differences in their political and economic systems. We tend to think of regional collective security alliances in connection with the U.S.-Soviet cold war; certainly it was the cold war that has until now generated the regional collective security alliances. But if the real aim of regional collective security alliances is to maintain peace, there is no longer any need for them to have a common ideology.

REGIONS WHERE COLLECTIVE SECURITY ALLIANCES ARE POSSIBLE

Where might a regional security alliance be possible? What possibilities are there in Europe, East Asia, the Arab world, Central and South America, and Africa? Little needs to be said about the integration in Europe that has evolved into the European Community, which has already gone beyond the level of a security alliance to become general in character, and which includes economic integration. This integration, even if we limit ourselves to the period since the Second World War, is a result of the accumulated experiences, beginning with the Coal and the Iron and Steel Communities. Among these, however, there is no doubt that NATO was decisive in increasing the cohesion of the West European countries. The military alliance, maintained in the keen awareness of the possibility of invasion by the WTO, created what one might call a "destined community." On this basis, the integration of domestic tax systems and agricultural policies, and currency unification, are now making progress, albeit slowly. For Europe, the birthplace of the nation-state system, this integration has been a historic event, and NATO has promoted its rapid progress. The newest issue for European integration is whether the East European countries should participate. It is most interesting that it was the Conference on Security and Cooperation in Europe (CSCE) and the treaty on the reduction of Conventional Forces in Europe (CFE) that followed the Helsinki Accord. It seems to have been well understood that security maintenance is the first requirement in building regional cooperation.

The East Asian case is very interesting. (In the discussion below, East Asia refers to both Southeast and Northeast Asia but excludes China.) Economic interdependence within East Asia, even though it is not at the level seen in Europe or between Canada and the United States, is already greater than in any other region (Latin America, for example). Of course, this is due to the emergence of vibrant developmentalist countries in the region since the 1970s, and to the rapid and continuing surge in supply and demand. Korea, Taiwan, Hong Kong, and Singapore have already passed the take-off stage, and Thailand, Malaysia, and Indonesia are not far behind. These countries are all developmentalists and also face similar problems in the international economy. These economies differ in their levels of development, but as their growth continues it is possible that such differences will disappear. Some may grow more rapidly than others by implementing effective economic policies. For example, Singapore's per capita income is now close to those of neighboring Australia and New Zealand, long recognized as developed countries, and if current trends continue both Korea and Taiwan will soon enjoy per capita income similar to that of Singapore.

But there is no collective security alliance in East Asia. At first glance, it seems as if increasingly close economic relations have preceded the emergence of a security system. Certainly, there was the SEATO (the Southeast Asia Treaty Organization, an anticommunist alliance composed of Thailand, Pakistan, the Philippines, the United States, Great Britain, France, Australia, and New Zealand). But this alliance broke up in 1977 and can hardly be called an example of a successful regional alliance. Other bilateral security networks between the United States and several Asian nations had an indirect stabilizing effect in this region. In the past, Malaysia and Singapore relied on the military capabilities of Britain, and today Thailand and Singapore maintain a de facto military alliance with the United States. All of this is to say that the East Asian countries (except for the three countries in Indochina) have guaranteed their security, and achieved economic prosperity, mainly by relying indirectly on the U.S. military capability. But with the end of the cold war this security support now faces the possibility of disappearing.

That is, the diplomatic circumstances in the East Asian countries are now unstable. No country in this region wishes to see a vacuum emerge as a result of the withdrawal of the U.S. military from East Asia. At the same time, not one country openly acknowledges or is increasing its dependence on the U.S. military capability. Even in countries that have traditionally maintained strong military cooperation with the United States, such as Korea and the Philippines, there is a more and more apparent tendency to try to avoid strengthening their relationship with the United States. (Incidentally, the same is happening vis-à-vis Japan in the economic sphere. Not one country in East Asia wants to reject Japanese investment, but there is also not one country eager to increase its economic dependence on Japan.) The arrangement in East Asia up to this point that combined a tacit security system and substantial economic relationships may seem more precarious than its counterparts in Europe, but it has worked well. Now, however, there seems to be a cloud hanging over this arrangement.

THE STRANGE CASE OF ASEAN

ASEAN (the Association of Southeast Asian Nations, composed of six countries, Indonesia, Malaysia, the Philippines, Thailand, Singapore, and Brunei) is interesting in several respects. ASEAN is not a security alliance but curiously came into being not with a founding charter but with the abstract and ambiguous Bangkok Declaration in 1967, and for a long time it has seemed to have an indeterminate position in international law. Particularly in the first ten years of its existence, it was unclear, at least from the outside, what kind of regional cooperation it wished to achieve, and it even seemed as if it might break up.[14] During this initial period, ASEAN defined itself as simply an economic and cultural grouping, but in fact this was rhetoric to distinguish itself from SEATO and ASPAC (the Asian and Pacific Council), which were regarded as anticommunist collective security organizations. Actually, economic cooperation began to be achieved only in the latter half of the 1970s (beginning, one could say, with the signing of the intraregional preferential tariff agreement in 1977); the Southeast Asian Friendship and Cooperation Treaty in 1976 also advocated the peaceful settlement of regional conflicts, but there were no instances of this actually happening. (A security council for dealing with such conflicts has still not been created.[15]) Thus at first glance, ASEAN is an association with no function. Nevertheless, ASEAN has clearly maintained a fixed political stance. Its concentration on the economy and culture is a kind of paradoxical expression of this political stance.

The basic political stance of ASEAN has the following two characteristics. First, ASEAN has tried to achieve some kind of compromise between the two somewhat contradictory principles of nonaligned neutrality and being pro-Western. In fact, the governments in the countries that promote ASEAN, having considerable difficulty suppressing the influence of communism within their countries, adopted anticommunist policies; and the member countries depended militarily either on the United States (in the case of the Philippines, Thailand, and to a lesser extent Indonesia) or on Britain or Commonwealth countries (in the case of Malaysia and Singapore). ASEAN as an organization did not deny such military dependence. In theory, however, ASEAN proclaimed its nonaligned neutrality and was active in rebuilding Indochina and establishing diplomatic relations with China. This position was a reaction against interference by great powers from outside the region (which reminded the member countries of past colonialism) and a reflection of public opinion within each country. Most nonaligned nations faced diplomatic difficulties because of the loss of substance in their idealism (witness Indonesia until Sukarno's exit); but it is noteworthy how skillfully ASEAN has exploited the security capabilities of the West. This seeming contradiction is not, however, merely the double-faced diplomacy of a minor power. Given the conflicts within the region, it was the pragmatism of the political leadership in each country, concerned of course about development but also about security and independence, that overcame the contradiction between these two principles.

Second, ASEAN was formed even while regional disputes—such as the Sabah issue between Malaysia and the Philippines, Indonesian opposition to the planned Malaysian federation, and the question of Singapore's independence—had not yet been resolved. This is contrary to the existing common understanding of power politics between states, which posits that an alliance can be formed only once an agreement has been established on ends and means. Islam, Buddhism, Confucianism, and Christianity exist side by side in this region, but there have been no cases of religious confrontation causing wars.

Putting these facts together, one has to say that the existence of ASEAN runs contrary to the European understanding that such an alliance will emerge from the recognition of a single principle of justice, or of a shared goal concerning benefits to be collectively realized. To exaggerate somewhat, in this case both the end and the ideology have emerged after the fact—that is, after the creation of ASEAN. The approach that produced this result may be unique—what I would call a hermeneutic approach. It may perhaps also reflect a way of thinking common throughout East Asia, including Korea, Taiwan, and Japan. This diplomatic perspective is quite different from that in Europe, which sees international relations as a game of billiards in which inflexible rationalities collide with each other.

In any case, ASEAN is uneasy with great powers outside the region (the United States, China, Japan) but does not reject them. During the cold war, too, it did not support a single, justice-based approach. And ASEAN is not gathered under a single religion. It has been said that ASEAN is a form of solidarity among the Malay race, but this kind of emphasis on ethnicity has not been the mainstream. (In fact, seen anthropologically, such emphasis is untenable.) Even during the period when emancipation from colonialism still remained a passion, and the cold war doctrines of just war were yet dominant, the ASEAN countries were not caught up in ideological battles. But this was not necessarily due to aimlessness or isolationism on their part. Militarily, the Philippines, Singapore, and Thailand all in their own way had relationships with the United States, and economically, they actively welcomed investment and goods from countries outside the region, particularly Japan. One can say that ASEAN's aim was perhaps, while accepting these outside influences, to create an independence sufficient to cope with them.

A remarkable achievement of ASEAN has been its resolution of the long-standing intraregional disputes between Indonesia and Malaysia, the Philippines and Malaysia, and others over the course of 25 years. But what is most impressive is the measured but definite self-assertion against the great powers from outside the region, and the persistence of the unity that has caused this to be recognized. And, recently, ASEAN has come to proclaim as its objective a Southeast Asian Community. One might say that the way ASEAN has been organized satisfies the three conditions for a rule-based approach described at the beginning of this section—pragmatism, pluralism, and openness. ASEAN is a good example of an organization that has taken a diplomatic stance that is not justice-based and thus will be instructive for regional coalitions of the future.

DESIGNING A COLLECTIVE SECURITY ALLIANCE FOR EAST ASIA AND THE PACIFIC

Returning to the question of security for East Asia as a whole, it is good news that with the advent of peace in Cambodia, relationships among the three countries in Indochina seem to be stabilizing; there are almost no military disputes in East Asia at present (except for the guerrilla activity in the Philippines). But there are a number of causes for anxiety. The greatest problem in East Asia, the trends in China, will not disappear. A scheme is needed to prevent giving China the temptation to expand militarily even when it is politically destabilized. The possibility that the Russian Republic (or the Commonwealth of Independent States, which is centered on it) will attempt military expansion into East Asia cannot be totally dismissed. However, East Asia can no longer rely on U.S. security to provide a security umbrella as it did during the cold war. Thus, the question of revising the post-cold-war security system is particularly acute for East Asia. One imaginable solution is a regional collective security alliance including not only the Southeast Asian countries but also East Asia in the narrow sense (Korea, Taiwan, and Japan) as well as countries from outside the region (the United States, Australia, and New Zealand).[16]

I have already said that a collective security alliance should actively seek the participation of the great powers (particularly the great military powers). But all countries, whether they are great powers or minor powers, must have an equal right to speak. If this principle of equality is established as a rule, the alliance based on it will be able to function as a mechanism to oversee and control the actions of large countries such as the United States and Japan. The East Asian and Pacific countries are highly diverse, with varied histories, but in creating cooperation among them, the experience of ASEAN, with its demonstrated pragmatism, pluralism, and openness, will serve as a valuable precedent. In other words, the structure that will be most easily accepted is perhaps one that, while stressing economic and cultural cooperation, in fact promotes political cooperation for security. APEC (the original Asia-Pacific Economic Cooperation Council of Ministers) started to deal with economic issues, but it is quite possible that this could evolve as a basis for a system of cooperation in security. Indeed, if APEC is to continue to evolve, it would be prudent for it to learn from the experience of ASEAN. If Japan or the United States attempts to assume leadership—particularly with some idea of a justice-based approach—it will be difficult to establish cooperation in this region.

Together with, or rather before promoting a foreign policy of economic aid, Japan needs to show clearly that it will assume its responsibilities for security in East Asia. This will require establishing constitutionally the right to collective self-defense (by means of a constitutional amendment, or at least a revision in constitutional interpretation) and explicitly declaring that any overseas deployment of troops or participation in a PKO will be carried out under the restrictions imposed by the East Asian and Pacific Collective Security Alliance. It is often noted that the East Asian countries fear Japan's becoming a great military power; but no country either wants or expects Japan to adopt the principle of nonviolent resistance. (This would mean to experiment with a single idealism, at the sacrifice of the security of East Asia as a whole.) Nobody would believe that a country can be both egotistical in its economic behavior and altruistic in regard to security issues. This distrust is at the root of the misgivings people have about Japan. Even if the East Asian people can understand the Japanese people's war-weariness and deep-rooted psychology of dependence (*amae*), Japan's responsibility to make a substantive contribution to the security of the whole region (and also of the world) remains. If this contribution is only financial, Japan cannot but be discriminated against as an unfathomable outcast. Because the United States has the self-confidence of a great power, it was not hurt psychologically by the financial contributions it received from Japan for the Gulf War. But Japan's adoption of the same methods toward its neighbors in East Asia would provoke the strong psychological reaction of not wanting to become "Japan's mercenaries."

One cannot deny that for Japan, and for all the countries in East Asia, the issue of security has become extremely important because, even though the cold war has ended, there exists the possibility of conflict in Asia. During the cold war, East Asia weathered the security issue by using what one might call the jerry-rigged apparatus of the network of bilateral treaties and the stability provided by ASEAN. Fortunately or not, Asia's economic development during this period was the smoothest in the world. As a result the world has become somewhat complacent. Even the three great powers that have been extraordinarily interested in this region— China, the former Soviet Union, and the United States—are today either unable or unwilling to be actively involved in Asia. Of course, it is unlikely that they will continue to maintain this passive attitude. For example, given the force of its habits in the cold war period of managing bilateral relationships and assuming the leadership, the United States still has not withdrawn psychologically from the region. As symbolized by its abandonment of its bases in the Philippines, however, the United States has no choice but to reevaluate its existing security strategy in East Asia. U.S. foreign policy in East Asia today appears uncertain, and because of this, there is a distinct possibility that a sudden, violent, security-threatening crisis might result in the region. If their domestic economic situations stabilize, China and the Russian Republic too may throw their energy into their traditional geopolitical diplomacy.

More specifically, it is likely that problems such as the unification of the Korean peninsula, the relationship between China and Taiwan, and the position of the free market regions on the Chinese coast and in the coastal provinces will have to be dealt with in the near future. Moreover, if economic development among the East Asian countries progresses smoothly from here on, some among them may be tempted to increase their military capabilities for purposes other than defending their respective countries. And a government may even emerge in some country whose aim is to become the regional military power. Thus I would like to propose here an East Asian and Pacific collective security alliance that includes the United States, the great power that is least likely to be expansionist and that has had long relations with the region. Of course, the participation of the United States is desirable also to prevent worsening of economic friction between the United States and the East Asian countries.

This alliance would be a kind of collective self-defense alliance, but different from an alliance such as NATO for which the hypothetical enemy is clearly identified. Neither would it be a bilateral treaty such as the U.S.-Japan Security Treaty. It is easiest to imagine it as having the characteristics of a mini–United Nations and the ability to supplement U.N. peace-keeping functions. Let me begin by proposing the following set of rules for such a multilateral relationship; of course, this is nothing more than an idea to enable us to speculate on the course we could follow.

1. The member countries have equal voting rights. No large country may have special privileges.

2. When a member country's territory is invaded or attacked, the alliance's army may intervene militarily. The dispatch of the alliance army requires the agreement of all member countries other than those concerned.

3. The plan for the composition of the alliance army is always prepared. The member countries must always be ready to participate.

4. The alliance may request reports from the member countries regarding their military capability, military movements, and plans for military deployment.

5. The member countries must consult with each other on arms reduction.

Unlike the United Nations Charter, this alliance would not have the dual structure of a Security Council and General Assembly. Because the alliance would encompass a single region, one could expect it to be able to achieve a high degree of consensus and to implement its military interventions more promptly and effectively.

Some countries among the candidates for membership, including the United States, might hesitate to create the alliance. From Japan's standpoint, however, there is at least one major reason to promote its formation. Japan's economic advance into and economic aid to Asia have increased enormously. Unless it adopts a policy commensurate with such economic involvement in the region, demonstrating how Japan is to bear the burden of international public goods in the regional sense, violence may erupt in East Asia. Unless somewhere a framework for political cooperation, including cooperation in sharing the security burden, is created, I fear that the resulting situation will be detrimental to Japan and beyond its control. Japan must be the principal promoter behind the scenes of such an alliance.

THE PROS AND CONS OF A REGIONAL SECURITY ALLIANCE: THE ISSUE OF A SHARED ROOF

There is no question that a regional security alliance can react to events much more easily than the United Nations. This is because it can rapidly adopt military sanctions, regardless of the reactions of countries in other regions. Incidents such as Iraq's invasion of Kuwait, which attract the world's attention because of their concern with oil, are special cases. Other than these, there are frequent disputes that have great significance for the region concerned but not much global interest. One example is the unwillingness of the immediately neighboring EC countries to intervene in the Yugoslavian problem—one that, in a sense, concerns the EC more directly than the invasion of Kuwait. If Yugoslavia had been a member of the EC, other countries would have been more likely to intervene. For a long time, the reaction of the United Nations (the Security Council) was even more lukewarm than that of the EC. Regional security alliances provide the most effective solution for disputes like these, which the world heartlessly regards as insignificant.

Regional alliances, though, have the serious problem of increasing the likelihood of conflicts between alliances. For example, many fear that the EC will increase economic confrontation with other countries. Were the countries in East Asia and the Pacific to advance toward an alliance, would disputes between Europe and Asia and the Pacific not be exacerbated? In this case, though, at least for now, there is little possibility of either side's responding with military force because the hostility would for the most part be over economic issues. But the greater the unity of the regional security alliance, the more chance there is that the economic confrontation will escalate. We cannot very well dismiss as fantasy the idea that regional security alliances may be the starting point for disputes between large political blocs.

One way of avoiding this danger is for the great powers to participate responsibly in both alliances so that the roofs provided by the alliances overlap. For example, it is possible to imagine that the former Soviet Union will split into a Slavic federation and an Islamic federation. If this occurs, the Russian Republic might participate, as an exceptional case, in the Islamic federation as well. If this kind of interlocking participation could be implemented between the EC and the Slavic republics, or between a Central European and East European federation, then the same idea could be applied to the relationships between the latter two European federations and the EC. This idea of overlapping roofs may be difficult to accept in terms of the existing concept of an alliance as something that shares a single principle of justice, but it is in no way unnatural when considered from a rule-based approach.

Clearly the United States would have the main role in implementing this plan. It is realistic to think, I believe, that the United States would participate in the security aspects of all the alliances—the East Asian and Pacific alliance, a kind of Middle and Near East alliance including Israel, a Central and South American alliance, and the EC. Borrowing from what Mikhail Gorbachev called a "common house," let me here call this interlocking of the regional security alliances a system of overlapping, shared roofs. This system, by joining together the regional alliances, could cover the whole world in place of the United Nations.

Of course, an important question is whether the United States or the Russian Republic would be prepared to accept such a role. The reality, however, is that both are already involved with these multiple regions, and unless both countries suddenly revert to isolationism, they will be unable to extricate themselves from the existing involvements. Given that intervention on the grounds of an ideology of justice has become impossible, these interventions are most appropriately justified within the framework of regional security alliances. For example, the current Middle East peace talks are perhaps a prototype of such an alliance; once the parties involved reach an agreement they will surely have no choice but to create a security alliance that involves the United States. One final issue with regard to regional security alliances is their cooperation and interaction with economic alliances, which, depending on the circumstances, could exert substantial influence. I attempt an examination of this indispensable point in the next section.

Varied Patterns of Economic Alliances: Their Relationship with Developmentalism

There exist alliances for security reasons as well as alliances for economic purposes. These two types of alliance do not necessarily have identical goals and thus should be clearly distinguished. There is no one right answer as to which type of alliance is easier to form or which should precede the other. It may seem that economic alliances are easier to create given the trend toward a so-called borderless economy, but this is not always the case. Here we must consider general questions.

Of the various models for creating economic groups, a weak form might be cooperation on specific issues and policies, and a strong form the integration that shares rules on a large number of issues and policies. According to Bela Balassa, economic groups can be divided into five types, progressing from weak to strong: a free-trade area, a customs union, a common market, an economic union, and total economic integration.[17] There are many examples of the weak type, which should be called cooperation;

a typical contemporary attempt at the strong type is the integration of the EC. Here I refer to all the different types, from weak to strong, as economic alliances.

THE STANDARD PATTERN OF ECONOMIC ALLIANCE

The traditional theory provided by economists for economic alliances is the so-called theory of customs union. This theory analyzes the various possible groups that could be formed and compares the liberalizing (trade-creating) effects of abolishing tariffs within these groups with the protectionist (trade-diverting) effects of erecting tariff barriers to those outside the group, and thus examines what kind of group will bring the greatest benefits (for that group).[18] The most recent theories of customs union are overly concerned with intricate technical arguments. Their general conclusion, though, can be summarized as follows: a group made up of countries that are mutually complementary has more to gain from union or cooperation than a group of countries that are mutually substitutive (competitive).

In reality, however, protectionist policies are usually implemented within each country, and each country's protectionism is generally stronger in those industries that compete with the same industries in other countries. Thus in many cases a customs union between mutually substitutive countries would generate substantial benefits.[19] I should note, however, that this proviso is based on a static argument applicable only at the time that a union or cooperation is initiated. In a dynamic case, meaning that the efforts toward integration gradually increase from cooperation to union, ultimately the structural criterion of whether the relationship is complementary or substitutive becomes important.

Depending on which is dominant, complementarity or substitutability, one can distinguish between a vertical and a horizontal division of labor. For example, we can say that countries that produce the same commodities—that is, substitutes—and trade with each other will normally have a relationship based on a horizontal division of labor. Those countries that produce complementary commodities, such as raw materials and finished goods, will have a relationship based on a vertical division of labor. The relationship between countries that produce and trade various commodities cannot easily be distinguished as based on a horizontal or vertical division of labor, but let me here use this broad classification to advance the argument.

A typical example of a vertical division of labor between raw materials and manufactured goods was the imperialistic integration between colonies and their mother countries, or colonizers. In other words, imperialism was, or at least had an aspect of, an economically rational integration based on a complementary relationship. In this sense, imperialistic integration was economic integration; but, given that the colonies and their colonizers were distant from each other, it was clearly not regional integration. Imperialistic integration, though, had a tendency to generate disparities within the relationship. This was because there are great differences in the rate at which productivity increases and in the income elasticity of demand, between industries that extract raw materials and those that produce manufactured goods, and so the benefits of trade (both within and outside the region) return more to the industries in the mother countries. Thus the mother countries find it necessary to use military force to suppress the political discontent that arises from these disparities (as Britain did in its former relationship with India when the two clashed over the production of cotton goods.) Once military control is established, the pressure creates *noneconomic* exploitation.

The first among many economic blocs of the prewar period was the British Commonwealth, which adopted the preferential tariff system at the conference in Ottawa in 1932. Like others that followed, this was an economic integration in which the suzerain tried to vertically control all economic activities, from those involving resources (such as foodstuffs and raw materials) to the market for finished goods. Basically, it was the creation of groups that replicated the structure of imperialism. Following the Second World War, however, colonialism disappeared, and the use or threat of military force to protect economic interests has become impossible. The countries that became independent after the war were unwilling to participate in blocs at the cost of suffering the disparities a vertical division of labor tended to bring about.

Imperialism, of course, but also the blocs of the prewar types have now become quite impossible and are not likely to reemerge. The socialist bloc in the Soviet Union and Eastern Europe is the most recent example similar to these past blocs, but political, military, and ideological domination enabled this bloc to exist, and with the ideological collapse of socialism it has already become impossible for it to reemerge. Many voices warn against creating blocs, and at least the blocs of the prewar type based on a vertical division of labor and backed by military force will not reappear. We must not confuse the recent attempts at economic integration with the prewar endeavors that created the blocs of the past.

THE EC AS ECONOMIC INTEGRATION

Let us now examine the EC as an example of the horizontal model of the division of labor. The integration of the EC is the product of a long history, and its political and cultural character is distinct. Economic integration is a result of this history and is thus unique in that the framework for regional integration has been provided in advance. It is said that within the EC there is a strong trend toward the horizontal division of labor in manufactured goods. If this is the case, the economic integration of the EC should not generate a substantial benefit because, according to the traditional static theory (the theory of customs union), the horizontal division of labor is not a complementary but a competitive (substitutive) relationship. Let us consider the automobile industry or the electronics industry. If innovative changes are not expected in technology or the market, EC integration will simply reduce the number of firms in Europe through competition among them and will go no further than making a one-time increase in productive efficiency. Even if the number of European firms is reduced, there should be no great advantage gained by the EC firms in competing in international markets or by the consumers in the EC.

Nevertheless, immense effort is being made and a huge cost incurred to integrate the regional economic system (by closing not only customs but also each country's tax system, the system of subsidies, the currency system, and the credit system). Why? The only reason must be that the efforts and costs are justified in view of the EC's "dynamic" (as against "static") goal: realizing large-scale benefits by dismantling national boundaries and expanding the market, promoting technological innovation on the strengths of the benefits, and thereby enabling each country's firms to emerge as European and, finally, as genuine world-class companies. It is evident that one of the EC's important motivations is to try to reduce the technological gap between Europe and Japan that has widened rapidly within the past decade. In this sense, EC integration has as its original aim economic integration in pursuit of dynamic benefits; going one step further, one could even say that it is an attempt at a kind of EC-wide developmentalism. A static theory of economic integration is clearly inadequate to explain what one might call passion for the integration of the EC.

In the final analysis, the existing theory of economic integration considers only the issue of trade, and that only in a static analysis.[20] But economic interaction in the real world has many dimensions, including trade as well as investment, competition in or transfer of technology, the international spread of environmental pollution, and so on, and each has dynamic effects. Even in trade itself, with the emergence of many industries faced with decreasing cost, free competition either within or among industries becomes unstable, and a situation arises in which, potentially, cooperation (collusion?) might be required among firms or countries (as discussed in Chapter 7). The goal of present-day economic integration is to acquire complementary benefits (in the broad sense not considered in the past) from economic interaction that is becoming extraordinarily intensive, multifaceted, and dynamic.

Of course, many, even today, discuss the pros and cons of economic integration only from the static viewpoint of the costs and benefits of trade. The naive protectionists, who think only of protecting intraregional industry from imports, are an extreme example of such people. And they may be found even among those promoting economic integration or cooperation. Thus there are arguments warning that economic integration will hinder the development of world trade, and one cannot say that these fears are entirely groundless. However, if economic integration were merely protectionism, it could be implemented by individual countries and could establish more favorable tariffs (as taught by the so-called theory of optimum tariff). If economic integration were merely to erect protective tariffs (and other barriers) in common, it would be no more than a device of appealing to the masses and violating the rule of economic liberalism. The theoretical conclusion of this kind of protectionism is a mechanics of mutual retaliation, and the tragedy of a zero-sum game. But those among the theorists promoting economic integration who are adopting a dynamic way of thinking—perhaps the majority—are trying to avoid, and undoubtedly believe they can avoid, this kind of protectionism.

Their expectations may not come true, however, and the dynamic benefits may not be realized. This outcome would create a problem. The horizontal division of labor between the EC countries is in the main a competitive (substitutive) relationship; in other words, it is a relationship in which, if technological innovation does not progress evenly, the ties between each country, and with countries outside the region, would be broken. For example, if technological innovation in the United States, Japan, and East Asia were a success, and the efforts at technological innovation in Europe failed to bear fruit, there would be a flood of manufactured exports and new entrants into the European market from the United States, Japan, and the Asian NIEs, despite the tariff barriers. One result would be an increased horizontal division of labor with countries outside the region, causing ties within Europe based on the horizontal division of labor to break. From the political point of view, a strengthening of protectionism would become inevitable for the sake of protecting EC integration. If the EC failed to achieve technological innovation, EC integration would revert, in essence, simply to a protectionism appealing to the masses.

It is difficult to evaluate EC integration or to predict its future. However, given its political and cultural momentum, one may assume that it will progress. The question is which direction economic integration will take. If the EC withdraws behind protectionism, it will have no choice but to stop exporting to non-EC countries; and there will be no way of dealing with the desires for development of the countries in Central and Eastern Europe that hope to be members of an expanded EC. In the end, Western Europe would become a historical museum, recalling an age called the modern period. Seen in the long term (in the short term it could well become the trigger for a global recession), the global economy would be little affected should this scenario unfold. I believe, however, that Europe will continue to be energized by its desire to face up to the issues of the expansion of the EC and the reindustrialization of Eastern Europe and thus will not become a museum.

SHOULD THERE BE AN EAST ASIAN ECONOMIC INTEGRATION?

The intensive, multifaceted, and dynamic nature of economic interactions similar to those that created EC integration is today an impetus for integrating economies in regions throughout the world. Even in Latin America earnest attempts are being made at an economic integration that are somewhat different from the existing alliance centered on the United States. In North America there is the attempt at a North American Free Trade Agreement.[21] Each of these examples has its own characteristics, its own strengths and weaknesses. Here, though, let us consider the case of East Asia (Southeast Asia plus Japan, Korea, Taiwan, and Hong Kong).

There is a division of labor among the countries in East Asia, and also a complementary relationship in the supply and demand of capital within the region. This division of labor, though, unlike that in Europe, is neither horizontal nor vertical but exhibits "the flying-geese pattern in the division of labor."[22] In other words, there is a division of labor between the producers of parts and the parent firms that produce and market the final products, between low-tech and high-tech production, and between production of low-grade products and high-grade products—that is, there is a division of labor in manufacturing that is based on the level of technological competence. The competition to climb the ladder of technology is fierce because of differences in historical timing of economic development; but at present there is both stiff technological competition and a complementary relationship between those upstream (that are more technologically developed) and those downstream (that are less technologically developed); in other words, the flying-geese pattern in the division of labor—the horizontal relationship and the vertical relationship mixed together—has been created. In this sense, one could say that complementary economic relationships are stronger in East Asia than in Europe. (Incidentally, were Australia or New Zealand to enter these relationships of economic cooperation, for a time its participation would be complementary, as a supplier of raw materials.) Moreover, because productivity in the technologically backward countries generally increases more rapidly even within the same manufacturing industry, it is unlikely that the gap between the advanced countries (Japan, for example) and the backward countries would widen and thus give rise to criticism of exploitation. The potential benefits of economic cooperation or economic integration may therefore seem higher in this region than in the EC.

But would there be real benefits in the East Asian region's embarking on economic integration? The first step in economic integration is usually a combination of liberalization within the region and establishing barriers to countries outside the region. It would be unwise for East Asian integration to put priority on establishing trade barriers to countries outside the region because each country in East Asia has adopted its own developmentalist policies (some of which are protectionist) that have enabled the region to become the most dynamic in the world. Adopting a common protectionism, in effect adding another layer to the existing protectionism, aimed at countries outside the region would thus make little sense. Moreover, East Asia already faces growing protectionism from outside in reaction to its increasing success in the international market. In particular, unless the United States participates in this economic integration, the measures it will adopt in retaliation will become very harsh. In this sense, East Asia is the region most likely to be the spark that ignites global protectionism. It would be suicidal indeed for East Asia, where trade is expanding more rapidly than anywhere else, to raise the barriers of protectionism for the sake of short-term economic gains.

If the substance of East Asian integration were regional liberalization, it would be a policy prudent for East Asia itself. The liberalization of the Japanese market, in particular, would be of exceptionally great benefit to the East Asian economy; the liberalization of the economies of Singapore, Korea, and Taiwan too would have significant positive effects. By liberalizing their economies further, these nations would receive great economic benefits in the long term. If, however, the objective of the member countries were only liberalization, it could be advocated as a part of the global liberalization effort, and there would be no particular need to raise the banner of regional integration.

Economic integration can be much more than an instrument of liberalization. It could move toward monetary integration, for example. The significance of monetary integration is its potential to stabilize the intraregional exchange rate and to invigorate capital transfer within the region. As long as a high proportion of trade is with countries outside the region (the United States, for example), however, the stability of the intraregional exchange rate has no particular significance. There are, however, many things that should be done before monetary integration is begun. Harmonization of the financial system is necessary, and, above all, Japan's capital market must become open, free from the substantial interventions made today by the government. For now, however, monetary integration must remain a goal of the future. The first realistic goal should be to improve the institutions that can facilitate capital liberalization within the region. The conclusion to be reached from the foregoing is evident. At the present time, there is no need to aim for East Asian economic integration. The East Asian countries should now adopt policies to advance trade and capital liberalization.

ECONOMIC POLICY ALLIANCES

So far, I have discussed the question of cooperation or integration that is purely economic in character; the gains of such joint endeavors are realized mainly through trade or foreign investment between the countries that participate. But normally what is called economic cooperation includes elements that cannot be called economic in character. OPEC, for example, was formed to deal with the specific issue of oil. Because the OPEC countries do not trade oil among themselves, neither the issue of complementarity nor the issue of substitutability arises in relation to intraregional trade. OPEC aims to protect the interests of the oil-producing countries against countries outside the group, and in fact it has achieved significant results as an oil cartel in the global market. Put differently, OPEC is a political alliance, created only in an attempt to maintain the economic policy of a price cartel. If we call alliances that are not overly concerned with the types of policies adopted in realizing economic gains "economic alliances" (the EC is close to such an alliance), then we should call groups such as OPEC "economic policy alliances." It is important to distinguish between economic alliances and economic policy alliances.

Some groups, such as the OECD, try to adopt economic policies not for specific issues but for the economy as a whole. The OECD is a group of so-called advanced industrial nations and does not have any particularly distinctive common policies, but it functions well as a forum for debate among its members. This function is also expedited by the "summit meetings" of the advanced economies (such as the G-7 and the G-5). These groups of advanced countries, at various levels, generally work to stabilize the existing world economic order. Thus, they are examples of economic policy alliances in a loose sense.

In all such forums and alliances, the focal issue is (and will be) developmentalism. Because the leading nations are preoccupied with an ideology of classical economic liberalism, they still do not know how to deal with developmentalism, which has clearly grown beyond the stage at which it could be dealt with by escape clauses in the IMF or GATT. Developmentalism is not confined to East Asia; it could well spread to Latin America and is likely to be adapted by the former Soviet Union and Eastern Europe. Its success would be a kind of nightmare for many of the leading nations of today.[23] There is therefore a possibility that a group of leading countries will brandish the principles of classical economic liberalism in their attempt to repudiate developmentalism. Specifically, this group would probably rigorously criticize the tariff and nontariff barriers often seen in the initial period of developmentalism and urge strict observance of intellectual property rights. Confronted by such actions, the NIEs and the countries about to become NIEs might well be tempted to form an economic policy alliance and even to promote economic integration. In the next ten years, during which Latin America, the former Soviet Union, and Eastern Europe will not yet be ready to emerge as major exporting developmentalist economies, the East Asian region will probably have to bear the brunt of the attack by the classical liberalism of the leading nations. Of course, this is the worst scenario, but we cannot ignore the possibility. In other words, there is a danger that the North-South problem will turn into an East-West problem in this new sense, and that East Asia will become the focal point of confrontation.

How would the East Asian countries react to growing criticism from the United States and the EC about developmentalism? Developmentalism in follower countries must be publicly recognized as one of the rules of the world economy. At least that is the argument of this book. But such public recognition is not easily obtained and the East Asian countries might have no choice but to unite in protest. Japan too, as a country that has adopted developmentalism in the past, would probably be at a loss as to what to do if faced by this protest. In any case, forming a protest group is not the same as achieving economic integration, because such a group is likely to remain a political alliance. In this possibility, though, there would be a danger of cultural or even racial confrontation, which would be most destructive to world order.

Three factors will determine whether this problem becomes serious. One is the attitude of the East Asian countries themselves, other than Japan; the second is the attitude of the leading European countries and the United States; and the third is the attitude of Japan. Let us begin with Japan's attitude, since it is Japan that holds the key to this new East-West problem because of its economic power. For example, were Japan to join the side of the advanced European countries and the United States, the East Asian economic alliance would lose its greatest engine and thus any substantial influence. I discuss the attitude Japan should adopt again below, but what needs to be stressed is only that it should persuade East Asia not to promote an economic policy alliance (or economic integration), and it should urge the leading countries to recognize developmentalism. These efforts will require a patient, broad-gauged diplomacy, free of the confused diplomatic psychology typical of the Japanese, a mixture of inferiority and superiority complexes. But one cannot be certain whether Japanese parliamentary politics will permit this to happen.

Next, what should we expect of the attitude of the East Asian countries? Many leaders in East Asia now consider it dangerous to promote economic integration. And one cannot imagine that they would gamble on an economic order led by Japan and risk confrontation with the United States. I consider the idea of an East Asian Economic Community as articulated by Mohammed Mahathir, the prime minister of Malaysia, to be a minority opinion. Particularly in Korea, Taiwan, and Singapore, there are many opposed to economic integration under Japanese leadership. In East Asia the bad impression left by the Japanese before and during the war remains in the minds of many active politicians, and the impression survives in the minds of the younger generations who hear of the past deeds of Japanese in their countries. The precise facts about the Japanese "atrocities" may still not have been established, but it is certain that the actions of the Japanese in the territories they occupied would not have earned them respect as leaders. The overseas behavior of the present-day Japanese, too, is still not something that can be respected or welcomed. (Just as brutal war crimes are difficult to put in the past, so are images of Japanese men on sex tours of East Asia seen as shameful.) Thus, unless misunderstandings of policy between East and West continue to occur, the formation of an economic policy alliance will probably not gather majority support in East Asia.

But we cannot be certain that unfortunate policy misunderstandings will not occur. The United States' attachment to classical economic liberalism, or its fixation on being number one, can be a cause of misunderstanding. There are also reasons for anxiety on the East Asian side. One of these is the danger, in the midst of growing wealth, of a mass democracy that expresses its discontent and unrest only in anti-U.S. movements. Finally, there is the possibility that the Japanese will become mired in a similar psychological anti-Americanism. The worst scenario would be that all these possibilities become realities to create an Asian group in opposition to the leading Western nations.

With the example of the East Asian group, we have seen that there is a danger that it could form both an economic alliance and an economic policy alliance. However, today there are any number of possibilities for this kind of alliance throughout the world, and among these, the East Asian is not one of the likeliest. As an economic alliance, the EC is making an effort to be an open and a dynamic group, but there still exists the danger of its turning to a kind of protectionism that appeals to the masses, or in other words, becoming a protectionist economic policy alliance for protectionism's sake. The United States too, though it professes to protect the rule of liberalism, could turn toward alliances for protectionism's sake. U.S. efforts to embrace Latin America seem to be weakening, but some see signs of a protectionist alliance in the North American Free Trade Agreement, and others have warned that economic policy alliances could recreate the gloomy system of the economic blocs of the 1930s.

But the prewar situation referred to as the "bloc economies" and today's situation are quite different in character. The bloc economies of the prewar period were created by replicating the structure of colonial rule, or something similar to it, and aimed at an autarkic economy with a military hegemon at the apex of the bloc. Considered merely from an economic point of view, however, it was in some respects a rational arrangement that facilitated a vertical division of labor. Nowadays, however, when colonies have disappeared and the use of military force is restricted, it would be impossible to form an autarkic economy by force, either in North America or the EC, or in the hypothetical case of East Asia. Considered only in terms of economic rationality, these groups would naturally include the possibility of withdrawal or dissolution. As explained in the hypothetical example of East Asia, these groups could be formed only as economic policy alliances with a strong political character. Considered in terms of the strength of their political character, they are similar to the prewar bloc economies. In this sense the attempts to create economic policy alliances can be called attempts to create new blocs. If one were, somewhat irresponsibly, to envision an imaginary world made up of the new blocs, it would be one of confrontation among the three regions—led by the United States (promoting classical economic liberalism), the EC (pursuing classical protectionism), and East Asia (pursuing developmentalism). The massive confrontation of policies that is unavoidable in such a world is not likely to have an amicable solution. The only inevitable outcome of such a world is a catastrophe. To prevent this, an agreement on a set of global rules that can accommodate developmentalism must be reached.

The Rules for the New Economic Liberalism: Dealing with Developmentalism

In this section, I propose a set of rules for economic liberalism, principally to deal with developmentalism. Before embarking on this, I wish to add the following regarding the definition of developmentalism. In this book, for convenience, I have borrowed the expression "developmentalism," which may give the impression of a model that applies to follower countries' takeoff—that is, a transitional model applicable only to follower countries. As is clear from the preceding argument, however, what is meant by developmentalism in this book is broader. The essence of developmentalism is the way of thinking that sees decreasing cost as the basic state of affairs and attempts to best respond to that state of affairs; in contrast, classical economic liberalism is the way of thinking that is premised on a trend of increasing cost. One of main themes of this book is the confrontation between these two contrasting ways of thinking. Though a trend toward decreasing cost is more readily observed in follower countries that can exploit imported technology, it can also be seen in leading countries that are succeeding in technological innovation. Developmentalism in this broad sense is applicable to both follower and leading countries, even though it entails difficult problems specific to the latter.

AN EXPANDED DEFINITION OF DEVELOPMENTALISM

I will therefore give here another, expanded definition of developmentalism. In Chapter 6, I defined developmentalism as a national policy. In order for developmentalism to be effective for the country pursuing it, the policies adopted must be comprehensive; they must include industrial policy, a unique distributive policy, education policy, and other policies. But firms that consciously try to respond to the situation of decreasing cost also implement developmentalist management. This is a mode of behavior in firms not possessing a comprehensive national perspective. Developmentalism pursued by a country (as a policy) and developmentalism adopted by a firm (as a way of management) are of course not unrelated. National developmentalism generates developmentalism in firms, and indeed doing so is its aim. The reverse, though, is not true. Thus, national developmentalism and firm developmentalism are basically distinct phenomena.[24] In discussing developmentalism, it is essential for us to consider both national policies and the ways firms are managed.

As I have stressed often, the trend of decreasing cost includes the effects of technological innovation. Thus the essence of developmentalist management or policy is to fully recognize the reality of technological innovation and its effects. Standard economics treats technological innovation like manna from heaven, something that appears suddenly and unpredictably. But at least since the Second World War, technological innovation cannot be said to have been unpredictable; it became normal in many advanced countries for a firm's R&D investment to rival its plant investment. For example, in Japan, particularly since 1985, the average firm's investment in R&D has outstripped its investment in plant.[25] In the minds of managers, therefore, technological innovation has become as predictable as the workings of a plant. This is to say that, in the postwar economic environment, technological innovation has become constant and decreasing cost has become a characteristic of numerous industries. And since the latter half of the 1970s, in particular, there has been an advance toward superindustrialization centered on the production of information. The model of what I am calling developmentalism follows the logic of superindustrialization, in that it incorporates at its core the production of information as technological progress. Here I am suggesting that the logic of industrialization be taken to its ultimate. As a system for industrialization—only in that ultimate sense—developmentalism should perhaps be seen as having made more "progress" than classical economic liberalism.

DEVELOPMENTALISM IN FOLLOWER COUNTRIES

Given that developmentalism is the most "progressed" form of industrialization, one should not be surprised by the remarkable success of postwar Japan and the East Asian countries that have adopted it. If they follow the leading countries' pattern of development, countries attempting to take off toward industrialization will readily see which industries to introduce and how rapidly and in what order they should import technologies. Particularly following the Second World War, at both the firm and national levels, it was relatively easy to predict the direction of technological progress and the trends of the world market. This is to say that follower countries had little difficulty adopting a pattern of capitalism with a long-term perspective. The precedent of "developmentalism" in Japan offered useful guideposts.

Postwar Japan was the first developmentalist to succeed by adopting policies and managerial behavior for capitalism with a long-term perspective, and Taiwan, Korea, and Singapore adapted Japan's methods successfully. That is, the "four dragons" of East Asia, including Hong Kong, succeeded in the takeoff by adapting the developmentalist model to their own economies and became the NIEs (economies that are almost fully developed). Today the ASEAN countries as a whole, led by Thailand and Malaysia, are about to emerge as NIEs. Over the past several years, the rate of economic growth has exceeded 10 percent in Thailand and Malaysia and has been about 7 percent in Indonesia. The economic performance of the East Asian region is still today the best in the world.

Let me reemphasize that these countries' policies have not been exactly the same as Japan's. These countries are distinctively export-oriented; that is, they have become typical examples of nations built on trade. In Taiwan, for example, foreign markets and domestic markets are equally important. One cannot go so far as to say that Japan's policies were as export-oriented as Taiwan's. During the high economic growth period, the ratio of exports to GNP at its highest was about 10 percent, lower than that of most leading nations. While the size of its domestic market, 125 million people, allowed Japan to remain relatively closed, the other East Asian countries, more clearly trade-minded, have had to be more sensitive to demands to open their markets made by leading countries, the major importers of their products. Thus these countries have also generally been more open than Japan to foreign firms wishing to enter their markets. This is not to say that they impose no restrictions, but they, unlike Japan, in many cases welcomed foreign direct investment. In contrast to Japan, with its large domestic market and high saving rate (and therefore little need for foreign investment), the other Asian countries, with small markets and yet low saving rates, had no choice but to be highly export-oriented and to seek foreign investment.

A policy of developmentalism thus reflects the individual character of the respective countries. As explained in Chapter 6, developmentalism as a national policy has pillars of industrial policy and an anticlassical distributive policy. "Industrial policy" here, however, includes the three elements discussed earlier: indicative planning for each priority industry, the promotion of technological innovation, and the control of excessive competition over prices or investment. In other words, it supports a system of what I call "compartmentalized competition in priority industries."[26] It does not have to be a strongly restricted system as in the Japanese example. The "groupism" (or group-orientedness) peculiar to Japan—particularly the Japanese-style "closedness"—is not always necessary for developmentalism to succeed. Even the protectionist measures of the initial period can differ in content and length of time and, depending on the circumstances, there may well even be cases in which they are almost unnecessary. There are various—non-Japanese—models of developmentalism.

Of course, as can be learned from the experience of the East Asian countries, including Japan, a set of minimum conditions is necessary for developmentalism, beginning with stable politics and an impartial bureaucracy. Its essence, though, ultimately consists only of choosing priority industries by assessing the long-term prospects of both technology and demand, unswayed by the classical principles of comparative advantage or by short-term market signals of the moment. As this development strategy has come to be known more widely, examples of successful adoption of the strategy are likely to increase in many regions. To be sure, differences in each region's cultural characteristics will undoubtedly create differences in the specific methods adopted.

A review of the history of industrialization in the development that has been achieved to date shows that the leading countries maintained their technological leadership and monopolized the fruits of global economic growth. Because of this, far from being reduced, the disparities between the leading and follower countries have widened. In the periods of high growth seen frequently since the nineteenth century, the phenomenon of decreasing cost has undoubtedly been present. Its benefits, however, have gone to the leading countries that developed the new technologies, and almost all the other countries have had no share of them beyond a few meager gleanings. It cannot be denied that the rules of classical economic liberalism have a high degree of theoretical consistency. But at the same time, classical economic liberalism must accept the charge that it helped to rationalize the reaping of maximum benefits by the leading countries from their technological monopoly. In this sense, classical economic liberalism is severely deficient as a rule to be applied to the whole world. Thus, the system of free trade has not guaranteed equality or even efficiency. If technology had not been monopolized by the leading countries and instead been allowed to spread freely, world production as a whole would clearly have increased. The burden of the rule of classical economic liberalism has until now fallen on the follower countries.

The developmentalism that has been adopted by the follower countries is a means of rectifying this condition. Of course, before the Second World War a number of countries and colonies made efforts similar to developmentalism—Japan and some Latin American countries, for example. Until the war, though, the leading nations could suppress any discontent in the follower countries with military force. Political manipulation by means of various economic threats was also effective because of military force. But such methods, the relics of imperialism, are now obsolete; the democratic leading countries have lost their last great "justice" of opposing communism and cannot possibly decide to deploy military force for the sake of their economic interests. The method that remains available to them is economic sanctions justified on the grounds of a rule violation in the international economy. But with the number of developmentalist developing countries now rapidly increasing, it is becoming more difficult to implement such sanctions. The leading countries find it difficult to act in concert on such sanctions; and particularly with Eastern Europe and the former Soviet Union turning to developmentalism, the response of the Western countries will tend to be in disarray.

Will it be possible for a group of follower countries within a certain region—for example, East Asia—to be singled out as the object of sanctions? If it were, the group of follower countries in the region would form a political alliance for economic policy—a cause for the breakup of the international system. If there were enough developmentalist follower countries in that region, it would not be impossible for such an alliance to create its own independent economic area (the leading countries do not control the necessary resources to prevent the creation of such an alliance). It would also be possible for a country that had withdrawn from the group of leading countries (Japan, for example) to become the core of this economic area. And, if viable complementary relationships were built within the group (as discussed in the first section of the following chapter), then that economic area might develop more quickly than the economies of leading countries. The follower countries could also take the path of defiance, refusing to cooperate on the global problems of the environment and resources or in the prevention of nuclear proliferation. Finally, military confrontation between the regional groups might reach a very dangerous level.

Unlike in the bygone age of imperialism, however, it is now impossible to put a direct halt to such actions by the follower countries. Today developmentalism must have public approval because developmentalism in the follower countries has grown to be a problem too large to be tacitly approved. Public approval is necessary, not for the sake of some kind-hearted or humanistic equality of outcome but in order to maintain the world system. From now on, the rules for new economic liberalism must give some form of public recognition to developmentalist efforts by follower countries. When such recognition is given, economic liberalism can become for the first time a universal rule that should be applied to the whole world.

The essence of developmentalism is to select industries that clearly face a trend toward decreasing cost because of the advance of technological innovation. For the follower countries concerned, this means the transfer of technology from developed countries. Thus, as suggested in the previous chapter, the rules of the new economic liberalism must make it easy for technology to be transferred from leading to follower countries. In particular, the technology for environmental conservation and resource preservation with which the leading countries are greatly concerned should be transferred almost free of charge to the developing countries. Thus the recent position taken by the United States and other leading nations (a lead Japan has, regrettably, followed) in favor of expanding and strictly enforcing intellectual property rights is a mistake. As has been much discussed in economics, technology is not merely a private asset but clearly has the quality of a public good. Seen more broadly, contemporary technological innovation is nothing more than the leading edge of development in humanity's stock of knowledge. We owe much to various people in the past—for example, to the Native Americans for many agricultural products, to the Arabs for mathematics and astronomy, and to the Chinese for gunpowder and the compass.

Seen in this historical perspective, the patent system is nothing more than a system introduced along with capitalism. Though it is natural that the rights to intellectual creations should be recognized and recorded, their use should not be monopolized. For example, there should be an obligation to open their use to the general public for a fixed license fee. There might have to be a period during which monopoly is allowed, but its length should be sharply reduced. The length of the period during which the license fee for patents can be levied should also be short. In this connection, the proposal made by Secretary-General Arthur Dunkel in the Uruguay Round of GATT is mistaken in its basic orientation because it followed to the letter the demands of the leading countries to extend the life of patents and to recognize patents for materials.[27] As discussed in the preceding chapter, there is no need to be too concerned that weaker patent rights will destroy the incentive to invent.

The recent U.S. policy of strengthening and expanding intellectual property rights is misguided in that it persistently holds on to classical economic liberalism. The model here should not be its past experience of increasing production incentives by recognizing private property rights in land. Certainly a change in the thinking on intellectual property rights will encounter strong resistance from entrenched interests, but to create the rules for the economic liberalism of the future this is the only direction we can turn. To repeat, differences in economic levels are mainly due to differences in technological capability; thus unless there is a way to overcome the latter, the problem of economic inequality will not disappear. Of course, trying to remove inequality of outcomes is contrary to the liberalism I advocate in this book, but technology is not so much a "thing" as an opportunity. The spread of knowledge—technology—basically means creating equality of opportunity and supporting the advance of liberalism.

In addition, there may well be concerns arising out of self-interest and psychological obstacles that prevent the spread of technology. Leading countries of the past had little desire to aid development in countries they regarded as uncivilized. For example, in the nineteenth century, very few Europeans or Americans showed any interest in the economic development of Japan, a quaint island country in the distant Far East. Now circumstances are different. With the information revolution, the most distant countries seem near; Eastern Europe and Russia are embarking on reindustrialization. Already the United States and the EC countries have offered substantial capital aid to the former Soviet Union and the East European countries. These cannot be explained away as acts based on a cost and benefit calculation (for example, to prevent a flood of refugees from Eastern Europe and to nurture future markets). The Europeans share a feeling of solidarity with the former East Europeans, and the United States is home to many descendants of immigrants from Eastern Europe. When Eastern Europe and the former Soviet Union turn toward the path of developmentalism, Europeans and Americans will not be able to prevent it. And Japan has no choice but to help its many neighboring countries embark on a path it once took itself.

THE LEADING COUNTRIES AND DEVELOPMENTALISM

If, however, this developmentalism (developmentalism as a national policy) is publicly recognized as a rule, friction between that rule and the rule of classical economic liberalism will arise. Simply stated, to avoid repeating the preceding argument, from the standpoint of classical laissez-faire, developmentalism that relies on government intervention is necessarily a violation of the rules. However, in the existing provisions of the IMF and GATT, protectionism in follower countries has been recognized as an exception. The fact that the problem is on a scale that can no longer be dealt with by permitting exception was noted in the previous section. Even more serious than the problems between the leading and follower countries, though, may be the problems among the leading countries. For example, when follower countries become leading countries and begin to show evidence of overtaking the established leading countries, some kind of dispute over interpretation of the rules between the old and new leading countries becomes inevitable.

As the American historian David Landes vividly describes, in what is generally acknowledged to be his masterwork, this kind of dispute occurred between Great Britain and Germany 100 years ago, in the 1880s and 1890s.

> After 1870, . . . the British began to awaken to their new [German] rival. . . . There was the marked superiority of Germany in the newer branches of manufacture. . . . Above all, there were the "unfair" methods allegedly employed by the Teuton. . . . Complaints reached a peak during what Ross Hoffman called the "midsummer madness of 1896." Parliamentary orators exercised their eloquence on government purchases of Bavarian pencils, or the importation of brushes made by German convict labour.[28]

It is not yet 1996, but at least until now, the relationship described by Landes between Germany and Britain one century ago resembles to a surprising extent the present-day relationship between the United States and Japan. On such aspects as the character of entrepreneurs, the education system, the structure of credit, and the attitude toward technology, the parallels between these two relationships are almost uncanny. Though it is somewhat long, let me cite one more passage from Landes:

> In the meantime the German system had institutionalized innovation: change was built in. . . . Furthermore . . . these contrasts in receptivity to innovation were strengthened by differences in entrepreneurial rationality. The British manufacturer remained faithful to the classical calculus: he attempted to maximize return by making those investments which, given anticipated costs, risks, and sales, yielded the greatest margin over what existing equipment could provide. . . . He often made the mistake of tying investment to current operations and returns rather than to expectations of what the future might reasonably bring. . . . The significance of this pecuniary approach is best appreciated when it is contrasted with the technological rationality of the Germans. This was a different kind of arithmetic, which maximized, not returns, but technical efficiency. . . . The means had become end. The economist, to be sure, considering the situation *ex post*, will simply distinguish between two pecuniary calculations: the German entrepreneur simply had a longer time-horizon and

included in his estimates exogenous variables of technological change that his British competitor held constant.[29]

Note that this argument conforms precisely to the argument about developmentalism in this book—particularly the argument about a long-term perspective. What is now happening between the United States and Japan, a century later, closely resembles what happened between Germany and Britain. This correspondence is remarkable when one considers that Landes's book was written in 1969, before Japan's emergence as an economic power had become apparent.

The race in industrialization among the leading countries always repeats a similar pattern. In order to catch up with the leaders, the followers cannot simply learn from the leaders but must also make improvements of their own, and when they do, these will naturally incorporate the social characteristics of the follower. Thus there will appear differences between the systems of the leaders and the followers. And in fact, unless the system is sufficiently different to give the followers an advantage, they will not be able to catch up and overtake the leaders. As a result, though, the conceptual differences between the "rationality" or "rules" that each commonly accepts as orthodoxy will be emphasized and will become a catalyst for disputes. This is the general pattern for economic competition. It has been since the formation of the nation-state, between continental Europe and Britain, Holland and Britain, and Britain and France. And until now, it has been commonly understood that this quasi-theological dispute over ideology and rules does not end there but leads to actual war. In the case of the German and British relationship one century ago, the issue was settled once Germany, which seemed to be winning the economic battle, suffered defeat in diplomatic maneuvering and military conflict.

But history does not repeat itself exactly. The current relationship between the United States and Japan is not the same as the relationship between Britain and Germany 100 years ago. On one hand, it is certainly more evident than it was at the end of the nineteenth century that technological innovation is becoming "automatic," and the contrast between the two countries on this point is becoming so large as to be dangerous. Japan, the challenger at the end of the twentieth century, has made this contrast increasingly conspicuous, notably by fashioning a single system of developmentalist policies and management. On the other hand, it has now become almost impossible for this friction and confrontation to be resolved by means of a "war." Furthermore, one might add that the essence of American culture is clearly ideological, unlike that of Britain. The situation is therefore more intractable, in that the ideological character of the dispute is stronger. To solve this problem, do we have any choice but to grapple directly with the question of rules, even though this runs counter to the glorious tradition of cynicism in power politics, stretching back to the formation of the nation-state?

A PROPOSAL FOR THE AMENDED RULES

The United States, an ideological state, has already started a dispute over the rules. Article 301 in the Trade Act of 1974 and the "Super-301" clause of the Omnibus Trade Act of 1976 are two examples. Japan was the main target of these provisions, and this was to be expected. This friction between the United States and Japan, though, is only the first example. There is a fear that, as the East Asian countries steadily grow to become leading nations, there will soon be frequent friction between them and the United States. Already there have been signs of such friction between the United States and Korea, Taiwan, and Thailand. Russia and the East European countries have shown a strong interest in the East Asian model of development, and in Latin America countries will also follow the East Asian model. This cannot but mean that the confrontation between the rules of developmentalism and classical economic liberalism will intensify in all parts of the globe. In its belief that classical economic liberalism is correct, the United States is likely to repeatedly charge Japan and Korea with unfair trade. The majority of economists too, forgetting how their theory evolved in dealing with such problems as Marshall's problem, have rushed, almost ideologically, to justify economic liberalism. Given this state of affairs, some argue that the resulting confrontation will become as serious as that which once existed between the market economies and the planned economies.

Here we must reexamine the strengths and weaknesses of both economic liberalism and developmentalism from a broad perspective that goes beyond the viewpoint of economics. Let me begin by reminding readers of the following. The strength of developmentalism is that it can sustain the benefits of decreasing cost, but its weaknesses are, first, that once government intervention to implement developmentalism has begun, it tends to increase and become chronic. In particular, even when intervention has become unnecessary (that is, even when decreasing cost has come to an end in the targeted industries), the bureaucracy is reluctant to relinquish its power. At this point, developmentalism deteriorates into protectionism for stagnant industries, the economy as a whole loses its ability to grow, and the value of developmentalism is lost. A more fundamental weakness, however, is that developmentalism is effective only as long as there is a government able to implement both inter- and intra-industry coordination. Without a government to coordinate price-cutting and investment competition, developmentalism only creates a high-risk environment for firms. Furthermore, disparities between targeted and other industries, or distributive inequalities, occur under developmentalism. Unless these can be rectified by the government, developmentalism creates inequality (we should remember the dual structure that for a time became a problem in Japan) and invites political instability.

The central intent here, however, is to reexamine these issues from the perspective of the international economy. The conclusion is that two rules to deal with the two weaknesses are necessary. First, a "sunset" rule that terminates favorable treatment of follower countries needs to be adopted by international consensus. This will be difficult, but not impossible. The IMF and GATT have had similar rules for dealing with "exceptional" countries. Second, it is of decisive importance that *developmentalism cannot become the fundamental rule for the global economy.* This is because, given that there is no world government at present, there is no way of restraining international price-cutting and investment competition and there cannot be any international distributive policy to prevent disparities increasing among countries, or among industries that cross national boundaries.

Let us consider, for example, what would happen if the strongest economic power adopted developmentalism and raced ahead of its competitors. Increases in global inequality and political discontent would be even more likely than if developmentalism were forbidden to follower countries. That Japan is such a strong economic power is the substance of the criticism it is now receiving, even though the criticism is not based on coherently articulated theoretical analysis. Again, suppose that the United States became, in essence, a developmentalist country similar to Japan. Imagine how the competition and confrontation between the United States and Japan would destabilize economic and political order in the world. If developmentalism were taken as the only universal rule for the world economy, excessive competition on an international scale, more brutal than that under classical economic liberalism, would develop, crushing many countries' industries and distinctive firms. The result would be a world shaped by, and possibly resembling, Japan or the developmentalist United States. Surely nobody wants such a world.

These weak points of developmentalism are the strong points of economic liberalism. First, if economic liberalism is faithfully implemented, there will naturally be no government intervention or any difficult decision as to when and how to terminate bureaucratic intervention. Second, given that economic liberalism should be a self-regulating mechanism, there will be no need for any world government or a similar global coordinating mechanism. Thus, economic liberalism has the qualifications to be a universal rule for the global economy, even in a world without a world government. These are important strengths of economic liberalism. Its weak point is of course that it cannot fully exploit the latent growth potential of decreasing cost.

It is difficult to decide how these two models should be combined. In any case, we must first recognize that the trend toward decreasing cost is an undeniable fact. We must discard the groundless optimism about economic liberalism to which many of today's academic economists and others continue to give credence, uncritically and by force of habit. Accepting the reality of decreasing cost, we must reconsider how to combine the two rules and which institutions and practices of the two systems must be chosen. This choice between systems must be from a perspective that goes beyond merely economic issues. My own decision, for example, can be summarized in a proposed set of rules for polymorphic economic liberalism.

  1. The leading industrial nations must adopt economic liberalism and discard developmentalism. The most important reason for this is that to adopt developmentalism as the universal rule for the world economy is equivalent to assuming the existence of a world government.
  2. Developmentalism must be publicly approved for follower countries, and technology transfer should be promoted without hindrance. The key to this is the relaxation of patent rights. However, the "sunset" rule should be adopted to end such favorable treatment of follower countries.
  3. A certain degree of distinctiveness in each country's market rules should be recognized. But as long as foreign firms and individuals obey such domestic rules, they must be allowed to enter the domestic market, without exception, and must be treated in the same way that domestic firms and individuals are.

The third rule has a delicate relationship with the issue of universality in the first rule, but I consider this further in the following argument. The composite rule derived from these three is liberal but differs from classical economic liberalism in its polymorphic nature. To repeat, classical economic liberalism advocated economic liberalism (minimizing restrictions on economic action) in all cases; in other words, it was a unifaceted economic liberalism.

THE MEASURES JAPAN SHOULD ADOPT: ABOLISHING THE SYSTEM OF PERMITS AND LICENSES

Japan's actions hold the key to whether these three rules will be recognized internationally. According to these rules, Japan, as an advanced nation, should change from being a prototype of developmentalism to a country of economic liberalism, albeit of a new form. At the same time, it must accept the developmentalism of the follower countries. The impact on the world as a whole would be great if Japan were to transform itself from a developmentalist nation to a nation of economic liberalism. Here, however, we encounter the problem that always confuses researchers on the Japanese economy—that is, the extreme difficulty of defining Japan's developmentalism as a distinct system. This difficulty often causes researchers to make untenable arguments in trying to give institutional proof of Japan's developmentalism. The Japanese institutions (and practices) that would be clear proof of developmentalism had already to some degree disappeared by the latter half of the 1960s, and there has been little institutionalized systematic government intervention since the latter half of the 1970s.

To briefly trace the history of developmentalism in Japan, in 1960 the Japanese government adopted the basic framework for the liberalization of trade and exchange control and began to dismantle the developmentalist system (institutions and practices). In 1963 it became a member of GATT under Article 11, and government allocation of foreign exchange for import and export subsidies was abolished; in 1968 it became an Article 8 "developed" nation of the IMF and at the same time a member of the OECD, required to comply with those organizations' requirements. To some degree, the dismantling of the developmentalist system proceeded in the first half of the 1960s, and with the liberalization of the import of software in 1976, liberalization of trade and capital was almost completed. What remains unfinished at present is the elimination of the import restrictions on twelve products (mainly in agricultural, forestry, and marine products) and six national trade items (traded goods in which the state is significantly involved [under Article 17 of GATT]). There are no examples of invoking "safeguards" (Article 12) or "waivers" (Article 25).[30]

Seen internationally, Japan has extremely few import restrictions on products. Tariff rates vary depending on how they are calculated, but it seems Japan belongs in the group with the lowest rates among the advanced nations. Subsidies are normally counted as trade barriers, but the Japanese ratio of government subsidies to GNP is low among the advanced nations; almost half of the subsidies are related to rice production. Also, subsidies for research and development are unusually low, while subsidies for small and medium-sized firms are comparatively large. In short, there is scarcely any system left to liberalize. The clear exceptions are, first, the protectionism for rice production; second, policies such as a preferential tax system, subsidies, and government credit for small and medium-sized businesses; and third, the wide-ranging permit and licensing system, and particularly the way it is administered. It should be especially noted that this system involves the priority industries of the future, such as the financial industry and the transport and communications industries.

Thus the primary instrument of developmentalism in Japan is a system of informal practices that does not depend on formal institutions—the system of administrative guidance. Of course, during the period of high economic growth until the 1960s, there were clearly developmentalist institutions. As a consequence, various practices and patterns of behavior became established in the relationship between government and industry and in firms. Since then, this established government-firm relationship and patterns of firm behavior have continued to define the essential characteristics of Japanese-style developmentalism. Thus, were Japan to try to discard its developmentalism, there would be two issues to consider. First, what developmentalist institutions should be discarded, or rather, are there such institutions? And second, can (should) the developmentalism that has been established in firm management be changed? Since I discuss the second question in the next chapter, let us here consider the first.

Do any significant Japanese institutions still serve as the key to developmentalism? In terms of products or industries, the liberalization of oranges and beef (which were an issue in U.S.-Japanese relations) has been realized, and it seems that all that are left are the institutions involving rice. The liberalization of rice seems to be only a question of time; with the difficulties of finding the next generation of rice farmers, the number of rice-farming families with side employment will decrease rapidly from now on, significantly reducing the political pressure to maintain the current institutions (policies). Thus, the liberalization of institutions relating to specific products will proceed. But will Japan then succeed in abandoning developmentalism completely? Will foreign countries be persuaded that Japan has ceased to be a developmentalist? I believe the answer to both questions is no.

Administration can be seen as an institution, and administrative methods can be classified as (1) intervention that is passive but backed by the power of state, such as granting or denying permits or licenses; (2) intervention that is active and backed by the power of the state, such as government procurement, credit, subsidies provided by government, and preferential tax systems; (3) intervention not backed by the power of the state, such as administrative guidance.[31]

Passive intervention (1) is, so to speak, the stick, and active intervention (2) the carrot. For administrative guidance (3) to have played such a large part is a characteristic unique to Japan, but the role of (1) and (2) in acting as a basis for this cannot be ignored. As a means of intervention, the carrot of (2) does not have an immediate effect, and "prohibition," among the sticks of (1), was extremely weak in postwar Japan. As a result, the Japanese bureaucracy often used permission, from (1), and administrative guidance was implemented by using this as a kind of threat. The prevalent use of administrative guidance and the spread of a system of licensing were two sides of the same coin. Even in industries where the liberalization of product and capital is considered complete, the permit and licensing system remains as before in the vaguely defined public interest.

What does it mean to grant a permit or a license? According to a scholar of administrative law, granting a permit or license is an act rescinding a general prohibition in a particular case and allowing a specified act to be undertaken legally. In other words, it is to make an exception for something that is not allowed.[32] This legal principle, when applied for example to a certain kind of economic action, means that the action is basically not allowed; it is thus in conflict with the concept of liberalism. Of course, in cases of "congestion," where it can be readily predicted that a certain kind of activity originally approved will spread too widely and exert a substantial influence on society (a simple example would be driving cars), intervention to provide licenses to a limited range of economic actors can be justified, even on liberal grounds. But given that driving a car, for example, is not illegal, a qualifying examination and civil and criminal proceedings to deal with accidents are sufficient; there should be no room for bureaucratic decisions to be involved in individual cases. Similarly, from the standpoint of liberalism, no firm wishing to enter a market should be prevented from doing so if it fulfills certain qualifications. If a firm satisfies the qualifying conditions, applicants—whether Japanese or foreign—should be given permission automatically and promptly. It is perhaps not necessary, though, for the qualifying conditions to be made internationally uniform (rule 3 above for polymorphic economic liberalism).

A permit and licensing system is fundamentally "illiberal," and thus the clearest way of making Japan's economic institutions liberal is to abolish the system, or at least to make the approval of permits and licenses automatic. As with driving licenses, so with the qualifications for opening a factory or a shop, becoming a member of the Tokyo Stock Exchange, bidding on the construction of the new Osaka airport, and joining the bar. That is, any applicant who satisfies a prescribed standard, or passes a required examination, should be granted a permit or license within a fixed period of time. The impression would be created that foreign imports or the entry of foreign firms to Japanese markets had become greatly freer. Perceptions are important. If foreign firms believe, based on their experience with Japanese society, that the decision as to whether they can enter or invest in the Japanese market is made at the discretion of the bureaucracy, foreign desire to participate in economic activities in Japan will decline. For example, as long as the Tokyo Stock Exchange continues to be shackled by a unique and burdensome licensing system, it will never become an international market, even if it has a very large trading volume. Foreign firms are so discontented in Japan largely because of the fine net of permits and licenses that business activity encounters on all sides and the bureaucratism of the authorities concerned that is so distinctive of Japanese society.

Even more important is the Japanese political leaders' and bureaucrats' perception of fundamental characteristics and institutions. Even if the permit and licensing system were simplified and made less stringent, this alone would not be proof that Japan had abandoned developmentalism. In particular, relaxing the system preferentially for a country that applies strong pressure (as the United States has often done recently) would be contrary to the ideal of equality of opportunity. Such preference would increase rather than reduce the perception of all countries, including the United States, that Japan is a trustworthy country that plays by the rules. Unless foreigners become convinced that Japan had abandoned the system in principle, ad hoc relaxation of the criteria of the system would only exacerbate economic friction in the longer term. Liberalism is a principled set of rules, not an outcome. In many recent measures that Japan has adopted in response to foreign pressure, Japan strayed from this basic logic.

For example, the promise of a certain outcome in quantities of imports in the recent U.S.-Japanese negotiations on "structural impediments" created the impression, even for the United States, that Japan is an illiberal state controlled by the bureaucracy. It is not promises about outcomes that is required, but a declaration of intent to end the permit and licensing system. The major reason this cannot be made easily is the Japanese need to defend the bureaucratic system and the long tradition of the concept of *Kadi*-like "justice." For instance, the same Japanese who often criticize the "excessive" control exerted by police also criticize the inadequacy of police protection. Whether Japan can overcome these obstacles will be an acid test of the quality of Japan's present parliamentary democracy (including that of the electorate). It will also determine whether the Japanese will continue to live, as always, in their small pond, not seeing beyond what occupies them in their daily lives.

I have proposed a set of rules for polymorphic economic freedom (and their application in Japan), but these rules do not end the argument. What is decisively important is the forum or the organization that sets the rules, which clearly must be done with the unanimous consent of the economic powers. Any self-serving action by a single economic power would cause the collapse of the rules. Thus the forum for discussion can only be an economic summit or a conference of a small number of economic powers, such as the G-7. The Economic and Social Council of the United Nations, made up of 54 members, is a forum of unending debates and confrontation between the leading and follower countries. The U.N. General Assembly is, of course, inappropriate. Some may resist a decision made only by the leading economic powers, but since the new rules suggested above would be advantageous for the follower countries, they would perhaps eventually be accepted by the follower nations. The problem, therefore, comes down to forming a consensus among the leading countries—that is, to the parliamentary democracy in each leading country. This problem is the theme of the next chapter.

Here, let us imagine that this problem has been solved, and that Japan, for example, has left behind national developmentalism (as a policy). An important problem still remains: even if national developmentalism has vanished, developmentalism in the firm (as management strategy) will not necessarily disappear. What one might call the fundamental nature of the Japanese firm has become the target of recent criticism. For expository convenience, however, I address this issue in the next chapter as well.

WHAT IS A "GREAT POWER"? THE ROLES OF JAPAN AND THE UNITED STATES

Of course, responsibility for the future rests not only on Japan. Generally, world trends—at least for now and into the near future—will depend on the choices made by the so-called leading industrialized countries. This is not so much because the leading countries will be the driving force that ensures the success of the new world system but because they hold the key to whether it fails. Until the emergence of the Pax Americana, wars over hegemony produced the succeeding hegemon. The country that emerged victorious in these wars, demonstrating its superiority in all dimensions of national power, was the de facto architect of the succeeding world order. The driving force behind the success of the Pax Americana was the overwhelming national strength, in all dimensions, of the United States. Even when not as evident as in the case of the Pax Americana, the minimum requirements for a hegemon are usually superiority in economic and military power. Today, however, no great power possesses the requisite powers in all dimensions. The United States, Europe, and Japan, as well as China and the Russian Republic, all have substantial weaknesses in some dimension of national power. At the same time, they have sufficient strength in some other dimension of national power. What characterizes the contemporary world is not so much the much talked-about "multipolarization" of the great powers as the increasing imbalances in the structure of national power in all the great powers.

For example, the economic power of both the United States and Europe is limited. But the United States has political power based on the prestige of being a hegemon, its military power, and the size of its domestic market. Europe garners respect for having borne the burden of modernization for more than the past four centuries, and if the integration of the EC proceeds smoothly, the size of its regional market will become another weapon. Japan's strength is its ability to achieve economic growth, including its capacity for technological innovation; but Japan's experience on the international stage has been limited, and the policies it has adopted have not earned it the confidence of the international community. As a result, Japan's political influence is meager, especially in contrast to its economic power. China and Russia have military power, including nuclear capability and geopolitical advantage (they are difficult to attack but easy to defend), but their economic power (particularly their nonmilitary technological capability) is still very weak. Because each of these great countries has national power in a specific dimension that is sufficient to throw the world into confusion, we have reason to be discouraged in our efforts to create a new world order. I want especially to note for Japanese readers that, as I argue below, Japan's economic power (how its economy is managed—that is, its developmentalism) is also strong enough to significantly destabilize the political-economic order in the world. For some years the Japanese have been caught up in a small-country mentality and are not as yet sufficiently aware of this fact.

Of course, the growing ability of the follower countries to act freely is also a factor that could destabilize the world. For example, the economic power of the NIEs cannot be ignored; under the present circumstances, however, unless they form a shrewd alliance, these countries alone do not have the power to cause the collapse of the world system. There may emerge adventurist countries that cause regional conflicts, and international control of such local adventurism may well be weak. But without conventional military capability augmented by long-range ballistic missiles at least as powerful as Iraq's, such adventurism cannot directly disturb the world order as a whole. Thus only a small number of great powers have the capacity to bring about a catastrophe. From now on, we should perhaps understand "great power" to mean a country that, even acting independently, could make it impossible for the world to progress smoothly toward a new world system.

The countries named above are great powers in this sense; but if we follow this book's proposals, these countries will be required to take the initiative in implementing and preserving the new rule of polymorphic liberalism. Which countries' decisions will have particularly significant effects? In my opinion, it will be those of the United States and Japan. China and Russia would only bring about fatal chaos in the world if they embarked on military adventurism using nuclear missiles. However, unless extraordinary developments in their domestic situations compel such adventurism, these countries will be preoccupied with their own efforts at economic development and, at least in the immediate future, will take a passive attitude toward the outside world.

For the time being, the EC countries will have to concentrate on the integration of the EC and aid to Eastern Europe. Certainly the EC could turn toward a protectionist, closed economic policy alliance or a new bloc, and in the short term this might destabilize the world economy significantly. But as discussed earlier, unless the United States and East Asia created a new bloc of their own in response, European protectionism would invite only the economic enervation of Europe itself (as did the protectionism of the former Soviet Union and Eastern Europe). Thus, it seems unlikely that Europe would pursue such a course. Whether the United States and East Asia create their own new bloc depends on the choices made by the United States and Japan. Ultimately the United States and Japan, more than any other countries, now have the strength and sufficient freedom of action to bring about a collapse of the order in the world.

I believe that no one will disagree that the choices the United States makes will be crucial, but many may reject the idea that Japan is one of two "great powers." In particular many Japanese may be surprised by such an idea. But because those who do not know their own strength are prone to harm the world, we should no longer tolerate the self-indulgent wish of the postwar Japanese to preserve their own "corner of happiness." As I have already argued, if Japan continues its economic growth using developmentalist methods, it will continue to win one-sided victories in trade over other countries, particularly the leading countries that have espoused classical economic liberalism as their basic principle. Under a floating exchange rate system, even fluctuations in the rate cannot rectify this tendency. As a result, firms in other countries and eventually many industries may well be gradually destroyed. Even if this does not happen, the threat is real to many in the leading countries. This is the essence of what is frequently called "the Japan problem."

Since the theory and workings of developmentalism have not yet been adequately analyzed, the foreigners who have talked about the Japan problem to date have only an inadequate understanding of the problem. For quite a number of Japanese, the Japan problem is a reflection of the unjustified criticism of people in leading countries. Because the Japanese do not have the least understanding of the power of the monster they have created—developmentalism—they are prone to refute the existence of the Japan problem by arguing that there is nothing wrong with working diligently, saving, and being absorbed in technological innovation. But as I have argued throughout this book, the Japanese have brought into the world political economy more than simply the virtues of industrialism—hard work and thrift—and more than mercantilism or command economy; theirs is a new and strange system that has pushed the logic of industrialization another step forward.

In the next chapter I discuss which of the two systems, classical economic liberalism or developmentalism, is more desirable as an ultimate standard for human beings. But here let me sketch some parameters of the answer. If developmentalism were adopted as the universal rule, its logical consequence would be a world of borderless excessive competition. The superlarge corporations or their cartels that would dominate the world would destroy traditional national industries and firms and create a high mass consumption society which, though colorful, would never change. Governments would come under the influence of those corporations, the state would be substantially weakened, and people in the world, having forgotten race and culture, would form groups for the convenience of the moment. There are those who say that cosmopolitanism is an ideal, but complete domination of industrialization (developmentalism) is the shortest road to cosmopolitanism. To continue to insist on the validity of Japanese developmentalism is to march toward a new kind of "progressivism." The system the gray-suited business warriors of Japan are unwittingly bringing into existence is not a Japanese-style samurai empire but perhaps only an ultramodern, cosmopolitan society that will suffer from endless confusion.

There have been few attempts to seriously analyze this kind of future society. But the world described in "cyberpunk" science fiction, which appeared in the United States in the 1980s, comes close.[33] In this science fiction, ominously large megacorporations (frequently with Japanese names) dominate the cutting-edge industries and compete among themselves. In the midst of this economic whirlpool, people's lives and national cultures have little significance. The heroes, whose nationality is uncertain, succeed brilliantly and then disappear into the whirlpool. The novels of Aldous Huxley and George Orwell in the 1930s and 1940s were ultimately novels warning against a future of merciless industrialization. But they did not go so far as to envision the uncontrolled market competition and cut-throat economic wars we are seeing at the end of this century; and they did not offer ideas that could help prevent such competition. In contrast, the cyberpunk science fiction of the 1980s rides on the wave of super-industrialization and slides easily toward the future. A scholarly work that approaches this science fiction is perhaps Robert Reich's *Work of Nations*, which explicitly affirms the borderless world of the near future in which "symbolic analysts" play visible and important roles.

In reality, however, just as the world imagined by Huxley and Orwell has not materialized, the future described by cyberpunk science fiction too is unlikely to arise. People who today find the old-fashioned antifuture vision of Huxley and Orwell anachronistic are doing their best not to be swept away by the ongoing march of industrialization. The voices calling for the protection of the global environment are a sign of this kind of resistance. But there will be resistance motivated more directly by self-interest that will take the forms of protectionism safeguarding national economic interests, demands for redistribution to depressed regions and the un-employed, and the narrow-mindedly nationalist politics that will arise from the preceding two. Resistance to Japan's continuing developmental-ist growth too is a part of the unease felt as we plunge into superindus-trialization. In the final analysis, the reason for resistance is our distrust (that by now has become deep-rooted) in any unidimensional progressiv-ism. Are the Japanese prepared to accept responsibility for this distrust? How completely and how soon Japan ceases to be a developmentalist will surely be the greatest challenge for Japan as a great power. Even supposing that the Japanese were able to leave behind national developmentalism, the question of the developmentalism of firms remains. This is one of the main questions we must yet examine.

CHAPTER 9

Developmentalism, Heterogeneity, and Parliamentary Politics

The Future of Developmentalism

The question at issue in this book—and perhaps for humanity as a whole at the present time—might in the final analysis be summarized in the following question. In an age when there can be no politics of power—and particularly no wars—to determine which nation is to gain political supremacy, how is it possible for nations to continue to industrialize when that process necessarily entails the danger of differing paces of development for each nation?

This is a huge question, and it used to have a definite answer of modern progressivism: in the long term, the combination of power politics, under the name of the nation-state system, and classical free competition would lead the world to an ideal state. This could be called the nineteenth-century determinism represented by G. W. F. Hegel (and expounded by Francis Fukuyama). But this answer is no longer adequate.

There is no single answer to this question. Within a framework determined by the destructive capabilities of nuclear weapons and limited resources, and faced with the process of industrialization that is certain to gain further momentum of its own, humanity today for the first time must directly confront multiple possible outcomes. If we hope to see peace, order, and human fulfillment in the new century, or rather in the new millennium, we must reject the "violence" of a unitary argument, be it that of anti-industrialism, of environmentalism, or of finite resources.

The answer proposed in this book is a modest one that is medium term and transitional. This is neither a short-term analysis to predict what will happen in the next few years of the 1990s nor a long-term theory of civilization that tries to draw a map for the next centuries. As I have argued above, though the retreat of nationalism and industrialization, both in the classical sense, can be confidently predicted, it is not clear what form the phenomena we must call transnationalism and transindustrialization, which will replace them, will take.

The intellectual compass for this book is clear, as I have already indicated. It is to maintain the "liberal" world order in the sense explained in the first chapter. "Liberalism" here, as the fundamental law that makes human beings human beings, is a concept that goes beyond the confrontation between progressivism and conservatism. Unlike modern progressivism to date, it does not provide a single concrete standard of justice or image of the ideal society. The aim of this book has been to lay out a medium-term scenario that will enable us to move beyond this transitional period without straying from the goal of a liberal world order. In other words, my goal has been to discover which are the likely and desirable predictions and choices among the various possible alternatives. We must choose the scenario that will help us approach the ultimate goal. It is not my aim to provide an absolute answer, and I have no doubt that some will disagree with the views and analyses presented in many parts of this book. What I wish to stress, however, is that my argument is developed using *prediction and choice* (which means that I have chosen what seems to me the most desirable path among the range of possible choices). Thus it is possible that I have erred in my predictions and that a choice that requires a new set of rules may in fact be difficult to make.

THE POSSIBILITY OF MISTAKEN PREDICTIONS

Here, therefore, let me review the possible mistaken predictions and the choices that are likely to be difficult. There is a need to examine the possibility of my having been mistaken in my predictions, either explicitly or implicitly. Similarly, there is also the possibility that I have overestimated the capacity to make choices on the part of those who bear the main responsibility for the international political economy (the great powers). Among these possibilities, the following predictions are problematic:

1. The retreat of classical nationalism, particularly regarding the domestic politics of the former Soviet Union and China.
2. The retreat of classical economic liberalism, which in large part depends on the prediction about the vigor of developmentalism. The background common to both of these is simply a prediction concerning the possibility of technological development.
3. The ability of the great powers to overcome the friction among them (or to make the difficult choices). Particularly important is how the debate about differences in political and economic character between the United States and Japan develops.

4. The potential of liberal democracy (and relatedly, the difficulty of choosing liberal democracy).

Of the series of arguments about the retreat of classical nationalism that I have attempted in this book, the most criticism is likely to be made against my view that the United Nations will not be able to play a central role in the world order of the future. Since the Gulf War there have been a number of arguments reconsidering the United Nations in a more favorable light, but contrary to the majority opinion, I have taken a pessimistic interpretation of the United Nations because I predict the following. It is highly possible that, in serious international disputes from now on, there will be many cases connected to the breakup of, or internal upheavals within, the socialist quasi-empires of Russia and China. In these cases, these two permanent members of the Security Council will exercise their veto for the sake of defending their own interests—or even to preserve their own existence—even if doing so will weaken the ability of the United Nations to deal with international crises. This prediction clearly requires an in-depth analysis of the dynamics of domestic politics within Russia and China and, unfortunately, this book's analysis of these issues has been inadequate. Russia or China may unexpectedly be cooperative and make a substantial contribution in establishing the security functions of the United Nations. Seen from the outside, however, until it is recognized that the domestic institutions of Russia and China are stable, I—and perhaps everybody in the world—cannot place too much trust in the function of the Security Council. It may well be at least ten years before we are certain of the future of these countries and thus of the future of the United Nations. The last point to be made regarding the United Nations is that, even aside from the security issue, its ability to influence the global economy is at best weak.

I will now turn to examine the other issues: the question of developmentalism, the debate on differences between the United States and Japan, and the question of democracy. My aim in the following is to raise important questions rather than to offer conclusive analyses.

PREDICTIONS BASED ON THE ANTICIPATED DIRECTION OF ECONOMIES

Let us consider the prediction of the retreat of classical economic liberalism. We today clearly observe many phenomena of a retreat, such as rapid changes in the international distribution of economic power, the increase in protectionism accompanying these changes, and the economic policy integration (or the rise of new economic blocs). As argued already, the relative decline in U.S. economic power has brought on the collapse of the hegemonic system and weakened classical economic liberalism; the increase in the relative importance of national developmentalism, centered on the Asian NIEs, further accelerates this process. I have predicted that this trend will continue, but a counter prediction is possible—first, that the U.S. economy will be reinvigorated, braking the trend of relative decline, and second, that the success of developmentalism will not continue for long.

Both parts of this counterprediction require cautious analyses, but on the first part, I predict that as long as the U.S. economy focuses on industries that are easy for follower countries to promote in adopting developmentalism, then the U.S. economy will not regain its former importance in the world. The industries I have in mind here are such "old" industries of the twentieth-century model (in the sense that I describe below) as iron and steel, automobiles, and dynamic random access memory (DRAM) semiconductors. And even if brakes are put on the decline of the U.S. economy, its relative importance is unlikely to increase. Any chance of the U.S. economy's again leading the world surely lies in its making genuine developments in the new industries of the twenty-first-century model. The issues of when the dynamics of such development will begin and whether the United States will be able to seize the opportunity in a timely fashion are decisive.

The problems involved for the United States are many and include inadequate saving, undisciplined fiscal policy, the decline in entrepreneurial spirit, and the confusion about industrial policy. The first two are comparatively simple problems that can be solved by appropriate macro policies, and they are also necessary conditions for solving the latter two. Under the present state of American parliamentary democracy, however, even resolving these comparatively easy macroeconomic problems will not be easy.

Even if these are solved, the microeconomic structural issues need to be dealt with in a different way. It will not be easy to reinvigorate the management of U.S. firms, which are now seemingly beset with numerous weaknesses. Since the beginning of the 1980s, leading scholars in the United States, such as William Abernathy, Robert Hayes, and Robert Reich and the MIT group, have warned of stagnation in the management of large U.S. firms and advocated the need for substantive changes.[1] One has to say, however, that in the ten years since then, little improvement has been made, at least in the management of firms in "old" industries.[2] It is true that there has been rapid growth in U.S. exports since the latter half of the 1980s, but much of this is due to the continued decline of the dollar exchange rate during this period (as was intended by the Plaza Accord, a 1985 agreement reached by the finance ministers of the United States, Japan, West Germany, the United Kingdom, and France). This trend toward a cheap dollar, though, cannot continue indefinitely, and in fact since 1988 the exchange rate has more or less stabilized; as a result, the growth rate for exports ceased to climb. It should be noted that as long as the "old" industries are shielded by protectionism and supported by export-promoting measures, we cannot say that the economy has actually been revitalized.

Although industrial policy is discussed widely today in the United

States as a possible means of reinvigorating its economy, will it work? The United States has already been the world's leading industrial policy power, though its policy differed in content from that defined in this book. The government provided large subsidies, particularly to the defense industry. The proportion of federal government subsidies in total national expenditure for research and development is substantially larger than Japan's, for example, and much of this flows via the Pentagon. Further, protection for stagnant industries and aid for specific industries has frequently been implemented. The problem is that this U.S.-style de facto industrial policy differs significantly from the industrial policy considered in this book. It is a collection, in most cases, of various aid measures implemented from the perspective not so much of the national economy as a whole as of the interests of specific regions or firms. Thus it lacks consistency and transparency (outsiders in particular find it impossible to establish the precise magnitude and type of the various tax reductions and exemptions provided). Ira Magaziner and Robert Reich have stated that this de facto industrial policy in the United States is nothing more than the introduction of protectionism.[3]

In revitalizing the U.S. economy, what is necessary now is not introducing industrial policy but changing the perspective of industrial policy or, rather, bringing to an end the existing de facto industrial policy. If I am correct, the problem is the nature of the political process that determines government aid. Unless there is a fundamental change both in what Theodore Lowi called the "interest-group liberalism" of the legislative branch and in the amateurism of the administrative branch, it will not be easy to change the nature of this industrial policy.[4]

If the United States were to embark on a genuine industrial policy, the designation of priority industries—the "targeting" that is the essence of an industrial policy—would be of primary importance. There is little chance, though, of future technological innovation in those industries that have been the pride of the United States, such as automobiles and iron and steel. Even if they were designated as priority industries, the most that would be achieved would be to prevent them from falling behind other countries, but the relative position of the U.S. economy as a whole would not improve. The future of the U.S. economy does not rest in reviving these industries, but in taking the global lead in the key industries of the twenty-first century. No one can be certain which industries those will be, but if increasing specialization in the chemical industries with a high degree of dependence on basic research and totally new communication industries (for example, industries that use large-scale digital communication circuits) are to lead the new phase of superindustrialization, then there will be great changes in the distribution of each country's economic power. U.S. economic power will likely increase because the United States has the most accumulated strength in basic research. The question is when such developments are likely to occur.

We must also note that half the reason for the retreat of classical economic liberalism was the successful developmentalism in Japan and the follower countries. In this book I have predicted that this kind of developmentalism will continue to progress, but a counterargument is possible. For example, one could make the pessimistic argument that the dramatic development of the Asian NIEs since the 1970s was made possible by a coincidental combination of favorable conditions and that their prosperity will not continue for long. But whether or not their initial development was a lucky accident does not change the fact that the East Asian countries have already taken off into industrialization. In the history of capitalist industrialization, not one country that has taken off and demonstrated an ability to export industrial manufactured products has returned to its preindustrial state. This is because management capabilities, technological knowledge, and an industrious labor force for maintaining industries, once accumulated, become an endowment that sustains the march of industrialization.

The East Asian countries have already accumulated their human capital. From now on, these countries will inevitably use all the means at their disposal to maintain the impetus of economic development; to do this, they will continue for the present to adopt national developmentalist policies. Thus, even supposing that the impetus for development were to weaken in the near future, we cannot ignore the fact that these countries will continue to resist the ideology of classical economic liberalism. Latin America, Eastern Europe, and the countries of the former Soviet Union, too, will not defend classical economic liberalism faithfully. To protect their own economies, they will adopt developmentalist policies, at least in part. Thus even if we cannot call it the expansion and progress of developmentalism itself, a pattern of industrialization that is *not* classical economic liberalism will continue to be important in international political-economic relations.

This situation might be overturned by imagining a case in which the actions of developmentalist countries give rise to economic friction, encounter substantial resistance within the global economy one after another, and stagnate. A way of breaking through such resistance might be the comparatively little resisted, harmonious "flying-geese pattern" described in Chapter 4. There is also a worst-case scenario, however. The leading countries might collaborate to try to crush politically the progress of developmentalism. Faced with such a threat, the developmentalist countries would not stand idly by; confrontation would inevitably intensify between the group of leading countries and that of follower countries. As discussed above, this is, of course, a scenario of cataclysm in the world order. Thus I emphasize that to foresee the rapid decline of developmentalism is almost equivalent to foreseeing the world turning toward catastrophe.

DEVELOPMENTALISM IN FIRMS

What role, then, will developmentalism play within this set of circumstances at the end of the twentieth century? As discussed in the previous chapter, developmentalism best exploits a trend of decreasing cost, but this includes both developmentalism in the country (as policy) and developmentalism in the firm (as management)—in other words, both national and private developmentalism. In Japan's case, there is no question that national developmentalism should be abandoned. Were Japan, having achieved the rank of a leading nation, to continue its one-sided victory through developmentalism as national policy, it would cause global outbreaks of protectionist nationalism, and Japan would become completely isolated or have no choice but to create a new bloc. This would be a catastrophe for both Japan and the world. Fortunately, in Japan too, developmentalism as national policy has been almost entirely abandoned. A major remaining problem is bureaucratic intervention, which I have already discussed and suggested means to prevent.

Even if bureaucratic intervention is substantially curtailed and its undesirable effects are significantly reduced, it is doubtful whether this alone can eliminate the developmentalist character of the present-day Japanese economy. Developmentalism has become the ingrained substance of Japanese management and will not easily disappear, even if Japan abandons the national policy that provided the country with its start. Of course, like any other advanced country, whatever systems or policies Japan adopts, the reality of decreasing cost will not disappear. Even if there were a decisive means by which to prohibit the government of a leading nation from adopting a developmentalist policy, the individual firms in such a country would not be prevented from exploiting decreasing cost to the best of their abilities. That is, if certain specific industries are found to have good prospects for technological innovation and decreasing cost, the management of large numbers of firms in various countries will simultaneously become developmentalist. This means that the management of these firms will have the long-term view necessary to best exploit the long-run decreasing cost curve.

Such a development cannot but give rise to various new patterns in firm behavior. That is, under a long-run decreasing cost curve, firms engage in vigorous market-share competition, price-cutting competition that may well be interpreted as a new kind of dumping, investment competition to gain even the slightest cost advantage, and even more intense competition in R&D. The instability of this excessive competition has recently become the frequent target of criticism as a peculiarity of Japanese firms. Though arguments that link this to the peculiarities of Japanese culture persist, this kind of firm behavior, as I have already explained, is not unique to Japan. It is only that Japan happens to be a forerunner that has systematically developed a management style that exploits a trend of decreasing cost as effectively as possible. (This is not to deny that Japan's particular culture helped spread this kind of management style and enabled it to become as effective as it did.)

Kiyoshi Kojima and Paul Krugman have tried to analyze the issue of unstable competition under decreasing cost, not as a characteristic unique to Japanese firms but as the fundamental character of the present world economy. Interfirm competition of this nature is excessive competition and is often self-destructive. An international economic system in which such excessive competition is a normal state of affairs is not likely to be sustainable. On this point Kojima pins his hope on the establishment of a "consensual international division of labor" among these developmentalist firms. On the other hand, Krugman makes the pessimistic prediction that this kind of interfirm international competition will necessarily bring about monopoly or collusive oligopoly.[5] Krugman's analysis is clearly the same as that advanced earlier in this book (mainly for the domestic economy), but he goes one step further. He posits that eventually the adoption of some international rules to control this kind of firm behavior will become inevitable, and that, given the differences in views relating to these rules, countries will form a new kind of bloc (what I am calling economic policy alliances). It is not clear what kind of actual situation Krugman is hypothesizing, but it may be that he wants to say that the respective rules for controlling excessive competition in the North American alliance, the EC, and the East Asian alliance, for example, will become distinct, and that the three groups will become increasingly dissimilar.

On the one hand, Kojima's view is certainly too optimistic. But on the other, Krugman is overly pessimistic in concluding that the world will turn to creating "new blocs" because of international disagreement regarding how to deal with industries faced with the favorable prospect of decreasing cost. Even if economic policy alliances are created as a result of various misperceptions and misunderstandings, there will still be room for political negotiations, which need not be bound only by the logic of economic theory. When we see the frequent appearance of decreasing cost and the shift to a long-term view in firm management as inevitable trends, the reality for some time to come may well be a wavering between the two extremes indicated by Kojima and Krugman. In the meantime, it will not be easy to discover an international solution that will indicate the direction to take, and for now, the most severe economic friction will continue.

Many people may not be aware that this is so urgent an issue. Japanese firms, or their managers, in particular may well lack any sense of impending crisis. Two factors are at work here. First, at present, it is almost solely in Japan that this kind of management behavior dominates the cutting-edge industries; the same type of firm is rare in other countries. In the semiconductor industry, for example, this tendency can be seen in Korean companies, but they do not yet pose a threat to the Japanese firms. Second, the habit of cooperation within an industry (formed in the period when Japan actively pursued national industrial policy) still exists among Japanese firms, and so truly suicidal price-cutting and investment competition have not yet developed. But if the first factor were to disappear—suppose, for example, that U.S. firms adopted the same management strategies that Japan has—competition in a world market in which U.S. and Japanese firms confronted each other would become much more intense. The fact that only Japanese firms are conspicuous in their adoption of the developmentalist model conceals the seriousness of the situation. And for Japanese managers, this fact provides an excuse to ignore the situation. However, it is the Japanese themselves who must first become aware of its seriousness. It is the insufficient awareness by the Japanese of the nature of their own firms to which governments and businesses in other leading countries have strong critical reactions, even if most of their reactions are still more intuitive than based on articulated reasons.

Recently, conspiracy theories have even argued that Japan's firms are aiming at complete world domination. But the fact is that Japan's managers are now mainly "salarymen" managers who are simply following the dictates of organizational inertia, which force them to seek an ever larger market share for their firms. In short, they are only performing their duties earnestly and methodically. A result of this, however, is the emergence of a competitive psychology in Japanese industries. That is, as long as all other firms in an industry continue to pursue their market share, then no one firm in the same industry can stop doing so lest it fail. As long as such management attitudes inherent in developmentalism are not restrained, excessive competition among Japanese firms may continue to threaten, and indeed vanquish, their competitors in many markets in the world at great cost to the world order.

THE POSSIBILITY OF DEVELOPMENTALISM ABATING

Will such behavior by Japanese firms not be naturally constrained by market forces in the changing world economy? More generally, will developmentalism in firms not naturally abate? Here let us recall the arguments of Joan Robinson and E. H. Chamberlin from Chapter 5. During the Great Depression of the 1930s, they pointed out that there was increasing product differentiation on the part of the seller, and they believed that, by definition, monopoly dominated the market of each differentiated product. Their concern was with the undesirable effects of monopoly, but here let me note a particular effect of differentiated markets that they did not emphasize. In the market of each differentiated product, a monopolistic equilibrium will be established (monopoly price is set and maintained); in other words, the problem of unstable equilibria will most likely disappear. Similar products will compete indirectly, but since the competition occurs in the mind of the consumer, it will not be easily apparent to a monopolist firm. Estimating how future cost will be affected by technological change will become a more difficult and subtle task. Rather than trying solely to increase production and expand market share, firms will instead attempt further product differentiation and quality improvement by following their long-run average cost path (or a variant of it). It is unlikely that this kind of indirect competition will lead to destabilization of the market. As long as consumers are sufficiently discriminating, what Robinson and Chamberlin called "unstable competition" and "monopolistic competition" will satisfy the requirements for what this book has called "adequate competition," and firms will not need to be supported by industrial policy. In other words, in such a case, Marshall's problem, as raised in Chapter 5, would be solved.

Thus we see that in a situation of decreasing cost, there are two possible scenarios and two possible responses. One scenario is product differentiation, in which there is little danger of excessive competition. The only concern in this scenario is that indirect competition between differentiated products will be limited, and there will be a danger of monopoly, which concerned Robinson and Chamberlin. The other scenario is product homogeneity, in which excessive competition emerges to the extent that government intervention is required. There are also many intermediate cases, but we must try to predict which of these two trends will be stronger in the years to come.

Is the trend toward product differentiation nowadays stronger or weaker than in the 1930s, when Robinson and Chamberlin's theories were advanced? Although we do not have adequate evidence, at the moment this trend seems stronger today. In the advanced countries, industries that manufacture homogeneous products that are difficult to differentiate have passed beyond the stage of decreasing cost and are having difficulties. Iron and steel, some consumer durables (electrical goods and cars), petroleum and chemical products, and synthetic fibers are examples. Industrial policy is already of no use in these industries, which have been nicknamed the *jū, kō, chō, dai* (heavy, thick, long, and big) industries in Japan. The iron and steel and automobile industries have already entered an era of international cooperation, or in fact an era of collusive oligopoly; in iron and steel an international cartel has been established, and in automobiles, Japanese firms have accepted self-imposed controls on exports. In terms of long wave theory, the latter half of Kondratieff's maturation phase has come to an end, and the industries that led the phase are approaching a period of relative stagnation.

In place of these industries, those that carried the burden in the initial period of the fourth quarter-century period (that is, during the latter half of the 1970s and the 1980s)—and that will remain the key industries for at least a while longer—are those high value-added industries called in Japanese the *kei, haku, tan, shō* (light, thin, short, and small) industries. (High value added here refers to having a high ratio of the sum of R&D costs and profit to the combined material and labor costs.) These are the so-called multiproduct, small-lot production industries, or industries of highly differentiated products. If these industries occupy an important place in the leading countries' economies, there will be little need for a revival of Robinson and Chamberlin's arguments, or for anxiety about unstable equilibria and excessive competition.

Multiproduct, small-lot production techniques are possible, in part, because of circumstances on the supply side. There is the latent potential of the technologies of superindustrialization, which depend largely on the increase in information. One could call these the production technologies of the twenty-first-century system. Without the emergence of the so-called flexible manufacturing system (FMS) aided by computers (especially in the form of computer-aided design, or CAD) and numerically controlled machine tools and robots, firms would be unable to make frequent changes of model, maintain complex stock control, make precise and swift changes in the production process, and automate quality control. In short, had it not been for FMS, multiproduct, small-lot production techniques could not have become the mainstream of industrialization.[6] The strong desire of management to develop demand and bring down costs has also had a significant effect on supply. A good example is the automobile industry in Japan. Each firm has created a prototype for multiproduct, small-lot production techniques in what was originally a mass-production industry. Toyota's production and stock control system, in particular, known as the *kanban* (just-in-time) system, is famous worldwide. The impetus of developmentalism in Japanese firms has also contributed to the development of these techniques.

Changes in the structure of demand have also encouraged the emergence of multiproduct, small-lot production techniques. During the period of high mass consumption following the Second World War, which corresponded to the latter half of a Kondratieff wave of maturation, successive waves of demand built up for consumer durables such as the washing machine, refrigerator, and television (or vacuum cleaner), known in Japan as the "three sacred treasures," in the 1960s; demand grew for the color television, car, and air conditioner, which Japanese called the "three Cs," from the latter half of the 1960s. The rate of diffusion of each of these products approached the saturation point. Toward the end of the 1970s saturation was reached, and since then no mass product with a long cycle has appeared. Video, the Walkman, and karaoke come close, but it does not seem as if they will spread to 100 percent of the population. The word processor is perhaps the most likely to reach universal use in Japan.

Throughout the 1980s, product differentiation, which emphasizes minor differences in the function and appearance of each product, supported demand and enabled a semblance of continuing high mass consumption. In other words, a series of differentiated products was created and the boom in demand for each lasted no more than a year. It seems evident that the age of product differentiation follows the age of high mass consumption, which had reached a saturation point. But it also seems that product differentiation and the system of multiproduct, small-lot production are only filling the demand gap left by the end of high mass consumption. It is not yet sufficiently clear whether this phenomenon will last beyond this lean period or whether it will be linked to the twenty-first-century system.[7]

CONSUMPTION IN THE TWENTY-FIRST CENTURY

What form will high mass consumption take in the twenty-first-century system? Will there even be such a thing? It is nearly impossible to predict its exact form. Just as people in the eighteenth century could not predict the nineteenth century, nor people in the nineteenth the twentieth, so we cannot accurately forecast mass consumption in the twenty-first century. But if it is a part of the paradigm of superindustrialization, based on the rapidly increasing creation and use of information—"informatization"—we may be able to distinguish its contours.

Just as machinery and energy, respectively, symbolize the nineteenth- and twentieth-century systems, information will surely do the same for the twenty-first-century system. To borrow the expression of the "theory of input value," the input that represented the nineteenth-century system included the high volume of mechanical input embodied directly or indirectly within it. This is to say that human efforts without such a high content of mechanical input could have produced cotton goods, the machines that made cotton goods (spinning and weaving machines), the machine tools that made those machines, and even the steam engine and the steamship. The input that played the main role in the twentieth century (though again substantial investment in machinery was required) was characterized by the significant quantities of energy used. Energy played a role that could not be replaced by mechanical input. For example, the electric light, the telephone, and wireless communications do not merely provide mechanical input, as is evident in the wide range of functions performed by the electric motor and the internal combustion engine. Within this trend, the principal actor in the twenty-first century must surely be input characterized by a substantial quantity of information. If mass consumption goods are also to have twenty-first-century characteristics, they will clearly carry a greater volume of information than such goods have before now. To use the most extreme technological example at present, one could say that they will take the form of multimedia CDs, high-density disks, all kinds of networks (and participation in them), or products that combine all of these.

There are clearly distinct kinds of information. The difference, for example, between instrumental information and consummatory information is significant. Instrumental information is useful for some purpose (including creation of a world image)—information as raw material or intermediate product, information as investment. This type of information includes that for economic policy, management, diplomacy or military strategy, research, and technological know-how. But this kind of information will become increasingly embodied in capital goods and intermediate products. In contrast, the very possession of consummatory information gives pleasure; in other words, it is information for consumption. For example, the various kinds of knowledge accumulated in artistic and classical works such as novels, films, and music are the prototypes for consummatory information. But there are many others. Conversations in everyday life and common entertainment of all types also contain information that provides a certain pleasure. For consummatory information to be able to provide great pleasure, it must conform to the personality of the receiver of the information and match the receiver's particular worldview. In short, consummatory information must basically be differentiated information. In this sense, the majority of mass-consumption goods in the twenty-first century will probably have to be differentiated products.

It is doubtful whether all of these differentiated products can become mass consumption goods as such. Communication through personal computers and the development of multimedia have the potential to become the bridge between instrumental and consummatory information, but even here it is doubtful whether they have what it takes to become mass products. Moreover, there is a paradox. How can things that have been individually differentiated create mass consumption? It is the technologies of multiproduct, small-lot production that can bridge this gap to some extent. But surely this does not mean that these technologies will be able to create a production system to cater to the tastes of each individual. Thus, at the basic level there will be multipurpose infrastructures, such as high-volume communication circuits and satellites, and countless ways to use them will be developed. But there will be limits even to this vast infrastructure. At some point, differentiation to best meet the needs of the final consumer and expansion of infrastructure will become totally incompatible, and the capitalist economies will eventually be unable to support the impetus of "informatization." Superindustrialization will perhaps yield its place to transindustrialization.

For the time being, however, we are likely to pin our hopes on the possibilities suggested by the techniques of multiproduct, small-lot production. The effort to find products that can carry even larger quantities of information will continue. There seems to be no other way to create consumption demand for the twenty-first century. This fact—putting aside the question of whether it will succeed or fail—suggests that the main trend will be an attempt at product differentiation.

I anticipate that the major role occupied by developmentalism in the production of homogeneous products will at some point become minor. The trend toward long-term orientation in management perspective will continue, but the importance of devoting managerial efforts to a specific homogeneous product will be reconsidered.

Some may accuse me of making a bold prediction. But how likely is it that in the next century industries producing homogeneous products will continue to be most important and consumers will continue to be manipulated to keep buying "machines" that differ so little in function and appearance? This scenario would mean that important firms in each country had followed the precedent of Japan and turned, somewhat behind the times, toward developmentalist management. It would include the possibility, for example, that superlarge firms would skillfully manipulate the mass media and continue to manipulate consumers to buy what are ultimately only machines, however more elaborate they may be than their predecessors. This possibility seems unlikely, however, because firms are not likely to dominate politics, as was discussed by scholars from John K. Galbraith to Jean Baudrillard. Consumers too will exercise their rights not to buy and to lose interest in consumer products; mass communications will show a trend toward differentiation to better inform all subgroups of consumers, each with specific needs and tastes.

Generally, though, with demand at present showing signs of saturation, the trend toward product differentiation, supported by technologies for multiproduct, small-lot production, will substantially mute excessive competition and will likely significantly limit the global advance of Japanese firms. The question is how quickly Japanese firms, overcoming the momentum of success, can adapt to the genuine long-term-oriented management perspective, taking the best advantage of product differentiation and the development of FMS. At present, it seems that one can divide them into firms that are, as ever, pursuing the advantages of declining cost present in large-scale production (represented by makers of autos and DRAM semiconductors), and those aiming at differentiation and diversification (Sony and Matsushita, for example). But we have not yet become sufficiently aware of this division. The degrees of product differentiation and multiproduct, small-lot production that have been achieved to date are insufficient in themselves to change the basic nature of Japanese firms; there is a need for them to be implemented much more thoroughly.

THE POSSIBILITY OF INTERNATIONAL INDUSTRIAL POLICY

During the transitional phase when product differentiation is still incomplete, developmentalism may well maintain its advantages. Even in the long term, the possibility exists, however small, that new large-scale production industries will emerge to take maximum advantage of developmentalism. There is, therefore, a need for a policy to deal with this possibility. Theoretically, one solution is an international industrial policy for each leading industry, as discussed in Chapter 7. If domestic industrial policy is theoretically justified, there is no reason to reject international industrial policy. In other words, based on a consensus among the governments of all the leading countries concerned, it would be possible to have international intervention in an industry in order to control any too-sudden price-cutting, and investment competition to prevent multiple bankruptcies. Even in the United States, for example, Laura Tyson and others have recently made a similar proposal, but there also are no signs of a move toward such international intervention at present.[8]

To cite an internationally prominent recent example, competition in DRAM semiconductors has developed novel features. The primary reason is that the trend toward expanding chip memory is almost predictable, and unit cost declines very rapidly. Competition in technological development as well as strategy in investment timing and the ability to obtain capital are frequently matters of life and death. This kind of intense competition is precisely what I call excessive competition, and it has the potential to create a huge international monopoly or collusive oligopoly. Of course, it is not unimaginable that the problem will be solved naturally by the firms in this industry differentiating their products. It seems that American semiconductor makers are adopting the strategy of producing highly specialized products to survive. The Japanese manufacturers, though, are aiming solely at increasing memory capacity, and a situation has now developed in which it might be possible for the Japanese oligopolists to control the world market. Although they created the current situation, the Japanese manufacturers themselves must now be concerned with this possibility and ask how long they will be able to sustain this strategy.

Thus for semiconductors, international "administrative intervention" may be proposed as a solution, and in the "structural impediments" negotiations between Japan and the United States on semiconductors, intervention has already been discussed. The U.S. government has intervened in international semiconductor competition, frequently on the grounds of national security, and has protected its own semiconductor manufacturers. The Japanese manufacturers, too, are being made aware that they cannot reject international cooperation. The present situation is as yet confused, but it may be that an attempt at a borderless industrial policy is beginning. If this is the case, to see the MOSS (Market-Oriented Sector-Specific) talks on semiconductors between Japan and the United States as merely the collision of national interests is surely too narrow a perspective. Certainly this kind of international exchange has significance as a way of resisting the creation of the new blocs of which Krugman has warned. For specific individual industries, such as semiconductors, bilateral negotiations between Japan and the United States may achieve some results. But these negotiations will inevitably have to be extended to other industries and broadened into multilateral negotiations that include Europe and the NIEs. When many countries are yet unable to deal even with a domestic industrial policy, it is difficult to imagine how an agreement on global industrial policy could be reached. As I have remarked before, implementing developmentalist policy on a global scale will be extremely difficult.

This is not to say that in the past there has been no experience resembling an international industrial policy. In textiles, iron and steel, and televisions, there have been multilateral and U.S.-Japanese agreements, and on various electrical domestic appliances, automobiles, and machine tools, there have been international agreements, mainly in the form of voluntary export restraints (VERs). Many of these, though, have occurred because of the relative decline of industries in the leading countries and have been what one could call backward-looking industrial policies. Even if the follower countries have been able to adopt developmentalist policy more easily, one reason for the need for backward-looking industrial policy has surely been the inadequate effort on the part of industries in the leading countries to improve the quality of, and differentiate, their products.

To respond to the challenge of low wages by improving and differentiating one's products, and thus to sustain a flying-geese pattern, is an intelligent policy first adopted by the British textile industry and now being put into practice in East Asia. But the lessons have not been learned sufficiently well. For the leading countries in particular, to adopt protectionism in reaction to dumping and unfair trade is to demonstrate a lack of understanding of the mechanism of developmentalism (especially the significance of dumping under decreasing cost) and to be oblivious to the current global situation, which demands that leading and follower countries cooperate and coexist. This kind of protectionism toward stagnant industries in the developed countries cannot be allowed within classical economic liberalism or accepted from the standpoint of the polymorphic economic liberalism this book has proposed.

For example, the protection of rice farming had some sense as a distributive policy during Japan's developmentalist period, but it has none now when Japan must discard developmentalism. This kind of protectionism might be allowed as an emergency measure (for example, as a safeguard for Article 19 of GATT), but it must be replaced by a demand that protection of the same industry be discontinued by the exporting countries (for example, that the industry be completely liberalized). Generally speaking, in the case of Japan's rice production, Japan should oppose subsidies to rice farmers in the United States and other countries. If rice exports to Japan suddenly increase, Japan should be permitted to invoke the safeguard clause for a brief period but nothing else. Protectionism in the European countries and the U.S. policy in textiles, iron and steel, and automobiles are examples of the same protectionism for stagnant industries that is highly likely to lead to further protectionism.

It will be easy for an international policy of protecting such stagnant industries to be agreed upon when the major leading countries are suffering from stagnation. But its effects will be undesirable, both for the world as a whole and for the countries that have implemented the protectionism. Why is it that since the 1970s there has been not even one new breakthrough, technological or managerial, in the U.S. iron and steel or automobile industry? We need to think about these facts. The situation is fundamentally different, though, in the cutting-edge industries in which the leading countries are concentrating their energies and competing with each other. Here, worldwide excessive competition is the issue, and *it is fundamentally correct to adopt a borderless industrial policy in order to prevent such competition.* As with domestic industrial policy, there must be a schedule for price-cutting incorporated in this international policy. If it is only an agreement to maintain prices, the leading industries in the leading countries may well rapidly turn into stagnant industries, controlled by a collusive oligopoly, and not aspire to a flying-geese pattern of complementary development.

To repeat, it will not be easy to create an international consensus on industries to be designated as the object of international industrial policy. And with the emergence of new leading industries, and the remarkable rebirth of previously stagnant industries, it will be even more difficult to achieve such an international consensus quickly. Similarly, international consensus will be especially difficult if follower countries become new leading countries and the leading countries fall into stagnation. There will be a clash of opinion over the substance of the rules for such an international industrial policy. If groups of countries understand the substance of these rules differently, they may form new blocs, as Krugman has observed.

To avoid such a situation, there is no alternative but to make the effort to bring closer together all countries' understandings of developmentalism, and to create a set of rules that incorporates the rules of developmentalism as one of its parts. The rule of polymorphic economic liberalism described in Chapter 8 is my own tentative proposal for this purpose. I have already stressed several times that the United States and Japan will have the most important roles to play in adopting such rules.

The focus of debate between them, as is seen, prototypically, in the structural impediments negotiations, may well be discriminating between developmentalism in firms and the cultural particularity of each country. Even if it is clear that Japan has come to a point where it should control developmentalism, there remain its "Japanese" characteristics, a "natio-like" cultural particularity not directly connected to developmentalism but neither completely unrelated. Given that there is no firm understanding of developmentalism, the debate between Japan and the United States often involves a confusion of Japanese characteristics in general and the characteristics of developmentalism, which are only one part of the former. A good example of this is the recent confused discussion of U.S.-Japanese friction: rather than *the different character of Japan's policy as a nation*, it is *the different character of Japanese firm management* that has gradually become the focus of debate. Thus, for example, even those Japanese who doubt the wisdom of developmentalist practices may well suddenly become unreceptive to justified American complaints against Japanese trade practices if all Japanese characteristics are criticized by the United States.

In the following section, I take up the three issues of *keiretsu*, employ-ment structure, and the cost of capital and cross-shareholding, which have now been called into question, as representative examples of the question of heterogeneity; I discuss only the principal issues in each to support the road Japanese firms ought to take and the traps into which they could easily fall in making these choices.

On the Heterogeneity of Japanese Firms

If one were to summarize what Japan as a country should do for the new world system, leaving aside the issue of security, the rules would be (1) as a leading country, it should itself recognize economic liberalism as the primary rule; (2) as a leading country that has had experience with de-velopmentalism, it should promote the recognition of developmentalism in follower countries (it should particularly support the transfer of tech-nology); and (3) it should recognize the distinctive characteristics of other countries' (and its own) economic systems.

At first glance, these three rules may seem ordinary, but in fact they in-volve various problems. The third rule, in particular, raises difficult issues. It clashes with the existing classical economic liberalism, which has tac-itly assumed that the world will converge to become one civilization. It also resists the uniformity of the cyberpunklike future. If the world con-verges in a cosmopolitanism, or as a single civilization with no nationali-ties, people will lose what is important in their lives: a shared, subjective history that includes everything from nostalgia for one's birthplace to an attachment to the classical works of their own countries. Their gaze will become fixed on a future measured by the clock of technological progress, and their lives will be shaped only by the torrent of industrialization.

This is why respect for the differences in natio that support people's cultures is indispensable, and why there is a need to recognize to some de-gree differences in economic systems. The value of what I have been call-ing differences in natio should be reflected to some extent in recognition of differences in economic systems. To believe that an economic system is created independently of any shared subjective perceptions of customs and tradition of the people is the fallacy of modern progressivism.

THE INDIVIDUALITY OF AN ECONOMY

Throughout the half century since the end of the Second World War, the Japanese people have tried to model the Japanese economic system after the economic systems of the past hegemons (namely, the United States and Great Britain). But as I have mentioned in referring to Friedrich von Hayek and Milton Friedman, this Anglo-American system, considered to be the orthodoxy, is not the only or the most complete form of economic liberalism. Put differently, it is extremely narrow-minded to believe that the only rules are those derived from a "theory of natural rights." It is true that the British and the Americans in particular have contributed greatly in establishing institutions for, and refining the theory of, economic liberalism, but the history and cultural particularity of Britain and the United States have also been at work in these efforts. In short, there is no theoretical basis for positing the U.S. system as the only model for liberalism.

Still, the fact that Americans believe their own system to be the best is also a form of cultural individuality, and thus it is not to be blamed. The problem is that countries that have approached economic liberalism from a different historical experience—for example, the East Asian countries, including Japan—have not clearly presented their own interpretation of economic liberalism. We can understand, too, that because they have been dependent on U.S. hegemony, other countries have followed the U.S. interpretation of the rules. Now, however, when there is no hegemon, it has become essential not only for each country to assert its own individuality but also to understand the individuality of the others in order to achieve a stable and lasting international consensus.

The preceding, however, means that we will have great difficulty interpreting the rules because the three rules mentioned above generate two intertwined problems of discrimination—differentiating both between classical economic liberalism and developmentalism, and between developmentalism and each country's individuality. How to distinguish between Japan's developmentalist characteristics, which should be suppressed, and the individuality of Japan, which should be recognized and preserved, is a decisively important but extremely difficult issue. This very issue is the most important in the current debate over the U.S.-Japanese economic friction, as has been noted even in popular journalism. This issue has been further confused by the "theory of Japanese exceptionalism," which posits that Japanese developmentalism is an inevitable product of Japanese culture.[9] Of course, seen historically, there is a complementary relationship between the two. But this is not a unitary relationship of cause and effect, as has previously been argued, and it is possible to distinguish between, and separate, these two factors. I will clarify this in relation to three issues—*keiretsu*, employment practices, and financial structure.

ARE 'KEIRETSU' DISTINCTIVELY JAPANESE?

The phenomenon of *keiretsu* has been taken up as an important topic in the U.S.-Japanese negotiations over structural impediments, and the American side has expressed its discontent, viewing this phenomenon as a kind of conspiracy to prevent foreign firms' access to the Japanese market. The meaning of *keiretsu* (which used to be called a "grouping," but has now become part of the American vocabulary) is not always clear, but to take as an example what has (reportedly) been negotiated between Japan and the United States, the phenomenon can be defined as follows.

1. Financial *keiretsu* or *keiretsu* linked by cross-shareholding: there are extensive financial *keiretsu* such as the Mitsui group, the Mitsubishi group, and the Sumitomo group, centered on a large bank, that used to be called "one-set" (each group having one firm in various industries), and recently they have been said to be turning into *keiretsu* linked by cross-shareholding. In either case, they are criticized for erecting a barrier to entry by maintaining strong mutual trading relations within the group, that is, between group member firms in different industries.

2. Subcontracting *keiretsu*: typically seen in the automobile industry (Toyota, for example), subcontracting *keiretsu*, formed around a specific finished product (such as a car), have been questioned as a practice that restricts the entry of foreign parts manufacturers into the Japanese market.

3. Distribution *keiretsu*: the hierarchy of the distribution system, stretching from many different levels of wholesaler down to the retailer, has also been said to effectively exclude foreign firms (for example, Toys R Us) from Japan's retail business.

For convenience's sake, let us divide the above types of *keiretsu* into horizontal *keiretsu* and vertical *keiretsu*. I call vertical *keiretsu* those that are tied together by an "upstream-downstream" relationship that covers all stages from the acquisition of raw materials to final use, or a relationship maintained between inputs and outputs; those that are not, I call horizontal. The relationships in (1) are horizontal, and those in (2) and (3) are vertical. It is better to discuss these two kinds of *keiretsu* separately, as shown below.

To make the discussion clear, I broadly define *keiretsu* as a group of firms tied together by economic transactions that continue over a long period. Subcontracting *keiretsu* are the most easily definable *keiretsu* and are also easiest to form. One of the main reasons they are easy to form is that there are usually differences of scale and differences in negotiating power between the assembler (the parent) and the parts manufacturer; thus, they establish a leader and follower relationship with respect to setting prices. This relationship of bilateral monopoly (at times, monopsony) is stable (that is, it does not result in a Cournot-type outcome). This relationship, though, does not necessarily generate a one-sided advantage for the parent firm, or so-called exploitation. The outcome of the relationship depends on various factors, and at least in the long term this market relationship can be contestable.[10]

One can also regard the relationships seen in the distribution industry, between wholesaler and retailer, manufacturer and franchisee, as *keiretsu*. Here, too, for many individual products, a retailer will depend on a supply from a single wholesaler or manufacturer. Particularly in Japan there is a trend toward maintaining long-term transactional, or *keiretsu*, relationships. But because the dependency of the retailers on a specific wholesaler for each specific product is multifaceted in character, the relationship is not as stable as it is between a parent and its subcontractors. Thus one could say that the so-called distribution *keiretsu* between wholesalers and retailers is a weaker form of *keiretsu* than the subcontracting *keiretsu*. In addition, the dependency of the retailers on wholesalers has a tendency to turn into a hierarchy, of manufacturer-wholesaler-retailer, because of the differences in negotiating power noted above.

In contrast, horizontal *keiretsu*—financial or cross-shareholding *keiretsu*—deal with finance. Thus it may be better to be direct and call vertical *keiretsu* "tangible products *keiretsu*" and horizontal *keiretsu* "financial *keiretsu*." The financial industry has a particular character not seen in *keiretsu* that involve products: even among firms considered to belong to *keiretsu*, few obtain their financing from only one bank (the so-called main bank), and in virtually no case is the majority of a firm's shares held by a single corporate shareholder. This is to say that the mutual dependence among large firms that has become a cause of U.S.-Japanese economic friction is far weaker than that in the subcontracting *keiretsu*. Thus, if a *keiretsu* relationship (a long-term relationship of continuous transactions) emerges despite this, it cannot be only because of extensive mutual dependence. Rather, what is at work here is the uniqueness of the financial industry, but let me postpone detailed discussion of this point to a discussion of cross-shareholding.

In the trade talks between the United States and Japan, one recurring criticism of Japan is that its firms create barriers to U.S. imports by trading primarily within the *keiretsu* with which they have financial ties. Certainly, once a group of firms has become firmly established through financial ties, it is possible that, through the indirect influence of these ties, trade in products and services within the group will increase, continue over a long period, and stabilize. But as I discuss in detail later, this is an indirect by-product of forming the financial group. There is no direct reason why a long-term transactional relationship in products and services should emerge among firms simply because they share a main bank.

It is also possible for *keiretsu* involving products to yield by-products in the financial sphere. That is, the interdependence of firms dealing in products will frequently generate a relationship in which one firm guarantees another's debt. For example, a parent firm may hold stock in its subcontractors and act as an intermediary to help them obtain loans or to guarantee their debts. In the U.S.-Japanese debate over trade issues, the workings of a *keiretsu* as such and its by-products have been frequently misunderstood. The misunderstanding seems to be worsened by the recent emphasis on the "results" of the bilateral trade negotiations. But in discussing the rules of economic liberalism as I am attempting here, this misunderstanding is undesirable, even dangerous.

In discussing *keiretsu*, therefore, it is first necessary to distinguish clearly between horizontal and vertical *keiretsu*—that is, between financial and goods *keiretsu*—and to examine their respective characteristics. In this section, I deal mainly with vertical *keiretsu*. Certain parts of the argument also apply to horizontal *keiretsu*, but I deal with issues specific to horizontal *keiretsu* in the section on cross-shareholding below.

Let us turn from definitions to the actual points at issue. First, generally speaking, *keiretsu* are the result of activities freely engaged in by private Japanese firms in order to maximize their long-term, cumulative benefits. In only a few cases have administrative authorities such as MITI or the Ministry of Finance actively supported the development of financial or subcontracting *keiretsu*.[11] In other words, *keiretsu* did not emerge through government intervention but are a product of individual firms' long-term pursuit of economic efficiency. The reality is that long-term relationships based on continuing transactions are seen not only in Japan but frequently throughout Europe as well. Peter Katzenstein and the Schmiegelows, for example, have pointed out that Germany has a small number of large industrial conglomerates, and that the control of the three largest banks extends to the boards of almost all the leading firms. The German industrial conglomerates probably have both horizontal and vertical *keiretsu*.[12] If we were to consider *keiretsu* in themselves to be a violation of the rules, there would probably be very few economically liberal countries. It is a mistake to see *keiretsu* as a nonmarket phenomenon.

Of course, this is not to say that all market phenomena are socially desirable. Even some market phenomena are violations of the rules. Monopoly, in the standard interpretation, is one such instance, and thus every country implements controls through some kind of antitrust law. (The contrary opinion, such as Hayek's, is also possible.) As is well known, the neoclassical theory of market structure provided the theoretical basis for considering monopoly a violation. If there were a theory that could apply to the case of *keiretsu*, it would have to be one that could analyze the links between different kinds of productive activity, and in that sense it would be a "theory of organization."

Without resorting to a theory of organization, it is clear that *keiretsu* are formed by firms in different industries (in contrast to collusive oligopolies or cartels, which are formed among firms in the same industry, competing in the same market). Certainly, long-term cooperative relationships between firms in the same industry, or in the same market, may lead to collusive cartels. The ultimate form of cooperative relationships between firms in the same industry is merger. However, as is well known, merger between firms in the same industry is strictly supervised and is frequently prohibited by antitrust law.[13] In contrast, the ultimate form of *keiretsu* is vertical integration and conglomerates (merger between firms in different industries). Antitrust law cannot rule them per se illegal and prevent them from being formed, because if one were to sustain the legal view that vertical integration is illegal per se, one must argue also that each stage of production must be carried out by an independent firm. Even in extreme cases of vertical integration, such as in the first decades of the twentieth century when the Ford Motor Co. had the leading iron works in the United States and manufactured everything internally, from glass to rubber, the authorities did not raise the antitrust issue.[14]

In the context of vertical integration, it is clear that a *keiretsu* has more intragroup competition. And, through the workings of the market at each stage, firms outside the *keiretsu*, and therefore foreign firms, naturally have a chance to enter the *keiretsu*. The possibility of entering a *keiretsu* is at least higher than in the case of vertical integration, where such a possibility does not exist. Considered in terms of competition, it is not logical to permit vertical integration but to prohibit *keiretsu*.

It takes a long time, however, to enter the set of long-term cooperative relationships on which the *keiretsu* is based. Nowadays particularly, virtually all *keiretsu* are involved in joint development of technology, and this is clearly time-consuming. We should note, though, that joining and exiting from a *keiretsu* are two sides of the same coin, and the latter also takes time. Even when the cooperative relationship has become a disadvantage for the firm, or for the *keiretsu* as a whole, it cannot be easily terminated. All the conflicting interests of the parties involved cannot be resolved in the short term, and it is a characteristic of long-term interfirm cooperative relationships to become "sticky." For individual firms, this stickiness can be an advantage or a disadvantage, depending on the case. Thus it is unjustified to criticize *keiretsu* only on the ground of the length of time required to join it. In short, sticky relationships such as *keiretsu* occupy an intermediate position, somewhere between the relationships of a "spot market," in which everything is settled in a short period of time, and relationships such as vertical integration, which are in principle long-lasting. Michael Porter has called this kind of relationship "quasi-integration"; Ken'ichi Imai, Hiroyuki Itami, and Kazuo Koike have called it "intermediate organization."[15]

The functional characteristic of such an intermediate organization is precisely its being intermediate, a mix of the respective characteristics of relationships in a spot market and vertical integration. In a spot-market relationship, firms link up with and separate from each other instantaneously, in response to changes in economic conditions. In the United States, spot-market relationships are said to be the norm:

> Over the course of business cycles, suppliers were treated much as production workers were: as marginal assets to be utilized at times of peak demand but jettisoned during troughs. These arrangements could not foster loyalty and trust. Assemblers [in the automobile industry] feared that their suppliers might shift to competitors, revealing inside information like plans for future models. Hence, the assemblers kept their plans secret and did little to advance the skills of suppliers.[16]

The strength of spot-market interfirm relations is their speed of response to short-term changes. But this advantage is gained at the cost of long-run stability in the supply-demand relationship between firms, and cooperation in technology. In contrast, the strength of vertical integration is the absence of concern about the supply of intermediate products; this advantage is gained at the cost of making short-run costs inflexible; and in the long run, when technology and demand change, the firms involved will be saddled with a plant that produces intermediate products that are no longer required. In short, firms that rely on spot-market relationships come to think of tomorrow as uncertain and the future as unpredictable; firms that have implemented vertical integration expect that the future will be basically no different from the past.

The strong point of an intermediate organization such as a subcontracting relationship is that it enables a management policy somewhere between these two. A parent firm can expect to some extent a stable supply of good quality parts and can eventually cut its links with a subcontractor that fails to perform. In other words, both the parent firm and the subcontractor agree to a somewhat predictable scenario for the future and are prepared to cooperate in technological development and in a relationship of financial dependence. They also understand, though, that the cooperative relationship can be terminated. Clearly, the financial superiority of the three kinds of interfirm relationship—the spot market, intermediate organization, and vertical integration—depends on the degree of predictability in the economic environment. These three kinds of relationships are appropriate, respectively, to three kinds of situation: unpredictable, somewhat predictable, and quite predictable. As I have already pointed out, the years after the Second World War were characterized by a steady trend of technological innovation. In other words, although it was certain that technological innovation would continue, it was difficult to predict what the actual technological innovations would be. That is, because it was an intermediate situation in which the future was somewhat predictable, an intermediate organization was the most efficient form of interfirm relationship. The subcontracting keiretsu in Japan were not a prewar legacy but for the most part a product of the postwar period.

Today, the advantages of such an intermediate organization are gradually being recognized even outside Japan. For example, the MIT report cited above recommends strengthening long-term ties between firms in the automobile and textile industries. MIT has been one of the principal "temples" of the neoclassical school in economics (and in fact Robert Solow, leader of the school, added his name to that report as an editor), but the economists at this "temple" have recognized that keiretsu in themselves are not contrary to the rule of economic liberalism. Further, Michael Porter also actively recommends what he calls "quasi-integration,"[17] and, as I note below, Oliver Williamson has also turned toward recognizing quasi-integration. At least in general, the view that keiretsu are contrary to the rule of economic liberalism is weakening, and even in the United States there seems to be a move toward long-term cooperative relationships.

Even if there are signs of change, though, for the majority of U.S. firms, such as automobile parts manufacturers, it will not be easy to decide to adopt long-term, cooperative, interfirm relationships. They still argue that Japanese-style *keiretsu* practices prevent U.S. firms from entering the Japanese market. Recently, however, an increasing number of East Asian firms in the electronics industry have entered the subcontracting *keiretsu* of Japanese firms, demonstrating that entering a Japanese *keiretsu* from outside the country is not impossible. Why do U.S. parts manufacturers believe it is? Or, in the most general terms, why are U.S. firms not actively adopting long-term relationships in which there is a continuity of transactions? The answer to this question is that, even though an intermediate organization has functional advantages, it is not easy to create and sustain. An agreement to support an intermediate organization has long-term implications, is multifaceted, and is difficult to put into writing. At most, it is an implicit contract (or a pseudocontract). Each party must trust that it will be protected even by such a pseudocontract, and that its partner will adopt a cooperative attitude.

As a functional equivalent of this trust, one can imagine a lucky situation in which trading that began with trust continued to yield mutually beneficial results. To use the terms of game theory, a strategy of "tit-for-tat" (cooperation for cooperation, and noncooperation for noncooperation), which falls between a strategy of absolute noncooperation and a strategy of total cooperation, would become dominant and the parties involved would continue using this strategy to maintain lasting cooperation.[18] Certainly, the "tit-for-tat" strategy is closer to cooperation than to inflexible absolute noncooperation. If the strategy continues to produce economic prosperity, more firms are likely to trust their trading partners and to accept an implicit contract. Such a convergence toward a cooperative solution, though, can only be proved (or simulated) in an ideal state where the structure of the game remains unchanged, one knows one's partner's strategy, and the game is played repetitively (over the long term). If the economy enters a recession, the structure of the game will change, one's partner's strategy will also change, and one's own perspective will become short term; thus, the process leading toward a cooperative solution will be interrupted. In many cases the progress toward cooperation will be interrupted by such difficulties.

Even in the postwar decades during which most economies enjoyed continuous prosperity, fluctuations in economic performance could not be avoided. Thus cooperating in an implicit contract requires something more than economic prosperity. Normally this is an ethos of a trust in the society, or, more precisely, the society considers cooperation and trust to be virtues and has a mechanism to restrain or penalize actions that run contrary to those virtues. The tendency to trust is perhaps stronger in Japan than in the United States; thus it is easier for implicit contracts to be observed. In American society, this tendency may be perceived as conflicting with the tradition of individualism, and some U.S. parts manufacturers call Japanese transaction practices "groupism" and find the practices psychologically difficult to accept.

Until very recently, these issues relating to *keiretsu* have not been adequately acknowledged by neoclassical economics, which has relied on the model of the spot market. On reexamination, however, the *keiretsu* as an intermediate organization emerges naturally in the market; thus it cannot be said to contradict the concept of economic liberalism. The continuing postwar trend toward constant technological innovation will perhaps push firms in other countries to form similar alliances. Even in the United States, if economic prosperity continues, cooperation among firms will increase and more firms will take long-term management perspectives; as a result a phenomenon similar to *keiretsu* may emerge, as advocated by the MIT group. The possibility of intermediate organizations emerging, though, is different in each country, reflecting to some extent differences in what I have called the natio. And the danger that international friction will emerge from this fact was precisely the focus of debate in the previous section. Below I examine this problem, together with other similar problems, from the perspective of a general theory of organization.

IS THE JAPANESE EMPLOYMENT SYSTEM DIFFERENT? THE GENEALOGY OF THE THEORY OF ORGANIZATION

Beneath the economic friction between Japan and the United States lies an uneasiness with, or antipathy toward, Japan's tendency toward "groupism." This is primarily a result of the failure on the part of both sides to understand each other's natio. For example, there are various ways of interpreting Japan's groupism, and none seems to be accurate. Various impressionistic theories are being advanced, particularly in discussions related to the economy and the management system, involving such questions as what part or what pattern of groupism is at work and how does it influence the economy and the management system? As a result, extreme views based on misconceptions and preconceptions abound. Thus, it is necessary to clearly see Japan's groupism as a concept of historical analysis, and I too have my own view. However, without entering a historical analysis, let me discuss this issue from the standpoint of a general theory of firm organization.

In its weakest definition, management based on groupism is firms behaving as if they were a single corporate group. This expression is borrowed from British anthropology and refers to a group with a structure that outlasts its founding member. Since profit cannot be calculated, let alone maximized, over such a long period, the firms come to adopt a goal somewhat different from profit maximization, the standard of what one might call a kind of "utility." Thus, in the classical image of the firm, for example, which assumes that a single individual is both capitalist (owner) and manager, the firm exists only for the lifetime of the owner and therefore cannot be a corporate group. (Even if the owner has descendants, or there are joint owners, it is clear that this alone does not guarantee the firm's becoming a corporate group.) Surprisingly, this classical image of the firm has survived for as long as a century in both Marxist and neoclassical economics.

It is well known, though, that by the latter half of the nineteenth century, when Marx wrote *Das Kapital*, the scale of factory production had grown, the system of joint-stock companies had been established as a mechanism to obtain the industrial capital required to build such a factory, and ownership and management had begun to be divided. "Organized capitalism" or "corporate capitalism" on the twentieth-century model had already begun to emerge. A book that is informative on such maturation of managerial structure is Adolf Berle and Gardiner Means's famous *Modern Corporation and Private Property*, written in 1933. This book empirically demonstrated that stock ownership had become diffuse as the scale of firms increased and, as a result, the shareholders who could manage firms disappeared, causing managers to gain de facto control of firms.[19] Given this situation, in which ownership (stock ownership) had become diffuse, its transfer (the buying and selling of stocks) does not have any great influence on the substance of management, apart from those exceptional cases such as the takeover of a firm through buying up its stock. It is inevitable that this separation of ownership and management, in the weak sense defined above, should have come about, and that given this separation, management control should have grown stronger, particularly in day-to-day business operations. Berle and Means were also much interested in the important question of which direction this increased management control over business operations would turn. Would managers simply become representatives of stockholders, or would they assume an independent social role? In the 1930s, many hoped for a managerial revolution to affirm the latter role to replace the socialist revolution.[20] In the United States of today, too, those arguments that respect only the rights of the stockholder and criticize the division of ownership and management are not the mainstream.

What is now called "firm organization" or simply "organization" in economics and in the study of management is nothing other than the corporate group. Each firm develops its own individual organizational structure and practices, and a so-called corporate culture evolves. Regardless of who the stockholders are, and indeed who the managers are, GM is GM, Toyota is Toyota, and their natures will not change, at least not rapidly. As firms grew and corporate cultures developed, so did the theory of firm organization after the Second World War. First, in the 1950s and 1960s, Edith Penrose discussed the "growth of the firm," and Robin Marris, "managerial capitalism." What they assumed, though, was a principle not of profit maximization but of a kind of firm "utility"—that is, utility for managers.[21] At about the same time, Gary Becker's theory of "human capital" also began to analyze the trend toward corporate groups (in the sense that I use the term here) from a slightly different perspective.[22] But the theories of these forerunners did not evolve into a general theory of firm organization.

It was in the 1970s that substantive analyses on organization began to appear. Oliver Williamson's theory of "internal organization" is famous for its strongly theoretical character. Using the theory of transaction costs, he attempted to incorporate the theory of organization within the neoclassical framework. Continuous transactions and vertical integration were also important subjects of his analysis. Williamson had a great predecessor in Ronald Coase, and others in Williamson's generation contributed to the development of the theory of organization, but he must be seen as the scholar who has made the most significant contribution.[23]

The important research of Peter Doeringer and Michael Piore, built on the work of the institutionalist school, should be noted for its strongly empirical character. After demonstrating that worker mobility decreased following the Second World War, they explained this trend as one result of a quasi-competitive market allocation of labor due to intrafirm institutions and proceeded to develop the theory of what is called the internal labor market.[24] The research of Kazuo Koike in Japan reaches a similar conclusion. Mindful of the legacy of studies by the Marxist school, Koike concentrated on the allocation of labor by intrafirm institutions and developed a theory very similar to that of Doeringer and Piore. The substance of his theory clearly has a universal significance and its usefulness was not limited to the Japanese case.[25] Thus, soon after the Second World War—clearly before Japanese management began to attract global attention and the "Japan problem" began to be discussed—continuous transactional relations and permanence of organization were attracting scholars' attention.

The tendency for worker mobility to decline (for length of service by regular employees to increase), which Doeringer and Piore found in the United States and for which Koike made the contribution noted above, has become the foundation for analysis of the contemporary firm. The principal reason for declining mobility undoubtedly is the trend toward constant technological innovation, which became particularly conspicuous following the Second World War. That is, as the pace of technological innovation became steady and, so to speak, routinized, learning by doing became unavoidable for firms. While absorbing technology, firms were forced to train workers (and in certain respects, workers had to train themselves). It was difficult to establish school education or training programs to meet the need of the existing technology because technology was advancing so rapidly and was used in firm-specific ways. A melding of work and training, or in other words, the element of what is called on-the-job training (OJT), became more or less required. OJT, though, provides skills that are specific to an individual firm or workshop and thus are not "portable" to other firms. In order for workers to make the best use of their own skills, it is advantageous for them to stay with one firm.

Managers, too, fear losing the skilled labor that they have developed at some cost. Differences in the institutions created to prevent such loss of trained labor cause the forms of management in each country to diverge. The U.S. system of job-specific seniority (temporarily laying off new employees first while retaining longer-term employees) and the Japanese system of job rotation and lifetime employment (an effort to minimize layoffs) are examples of the results of this divergence. Both systems are economically rational, responding to the demands of the routinization of technological innovation and to the necessity of maintaining a stable skilled labor force. In a sense, management in the United States has also become group-oriented.

But even if these two systems share the goal of creating and retaining a skilled labor force, their substance is strikingly different. For example, in the United States jobs under the job-specific seniority system are narrowly defined; in Japan jobs are defined only broadly, and how and when the transfer of workers from one job to another is made is not clearly predetermined. Because of these differences, the two systems also provide different levels of job security; in the United States, layoffs are often used, but in Japan layoffs are avoided.[26] All of the above is to say that, although both systems adopt internal promotion, in the U.S. system there remains a structure comparable to the market (negotiations on wages and promotion specific to the individual), while in the Japanese system this market element is absent. Neither Doeringer and Piore nor Koike offers an adequate explanation of this difference. Doeringer and Piore did not examine the Japanese case, and Koike, who is a strict empiricist, refrained from applying his theory to other countries. Koike seems to suggest that—as long as technological innovation progresses smoothly—the Japanese system is superior in increasing productivity, and thus more advanced.[27] But in the end, he does not explain why these differences in the two systems developed. Below I attempt a somewhat speculative explanation.

THE QUESTION OF GROUPISM

Let us use Oliver Williamson's framework to discuss the differences between Japan and the United States. Most important, he posited that, in order to prevent an increase in the trouble caused by people's "opportunism" (related to both capital and labor), it was necessary for the firm to be organized hierarchically. What he meant by opportunism was egoism, or adopting a strategy of outmaneuvering others in "the game" to pursue one's own self-interest. In other words, Williamson assumed economic transactions involved antagonism and distrust on the part of the parties involved. In order to overcome opportunism—that is, to control the elements of antagonism and distrust—he believed that economic liberalism required not only a "market" but also "organization." In any case, Williamson's way of thinking could be said to be founded on self-love and is far removed from Adam Smith's generous optimism, which did not give serious attention to the possibility of action designed to ensnare others. It may be that it symbolizes the distress of the present-day United States, or of neoclassical economics.

Let us return for a moment to the example of choosing between vertical integration and an intermediate organization such as a *keiretsu*. Williamson believed that long-term relationships for which it was difficult to stipulate a clear content—a relationship such as a *keiretsu*, which is insufficiently hierarchical—would typically be wracked by opportunism and could not possibly last (although recently, he seems to have turned somewhat in the direction of recognizing the possibility of intermediate organization).[28] Certainly, in such cases as joint R&D projects between parent firms and subcontractors, seen often in Japan, either one can easily "cheat" the other, as the MIT report cited above also mentioned. Similarly, in Japan up until the present there has a been a tacit understanding that, when a subcontractor faces financial difficulty, the parent firm will provide financial aid. But this promise could be easily broken. In other words, what established the *keiretsu* in Japan was the expectation of harmony and trust, that these kinds of tacit promises would for the most part be honored.

This does not mean that the Japanese are an ethical people who keep their promises and that Americans are schemers, not to be trusted. Rather, in adopting an ideology that recognizes freedom of individual action, Americans have to consider the possibility of opportunism; the Japanese, on the other hand, do not openly recognize the existence of opportunism, having been brought up within an ethos that tries to increase mutual understanding and harmony among individuals. In addition, during the postwar period of high growth, there existed conditions favorable to maintaining harmony and trust. At least in the economic sphere, the postwar Japanese conception of society and the favorable Japanese economic environment helped to better establish this standard of "trust" socially.

The question of employment structure can be examined in a similar way. The substance of lifetime employment is nothing more than a tacit understanding that workers will not be laid off; but this agreement requires trust that the management will do everything possible to avoid layoffs and will not use that trust as an excuse to hold down wage increases. Similarly, the extensive use of job transfer requires employees' confidence that transfers will not be used to separate them from a familiar workplace and isolate them. Both of these implicit rules can be abused opportunistically by both capital and labor. Nevertheless, the fact that this system has functioned is due to the expectation that the implicit agreement would be honored. Of course, an important reason why the agreement could be honored was the continuous postwar economic prosperity. But we cannot ignore the part played by the binding power of an ethos that prized harmonious relationships between individuals (it is highly possible that this was nurtured in farming communities engaged in rice cultivation). From the perspective of an American sense of values, which prizes the demonstration of the individual's will, such harmonious relations seem coerced, and it is easy to think that there must be some hidden relations of dominance supporting them. Harmonious relations are, of course, an ideal, not a reality, and there must be cases where they are used as a cover for the exercising of power by capital. But to view concealed relations of dominance as the Japanese norm is to err by being overly influenced by a perspective that values the demonstration of the individual's will.

I have described this situation by saying that "the mode of social exchange has diffused . . . significantly into the economic sphere in [Japan]."[29] "Social exchange" refers to exchange that finds value in the act of exchange itself rather than in the benefits provided by the object of exchange, and its objective is the creation of mutual trust. Forms close to genuine social exchange are *kula* and potlatch exchanges, well known in anthropology; the etiquette of exchanging presents, which has flourished in Japan recently, is also close to these types of exchanges. In Japan this kind of mechanism has been adapted into the economic sphere. In both the Japanese *keiretsu* and the employment system, elements of social exchange are clearly at work. In the eyes of the average American, though, it is difficult to think of social exchange that is not linked to hierarchical control; thus to introduce elements of social exchange into economic action is to insert what should not be involved.

However, it is surely dangerous to explain such differences in practice by a naive cultural determinism. The Japanese management system is a composite of various factors; certainly one cannot deny the influence of comparatively long-term factors such as Japan's unique historical background and its position as a late-developing country. At the same time, one cannot ignore comparatively short-term factors such as the wartime experience of the command economy, the postwar economic environment, and the nature of changes in the society. Analogous observations can be made about the American system. It would be perverse to deny that the uniquely American idea of freedom and equality that de Tocqueville noticed in the first half of the nineteenth century had a hand in creating the American system. But at the same time, we cannot forget the effects of the experience of management of the large American firms, which achieved remarkable success in the first half of the twentieth century in surviving the prewar depression, regaining their vigor during the war years, and again overpowering firms in other countries in the postwar period.[30] It is quite possible that such great success led American firms to limit their responses to the postwar trend that demanded the development of the corporate group. This was perhaps the price paid for being the leader of the world economy. That is, in the cases of both the United States and Japan, historical accidents were at work to some extent. As Koike has emphasized, Japanese management was a rational solution given the conditions Japan faced. American management too is surely a rational outcome given the conditions that confronted the Americans.

Of course, these differences in conditions include differences in long-term factors close to what one could call culture or, to use an expression employed frequently in this book, differences in the natio of our time. These differences, though, were in adapting to the trend toward a firm's becoming a corporate group, seen throughout the twentieth century, and were not rejections of this trend. Neoclassical theory, which tries to reduce organization to a bundle of spot-market transactions, tends to ignore this trend, or at least its theoretical structure has been unprepared to address this question. When such neoclassical preconceptions are discarded, there is no doubt that both the American and Japanese systems of inter- and intrafirm relationships have shown a general trend toward the corporate group. In other words, as I suggested earlier, American firms are in a functional sense becoming more group-oriented. What has caused these systems to diverge are the differences in timing between early and late developers and differences in natio. Cultural differences do exist, but to stress only them and to emphasize differences in character fails to take the balanced approach necessary to better understand the issues.

Are Japanese Firms Different? Cross-Shareholding and Monetary Policy

Keiretsu and the Japanese employment system are frequently identified as sources of friction in U.S.-Japanese economic relations. But recent arguments have cast doubt on even the so-called long-term orientation of Japanese management. As long as the logic of industrialization is taken as a premise, however, it is logically self-evident that an increasingly long-term orientation in management's outlook is itself desirable for individual firms, and one cannot criticize it as a violation of the rules of economic liberalism. However, if there are striking differences between Japan and the United States in the conditions under which such long-range plans are implemented, for example in the supply cost of investment capital (I call this the cost of capital), it is inevitable that this should become the source of economic friction.

Some critics on the U.S. side have argued recently that the low cost of capital in Japan is supported by the practice unique to Japan of cross-shareholding within the *keiretsu*, and some people have even gone so far as to call this practice unfair. Certainly in Japan some large firms engage in cross-shareholding and do not demand large dividends (particularly in relationships between financial institutions and nonfinancial firms). When the proportions of the stock ownership of leading firms are examined, we find that financial institutions, nonfinancial firms, and individuals each hold about one third, and the total amount of stock held by firms is unusually large by international standards. When cross-shareholding relationships are examined, for example, we discover that among the firms that belong to the Friday Club of the Mitsubishi *keiretsu*, on average a little less than 27 percent of their stock (in 1988) was held by other members of the Friday Club.[31] The dividend rate in Japanese firms is clearly lower than that in other advanced countries.

Stockholders in the United States are extremely sensitive to dividend earnings. This tendency has become particularly striking since the 1970s, when financial investors such as pension funds became the leading investors. This attention to dividends has restricted American managers' ability to carry out their investment plans unless they are able to produce an adequate profit during each period; in contrast, their Japanese counterparts can embark on investment with little attention to the (short-term) interests of stockholders. It is from this difference that the complaints emerge that there is a handicap against U.S. firms, and that they cannot win a handicapped race. Recently a number of economists too considered these criticisms or objections to be reasonable. I do not agree with this critique, except on the issues surrounding administrative intervention mentioned below (to achieve a monetary policy oriented toward stability).

DIFFERENCES IN THE COST OF CAPITAL

Let us examine whether there are differences in the real cost of capital. Calculating the real cost of capital is extremely difficult; because it involves the deflator, evaluating the effective tax burden, and adjusting for differences in accounting practices, one has to be extremely cautious, particularly in making international comparisons. To date, although more research findings seem to suggest that the cost of capital (the sum of the cost of shares and the cost of borrowing) is lower in Japan than in the United States, there have been no unequivocal conclusions.[32] The cost of equity (share) financing since the beginning of the 1980s has been lower in Japan, and unusually low (with an unusually high price-earnings ratio) in the latter half of the 1980s; the cost of borrowing seems to have been higher in the United States, particularly on a pretax basis. But comparing only Japan and the United States is not sufficient. The economists of the Federal Reserve Bank of New York agree that there are differences between Japan and the United States, but in comparing Japan and Germany they have estimated that, since the beginning of the 1980s, the real cost of capital after taxes has been almost the same in both countries.[33]

Certainly the international mobility of capital has greatly increased recently, but differences in the cost of capital between advanced countries continue to persist. Thus it cannot be said that the cost in Japan differs distinctively from that in many other countries. Generally speaking, the cost of capital in each country depends on its system of financial institutions, factors determining capital supply (such as the propensity to save), the stability of macroeconomic policy, and the probability of firm bankruptcies, and the cost also changes over time. Clearly, the fact that the cost of capital is low is not, in itself, evidence of a violation of the rules of liberalism. If this were not the case, not only Japan, but also Germany until recently and probably most of the capital-rich countries (that is, countries with a surplus in their balance of payments) would all be in violation of the rules. This is an obvious point, but it needs to be stressed.

Moreover, it is dangerous to discuss differences in the cost of capital between Japan and the United States only for the 1980s. For example, there was no substantial difference between the cost of capital in Japan and the United States in the 1970s. It seems, rather, that the effective cost of capital was lower in the United States and that there was almost no difference in the cost of equity capital. And the corporate tax rate, too, was higher in Japan. Put in the most conservative terms, differences between the cost of capital in Japan and the United States in the 1970s were smaller than in the 1980s. Even in the 1970s, though, the relative decline of such industries as iron and steel and automobiles in the United States continued, and conglomerates (corporations made up of widely diversified firms) became prevalent as firms acquired other firms in unrelated fields of business. The largest firms also followed this example, and they made little industrial investment. In the latter half of the 1980s industrial investment in the United States began to increase rapidly, but it was in this period that the difference between the cost of capital in Japan and the United States diverged. In any case, there is no consistent relationship between differences in the cost of capital and differences in investment activity; that is, apparently one cannot use the former as the main explanatory factor for the latter. Differences in investment activity, or more generally, in management behavior, seem to be based more broadly on structural factors.

SHORT-TERM AND LONG-TERM ORIENTATIONS OF MANAGEMENT

With the comparison with Japan perhaps playing some role, many in the United States are today criticizing the short-term orientation of American management, and, as its cause, many scholars suggest the short-term orientation of institutional investors. As discussed above, the general trend among academics and editorial-page contributors—Robert Hayes and William Abernathy, the MIT group, Robert Reich, and others—is to criticize the short-term orientation of management and the preoccupation of institutional investors with short-term earnings.[34] Certainly when their investment behavior is examined, it is difficult to deny the short-term orientation of management in American firms in many important industries, such as textiles, iron and steel, automobiles, electrical machinery, and machine tools.

But what are the reasons for this? First, is it true that institutional investors are preoccupied with short-term earnings? If so, they are going against the trend toward long-term orientation in economic outlook seen in industrial society as a whole, as discussed above. This is an unfortunate situation for American managers, but it does not mean that responsibility for it lies with other countries such as Japan. The question is whether U.S. institutional investors as a whole are really short-term in their orientation. The answer is far from evident because there is considerable research that argues the opposite.[35] If this counterargument were correct, the short-term orientation of management in many leading U.S. industries would become the primary responsibility of the managers themselves. One must not be hasty in judging, but it seems impossible to deny that the problem lies in the structure of American-style management to date.

Various diagnoses of American-style management are possible, but the situation in the United States in the 1970s provides much useful input for a diagnosis. As noted above, in the 1970s, when the cost of capital in the United States and Japan differed little (or at least less than in the 1980s), the main actors were the highly heterogeneous conglomerates that grew rapidly by making acquisitions in many related business fields.

In retrospect, it is evident that the goal of management in making such acquisitions was not to develop productive businesses but to make financial gains that could be realized for tax reasons and/or by reselling some or all of the acquired firms. The high risk involved in such acquisitions required a high return and increased the interest rate. One result was that less capital was available for industrial investment; and managers, in order to prevent takeovers, began focusing on short-term profits and adopting strategies to prevent takeovers. Into the 1980s, this trend grew stronger, and means such as junk bonds came to be used to make leveraged buyouts (acquisition using loans made by mortgaging the assets of the firms to be acquired). In other words, the difference in the cost of capital in the 1980s may well have been the effect, not a cause, of a shift from productive investment to speculative investment. Why did the management of so many firms become absorbed in manipulative financial dealings? One can offer various answers, beginning with the tradition of respecting the individual's freedom of action, but the most important answer must be that *firms did not have effective means of resisting takeover*. This was a manifestation of a conflict between the trend toward the firm's becoming a corporate group, required by the present stage of industrialization, and the rights of stockholders.

THE HISTORY OF CROSS-SHAREHOLDING

Leaving aside the problems of comparing the United States and Japan (particularly in terms of differences in the cost of capital), let us turn to why cross-shareholding emerged in Japan. It is important to note that the rising trend in share prices (as well as the high growth of the Japanese economy) cannot be a reason for cross-shareholding. Generally speaking, following the 1950s there were of course capital gains that were very large by international standards (due specifically to an increase in unrealized profit that resulted from rising share prices, and to de facto preferential buying rights of new issues), and many firms had substantial cash flow (internal reserves). But if these kinds of capital gains alone were the reason for shareholding by firms, when share prices slumped one would have expected their shareholdings to decrease. On the contrary, after both the securities panic of 1966 and the oil crisis of 1974, the proportion of stock held by firms increased. Moreover, even if we suppose that firms hold stock to realize gains (dividends or capital gains), there is no reason for cross-shareholding. Instead, we would expect a firm's holdings to be concentrated in blue-chip stocks. Certainly the rising trend in share prices is a factor promoting cross-shareholding, but the above explanation makes clear that this cannot be the principal factor.

Cross-shareholding in Japan has a long history, and the practice was already well established in the 1950s. Instead of discussing the many explanations for this development, I only enumerate them, going from indirect and less important to direct and significant. First there is the well-known high saving rate of individuals in Japan (the household saving rate), which has remained at a consistently high level since soon after the war. Large amounts of capital flowed from the individual sector to the corporate sector, enabling high growth in the Japanese economy. Second, these individual savings were not invested in stocks. During the 1950s, almost all of the prewar rich lost their wealth, and the distribution of assets and income among individuals became more equal, but at an extremely low level. Given such poverty, it was natural for individual savers to avoid high-risk investment in stocks and to turn toward deposit accounts. As a result, "indirect financing," the channeling of individual savings through the banks to finance firms, became predominant.

Third, the individual preference for assets in the form of bank deposits meant that firms were the only main holders of company stocks. As a result, cross-shareholding gradually increased because it was the lowest-cost means of increasing shareholding by firms. Because cross-shareholdings offset each other, no effort is required to obtain new equity capital. From the latter half of the 1950s until the first half of the 1960s, the proportion of firms' capital that was supplied through issuing shares was seemingly as high as in the advanced countries, but almost all of this was through cross-shareholding ("third-party allocation").[36] In short, firms were able to grow with only limited equity capital because of indirect financing, which continued to supply capital. Indirect financing was a very significant reason for cross-shareholding.

But indirect financing itself does not explain why cross-shareholding persisted. Surely it might have been possible to change from a combination of indirect financing and cross-shareholding to direct financing and individual share ownership (what is called democratization of shareholding). In reality, however, the incentive to increase equity capital remained weak. As reasons for this, one cannot ignore the effects of the persistent strong interest of the monetary authorities in maintaining indirect financing (for the sake of industrial policy) and the effects of a serious slump in the stock market that began in 1965. Despite the increase in real assets due to the growth of firms, the increase in capital thus lagged behind, and the ratio of equity capital to real assets became extremely small and could not be readily raised even by rising share prices. (The investment boom in stocks to capture the unrealized capital gain did not occur until the beginning of the 1980s.) The potential danger of takeover was greater than in cases where there was no such lag, and cross-shareholding took on increased significance as a means of resisting such takeover. This is the fourth and most important reason for cross-shareholding.

In fact, in the first half of the 1950s, there were frequent sizable acquisitions of shares by speculative groups, causing increases throughout the decades in the proportion of stock held by firms as a means of defense against possible takeover. Also during this period, both the proportion of equity capital and that of stock held by corporations increased, indicating a desire by firms to increase equity capital. With the beginning of the 1960s, however, the proportion of equity capital declined, and only the proportion of stock held by firms rose, indicating an increase in cross-shareholding. In other words, cross-shareholding was no longer a means of obtaining capital but had become a means of preventing takeover. The 1960s through the first half of the 1970s was the zenith of indirect financing. Moreover, the indirect benefits realized by members of the cross-shareholding groups promoted cross-shareholding still further. The proportion of stock held by firms has continued to rise until very recently, because of the acquisition of shares that had ceased to be traded as a countermeasure against the slump in the stock market beginning in 1965, because of the efforts to further "stabilize" shareholders in preparation for capital liberalization in the 1970s, and also because of acquisition of firms that occurred against the background of excess liquidity in the 1980s. (The figures for 1991 are not yet known, but there are rumors that firms are beginning to sell shares they hold.) There was, however, one great change during this period. The preferences of individual Japanese investors finally began to shift away from deposit accounts. With the 1970s as the turning point, trading newly issued stock at the market price (instead of par value) became an established practice, and the proportion of equity capital to total capital began to rise. Thus three periods can be distinguished. In the 1950s, there was an increasing proportion of equity capital and an increasing proportion of stock held by firms. The 1960s and the first half of the 1970s saw a decreasing proportion of equity capital and an increasing proportion of stock held by firms. And the second half of the 1970s and the years following were marked by increasing proportions of equity capital and stock held by firms.

Since the latter half of the 1970s, the assets of individual investors have also grown substantially, and all newly issued shares can be easily sold in the open market. Why then has cross-shareholding increased still further? The answer can only be to prevent takeovers and to form groups. At the same time, indirect financing is clearly weakening. The "flow" version of the proportion of borrowed capital—"leverage" or the "debt-equity ratio"—was lower than that in the United States at the end of the 1980s. The basis of financial *keiretsu* in Japan is gradually shifting from bank financing to cross-shareholding, and as a result the cohesiveness in financial *keiretsu* is also becoming indirect and seems to be weakening. In sum, cross-shareholding today should be regarded as an action taken to prevent takeover or to form a group.

IS THE PRACTICE OF CROSS-SHAREHOLDING REALLY SO UNUSUAL?

Is cross-shareholding permitted under the rules of economic liberalism? In the previous section, I pointed out that there is inadequate proof that cross-shareholding reduces the cost of capital. I argued that differences in investment behavior between Japan and the United States should be explained not only as a reflection of the "heterogeneity" of the Japanese economy but also by structural factors such as the abundance of capital (a high propensity to save), the stability of macroeconomic management, and the developmentalist nature of firm management. Apart from this, however, one can raise the question of whether cross-shareholding violates the rules of economic liberalism. This has been my central topic since the preceding chapter.

This question is linked to, indeed is the obverse of, the question of whether takeovers are a violation of the rules. In terms of the classical conception of the firm, shareholders are the owners and substance of the firm (the theory of the firm as a legal person). Certainly, therefore, a takeover through the buying of stock would be the just exercising of the shareholders' freedom, and is a right that is fundamental to economic liberalism. This is the commonly held classical opinion. Of course, a takeover has the effect of providing managers with discipline (though recently this is questioned by a number of theorists).[37] On the other hand, when managers try to implement management plans for the long term, it is natural that they should create a strategy for defending against takeovers. Is this a violation of the rules? In the most classical theory of the firm, managers are no more than representatives who implement the will of the shareholders. The managers themselves have no right to prevent a takeover by someone who has already acquired stock. This classical theory, though, clashes with the trend toward the firm's becoming a corporate group. Many in the United States today believe the unusual boom in mergers and acquisitions was a serious error. Hypothetically, if the practice of cross-shareholding had not existed in Japan in the 1970s, a large number of leading Japanese firms might have been acquired and merged, giving rise to conglomerates of the American type. Had this occurred, Japanese firms, like U.S. firms, might not have been able to make productive investment. The question is whether we see this situation as unavoidable.

In this book, I have pointed out the possibility of conflict between classical economic liberalism and industrialization. The preceding discussions, too, have raised one of the most important contemporary issues. In terms of shareholding, we must ask what the common set of rules should be for the world of the future. First, for example, we should not make the legal position of the shareholder absolute. One of the critiques of cross-shareholding makes the legal argument that it infringes on the rights of the shareholder and is contrary to the spirit of the present law. However, seen from the perspective of the argument I am advancing, this critique puts the cart before the horse, as it were. What is at issue is the classical concept of ownership, which is the basic concept of the existing law, in which doubts have been raised as to whether a firm is the same kind of "thing" as any other material asset. In other words, are the rights of the limited-liability shareholder, established in the latter half of the nineteenth century, the same as ownership?

Article 200 of the Commercial Code of Japan states that "the responsibility of the shareholder is limited to the value of shares held," thus exempting the shareholder from criminal or civil liability for any serious loss. Those responsible for management (or middle management), for example, are responsible for any violation of labor relations law or the laws relating to environmental pollution, and they are subject to fines or imprisonment. Stockholders never receive such penalties. The shareholders' responsibilities are less than those of the average owners, and it is possible to think that their rights should be similarly restricted. In fact, the law has wavered for a long time between protection and restriction of the rights of shareholders; that is, the law does not provide sufficient direction on this point. The debate has shifted between the theories of the corporation as a legal person and the corporation as a real entity, without reaching any conclusion. Perhaps in the twenty-first century we will have to reconsider the rights of the shareholder and bring the debate to a conclusion.

Second, whether one supports or opposes the concept of cross-shareholding, one should not be nationalistic in discussing it. The argument is often made that cross-shareholding should be abandoned because it is "uniquely Japanese" and fundamentally "different." But to reject cross-shareholding only on these grounds is naive. Rejecting national characteristics is not synonymous with promoting universality. This is the same kind of thinking that earlier tried to reject the Japanese employment structure. We should remember that today many around the world believe that the Japanese employment structure has strong points, even though they may not wish to adopt the structure for themselves. Even in the U.S.-Japanese structural impediments negotiations, the Japanese employment structure has not been an issue. Conversely, it is not right for the Japanese to affirm cross-shareholding only because eliminating it would weaken Japan's economic power. An appropriate course of action to prevent takeovers cannot be founded on the basis of this nationalistic concern or of the legalistic interpretation. Once one has recognized the trend toward superindustrialization, as I do in this book, one must search for a set of rules that will allow nations in the world as a whole to coexist in the long term (although, to be accurate, one should allow for exceptions for developing countries). (Recall that I consider that the society of transindustrialization, going beyond superindustrialization, has not yet evolved.)

The trend toward superindustrialization is necessarily accompanied by the trend of the firm's becoming a corporate group. Thus the continuity of the firm should to a certain extent be protected. This implies a perspective that does not see the firm merely as an object to be possessed or the shareholder as an owner in the usual sense. Seen from this perspective, methods designed to prevent takeovers should not necessarily be prohibited. Various methods other than cross-shareholding can be imagined. Allowing a firm to hold its own shares, which is permitted in the United States but not in Japan, is one such method. In Europe there are many firms that are not stock companies, or whose shares are not dealt publicly, and this also has the general effect of avoiding takeover (though there are problems over the inheritance of shares). In Germany there are a number of examples of cross-shareholding (for example, Deutsche Bank and Daimler-Benz), and the boards of directors in leading firms almost always include representatives of a major bank. In the United States, some firms issue shares that carry only half the ordinary voting rights. Each country creates its own methods of dealing with the dilemma of industrialization and classical economic liberalism. And it is quite possible that in developmentalist follower countries in the future, a combination of direct financing and cross-shareholding will appear as a means of preventing takeover by foreign capital, for example.[38] It has been shown that cross-shareholding is perhaps one of the most effective methods.

THE SIDE EFFECTS OF CROSS-SHAREHOLDING

There are problems, however, with cross-shareholding. When cross-shareholding creates a group of firms in a large number of markets in diverse industries, it has the effect of preventing competition because of the influence of *keiretsu* in the individual markets. (This is an example of the secondary effects of financial *keiretsu* in market activities other than financial.) Criticism of Japan from the U.S. side in the end seems to come down to this, and, as a specific countermeasure, the United States demands stronger enforcement of the antitrust law in Japan.

I note in passing that the period from the latter half of the 1960s through the first half of the 1970s was what one might call a golden age in American antitrust law. The law was enforced strictly in various respects, especially against mergers between firms in different industries.

The argument that flourished then in support of such enforcement is now used in the criticism of Japan. But we need to recall that, starting with the Supreme Court's judgment in the General Dynamics case of the early 1960s, a clear trend toward more lax enforcement of the antitrust law emerged, and with the Reagan administration, U.S. antitrust law changed completely. Mergers between firms in different industries were tolerated, or more accurately, the effort to prohibit them was rarely made. Thus, for the Republican administrations from Reagan's time, criticizing Japan's enforcement of its antitrust law was akin to telling Japan to "do as I say, not as I do." Here, however, disregarding the changes in antitrust policy in the United States, we must examine the problem of side effects of mergers between firms in different industries.

Certainly, if there is an increasing awareness of common interests and a growing sense of trust within the cross-shareholding group, it is possible there will be a tendency to give priority in placing orders to firms within the group. There is no clear proof of preferential dealing, but research has demonstrated that the proportion of intra-*keiretsu* transactions to total volume of transactions is high. The question, though, is how significant this fact is. Certainly, considered in terms of static neoclassical theory, firms that do not belong to *keiretsu* (foreign firms, for example) will be at a transactional disadvantage, and the so-called perfect competitive equilibrium will not be achieved. But it is a mistake to view antitrust law as a means of achieving perfect competitive equilibrium. For example, neither the Harvard school, which emphasizes the distribution of economic power, nor the Chicago school, which stresses the freedom of individual firms for the sake of efficiency, is especially concerned with the concept of static equilibrium. In reality, one would not be able to implement the antitrust law by drawing upon neoclassical theory; one would run up against any number of serious problems in applying it. To give a much-discussed example, neoclassical analysis can provide no clear criteria for how to deal with nonprice competition (advertising competition, for example) and product differentiation.

Even more important, as I have argued throughout this book, in a dynamic situation where technological innovation occurs steadily, the static concept of perfect competitive equilibrium is meaningless. Thus the actual role of antitrust law can only be to maintain competition in the broad sense. How to define "maintaining competition" is difficult. The neoliberal Chicago school has adopted the clearest position on this point. They believe that only cartels that make price competition impossible should be prohibited, and all other market phenomena should be allowed. I am not adopting the position of the Chicago school here, but their analyses demonstrate effectively that the neoclassical approach, reliant on a static, perfect competitive equilibrium, provides no basis for antitrust enforcement. Japan's antitrust law prohibits stock acquisition only in "those cases that would substantially reduce competition" (Articles 10, 14), and although the interpretation of the American antitrust law—the model for the Japanese law—changes by period, we could not expect the current Japanese anti-trust law to be able to do much more.

Does cross-shareholding in Japan substantially restrict competition, as is commonly believed? To answer this, one has to take into account a number of factors. First, generally speaking, a firm that places priority on obtaining parts within the keiretsu will restrict its transactions and (at least in the short term) sacrifice efficiency. The firm receiving the order benefits, but the efficiency of the keiretsu as a whole will be lowered over time. Financial keiretsu cannot be designed to pursue efficiency in trans-actions involving products.[39] A firm that persists in trading only within the keiretsu when outside firms could supply cheaper parts will suffer a decisive disadvantage, at least in growing markets (particularly foreign markets). Thus there are clearly limits to preferential transactions within the keiretsu.

Second, whether intra-keiretsu trading substantially limits competi-tion depends on the circumstances in individual markets. To take an ex-treme example, if a firm that already has a substantial share of the market (30 percent, for example) joins a cross-shareholding keiretsu and thereby increases its market share, its influence on the market will become de-cisive enough to substantially restrict competition. Such a firm could be-come the target of the antitrust law (Article 10). But when competition in the market is vigorous, the side effects of cross-shareholding keiretsu will be limited, in the sense noted above. In Japan there are at least six cross-shareholding keiretsu and many major firms that do not belong to any keiretsu, and competition among them is vigorous. In other words, there are at least seven or eight firms of similar size and competitive ability competing with each other. One could see this as the preservation of what I call "polypolistic" competition. Generally speaking, the likelihood that cross-shareholding keiretsu will have negative effects on trading varies ac-cording to the individual market, and we need empirical research for each market. The findings might show that antitrust law could and should be applied to a particular market. Prohibiting cross-shareholding outright, however, on the grounds that its side effects restrict competition, cannot be considered a judicious act.

Cross-shareholding keiretsu (and the financial keiretsu that preceded them) do have a long-term advantage in that they act as a kind of safety net for the firms within the keiretsu. In many instances the main bank has come to the aid of a member firm in the same keiretsu facing a tem-porary difficulty. A famous example is the rescue of Mazda by Sumitomo Bank, which sought the cooperation of firms within the keiretsu. This is often compared to the U.S. government's dramatic rescue of Chrysler.[40] In this sense, one can think of keiretsu membership as a mutual insur-ance mechanism between private firms. The insurance premiums are the potential costs of preferential transactions within the keiretsu and the potential capital losses that can arise from having to hold the stocks of fellow *keiretsu* firms. In the long run, though, a firm cannot continue to sustain a clear disadvantage. There is the serious problem of share price, for example. From the beginning of the 1970s, share prices in Japan have continued to rise (except during the widespread recession caused by the oil crisis), and capital gains have also seemed to increase. Now, however, this trend has collapsed, and there are signs of uneven performance among firms. If these warning signals are accurate, cross-shareholding will become impossible because of the danger of a decline in the value of assets. Recent announcements of the sale of shares by firms may be a sign of change. Cross-shareholding *keiretsu* depend on the economic environment, and their effectiveness is limited. In future, maintaining cross-shareholding *keiretsu* may become significantly more difficult than it is at present.

In sum, cross-shareholding, like subcontracting *keiretsu* and the Japanese employment system, relies on an implicit contract. There have been no examples of using a written contract to implement cross-shareholding. Even if there is preferential trading by firms within the *keiretsu*, its continuation is based on implicit understanding; the safety-net effect of the *keiretsu*, too, is not promised in advance. Whether such an implicit contract is stable and continues depends on both the economic environment and the presence of an ethos that values trust and harmony. The mere presence of this ethos alone cannot guarantee that the implicit contract will be maintained. Without the postwar financial environment, symbolized by methods of indirect financing, cross-shareholding might well have been impossible. And now it seems as if the economic environment (including the trend in stock prices) is turning from favorable to unfavorable. In a sense, cross-shareholding, even if it is not unique to Japan, is a distinctive phenomenon most prevalent in Japan. Even there, it may only be a transitional phenomenon of Japan's "developmentalist stage." Developing countries of the future may wish to adopt the practice, and thus to consider it a violation of the rule of liberalism is to go too far.

ADMINISTRATIVE INTERVENTION IN THE FINANCIAL MARKETS

The popular belief that the financial system in postwar Japan was designed and instituted by the government is particularly strong abroad. I have already argued that this is a serious misperception, but here let me again summarize this argument from the perspective of government policy. There have been two aspects to financial policy in postwar Japan. One aspect has been to protect the banks, in order to also protect small depositors; this aim has been substantially achieved. The other aspect of financial policy has been to enable banks to make the largest possible proportion of loans for industrial investment so that the government, which controls the loans, can indirectly implement an industrial policy. This goal was pursued by such practices and policies as "window guidance" (imposing lending limits on individual financial institutions, especially the largest city banks) by the Bank of Japan, stringent control over private bond issues, the passive attitude to so-called "democratization of shareholding" (for example, making large-lot trades of shares more advantageous by fixing traders' commissions), and prohibiting the securitization of certificates of deposit (CDs). As is noted below, though, even from the perspective of developmentalism, it is doubtful whether this industrial-policy-like attitude, present in the financial policy of the Ministry of Finance and the Bank of Japan, was necessary. And it is even less necessary now, when national developmentalism should be discarded. It will be difficult, however, to separate these two aspects of financial policy and discard only the latter.

In all countries, the financial industry is the most heavily regulated. There are strict regulations in the United States and Germany, and it is not evident that regulation in these countries is less stringent than in Japan. Clearly, the policy of protecting depositors or investors is common to all these countries, but there are also other policy considerations at work (housing policy in the United States, for example). Because of this, in all countries, it is difficult to separate out the policy of protecting depositors. For these reasons alone, administrative intervention in the financial markets is strong in any country. This is to say that financial markets have a unique character that is difficult to deal with using the classical (or neoclassical) conception of the market.

Recently, financial economists have labeled this characteristic of financial markets "informational asymmetry." In other words, there is a substantial disparity in the amount and quality of information possessed by the individual who is the ultimate lender and the ultimate borrower (in many cases, the firm, in Japan). The borrower has a careful investment plan and a thorough understanding of the risks involved, but the lender usually has much less information and thus is frequently deceived. Clearly this is an example of the opportunism discussed earlier. If this kind of experience were to accumulate, the flow of capital would dry up while lenders would be forced, in effect, to hold cash and precious metals yielding no interest. The raison d'être of financial institutions is, by examining and screening the investment plans of the borrower on behalf of the lender, to reduce or eliminate this information gap and to mediate between the borrower and lender. Banks are a typical example of an institution that functions as a financial intermediary, employing the resources of its substantial examining and screening departments; the investment trust and bond-underwriting businesses of securities firms also act as financial intermediaries. Trust banks and insurance firms, in the process of supervising their depositors' assets, also perform substantially the same function.

Where institutions that act as financial intermediaries have been established, the flow of capital involves three parties: the ultimate lender, the financial intermediary, and the ultimate borrower. The information gap does not disappear but remains as before for all parties. First, there is a substantial information gap between the financial institution and the ultimate lender (that is, between the bank and the depositor, the securities firm and the investor). For example, there are inevitably substantial disparities in information between a large bank or securities firm and an individual depositor or investor. When new financial products appear in rapid succession as they do today, the individual investor's knowledge almost never catches up with the situation. Second, an information gap also often re-emerges between the financial institution and the ultimate borrower (the bank and its borrower, the securities firm and the bond issuer). The financial institution probably has a wealth of information about the general financial situation, and the borrower or the bond issuer (in Japan, often the firm) naturally has good information about its own investment plans. The gap in this case could perhaps rather be called a difference in the substance of the information. Thus, despite the appearance of financial institutions, information asymmetry will not disappear. As always, there reappears the possibility of "cheating," or opportunistic behavior to exploit the information gap.

One way of reducing the information disparity is to build a long-term relationship based on the continuity of transactions between the financial institution and the firm. As the relationship develops, each party will get to know the other well. Thus there emerges a characteristic of financial transactions: they will be long-term one-on-one transactions, or face-to-face negotiations.[41] Financial institutions were originally service firms, nothing more than suppliers of differentiated information to individual clients to supplement information clients already had. This characteristic is less evident between financial institutions and small lenders, but still remains, even today, between financial institutions and large borrowers. Thus financial markets are a bundle of individual face-to-face negotiations. In each such negotiation, there is, at least potentially, a substitutive or competitive relationship, but there is no guarantee that these negotiations as a whole can provide the effect of perfect competition. Therefore, it is difficult for financial markets to be perfectly competitive.

The problem is the relationship between the financial institution and the individual depositor or investor. Here the information gap is one-sided. For example, there is no way for the average depositor to know if a bank is facing financial difficulties. If the investment trust is not investing its funds most profitably, there is, again, almost no way for the individual investor to be certain of this fact. In analyzing such instances, some economists use "principal-agent" theory. That is, it is expected that the bank or the securities firm, as the agent, will act to the best of its ability in the interests of the individual depositor or investor in a fashion analogous to the relationship between a patient and doctor or a client and lawyer.

The bank or securities firm, however, does not usually act in this manner. The depositor, for example, wants to be able to receive interest payments and withdraw deposits as safely as possible, while the bank is most interested in maximizing its profit or (if there are increasing returns to scale) in expanding the scope of its business. The same can be said about the investment trust business of securities firms. The individual investor and the securities firm do not have the same attitude toward risk. This difference is apparent when a bank or securities firm goes into bankruptcy, or, to take a somewhat less striking example, when the value of total assets of an investment trust falls below that of the total funds invested.

One way of bringing the principal-agent relationship closer to the ideal is to introduce an incentive system (for lawyers, for example, a bonus for winning the case). In the case of the financial system, however, it is impossible to devise a good incentive system, and we resort to government regulations on entry and activity, as in licensing systems for doctors and lawyers. This is why all countries regulate financial institutions. Both the United States and Japan have implemented strict regulations. With regard to banks, entry, interest rates, the field and types of activity (inter- or intrastate in the United States, and the number of branch offices in Japan), and types of permissible portfolio and structure of capital (for example, the proportion of the bank's own capital) are all regulated. Specific regulation may be stronger or weaker in one country, but one cannot simply say that there is less regulation in the United States than in Japan. For example, state regulation of business in the United States has substantial effects, both good and bad. In any case, regulation on the U.S. or Japanese model, or regulation in some other country, originates in informational asymmetry.

Among the various forms of regulation, the most important, particularly for the individual depositor, is the rescue system, the so-called safety net (measures for rescuing depositors when a bank fails). According to popular belief, the safety net in the United States is centered on a government-guaranteed, large-scale deposit insurance system, while the safety net in Japan is thought to be the strict formal and informal supervision of the banks by the financial authorities and the strength of the large banks themselves. But these contrasting characterizations are not accurate. For example, the U.S. deposit insurance system, comprising a huge staff of 2,500, has authority to supervise and inspect banks and to effect such measures as closure, liquidation, absorption by other financial institutions, assumption of deposits, and rescuing banks. (There is a small-scale deposit insurance system in Japan too.) These kinds of authority, which supplement the deposit insurance system itself, are similar in many respects to those seen in the Japanese system and practices. Kazuto Ikeo, for example, has stated that "despite the apparent differences in the institutional arrangements, both in functions and substance, the ways by which the safety net is provided in Japan and the United States are remarkably similar."[42] Certainly in the 1980s deposit insurance payments in the United States grew extremely large and drew much attention, but this was rather a sign that the system had failed. The reasons for this failure were perhaps the dismantling of the supplementary controls cited above and rapid deregulation by the Reagan administration. Even the United States has not managed to provide an adequate safety net that relies only on the deposit insurance mechanism.

In any case, there has not been a single bank bankruptcy in Japan, even though there have been some mergers and absorptions to rescue small and medium-sized banks in difficulties. It is undeniable that the safety-net system in Japan has worked unusually well, in large part because of the rigorous, formal, and informal intervention by the financial authorities. Another important factor seems to have been the large size of the banks and the substantial effect this has had in spreading risk and reducing the cost of risk assessment. But the strength of the large banks in Japan is not only due to their size. What should not be forgotten is that financial *keiretsu* stand behind the large banks, and that the banks, acting as main banks, can rescue borrowers in difficulty with the aid of the firms in the *keiretsu*. A long-term side effect of this is that the main bank itself remains stable (without aid from government coffers). The present cross-shareholding *keiretsu*, having inherited the interfirm ties of the financial *keiretsu*, have become a part of the safety net in Japan. Japanese banks are extremely stable because of the safety-net mechanism supported by the *keiretsu* and by the Ministry of Finance and the Bank of Japan. In terms of the safety-net effect, the Japanese system until now has clearly been superior to the U.S. system, particularly since the Reagan administration.

One of the main reasons for this difference is that the Japanese safety-net system has been based, in part, on a nonneoclassical distributive policy. As the neoclassical school would be likely to express it, optimum results are supposed to be achieved by the combination of a freely competitive market (financial deregulation) and a redistributive policy independent of the market (a deposit insurance mechanism). As noted in Chapter 6, however, because the market and distribution are linked by incentives, this dividing of policy does not work as expected. Deposit insurance is a kind of redistributive system, but it clearly gives rise to opportunism—what is normally called moral hazard—and negative incentives. As is shown in the standard analytical model, under conditions of deposit insurance, the outcome of profit maximization on the part of banks is frequently bankruptcy, and this is the case in which the effects of redistribution as negative incentive are made evident.[43] In cases where there is such a negative incentive, the neoclassical combination of market and redistribution will be of no use. In many cases discretionary intervention would yield better results.

This mixing of policy objectives is not limited to safety-net policy. In the United States, various forms of financial regulation have been introduced since the Great Depression, and among these many have been designed to guarantee security and safeguard the interests of the individual, even at the sacrifice of competition in the market. Examples are regulation of interstate business, fields of business (as represented by the Glass-Steagall Act of 1933), and the deposit rate (known as Regulation Q). But no one can reasonably argue that this collection of regulations, accumulated through trial and error, provides the optimum mixture of competition and security. For example, since the securities firms invented money market mutual funds (MMMFs) in the 1980s, the regulatory divisions between banks and securities firms have become meaningless and are being abolished. Theoretically, however, it is impossible to decide which of the three plans being considered as replacements—the EC model of the universal bank, the U.S. model of the bank holding company, or the Japanese model of the bank as quasi-parent firm—is superior.[44] Bank holding companies are still supported in the United States at present, but we should recall that they have frequently been criticized severely since the Great Depression, during which period the efforts to enact or revise the regulatory laws have sometimes been active and sometimes not.[45] In the future, it is quite possible that there will be a resurgence of regulatory activity toward the bank holding companies that have incorporated securities business. This variety in regulation, particularly the great wavering in regulatory activity seen in the United States, speaks to the difficulty of regulating the financial industry and the absence of a consensus on the best course to follow.

There can be no clear, universal solution to informational asymmetry. As is apparent in the different responses of Europe, the United States, and Japan in dealing with the abolition of regulatory divisions within the financial industry, the financial system reflects differences in historical experience. The universal bank model in Europe, particularly in Germany, is a tradition stretching back to the nineteenth century. The bank holding company in the United States emerged rapidly in the 1930s in response to state-level regulation, which valued state autonomy. Japanese banks as quasi-parent firms are a product of the antitrust law introduced by the Allied occupation (its provisions prohibiting holding companies). In short, these outcomes are due to a significant extent to differences in historical conditions, which may even be accidental.

In any case, the superiority or inferiority of these financial systems cannot be decided on the basis of which is the most economically liberal. For example, it is untenable to argue that, as a safety net, the deposit insurance system in the United States is more liberal than the Japanese system. Everyday government intervention may be more prevalent in Japan, but the impact of the government's decision whether to rescue a bankrupt bank is stronger in the United States. What is most decisive is whether the federal government will provide financial support to the insurance system. This decision is made by discretion, not by rules. It is also impossible to judge which is the most economically liberal of the three responses to the abolition of regulatory divisions of the financial industry. We have no choice but to recognize international differences in financial systems.

THE INFLUENCE OF INTERNATIONALIZATION

This is not the end of the story. The financial industry is not characterized only by "information asymmetry"; it has other distinctive characteristics as well. Today, two of the most significant are the trends toward globalization and securitization, which in the broad sense have a similar structure. Put simply, money (or, more precisely, financial assets) crosses national boundaries because it is the asset with the most power to overcome barriers between assets. Financial assets flow through all the cracks. Or rather, one should say that by discovering all the loopholes, they invade other territories. In the 1970s and 1980s the United States discovered such loopholes, created new opportunities, and became the stage for a huge contest to acquire large fortunes. For example, large numbers of new financial products, such as certificates of deposit, sales of loans, and MMMFs were created during this period.

What matters in the world of finance is not national boundaries but differences in institutions of law, tax, and customs; as long as there are institutions, there will be the chance of financial profit through exploiting these differences. The most recent important examples of this are the so-called offshore markets, such as the Euro-dollar market, which have become huge, avoiding any country's taxes on interest income. As the flow of capital to these markets increased, they set interest rates and thus became increasing stable. But we should recall that during the initial period these markets had substantial destabilizing effects on the financial industries and capital markets around the world. Recently, the Euro-dollar market ceased to be a topic of concern or discussion, but this does not mean that the trend toward a borderless economy has disappeared. For example, "interest rate swaps," which have become firmly established recently, are the trading of rights to future interest earnings on bonds (the securitization of bond earnings); it now no longer matters in which currency a bond is denominated. Without transferring the substance of financial assets, financial influence is crossing national borders. Perhaps there are no longer financial national boundaries. This cannot but cause the earning of profits through exploiting differences in institutions. (This too is rent-seeking.)

The reach of securitization goes even further. Financial instruments are many and diverse, and their various creditor-debtor "derivatives" become the object of financial transactions. The very fact that there is a creditor-debtor relationship itself becomes the object of financial transactions. This is a world of what one could call meta-securitization. If the world economy continues to develop, disequilibrium will become the normal state of affairs, and some will attempt to securitize it for profit. If this trend continues, the financial industry will become awash with countless technological innovations, where the increasing returns to scale of spreading risk play an ever more important role. If this happens, it will become an industry with increasing returns—that is, decreasing cost—and the large financial institutions will devote themselves solely to increasing the scale and scope of their activities. International cooperation in an industrial policy for finance may well become necessary. In any case, the future of each country's economy will be significantly affected by ongoing trends in the financial industry.

THE DESIRABLE FINANCIAL POLICY FOR JAPAN

What policy should one adopt in dealing with this situation? If one considers the stability of the domestic economy as primary, one could imagine binding the domestic financial system in a web of informal, discretionary regulations to ward off all foreign financial influence—in other words, isolating the economy. The past behavior of the Japanese financial authorities has been of this type. But should Japan now adopt this pattern of response? My answer, based on the rules of polymorphic economic liberalism, is that such a response would be a mistake. Each country's rules can differ from others', and thus Japan can have cross-shareholding and the United States holding companies. Foreigners who want to do business within the country should be given "resident treatment" and not discriminated against ("transparency" in the implementation of laws will follow from this). Abolishing the licensing system, or making approval for licenses automatic, is necessary to guarantee such treatment. Of course, a system that does not provide "resident treatment" to foreigners is a de facto closed system. Japan today cannot be allowed to have such a closed system because it is not still in an early stage of development in which foreigners could dominate the domestic economy.

The regulations to date of Japan's financial authorities do not respond adequately to the demands for "resident treatment," which is essential for openness. This does not mean that various current regulations in themselves are less desirable than those of the United States and Germany. There is a high possibility that such international disparities in regulations will soon be reduced, but for the time being differences between each country's regulatory methods are unavoidable. The problem is whether these regulations are applied equally to foreign firms (firms with their head offices in foreign countries). If such firms are accorded "resident treatment," one cannot rely on the current practices of the closed regulatory system. Foreigners do not operate on the basis of trust and harmony to the same degree that Japanese firms do. On the other hand, it will not be easy for Japanese financial institutions to part with existing intraindustry and intra-*keiretsu* practices.

For example, both the Recruit scandal of 1986, involving the distribution of newly issued shares before they were offered for sale on the stock market, and the compensation in the early 1990s provided by Nomura and other securities firms for losses of specific clients were nothing more than an unsavory legacy of past practices of the securities market. The *amakudari* of bureaucrats to financial institutions is a payoff for their past relationship and is only one step short of bribery.[46] To give "resident treatment" to foreign firms would mean that all practices become transparent to everyone and implicit regulations would become ineffective. The influence of the authority in administering the permit and licensing system remains strongest in the financial industry. The United States also has regulations, but as long as the laws are obeyed, its permit and licensing system works automatically. If Japan's financial firms are to continue to seek investment opportunities overseas, Japan cannot continue to be allowed to persist in its self-serving policy of "regulation at home, freedom abroad."

The problem is even more difficult. If there are differences between the rules in each country, or to put it directly, in each important financial center, then financial transactions may well flourish in the cracks thus created. Therefore, the financial rules will have to become uniform at least in the three great financial centers. Clearly, there are two choices: to completely deny foreign entry and preserve as much as possible the lack of transparency, or to permit foreign entry and provide foreigners the same treatment as residents. There can be no middle course because the unstable dynamic of the financial industry will not allow it. Once a hole opens in the dike, there will be changes in the financial structure, and at times there could be major changes affecting the entire world.

Exporting large amounts of capital while keeping one's country closed to the outside is nowadays no more thinkable than completely closing one's country. Both choices are impossible in terms of international politics. This means that the only choice for Japan is to allow free entry into its financial industry, to clarify domestic financial rules, and above all to minimize its permit and licensing system. This course should be followed with regard to all industries, but it is particularly necessary in the financial industry because of its unique character. However, this does not mean that Japan's domestic financial rules should be made to conform to those of the United States. There is no need to legally prohibit *keiretsu*, but any foreign entrant must be treated in the same manner as residents. The changes suggested above will serve as a beachhead for the rule of polymorphic economic liberalism.

As was shown in the above examples, the rules of economic liberalism allow a number of variations. This is necessary if each country's traditional methods are to be made harmonious with the rules of economic liberalism—a difficult task. If we avoid this task, however, we will not be able to create economic rules between the advanced countries, and an international economic order will be impossible. Such an international order, starting from equal treatment for all, however, may well ultimately differ from the classical ideal and be somewhat different from what the United States now considers to be the rule. The characteristics of an age of polymorphic economic liberalism will necessarily differ from those of the present classical economic liberalism. The Japanese must do their best to abandon their current practices and contribute to the creation of the new rule. Going one step further, I believe that there is a need to construct a uniform set of rules for international finance, even if some countries have to be persuaded to do so. I would like to see Japan exhibit sufficient interest in this effort and take the initiative at least in organizing a conference to begin the necessary task. A major prerequisite for Japan to be able to assume such a role perhaps is to abolish the implicit and usually unwritten administrative guidance and to demonstrate its willingness to accept the scrutiny of an impartial international body (such as an international securities and exchange commission). In any case, if there is to be any visible progress in the difficult task of harmonizing the rules, it will begin in the financial industry, and particularly among its three centers in New York, London, and Tokyo.

A Critique of Democracy: Freedom and Equality

The importance of the questions I have raised in this book for the contemporary world depends on the workings of liberal democracy, or more accurately, parliamentary democracy, in each country. Broadly speaking, I have proposed the realization of two ideas—the rule of polymorphic economic liberalism, and overlapping security alliances. But the political system to which the duties of realizing these ideas must be entrusted is clearly, at present, none other than parliamentary democracy, and it will not be easy for parliamentary democracy to discharge these duties. If the parliamentary democracies, particularly the great powers, continue to fail in dealing with these issues, a worldwide crisis that I have not even attempted to describe will begin to unfold. Where this crisis might lead is clearly even more difficult to foretell than progress premised on the hope that parliamentary democracy will respond to the duties it must perform. Thus placing our hope in parliamentary democracy, let me point out what I believe are its weaknesses and suggest ways it could be strengthened.

In this book I have taken liberalism as the basic premise. I have called an economic system based on this premise polymorphic economic liberalism. What form should a liberal domestic political system take? To recapitulate, to be "liberal" in this book means to respect and value the unceasing efforts of human beings in remaking their image of the world. I have called this effort of creating new images, among other things, "reflection" in the broad sense, self-reference, and reinterpreting the world. Thus, given that only individuals themselves can act as the creators and remakers of the image, liberalism is also an "individualism" that respects the individuals creating and remaking the image of the world. By "individual" I do not mean an isolated or self-sufficient individual, but one who exchanges views and debates with others in forming an image of the world, and who has inherited a historical wisdom. True liberalism must be an individualism rooted in a shared view of the world.

The question raised above—what form should liberalism of a domestic political system take?—can be rephrased as follows. What institutions produce the decision of a society from the various images, opinions, and ideas held by individuals? Clearly, there is no single answer to this question. Political institutions, or at least liberal political institutions, are not simply a mechanism for aggregating individuals' pursuit of their own interests; they must be institutions that attempt to discover points of agreement among the collection of their worldviews. Various institutions can respond to the basic demands of liberalism, yet they are all in their own way incomplete. The unquestioned choice of a single liberal set of institutions would be contrary to liberalism itself, because being able to "remake" any set of institutions is what freedom means. Liberal democracy (in its specific form, parliamentary democracy) is an example of such an incomplete political institution. Parliamentary democracy in each country is only one of its many possible variants.

LIBERALISM AND DEMOCRACY

Since ancient times, there have been many debates about political institutions. This was especially true in regions where many states coexisted and a choice among several types of institutions was possible, as in China during the warring states period, Greece during the city-state period, and Europe at the birth of the nation-state.[47] For example, the Hundred Schools of philosophy in China included various political ideologies, from the government of the wise (Confucianist) to a kind of democracy. But their theories of institutions seem not to have been sufficiently systematic. In the classical age, it was Aristotle who excelled in systematization. He attempted a theory of institution that divided political institutions into three types—monarchy, aristocracy, and democracy—and this theory was subsequently inherited by John Locke and Jean-Jacques Rousseau.[48] What was common to all these classical theories of political institutions was, on the one hand, a lament that an ideal monarch or leader did not exist, and on the other, a strong skepticism about democratic government. Locke, Rousseau, and John Stuart Mill, the founders of modern parliamentary democracy, also shared this concern.

Democracy, the combination of *demos* and *kratia*, means the people (*demos*) having the power (*kratia*) of decision. And as a matter of experience, its only form has been the system of majority decision. Thus democracy is normally thought of as election and decision by majority vote. Hans Kelsen, an empiricist and legal scholar, declared that democracy is nothing more than the formal process of election.[49] At least as it was originally understood, however, a system of majority decision was not simply a system in which voting took place and votes were counted. Before the voting, there was supposed to be some debate, and voting was meant to take place after one had learned new things and possibly even changed one's opinions in response to the debate. A mechanical system of majority decision, in which people's opinions were considered to be uninfluenced by debate, would not be in the interest of the society but would become an aggregation of self-interest. In such a system even the wisest individuals would naturally be preoccupied with their own immediate interests; a people who did not learn the lessons of history or understand others' opinions would find it impossible to rise above a narrow concern for their own welfare. Thus a mechanical system of majority decision would enable the majority (by uniting in a faction) to gain private benefit. In other words, it would be a mechanism for achieving not only individual equality of opportunity to vote but also equality of outcome in what individuals received. Larger social or long-term interests would be forgotten, and the democratic society would deteriorate.

Here let us return to the earlier question of liberalism. When society's view clashes with one's own image of the world, one *might* choose to express one's own opinion in the voting. This is nothing other than a demand for freedom of thought. (I say "might" because not to express oneself is also a kind of freedom of thought.) Liberalism in this sense is to provide at all times and to everyone the opportunity to participate, or in other words, to accommodate a demand for equality of opportunity. In the main, equality of opportunity is an indispensable attribute of liberalism, although as I note below, there are various interpretations of "opportunity." Thus liberal political institutions must be "democratic," in the weak sense of being open to anybody's participation.

This does not necessarily mean, however, that a system of majority decision is the essence of liberalism; in fact, the system is nothing more than a convenience, adopted for lack of an ability to devise a better system. Since ancient times, many have made this observation. In this century, Hayek said: "While individualism affirms that all government should be democratic, it has no superstitious belief in the omnicompetence of majority decisions, and in particular it refuses to admit that 'absolute power may, by the hypothesis of popular origin, be as legitimate as constitutional freedom . . .'; and it is particularly opposed to the most fateful and dangerous of all current misconceptions of democracy—the belief that we must accept as true and binding for future development the views of the majority."[50]

As Hayek notes, from the standpoint of individuals, or liberalism as I am using the term, what is important is that, at the same time that there is a sphere that can be controlled by majority decision, there is a sphere in which majority opinion must on no account intervene. The most important example of this is freedom in the expression of thought. It is often asked whether one should also provide freedom to thought that denies freedom of thought. The answer can only be "of course." Although thought that denies freedom of thought disrupts the dynamic of free thought, allowing its free expression is the essence of liberalism. Majority decision can have nothing to do with what we call the sphere of human rights, including freedom of thought. The need for restrictions on the spheres into which a system of majority decision can intrude seems to be comparatively well understood.

Where understanding is comparatively lacking is that liberalism is in principle incompatible with a mechanical system of majority decision that is not accompanied by adequate debate. Remaking one's own worldview, reflecting self-referentially to do so, and reinterpreting the world are the meaning of having freedom. In encountering others' opinions and confronting one's own deficiencies, one recaptures the value of human beings as human beings. A system of majority decision is liberal when debate plays an essential role. If democracy becomes a mechanical system of majority decision, in which debate is regarded as of secondary importance, liberalism and democracy will become conflicting ideas. Liberal democracy, in the sense that it contains this possibility of confrontation, is nothing more than compromise. This is symbolized in the confrontation between equality of opportunity and equality of outcome. A mechanical system of majority decision is transformed into a tool for equality of outcome. Although liberalism acknowledges equality of opportunity, it has no connection to equality of outcome. It is not that it rejects equality of outcome but that it has no interest in it.

In the realities of political history, the relationship between liberalism and democracy, freedom and equality, has passed through various phases, ranging from confrontation to harmony. In principle, what should the relationship be between freedom and equality? A common answer is that both are necessary. Certainly there are circumstances in which this answer is correct. For example, proscriptions such as status systems and racially discriminatory laws forbid the participation and the advocacy of interests of those outside a particular class, restrict expressive action, and create inequality of opportunity. Such proscriptions clearly prevent equality of opportunity and thus injure freedom. It was under such conditions that the concepts of freedom and equality were always proclaimed together, and won people's consensual support, in the charters of the "citizens' revolutions," beginning with the French Revolution. (In this connection, it is worth noting that a third concept of fraternity was proclaimed together with freedom and equality.)

In a stage when there remain status systems and racially discriminatory laws, the demand for freedom and the demand for equality can coexist. Eighteenth-century thinkers such as Locke, Rousseau, and James Madison, who battled with discrimination based on status or rank, for the most part thought in terms of this coexistence. However, in doing so, they were strongly concerned about the forum for debate being lost and democracy deteriorating. For example, what Locke had in mind was a society of "reasonable people" where debate was possible, and he clearly considered education and property (the rights of ownership) to be requirements for membership;[51] that is, he advocated a restricted electoral system. Rousseau, in *The Social Contract*, also strongly warned of the danger of democratic government degenerating into mob politics: "If there were a nation of Gods, it would govern itself democratically. A nation so perfect is not suited to men."[52]

DEMOCRATIZATION IN THE NINETEENTH CENTURY

The period during which freedom and equality were assumed to co-exist did not last long. The industrial societies of Europe, which began in the eighteenth century, required large, mobile labor forces and a spirit of creative entrepreneurship and had no choice but to provide freedom across a broad range of action (interregional mobility, changes of occupation, and creation of productive units of many types) to all social classes. The result was that large numbers of individuals, as never before, enjoyed freedom of action and demanded a freedom no less than that accorded to others. The force that expanded this freedom of action for an ever-increasing number of the populace was ultimately no more than a desire for material gain. To paraphrase Jacob Burckhardt, who foresaw the coming of the mass society, an age of unlimited, furious trade and communications had begun, repeating the pattern of England.[53] But this freedom of action was a bitter victory for most of the "mass" because it was frequently accompanied by poverty and a loss of dignity. Resulting from this were social instability and increasing political discontent among the newly emerged working class. In order to deal with this situation, the government in each country, in the latter half of the nineteenth century, had no choice but to adopt some policies for "equality of outcome," policies that are today called income redistribution and welfare policies. In Britain, various pieces of social legislation were successively enacted and repealed. In late-developing countries such as Germany, social legislation was adopted more systematically. In other words, various prescriptions were attempted, from those of Robert Owen to those of Otto von Bismarck. Perhaps on middle ground was John Stuart Mill, who theorized a path of compromise leading to equality of opportunity by separating the issue of production and the issue of distribution. This was the beginning of the neoclassical theory of distribution.

Furthermore, as emphasized in Chapter 2, the wars between nation-states necessitated the creation of national armies and the emergence of patriotism. Industrialization and nationalism required mobilization of the masses and made inevitable both a rapid increase in political participation (universal suffrage) and an equalization of economic distribution. Conservative administrations in each country already could no longer defend the principle of restricted suffrage, with education and ownership of a certain amount of property as its requirements. The nationalist movements laid the groundwork for a politics of "mass autocracy." Thus the preeminence of democracy was established under the pressures of industrialization and nationalism. The linkage between the liberalism of a system and majority decision premised on debate grew increasingly weaker as democracy advanced.

Soon, in the latter half of the nineteenth century, the critique of inequality became the dominant voice, and the argument that inequality brought about deficiencies in freedom grew stronger. To some extent this argument is true. During this period, discriminatory systems still remained, beginning with restrictions on suffrage and the education system, divided by class. It is precisely in those cases where equality of opportunity is lost through a discriminatory system that equalization of opportunity can be the path toward freedom. This argument, however, also can be extended indefinitely. For example, the argument can be made that, even if the right to vote is provided, participation in politics is not equal if some have more resources than others to support the candidates of their choice. And it can be argued that even if school entrance is determined by perfectly competitive examination, poor people are disadvantaged by their home and social environments, and thus educational opportunity is unequal. This reasoning leads to the conclusion that equality of opportunity is virtually identical to equality of outcome. But at least in those social systems with which we are familiar, guaranteeing equality of outcome requires extensive as well as intensive government intervention. A market economy, however, is a system in which unequal outcomes are inevitable; thus, if we pursue the argument based on the theory of equal opportunity to its logical conclusion, we will not be able to expect a solution in our existing social system.

On this point, Marxism follows this logic to its conclusion. Freedom is impossible in a capitalism of exploitation that structurally incorporates inequality of outcome. Democracy based on debate or persuasion between different social classes is in essence impossible, and the success of so-called bourgeois democracy is impossible. Finally, it is the private interests of the working class who are the majority that is "society's interest," and the efforts of the capitalist class to suppress this interest will eventually be overcome to establish true democracy. The revolution and subsequent dictatorship of the proletariat are the realization of a true democracy in which no room for debate exists. Because of such facts as the rejection of debate, the victory of majority decision, and the victory of private interests, socialism is the final form of a mechanical system of majority decision, and in this very fact the structure of the confrontation between liberalism and democracy is fully exposed. Thus the trend toward democratization accelerated still further with the beginning of the twentieth century, and Marxism's use of the concept of class struggle as its principal weapon to achieve the equality of outcome inflicted a mortal wound on the democracy of debate.

As equality of outcome becomes an increasingly dominating objective, all other objectives fall by the wayside and it soon becomes the sole goal to be achieved in an ever more literal and strict sense. Thus, even supposing that an assessment (by some external standard) is made to the effect that differences in the standard of living or in educational standards have narrowed, this is not yet likely to be regarded as achievement of the goal. Even though these standards rise, the demands for equality will continue. With increases in income and knowledge, the consciousness of disparities rises even further to sustain the demands for equality. But to let equality itself become the objective is very close to justifying the primitive emotions of jealousy and envy. A democracy of interests is transformed into a democracy of emotions.

Perfect equality of outcome is impossible. Certainly there have been ages in which discriminatory restrictions have created and maintained inequality, but if such restrictions are removed beyond a certain extent, then subsequent restrictions for equality soon become necessary. As long as there are differences between human beings, there is no likelihood of naturally achieving a perfect state of equality without discretionary restrictions, whatever the social system. And as long as we are preoccupied with equality of outcome, the definition of equality will become polymorphous and complex, causing the necessary restrictions to become detailed and complex. Again, whether a certain, specific restriction promotes or hinders equality will become a troublesome and protracted debate because the views on the complex workings of the social system often differ substantively. (For example, will so-called reverse discrimination on behalf of minorities and women eliminate discrimination against them in the long term?) It will be leaders' judgment, and in fact bureaucrats' discretion, that will determine how specific restrictions are interpreted and enforced.

In a sense, life in the former Soviet society was equal, and in another sense it was extremely unequal. The communist bureaucracy determined these outcomes. Its dictatorship emasculated even the pettiest freedom of action. In such a situation, however "freedom" is defined, the dilemma between equality and freedom continues to persist. Even supposing that one were not overly insistent on a liberal viewpoint, one could not believe that human beings live only for equality. Human beings would surely not be satisfied in a society of clones.

Thus, during the period since the objectives of the nineteenth-century "citizens' revolution" were, to some extent, achieved, the dilemma of freedom and equality has become a problem that cannot be ignored, and democratic equality has become a predominant ideal. What Karl Mannheim called the trend toward "fundamental democratization" has been established as an indivisible element of the twentieth century. In 1934 Mannheim said: "Today a growing number of social groups strive for a share in social and political control and demand that their own interests be represented."[54] Clearly he had in mind the Nazi and communist dictatorships (before the publication of the work cited here, he was expelled from Nazi Germany), but he called these political systems "negative democratization," considering them to be a pathological subversion of democracy through the "irrationality" of the masses. His prescription for this pathological phenomenon was a revival of democracy through the return of rationality, but there are still problems with such a progressive proposal; as in all social democracies, the problem is what "rationality" is. It is clear, though, that even Mannheim considered the Nazi and communist dictatorships to be a result of democracy. One could include with these the system of military rule in Japan. What can be seen in the authoritarian system that emerged in the 1930s, however, is not a lack of democracy, even if it is a shortage of liberalism.

MASS DEMOCRACY FOLLOWING THE SECOND WORLD WAR

During the first half of the postwar period until the 1970s the many social democratic governments adopted progressive policies in their introduction of planning. In other words, in this period the ideas that determined policy, even in conservative governments, were progressive; that is, it was an age of policy-based progressivism. Of course, the West during the postwar period strongly opposed economic planning and one-party dictatorship of Soviet-style socialism and denounced the lack of "freedom" in the East. At the same time, in order to oppose the East, the policies the West adopted were intended to correct the "excesses" of freedom in the market (capitalism) and to emphasize the concept of equality. These took concrete form in Keynesian unemployment policies (effective demand management) and welfare state policies aimed at equality. Though freedom was the ostensible goal, it was instead government intervention and equality that played predominant roles in policy formulation, and one result was the appearance of big government.

Any number of factors were related to this postwar trend toward progressivism. First, of course, was the long-term trend toward fundamental democratization. One could say, as Mannheim, for example, suggested, that postwar progressivism attempted to overcome the various interwar trends toward "negative democratization" by moving toward democratic socialism. Second, the political influence of the Second World War worked to strengthen the trend toward fundamental democratization. In one respect, the general mobilization seen in the war led to the adoption of various egalitarian policies that shaped postwar policy in defeated countries such as Japan as well as in Britain. For example, the War Cabinet in Britain, as compensation for the cooperation of the Labour party and the colonies, promised social insurance and colonial emancipation after the war, and this substantially determined the course of postwar Britain. One should also mention the direct influence of the East-West confrontation, for example, in competition over living standards.

I particularly want to point out the unique economic conditions in the postwar period of high growth until the 1970s. As noted earlier, this period was the latter phase of a half century of maturation of the twentieth-century system during which the growth of high mass consumption was the main driving force enabling the Western world to maintain remarkable high growth. The growth rate in per capita income (that is, the material standard of living) reached perhaps the highest levels in human history, and the growth rates of trade were even higher, which helped increase global economic interdependence to an unprecedented level. The key phrase, closely linked with this epochal high growth, is "high mass consumption." That is, on the demand side the postwar pattern of development was supported by the full-scale spread of consumer durables such as cars, home electrical appliances, and electronic products, and on the supply side by more effective adaptation, larger-scale uses, and systematization of existing technologies. The technological preparation for this had already been made to a substantial extent in the first half of the twentieth century. For example, technologies for such products as the automobile, radio, television, and air conditioner had all (with the exception of color television) been discovered before the war. Since I have already discussed this point, I only reemphasize that high mass consumption was consumption of consumer durables that were neither necessities nor luxuries but somewhere between the two.

Equalizing income distribution among the masses (the whole population) is effective in increasing demand for such consumer durables. If this is done, a vast number earning the average income or near it become the buyers of these products. For this mass market, electrical appliances and cars of a certain type and quality can be mass produced. Such a homogenized lifestyle strengthens still further the psychological impetus to "keep up with the Joneses" and sustains the slow but steady shift in demand toward higher quality consumer durables.

Thus, one of the main policies supporting high mass consumption was the policy of equalizing distribution, particularly establishing workers' share in the distribution of the benefits of technological progress. Even for conservative governments, which are usually skeptical of equality, the economic benefits of a policy of equalizing distribution became impossible to ignore. In every country, the effects of the pattern of income distribution on demand became a constant topic in economic planning and government white papers. To say that conservative governments consciously pursued such policies is perhaps going too far, but if as a result of their having adopted equalization policies, however reluctantly, mass demand became dependable at all times, firms continued to earn good profits, and the economy as a whole remained prosperous, there was no reason not to continue such policies. During the decades immediately following the end of the Second World War, policies of distribution equalization and economic growth were compatible and even mutually reinforcing. Generally, though, these two policies are not always compatible. What allowed them to be compatible were the unique conditions of the latter phase of a half-century cycle of maturation.

Similar observations can be made regarding Keynesian policies. Conservative governments have no reason to oppose improving the business climate, even if they must temporarily forget the principles of classical economic liberalism. There were, however, substantial problems in J. M. Keynes's original policy proposals. For example, even if one attempts to stimulate the economy through large-scale public investment, such investment will have to continue indefinitely (at an increasing rate if one hopes for growth), unless there is a so-called priming effect that induces private investment. But because private investment depends on the long-term outlook and the social psychology it is not certain that the desired effect will occur. If it does not, implementing a Keynesian policy will cause the national debt to rise. In cases where there is a structural trend toward recession in the economy, as before the war, the benefit of such a policy will be limited to providing a brief boost to the economy.

The success of Keynesian policies in the postwar period was due not to large-scale investment that could easily increase debt but to the structure of demand (demand could be easily generated) and to preserving the principle of fine tuning, in the form of reducing budget surplus by reducing taxes and lowering the official discount rate. Keynes himself would surely have been skeptical of tax reductions under a balanced budget and the reduction of the discount rate as a means of stimulating investment. In the unique conditions of the 1950s and 1960s, however, there was a huge potential for an explosion in high mass consumption and related investment that could be triggered by tax reductions and a decrease in the official discount rate to bring about favorable economic conditions quite easily. This was adopting a Keynesian-style policy in a non-Keynesian situation to help achieve steady growth.

When the pattern of distributing the gains of technological progress to workers becomes established, the workers' demands will turn toward consumer durables and begin a series of linked expansions. The proportion of consumer durables in consumer spending will increase, becoming the most important item. For Karl Marx and David Ricardo, workers commuting by car, storing the food they have bought in supermarkets in large refrigerators, wearing neat, clean clothes every day, talking over the telephone, and enjoying the communication of images on television would have been quite unimaginable. Although consumer durables can be viewed as things that meet human beings' biological needs, they are not indispensable to existence. They are the product of the socialization to a particular mode of living, and this mode has been established on the interdependence of people's images of the world. To borrow terms used by economists, the elements of interdependent consumption, demonstration effects, and conspicuous consumption are essential pillars of high mass consumption. These pillars refer not simply to a world of things but to a world of images.

The logic of industrialization on the twentieth-century model achieved remarkable success and has accelerated equality of outcome. But as a result, private interests have begun to exercise their right to veto, and a trend has increased toward a mechanical system of majority decision, with no debate, dominated by the majority who are the "weak." This was the typical state of affairs in the advanced industrial countries in the third quarter of the twentieth century, when there was a high rate of economic growth and egalitarianism of outcome could be achieved comparatively easily. In the final quarter of this century, when demand and technology reached their saturation point, the progressive postwar policies collapsed and neo-conservatism emerged as a remedy for all that was ailing the advanced industrial economies.

THE DEVELOPMENTALIST, EGALITARIAN SOCIETY

The structure of high mass consumption particular to the first half of the postwar period and the constant technological innovation that supported it have brought the twentieth century to an end. The nineteenth-century mixture of industrialization and fundamental democratization reacted and became linked more securely, and these trends themselves underwent internal transformations. Throughout the latter half of the twentieth century these transformations gradually progressed, and super-industrialization is about to emerge. Since I discuss superindustrialization below, here let me consider the transformation to date, linking it to the developmentalism that emerged in the late-developing countries. To borrow the words of Carl Schmitt's remarkable, prophetic essay of 1929, this transformation was a change from the "industrialism" of the nineteenth century to the "technologism" of the twentieth.

> The belief in technology that is spreading at present is based on the belief that we have discovered ultimate, absolute, neutral. . . . Certainly there seems to be nothing as neutral as technology. . . . Technology serves thousands of people . . . regardless of nation, race, class, creed, generation, or sex. . . . And since this is the case, it seems we could say this is the basis for a universal reconciliation. . . . The neutrality of technology, though, is different from the neutrality of the existing disciplines [meaning theology, metaphysics, Enlightenment thought, and economies]. Technology is always a tool, and can even be a weapon. It is something that serves thousands of people, and precisely because of this it is not neutral.[55]

In contrast to the nineteenth century, when it was thought that all problems were economic problems, in the twentieth century it is believed that technology can solve everything. To use the language of this book, this change is equivalent to the trough of the century-long wave cycle of industrialization. Schmitt discerned very early, in the 1920s, the subtle but important difference between the waves of the nineteenth and twentieth centuries and predicted the gravity of the problems the latter wave was to encounter. Below I discuss the anthropology of the impasse to which technologism is leading.

Signs of technologism have been seen in various countries. As noted in the discussion of Anglo-German rivalry in the previous chapter, this tendency was more noticeable in Germany than in Britain. The technologism of the Soviet Union was also feared by all countries. It was the United States, though, that was representative of this technologism, at least during its initial period. The mass production business, supported by "scientific management," was created in the United States, and many engineering technologies (including atomic energy) were first realized there too. But the United States had its fetters. To borrow Burckhardt's words, the United States arrived at technologism through an "Anglo-American compromise between Calvinistic pessimism in theory and ceaseless money-making in practice,"[56] but the tradition of Puritanism finally prevented technologism from being carried through to its logical conclusion. It is clear, however, that the United States was more technologist than the European countries.

But it is no exaggeration to say that Japan, in the latter half of the twentieth century, was the most earnest devotee of technologism and "discovered" industrial policy as a means of pursuing technologism. That this was possible was due to a unanimous decision that the advancement of technology was the key to recovering from the double handicap of being both a late-developing country and a nation defeated in war. That Japan could pursue such a course was largely due to its not being burdened by the history of a journey through the Enlightenment, industrialism, and technologism. Subsequently, the East Asian NIEs, having similar historical backgrounds, have also seen that technology is the key to catching up with the advanced countries. The policy of these East Asian countries, including Japan, has been to ignore the conventional classical understanding of industrialization, from the nineteenth century, and to push technologism to its limit. The United States took the lead in technologism, but Japan and East Asia are following in the footsteps of the United States and attempting to perfect it.

As I indicated in Chapter 6, developmentalism consists of industrial policy and a distributive policy, and the latter frequently takes the anti-neoclassical form of protection of and assistance for traditional industries such as agriculture and small and medium-sized business. As a result, in the East Asian NIEs and Japan, there have been few or no phenomena such as the emergence of huge slums in the megalopolises, the accumulation of persistent disguised unemployment, and the loss of dignity of workers. Those who refuse to see the realities of these countries frequently predict and warn of the danger of unequal distribution of income in East Asia. But in Korea, Taiwan, Hong Kong, and Singapore, as well as in the rapidly developing ASEAN countries (the Philippines may be an exception), the situation does not seem to suggest that the problem of distribution will become insurmountable. In the emerging societies of East Asia there is a high degree of economic equality, and the class structure has dissolved. When I noted this phenomenon in the 1980s as the emergence of a "new middle mass," a number of people were skeptical and, particularly in the West, many disagreed with the image of Japan as a society in which equality had advanced. However, the reality is as I described, and similar phenomena seem to be spreading throughout East Asia.[57]

In Japan the tendency toward "equalization of outcome" is evident, as seen in phenomena such as the smallness of intrafirm wage differentials, the broad egalitarianism manifested in many ways within the firm, and the keeping-up-with-the-Joneses pattern of consumption (interdependent consumption). There are influences here from the traditions of preindustrial society, but fundamentally much is due to developmentalist policies and management and the structure of high mass consumption they promoted. As noted in the previous section, developmentalist management in Japan was a means of dealing with constant technological innovation. Developmentalism is a system in which technologism is pursued successfully because attempts are also made continuously to limit distributive problems. Thus technologism and egalitarianism of outcome are linked by way of developmentalism. In the popular majority opinion, both technologism and egalitarianism of outcome are considered desirable and thus within the limits of this common view. Developmentalism is something to be welcomed.

However, technology is a tool, not a value. Technologism cannot be a system of values. When late-developing countries embark on technologism, there is present the higher value of nationalism. But when advanced countries such as Japan and the United States pursue technologism single-mindedly, it becomes a soulless monster. Other countries wonder whether they are aiming at world domination, with technological power replacing military power. The politics of technological domination, though, does not have the inspirational power to mobilize the masses. Thus the politics of countries that have nothing but technologism will be a soulless politics, perhaps becoming nothing more than the process of mediating various interests. Results of this are dilution of common values and the loss of forums for public debate. Tendencies emerge such that, politically, the principle of majority decision, which has forgotten debate, and the scramble for redistribution become predominant. The accumulation of political compromises continues. That until now these weaknesses in postwar Japanese politics have not become prevalent is largely due to the economic success of developmentalist policies and management. Large-scale redistributive policies (to achieve equality of outcome), such as aid to the agricultural sector and small and medium-sized firms, stability of employment, and rapid improvements in the welfare system, were made possible by the size of the surplus produced by economic growth. And that a consistency in policies was well preserved was largely due to the bureaucracy's having learned much from the experience of the advanced Western countries (including their failures).

Now, however, when economic growth has substantially slowed and there are no examples from which to learn, Japan is beginning to show latent deficiencies. Its present parliamentary politics shows tendencies of being on the one hand an aggregation of the interests of electoral districts, and becoming on the other an accumulation of ex post facto, ad hoc, temporary remedies. Given this kind of inertia, making any substantive change of the existing political system from a long-term perspective is extremely difficult. For a certain time, the method of the conservative politicians pushing policies proposed by bureaucrats through the Diet has worked well. Now, however, there is an increasing tendency for each ministry to be caught up in its particular organizational interests rather than actively devising new policies. The politicians, too, have become even more intent on reelection and thus are serving the interests of their electoral districts and sources of funding more eagerly.

This problem with Japan's politics at present is an example of a problem common to all advanced countries, and is in fact a problem connected to parliamentary democracy in general. Since the 1970s in the United States too, the evils of interest group liberalism have been frequently noted by Theodore Lowi and others.[58] Even in the Senate, which used to be considered the conscience of Congress, there is an increasing tendency toward mechanical democracy, as seen in the abolition of the custom of observing various privileges of the senior senators. The institution of the presidency has preserved the consistency of U.S. politics, but little exaggeration is involved in saying that it is at the mercy of the mass media; the fact that often less than 50 percent of the electorate chooses to vote indicates the danger that U.S. politics will become more and more a politics of emotions. European corporatist politics too—much of whose origins are in class warfare—may not be able to check the demands of what I am calling the "new middle mass" and faces the danger of adopting conflicting policies. In all these cases, there can be little expectation of a politics with any long-term consistency in its choices.

This deficiency in parliamentary democracy has long been predicted. The classical prescription for dealing with it has been the idea that those chosen by the electorate should not be delegates but representatives. Edmund Burke's speech to the electors of Bristol is perhaps the earliest example of this position, but the idea was also adopted in the French constitution of 1774 and was clearly theorized in J. S. Mill's *Considerations on Representative Government*.[59] Thus, it is no exaggeration to say that the present standard theory of parliamentary democracy has adopted the "representative principle" as one of its fundamental principles. For example, the Weimar Constitution (Article 20) stipulates it unusually clearly: "The Reichstag is composed of the representatives of the German people. The deputies are, each of them, representatives of the whole people. They are subject to their conscience alone and not bound by instructions." It is also not impossible to read Article 43 of the Japanese Constitution in this way. But that this "representative principle," so long respected, should still need to be debated shows that the classical prescription has not always been effective.

Can Japanese politics avoid the pitfalls I have indicated above? More specifically, can it actively tackle the steadily mounting issues of abolishing or substantially relaxing the permit and licensing system, promoting technology transfer, and cooperating in an international industrial policy? For Japan itself, I have already explained the necessity of abolishing the permit and licensing system and providing foreigners with "resident treatment," but controlling the organizational interests of the bureaucratic system (the ministries), which are becoming an obstacle in making these necessary changes, is also an issue for the political system because the bureaucratic system is not able to reform itself. To ensure that these issues will be solved, some kind of "political reform" is necessary. By political reform, however, I do not mean reforms to ensure politics free of dependence on money, concentrating on a system of small electoral districts and regulating political funding, as are being proposed at present. All political systems have their good and bad points. For example, the question of whether a system of proportional representation or a system of small electoral districts is better will never be settled in debates among political scientists. The problem is not money itself but electing people who are unduly influenced by money and/or excel in raising money. Were I to propose reforms, most important, I think, would be a drastic strengthening of the penalties against those involved in illegal electoral activities (including prosecution of a successful candidate whose campaign manager is implicated in the violation of election laws) and an increase in the annual salary and expense allowances for members of the Diet. As a result, one could perhaps expect the emergence of a new type of politician. But when one considers that it is the present members of the Diet who will be deciding on these reforms, one should not be overly optimistic about their prospects.

RECONSIDERING LIBERALISM

Throughout this book, I have tried to show that the two concepts of classical nationalism and classical economic liberalism no longer have the power to guide our age. A significant theme running through this argument has been the importance of technological development. In advancing the argument to this point, I must point out that its logic has been both necessary and at the same time inadequate. Certainly the historical role that constant technological progress has played has not been explicitly evaluated until now. This corresponds to the fact that capitalism (private property and the market economy) and industrialization (in which technological progress plays an important role) have not been distinguished—despite the fact that some have tried. For example, Fernand Braudel thought in terms of three layers: "capitalism," the "market economy," and the "structures of everyday life." His terminology is somewhat difficult to understand, but in brief, he contrasted the "market economy," a system of competitive economic exchange seen in many societies and historical stages, with "capitalism," a self-propagating system that includes elements of monopoly and speculation.[60] Carl Schmitt had a similar idea in mind in distinguishing between "industrialism" and "technologism." Although it is inconvenient that each analyst adopted different terminology, they share the attempt to distinguish between the market, which one could say is as old as history itself, and the self-propagating system that has emerged since the industrial revolution. They also seem to share the view that this difference is due to steady technological innovation.

To make this point clear, I have adopted a technology-centered argument in this book. The phenomena of decreasing costs generated by constant technological innovation and developmentalism as a policy to exploit it express most clearly the vigor of an industrialization that has progressed from a nineteenth-century system to a twentieth-century system, and correspond to the emergence of technologism. By emphasizing these, I have tried to make clear the momentum, and inertia, of 200 years of industrialization. Both classical nationalism and classical economic liberalism are not enough to explain this momentum. In this sense, one could say that the world system is lagging half a century or more behind its basic undercurrents and at most can only deal with the stages before technologism. If the only problem were the abdication of the classical ideal, the story could end here.

Ideas such as developmentalism, however, which I have brought forward as a critique of the classical concepts, contain a substantive problem that demands that the story continue. National and firm developmentalism are powerful manifestations of what I am here calling technologism, and in this sense Japan is perhaps the most technologist of countries. The problem is whether technologism is merely the unruly offspring of industrialism and thus nothing more than a transitional phase that must soon quickly disappear, or is itself becoming something that will support the twenty-first-century system (or at least superindustrialization). And this must be answered together with the question of how technologism should be evaluated from the perspective of genuine liberalism. Providing answers to such long-term questions is impossible and is not the goal of this book, which has been to analyze them in a medium-term perspective. To bring the argument to an end, though, let me here make a number of guesses from the perspective of the internal consistency of a long-term civilization.

Predicting the future map of civilization given only the materials now at hand is a complicated task. The paradigm of technologism / developmentalism is rising from the landscape of industrialization, but the phenomenon of superindustrialization appears to be an even higher peak to climb. In the background there is the still-higher mountain of transindustrialization, at times vaguely visible but often hidden in the mist.

The key concept in tracing this topography is perhaps not technology, but information, and information in the broadest sense. What I have called the information revolution has the latent capacity to go beyond technologism, bridging the gap from superindustrialization to transindustrialization. The phenomenon of the information revolution is now the driving force of superindustrialization, acting either symbiotically or parasitically; conversely it seems to possess the ability to drive humanity even beyond superindustrialization toward a society of transindustrialization. Aggressive opposing ideologies such as environmentalism or globe-as-resource-ism are often mentioned as transcending industrialization, but their corrosive power is probably much weaker than the power that will arise from within the information revolution.

Certainly technology is a kind of information, and technologism is a kind of information revolution. But information spreads even further than technology. Information is perhaps a part of what, in the broad sense, one could even call "knowledge." Reflecting, self-referencing human beings are always trying to transcend the self. Industrialization is perhaps no more than a manifestation of this process of self-transcendence. As long as human beings are human, there will surely be no end to this labor of self-transcendence. Human beings cannot but advance in this direction even not knowing what lies ahead.

The information revolution now appearing is a revolution in what I have called "instrumental information," and superindustrialization is advancing by means of its capabilities. It has already had a substantial impact, in all aspects of society. Even in its influence on economic aspects, its impact in some ways goes beyond our present powers of imagination. Phenomena such as product differentiation, which will likely emerge in many products and services that include information, and securitization, which will be seen in financial operations, go beyond our current understanding of the market and show a tendency one should perhaps call a kind of networking. Here the existing neoclassical framework (of general equilibrium analysis) becomes invalid and it becomes less meaningful to discuss the phenomenon of declining cost in each market. A network will appear with the differentiated markets (monopolistic markets, in the expression used to date) as its nodes, and the difference between economic exchange and social exchange (including political exchange) will become indistinct. With what we now think of as markets at the periphery (for example, the financial market) leading the way, there will be a restructuring of the economic and political systems. If this is the world of superindustrialization, with the revolution in instrumental information as its support, technology, which has been defined with a homogeneous market in mind, and developmentalism, as a means of dealing with technology, will have much reduced roles. Technologism and developmentalism must surely then become merely phenomena of the lean, transitional period leading to the twenty-first century. Japanese management, which is now at its peak, in its present form will not be exerting power around the globe in the twenty-first century.

It is certain that classical economic liberalism will become inappropriate as an economic principle under superindustrialization, but the form of liberalism that will replace it is perhaps beyond our present powers of imagination. The polymorphic economic liberalism proposed in this book is no more than a plan with which to negotiate the transitional period. But if it is a plan for the transitional period, with no connection to the future, it loses all meaning. To return to the argument of Chapter 1, human beings are animals who cannot exist without freedom in the broad sense. But the significance of this has been that human beings are always changing their images of the world, through intercourse with others in the past and present. Included in this process at a fundamental level is the element of a sense of "pleasure, beauty, and truth" in sharing information with others. That is, information is not only "instrumental," but expands into something "consummatory." With the development of the means of the revolution in "instrumental information" now being attempted, and the increasing interest in information, there will also be increasing interest in consummatory information, or more understandably, such things as wisdom and sensibilities.

The change from industrialism to technologism is linked to the change from technologism to informationalism, and informationalism may become a fundamental human occupation that cannot merely be called an -ism. This series of changes could also be called the chain of transformations from economic liberalism to technological liberalism to informational liberalism. The development from economy to technology to information is in a sense a process of abstraction and generalization. If this is the case, we may come to speak of this process as a detour by which liberalism reached a better stage.

This process is not likely to move forward easily, but in it there is clearly one basic theme: the forum for individual exchange will move from an exchange of things to a mutual understanding of systems that produce things (technology), and subsequently to an understanding of systems that understand systems (information). This is a path of universalization expanding outward, and it is also a path of enrichment within. Without a capacity to incorporate its various elements, the future world system will not be established. This applies to the argument for polymorphic economic liberalism and, more specifically, to the friction between Japan and the United States. We must grope our way toward a single set of rules that can incorporate heterogeneity. There are many difficult issues ahead, such as questions of institutions and politics, but our touchstone for the twenty-first century is surely understanding between cultures.

CHAPTER 10

Understanding "Understanding"

Three Types of Cultural Explanation

TOWARD A GENERAL FRAMEWORK

At the end of the previous chapter, I emphasized the importance of different cultures understanding each other. But what is "understanding"? So far in this book, this question has been always in the background. The themes to this point—conservatism versus progressivism, true liberalism, anthropocentrism, justice and rules, commensurability, knowledge and information, a unitary versus a pluralistic view of history, classical economic liberalism and polymorphic economic liberalism, liberalism and democracy—are all connected at a profound level to "understanding." It is difficult, though, to deal with this question fairly from a sufficiently broad perspective. The main current of Western thought, which has dominated the early modern and modern periods over the past 500 years, has had a strong inclination toward enlightenment and progressivism, in which humanity will in the end achieve a single true understanding and build a just society. It has considered that the logical or rational understanding of enlightenment is the true understanding; but this way of thinking must now itself be made the object of criticism. An unusual breadth of vision is demanded of anyone attempting such an undertaking.

At present there is substantial proof that people are less than satisfied with enlightenment rationality and progressive thought. To probe what is unsatisfying, we must establish a perspective that goes beyond this modern rationality. Among the thinkers of the past who took varying positions on modern rationality, there are on one side the countless giants of rationalism from René Descartes to Gottfried Wilhelm Leibniz, Baruch Spinoza, and Isaac Newton who have embellished the intellectual history of the modern age; on the other are the always-present minority who opposed this mainstream viewpoint, including such first-rate thinkers as Giambattista Vico, David Hume, Edmund Burke, Alexis de Tocqueville, Jacob Burckhardt, Wilhelm Dilthey, José Ortega y Gasset, Friedrich von Hayek, and Georg Gadamer. To pinpoint what those in this minority actually had in common would be to discover a new way forward, but doing so is difficult. To define them negatively as being antiprogressive and antirationalist is clearly inadequate. What is required for a positive definition is nothing other than a reconsideration of the conceptual framework in the most fundamental sense.

Even in Europe itself, attempts to reconceptualize the basic framework began at the end of the nineteenth century. One could say that Cartesianism (as I note below) has been representative of modern thought, but since the end of the nineteenth century, even in the West, there seem to have emerged a series of philosophical positions that are anti-Cartesianism. The first among them was the phenomenology of Edmund Husserl. His methodological position, at least, was anti-Cartesian in trying to analyze the condition in which there is not yet any distinction between subject and object. Martin Heidegger amplified Husserl's phenomenology to suggest a "hermeneutik des Daseins," but not stopping with this, he called the condition of a humanity that could not be confined to hermeneutics "existence" and attempted to analyze it. This course toward a so-called existentialism was inherited by Jean-Paul Sartre, who demonstrated a strong attachment to ontology, and Jacques Merleau-Ponty, who was interested in developing a richer, more complete hermeneutics. Their successors too, such as Paul Ricoeur, Jacques Derrida, Gilles Deleuze, and Felix Guattari, all intersect somewhere with phenomenology, or with a hermeneutics modeled on phenomenology. The main line of twentieth-century philosophy has been anti-Cartesianism, especially in several perspectives, and an attempt toward a phenomenology and/or hermeneutics has formed its backbone. Anti-Cartesian elements can clearly be seen even in other philosophical schools that seem at first glance to be removed from anti-Cartesianism, such as pragmatism (C. S. Peirce), logical positivism and analytical philosophy (the later Ludwig Wittgenstein and Richard Quine), and structuralism (which highlights the structures of the unconscious or of group consciousness).[1]

Inasmuch as they are steeped in the Western intellectual tradition, though, these attempts to break through that tradition do not seem able to achieve decisive results. Even Husserl sought ultimately to return to the thesis of a transcendental subjectivity, by suggesting the need for what in substance is a new Cartesianism.[2] It is symbolic that subsequently the line stretching from Merleau-Ponty to Deleuze, while taking an anti-

Cartesianism position, could only adopt the negative position of "deconstruction." There is no doubt that Westerners have groped for a position that goes beyond Cartesianism. But it is doubtful whether, in actively developing this line of inquiry, they can emerge onto new ground for thought. In question here is the hesitation before and fear of the void after the disappearance of Cartesianism.

In fact, Westerners also often betray an ambivalent position in trying to understand non-Western societies and cultures—for example, in trying to comprehend Japanese society. Among Westerners a number of scholars are aware of the limits of Cartesianism and are dissatisfied with enlightenment thought, but their interest in things anti-Cartesian does not always turn toward conquering their sense of incompatibility to non-Western cultures (with such notable exceptions as Clifford Geertz and H. Gerfinkel). Furthermore, intellectuals in non-Western societies show a tendency to criticize the "backwardness" of intellectual conditions in their own countries, and to justify their own intellectual authority, by borrowing Western models. Progressive intellectuals in postwar Japan were typical in doing so, and in many cases they described their own country's non-Western culture in negative terms—as irrational, unintelligible, illogical, lacking univocity, situational, and so on—and believed that by agreeing with Western scholars they had achieved a universal understanding.

But the non-Western cultures and civilizations, with their long history, have at least a certain degree of consistency. This, however, will not be apparent through the spectacles of modern progressivism. What will be apparent will only be the logic of a "state of deficiency," which is to say that the observer is aware that something remains unobserved when seen through these spectacles. Of course, the spectacles of modern progressivism are excellent, but they cause a number of biases and oversights. In the first place, it is impossible for humanity to have absolutely clear spectacles. And if this is the case, there is no way to proceed but to compare and contrast what we see by wearing the various spectacles.

Until now, the overwhelming military and economic force of Western culture has blocked viewpoints (spectacles) other than those originating in the West. From now on, however, with the decline in the significance of military force and the spread of economic power, if humanity is to continue to exist, all cultural units (natio) will have to search for a way to coexist and understand each other. Non-Western countries will have to create societies unlike the West, and Westerners will have to accept the polymorphism of such a future world. The societies of East Asia, Islam, and Russia will surely never become identical to the societies of the West. On points such as interfirm relations and employment practices discussed in the previous chapter, all countries will not adopt the institutions and organizations of the United States. It is erroneous to imagine that in a world with thousands of, or rather ten thousand, years of history, all societies will gradually become identical. The rule of polymorphic economic liberalism is a device to deal with a world that is not converging simply toward homogenization. No doubt "mutual understanding" is necessary, but simply repeating this mantra is insufficient. What is really necessary is to reconsider what "understanding" is, and to do this we must search for a general framework capable of criticizing both the existing mainstream of Western thought and, of course, non-Western thought. A methodology must be created that demands tolerance for the wearing of spectacles other than those produced in the West. This will of course not be easy, but it is perhaps the core of "understanding."

THREE TYPES OF ACTION AND CULTURE

Let us take "culture" to signify the patterns common to the actions of individuals who belong to a certain group. *Action* is not only a concrete phenomenon apparent externally but also incorporates the workings of the mind. From another perspective, culture is the framework for the image of the world shared by the individuals of a particular group or society. To use expressions much employed by philosophers, culture is the subconscious fundamental structures common to the *Lebenswelt* (Husserl) or *monde vécu* (Merleau-Ponty) of individuals. At a subconscious level, culture regulates and supports the fundamental patterns of human action.

As philosophers often say, our *Lebenswelt* is structured by that which attracts our interest, that is, by objects, which include things (including the body), others, and the self. The self as an object has a special character, and I discuss this in detail later. One should thus distinguish three spheres of action: action oriented toward things (action aimed at nature, which includes the body), action oriented toward others, and action oriented toward the self (or reflexive action).

Correspondingly, one should also distinguish three aspects of culture: a culture of nature (a culture of technology), a culture toward others (a culture of the group or organization), and culture as reflexive action (culture in a narrow sense or cultural expressions). These three aspects overlap in influencing actual human action, and at many points they are similar in their basic patterns. Claude Lévi-Strauss, for example, cites examples where fundamental structures such as hierarchical (concentric) and symmetrical (diametric) patterns are seen to be common to all three aspects of tribal society.[3] Generally speaking, however, the three aspects are not normally adequately integrated. Certainly the effort of interpretation and reflection appears as cultural expression and includes an effort to integrate these three aspects, but there are few cases where perfect integration is achieved. Human beings normally inhabit a shared, eclectic landscape—a landscape that is incompletely integrated. In discussing culture, therefore, it is frequently effective to distinguish these three types. If we consider them to be integrated, it is easy to overvalue other countries' cultures; and if we focus only on the aspects individually, we tend to have a biased understanding of a culture.

For example, one can identify three kinds of explanation in theories of Japanese culture. First, there are explanations that consider the common characteristics in action toward nature as primary; as examples one could mention the model that emphasizes the mild and humid climate, the geographical or geopolitical model that points out Japan's island-country character, and the agricultural technology model that stresses the characteristic of rice as the staple foodstuff. Second, there are what one might call the models of organizational theory, which consider action toward others as primary. Numerous models have been offered and are debated by specialists. There are many examples of this, such as the *dōzokudan* model (Hiroshi Oikawa and Kizaemon Aruga), the *mura* (village) model (Thomas Smith), the model of the *tate-shakai* (the vertical society) (Chie Nakane), the *ie* or *iemoto* model (Shumpei Kumon, Seizaburō Satō, and myself, or Francis Hsu), and the social exchange model (Ruth Benedict, Harumi Befu, Thomas P. Rohlen, and myself, and others).[4] Third, there are explanations that take human reflexive action as primary and point to an interpretation stressing philosophy or religion. As noted below, these include, for example, a model of intellectual confrontation between East and West, the Confucian model, and a model that emphasizes the survival of ancient patterns of thought. Takeo Doi's and Hayao Kawai's psychoanalytical models fall into this category.

In many arguments, these different explanations are jumbled together, and there is a need to clearly distinguish among the kinds of explanation. Though distinguishing differing explanations is desirable, attempts to explain Japanese culture by such efforts as those made in the so-called *Nihonjinron*, focusing only on one kind of explanation, are intrinsically pointless. For example, although theories of what it means to be American, British, or German may make interesting reading, they will never become the object of debate because it is quite clear to Europeans and Americans that these so-called theories are simply foolish overgeneralizations. That *Nihonjinron* has become established is a temporary phenomenon, brought about because of the limited understanding of Japan by non-Japanese and of foreign nations by Japanese. The widening ripple that began with this ignorance, however, has now reached the point where it is linked to political and economic issues and could cause political problems.

Some Philosophical Underpinning

The general framework I set up below for understanding "understanding" could be characterized in a broad sense as "phenomenological." Normally, in living our everyday lives, we all experience what can be called a naive state of consciousness. In this naive state, our consciousness is oriented toward, and preoccupied with, "objects." Or, in phenomenological terms, it "intends at" objects. What are here called "objects," though, are objects as images, or precisely, as phenomena. The naive conscious-ness does not consider whether these objects have an actual existence, in the sense used by philosophers. And the naive consciousness considers it natural that these objects should be made up of our own bodies, others, and other things. It is not medical science or psychology that teaches us the distinction between the body and other things. And it is not physics or biology that teaches the distinction between others and things. This kind of distinction is born with the consciousness itself. Specialized scientific taxonomical criteria are nothing more than derivative elaborations.

Of course, one can doubt these things philosophically (doubt in the sense of Descartes's "I doubt"), but for the naive consciousness, they are only "evident." In the sense that without what is "evident," even philo-sophical skepticism would be impossible, this naive consciousness is the starting point for everything. If the naive confidence even in this fact were to be lost, we would be shaken from our foundations to such an extent that everyday activities would become impossible and would find ourselves in the world of schizophrenia or depression with which psychiatrists grapple.[5] For example, in contrast to the anxiety of schizophrenics, the skepticism of philosophers is a luxury.

What is important is that our attention is oriented toward objects, and not toward the "internal self." When we are involved in normal, everyday action, we naturally distinguish between our body, others, and things, but at the same time we are quite oblivious of the self that is acting. This is the attitude toward the world that emerges in the naive, everyday conscious-ness, what Husserl called the *Lebenswelt* and Merleau-Ponty the *monde vécu*.[6]

THE 'LEBENSWELT' AND REFLECTION

The *Lebenswelt* is also a single whole accumulated in various contexts. No sensation, perception, or judgment is ever isolated. At their respective levels, they are all, always, situated in some kind of context; the context itself is also placed in a larger context, in turn set in an even larger con-text. Thus, although the *Lebenswelt* focuses on a specific object, its hori-zons always extend beyond that object. Although for empiricists such as John Locke, our awareness of the world can be reduced to a collection of elements designated as sensations, this is only to conduct an autopsy on a *Lebenswelt*, which is in fact a single, amorphous whole.

To summarize, the nature of the *Lebenswelt* might be expressed in the following premises:

> *The premise of intentionality* (what Lujo Brentano and Husserl called *In-tentionalität*): the naive consciousness "intends at" objects. The naive consciousness is not aware of the internal self.
> *The premise of corporeality*: the naive consciousness distinguishes its own body from other things.

> *The premise of alterity* (the premise of intersubjectivity): the naive con-
> sciousness believes it can communicate with other beings that have con-
> sciousness.
>
> *The premise of contextual totality* (what Heidegger called *Bewandtnisgan-*
> *zheit*): the naive consciousness is a whole made up of the accumulation of
> various contexts; in other words, it is a holistic image with open horizons.

These premises are well known in the debate surrounding phenomenology. For the contemporary individual, facing issues such as the conflict
between science and antiscience, disputes between worldviews, and the
contrast between East and West, there is perhaps a need to return to the
naive state of consciousness that is the ground for all thought. Even
the modern worldview, or what is called Cartesianism, is ultimately derived from this naive consciousness.

It would be inadequate, however, to describe the originality of the
human state of consciousness using only the above four premises. The following key premise becomes necessary: human consciousness does not
stop in this naive state, but always reflects on itself. "Reflection," here, is
of course not meant in an ethical sense, but in an extremely broad sense,
and signifies the fact that consciousness looks at consciousness. In fact,
my attempt to describe consciousness is itself already a kind of reflection. In trying to describe naive consciousness in words, human beings are
already looking down on, reviewing, and without being aware of it, recre-
ating and reinterpreting this naive consciousness. In other words, they are
occupying the standpoint of what one could call a higher-order consciousness. Thus expressive action, stretching from everyday conversation to science and philosophy, always includes an element of reflection. Even when
it does not emerge as expression, the consciousness is always to some extent reflecting. To use a fashionable expression, reflection is nothing more
than the "self-referencing" of human consciousness. Thus we must add the
following fifth premise:

> *The premise of reflection*: human consciousness is, essentially, reflective.
> That is, human interpretation of the world from the first refers to inter-
> pretation itself, creating a series of reinterpretations. The self comes to be
> revealed through reflection.

The human individual is a reflecting animal. In reality, there is no
such thing as a perfectly naive consciousness. The reality is a reflected
consciousness being further reflected. In this sense, naiveté is relative.

Reflection is consciousness referring to consciousness. The two con-
sciousnesses, however, are not the same. Accurately speaking, reflection
is a postreflective consciousness referring to a prereflective consciousness.
The postreflective consciousness looks down on the form of the prereflective self-consciousness, oriented toward (intending at) various objects, including its own body, others, and other things. In this way, beginning
with reflection, the prereflective internal self becomes an object and thus

comes to be revealed. But at this point the postreflective self is not yet objectified or revealed. In reflective action, therefore, the self has a double significance, as a revealed, prereflective self, and an invisible, postreflective self. To use a common metaphor, often employed in reference to the self, the prereflective self is an actor and the postreflective self the audience or stage director. The actor is oriented toward the context called the stage (and thus toward other actors and the stage apparatus) and must perform oblivious to the self. For the audience and the stage director, the actor is an element on the stage, nothing more than an object to be evaluated from the perspective of the play as a whole. A good actor, though, possesses some of the vision of a stage director, and a good stage director has a part that can empathize with the actor.

As this metaphor demonstrates, the self could be said to be a split personality. One cannot say which personality is more genuine. In a sense, the prereflective and postreflective are reflections of each other. But we cannot say that the concept of the self is unimportant, simply because it is something like a reflection. This way of understanding the structure of consciousness is of course not my own creation.[7] Inasmuch as I understand them, it is this kind of understanding that is common to various phenomenological approaches. And outside Western philosophy, the thinking of Dignāga and Dharmakīrti also seems to be extremely close to this.[8]

Reflection can be classified in any number of ways. The first important distinction is between comprehensive reflection and partial reflection. Comprehensive reflection signifies that the reflexive action extends to all objects. And the prereflexive self is naturally included among those objects. The humanities and the majority of the social sciences try to include the internal self among their objects of study, and thus these disciplines are in essence attempts at comprehensive reflection. Partial reflection signifies that reinterpretation through reflection is limited to a particular class of objects; particularly important here is that this reflection does not refer to the internal self. The natural sciences, which exclude the self, are a typical example of partial reflection on this pattern; the self (that is, the scientist) is placed outside the range of objects to which reflection applies, considered as an observer with no involvement in the world the self is analyzing, and thus plays the role of a quasi-transcendental subject. To restrict reflexive action to partial reflection on the model of self-exclusion in this way, the assistance of a specific philosophical position (normally called Cartesianism) becomes necessary. With recent, cutting-edge theories in physics and biology, there seems to be a trend, even in the natural sciences, to break through what I am here calling "partiality"; but in summarizing their development to this point, one has to emphasize the partial character of thinking in the natural sciences.

Next, let us consider the classification that is the core of this argument. By considering which of the split personalities of the self is more genuine, we can divide comprehensive reflection into two kinds: emphasizing the postreflective self, and separating from the *Lebenswelt* the "self" as a conscious subject that transcends the *Lebenswelt*; or emphasizing the prereflective self, and reembedding the "self" in the *Lebenswelt* as an element that constitutes the *Lebenswelt*. Thus we can divide comprehensive reflection (or reflection as a whole, which is not self-exclusive) into two; here I will call these respectively transcendental reflection and hermeneutic reflection. I explain the significance of these designations below.

Let me clear up a misunderstanding that may arise from using the term "reflection." For example, the Japanese expression *hansei* may carry an echo of quietism in the form of contemplation or meditation. What I am here calling reflection, however, is extremely dynamic, intended on the one hand to be creative (for the self) and on the other to have the possibility of being destructive (in the broader context). Animals and plants likely do not reflect in this sense. Though they may be able to reconsider the world, this is surely only on a small scale or as environmental adaptation. Only human beings are continuously challenging the landscape of their world, plunging themselves and their bodies into dynamism. In this sense, human beings are "reflecting animals," as mentioned in Chapter 1, but this means that a fundamentally nonadaptive, discordant element is planted in humanity.

This nonadaptive, discordant aspect of humanity has long been the object of warnings, as in Buddhism, for example. At the present, what is called environmentalism could perhaps be cited as a leading source of such warnings. The substance of environmentalist warnings, however, is that for almost 400 years human beings have been absorbed in their efforts at "partial reflection" (natural science) particularly concerned with the class of objects that is nature (things); in other words, environmentalist warnings are nothing more than a critique of industrialization. The partiality of the "reflection" seen in natural science and industrialization may be able to change to some extent, but it is impossible for the creative as well as destructive character of human reflection to change. Thought such as environmentalism does not have the power to do this. Industrialization may change into transindustrialization, but even then human beings will discover, or rather create, the opportunity of challenges in new creation and destruction.

"Reflection," here, has this active sense. Why is it that human beings try to create and destroy in this way? It may involve substantial sacrifices. Here is what one might call the dark side of human characteristics, which Buddhism, for example, has called "karma." But one can also discover a bright side. Human beings have a drive that never stops searching for an ultimate, final state that can be designated as true, good, and beautiful. From this comes the mind that seeks "integrity." But to achieve this, human beings in real life create and destroy, doubt, challenge, and struggle. The yearning for an ultimate existence, and the practice of creation and destruction, are two sides of the same coin. Human beings, one could say, are both noble and frequently extremely foolish.

In modern progressivism, there is a tendency to think of folly as a deviation in a progress that advances in search of the sublime. Today, though, when modern progressivism has come to an end after countless attempts at creation and destruction, we have to confront again these two aspects of dark and light. Let me give one or two examples. There seem to be people who consider environmentalism and pacifism as candidates for a new progressivism, but there is a distinct danger of their lapsing into foolish disputes among self-satisfying overbearing views of nature, and among stubborn views of society. To deal with the problem of this dual aspect, we have to go back to the human karma of "reflection" and thus reexamine the two basic ways of thinking, transcendental and hermeneutic reflection.

TRANSCENDENTAL REFLECTION

In transcendental reflection, the self takes up a position that transcends the prereflective, naive consciousness and tries to relativize, or rather subordinate, the naive consciousness. To return to the metaphor used above, in assuming the standpoint of an audience or stage director, the self no longer attempts to return to the stage, or to the position of an actor performing the actual drama. "Objects," for this transcendental self, are no longer objects in the original sense such as things and others. Various (prereflective) world images, including as elements these things and others, become the "object"; the object of reflection moves to a higher level. In the eyes of the transcendental self, the image held by consciousness before reflection is classified as nothing more than an example of countless, as-yet-naive interpretations of the world. What the transcendental self faces is the system that develops from the collection of the various possible interpretations, the system of the system, or the meta-system. The individuality of the separate images of the world (and thus of the original objects in these) is of no significance. What is sought, by going beyond the individual images, is the meta-system common to all individual images. This meta-image is what is called a "law"; in other words, transcendental understanding is nothing more than an "understanding of laws."

In the process of reaching transcendental understanding/understanding of laws, what kind of position does the self occupy? As noted in the "premise of intentionality," the understanding is oriented toward objects, not the self. Nor is transcendental reflection oriented toward the transcendental (postreflective) self. For the transcendental self to be revealed, the perspective of a trans-transcendental self would be necessary, which could even transcend and so look down on the transcendental self; that is, reflection at the level of a meta-meta-system would be required. As long as we try to make the self clearly aware of itself, this process of transcendence will continue without end. In fact, that the self continues

to move to a higher level in this way is because transcendental reflection in essence tries to be "comprehensive," or in other words, to consider
the totality of the world as its object of reflection. But at no time is the
postreflective (transcendental) self contained within the world it observes.
Thus, after exiting from the world it observes, the postreflective self attempts to reenter the world in an effort to be comprehensive. This means
that transcendental reflection has no choice but always to trace a process
of transcendence.

This continuous process of transcendence could be called, metaphorically, an upward, even vertical, process. There have been a number of
attempts to formularize this process of transcendental reflection. For example, Buddhist philosophy of the Consciousness-Only School sets up a
fourfold scheme of the consciousness: the self or subjective portion (the
observer), the other or objective portion (the observed), the self-witnessing
portion (that which is conscious of this observation), and the rewitness-
ing portion (that which is conscious of this consciousness). It expounds
the stages through which consciousness moves to higher levels using a
model of progression from the five sense-consciousnesses (eyes, ears, nose,
tongue, and body) to the sense-center consciousness (*manovijñāna*) to
the thought-center consciousness (*manasvijñāna*) to the storehouse consciousness (*ālaya*) to enlightenment.[9] In Japan, Kūkai expounded a kind
of ladder of consciousness, leading to the realization of *sokushin jōbutsu*
(bodhisattva-hood), in his famous *Jūjūshinron*.[10] These treatises can be seen
as attempts to describe the movement of the transcendental consciousness to a higher level. Such an unending upward progression of consciousness, though, is beyond the normal abilities of human beings. Thus the
ladder of consciousness must change, either yielding its place to a form
of gnostic practice (in terms of the Buddhism of the Consciousness-Only
School, yogic practice), or introducing an absolute being, which can serve
to interrupt the endless upward progression. The "historical religions,"
which began to emerge throughout the world in the first millennium B.C.,
all incorporated this kind of attempt.

Historical religion is Robert Bellah's term; in his theory religion
evolves from primitive religion to archaic religion to historical religion.[11]
What Bellah calls "archaic religion" is a belief system based on cosmological myth, which gives an account of the origins of the world and society,
and particularly of a genealogy stretching from the ancestral gods to the
people of the present day. Archaic religion existed throughout the world,
in Mesopotamia, Egypt, the Indus Valley region, the Aegean Sea, the area
surrounding Crete, the Mayan and Incan civilizations, Mexico, and Japan
before the adoption of the *ritsuryō* codes; and for each historic religion
one can identify an archaic religion that was its forerunner. Examples of
this are the systems of myth and divination in China before the Chou dynasty for Confucianism, Hinduism during the early Rig Veda period for
Buddhism, and ancient Judaism for Christianity. In archaic religion, the

contemporary social system is made sacred, the ruling authority divine, and in its final state, a theocracy is established. The possibility of salvation is restricted to a specific race or region that shares the same ancestral gods. Society under archaic religion is precisely what Henri Frankfort called society "before philosophy."[12]

In contrast, during what Karl Jaspers has called the "age of the axis," in about the middle of the first millennium B.C., systematizations of transcendental thought emerged in three places—the Mediterranean region centering on Greece, the Asian continent, and the Yellow River region. Greek philosophy, Hindu philosophies such as Buddhism, and the Hundred Schools of philosophy including Confucianism are the respective examples of this, and it was at this time that "philosophy," in the sense we speak of it today, was born. These systems of thought were either "historical religions" or the bases for such religions. Christianity and Islam, too, were historical religions that emerged somewhat later as a result of hybridization between the various religions and philosophies.

The substance of a historical religion is first a systematization of transcendental reflection, but with this alone it would be no more than a contemplative philosophy. What is particularly important is its role in the urgent question of the ultimate meaning of human existence. This role, though, is not a simple one. At first glance, the unlimited upward potential that transcendentalism connotes may seem to lead human beings to an ultimate meaning. However, average human beings do not have the intellectual capacity or the patience to realize completely the upward progression of transcendental thought. By introducing in some form an absolute transcendence (which transcends even the transcendental method), or more concretely, by bringing onto the stage an absolute god or principle, the historical religions provided practical guidance about transcendental or quasi-transcendental thought for human beings. In other words, the historical religions were a prescription for sharing the effects of transcendental thought with the average person, or, to borrow Nietzsche's acerbic description, nothing more than "Platonism for the masses."[13]

In archaic religion and primitive religion, the sacred and the profane were mixed together, and the divine was continuous with the human. But when a cosmological principle was established in the faraway place to which unlimited upward progress would lead, or when an absolute god was introduced who might set at rest, and interrupt, the unlimited upward progress, there appeared for the first time the concept of a world transcending this world of the profane, a world beyond, a world of the sacred. Historical religions, through the image of transcending this world, provided for the first time the concept of a universal salvation unconnected to race or region. This was an event of incomparable significance in human history.

As I discuss again below, there are various differences among the historical religions. The one that paid the most concern to analysis of the actual, everyday world was Christianity, which significantly determined the character of those civilizations with a Christian ancestry—the Western civilizations. It seems that much of their character was due to the structure of Christianity, but since I discuss this later, let me here mention Descartes, who opened the way in Western civilization for interest to turn from religion to the temporal world. In Christianity, human beings are special, created "in the likeness of God," but it was the Cartesian dualism of spirit/matter, active understanding/passive acceptance, and subjective/ objective that provided a conceptual framework for expressing this special relationship between man and God, establishing the authority of human understanding over the world of matter (corpus). With his own capacity for understanding established in this way, man was freed from the task of tracing the unlimited upward progress of transcendental thought and, turning away from that path, could now concentrate his energies on the understanding of matter. The greatest product of this was of course natural science.

Strictly speaking, natural science is a form of partial reflection, in the sense that it does not make the reflecting self (the scientist) an object of reflection and thus is not genuine transcendental reflection. But it is quite clear that natural science aims not at individual everyday events (that is, individual things and others), but at laws of understanding, as a meta-system that one could say looks down on these from above, and in so doing it attains an attitude of transcendentalism. The natural scientist does not investigate the individuality of each event (the appearance of the system), but flushes out the "regularity" seen to be common to the individual events. It is believed that the partial scientific theories thus achieved should be transcended by a yet more unified theory, and eventually a single, completely unified "science" will be perfected. There are no examples in the civilizations based on other historical religions of such a thorough pursuit of all that relates to the temporal world. It is perhaps clear that the advance of these efforts to understand the material world generated the progressivism that originated in Europe.

Descartes provides four famous rules as a guide for advancing his own analysis: "never to accept anything as true that I did not know to be evidently so[,] . . . to divide each of the difficulties that I was examining into as many parts as might be possible and necessary in order best to solve it[,] . . . to conduct my thoughts in an orderly way, beginning with the simplest objects and the easiest to know, in order to climb gradually . . . as far as the knowledge of the most complex, . . . and the last, everywhere to make such complete enumerations and such general reviews that I would be sure to have omitted nothing."[14] By following these rules, matter was divided into atoms, possessing only extent and movement, and the so-called atomic, mechanistic approach was created, becoming the basic method of analysis in subsequent natural science. The mind was considered to be embodied in the transcendental self of "I think, therefore I am," and it was from this that individualism was created. This Cartesian philosophy created on the one hand analytical thinking about, and treatment of, nature—that is, the mode of action toward nature that has brought about modern science and technology; on the other, it gave rise to individualistic action and the system that conforms to it—in other words, the action toward others that has fostered the system of contract and competition. Even if it is an exaggeration that Cartesianism created the capitalist, industrial society we see today, it is true that Cartesianism was instrumental in maintaining and developing it.

HERMENEUTIC REFLECTION

Within the tradition of modern philosophy, one is apt to forget that transcendental reflection is not the only possible form of reflection, or the only way for reflection to move to a higher level. Here, there is a need to note another pattern of reflection, which I called above "hermeneutic reflection." In this second form of reflection, the higher-order (postreflective) self is recalled to the lower-order (prereflective) self in the system it has just now transcended, and the new and old images of the world are made to overlap. The higher-order self dissolves, and the overlapping "selves" discover their own new location or position at the level of the original *Lebenswelt*. If one sees this "self" as an unmoving point, one could say that the "self" has changed its interpretation of the world, or even that the images of the world successively overlap and are constantly recreated.

Let us consider, for example, a mountaineer who has lost his way in a fog through which he cannot see even one meter ahead, and who, on eventually emerging from the forest, pauses to take a breath. Up to that point, he had been consumed by the act of walking; his consciousness had forgotten the self, quite unaware of its own position, and intending solely at objects. At that point the fog suddenly clears and his surroundings are revealed. When he looks around, he sees that he is in a position to have stepped off a precipice. At such a time, when one discovers one's own position, a new prospect opens up. In other words, when the self's position in the world becomes clear, a new world landscape opens up. To plot one's own position on the map, thus reinterpreted, and again start out as a mountaineer is what I am calling here "hermeneutic reflection." In contrast, one could say that the position of "transcendental reflection" is to examine the reasons for having been lost by referring to one's existing knowledge and experience and to try to create a science of mountain climbing.

Transcendental reflection may be useful in the long term, but it cannot solve the immediate problems faced by the mountaineer. The mountaineer must rely on hermeneutic reflection, and he must continue to rely on it to find ways to return to the town at the foot of the mountain. In reality, the two kinds of reflection are mixed in the mountaineer's mind. As long as he wants to continue living, the position I have called hermeneutic reflection is indispensable, or rather, must take first place. This process of reinterpretation that hermeneutic reflection generates is the very course most befitting the human life and is always repeated in the lives of individuals or the histories of groups (states, regions, lineages, households). The wisdom of the living is an accumulation of this kind of reflection and is more natural as a way of reflection.

The core of what I am calling here hermeneutic reflection is superimposing the postreflective image on the prereflective image or creating an overlapping image. The problem is the significance of this overlapping. In transcendental reflection there is no process that could be called overlapping; the postreflective image must transcend the naive, prereflective image. The lower-order (prereflective) image is placed at a lower level as a specific, concrete example of the higher-order (postreflective) image, thus forming the base of a hierarchy made up of various interpretations of the world. That is, a general system that incorporates the specific systems is created, and the specific instances are, one could say, inserted into, without overlapping, the general law. In hermeneutic reflection, in contrast, the images of the world before and after reflection are made to overlap, and in a concrete way, on specific points, they are similar in character. There is no hierarchical relationship of specific and general, or concrete and abstract, between the two.

In overlapping, the two images do not immediately fit together perfectly. But the postreflective image of the world requires a different reading of the prereflective image, the postreflective image itself is transformed, and thus the overlapping of the images is accomplished. When the fog clears, the mountaineer who discovers himself on the edge of a precipice does not discard entirely the mental image of the mountain he had drawn up to that point. For example, he fits the route he had drawn on the map to overlap with his new discovery, revises his reading of the map, and decides to follow a new route.

This second form of reflection is connected at a deep level to what philosophers have called hermeneutics. When one talks of hermeneutics in the modern period, Wilhelm Dilthey's name springs immediately to mind, but others have since offered various definitions of hermeneutics. Opinions concur, however, that its original meaning was the interpretation, and so-called *Nacherleben* (vicarious experience), of great works of the past (the most prominent being the Bible) in the present context. In other words, as an author I embed the interpretation of the world made in past works in my own image of the world and make them overlap. If I can believe that I and past authors share a sphere of communication (what allows this is the above-mentioned "premise of alterity"), hermeneutics is nothing more than a natural extension of what I am calling the second form of reflection.

Looking back from this point, the second form of reflection is a hermeneutics of oneself, providing a basic method for hermeneutics in the sense that the term has been used. That is, hermeneutics is a self that has vicariously experienced works of the past, making them overlap with its self before that experience. By vicariously experiencing, so to speak, not only others and their works but also one's own former self, and only by doing so, human beings can have a "history" that extends beyond their own lives. Though it is a somewhat stilted expression, in the sense that we are aware of this possibility of an increase in the scope of application, I would like to call this second form of reflection "hermeneutic reflection," or "historiological reflection."

In hermeneutic reflection, the split personalities of the self are not divided but overlap, however unsteadily. Thus there is no higher-order subject of understanding, towering above the rest, evaluating and justifying the effort at interpretation. Transcendental understanding (historical religion) was not born from this form of reflection, and it would be hard for quasi-transcendental understanding (natural science) to be created from it. Hermeneutic reflection is not an understanding of laws such as those in natural science. Thus one's effort to interpret has no way forward other than to ground the self by relying solely on one's own endeavor. Since Heidegger, the discussion of this point has been often known as the question of the hermeneutic circle.

> What is decisive is not to get out of the circle but to come into it in the right way. This circle of understanding . . . is the expression of the existential *fore-structure* of Dasein itself. . . . In the circle is hidden a positive possibility of the most primordial kind of knowing. . . . Because understanding, in accordance with its existential meaning, is Dasein's own potentiality-for-Being, the ontological presuppositions of historiological knowledge transcend in principle the idea of rigour held in the most exact sciences.[15]

In contrast to transcendental reflection—which traces an endless, vertical, upward progression, intending to reach a divine other-world—hermeneutic reflection, while remaining at the level of the profane world, tries to sustain a reinterpretation without limits. Seen from a perspective accustomed to the historical religions and natural science, this process, in which interpretation generates interpretation, may even seem like a vicious circle. But within this endless circle, while trying to reflect on their own image of the world, understand other people's images of the world, and particularly, experience vicariously the great linguistic inheritance of the past, individuals repeatedly reinterpret the world. Clearly this process advances as the self incorporates the *Lebenswelt* of others. This repeated reinterpretation is a process of digesting the life experience common to human beings and discovering fulfillment in the process. If this shared fulfillment comes to the surface, this would be precisely the "positive possibility of the most primordial kind of knowing," and the endless circle would come to have significance.

What Gadamer calls *Gemeinsein* (common sense) is one expression of this shared fulfillment. Predating this are Immanuel Kant's *Urteilskraft* (ability to judge) and *Geschmack* (taste) (as differentiated from *Vernunft* [rationality]), and Blaise Pascal's *esprit de finesse* (as something opposed to an *esprit géometrique*), also similar concepts. What is perceived by means of this sense, capability, or spirit is *Bildung* (culture), tradition, taste. And what is common to these concepts is a concern with the observed nature of humanity as a whole.

Hermeneutics began by being applied to the literary and aesthetic spheres, but it is precisely a concern with the aesthetic sphere that brings to the surface the characteristics of what I am calling here hermeneutic reflection, in the broadest sense. This is because a sense of beauty and a feeling of enjoyment are things that are discovered within the totality of the naive consciousness and normally escape in the process of transcendental reflection. In transcendentalism, as one's understanding moves to a higher order, the details of the *Lebenswelt* are washed away and the process of abstraction continues. For example, in the case of Max Weber, who sought the "scientization" of social analysis, the image of the world obtained under the constraints of a "suspension of value judgments" and "objectivity" was a somewhat alienated, monochrome world.[16] The interpretation of the world obtained by what Husserl called "phenomenological reduction" is a neutral image, once it has passed through the sieve of *Geltungsvariation* (appropriate variation). Neither Weber nor Husserl offers arguments as to how beauty is created.

Again, for any historical religion, for example, idol worship was originally a deviation, and there was no room to allow a dependence on a sense of beauty or enjoyment. In contrast to the human nature in which transcendentalism is interested and that is an abstract concept seen from a specific perspective, the hermeneutic method is interested in precisely the whole of human nature as it is lived, and by passing through this totality, one can expect to achieve the true, good, and beautiful.

The form of transcendental reflection itself is best expressed in the natural sciences. But they are no more than a kind of partial reflection, as I have already noted. Thus the historical religions are the legitimate representatives of transcendental reflection; one could say that history (as something spoken and written) represents hermeneutic reflection. In the period before historical religion, religion and history were fused together as mythological history. But since the time of historical religion, religion has been supported by transcendental concepts (an absolute god or dharma), and thus there has no longer been a need for historical justification in the previous sense. ("Historical religion" is in fact an ironic designation, meaning religion during the age when history acquired its independence from religion.) There is no way for the validity of religion to be compromised. As is well known, the Indians, who created historical religion in its most completely transcendental form, show very little interest in history. Human beings who demonstrate an interest in their own history perhaps engage to some extent in sacrilegious behavior.

Thus religion and history form two different axes for reflexive action, and although one cannot say they are unconnected, they cross each other at right angles, so to speak. At present, science and technology are attempting to serve in place of religion. In any case, in reality, the two forms of reflection labor in tandem, each tangled up in the other, and human beings live their lives in the midst of this entanglement. The metaphor that posits that a good stage director has a side that is a good actor, and vice versa, applies here too. Even in historical religion itself, transcendentalism and the hermeneutic method are in fact confused. For example, many more hermeneutic elements can be discovered in Confucian thought than in Hindu thought.

Even Descartes himself confessed, in the *Discourse on Method*, "I formed a provisional moral code." In his own words, the code consisted of three maxims:

> The first was to obey the laws and customs of my country, firmly preserving the religion into which God was good enough to have me instructed from childhood, and governing myself in all other matters according to the most moderate opinions and those furthest from excess. . . . My second maxim was to be as firm and resolute in my actions as I could, and to follow . . . constantly the most doubtful opinions, once I had determined on them. . . . My third maxim was to try always to conquer myself rather than fortune, and to change my desires rather than the order of the world.[17]

What enabled the intellectual revolutionary Descartes to write the *Discourse on Method* was this code for living, which could even be called moralistic in style. It was not something deduced from his principles of understanding, beginning with "I think, therefore I am." As is most clearly apparent in the first maxim, these maxims were learned from "the most prudent people with whom I should have to live";[18] to borrow the terms we are using here, they were the result of hermeneutic reflection. Descartes recognized that there were two forms of human reflection. One has to say that he had a profound understanding of human nature. He himself would have frowned, perhaps, at the subsequent hypertrophy of "Cartesianism." Transcendentalism and the hermeneutic method are in fact always used together.

Both religious practice, at least as it is seen at present, and the attempt to understand tradition seen in historiology have their respective limitations. In the creation or reform of religion, a massive (transcendental) reflexive ability is considered necessary, but in fact, even with the abilities of religious founders or reformers, the reflection is inevitably incomplete, and the substance of practical doctrine diverges. Thus there are intense struggles between religions, and between orthodoxy and heresy within religions, frequently paving the way for bloody repression and war. It is ironic that religion, which is supposed to obviate human anxiety, leads to slaughter, but this fact symbolically exposes the contradiction that transcendentalism incorporates in its layer of the reality. Transcendentalism, in causing a relentless pursuit of concepts, is in essence reformatory or revolutionary. On the other hand, history, as an attempt to understand tradition, limits its field of vision to the concrete experience of the society based on that tradition. In this sense, an interest in history is conservative in the original sense, or traditionalist. In the hermeneutic aspects incorporated in history, there may be a weakness in being caught in the yoke of the past.

For human beings from the time of historical religion, history and religion (tradition) have frequently been presented as choices. Both of these orientations, at least at present, have their respective deficiencies and should be relativized. In our existing general understanding, it seems to be believed that historical religion is the highest human achievement. Even those who believe in science do not try to hide the legacy they inherited from historical religion. As I have argued here, however, just as historical religion is not an absolute, neither is the pursuit of history, tradition, culture, or taste. To describe this relativity from another perspective, just as it is possible for a religion to cut across any number of social traditions, one should also consider that human traditions and culture cut across any number of religions. Unless this is the case, in today's global society, where conflicting religious traditions still have strong roots, the ties linking the human race together may be too weak. For example, can there be anywhere else a basis for freedom of belief and ecumenicalism?

VARIOUS HISTORICAL RELIGIONS: THE UNIQUENESS OF CHRISTIANITY

Here, though it is somewhat of a side issue, let us consider the differences among the historical religions. These differences appear especially in the ways they set up "absolute transcendentalism." The historical religions belonging to the Hindu tradition (represented by Buddhism and including the Jain religion), Confucianism, and Christianity (to which Islam is close) can be clearly distinguished on this point.

First, in the case of Hinduist Buddhism, there are no clear constraints placed on the upward trend of transcendental speculation. It is only taught that, far removed from our thoughts relating to our mundane daily existence, there may be an ultimate limit to a transcendental upward progress. When one thinks of absolute transcendentalism, one can only talk of "dharma" as the ultimate limit of such an understanding. In Buddhism, at a high level, this is the abstract principle of "origin"—the principle that all beings necessarily depend on others and exist in relativity to others.

Second, Confucianism in China attributes the role of absolute transcendence to human beings in history, and with this tries consciously to interrupt the endless upward progress of speculation.[19] Confucius considered King Wen, King Wu, and the Duke of Chou of the Chou dynasty to be the ideal sages, but Mo Di went still further, citing King of Yu of the Xia dynasty, and Mencius opposed even this, considering Yao and Shun who preceded Yu to be the ideal. In fact, there is a question whether these sages were actual historical figures. In particular, Mencius's citing of probably fabricated figures such as Yao and Shun was a reaction to the ideas of Confucius, who had tried to interrupt the endless upward progress of speculation by relying on the historical past. Although for all schools of Confucianism these sages were clearly human, they were considered nothing more than that. This was what one might call an absolutization of the historical past, and any attempt "to speak of gods of supernatural powers" transcending this framework was repressed. But it was impossible to avoid the intrusion of hermeneutic thought in speaking of the historical past.

Third, Christianity (and to a certain extent Islam) has a structure unlike either Buddhism or Confucianism. Jesus of Nazareth, unlike Yao and Shun, was a man who clearly existed, but it is his existence as the "son of God" and as testament of the "sacraments" that is the key to the Christian faith. Christianity is unique among the historical religions in that its divine nature was made manifest, not in the dim mists of a mythological past or in the farther reaches of meditation, but directly, in the midst of the everyday world. That is, transcendental thought is absorbed in a faith in "Our Lord Jesus Christ," who actually appeared in the midst of everyday experience (in the contemporary kingdom of Judea), and in this the unlimited upward progression of transcendental thought is terminated. In Christianity, the absorption in transcendental thought seen in Hindu civilization (particularly Buddhism) is not allowed. In fact, the monastic inclination toward meditation, for example, has always been considered dangerous in Christianity. One can say that Christianity, and the civilizations based on it, have a strong, latent, this-worldly orientation.

The granting of divinity to the founder of a religion is a phenomenon often seen with the popularization of a religion during its period of diffusion (for example, with Gautama Buddha), but only in orthodox Christianity has this been made so strictly a tenet of faith. In fact, as is well known, there are great problems with the doctrine that makes one and the same the Jesus who was a human being and the divine, difficulties apparent in the controversies surrounding the doctrine of the Trinity. For example, the Council of Nicaea in 32 A.D., which rejected the Aryan heresy (that Christ and God were not exactly the same), and the Council of Ephesus in 431 A.D., which rejected the Nestorian heresy (that Christ was not born as God), are both famous attempts to determine the doctrine on this point. One has to say that, in contrast to the impenetrability of the doctrine of the Trinity in Christianity, Islam, which considers both Jesus and Muhammad to be merely prophets, clearly has an easy structure.

On the other hand, Christianity and Islam are similar in that both inherited the ancient Jewish myth of cosmological creation (as told in the Old Testament). Buddhism and Confucianism both separated fundamentally from the ancient religions that preceded them (the Rig Veda myths; the myths of Fu Xi, Shen Nong, and Huang Di; and the system of divination), in not having the concept of a creator, but both Christianity and Islam inherited and sustained the ancient religious concept of a creator. For example, in the world of the Old Testament, while there are episodes about paradise, there is no concept of a heaven (or hell). The transformation from this world of the Old Testament, typical to an ancient religion, to the world of the New Testament as a historical religion was possible only through an abrupt break, which was provided with the appearance of Jesus, the son of God, as a historical figure. It is from this that the importance of the "doctrine of the Trinity" derives, linking God and His son.

In any case, by God's manifesting himself in the midst of everyday reality, the common, everyday world was also affirmed in Christianity in its actuality as God's creation, becoming an object worthy of making an effort to understand. Thomas Aquinas built a complete system of a kind of "social science," independent of a theology connected to Christianity itself. The comprehensiveness and elaborateness of this system was unprecedented among thinkers, including Aristotle, in the East or West up to that time. Joseph Schumpeter, for example, considered that modern "social science" would have been impossible without the medieval Scholastics, represented by Thomas Aquinas.[20] There is no disputing that, in the past several centuries known as the modern period, those who have believed in Christianity have desired most to understand the world in which we live, but even in the Middle Ages, this enthusiasm surpassed that in other historical civilizations. This fact is certainly not unconnected to the particular concept of God in Christianity. It was because of the unambiguous termination of the limitless upward progress of transcendental thought that Christianity, and the civilizations based on it, turned to a this-worldly orientation.

As a contrasting example, let me again mention Buddhism. From the first, Buddhism, marked by what are together called the *sanbōin* (the three dharma seals: all things are transient, all things are selfless [insubstantial], and Nirvana is the state of tranquillity), has had no interest in the vulgar world. Particularly with the development of Mahayana Buddhism, the understanding clearly increased that: "Man has no self, . . . it is impossible for there to be a subject who is the only observer, the only perceiver. Foolish men imagine the substance of such things as subjects and objects."[21] Buddhist thought vividly demonstrates that concepts such as self, subject, and object cannot withstand a thorough critique of understanding, which intends at unlimited upward progression. Conversely, in Christianity, which has suppressed this endless upward progress, concepts of self and subject/object can appear easily, and as the actual world of everyday behavior becomes a place where salvation is possible, a this-worldly activism emerges.

The thought of Max Weber, who considered activism to have emerged first with Protestantism, was perhaps overconcerned with the question of industrialization because in the Middle Ages too there was no lack of divinely inspired industriousness. The Cartesian formulation, which posited that the division between the transcendental subject (the mens) and the objective object (the corpus) had been instituted by God, clearly established a method of understanding that terminated the upward transcendental progression and became the starting point for the massive development of the practical application of transcendentalism in the modern West. The historical religion—Christianity—created Cartesianism, and through its formularization as Cartesianism it brought about the absolutization of the comprehending subject and a thorough inquiry into the comprehended object (science). "God"-less transcendentalism, in contrast, as seen in much twentieth-century thought, has brought humanity unlimited anxiety. The introduction of the concepts of "death" and "nothingness" by Heidegger and Sartre symbolizes this fact. Ultimately, the modern age would have been impossible without Christian, Cartesian transcendentalism.

CONSERVATISM, PROGRESS, LIBERALISM, AND INDIVIDUALISM

Let us turn again to observed social phenomena. As discussed in Chapter 1, modern progressivism has lost its significance, as seen in the failure of socialism; and with this, modern conservatism is also about to lose its raison d'être. Francis Fukuyama has expressed this situation as the "end of history" and has said that the dialectic of thought is no longer possible. But when human beings are no longer engaged in thought, they are surely no longer human. As I explained above, the confrontation in the most general sense between progressivism and conservatism is a dialectical relationship between transcendental and hermeneutic thought and can always be discovered in human beings as reflecting animals. Karl Mannheim argued that only under the dynamism that modern society possesses is the confrontation between progressivism and conservatism possible. Given, however, that the modern age has been characterized by the dynamics of a thought whose keynote has been transcendentalism, modern progressivism has been a progressivism subsumed under progressivism, and the modern conservatism that has opposed it has been a conservatism subsumed under progressivism. It is not history that is about to end, but the modern age of Western origin; even after its demise, the dynamic inherent within human beings will continue to manifest itself, and the dialectic between hermeneutics and transcendental thought (conservatism and progressivism) as intellectual orientations will remain.

For example, in response to the questions of how to move beyond the modern, and how to move beyond industrialization, naturally two different attitudes are possible. But given our present intellectual situation, the influence of transcendental thought, which the modern age has fostered, is as ever deeply rooted in our consciousness, despite its various deficiencies that are being continuously exposed. To counter this, pointing out that hermeneutic thought in the general sense exists may serve as an antidote. The reason the manner of argument in this book may appear inclined to conservatism is because of the inertia of progressivism due to the influence of transcendentalism. The real focus of the argument, though, must be on the basic structure that generates the confrontation between these two positions. In this book, I have defined this as "liberalism." True liberalism is a fundamental characteristic of human beings, which goes beyond even the confrontation between hermeneutics and transcendental thought.

As discussed in Chapter 1, the most fundamental sense of "freedom" for human beings is that reflexive action and self-referential action can be sufficiently carried out. Freedom is nothing other than a dynamic state of being in which one reinterprets and reconsiders the world. "Freedom of action" in the normal sense is a derivative product of this labor at re-interpretation, and nothing more. For example, in Buddhist practice, it is considered that even though freedom of action is severely restricted, or rather, because it is so restricted, true freedom will be attained. Lao-tse and Zhuangzi also preached that it was by restricting freedom of everyday action to a minimum that freedom of spirit and thought would be attained. But even though this may be applicable for exceptionally religious men and women or seekers after truth, this is too difficult for others. Generally speaking, therefore, freedom of action and freedom of thought have instead a proportional (or positively correlated) relationship, and freedom of thought cannot be preserved under imprisonment or torture. But freedom of faith, expression, and assembly are all kinds of freedom of action, linked almost directly to freedom of thought. In terms of our prior historical experience (hermeneutically), freedom of action should be greatly respected. In this sense, from the standpoint of true liberalism, there can be no objection to liberalism of action. To believe, however, that liberalism of action guarantees liberalism of thought is an illusion.

Furthermore, liberalism of action does not have only one form. One cannot derive a specific form of liberalism of action, specific to a particular field of activity, from the principles of liberalism. For example, as I have noted in this book, there are different varieties of liberalism of economic action, ranging from classical to polymorphic. Even different varieties of parliamentary democracy, the most generalized systematization of liberalism of political action, can be identified. And there are various possible combinations of liberalism in politics and liberalism in the economy. Thus, even in Anglo-American thought, which considers a combination of classical economic liberalism and two-party parliamentary democracy to be optimal, there is no absolute orthodoxy.

At the same time, to believe that combining the options of liberalism of action in various fields always works well surely runs counter to historical experience (hermeneutic knowledge). For example, in the debate on economic planning in the 1920s, a defense of socialism was made, arguing that the establishment of parliamentary democracy (liberal democracy) would adequately make up for the deficiencies in freedom of economic action seen in economic planning. The danger, though, in believing that freedom of political action can be established independently of freedom of economic action is clear from the experience of socialism in the former Soviet Union and Eastern Europe. Historically (hermeneutically) speaking, it is appropriate to believe that freedom of action in various fields is positively correlated. But generally speaking, the idea of liberalism until now has been conceived in somewhat too rigid a form, within the framework of modern progressivism. My emphasis on polymorphic economic liberalism in this book has been an attempt to redress this imbalance. History is about to unfold still more new possibilities. For example, one of the questions awaiting us is: what will thought be like in the transindustrial society imagined on the far side of "informatization"? In such a society, the method that divides politics and the economy may finally become invalid, and the spaces in our lives where freedom of action is established may become quite different. But I will not venture into a discussion of transindustrial society in this book.

The question of the polymorphism of liberalism of action has been debated for a long time. The first example was perhaps the argument of Locke, who discussed freedom of religious action in British society after the Puritan revolution, advocating the need for "toleration" between the various sects. In fact, freedom of belief is the argument easiest to draw directly from freedom of thought. But what Locke was talking about was something more than simply freedom of religious action. He was discussing something more than "relativism" as regards religion. He argued that each religion is orthodox (not a heresy), and that there should be "charity, meekness, and good will in general towards all mankind"—in other words, that "mutual toleration . . . [is] the chief distinguishing mark of a true church."[22] Locke's concept of toleration was derived by believing in a communality that transcends religious positions and differs from ordinary relativism. Though problems arise in applying this logic of toleration beyond the religious sphere, the principle itself should surely be respected in all spheres of freedom of action. When the link provided by God at its core is lost, the philosophy of natural rights, which posits that human beings have an innate right to freedom, easily becomes a relativism with no interest in relationships with others. At present, liberalism is globally exposed to this danger. It is only "mutual toleration" among all mankind that has the capacity to save us from this danger and mutual understanding that can cultivate this toleration. We cannot rediscover a just criterion for action that should be applied to the whole world.

In a sense, the assertion that human beings are the same, or should be the same, is dangerous because it can be too easily betrayed and tends to foster indifference. Our starting point should be to believe that human beings, or societies, are different but that they have some commensurability. The key to ensuring that liberal societies continue should be not relativism but mutual toleration, not a shared character but the possibility of commensurability, and the creation of a rule based on this perception. This is the substance of the "understanding" for which I have consistently argued. Depending on the individual, this may be minimal, or unreliable. But given the present conditions, even such an understanding is difficult to obtain. Is it now necessary to start out from such a minimum understanding? Adam Smith, for example, sought in "sympathy" the way to achieve this minimum understanding.[23] In the terms of this book, this would mean to control the impatient predilection for a single justice and universal principle, and to make an effort to seek common ground, and points of agreement, between individuals and societies. That is, a hermeneutic rather than transcendental attitude should be dominant. The key to polymorphism in liberalism is surely nothing other than hermeneutic reflection.

The concept of individualism too is deeply intertwined with the question of liberalism. That acts of reflection and self-reference are undertaken by each human being as a biological entity will not change. Thus a respect for individuals' thought derives almost inevitably from true liberalism. It is a universal truth that speech and religious belief treat each individual as a unit, and from now on as well, this must be always recognized and respected. Clearly therefore, that people should rely on the mass to determine their opinions—the phenomenon of the mass society—is fundamentally undesirable.

There is room for argument, though, about how much significance individualism should have in the actions of individuals. Following the reasoning thus far, there is an undeniable correlation between individualism in thought and individualism in action. But action always goes with a re-reflection in thought. And the landscape of the world woven by thought is essentially intersubjective. Individual action is, to a varying extent, affected by others and is frequently undertaken on another's behalf. Unless individualism in action goes with reflection (particularly hermeneutic reflection)—that is, unless it is rooted, to some extent, in an intersubjective intellectual context—it will contradict liberalism. Recently, there has been much advocacy of "enlightened self-love," but at least as an expression this concept is inappropriate. Self-love or individualism should not be guided or shaped by an enlightenment toward a single, correct image of the world but should reflect "toleration" and be reexamined within an intersubjective framework. "Enlightened self-love" creates an expectation of a convergence toward a single landscape of the world. The reality we will face in the history to come will demand that we work patiently to find common ground between pluralistic images of the world. What will be required is not "enlightened self-love" but rather Adam Smith's principle of "sympathy."

The "Ambiguous Nature" of Japanese Culture

On the basis of the above argument, let us consider the characteristics of Japanese culture. This means attempting to explain Japanese culture from the religious and philosophical perspective (what was called in the first section the third type of cultural explanation). Making such an attempt is not a rejection of the other two types of explanation—namely, explanation derived from attitudes toward nature and toward others (explanation based on organizational theory), as I discuss below.

It is often argued in explaining Japanese culture that Japanese thought is ambiguous and lacks the clarity and consistency of the Western intellectual tradition. Indeed, Japanese self-reflection has often been unclear and inconsistent since the Meiji period, and particularly among progressive intellectuals since the Second World War. Western critiques of Japanese culture have also often noted a lack of principles; a situational, two-faced lack of morals; and untrustworthiness. But it is impossible that the culture of a country comprising more than 100 million people, which is a first-rank economic power and, in international comparison, safe and stable, should be merely unprincipled and full of contradictions. That it should appear so is likely because the principles of Japanese society and the logic of Japanese thought are not readily apparent to people from other countries. Japanese people too, in the rush toward modernization since the Meiji period, have come to look at themselves through other people's eyes, and their own logic has become not readily apparent. These "eyes" are nothing more than the perspective of transcendentalism and progressivism that originated in the West. But as I have already noted, transcendentalism is not an absolute.

From the perspective of comparative religion, this model of criticism of Japan emphasizes not so much the influence of historical civilization (the civilization based on historical religion) as the fact that this influence has not borne fruit. It is asserted that the particular belief of the Japanese people is a strange mixture of historical religions (Buddhism and Confucianism) and archaic religion (foreign researchers often use the term Shintō). Since I have already explained archaic religion, I will not go over it in detail here, but simply put, it is nothing more than the belief system before the systematization of transcendental thought. If one were to conjecture from the *Kojiki* and *Nihon shoki*,[24] and from works in archaeology, the belief system held by the Japanese before the seventh century certainly had all the characteristics of archaic religion; one could say that its influence remains even today.

THE PHENOMENON OF RELIGIOUS COEXISTENCE

The first half of the first millennium B.C. was a period of transition from archaic religion to historical religion. One can imagine various origins of historical religion. As Hideo Suzuki has indicated, however, it is

perhaps closely linked to the fact that, as a result of the glaciation that occurred in about the middle of the second millennium B.C. (3,500 years ago),
the nomadic tribes from the Central Eurasian steppes (whom we can assume to have belonged to the so-called Aryan linguistic group) swept south
and had major encounters with the agrarian tribes in southern Eurasia.[25]
These encounters occurred in three areas—from the eastern Mediterranean to Greece, from the Indus Valley region to the Ganges delta region,
and in the Yellow River region—and the emergence of the three types
of historical religion (or philosophy) clearly correspond to these three encounters. The historical religions were perhaps an effort to integrate different cultures and to enable two kinds of people to coexist, by universalizing
from the nomadic and agrarian experiences of life to abstract concepts and
universal principles. In other words, these major encounters seem to have
created a situation with which mutual toleration based on hermeneutic
thought could not cope, and to have made inevitable a systematization of
transcendental thought that could oversee and dominate different interpretations of the world.

Once established, historical religions created and enlarged mass societies on an unprecedented scale, through the concept of justice created
by transcendental thought and the power of abstract thought, influencing
and conquering the primitive or archaic religions of neighboring societies.
In the majority of cases, these secondary encounters were made with what
one might call a physical impact, through military invasion or by achieving economic dominance through trade. The encounter between the archaic religion of Japan and the historical religions of China was an example
of this secondary encounter, but exceptionally, the aspect of physical impact was minor. There was a substantial geopolitical distance, including a
sea, between the cities of the Yellow River region, which were the center
of the civilization, and the Japanese archipelago, and the threat of military
invasion of Japan was not sustained because of the cycle of dynastic rise
and fall in Chinese history. Thus one can suppose that the influence of historical religion on Japan was purely conceptual, with no physical support,
and that this is a reason for its weakness.

This situation was not unique to Japan. The situation when the ancient
German belief system encountered Christianity is to some extent comparable to the Japanese case. One could even say that the case of the German
tribes is more thoroughgoing, because the influence of the mother civilization (the Roman civilization) collapsed following the encounter, rendering its physical influence virtually nonexistent. The timing and place of
the encounters were also similar. In both regions, there were sweeping
ethnic migrations until about the fifth century (the rapid migrations of the
German tribes are well known, but there were also substantial migrations
from southern China and the Korean peninsula to Japan). After this fluid
situation had settled down, the peoples established substantial ties with
historical religion and its institutions. Both the Merovingian and Carolin-

gian dynasties tried to establish their legitimacy with the aid of Christianity, and the change from the Yamato court to the Ritsuryō state too is unimaginable without the introduction of culture from China. In both cases this was the period between the fifth and eighth centuries. That both secondary encounters should have taken place at the edges of the Eurasian continent is also suggestive. And in both cases, as a result of the lack of physical influence, there was no inheritance of a powerful macropolitical order from the historical civilization. This seems to have been a major reason for the simultaneous emergence in both regions of decentralized political-economic structures that can be summarized broadly as a "feudal system."

Their subsequent processes of religious (intellectual) development, however, were substantially different. In Europe, Christianity grew dominant independently of its originary context in the Near East. The Roman Catholic Church interdicted all the pagan religions, including the ancient German faith, and suppressed heresies, beginning with the Aryans and moving on to the Nestorian and Cathar sects. The prosecution of heretics continued until the Inquisition of the fifteenth century. The Reformation and the religious wars that followed it also symbolized the fierce desire to seek a single orthodoxy. In Japan, in contrast, various systems of belief, such as various kinds of Buddhism, Confucianism, and the new Kamakura Buddhism, which should perhaps be called Japan's Protestantism, coexisted without any large-scale suppression or war. In the sixteenth century, religious groups of the Ikkō sect (Jōdo Shinshū) attempted large-scale military resistance to the dominance of the warrior class (*bushi*), but it is valid to consider that fundamentally this was a struggle between the clerical and the secular, or between the secular and the secular, and not a war between religions. Symbolic evidence is that though the imperial court (even today) performs festivals that originated in archaic beliefs, the majority of emperors have themselves been adherents of Buddhism. This phenomenon of religious coexistence is unimaginable in Europe and is often considered to demonstrate that the historical religions never took root in Japan.

It is necessary to note, however, that the bitter religious confrontation symbolized in the suppression of heresies and religious wars is a characteristic limited to the Western historical religions (Christianity and Islam). In India, various Hinduistic beliefs, including Buddhism and Jainism, have coexisted, for the most part peacefully. In China too, though Confucianism, Taoism, and Buddhism have occasionally contended for the position of state religion, generally speaking they have intermingled because of the shared belief in ancestor worship. Perhaps this tendency is common to Eastern transcendental thought, which lacks any clear break, or point of termination, in the form of an absolute God in human form. As Max Weber pointed out, the essential form of Eastern historical religion requires a high-level "intellectual understanding," in that its core is not a human God but an abstract cosmological principle.[26] For the common people, meeting this requirement is difficult. Thus they seek salvation in a mixture of forms of belief, oriented toward benefit in this world. The division into a high-level intellectual form and a vulgar popular form is characteristic of Eastern historical religion. In contrast, in Western historical religion, there is little of this tendency toward division. One of the reasons for the phenomenon of religious coexistence in Japan is this characteristic common to religious structures of the Eastern type.

HISTORICAL RELIGION IN JAPAN

There are problems, though, in subsuming the Japanese phenomenon of religious coexistence under Eastern culture in general. For example, Hajime Nakamura, an authority on Indian philosophy, has argued that the Japanese way of thinking is more ambiguous and eclectic than that of Indians or Chinese. In his view, in terms of the degree to which they prefer abstraction over concreteness, or metaphysics over pragmatism, the order is Indians, Chinese, and then Japanese. Robert Bellah and S. N. Eisenstadt hold similar views.[27] To quote Nakamura: "In the first place, we should notice that the Japanese are willing to accept the phenomenal world as Absolute because of their disposition to lay a greater emphasis upon intuitive sensible concrete events, rather than upon universals. This way of thinking with emphasis upon the fluid, arresting character of observed events regards the phenomenal world itself as Absolute and rejects the recognition of anything existing over and above the phenomenal world."[28] Nakamura, in short, argues that the Japanese do not have a concept of another world as something with which to confront this world and that they have not really believed in historical religion.

Saburō Ienaga argues the opposite.[29] He acknowledges that in ancient Japan, before the sixth century, there was a "continuous worldview," with no distinction between this and another world, and that an "affirmative worldview" toward reality was dominant. This was precisely the boundless optimism common to cultures based on archaic religion. Ienaga, though, maintains that with the introduction of Chinese culture linked to the establishment of the Ritsuryō state, the standpoint of a rejection of this world clearly came to take hold of the Japanese mind.[30] During the period when the Ritsuryō state was being established in the eighth and ninth centuries, tensions and expectations temporarily concealed this keynote of pessimism. Kūkai and Saichō, particularly the fearless strength of the former, have been unparalleled in Japanese intellectual history.[31] From the tenth century onward, however, a Buddhist pessimism—onri edo, "to dislike and seek to leave this defiled world"—fully aware of the finite nature of this world, became the dominant theme in almost all literary works. In a representative religious work from this period, Ōjoyōshū by Keishin-In Genshin, we find a naive example of transcendental thought reflecting the teachings of the Jōdo sect: human beings are to do their utmost to transcend reality by envisioning Nirvana in contrast to the ghastliness of Hell.

From the thirteenth century, once the warrior government had come to power, Buddhist pessimism intensified still further. It seems the climate too grew colder from the thirteenth century.[32] Though it was inevitable that the court aristocracy, seeing the decline of a dynastic system that had lost its power, should have lamented the age as the end of the world, many of the newly risen warriors also converted to Buddhism, and once converted many became truly devoted. This may well have been because their profession required killing, and they could not but experience the terrors of a life that involved slaughtering even their own kinsmen. The collapse of the order and civil wars must have inflicted grave suffering on the common people. The new Buddhist sects in the Kamakura period (such as Jōdo Shinshū, Nichiren, and Zen) were attempts to reform the existing doctrines, responding to a situation in which the Buddhist faith had spread from the warrior class and diffused broadly among the common people. In the sense that they aimed at direct salvation (unmediated by a priest) for all people, they can be compared to Protestantism in Western Europe. The struggle with transcendental thought attempted by several leading Buddhist priests, such as Shinran, the founder of Jōdo Shinshū, and Dōgen, the founder of Sōtō Zen, can no longer be called naive. In the sixteenth century, followers of Jōdo Shinshū controlled a large number of areas; they engaged in fierce conflict with the ruling warrior class, and a large number of believers gave up their lives. Moreover, from the sixteenth to the seventeenth centuries, within a span of several decades, almost a million Japanese converted to Christianity. This too met with suppression by the warrior government, and countless people sacrificed their lives. (The Roman church canonized 26 of those crucified.) These facts show that the Japanese people have not simply preserved from ancient times an affirmative stance toward this world. The words and deeds of the medieval Japanese recall the attitude of West Europeans in the Middle Ages described by Johan Huizinga, particularly the famous phrase *memento mori*.

Despite all of the above, the argument of Nakamura and others contains a certain truth. All Japanese religious leaders, from Kūkai, Saichō, and Ennin, to Hōnen, Shinran, Dōgen, Nichiren, and Ren'nyo, tried to discover a transcendental Absolute that might bring about salvation, a becoming-one with the Buddha, or enlightenment in this world—that is, in the actual human experience of the common individual. Certainly Buddhism (unlike Christianity, in which it is quite impossible for the individual to become "God") affirms that it is possible for people to become "Buddha," by grasping the ultimate truth (achieving Nirvana or *satori*, enlightenment). In India and China, however, it is considered that there is no one other than Gautama Buddha who can realize this possibility. In contrast, the Japanese Buddhist leaders mentioned above believed that anybody (even animals and plants) can become "Buddha." Kūkai and Saichō in the ninth century believed that if they persevered in strict practices, individuals could become "Buddha." Dōgen in the thirteenth century, in developing what would today be called a phenomenological method, preached that (through Zen meditation) the ultimate truth would become apparent in the midst of the world of phenomena itself.

In a sense it was Shinran who was the most thoroughgoing in this approach. John Calvin's doctrine, that it was man who defied the transcendental nature of God by believing that God would save man, is well known, but Shinran's doctrine is exactly the opposite; he believed that doubting that Buddha would save human beings was in itself contrary to absolute faith in Buddha, as shown in his well-known aphorism, "If a good man could live his life fully, why not let a wicked one do so as well." Shinran's Buddha embraced humanity, in contrast to Calvin's God, who rejects humanity. Both Calvin's and Shinran's positions are theoretically possible as structures of transcendentalism. In neither case can the divide between ultimate, transcendent truth and this world be gauged by the measure of human consciousness; it is both infinitely far and infinitely near.[33] The God of Christianity, who once appeared in this world, strictly demands that the divide between God and man be infinite. But when the theoretical possibilities of the Eastern religions are pursued, which allow unlimited upward speculation, there appears a tendency, seen in Mahayana Buddhism and common to Japanese Buddhist thinkers, to see the possibilities of salvation in the world as manifested. Thus it is not a fair evaluation to see Mahayana Buddhist philosophers, including Shinran, as having abandoned transcendentalism. It is more correct to say that they have penetrated its specific possibilities. There have been none as alert as Shinran to the dangers of faith. But one cannot deny that this doctrine, of an embracing Buddha, tends to be linked directly to an easy affirmation of this world in the understanding of the common people.

THE RELATIVIZATION OF TRANSCENDENTALISM

There are substantial problems in generalizing, as does E. B. Taylor, the development of historical religion as merely the internal evolution of human reflexive thought. For example, as already explained, one of the initial reasons for the emergence of historical religion was that the two different, competing cultures of the nomadic and agrarian types encountered each other quite suddenly (measured in terms of the efficiency of communication at the time). Each of the three aspects of these cultures—action toward nature, action toward others, and philosophy and religion—influenced the other, and it is impossible to determine which was cause and which effect. We must also consider this interaction between cultural aspects with regard to Japanese culture, particularly how the culture in the broad sense (vis-à-vis nature) and the culture of organization (vis-à-vis others) are connected historically to religion and philosophy.

Let us start by considering the first aspect of culture, its relation to nature. The climate of the Japanese archipelago can be summarized as having distinct seasons. Because it is surrounded by the sea and has a central mountain range, there is heavy rainfall, and the Japanese islands as a whole almost never suffer from drought; thus plant growth is so luxuriant as to nearly be a problem. Generally speaking, one could say that the climate in the Japanese islands is temperate. But in the shorter run, the Japanese islands are not free of such natural events as typhoons and local flooding, earthquakes, and volcanic eruptions. Roughly speaking, one can say that the climate of the Japanese archipelago is in general temperate in the long term but changeable at the local level and in the short term.

Human beings' image of the world is of course influenced by their relationship with nature. The people who have lived in the Japanese islands, though, have not been threatened with dying of cold, starvation, or dehydration in the desert, for example. Thus even among the divinities of Japan during the period of archaic religion, one can find no divinity who symbolizes the threat of nature. For example, there was no concept of a divinity whose anger took a cosmological scale, such as a water, sun, or fire divinity. (Contrary to common belief, Amaterasu Ōmikami was not originally the sun divinity.) Only the divinities who symbolized local disaster were feared, such as the divinities of swamp, river, and mountain, who might curse the local people. The climate did not generate an interpretation of the world that sees nature as a whole as hostile to human beings. It was hard for the idea of a single deity who enforced submission through absolute authority to emerge. This is one reason why, when the Japanese people learned transcendental thought, it was easy for them to turn to a welcoming, forgiving god—that is, to a belief in Amida or the bodhisattvas—rather than to an absolute deity. Even the Japanese sense of transience was not understood as the evanescence of this world as a whole, but as the vicissitudes of individuals' fortunes and seasonal changes, akin to unexpected natural disasters. Within these limits, though, the Japanese sense of transience was vivid, and this was one reason they took to Buddhism rather than Confucianism. But the reality of the nature that surrounded the Japanese at least could not be a factor promoting the complete rejection of this world.

Second, let us consider the culture of organization.[34] Religion, particularly historical religion, is not only concerned with the salvation of individuals but in fact works as an ideology legitimizing political integration. And such political integration helps to sustain the continued existence of historical religion. As mentioned above, historical religion has played a historical role in integrating different cultures, and the fact that politics has required historical religion should not be ignored. In terms of this political perspective, during the more than 1,000 years between the Ritsuryō codification of the seventh century and modernization in the nineteenth century, the Japanese people never once had to confront wholesale, macropolitical integration.

The Ritsuryō state of the seventh century was in large part an attempt to unify the country and set up institutions to prevent an invasion by the Tang dynasty, which was believed to be imminent. The Japanese at that time, with Prince Shōtoku and the Soga clan as their first leaders, tried to establish Confucian and Buddhist Chinese models as the basis of the social structure. But the Tang invasion never arrived, the integration of the basic ideas for social institutions was left unfinished, and the institutional inheritance of the ancient past was preserved, somewhat modified. During the millennium that followed, Japanese society never experienced the physical impact of a different civilization, either military invasion (the exception is Kublai Khan's two attempts at invasion in the fourteenth century) or immigration on any significant scale. The Ritsuryō state was naturalized as what is called the dynastic system. The court culture of the Heian period from the tenth century, which was generated from this system, resulted in the creation of outstanding literary works in poetry, essays, and *Genji monogatari*, perhaps the world's oldest novel, but it has to be said that their content—aesthetic absorption in the life of the court— symbolized among the aristocracy an escape from the actual structure of society, which concealed an as-yet-unresolved conceptual dilemma and the self-satisfaction that was its corollary.

As a result of the self-satisfaction of the court government in Kyoto, regional administration became lax, the Ritsuryō system disintegrated, and the provinces became anarchic. In response, a new type of organization began to emerge in eastern Japan, far away from Kyoto. This new organization resembled the feudal system of Europe; its leaders were the so-called samurai (warriors), and its basic unit was a lineage group with multiple functions, agricultural and military. This was what Kumon, Satō, and I have called the *ie*. In the thirteenth century, a federation of *ie* known as the *bakufu* became firmly established, over time coming to function as the government, at first in the east, and then gradually throughout the country. Throughout the almost 700 years that followed, until the nineteenth century, the coexistence of warrior and court governments continued. It is indisputable that the warrior government enlarged its actual authority and that the court government gradually became nominal, but the warrior government was never able to deprive the court government and the emperor as its center of its nominal, but in theory ultimate, legitimacy. Occasionally the legitimacy of the warrior government itself was threatened, but not once was the position of the emperor denied. Among Japanese nationalists are those who make a mystery of this historical fact, though it was surely due to the absence of the danger of foreign invasion and thus required no complete political integration. For example, if Kublai Khan's attempts to invade had been more persistent, a more unified government might have been established under warrior leadership. But the warrior government never faced the need to confront a historical *fait accompli*. Throughout world history, such states, with two heads, seem to have been rare.

This dyarchy was unlike the division between the secular and religious orders seen in medieval Europe. The court government in Japan can in no way be regarded as a religious organization. It is noteworthy that intellectual attempts to resist this reality and search for the unifying principle of the political structure did not appear until the nineteenth century. Even two works by historians-*cum*-intellectuals from the court—Jien's *Gukanshō* and Chikafusa Kitabatake's *Jinnō shōtōki*[35]—ultimately recognized that the warrior government actually had a raison d'être. This dyarchic state continued until, confronted by the physical threat of the West European powers, it had to be abandoned.

The lack of macropolitical integration, however, did not lead to social disintegration. Groups that were small but had their own vitality formed the classes of society. These were mainly what I have called the military-agricultural groups of the *ie*. In the sixteenth century, they were joined by the *sō* (which can also be thought of as armed villages), which were characterized more strongly by self-government by the peasants. As long as these groups continued to exist, a reasonably firm foundation was provided for the livelihood and psychological security of individual Japanese. In this sense, groups such as the *ie*, *sō*, and *mura* have a decisive significance in the historical experience of the Japanese (during the Tokugawa period, the semifeudal *mura* was institutionalized as the substructure of the *ie*, which had increased in size; the *sō* also were absorbed by the *ie* and became *mura*).[36] Thus the life of the average Japanese was incorporated within the microcosm of these groups, in a macrosocial environment that was generally unstable. The majority of religious reformers in the Kamakura period were trying to provide a path toward salvation for the average Japanese living within this micro perspective, not to offer a new conception of society as a whole. In Japan the political demands for transcendental thought were not powerful.

Japan's case is clearly different from that of the Asian NIEs, which have recently frequently been called Confucian. It is clear that Confucianism has long played an important role in Japan, since the seventh century, even if not as important as Buddhism. One cannot say, however, that Tokugawa society, for example, the final period of premodern Japan, was Confucian. Certainly, if the Tokugawa government (the *bakufu*) had an official ideology, it was not Buddhism or Shintō but a transformed Confucianism. And in the schools and schoollike institutions of Tokugawa Japan, the Confucian classics were frequently used as textbooks. But many of the Confucian principles of conduct were not observed. In a revealing example, as the seventeenth-century Confucianist Keisai Asami criticized, the practice of adopting nonfamily members, which had spread among the warrior class, violated both official and Confucian norms and would not even be considered in China or Korea. To give another example, for the warrior, loyalty to one's lord preceded filial piety toward one's parents, the most important Confucian virtue.

More generally, the warrior virtues of bravery and loyalty to the military group were fundamentally incompatible with the Confucian ideals of moderation and a harmonious order. From the thirteenth century on, it was the warriors who actually controlled Japan, and their virtues gradually spread to the general population to the extent that their warrior virtues became the backbone of the Shingaku (a school of ethics) that had such an influence on the populace. Of course, there were points in common between the warrior virtues and Confucianism, such as loyalty toward the group and a sense of hierarchy. But in a certain respect, it was the differences that were decisive. The warrior group (below I call this the *ie*), from its origins in eastern Japan in the eleventh and twelfth centuries, was an achievement-oriented, artificial organization; that it was so cohesive was a product of its long history of conflict with neighboring warrior groups. The house or family in the Confucian context was a natural, ascriptive group that could not respond easily to the functional requirements of industrialization, for example. In contrast, the tradition of the achievement-oriented organization in Japan—the *ie*—was a positive asset in the creation of the modern bureaucracy and firm. In this sense, one of the reasons for Japan's success in industrialization was that the organizational tradition at the micro level of society was not Confucian in any real sense.

The development of historical religion requires a certain kind of situation with respect to action toward nature and toward others (harsh natural conditions and a chance encounter between different tribes). Certainly, though, the triumph of historical religion is frequently achieved by ignoring the internal conditions of neighboring societies. In order to achieve a high level of abstraction, historical religion frequently understands the thought of neighboring societies as something with limited universality. This ability to abstract is all the greater if it can apply directly to an interpretation of action (such as science and law) toward nature (technology) and toward others (organization). The large-scale societies of historical civilizations had substantial capability for physical, military conquest. But from the seventh to the nineteenth centuries, Japan was by chance almost isolated geopolitically from the historical civilizations and therefore had little need for domestic political integration. Also, the natural environment provided only limited incentives for Japanese society to turn to transcendental thought.

Because of these geopolitical and domestic conditions the control of transcendental thought/historical religion over Japanese society was not total. But to link this to the survival of archaic religion is simplistic. The survival of the court government centered on the emperor was, in many ways, an accidental result of changing political dynamics. The *ie*-type group of the samurai, which was dominant in Japanese society from the Middle Ages, was not simply a revival of the ancient clan. Over more than 1,000 years, the social structure was transformed by more than a simple change in rulers. During this period cultural inheritances were created that cannot be called entirely archaic (the culture of the Heian court, the new Kamakura Buddhism, the Muromachi city culture, and the Tokugawa townspeople's culture) and that are globally recognized as more than simply popular culture. Not just since modernization but throughout history, one can say that the Japanese people's response to the changing environment has been traditionalist and at the same time accepting of change. This duality of tradition and change reflects the diffusion of a particular worldview, not through theoretical innovation but through gradual growth.

These are precisely the characteristics of what I have called hermeneutic thought, which has deep historical roots in Japan. For example, the acceptance of Chinese civilization from the seventh century, the response to the advance of Western Europe in the sixteenth, the adaptation of all that was Western and modern in the nineteenth, and the acceptance of American civilization following defeat in the Second World War were all self-reforms on the part of Japanese society, implemented through the "interpretation" of other civilizations. Clearly a common form can be discovered in these changes. In terms of a transcendentalism that advocates a single justice and unified principles (enlightenment thought and modern progressivism, for example), relations between cultures are those of the doctrine of just war, where the question is whether one will conquer or be conquered; and the conquered culture has no option other than faithfully to copy, and become the same as, the conquering culture. As a culture lower than the conquering culture, the conquered culture can only "fit in" as a part of it. Japan's acceptance of other cultures, however, has not been imitative in this sense, and above all, Japan has not fit in. It has never fit in as a lower culture, whether to Chinese civilization, the civilization of early modern Europe, modern European civilization, or American civilization. Japan's form of acceptance has not been fitting in but "overlapping." From the innovation of the phonetic syllabary (the various kinds of *kana*) in the eighth and ninth centuries, to industrial policy and Japanese management following the Second World War, foreign patterns and traditional patterns have been made to overlap and rub together, and a fixed, compound pattern has been created, unlike either of the other two. This common form is precisely what I have explained above as hermeneutic thought.

Typically, transcendentalism criticizes this pattern of response to other cultures as lacking in principles and relying too much on pragmatism. Both the existing Western critique of Japan and progressive Japanese intellectuals' critique of their own culture have been based on the belief that a single justice and the future history of progress can be predicted. This kind of critique is inevitable, as long as one relies on the transcendental viewpoint of progressivism. The problem, however, is that transcendental thought is not the only pattern of human reflection, and that the form that is modern progressivism, in particular, is failing as a response to the issues of the contemporary world. As I have explained in this book, what is now needed is to understand and respond to other countries' cultures without discarding one's own. The basis for such a method is in hermeneutic thought, and one example of this is Japan's historical experience, though achieved under limited conditions. Nowadays, when cultural conquest through military force and the concept of justice has become impossible, it is hermeneutics and not transcendentalism that will save international relations from catastrophe.

Furthermore, the historical background of hermeneutic thought in Japan is both deep and extensive. For example, Japanese ideas about culture and taste are unique. In any society, the aristocracy has a "culture" and "taste" that makes its own position prominent. But Japan has cultural forms such as *waka* and haiku (poetic forms), *nō* theater, *sado* (the tea ceremony), and *ikebana* (flower-arranging), "tastes" that cut across the vertical classes. This is an indication that over a long period a common sensibility was formed, and diffused, among the Japanese people. But one should say that this is a characteristic, not of the Japanese disposition, but of an isolated society blessed by certain natural conditions.

THE NEED FOR UNDERSTANDING IN CONTEMPORARY POLITICS

One can look at the contemporary world too from both transcendental and hermeneutic perspectives. For example, the United States, which even today faces major encounters between various races and cultures, can be regarded as representative of a culture that pursues transcendental thought. The starting point for the founding of the United States was the emigration of the most radical wing of Puritans from Britain. Transcendentalism in its purest form was cultivated in the rich soil of the new country and developed into the basis for the United States as a country of ideals and justice. Alexis de Tocqueville, who visited the country in the 1830s, wrote: "So, of all countries in the world, America is the one in which the precepts of Descartes are least studied and best followed. No one should be surprised at that. The Americans never read Descartes's works because their state of society distracts them from speculative inquiries, and they follow his precepts because this same state of society naturally leads them to adopt them."[37]

Even now, more than any other country in the world, the United States is a country in which transcendental thought is strong and a country that believes in a single justice, does not doubt progress in the modern sense, and has a strong Cartesian tendency. Until very recently, the Soviet Union, which raised the banner for another concept of modern progress, was a worthy opponent, but now neither Japan nor the European countries can challenge the force of this belief in progress. As noted above, the trend of Japan's economic development, as the automatic result of a social system adopted in the process of catch-up, did not lead to the emergence of progressivism as an ideology. As long as the United States tries to sustain its progressive/transcendentalist tendency, there will be no means for the American people to orient their own intellectual position other than as either an intellectual conversion of the world or intellectual isolation. Thus there is a danger that the United States, in dealing with international questions, will rely on abstract concepts and reject other kinds of ideas.

On the other hand, Japan may represent the hermeneutic orientation among the industrialized countries or may be seen as a country that relies on the hermeneutic method. Is it because of this quality, which does not start with a single idea of justice, that the United States became particularly irritated with the Japanese way of thinking? The hermeneutic method, however, is clearly one pattern of human reflection and should not in itself be criticized.

But the hermeneutic position does have the shortcoming of being restricted to the historical experience of the past and is closed in on itself. Japan is in no way a country that rejects change; it adapts to change. But the adaptive changes Japan makes do not follow previously determined principles. The so-called American revisionists always point this out as Japan's problem. Certainly, given the present rapidly changing international situation, there is a danger that the Japanese pattern of gradual adaptation will cause serious friction. At the same time, dealing with specific problems one by one, without rejecting them ideologically, may be Japan's strong point. Considering the question more broadly, with reference to the United States and Japan, what is now most necessary to create an international society that incorporates various cultures and races? Until now, the usual answer has been that an abstract, universal framework is needed, which can accommodate the uniqueness of individual cultures. Even if such a framework could be developed, it would bring with it difficulties almost like those of a new "superreligion." Is it not the hermeneutic position, therefore, which tries to experience other cultures as its own, that is now most needed? Its effectiveness seems to be increasing remarkably with the recent, extraordinary growth of new methods of communication. In other words, instead of a common religion or science, is not what humanity now needs a toleration of different patterns of tradition and culture and an increase in commensurability?

Afterword

The various problems raised in this book share a broad similarity. In Chapter 1, I set out the three axes connected, respectively, to industrialization, nationalism, and economic freedom and equality; but from these axes there naturally arise similar problems.

First, what becomes apparent from the axis connected to nationalism is the difficulty of achieving both justice and peace. Certainly, it has been an eternal human desire that justice and peace be brought into accord with each other, that a perfect order in which justice had been realized might be peaceably maintained. But as Augustine said in *The City of God* (book 19, ch. 27), the accord of justice and peace is possible only in the "kingdom of God," not in the "kingdom on earth." To our regret, in the real world, there will always be a conflict between justice and peace. This is a general conclusion that cannot be disputed. On the one hand, the justice human beings advocate—even in its most complete form as historical religion—is self-centered, and multiple justices come into dispute; on the other, a pacifism intent on abandoning the advocacy of justice comes back to an abandonment of freedom of action, and thus, almost always, of freedom of thought. Other than those high-level thinkers who have escaped the dimension of action, no one has the capacity to transcend this conflict. If one follows the orthodox line of Christian theology that began with Augustine, a kind of *convergence theory* comes to be expected, in which an effort intended toward the "kingdom of God" sooner or later yields a single justice. One could say that this was the prototype for modern progressivism. As has been made clear throughout this book, however, although history has accommodated the doctrine of nonjust war, the combination of this with cultural imperialism, and the doctrine of just war in the cold war, expectations of convergence continue to be betrayed by modern and contemporary political events.

If one were to annotate this, one could say that this argument represents in concentrated form the more wide-ranging conflict between freedom of action and order. Harmony between individual freedom of action and social order is possible only in an ideal society that one might, if one were a theologian, call the "kingdom of God." It may be that during certain historical periods (the modern period in Western Europe, for example), and within a limited sphere (the economic sphere, for example), there has been harmony. But there have been no examples in human history of such harmony prevailing in all spheres and increasing over time. I am not saying we should abandon all hope, only that we should be cautious of any too-great expectation at this point in human history.

A similar problem appears as the conflict between freedom of economic action and the market system on the axis of industrialization. In the view that has become mainstream in modern Western Europe, it has been argued that the self-regulating and self-maintaining capability of the market is sufficient, that it can absorb technological progress, and that it can achieve harmony. The material abundance seen in the leading countries at present seems to endorse this view, and since the collapse of the socialist bloc this argument has seemed to gather still more force. But market-oriented industrialization eradicated many preindustrial cultures that may well have had merits, and the takeoff to industrialization, with each successive wave of technological innovation, injured the previous way of life and ethos. Particularly in the international context, because of an unbridgeable technological gap, the disparity between the developed and developing countries until recently was widening still further. The position that the market mechanism will bring equilibrium and harmony to the world is nothing more than a myth.

There has recently also appeared what at first glance seems to be the reverse phenomenon. With technological innovation becoming constant, developmentalism has become established, seeking consciously to exploit this fact; and the substance of the market system has changed significantly and instability has increased. A number of "developmentalist" late-developing countries are rapidly achieving economic growth; but this is a sign of instability. In general, it is gradually becoming harder to integrate economic freedom in the classical sense and maintain the market system (including the social environment that supports it). We see here, again, a conflict.

What has long made me consider this a conflict is the enlightenment concept of "human progress," or the power of the convergence model since Adam Smith, which has posited that economic progress will lead human society as a whole toward a specific, fixed, and desirable state. The constant technological innovation of the past two centuries has surprised and confused people and has supported this ideology of progress. But at present, this classical convergence model of unitary progress is at most a model of convergence among the leading countries and cannot guarantee the convergence of progress for humanity as a whole, including the late-developing countries. As I have argued throughout this book, many signs now demonstrate this deficiency, and there is no need to go over them again here.

In short, "God" is dead, and so is the concept of "progress." Of course, what I am here calling "God" signifies the somewhat exclusive, narrow idea that appeared typically in Christianity; and "progress," similarly, signifies the unilinear, narrow idea connected to natural science and industrialization. It is not impossible that a broader concept of god will appear to capture the human spirit. A more pluralistic concept of progress is both possible and desirable. The emergence of a progressivism that is not narrow may be possible in the distant future.

However, leaving aside dreams of the future, the most important issue today is to get rid of the concepts of justice and progress in their existing senses, and this has been the theme throughout this book. As I mentioned in Chapter 1, the starting point for this theme is liberalism of thought in the sense that I have defined it. There may be some objections to making liberalism in this sense the first principle. If this liberalism of thought gains general support, in order to make it possible we need a model that goes beyond unifaceted justice and unilinear progress. There is substantial inertia in the old progressivism, however, and under the present circumstances we cannot ignore the symptoms of intellectual thirst for the simple, clear concepts of justice and progress. The dangers of vehemently advocating justice and progress have to some extent become clear in the failure of the attempt at socialism. But in the United States, the same danger exists in its forceful position taken in advocating a return to the classical model (Francis Fukuyama's, for example). Its frequent stifling of freedom within and outside the country was socialism's greatest failure, but the international imposition of the classical model (the model combining classical economic liberalism and nationalism) also has a danger of stifling freedom globally. The new model must provide an adequate forum for debate between various justices and various progresses, and for intellectual debate generally. We must agree on the "rule" (distinct from justice) that can establish such a forum and search for a model of what might be called meta-liberalism.

At the moment, however, people do not seem to have the imaginative powers sufficient to discover such a model. The model of polymorphic economic liberalism and an overlapping, shared roof is my own attempt to stir up such an imaginative capacity, and it is as yet incomplete. There is a need for such an attempt by many people, and we must be especially careful to avoid intellectual or ideological positions, advanced without sufficient analysis, that seek to return to the existing, classical ideas of progress. To stress the point, let me present a few examples.

This kind of danger exists in the environmentalism and idea of conserving global resources that have recently attracted people's attention. Of course, it is necessary to implement controls on productive and consumer activity that visibly destroys the environment, and in this sense, all nations, including late-developing countries, are now environmentalists. For example, there seems to be a high level of agreement that the growth of the hole in the ozone layer through the use of freon, global warming through the increase of carbon dioxide, the unsafe disposal of radioactive materials, and the increase in acid rain should be dealt with as dangerous problems. The technology for dealing with these exists for the most part; thus, the problem is how to enable a politics to change social institutions, given these technologies. Environmentalism of this kind, calling for use of our scientific and engineering capabilities on a piecemeal or gradual basis, should naturally be incorporated in all future political programs.

But even on these problems, where agreement is easy, there are potential differences of opinion. For example, different races have different amounts of the skin pigment (melanin) that reduces the harmful effects of ultraviolet rays, and this could lead to each country's having a different opinion about the urgency of the problem of the ozone layer and about the amount of resources that should be devoted to solving it. Depending on whether one lives in a cold or warm area or on the coast or inland, opinions may vary on the carbon dioxide problem. One proposal is to merely prevent the problem from worsening, but, as discussed below, a kind of distributive issue would arise if this proposal were adopted. Ultimately, these questions will give rise to a fundamental debate about what is a good or bad global environmental order.

Any such debate must begin with who is to take the leadership, whose view is just. It goes without saying that each country and each region has its own particular historical memory. People's images of the "greening of the earth" differ depending on whether they are part of a rice-growing society, a wheat-raising society, a society that cultivates root vegetables, or a nomadic society. For example, the Japanese perceive a "greenness of nature" with which they have become intimate through their rizoculture; in contrast, Europeans may see the "greenness of nature" as something toward which human beings must carefully preserve an attitude of confrontation. Similarly, the peoples of the steppe, the oasis, and the savanna have differing images of the "greenness of nature." Also, the concept of the natural order as a whole, including animals, differs greatly depending on how much one engages in cattle-ranching or fishing. Concepts of cruelty toward animals also differ for the same reason. In this world, we have both those who refuse to eat dolphin or whale and many who cannot understand offering a lamb or cow as a sacrifice to a god. In sum, what the ideal ecological order should be differs by country and region. Only a powerful world authority will be able to unify the varying ideas of an ideal order of the environment.

In the final pages of this book, there is no need to discuss the political difficulties connected with realizing environmentalism, whether through scientific and technological means or by resorting to full-blown anti-industrialization. The confrontation between the developed and developing countries will be especially difficult. For example, as regards the problem of carbon dioxide, if a ban on logging in the tropical rain forest is to be enforced on the developing countries, the developed countries should first sharply reduce their own energy consumption; but it is rare for the developed countries (particularly the United States, for example) to show the will to implement such a policy. If we are to prevent acid rain, the developed countries should give the developing countries the means to prevent pollution. There is a proposal for auctioning internationally the "right" to pollute with carbon dioxide, but the effect would probably be to widen still further the disparity in industrialization between developed and developing countries. In any case, as long as there is no advance in the international equalization of economic strength, there will be no way to implement such policies. The likelihood of such policies being adopted is very different from what progressivism has anticipated to date, using various scientific theories enlisted to make predictions. Environmentalists must at least accept the reality of industrialism in late-developing countries; simply advocating the principles of environmentalism will have no substantial effect internationally. Unless those who advocate environmentalist principles fully recognize the fact of industrialization, we will be committing the irreparable mistake of placing the cart before the horse. Think of the fearsome agrarianism of Mao Tse-tung.

Advocating total dependence on the United Nations and democratic socialism would have similar consequences. Given the belligerent tendencies shown by the nation-state system, advocating the principle of a world-state and turning toward dependence on the United Nations as a substitute is a temptation to which it is too easy to succumb. The weaknesses of the United Nations as an organization reveal the dangers of attempting to maintain the world system by relying solely on it. Those who wish to make the best uses of the United Nations must recognize that it requires support at least by a regional security system. Democratic socialism, too, if it pursues distributive equality as a principle, will become embroiled in welfare bureaucracy and systems of economic planning. Distributive justice cannot be the only guiding principle of the society that is to come.

In the end, the key to the twenty-first century cannot be a hasty revival of progressivism or an unyielding adherence to the prevailing conservative opinion (through rediscovery of classical economic liberalism and nationalism). A meta-liberalism is needed, in which the advocacy of various progresses and justices can compete and the rules that make it possible are created through "understanding." Throughout the world, many are calling for a new world order, but we can acquire such an order only if each individual is able to think and act freely. Perhaps, even without the extended arguments offered in this book, all those concerned with the future of our world are fully aware that "understanding" is the basic condition necessary for humanity in its journey toward achieving order. However mundane it may sound, the key to the twenty-first century can only be for each of us, as individual human beings, to have our own thoughts and beliefs and to "understand" each other. The task, however, is as challenging as it is obvious.

Reference Matter

Notes

CHAPTER I

1. Ludwig Wittgenstein, *Vermischte Bemerkungen*, ed. Georg Henrik von Wright (Frankfurt am Main: Suhrkamp Verlag, 1977).

2. Martin Heidegger, *Die Technik und die Kehre* (Pfullingen: Günther Neske, 1962).

3. George Herbert Mead, *Mind, Self and Society, from the Standpoint of a Social Behaviorist*, ed. C. W. Morris (Chicago: University of Chicago Press, 1934).

4. The problem of "predictions being subverted" in historical theory usually cannot be handled head-on by progressivists. By beginning to give careful consideration to all the possibilities of predictions being subverted, of predictions of predictions being subverted not coming true, and so on, a determinism toward social phenomena might be realized. Given what I have said so far, it may be better to call this ultradeterminism. But there is no such usage in the historical theory of progressivism.

5. A pluralistic or multilinear view of history that envisages various non-convergent paths of history is not progressivism. This is because when one envisions the existence of diverse paths that can be taken to achieve varying levels of progress, there cannot but be differences in the levels of progress achieved depending on the path chosen—that is, a difference between progress and regress. The continued existence of an inferior path, or a regressive path, would be contrary to the idea of progress.

6. For example, in the opinion of John Rawls, who has considered these kinds of problems carefully, equality of outcomes is nothing more than a third-level consideration and nothing more than what is produced by the so-called

maximim solution, which maximizes the minimum outcome. John Rawls, *A Theory of Justice* (Cambridge, Mass.: Harvard University Press, 1971), ch. 2, sec. 13, and ch. 3, sec. 26.

7. For example, Yoshiaki Ito, Norio Yamamura, and Masakazu Shimada, *Dōbutsu seitaigaku* (Tokyo: Sōju Shōbo, 1992), ch. 13.

8. One example of this argument is found in Robert Reich, *The Work of Nations* (New York: Knopf, 1991).

9. Sacred and profane here follow the usage of Mircea Eliade, *The Sacred and the Profane: The Nature of Religion*, trans. Willard R. Trask (New York: Harcourt, Brace, 1959).

10. Isaiah Berlin, *Four Essays on Liberty* (London: Oxford University Press, 1969).

11. Asvaghosha, *Daijōkishinron*. A free translation of the title might be "An invitation to the teachings of the great vehicle." See *The Awakening of Faith*, attributed to Asvaghosha, trans. and with commentary by Yoshito S. Hakeda (New York: Columbia University Press, 1967).

12. Max Weber, *Gesammelte Aufsätze zur Religionssoziologie*, Band II: *Hinduismus und Buddhismus* (Tübingen: J. C. B. Mohr, 1923), pp. 363–78.

13. In the words of the *Daijōkishinron*, this refers to an "ingrained compunction."

14. Karl Mannheim, *Essays on Sociology and Social Psychology*, ed. Paul Kecskemeti (New York: Oxford University Press, 1953), pp. 74–164.

15. It is necessary to be particularly cautious about where one places the conservatism seen in the countries that were late in industrializing. The conservative postwar politics of Japan is also an example of this; "late-developer conservatism" is a kind of compromise between progressivism and conservatism, and while clearly aiming at progress in the name of becoming an advanced industrialized country, it also has an aspect that puts a brake on the speed with which that is achieved. Late-developer conservatism, while commonly criticized by progressivists for its backwardness, and by anachronistic orthodox conservatives for its blind faith in change, in the main is clearly a subspecies of progressivism. The governments in all the Asian NIEs (newly industrializing economies) show strongly the character of late-developer conservatism. See Yasusuke Murakami, "The Japanese Model of Political Economy," in Kozo Yamamura and Yasukichi Yasuba, eds., *The Political Economy of Japan*, vol. 1: *The Domestic Transformation* (Stanford, Calif.: Stanford University Press, 1987), pp. 64–65.

16. One can cite Mannheim as an example of someone who used "orthodoxy" in a similar sense. Karl Mannheim, *Freedom, Power, and Democratic Planning* (New York: Oxford University Press, 1950), p. 308.

17. Francis Fukuyama, "The End of History?" *National Interest* 16 (Summer 1989): 3–18.

18. Friedrich Engels, "Introduction to the First (1884) Edition," in *The Origin of the Family, Private Property and the State* (London: Lawrence and Wishart, 1972). One can imagine that Marx was also thinking of similar rules, but here there is the question of confusion or contradiction between the "homo laborans" and "homo faber" pointed out by Hannah Arendt. Cf. Hannah Arendt, *The Human Condition* (Chicago: University of Chicago Press, 1958), chs. 3 and 4.

19. What I am calling here "philosophical hermeneutics" is distinct from

the hermeneutic object characteristic of scriptural and classical hermeneutics but points to the research into the general rules of how people understand and interpret others (and themselves). Representative philosophers are Wilhelm Dilthey, Martin Heidegger, and Hans-Georg Gadamer. See, for example, Martin Heidegger, *Being and Time*, trans. John Macquarrie and Edward Robinson (New York: Harper and Row, 1962), pp. 61–62.

20. Adam Smith, *The Theory of Moral Sentiments* (1759). His concept of the "impartial spectator," however, is a sudden intrusion of transcendental thought.

21. That is, *ryakugateki*, in the sense in which the expression is used in Shōzō Ōmori, *Chishiki to gakumon no kōzō* (Tokyo: Ōbunsha, 1983).

22. Daniel Bell, *The Coming of Post-Industrial Society: A Venture in Social Forecasting* (New York: Basic Books, 1973), p. 52.

23. To use the concepts in this book, "knowledge" indicates in general that which a world image has accumulated through "reflection."

24. *Translator's note*: Chapter 9 offers a full discussion of how this should occur and why Murakami was prompted to use the strong phrase "developmental dictatorship."

CHAPTER 2

1. Richard Rosecrance, *The Rise of the Trading State* (New York: Basic Books, 1986), p. 77.

2. *Translator's note*: Not "unjust wars," but wars from which had been removed the issue of which party had justice on its side; that is, a-just, or perhaps better, nonjust wars.

3. Thus, depending on the individual, the nation-state and nationalism were generated not by the Treaty of Westphalia but by the Napoleonic Wars. Edward Hallett Carr's *Nationalism and After* (London: Macmillan, 1945) pays no attention at all to the Treaty of Westphalia (see p. 6). However, as I have already noted, it is clear that the doctrine of the nation-state system was created in the seventeenth century. What was generated in the nineteenth century was, so to speak, the democratization or popularization of nationalism.

4. John Maynard Keynes, *The Economic Consequences of the Peace* (New York: Harcourt, Brace and Howe, 1920).

5. Morton A. Kaplan, for example, in *System and Process in International Politics* (New York: John Wiley, 1957), p. 23, simply formulates the rule of what he calls "the balance-of-power system," but his sixth rule requires the restoration of the vanquished.

6. A. J. P. Taylor, *The Origins of the Second World War* (New York: Atheneum, 1962), p. 30.

7. *Translator's note*: "The Western world" or "the West" is used to refer to Europe and North America.

8. For a superb introduction to this literature, see Benedict Anderson, *Imagined Communities: Reflections on the Origin and Spread of Nationalism* (London: Verso, 1983; revised and extended edition, 1991), ch. 2.

9. Various representative Meiji intellectuals—such as Yukichi Fukuzawa, Chōmin Nakae, Sohō Tokutomi, Setsurei Miyake, and Kanzō Uchimura—in at least some period during their careers expressed these points of view.

10. The phrase "The Greater East Asia Co-Prosperity Sphere" appeared just

one year before the outbreak of the Pacific War, in 1940 (in a news conference given by Foreign Minister Matsuoka in August). See Noboru Yano, *Nihon no nanshin shikan* (Tokyo: Chūō Kōronsha, 1979). It is often noted that the philosophies of Kitarō Nishida and the so-called Kyoto school provided an intellectual basis for the thinking about the Greater East Asia Co-Prosperity Sphere. These philosophies, as criticisms of European philosophy up to the nineteenth century, were in a certain sense quite standard, and at the very abstract level even their concepts such as *hakkō ichiu* can be understood as a version of "universal brotherhood." These philosophies, however, gave insufficient answers at the level of concrete social analysis to the most urgent questions, such as: why, while opposing Euro-American imperialism, does Japan adopt imperialistic actions and policies that are difficult to distinguish from those of Western imperialism? And, if there is a point on which the two can be distinguished, what is it? If the point of distinction is in the unique historical experience or memory of an unbroken imperial line, then it cannot be a universal principle. If one argues that this is a transitional but necessary evil, then this is not a philosophical answer.

11. *Translator's note*: "Progressive" refers to the Marxists, social democrats, and others on the left.

12. See Augustine, *The City of God*, book 4, ch. 15, and book 5, chs. 12–21. The quotation is from the title of book 5, ch. 21, as translated by William M. Green in *The City of God Against the Pagans* (Cambridge, Mass.: Harvard University Press, 1963), vol. 2, p. 249.

13. Ibid., vol. 6, p. 141 (book 19, ch. 5).

14. Ibid., vol. 6, p. 195 (book 19, ch. 17).

15. Thomas Aquinas, *Summa Theologica*, trans. Fathers of the English Dominican Province, First Complete American Edition, 3 vols. (New York: Benziger Bros., 1947).

16. For example, see the description of the "powerful, but enlightened race," in Immanuel Kant, *Kleinere Schriften zur Geschichtsphilosophie, Ethik und Politik*, ed. Kurt Vorlander (Leipzig: F. Meiner, 1913), pp. 356–61. For Kant's critique of colonialism, see Immanuel Kant, *Eternal Peace and Other International Essays*, trans. W. Hastie (Boston: World Peace Foundation, 1914), pp. 286–89. For Rousseau, see Jean-Jacques Rousseau, *Œuvres Complètes de J. J. Rousseau*, tome 4 (Paris: A. Baudouin Editeur, 1826), pp. 407–47 and 448–63. Both Rousseau and Kant believed that if one were to abandon absolute monarchy and take up a constitutional system, this would have the result of stopping war. This expectation has been betrayed, however, by history from the Napoleonic Wars to the Second World War. The common masses have often been more prowar than their governments. This too has been one of the limitations of pacifism on the eighteenth-century model.

17. *Translator's note*: The original is *jikkan*, to have a real sensation of.

18. *Translator's note*: The original term used is *seikatsu*, a broad term meaning the way of life, living, livelihood, or existence.

19. Anderson, *Imagined Communities*.

20. This is an argument of Naoki Kobayashi, as quoted by Masanori Ishibashi, a former secretary general of the Japan Socialist party and a forceful advocate of unarmed neutrality, in his *Hibusō chūritsu-ron* (Tokyo: Japan Socialist Party, 1983), p. 67.

21. Karl Polanyi, *The Great Transformation* (New York: Farrar and Rinehart, 1944).

22. Rosecrance, *Rise of the Trading State.*

23. Polanyi, *Great Transformation*, pp. 65–66.

24. Ernst B. Haas, "What Is Progress in the Study of International Organization?" *International Relations 76: International Organization and Regime Change* (Tokyo: Japan Association of International Relations, 1984); and Ernst B. Haas, "Why Collaborate? Issue-Linkage and International Regimes," *World Politics* 32, 3 (1980): 357–405. On regimes, see Stephen D. Krasner, ed., *International Regimes* (Ithaca, N.Y.: Cornell University Press, 1983).

CHAPTER 3

1. Robert Gilpin, *The Political Economy of International Relations* (Princeton, N.J.: Princeton University Press, 1987). This is what I believe to be the best summary of his position, but it is not quite faithful to his phrasing.

2. Susan Strange, "International Economics and International Relations: A Case of Mutual Neglect," *International Affairs* 46, 2 (April 1970): 304–15.

3. There is in fact something called a neoclassical theory of development. However, among the various paths this theory describes, the only one that can stand up to analysis is the so-called balanced growth path and its equilibrating characteristic. On this path, although the quantity of production can increase, the production per unit of scarce resource (for example, labor)—that is, per capita GNP—stays fixed. In the normal understanding of the theory of economic development this set of circumstances is not development, but stasis. Recently, there have been attempts at a theory of internal development, and this in itself should be welcomed. See, for example, R. E. Lucas, Jr., "On the Mechanics of Economic Development," *Journal of Monetary Economics* 22, 1 (June 1988): 3–42. However, to try, for example, to capture technology as a whole only mechanically, with macro variables such as capital and total production, makes no sense. To have only added, as is often done to the model, an aggregate function of the "induced technology" is meaningless. The first problem is whether or not the relevant functions that determine technology can be formulated using a meaningful parameter as an axis. The second, and more important, as I discuss in Chapter 5, is that technological innovation in fact brings about the phenomenon of declining marginal costs, but the instability of equilibria and the indeterminateness of distribution this generates cast doubt on the existence of stable, comprehensive production variables. Third, in handling this kind of problem, it is inappropriate to deal with what is essentially unpredictable by positing rational expectations as a premise.

4. Gilpin, *Political Economy of International Relations*, p. 82.

5. H. J. Morgenthau, *Politics Among Nations: The Struggle for Power and Peace* (New York: A. A. Knopf, 1948) is always cited as a representative work.

6. See, for example, Miyoko Kuroda, "Minzoku kokka no kyokōsei," in Toshio Kuroda, ed., *Kyōdōtai-ron no chihei* (Tokyo: Sanshūsha, 1990).

7. Famous recent examples are Robert M. Axelrod, *The Evolution of Cooperation* (New York: Basic Books, 1984), and Robert M. Axelrod and Robert O. Keohane, "Achieving Cooperation Under Anarchy: Strategies and Institutions," *World Politics* 38, 1 (1985): 226–54. There are many things one should say about

Axelrod's model, which posits that the repeated strategy of "an eye for an eye" will eventually lead to cooperation, but here I only want to point out that a nonfinite supergame requires perseverance on the part of the participants beyond momentary cooperation. When the strategy of "an eye for an eye" exceeds the bounds of mutual patience and brings about a catastrophe, it is because there is an end to the game, and a new supergame begins.

8. Charles P. Kindleberger, "Dominance and Leadership in the International Economy: Exploitation, Public Goods, and Free Rides," *International Studies Quarterly* 25, 2 (1981): 242–54. Gilpin, *Political Economy of International Relations*, ch. 2.

9. Yoshinobu Yamamoto, *Kokusaiteki sōgo izun* (Tokyo: University of Tokyo Press, 1985), p. 169. For problems about definitions of regimes and other problems, see chapter 5 in the same book. The following is one definition. "A regime is made up from a single set of clearly stated or suggested principles, criteria, rules, or procedures of policy decision, and by attaching importance to this, the expectations of the interested parties converge as to the extent of a problem in international relations." Ernst B. Haas, "What Is Progress in the Study of International Organization?" *International Relations 76: International Organization and Regime Change* (Tokyo: Japan Association of International Relations, 1984), and Ernst B. Haas, "Why Collaborate? Issue-Linkage and International Regimes," *World Politics* 32, 3 (1980): 357–405.

10. Haas, "Why Collaborate?"

11. George Modelski, *Long Cycles in World Politics* (Seattle: University of Washington Press, 1987).

12. In fact, the neoclassical explanation of these differences is complicated. If one abandons the hypothesis of the production function having constant returns to scale and assumes diminishing returns, then one gets the somewhat strange result of countries with little labor or capital having higher real wages. If one allows the international transfer of capital, then there is a high possibility of an equalization of real wages—that is, a disappearance of disparities in wage levels. As I show later, if technological differences between economies are assumed, varying growth rates can be explained.

13. The Prebisch Report and so-called dependency theory contain examples of such expressions of discontent. Raúl Prebisch, "Commercial Policy in the Underdeveloped Countries," *American Economic Review* 49 (1959): 251–73. There are those who offer qualified support for this argument. For example, Paul Bairoch, "International Industrialization Levels from 1750 to 1980," *Journal of European Economic History* 11, 2 (1982): 269–333. See Akihiko Tanaka, *Sekai shisutemu* (Tokyo: University of Tokyo Press, 1989).

14. This theory is developed in, for example, Immanuel Wallerstein, *The Modern World-System*, 2 vols. (New York: Academic Press, 1974, 1980).

15. Kaname Akamatsu, *Sekai keizai-ron* (Tokyo: Kunimoto Shobō, 1965). He summarizes his theory in English in "A Theory of Unbalanced Growth in the World Economy," *Weltwirtschaftliches Archiv* 86, 2 (1961): 196–215.

16. Ronald P. Dore, *British Factory–Japanese Factory* (Berkeley: University of California Press, 1973).

17. For the details of the above argument, see: Yasusuke Murakami, *Shinchūkan taishū no jidai* (Tokyo: Chūō Kōronsha, 1984), ch. 8, and Yasusuke Murakami, "Nijūseiki no sōzōsha Amerika," in Masakazu Yamazaki, ed., *Hana*

sakeru shin-bunka; bunmei to shite no Amerika 1 (Tokyo: Nihon Keizai Shin-bunsha, 1985).

18. Akamatsu, *Sekai keizai-ron*. The argument of Nicole Bousquet, who is regarded as a member of the Wallerstein school, is similar. However, she tries to separate the argument about the processes of attaining the lead and catching up from the argument about long-term economic cycles. If one thinks in units of a century, however, then the two dynamics are clearly connected. Nicole Bousquet, "From Hegemony to Competition: Cycles of the Core?" in Terence K. Hopkins and Immanuel Wallerstein, eds., *Processes of the World-System* (Beverly Hills, Calif.: Sage, 1980). Tanaka, *Sekai shisutemu*, provides a useful summary of this kind of argument.

19. In Japan, for example, this kind of description can be found in Masahiro Sakamoto, *Pax Americana no kokusai shisutemu* (Tokyo: Yūhikaku, 1986), p. 37.

20. See Paul Kennedy, *The Rise and Fall of the Great Powers* (New York: Random House, 1987), p. 515. He uses the expression "overstretch" to describe Napoleon (p. 135), Hitler (p. 352), and the Japanese military (p. 352). One can see another example of this kind of assertion about the former Chinese empire in Mark Elvin, *The Pattern of the Chinese Past: A Social and Economic Interpretation* (Stanford, Calif.: Stanford University Press, 1973).

21. Peter F. Drucker, *The New Realities: In Government and Politics, in Economics and Business, in Society and World View* (New York: Harper and Row, 1989). His argument makes many of my principal points.

22. Gilpin, *Political Economy of International Relations*, ch. 10.

CHAPTER 4

1. Samuel P. Huntington, "Transnational Organizations in World Politics," *World Politics* 25, 3 (1973): 333–68.

2. Ibid., p. 343. See also Nagayo Honma, *Rinen no kyōwakoku* (Tokyo: Chūō Kōronsha, 1976), ch. 2.

3. Representative of this kind of criticism is George F. Kennan, *American Diplomacy 1900–1950* (Chicago: University of Chicago Press, 1951), ch. 6.

4. *Translator's note*: The article reads: "The Members of the League undertake to respect and preserve as against external aggression the territorial integrity and existing political independence of all members of the League."

5. *Translator's note*: The article reads: "Except where otherwise expressly provided in this Covenant or by the terms of the present Treaty, decisions at any meeting of the Assembly or of the Council shall require the agreement of all the Members of the League represented at the meeting."

6. *Translator's note*: The full article reads: "Should any Member . . . resort to war in disregard of its covenants . . . it shall, *ipso facto*, be deemed to have committed an act of war against all other Members of the League, which hereby undertake immediately to subject it to the severance of all trade or financial relations, the prohibition of all intercourse between their nationals and the nationals of the Covenant-breaking State, and the prevention of all financial, commercial or personal intercourse between the nationals of the covenant-breaking State and the nationals of any other State, whether a Member of the League or not."

7. In the League of Nations, the council did not have much power. The permanent council did not have the right of veto, and for approval and release of the written recommendations, unanimity or majority support among the countries on the council (excluding the parties involved in the dispute) was necessary. However, dispute investigations could be transferred to the assembly of the league on the decision of the council, or at the request of one of the countries involved in the dispute (Article 15.9). In dispute enquiries, each country in the General Assembly, excluding the countries involved in the dispute, had the right to one vote, and the written statement could be adopted with the support of all the members of the council and a majority of those countries not on the council (Article 15.10). This was, so to speak, a rule of conditional majority, and given that it was very flexible as a rule for decision making, the authority of the assembly in dispute enquiries was substantial (Article 15.10). In this connection, in decision making by the council and the assembly on general items, there was the strict requirement of unanimity (Article 5.1). Thus it was comparatively easy to issue decisions on dispute enquiries. Though this was a carefully crafted process, it had the deficiencies mentioned in the text.

8. The Geneva Protocol of 1924 allowed the parties in enquiries that ended in failure to participate in a subsequent procedure, close to arbitration, that obliged them to submit to a binding decision. However, as is well known, this protocol was a failure. A similar process was included in the General Protocol of 1928, and new members were to choose which process to abide by at the time of their admission to the league. It is hard to say that such efforts solved the problems at issue in the Covenant of the League of Nations.

9. In this connection, if one interprets Article 9 of Japan's Constitution as a complete renunciation of military force, it contradicts Articles 42 and 43 of the United Nations Charter, and Japan should not be a legitimate member of the United Nations. The "original drafters" of the constitution probably did not give serious thought to Japan as a war criminal actually becoming a member of the United Nations. As is well known, it is said that the intentionally ambiguous expression in the opening paragraph of Clause 2 of Article 9 was added by the Japanese team (the committee headed by Hitoshi Ashida) in anticipation of this contradiction.

10. Here I distinguish between collective security as seen in the United Nations, and what we might call collective security based on collective self-defense.

11. If one wants to be exact, the last occasion was the hostility surrounding the return of Damansky Island, which broke out between China and the USSR in March 1969. However, this was really nothing more than a small-scale dispute over national boundaries in which the total of both sides' casualties was less than 100.

12. Akira Iriye, in *Nichi-bei sensō* (Tokyo: Chūō Kōronsha, 1978), gives a dispassionate account of this development.

13. Anthony Reid and Lance Castles, eds., *Pre-Colonial State Systems in Southeast Asia*, Monographs of the Malaysian Branch of the Royal Asiatic Society, no. 6 (Kuala Lumpur: Rajiv Printers, April 1979). O. W. Wolters, *History, Culture, and Region in Southeast Asian Perspectives* (Singapore: Institute of Southeast Asian Studies, 1982). On "port state," see Harry J. Benda, "The

Structure of Southeast Asian History," *Journal of Southeast Asian History* 3, 1 (1962): 106-38.

14. "The single ocean" is taken from Wolters, *History, Culture, and Region*, and refers to "the vast expanse of water from the coasts of eastern Africa and western Asia to the immensely long coastline of the Indian subcontinent and on to China" (p. 38).

15. The original version was presented in Yasusuke Murakami, "Tenkan suru sangyō bunmei to 21 seiki e no tenbō," *Ekonomisuto*, Apr. 5, 1983, and an expanded version was included subsequently in Yasusuke Murakami, *Shinchūkan taishū no jidai* (Tokyo: Chūō Kōronsha, 1984), ch. 8. See also in English, Yasusuke Murakami, "Technology in Transition: Two Perspectives on Industrial Policy," in Hugh Patrick, ed., *Japan's High Technology Industries* (Seattle: University of Washington Press, 1986), pp. 211-41.

16. Nikolai Kondratieff, *The Long Wave Cycle* (New York: Richardson and Snyder, 1984); Joseph A. Schumpeter, *Business Cycles: A Theoretical, Historical, and Statistical Analysis of the Capitalist Process* (New York: McGraw Hill, 1939); Fernand Braudel, *Civilization and Capitalism, 15th-18th Century*, vol. 3: *The Perspective of the World* (London: Collins, 1984); T. K. Hopkins and I. Wallerstein et al., "Cyclical Rhythms and Secular Trends of the Capitalist World-Economy," *Review* 2, 4 (1978).

17. C. Perez's "theory of a mismatch in technological innovation" is close to the observation just made. C. Perez, "Structural Change and the Assimilation of New Technologies in the Economic and Social System," *Futures* 15, 5 (1983): 357-75.

18. Kaname Akamatsu, *Sekai keizai-ron* (Tokyo: Kunimoto Shobō, 1965).

19. *Translator's note*: Polymorphic is Murakami's own translation of *tasōteki*. However, *tasōteki* can mean both multiphase and multifaceted, depending on whether the context is diachronic or synchronic. Thus, hereafter, when Murakami is discussing technological catch-up, we will use "multiphase," and when referring to the new system of economic liberalism, "multifaceted" or "polymorphic."

20. Tetsurō Nakaoka is an example of someone who is aware of this possibility but pessimistic in his judgment of its chances; see Tetsurō Nakaoka, "Shin-gijutsu to Kondorachefu no dai-5 no nami no kanōsei," in Miyohei Shinohara, ed., *Kokusai tsūka: gijutsu kakushin: chōki hadō* (Tokyo: Tōyō Keizai Shinpōsha, 1988). Certainly this mechanism of interdependence has not worked very well so far between the United States as the leader and Japan as the follower. This is due to Japan's restricting foreign investment and the United States' lack of enthusiasm for transferring technology. But the relationship between Japan and the East Asian countries does not seem to be repeating this pattern.

21. Richard Rosecrance, *The Rise of the Trading State* (New York: Basic Books, 1986).

22. Ibid., p. 24.

23. Friedrich List, an enthusiastic proponent of the construction of a unified rail system in Germany, wrote frequently on the political and economic significance of railroads. See, for example, *Das deutsche Eisenbahnsystem als Mittel zu Vervollkommung der deutschen Industrie, des deutschen Zollvereins*

und des deutschen Nationalverbandes überhaupt (Stuttgart: J. G. Cottascher Verlag, 1841).

24. Rosecrance, *Rise of the Trading State*, p. 40. "Trading system" is Rosecrance's way of referring to those countries that rely on industrialization and trade rather than on military power and territorial advantage.

25. See Chalmers Johnson, *MITI and the Japanese Miracle: The Growth of Industrial Policy, 1925–1975* (Stanford, Calif.: Stanford University Press, 1982), p. 20. He views developmentalism as a distorted pattern of the later developers.

26. Friedrich A. von Hayek, *Law, Legislation and Liberty*, 3 vols. (London: Routledge and Kegan Paul, 1973, 1976, 1979).

27. Friedrich List, *Das nationale System der politischen Ökonomie* (Stuttgart: J. G. Cottascher Verlag, 1841), ch. 29.

28. John Maynard Keynes, *The General Theory of Employment, Interest and Money* (New York: Harcourt, Brace, 1936), ch. 23.

29. Simon Kuznets, *Economic Growth of Nations: Total Output and Production Structure* (Cambridge, Mass.: Belknap, 1971); W. W. Rostow, *The Stages of Economic Growth* (Cambridge, Eng.: Cambridge University Press, 1960). See also the first section of Chapter 2 in this book.

30. Douglass C. North, *Structure and Change in Economic History* (New York: W. W. Norton, 1981), p. 110.

31. "Proto-industrialization" was coined by Franklin Mendels, and "industrialization before industrialization" is the phrase used by the Göttingen group, which accepted this way of thinking. See Osamu Saito, *Puroto-kōgyō-ka no jidai* (Tokyo: Nihon Hyōronsha, 1985), pp. 50–51.

32. Lujo Brentano, *Die Anfänge des modernen Kapitalismus* (Munich: Akadamie der Wissenschaften, 1916); Max Weber, *Wirtschafts-geschichte* (Berlin: Duncker and Humblot, 1958), ch. 4; Werner Sombart, *Der moderne Kapitalismus* (Munich: Duncker and Humblot, 1916), 2 vols.

33. See Hisao Otsuka in *Shihon-shugi no keisei 1*, vol. 4 of *Otsuka Hisao chosakushū* (Tokyo: Iwanami Shoten, 1969), p. 8, for an argument that uses a similar definition. "System," in the sense I use it here, is a collectivity formed by people, and not necessarily the nation-state, for example. Thus regional capitalism and global capitalism are both possible in this definition. In fact, however, where capitalism and the nation-state are not coterminous, various frictions arise.

34. North, *Structure and Change in Economic History*, p. 159.

35. In Latin, *proletarius* refers to the class that could serve the state only by increasing progenies, *proles*—not by making their property available to the state.

36. Benedict Anderson, *Imagined Communities: Reflections on the Origin and Spread of Nationalism* (London: Verso Editions, 1983), p. 13.

37. See, for example, Alan Macfarlane, *The Origins of English Individualism: The Family, Property and Social Transition* (Oxford: Basil Blackwell, 1978), pp. 138, 174; and Chie Nakane, *Kazoku no kōzō* (Tokyo: University of Tokyo Press, 1970). What I am here calling the "small family" are those in which children other than the heir (most often the eldest son) leave their parents' house even before they come of age; in this sense, the small family is even smaller than the nuclear family.

38. Marshall McLuhan, *The Gutenberg Galaxy: The Making of Typographic*

Man (Toronto: University of Toronto Press, 1962); Leslie White, *The Science of Culture* (New York: Noonday, 1949).

39. E. J. Hobsbawm, "The Crisis of the Seventeenth Century," in Trevor Aston, ed., *Crisis in Europe 1560–1660* (New York: Basic Books, 1965), p. 14; originally published in *Past and Present*, nos. 5 and 6 (1954).

40. *Translator's note*: At this point the author inserted the following: "In a supplementary section through a critique of this kind of acrobatics, I present a model to explain the early modern period in Britain." This was a section that Murakami hoped to write to take the place of Chapter 6 (in the original Japanese version of this book), but he was unable to do so before his death.

CHAPTER 5

1. See, for example, Edward F. Denison, *Accounting for Slower Economic Growth: The United States in the 1970s* (Washington, D.C.: Brookings Institution, 1979), table 7.3, and Kazushi Ohkawa and Henry Rosovsky, *Japanese Economic Growth* (Stanford, Calif.: Stanford University Press, 1973). In these and other similar analyses, an improvement in the quality of capital, including technological progress, was accounted for.

2. David Ricardo, *The Principles of Political Economy and Tax* (New York: Dutton, 1911), ch. 31.

3. Alfred Marshall, *Principles of Economics*, 8th ed. (London: Macmillan, 1925), pp. 318–19 (book 4, ch. 13, sec. 2). Original emphasis.

4. Ibid., p. 501 (book 5, ch. 15, sec. 4).

5. Piero Sraffa, "The Laws of Returns Under Competitive Conditions," *Economic Journal* 36 (1926): 535–50; Joan Robinson, *The Economics of Imperfect Competition* (London: Macmillan, 1933); Edward Chamberlin, *The Theory of Monopolistic Competition: A Re-Orientation of the Theory of Value* (Cambridge, Mass.: Harvard University Press, 1933). It is not clear, however, whether Chamberlin was under Sraffa's influence.

6. Kojima's attempt started with Kiyoshi Kojima, "Kaigai chokusetsu tōshi no riron: Amerika-gata to Nihon-gata," *Hitotsubashi ronsō*, June 1971. More recently, there is Kiyoshi Kojima, "Wagakuni kaigai chokusetsu tōshi no dōtai to Kojima meidai," *Sekai keizai hyōron*, Nov. 1988. Representative of Krugman's work is Paul R. Krugman and Maurice Obstfeld, *International Economics: Theory and Policy* (Glenview, Ill.: Scott, Foresman, 1988). The most recent work of Dosi and his group is Giovanni Dosi, Keith Pavitt, and Luc Soete, *The Economics of Technical Change and International Trade* (New York: Harvester Wheatsheaf, 1990).

7. There are a number of arguments as to whether the production function is something that applies to firms or factories, but at least in the initial stage when an industry is being formed, the norm is one firm, one factory. I therefore treat the production function here as applying to firms.

8. Motoshige Itō, Kazuhara Kiyono, Masahiro Okuno, and Kōtarō Suzuki, *Sangyō seisaku no keizai bunseki* (Tokyo: University of Tokyo Press, 1988), chs. 4, 5, and 6, is one of many theoretical works in Japan that, starting from a neoclassical perspective, has provided support for government intervention that goes beyond the theory of infant industries. To mention only one of various points on which I would like to take issue with their argument, my argu-

ment below differs from theirs in that it gives serious consideration to the positive contribution made by factors such as instability of competition that cannot be restored to a Nash equilibrium, and technology. My argument was first published in Yasusuke Murakami, "Sengo Nihon no keizai shisutemu," *Ekonomisuto*, June 14, 1982, and was restated, in an expanded form, in *Shinchūkan taishū no jidai* (Tokyo: Chūō Kōronsha, 1984), pt. 1.

9. In terms of technological limits, the average cost function cannot decrease indefinitely; that is, some would argue that infinite output cannot be the solution. But it is often assumed, in the theory of monopoly, for example, that if the demand curve were to shift far enough to the right (which would seem possible in an infant industry), then it would not be erroneous to see infinite output as a "solution" for profit maximization.

10. For example, when one considers the case where a firm decides to maximize its market share, it soon becomes clear that the form of the reaction function derived from Cournot is not settled. For the Cournot analysis of oligopoly, see Kōichi Okuguchi, *Kasen no keizai bunseki* (Tokyo: Kōbundō, 1960), or Motoshige Itō, Kazuhara Kiyono, Masahiro Okuno, and Kōtarō Suzuki, *Sangyō seisaku no keizai bunseki* (Tokyo: University of Tokyo Press, 1988), ch. 8. Even in these passive models, the relatively strong condition of stability is required in order to achieve a Nash equilibrium, and one should note that this is closely connected to increasing marginal cost. See Okuguchi, *Kasen no keizai bunseki*, pp. 22–23. The argument of Itō et al. is a typical example of an analysis premised on the formation of a Nash equilibrium.

11. An expansion of a public utility (an expansion in its supply network and capacity) frequently imposes huge additional investment costs. In other words, the *long-run* marginal cost increases. The contrast between costs decreasing in the short term and increasing in the long term is characteristic of public utilities. Since there is little chance of international competition in the utility industry, few analyze this industry as an infant industry. In fact, however, during the initial period for a public utility, there is domestic competition with traditional industries (lamp oil and firewood against electricity and gas, for example), and when it expands its facilities, there is frequently inadequate demand—that is, underutilization of facilities. In this sense it is not impossible to look at public utilities as infant industries.

12. Keynes himself was not much interested in the possibility of decreasing costs. See John Maynard Keynes, *General Theory of Employment, Interest and Money* (New York: Harcourt, Brace, 1936), pp. 9–10. Someone who has paid attention to this possibility is Masaru Yoshitomi, *Nihon keizai* (Tokyo: Tōyō Keizai Shinpōsha, 1971), p. 158.

13. This is the cost usually incurred by firms exiting a market, thus rendering the theory of contestability invalid. It is rare that the exiting firms can sell their secondhand productive capacity, and the organization created by the firms—in a sense, the human capital—is completely lost. Note that the loss of such organization is detrimental to technological innovation because technological innovation requires innovations in the organization.

14. When the slope of the supply function is negative, there is a possibility that the supply and demand curves will not intersect. Here, though, let us assume that they do intersect. When they do not intersect, we will apply the

following analysis as though the intersection occurs outside the nonnegative quadrant.

15. Shinya Sugiyama, *Japan's Industrialization in the World Economy 1859–1899* (London: Athlone Press, 1988), p. 34.

16. Marshall, *Principles of Economics*, pp. 502–3 (book 5, ch. 15, sec. 5).

17. Takashi Negishi, *Bōeki rieki to kokusai shūshi* (Tokyo: Sōbunsha, 1971), ch. 7, clearly models this theory. However, by using a two-period model, he avoids the problem of instability examined in this book's argument. In particular, see pp. 143–51.

18. Kenneth J. Arrow, "The Economic Implications of Learning by Doing," *Review of Economic Studies*, 29 (3), 80 (1962), pp. 155–73.

19. Marshall, *Principles of Economics*, p. 314 (book 4, ch. 13, sec. 2). Original emphasis.

20. Ibid., p. 318 (book 4, ch. 13, sec. 2).

21. Ibid. Original emphasis.

22. See, for example, Richard R. Nelson, "Aggregate Production Functions and Medium-Range Growth Projections," *American Economic Review* 54, 5 (1964), pp. 575–606.

23. For a discussion of this point, see Richard J. Gilbert and David M. G. Newbery, "Preemptive Patenting and the Persistence of Monopoly," *American Economic Review* 72, 3 (1982), pp. 514–26.

24. I may have been the first to use economic theory to advance the concept of excessive competition. See my "Sengo Nihon no keizai shisutemu," restated in Murakami, *Shin-chūkan taishū no jidai*, part I. The first to recognize the significance of excessive competition from a standpoint close to that of neoclassical orthodoxy were Itō et al., in *Sangyō seisaku*, ch. 12. Also, see Yūsaku Futagi, "Katō kyōsō no mekanizumu," in Miyohei Shinohara and Masao Baba, eds., *Gendai sangyōron, 2: sangyō soshiki* (Tokyo: Nihon Keizai Shinbunsha, 1974). (*Translator's note:* Since *katō kyoso* is usually translated as "excess competition," this expression is retained in lieu of "excessive competition" which perhaps is better English.)

25. Yasuo Takeuchi provides a comprehensive survey of the debate on excessive profit in *Shijō no keizai shisō* (Tokyo: Kōbunsha, 1991).

26. Joseph A. Schumpeter, *Capitalism, Socialism, and Democracy*, 3d ed. (New York: Harper and Row, 1950), pp. 101–2.

27. See, for example, ibid., p. 101. Richard J. Gilbert and David M. G. Newbery, in "Preemptive Patenting," posit that monopoly increases its dominance during the process of technological innovation. On the other hand, for the argument that in some cases monopoly causes technological innovation to stagnate, see Kenneth J. Arrow, "Economic Welfare and the Allocation of Resources of Invention," in R. R. Nelson, ed., *The Rate and Direction of Inventive Activity* (Princeton, N.J.: Princeton University Press, 1962).

28. Marshall, *Principles of Economics*, pp. 285–86 and 298–300 (book 4, ch. 11, sec. 5, and ch. 12, sec. 6).

29. Joseph Steindl, *Maturity and Stagnation in American Capitalism* (Oxford, Eng.: Basil Blackwell, 1952), and Joseph Steindl, *Small and Big Business: Economic Problems of the Size of Firms* (Oxford, Eng.: Basil Blackwell, 1945).

30. Edith J. Penrose, *The Theory of the Growth in the Firm* (London: Basil

Blackwell, 1959); Robin Marris, *The Economic Theory of Managerial Capitalism* (New York: Free Press of Glencoe, 1964).

31. *Translator's note*: This is the term Murakami coined to refer to competition maintained by more than seven oligopolistic firms in a market.

CHAPTER 6

1. As an introduction to the various arguments, see, for example, John Zysman, *Governments, Markets and Growth: Financial Systems and the Politics of Industrial Change* (Ithaca, N.Y.: Cornell University Press, 1983); George C. Eads and Kozo Yamamura, "The Future of Japanese Industrial Policy," in Kozo Yamamura and Yasukichi Yasuba, eds., *The Political Economy of Japan*, vol. 1: *The Domestic Transformation* (Stanford, Calif.: Stanford University Press, 1988).

2. See Zysman, *Governments, Markets and Growth*. Bhagwati considers domestic policy targeted at specific industries to be more desirable than a policy of tariffs and demonstrates ideas similar to the argument here. Jagdish Bhagwati, *Political Economy and International Economics*, ed. Douglas A. Irwin (Cambridge, Mass.: MIT Press, 1991), p. 11.

3. The phrase "compartmentalized competition" is my own. See Yasusuke Murakami, "The Japanese Model of Political Economy," in Yamamura and Yasuba, eds., *The Political Economy of Japan*, vol. 1.

4. *Translator's note*: Here and in the section on education policy below, Murakami divides education into *shōtō* (primary or elementary), *chūtō* (secondary or middle), and *kōtō* (higher or, perhaps, tertiary) levels. I have used the first set of English equivalents.

5. "Self-regulating" is Polanyi's phrase. See Karl Polanyi, *The Great Transformation* (New York: Farrar and Rinehart, 1944).

6. Ministry of International Trade and Industry, *Sangyō kōzō chōsakai tōshin* (Tokyo: MITI, 1983).

7. See Murakami, "Nijūseiki no sōzōsha Amerika," in Masakazu Yamazaki, ed., *Hana sakeru shin-bunka; bunmei to shite no Amerika 1* (Tokyo: Nihon Keizai Shinbunsha, 1985), particularly p. 244.

8. For an almost unique example among theories of economic development of someone who is sympathetic to the neoclassical school or tradition, see D. W. Jorgenson, "The Development of a Dual Economy," *Economic Journal* 71 (June 1961): 309–34. The significance of his argument ends, however, with pointing out that neoclassical development, theoretically, is not impossible.

9. Georgescu-Roegen and Sen make arguments that emphasize the significance of the family. See N. Georgescu-Roegen, "Economic Theory and Agrarian Economics," *Oxford Economic Papers* 12, 1 (Feb. 1960): 1–40; Amartya K. Sen, "Peasants and Dualism with or Without Surplus Labour," *Journal of Political Economy* 74, 5 (Oct. 1966): 425–50. I have also attempted a similar argument; see Machiko Kubo and Yasusuke Murakami, "Wagakuni nōson kōzō ni kansuru ichibunseki—toku ni gisō kinkō riron o chūshin ni shite," in Yoshirō Tamano and Tadao Uchida, eds., *Nijū kōzō no bunseki* (Tokyo: Tōyō Keizai Shinpōsha, 1964).

10. Max Weber, *Economy and Society: An Outline of Interpretive Sociology*, ed. Guenther Roth and Claus Wittich; trans. Ephraim Fischoff (New York: Bed-

minster Press, 1968), ch. 9, sec. 3. For the three conditions for the establishment of a bureaucracy, see pp. 956–73.

11. Ibid., p. 225.

12. On the *Kadi*-esque character of the bureaucracy, see ibid., p. 976. *Kadi* is the name for the judge in an Islamic religious state.

13. Weber, *Economy and Society*, p. 976.

14. Ibid., p. 290.

15. See, for example, ibid., p. 972.

16. The 1968 "Report of the Fulton Committee" in Britain and the 1978 revision of the law on public service in the United States seem for the most part to have done away with this kind of idiosyncrasy. See Geoffrey K. Fry, *Reforming the Civil Service: Fulton Committee on the British Home Civil Service of 1966–1968* (Edinburgh: Edinburgh University Press, 1993).

17. Chie Nakane, *Shakai jinruigaku—Ajia shoshakai no kōsatsu* (Social anthropology—an inquiry into various Asian societies) (Tokyo: University of Tokyo Press, 1987), p. 223. Nakane mentions China, Korea, and Japan, but in Thailand too the bureaucracy is considered to function effectively, albeit in a somewhat different form. For example, Akira Suehiro, *Capital Accumulation in Thailand 1855–1985* (Tokyo: Centre for East Asian Cultural Studies, 1989), contains a wealth of indirect information on this point. Minoru Ōuchi and Eiji Shimoyama, eds., *Kaihatsu tojōkoku no kanryōsei to keizai hatten* (Tokyo: Ajia Keizai Kenkyūjo Kenkyū Sōsho No. 328, 1985) provides much basic information.

18. See Yasusuke Murakami, "The Age of New Middle Mass Politics: The Case of Japan," *Journal of Japanese Studies* 8, 1 (Winter 1982): 29–72; Yasusuke Murakami, *Shin-chūkan taishū no jidai* (Tokyo: Chūō Kōronsha, 1984).

19. Many make this kind of argument intuitively, but more systematic examples of this argument are Michio Morishima, *Naze Nihon wa "seikō" shita no ka* (Tokyo: TBS Buritanika, 1984), and Leon Vandermeersch, *Le nouveau monde sinise* (Paris: Presses Universitaires de France, 1986).

20. Friedrich A. von Hayek, *Denationalisation of Money—The Argument Refined: An Analysis of the Theory and Practice of Concurrent Currencies* (London: Institute of Economic Affairs, 1976).

21. Friedrich A. von Hayek, *Capitalism and Freedom* (Chicago: University of Chicago Press, 1962), ch. 3.

22. The work of Robert A. Dahl, *A Preface to Democratic Theory* (Chicago: University of Chicago Press, 1956), is well known as a careful analysis of liberal democracy (which Dahl calls polyarchical democracy), but I will not go into such a detailed argument here. On the various possibilities of democracy, see David Held, *Models of Democracy* (Stanford, Calif.: Stanford University Press, 1987).

23. Joseph A. Schumpeter, *Capitalism, Socialism, and Democracy*, 3d ed. (New York: Harper and Row, 1950).

24. Peter Laslett, *The World We Have Lost* (London: Methuen, 1983), pp. 122–52.

CHAPTER 7

1. Samuel P. Huntington, "Transnational Organizations in World Politics," *World Politics* 25, 3 (April 1973): 333–68.

2. Richard Rosecrance, *The Rise of the Trading State* (New York: Basic Books, 1986).

3. Ibid., p. 141.

4. See for example, Yōichi Shinkai, *Tsūron kokusai keizai* (Tokyo: Iwanami Shoten, 1991), p. 86. The figures were obtained by multiplying his estimation of the average monthly fluctuation by twelve. Thus, the monthly variations (standard deviation) need to be summed. The monthly standard deviation is a little less than 3 percent, and so it would be possible, for example, for there to be a change of 10 percent in one direction over a three-month period (with the probability of 3 percent). It is common for the profit-to-sale rate to be 2 to 3 percent for all industry, and 3 to 4 percent for manufacturing industry as a whole. The fluctuation in sales can be offset only by the cost of imported raw materials. Normally, there is little trade in raw materials between the leading industrial countries, but countries that export raw materials frequently tie their exchange rates to the dollar. For manufacturing industry seen as a whole, the proportion of the cost of raw materials is not enough to change the observation made in the text.

5. It is commonly and erroneously thought that the United States, which conducts much of its trade in its own currency, can escape the influence that fluctuations in the exchange rate exert on trade. The reality is that U.S. firms transfer all the risk to the foreign firms with which they deal. The effects of this depend on the management of the exporting or importing firms of the countries concerned (or of U.S. companies in those countries). For example, to the degree that importing firms in these countries are risk-averse, U.S. exports will decrease, and if exporting firms in these countries are risk-takers then their imports are less likely to decline. But unless all of the firms with which the United States trades are risk-takers, U.S. trade will also decline because of the fluctuation.

6. Shinkai, *Tsūron kokusai keizai*, eh. 11. The citation is the title of the second section of that chapter.

7. Mathematically, such a model will be a differential equation of higher degree; unless it makes highly specific hypotheses about economic structure and the framework for forming expectations, it will not be able to avoid unbounded solutions. The hypothesis of so-called rational expectation is no help on this point.

8. Since the adoption of the system of floating exchange rates, it has been well known that purchasing power parity does not hold. See for example, Shinkai, *Tsūron kokusai keizai*, p. 87.

9. In the tables for Japan's balance of international payments, changes in foreign currency reserves and short-term foreign assets held by banks are treated as a financial account separate from the capital account. The capital account, referred to in the text, must include some part of banks' short-term foreign assets.

10. If the rate changes from 120 to 140 yen to the dollar, there will be specu-

lation assuming that the yen will decline in value. For example, people will expect to make a profit on buying dollars at 120 yen and selling them at 140 yen. There will be dollar buying on the basis of these expectations, making the yen still cheaper. However, since there will be a tendency toward an excess of capital in the United States with this inflow of speculative capital, the interest rate in the United States will go down, restricting the capital inflow to some extent. This change in the interest rate may also have many other effects.

11. Francis Fukuyama, "The End of History?" *National Interest* 16 (Summer 1989): 3–18.

12. On technological and management guidance, Kazuo Koike and Takenori Inoki, eds., *Jinsai keisei no kokusai hikaku—tōnan Ajia to Nihon* (Tokyo: Tōyō Keizai Shinpōsha, 1991), is worth careful reading.

13. Michèle Schmiegelow and Henrik Schmiegelow, *Strategic Pragmatism: Japanese Lessons in the Use of Economic Theory* (New York: Praeger, 1989), p. 56.

14. For television exports, however, there were major lawsuits against dumping by Japanese firms; the lawsuits became a significant trade issue in the 1960s.

15. Paul R. Krugman, "Is Bilateralism Bad?" (Working Paper, National Bureau of Economic Research, 1989).

CHAPTER 8

1. "Indirect aggression" is discussed in detail in the definition of invasion adopted by the General Assembly of the United Nations in 1974. U.S. interference in the domestic affairs of Nicaragua subsequently became a frequent issue in connection with this idea. See the decision by the International Court of Justice on September 27, 1984, and Wakamizu Tsutsui, *Gendai shiryō/Kokusaihō* (Tokyo: Yūhikaku, 1987), p. 166.

2. See, for example, Akio Hosono and Keiichi Tsunekawa, *Raten Amerika kiki no kōzu* (Tokyo: Yūhikaku, 1986), pp. 138–41.

3. See the essays in Toshio Kuroda, ed., *Kyōdōtai-ron no chihei* (Tokyo: Sanshūsha, 1990); for example, Toshio Kuroda, "Isuraamu sekai no shakai hensei genri," and Miyoko Kuroda, "Minzoku kokka no kyokōsei."

4. Balassa provides an apt classification of the conceptual distinction between integration and cooperation. See Bela A. Balassa, *The Theory of Economic Integration* (Homewood, Ill.: R. D. Irwin, 1961), pp. 1–3.

5. It is noteworthy, though, that since 1979 the European Parliament has been elected by the direct votes of the people in the member countries.

6. Some member countries have populations of less than 100,000, including island countries such as the Seychelles in the Indian Ocean and, in the West Indies, Antigua and Barbuda, the Dominican Federation, and Saint Christopher and Nevis. There are also small countries in the Gulf of Mexico such as Belize (population 170,000). The identity of the member countries here is as of February 1990, and the population figures are as of 1988.

7. Cicero, *De legibus* 3. xii. 28; in Cicero, *'De re publica' and 'De legibus,'* trans. Clinton W. Keyes (London: Heinemann Ltd., 1928), p. 493.

8. For example, in the case of the events in Grenada, the U.N. General Assembly resolved to criticize the U.S. invasion.

9. In the United States there is a strong demand for this kind of reform of the United Nations. In 1985 the U.S. Congress resolved, albeit as an amendment to the budget (the Kassebaum amendment), that unless the number of votes each country had in the General Assembly was changed to reflect its financial contribution to the United Nations, it would reduce its contribution. In the U.N. General Assembly in 1986, this did not result in a change in voting procedure, but a reform was approved to make it easier for the ideas of those countries that made substantial financial contributions to be reflected in the composition of the budget.

10. Of course, the U.S.-Japan Security Treaty states that it complies with the Charter of the United Nations. But when the permanent members of the Security Council, who have the right of veto, are parties to a treaty, it is in fact possible for the treaty to be managed without any restriction from the United Nations (see the U.N. Charter, clause 51). This applies to the U.S.-Japan Security Treaty and to other similar mutual defense treaties—for example, the treaty of the Warsaw Treaty Organization.

11. To be precise, the military clash between China and the Soviet Union over the return of Damansky Island was the last such confrontation between major powers. But this was nothing more than a small-scale boundary dispute, in which both sides combined suffered fewer than a hundred casualties. This should not perhaps be called a war.

12. The nonaligned conference was proposed by Tito, Nehru, and Nasser; the first conference was held in 1961 in Belgrade (with 25 countries participating) and advocated easing international tension and opposing military blocs, banning atom and hydrogen bombs, overthrowing colonialism, and supporting struggles for popular emancipation. (At present there are 99 member countries.) The African-Asian conference was proposed by India, Indonesia, Burma, Ceylon, and Pakistan; the first conference was held in 1955 in Bandung, Indonesia, and China also actively participated. (There were 29 participants in total.) It advocated opposition to colonialism, the establishment of human rights and popular self-determination, opposition to nuclear weapons, complete disarmament, and ten principles for peace.

13. China attended the Bandung conference that was the beginning of the African-Asian conference but did not participate in the nonaligned summit conferences. It is clear, however, that China sympathized with the principle of nonaligned neutrality and the African-Asian nations.

14. See Susumu Yamakage, *ASEAN—Shinboru kara shisutemu e* (Tokyo: University of Tokyo Press, 1991), p. 9.

15. Ibid., p. 241. Yamakage refers to Deputy Foreign Minister Ghazali of Malaysia. There were many similar pronouncements by those related to ASEAN. On the Friendship and Cooperation Treaty, see ibid., p. 205.

16. The participation of Taiwan might bring about friction with China. But one cannot neglect the position of Taiwan, uncovered by the U.N. security umbrella as it is. Taiwan's participation should be recognized in a way that does not foreclose the possibility of union with China.

17. See Balassa, *Theory of Economic Integration*, p. 2.

18. For a book on international economics arranged around this theme, see ibid.

19. An example of this is the famous counterargument of Jacob Viner, who posits that the benefits of tax union would be rather high between competitive economies. Jacob Viner, *The Customs Union Issue* (New York: Carnegie Endowment for International Peace, 1950).

20. Balassa's *Theory of Economic Integration* is an attempt to analyze dynamic issues. But it seems there are no examples, in this or in other books since, of having succeeded in systematizing the issue, including my own argument here.

21. *Translator's note*: Murakami died before the formal ratification of NAFTA in late 1993.

22. *Translator's note*: Kaname Akamatsu, *Sekai keizai-ron* (Tokyo: Kunimoto Shobō, 1965).

23. The world economy is in fact under the rule of a floating exchange rate system. As demonstrated in Chapter 7, this rule conceals a structure that sustains and amplifies the instability between the capital-deficient countries and the capital-rich countries. If this instability continues for any length of time, each set of countries may well form its own group. At present, the Asian NIEs and Japan have become powerful capital-exporting countries; and, in addition to the fact that they can cause powerful trade disturbances, as they have up to now, they have the potential to form a group that could use capital flow as a lever to dominate the world's economy. This is another reason we cannot ignore the East Asian economic region.

24. For a national developmentalist policy to succeed, there must exist in sufficient numbers individual developmentalist firms that are trying to sustain a trend of decreasing cost. It is possible for a national policy to foster this kind of firm, but there is no guarantee that it will always succeed. Conversely, even if there is no such national policy, in an industry that is clearly faced with decreasing cost, it is possible for firms to be, independently, developmentalist.

25. Fumio Kodama, *Haiteku gijutsu no paradaimu* (Tokyo: Chūō Kōronsha, 1991), pp. 63–65. He is careful not to count the same investment under both headings.

26. For a full discussion of "compartmentalized competition," see Yasusuke Murakami, "The Japanese Model of Political Economy," in Kozo Yamamura and Yasukichi Yasuba, eds., *The Political Economy of Japan*, vol. 1: *The Domestic Transformation* (Stanford, Calif.: Stanford University Press, 1987).

27. For example, patents in China last for fifteen years and in India for fourteen years. China, India, and Thailand do not recognize material patents. Under Dunkel's proposals, patents would last for twenty years, and material patents would be recognized.

28. David S. Landes, *The Unbound Prometheus: Technological Change and Industrial Development in Western Europe from 1750 to the Present* (Cambridge, Eng.: Cambridge University Press, 1969), pp. 326–58. The quotation is taken from pp. 327–28.

29. Ibid., pp. 352–54.

30. The list of remaining import restrictions stood at 21 products in 1989 — coal and twenty other agricultural, forestry, and marine products; there has been rapid liberalization in the two years since then, and seven products such as oranges and orange juice were liberalized before 1992. The "traded goods in

which the state is significantly involved" are rice, wheat, barley, condensed and powdered milk, butter, and raw silk; beef, which was included in this list for a long time, was liberalized in 1991.

31. Hiroya Ueno, *Nihon no keizai seidō* (Tokyo: Nihon Keizai Shinbunsha, 1978), p. 19. For the original classification, see Yoshio Kanezawa and Shigekazu Imamura, *Keizaihō, dokusen kinshihō*, rev. ed. (Tokyo: Yūhikaku, 1967), p. 37.

32. On the question of licensing, see Akira Morita, *Kyoninka gyōsei to kanryōsei* (Tokyo: Iwanami Shoten, 1988), a work unique in Japan.

33. See, for example, William Gibson's novels, *Neuromancer* (New York: Ace Books, 1984), *Burning Chrome* (New York: Ace Books, 1987), and *Count Zero* (New York: Arbor House, 1986). Mysterious Japanese "zaibatsu," Tokyo, and Japanese-manufactured cutting-edge technologies make frequent appearances in these. The picture of Japan that these books create is not, of course, the real thing.

CHAPTER 9

1. Robert H. Hayes and William J. Abernathy, "Managing Our Way to Economic Decline," *Harvard Business Review* 58 (July–Aug. 1980): 67–77; William J. Abernathy, Kim B. Clark, and Alan M. Kantrow, *Industrial Renaissance: Producing a Competitive Future for America* (New York: Basic Books, 1983); Robert B. Reich, *The Next American Frontier* (New York: Times Books, 1983); Michael L. Dertouzos, Richard K. Lester, Robert M. Solow, and the MIT Commission on Industrial Productivity, *Made in America: Regaining the Productive Edge* (Cambridge, Mass.: MIT Press, 1989).

2. Ken Yoshimori, *Amerika kigyōka seishin no suitai* (Tokyo: Japan Times, 1991), is detailed on this point. See, for example, p. 22.

3. See ibid., ch. 3. Ira C. Magaziner and Robert B. Reich, *Minding America's Business: The Decline and Rise of the American Economy* (New York: Harcourt Brace Jovanovich, 1982).

4. Theodore J. Lowi, *The End of Liberalism* (New York: Norton, 1969). His liberalism, as the antithesis to conservatism, has the strong nuance of a usage particular to the United States.

5. See Kiyoshi Kojima, "Wagakuni kaigai chokusetsu tōshi no dōtai to Kojima meidai" *Sekai keizai hyōron* 32, 11 (Nov. 1988): 22–39; Paul Krugman, "Is Free Trade Passé?" *Journal of Economic Perspectives* 1, 2 (Fall 1987): 131–44; Paul Krugman and Maurice Obstfeld, *International Economics, Theory and Policy* (Glenview, Ill.: Scott, Foresman, 1991); and Paul Krugman, *The Age of Diminished Expectations: U.S. Economic Policy in the 1990s* (Cambridge, Mass.: MIT Press, 1990). For a critique of Krugman, see Jagdish Bhagwati, *Political Economy and International Economics*, ed. Douglas A. Irwin (Cambridge, Mass.: MIT Press, 1991), pp. 4 and 24.

6. Fumio Kodama, *Haiteku gijutsu no paradaimu* (Tokyo: Chūō Kōronsha, 1991), pp. 44–73, is at present the best account of flexible manufacturing. A work with similar interests in the United States is Dertouzos, Lester, and Solow, *Made in America*. As far as I know, the earliest work to point out this fact was Michael J. Piore and Charles F. Sabel, *The Second Industrial Divide: Possibilities for Prosperity* (New York: Basic Books, 1984).

7. In the United States, Piore and Sable, in *The Second Industrial Divide*,

presented a forerunner of this type of argument. A similar argument was also made by Dertouzos, Lester, and Solow in *Made in America*. Nowadays this argument is much in fashion in Japan.

8. Laura D'Andrea Tyson, "Managed Trade: Making the Best of the Second Best," in Robert Z. Lawrence and Charles L. Schultze, eds., *An American Trade Strategy: Options for the 1990s* (Washington, D.C.: Brookings Institution, 1990), pp. 163–65.

9. I have discussed this point before, in Yasusuke Murakami, Shumpei Kumon, and Seizaburō Satō, *Bunmei to shite no ie shakai* (Tokyo: Chūō Kōronsha, 1979). For a condensed version of this in English, see Yasusuke Murakami, "Ie Society as a Pattern of Civilization," *Journal of Japanese Studies* 10, 2 (Summer 1984): pp. 281–363. This book argued that there was a consistent similarity of organizational pattern, stretching from the *ie* of the samurai in the twelfth century to large firms in the latter half of the twentieth, but it did *not* posit Japanese management as an inevitable result of the principle of *ie* organization. However, our argument was frequently misunderstood simply as a theory of Japanese exceptionalism and became the target of criticism. Inadequacies in the way we expressed this argument may well also be responsible. My original point is made more clear in a subsequent essay, Yasusuke Murakami and Thomas P. Rohlen, "Social-Exchange Aspects of the Japanese Political Economy: Culture, Efficiency, and Change," in Shumpei Kumon and Henry Rosovsky, eds., *The Political Economy of Japan*, vol. 3: *Cultural and Social Dynamics* (Stanford, Calif.: Stanford University Press, 1992).

10. "Contestable" points to the fact that, because entry to the market is free, competition is preserved, at least latently. The original formulation was made in William J. Baumol, John C. Panzar, and Robert D. Willig, *Contestable Markets and the Theory of Industry Structure* (San Diego, Calif.: Harcourt Brace Jovanovich, 1982).

11. The exceptions are those cases in which the large nationalized corporations (Japanese National Railways [JNR] and Nippon Telegraph and Telephone [NTT], which were under the supervision of the Ministry of Transport and Communications) protected an influential group of firms—the so-called NTT family and the JNR-related firms—with which they had a relationship close to subcontracting. Rather than cost, their concern was with a secure, stable supply. This phenomenon is similar to the government's relationship to its suppliers becoming fixed, as seen in many countries' defense industries. Now, however, the railways and the telephone company have been privatized, and the fixed character of their subcontracting relationships has largely disappeared. As another example, MITI to some extent supported maintaining the distribution *keiretsu* (by regulating branches that large stores are allowed to create), in order to protect small retailers. This, though, was a result of distributive policy, and MITI itself seems to have supported this policy rather passively.

12. Peter Katzenstein, "West Germany as Number Two," in Andrei S. Markovits, ed., *The Political Economy of West Germany: Modell Deutschland* (New York: Praeger, 1982). Michèle Schmiegelow and Henrik Schmiegelow, *Strategic Pragmatism: Japanese Lessons in the Use of Economic Theory* (New York: Praeger, 1989).

13. Before Japan's antitrust law was amended in 1953, "undue disparity" in

assets and/or market share of firms due to mergers was itself prohibited. U.S. antitrust law, which was the model for this, wavered between a strict interpretation that considered a large market share in itself a violation of the law, and a loose interpretation, which only considered aiming at market control a violation. There were few cases in which judgment was passed on the former model.

14. The period from the 1960s to the early 1970s was what one might call the "golden age" of U.S. antitrust law. Even though attempts were made to check mergers between firms in different industries, it seems it was impossible to establish an integrated law. After this, starting with a Supreme Court judgment in favor of General Dynamics in the early 1960s, there was a clear tendency toward a loose application of the antitrust law, and during and after the Reagan administration this tendency increased still further. One could say that this was the inevitable result of the basic theory that antitrust law is only a theory of a separate market structure for each individual business.

15. Michael Porter, *Competitive Strategy* (New York: Free Press, 1980). Ken'ichi Imai, Hiroyuki Itami, and Kazuo Koike, *Naibu soshiki no keizaigaku* (Tokyo: Tōyō Keizai Shinpōsha, 1982), p. 60.

16. Dertouzos, Lester, and Solow, *Made in America*, p. 177.

17. Michael Porter, *Cases in Competitive Strategy* (New York: Free Press, 1983).

18. Robert Axelrod, *The Evolution of Cooperation* (New York: Basic Books, 1984). To me, Axelrod's proof suggests instead how difficult it is for cooperation to arise among egoists.

19. Adolf A. Berle and Gardiner C. Means, *The Modern Corporation and Private Property* (New York: Macmillan, 1933).

20. James Burnham, *The Managerial Revolution* (Bloomington, Ind.: Indiana University Press, 1941); Tadaharu Miyamoto, *Kigyō to soshiki no keizaigaku* (Tokyo: Shinseisha, 1991), ch. 7. Miyamoto's popular work clearly sets out the kind of argument being attempted here.

21. Edith T. Penrose, *The Theory of the Growth in the Firm* (London: Basil Blackwell, 1959); Robin Marris, *The Economic Theory of Managerial Capitalism* (New York: Free Press of Glencoe, 1964); Adrian Wood, *A Theory of Profits* (Cambridge, Eng.: Cambridge University Press, 1975) is a work with the same ideas.

22. Gary S. Becker, *Human Capital* (New York: Columbia University Press, 1964).

23. Representative of his work is Oliver E. Williamson, *Markets and Hierarchies: Analysis and Antitrust Implications* (New York: Free Press, 1975). A famous, classic essay by Coase is Ronald H. Coase, "The Nature of the Firm," *Economica* 4 (Nov. 1937): 386–405.

24. Peter B. Doeringer and Michael J. Piore, *Internal Labor Markets and Manpower Analysis* (Lexington, Mass.: Heath, 1971).

25. Kazuo Koike, *Shokuba no rōdō soshiki to keiei sanka—rōshi kankei no Nichibei hikaku* (Tokyo: Tōyō Keizai Shinpōsha, 1977); Kazuo Koike, *Understanding Industrial Relations in Modern Japan*, trans. Mary Saso (New York: St. Martin's Press, 1988).

26. Ibid., p. 213. Koike is more cautious and does not draw as striking a contrast between their characteristics as I have here, but I believe even this kind of description is justified.

27. Ibid., pp. 218, 240.

28. Also see Masahiko Aoki, *Nihon kigyō no soshiki to jōhō* (Tokyo: Tōyō Keizai Shinpōsha, 1989), p. 19; Williamson, *Markets and Hierarchies;* and Oliver E. Williamson, *The Economic Institutions of Capitalism* (New York: Free Press, 1985).

29. Murakami and Rohlen, "Social-Exchange Aspects," p. 77.

30. Piore and Sabel, in *The Second Industrial Divide,* suggest that in the United States, too, another form of employment might have been possible.

31. Hidenobu Nakashima, *Kabushiki no mochiai to kigyōhō* (Tokyo: Shōji Hōmu Kenkyūkai, 1990), p. 75.

32. Kumiharu Shigehara and Setsuya Sato, "Kigyō no shihon cosuto o meguru mondai ni tsuite," in Nihon Ginkō Kin'yū Kenkyūjo, *Kin'yū kenkyū* 9, 2 (July 1990), provides a convenient summary of the research so far. Among American economists, too, there are those who argue that there are, and those who argue that there are not, differences between Japan and the United States.

33. Robert W. McCauley and Steven A. Zimmer, "Explaining International Differences in the Cost of Capital," *Federal Reserve Bank of New York Quarterly Review* 14, 2 (Summer 1989): 7–29; James M. Poterba, "Comparing the Cost of Capital in the United States and Japan: A Survey of Methods," *Federal Reserve Bank of New York Quarterly Review* 15, 3–4 (Winter 1991): 20–33.

34. See, for example, Dertouzos, Lester, and Solow, *Made in America,* pp. 53–60.

35. Yoshimori adopts the clearest position on this point. Yoshimori, *Amerika kigyōka seishin no suitai.* On p. 103, he introduces the counterargument to the thesis that blames institutional investors.

36. See, for example, Megumi Shudō, *Nihon no shōkengyō* (Tokyo: Tōyō Keizai Shinpōsha, 1987), p. 14.

37. See, for example, Joseph Stiglitz, "Credit Markets and the Control of Capital," *Journal of Money, Credit, and Banking* 17 (1985): 135–52.

38. Michel Albert, *Capitalisme contre capitalisme* (Paris: Editions du Seuil, 1991).

39. Nakatani argues that it is in the character of financial *keiretsu* to pursue stability over efficiency. Iwao Nakatani, "The Economic Role of Financial Corporate Grouping," in Masahiko Aoki, ed., *The Economic Analysis of the Firm* (Amsterdam: North-Holland, 1983).

40. Richard Pascale and Thomas P. Rohlen, "The Mazda Turnaround," *Journal of Japanese Studies* 9, 2 (Summer 1983): 219–63.

41. Shōichi Rōyama, *Nihon no kin'yū shisutemu* (Tokyo: Tōyō Keizai Shinpōsha, 1982), p. 14. Here I am using the phrase "one-on-one" transactions in a broader sense than Rōyama, however.

42. Kazuto Ikeo, *Ginkō risuki kisei no keizaigaku* (Tokyo: Tōyō Keizai Shinpōsha, 1990), p. 150.

43. Ibid., p. 28. Ikeo, though, recommends avoiding this problem with a system of variable insurance premiums; implementing this would surely be difficult, however (see pp. 130–31).

44. Ibid., p. 211.

45. Noritoshi Mabuchi, *Amerika no ginkō mochikabu gaisha* (Tokyo: Tōyō Keizai Shinpōsha, 1987), ch. 2.

46. *Translator's note:* Literally "descent from heaven," *amakudari* refers to

the practice of senior bureaucrats', on retiring from their respective ministries, taking up senior, and often lucrative, positions in firms over which they have often previously exercised administrative jurisdiction.

47. In Japan too, during the Kamakura period, when there was a continuous rivalry between the court government and the warrior government, there appeared works such as Jien's *Gukanshō* and Kitabatake Chikafusa's *Jinnō shōtōki*, which argued about how politics should be organized.

48. Aristotle, *The Politics*, book 3, chs. 6 and 7.

49. Hans Kelsen, *Foundations of Democracy* (Chicago: University of Chicago Press, 1955), pt. I, chs. 1–3.

50. Friedrich A. von Hayek, *Individualism and Economic Order* (Chicago: University of Chicago Press, 1948), p. 29; citing Lord Acton, "Nationality" (1862), reprinted in J. E. E. D. Acton, *The History of Freedom and Other Essays* (London: Macmillan, 1907), pp. 280–300.

51. John Locke, *Two Treatises of Government: A Critical Edition with an Introduction and Appartus Criticus* (New York: New American Library, 1963), chs. 5 and 6.

52. Jean-Jacques Rousseau, *The Social Contract*, trans. Maurice Cranston (Harmondsworth, Middlesex, Eng.: Penguin, 1968), p. 114.

53. Jacob Burckhardt, *Historische Fragmente* (Stuttgart: Deutsche Verlags-Anstalt, 1957), p. 281.

54. Karl Mannheim, *Man and Society in an Age of Reconstruction*, rev. ed., trans. Edward Shils (London: Routledge and Kegan Paul Ltd., 1940), pp. 44–45.

55. Carl Schmitt, "Das Zeitalter der Neutralisierungen und Entpolitisierungen" (1929), as translated and included in Ikutarō Shimizu, ed., *Gendai shisō I, Kaaru Shumitto—kiki no seiji riron* (Tokyo: Daiyamonda-sha, 1973), pp. 144–45.

56. Jacob Burckhardt, *Reflections on History* (London: G. Allen and Unwin, 1950), p. 132.

57. Yasusuke Murakami, "The Age of New Middle Mass Politics: The Case of Japan," *Journal of Japanese Studies* 8, 1 (Winter 1982): pp. 29–72. Murakami, *Shin-chūkan taishū no jidai*, pt. II. The argument first appeared in "Shin-chūkan taishū seiji no jidai," *Chūō kōron*, Dec. 1980. In my previous works, however, I did not indicate sufficiently the closeness of the relationship between this phenomenon and developmentalism.

58. Lowi, *The End of Liberalism*.

59. See Edmund Burke, *Reflections on the Revolution in France and Other Writings* (London: Oxford University Press, 1950); John Stuart Mill, *Considerations on Representative Government* (1861), especially ch. 3, "That the Ideally Best Form of Government Is Representative Government."

60. Fernand Braudel, *Une leçon d'histoire de Fernand Braudel* (Paris: Arthaud-Flammarion, 1986).

CHAPTER 10

1. There is of course opposition to this phenomenology-centered view. See, for example, Richard Rorty, *The Linguistic Turn* (Chicago: University of Chicago Press, 1967); and Richard Rorty, "Philosophy in America Today," in *Con-*

sequences of Pragmatism (Minneapolis, Minn.: University of Minnesota Press, 1982).

2. Edmund Husserl, *Cartesian Meditations* (The Hague: Martinus Nihjoff, 1960), pp. 17–18.

3. Claude Lévi-Strauss, *Structural Anthropology*, trans. Claire Jacobson and Brooke Grundfest Schoepf (New York: Basic Books, 1963), ch. 8, p. 133.

4. Hiroshi Oikawa, "Dōzoku-soshiki to kon-in oyobi sōrei no girei," *Minzokugaku nenpō*, vol. 2 (Dec. 1940); Kizaemon Aruga, *The Collected Works* (Tokyo: Miraisha, 1968); Chie Nakane, *Japanese Society* (Berkeley, Calif.: University of California Press, 1970); Ruth Benedict, *The Chrysanthemum and the Sword: Patterns of Japanese Culture* (New York: Houghton Mifflin, 1946); F. L. K. Hsu, *Iemoto: The Heart of Japan* (New York: Schenkman, 1975); Thomas C. Smith, *The Agrarian Origins of Modern Japan* (Stanford, Calif.: Stanford University Press, 1959).

5. A reference for the psychiatric implications of evidentiality is Wolfgang Blankenburg, *Der Verlust der natürlichen Selbstverständlichkeit* (Stuttgart: Ferdinand Enke Verlag, 1971).

6. Husserl argued that, in order to understand the *Lebenswelt* honestly and fully, "suspended judgment" was necessary. I believe, however, that such a position is possible only as a series of extremely high-level hermeneutic reflections by a philosopher, and not something that can be easily achieved by the average individual. Generally, the *Lebenswelt* should be defined as a pre-reflexive, relatively more naive image of the world, as I show below. It is no accident that Heidegger did not use the concept of suspended judgment.

7. See, for example, Husserl, *Cartesian Meditations*, pp. 34–35.

8. Moksakara Gupta, *Tarkabhasa and Vadasthana of Moksakaragupta and Jitaripada*, 2d ed., ed. H. R. Rangaswami Iyengar (Mysore, India: Hindusthan Press, 1952).

9. *Translator's note*: The Consciousness-Only School—*vijñaptimātra* in Sanskrit, *wei-shih* in Chinese, and *yuishiki* in Japanese—was founded in the later fifth century A.D. It was systematized and developed philosphically by Vasubandhu (c.420–c.500), the younger brother of the founder, and its essentials are summed up in his *Vijñatimātratātriṁ'sikā*, which has been translated together with other major works by Stefan Anacker, in *Seven Works of Vasubandhu, the Buddhist Psychological Doctor* (Delhi: Motilal Banarsidass, 1984), pp. 186–89. Both the doctrine and the school are perhaps more accessible through the subsequent Chinese interpretations. Hsüan-tsang's famous *Ch'eng-wei-shih lun* was itself subsequently annotated by his pupil K'uei-chi (632–682). A convenient introduction to and translation of selections of Hsüan-tsang's work are provided by Wing-tsit Chan, in *A Source Book in Chinese Philosophy* (Princeton, N.J.: Princeton University Press, 1963), pp. 370–95, from which this account is drawn.

10. *Translator's note*: A convenient reference work for Japanese Buddhism is Hisao Inagaki, *A Dictionary of Japanese Buddhist Terms* (Kyoto: Nagata Bunshodo, 1984). Kūkai (774–835) was the founder of the Shingon sect of Buddhism, also known as the "esoteric sect" (Himitsu-shū). *Sokushin jōbutsu*, its essential doctrine, is translated more literally as "becoming a buddha with one's present body." The *Jūjūshinron* was later condensed by Kūkai into "The

Precious Key to the Secret Treasury," trans. Yoshito S. Hakeda in *Kūkai: Major Works* (New York: Columbia University Press, 1972), pp. 157–224.

11. Robert N. Bellah, "Religious Evolution," *American Sociological Review* 29, 3 (1964): 358–74.

12. Henri Frankfort, H. A. Frankfort, John A. Wilson, and Thorkild Jacobsen, *Before Philosophy: The Intellectual Adventure of Ancient Man* (Chicago: University of Chicago Press, 1946).

13. From Nietzsche's preface to *Beyond Good and Evil*, trans. Walter Kaufmann (New York: Vintage Books, 1966).

14. René Descartes, *Discourse on Method*, trans. F. E. Sutcliffe (Harmondsworth, Middlesex, Eng.: Penguin, 1968), p. 41.

15. Martin Heidegger, *Being and Time*, trans. John Macquarrie and Edward Robinson (New York: Harper and Row, 1962), p. 195. Original emphasis.

16. This phrase is borrowed from Shōzō Ōmori, "Shintai dōsa to ishi-teki mirai," *Shisō*, Aug. 1982, p. 7.

17. Descartes, *Discourse on Method*, pp. 45–47.

18. Ibid., p. 45.

19. *Translator's note*: I have translated Murakami's word *shisaku* as "speculation"; it can also mean contemplation or thinking.

20. Joseph A. Schumpeter, *History of Economic Analysis* (New York: Oxford University Press, 1954), pp. 82–107.

21. Sylvain Levi, *Vijnaptimatratasiddhi, deux traites de Vasubandhu* (Paris: H. Champion, 1925).

22. John Locke, *Epistola de Tolerantia: A Letter on Toleration*, ed. Raymond Klibansky, trans. J. W. Gough (Oxford, Eng.: Clarendon Press, 1968), pp. 58–59.

23. Adam Smith, *The Theory of Moral Sentiments*, ed. D. D. Raphael and A. L. Macfie (Oxford, Eng.: Clarendon Press, 1976).

24. *Translator's note*: The *Kojiki* and *Nihon shoki* are Japan's earliest extant chronicles, compiled in 712 and 720, respectively. Based on historical memories and genealogical traditions, and also myth and legend, they cover events from the mythical age of the gods up to the seventh century.

25. Hideo Suzuki, "3500 Years Ago," *Bulletin of the Department of Geography*, Faculty of Science, University of Tokyo, October 1979.

26. Max Weber, *Gesammelte Aufsätze zur Religionssoziologie*, Band II: *Hinduismus und Buddhismus* (Tübingen: J. C. B. Mohr, 1923), pp. 363–78; Max Weber, "The General Character of Asian Religion," in Hans H. Gerth and Don Martindale, eds. and trans., *The Religion of India: The Sociology of Hinduism and Buddhism* (New York: Free Press, 1967), pp. 329–43.

27. Robert N. Bellah, "Values and Social Change in Modern Japan," *Asian Cultural Studies* 3 (1962): 13–56; S. N. Eisenstadt, *Revolution and the Transformation of Societies: A Comparative Study of Civilizations* (New York: Free Press, 1978), pp. 66, 144.

28. Hajime Nakamura, *Tōyōjin no shii hōhō* (Tokyo: Shinjūsha, 1962), p. 11.

29. Saburo Ienaga, *Nihon shisōshi ni okeru hitei no ronri no hattatsu* (Tokyo: Kōbunsha, 1940).

30. Ienaga cites the "Seventeen-Article Constitution" and "Sankei Giso" of Shōtoku Taishi, the first philsophical works by a Japanese, as proof of this.

31. *Translator's note*: On Kūkai, see note 10 above. Saichō (767–822), post-

humously known as Dengyō Daishi, and a contemporary of Kūkai, was the founder of the Tendai sect. Inagaki, *Dictionary*, pp. 258–99.

32. See Yoshinori Yasuda, *Kikō to bunmei no seisui* (Tokyo: Asakura Shoten, 1990), vol. 1, p. 289.

33. The following line about Kūkai comes from Katsuichirō Kamei, *Ōchō no kyūdō to irogonomi* (Tokyo: Bungei Shunjū, 1962), p. 40, which even today has not lost its originality. "Can we declare that the self-consciousness of the divide between Budda and man is not itself a delusion?" There is a similar discussion of Shinran in idem., *Chūsei no seishi to shūkyōkan* (Tokyo: Bungei Shunjū, 1964), p. 154.

34. *Translator's note*: Readers will find Murakami's article, "Ie Society as a Pattern of Civilization," *Journal of Japanese Studies* 10, 2 (1984): 281–363, useful; it contains more detailed discussion of natural developments and analyses dealt with in this section.

35. *Translator's note*: The former has been translated by Delmer M. Brown and Ichiro Ishida as *The Future and the Past* (Berkeley, Calif.: University of California Press, 1979), and the latter by Paul Varley as *A Chronicle of Gods and Sovereigns* (New York: Columbia University Press, 1980).

36. The *sō* were agricultural communities that began to appear after the mid-fourteenth century. They evolved into self-governing entities that owed taxes to their respective samurai overlords. In the Tokugawa period, they were formally institutionalized as the *mura* and incorporated into the *bakufu*-domain system of the period.

37. Alexis de Tocqueville, *Democracy in America*, ed. J. P. Mayer, trans. George Lawrence (New York: Harper and Row, 1966), p. 393.

Index

In this index "f" after a number indicates a separate reference on the next page, and "ff" indicates separate references on the next two pages. A continuous discussion over two or more pages is indicated by a span of numbers. *Passim* is used for a cluster of references in close but not consecutive sequence.

Murakami, Yasusuke.
[Han koten no seiji keizaigaku. English]
An anticlassical political-economic analysis : a vision for the
next century / Yasusuke Murakami ; translated with an introduction
by Kozo Yamamura.
   p.   cm.
Includes index.
ISBN 0-8047-2646-9 (cloth : alk. paper)
   1. Economics—History.   2. Economic policy—History.
   3. Neoclassical school of economics—History.   I. Title.
HB75.M87713   1996
330—dc20   95-48950
                                                           CIP

⊚ This book is printed on acid-free, recycled paper.

Original printing 1996
Last figure below indicates year of this printing
05   04   03   02   01   00   99   98   97   96